Financial
EIGHTH RATE
MORTGAGE TABLES

PUBLICATION NO. 267
APRIL 1984

Computed and
Published by

FINANCIAL
PUBLISHING
COMPANY
82 Brookline Avenue
Boston, Massachusetts 02215
(617) 262-4040

PUBLICATION NO. 267
COPYRIGHT © 1984 BY
FINANCIAL PUBLISHING COMPANY

PRINTED IN THE
UNITED STATES OF AMERICA

ISBN 0-87600-267-X

TABLE OF CONTENTS

Page

Mortgage Payment Tables **4**
— *Show the monthly payment necessary
to amortize a loan.*
RATES: 7% to 18% by ⅛%.
TERMS: 1 year to 5 years by each year,
        7, 8, 10, 12, 15, 18, 20, 25,
        28, 29, 30, 35 and 40 years.
AMOUNTS: to $150,000.

Points Discount Tables **184**
— *Show the APR when points are
taken on a loan.*

Loan Progess Charts **200**
— *Show the dollar balance remaining on
a $1,000 loan for various elapsed terms.*

Basic Payment Tables **210**
— *Show the monthly payment per $1,000.*

Constant Annual Percent Tables **254**
— *Show the annual constant per $100
for monthly payments in arrears.*

Down Payment Tables **256**
— *Show the net loan amount given
various down payment requirements.*

7% MONTHLY PAYMENT
NECESSARY TO AMORTIZE A LOAN

AMOUNT	1 YEAR	2 YEARS	3 YEARS	4 YEARS	5 YEARS	6 YEARS	7 YEARS	8 YEARS	10 YEARS	12 YEARS
$ 50	4.33	2.24	1.55	1.20	1.00	.76	.69	.59	.59	.52
100	8.66	4.48	3.09	2.40	1.99	1.51	1.37	1.17	1.03
200	17.31	8.96	6.18	4.79	3.97	3.02	2.73	2.33	2.06
300	25.96	13.44	9.27	7.19	5.95	4.53	4.10	3.49	3.09
400	34.62	17.91	12.36	9.58	7.93	6.04	5.46	4.65	4.12
500	43.27	22.39	15.44	11.98	9.91	7.55	6.82	5.81	5.15
600	51.92	26.87	18.53	14.37	11.89	9.06	8.19	6.97	6.18
700	60.57	31.35	21.62	16.77	13.87	10.57	9.55	8.13	7.20
800	69.23	35.82	24.71	19.16	15.85	12.08	10.91	9.29	8.23
900	77.88	40.30	27.79	21.56	17.83	13.59	12.28	10.45	9.26
1000	86.53	44.78	30.88	23.95	19.81	15.10	13.64	11.62	10.29
2000	173.06	89.55	61.76	47.90	39.61	30.19	27.27	23.23	20.57
3000	259.59	134.32	92.64	71.84	59.41	45.28	40.91	34.84	30.86
4000	346.11	179.10	123.51	95.79	79.21	60.38	54.54	46.45	41.14
5000	432.64	223.87	154.39	119.74	99.01	75.47	68.17	58.06	51.42
6000	519.17	268.64	185.27	143.68	118.81	90.56	81.81	69.67	61.71
7000	605.69	313.41	216.14	167.63	138.61	105.65	95.44	81.28	71.99
8000	692.22	358.19	247.02	191.57	158.41	120.75	109.07	92.89	82.28
9000	778.75	402.96	277.90	215.52	178.22	135.84	122.71	104.50	92.56
10000	865.27	447.73	308.78	239.47	198.02	150.93	136.34	116.11	102.84
15000	1297.91	671.59	463.16	359.20	297.02	226.40	204.51	174.17	154.26
20000	1730.54	895.46	617.55	478.93	396.03	301.86	272.68	232.22	205.68
25000	2163.17	1119.32	771.93	598.66	495.03	377.32	340.85	290.28	257.10
30000	2595.81	1343.18	926.32	718.39	594.04	452.79	409.02	348.33	308.52
35000	3028.44	1567.05	1080.70	838.12	693.05	528.25	477.19	406.38	359.94
40000	3461.07	1790.91	1235.09	957.85	792.05	603.71	545.35	464.44	411.36
45000	3893.71	2014.77	1389.47	1077.59	891.06	679.18	613.52	522.49	462.78
46000	3980.24	2059.54	1420.35	1101.53	910.86	694.27	627.16	534.10	473.06
47000	4066.76	2104.32	1451.23	1125.48	930.66	709.36	640.79	545.71	483.34
48000	4153.29	2149.09	1482.11	1149.42	950.46	724.45	654.42	557.33	493.63
49000	4239.82	2193.86	1512.98	1173.37	970.26	739.55	668.06	568.94	503.91
50000	4326.34	2238.63	1543.86	1197.32	990.06	754.64	681.69	580.55	514.20
51000	4412.87	2283.41	1574.74	1221.26	1009.87	769.73	695.32	592.16	524.48
52000	4499.40	2328.18	1605.61	1245.21	1029.67	784.82	708.96	603.77	534.76
53000	4585.92	2372.95	1636.49	1269.16	1049.47	799.92	722.59	615.38	545.05
54000	4672.45	2417.72	1667.37	1293.10	1069.27	815.01	736.23	626.99	555.33
55000	4758.98	2462.50	1698.25	1317.05	1089.07	830.10	749.86	638.60	565.61
56000	4845.50	2507.27	1729.12	1340.99	1108.87	845.20	763.49	650.21	575.90
57000	4932.03	2552.04	1760.00	1364.94	1128.67	860.29	777.13	661.82	586.18
58000	5018.56	2596.81	1790.88	1388.89	1148.47	875.38	790.76	673.43	596.47
59000	5105.08	2641.59	1821.75	1412.83	1168.28	890.47	804.39	685.05	606.75
60000	5191.61	2686.36	1852.63	1436.78	1188.08	905.57	818.03	696.66	617.03
61000	5278.14	2731.13	1883.51	1460.73	1207.88	920.66	831.66	708.27	627.32
62000	5364.66	2775.90	1914.39	1484.67	1227.68	935.75	845.30	719.88	637.60
63000	5451.19	2820.68	1945.26	1508.62	1247.48	950.84	858.93	731.49	647.89
64000	5537.72	2865.45	1976.14	1532.56	1267.28	965.94	872.56	743.10	658.17
65000	5624.24	2910.22	2007.02	1556.51	1287.08	981.03	886.20	754.71	668.45
67500	5840.56	3022.15	2084.21	1616.38	1336.59	1018.76	920.28	783.74	694.16
70000	6056.88	3134.09	2161.40	1676.24	1386.09	1056.49	954.37	812.76	719.87
75000	6489.51	3357.95	2315.79	1795.97	1485.09	1131.96	1022.53	870.82	771.29
80000	6922.14	3581.81	2470.17	1915.70	1584.10	1207.42	1090.70	928.87	822.71
85000	7354.78	3805.67	2624.56	2035.44	1683.11	1282.88	1158.87	986.93	874.13
90000	7787.41	4029.54	2778.94	2155.17	1782.11	1358.35	1227.04	1044.98	925.55
95000	8220.05	4253.40	2933.33	2274.90	1881.12	1433.81	1295.21	1103.04	976.97
100000	8652.68	4477.26	3087.71	2394.63	1980.12	1509.27	1363.38	1161.09	1028.39
105000	9085.31	4701.13	3242.10	2514.36	2079.13	1584.74	1431.55	1219.14	1079.81
110000	9517.95	4924.99	3396.49	2634.09	2178.14	1660.20	1499.71	1277.20	1131.22
115000	9950.58	5148.85	3550.87	2753.82	2277.14	1735.66	1567.88	1335.25	1182.64
120000	10383.21	5372.71	3705.26	2873.55	2376.15	1811.13	1636.05	1393.31	1234.06
125000	10815.85	5596.58	3859.64	2993.29	2475.15	1886.59	1704.22	1451.36	1285.48
130000	11248.48	5820.44	4014.03	3113.02	2574.16	1962.05	1772.39	1509.42	1336.90
135000	11681.12	6044.30	4168.41	3232.75	2673.17	2037.52	1840.56	1567.47	1388.32
140000	12113.75	6268.17	4322.80	3352.48	2772.17	2112.98	1908.73	1625.52	1439.74
145000	12546.38	6492.03	4477.18	3472.21	2871.18	2188.44	1976.89	1683.58	1491.16
150000	12979.02	6715.89	4631.57	3591.94	2970.18	2263.91	2045.06	1741.63	1542.58

AMOUNT	15 YEARS	18 YEARS	20 YEARS	25 YEARS	28 YEARS	29 YEARS	30 YEARS	35 YEARS	40 YEARS
$ 50	.45	.41	.39	.36	.34	.34	.34	.32	.32
100	.90	.82	.78	.71	.68	.68	.67	.64	.63
200	1.80	1.64	1.56	1.42	1.36	1.35	1.34	1.28	1.25
300	2.70	2.45	2.33	2.13	2.04	2.02	2.00	1.92	1.87
400	3.60	3.27	3.11	2.83	2.72	2.69	2.67	2.56	2.49
500	4.50	4.08	3.88	3.54	3.40	3.37	3.33	3.20	3.11
600	5.40	4.90	4.66	4.25	4.08	4.04	4.00	3.84	3.73
700	6.30	5.71	5.43	4.95	4.76	4.71	4.66	4.48	4.36
800	7.20	6.53	6.21	5.66	5.44	5.38	5.33	5.12	4.98
900	8.09	7.34	6.98	6.37	6.12	6.05	5.99	5.75	5.60
1000	8.99	8.16	7.76	7.07	6.80	6.73	6.66	6.39	6.22
2000	17.98	16.32	15.51	14.14	13.60	13.45	13.31	12.78	12.43
3000	26.97	24.47	23.26	21.21	20.39	20.17	19.96	19.17	18.65
4000	35.96	32.63	31.02	28.28	27.19	26.89	26.62	25.56	24.86
5000	44.95	40.78	38.77	35.34	33.99	33.61	33.27	31.95	31.08
6000	53.93	48.94	46.52	42.41	40.78	40.33	39.92	38.34	37.29
7000	62.92	57.09	54.28	49.48	47.58	47.05	46.58	44.72	43.51
8000	71.91	65.25	62.03	56.55	54.37	53.78	53.23	51.11	49.72
9000	80.90	73.40	69.78	63.62	61.17	60.50	59.88	57.50	55.93
10000	89.89	81.56	77.53	70.68	67.97	67.22	66.54	63.89	62.15
15000	134.83	122.33	116.30	106.02	101.95	100.82	99.80	95.83	93.22
20000	179.77	163.11	155.06	141.36	135.93	134.43	133.07	127.78	124.29
25000	224.71	203.88	193.83	176.70	169.91	168.04	166.33	159.72	155.36
30000	269.65	244.66	232.59	212.04	203.89	201.64	199.60	191.66	186.43
35000	314.59	285.43	271.36	247.38	237.87	235.25	232.86	223.60	217.51
40000	359.54	326.21	310.12	282.72	271.85	268.86	266.13	255.55	248.58
45000	404.48	366.98	348.89	318.06	305.83	302.46	299.39	287.49	279.65
46000	413.47	375.14	356.64	325.12	312.62	309.18	306.04	293.88	285.86
47000	422.45	383.29	364.40	332.19	319.42	315.91	312.70	300.27	292.08
48000	431.44	391.45	372.15	339.26	326.22	322.63	319.35	306.66	298.29
49000	440.43	399.60	379.90	346.33	333.01	329.35	326.00	313.04	304.51
50000	449.42	407.76	387.65	353.39	339.81	336.07	332.66	319.43	310.72
51000	458.41	415.91	395.41	360.46	346.61	342.79	339.31	325.82	316.93
52000	467.40	424.07	403.16	367.53	353.40	349.51	345.96	332.21	323.15
53000	476.38	432.22	410.91	374.60	360.20	356.23	352.62	338.60	329.36
54000	485.37	440.38	418.67	381.67	366.99	362.96	359.27	344.99	335.58
55000	494.36	448.53	426.42	388.73	373.79	369.68	365.92	351.38	341.79
56000	503.35	456.69	434.17	395.80	380.59	376.40	372.57	357.76	348.01
57000	512.34	464.84	441.93	402.87	387.38	383.12	379.23	364.15	354.22
58000	521.33	473.00	449.68	409.94	394.18	389.84	385.88	370.54	360.44
59000	530.31	481.15	457.43	417.00	400.97	396.56	392.53	376.93	366.65
60000	539.30	489.31	465.18	424.07	407.77	403.28	399.19	383.32	372.86
61000	548.29	497.46	472.94	431.14	414.57	410.00	405.84	389.71	379.08
62000	557.28	505.62	480.69	438.21	421.36	416.73	412.49	396.10	385.29
63000	566.27	513.77	488.44	445.28	428.16	423.45	419.15	402.48	391.51
64000	575.26	521.93	496.20	452.34	434.95	430.17	425.80	408.87	397.72
65000	584.24	530.08	503.95	459.41	441.75	436.89	432.45	415.26	403.94
67500	606.71	550.47	523.33	477.08	458.74	453.69	449.08	431.23	419.47
70000	629.18	570.86	542.71	494.75	475.73	470.50	465.72	447.20	435.01
75000	674.13	611.63	581.48	530.09	509.71	504.10	498.98	479.15	466.08
80000	719.07	652.41	620.24	565.43	543.69	537.71	532.25	511.09	497.15
85000	764.01	693.18	659.01	600.77	577.67	571.32	565.51	543.03	528.22
90000	808.95	733.96	697.77	636.11	611.65	604.92	598.78	574.98	559.29
95000	853.89	774.73	736.54	671.45	645.63	638.53	632.04	606.92	590.36
100000	898.83	815.51	775.30	706.78	679.61	672.14	665.31	638.86	621.44
105000	943.77	856.28	814.07	742.12	713.59	705.74	698.57	670.80	652.51
110000	988.72	897.06	852.83	777.46	747.57	739.35	731.84	702.75	683.58
115000	1033.66	937.83	891.60	812.80	781.55	772.95	765.10	734.69	714.65
120000	1078.60	978.61	930.36	848.14	815.54	806.56	798.37	766.63	745.72
125000	1123.54	1019.38	969.13	883.48	849.52	840.17	831.63	798.58	776.79
130000	1168.48	1060.16	1007.89	918.82	883.50	873.77	864.90	830.52	807.87
135000	1213.42	1100.93	1046.66	954.16	917.48	907.38	898.16	862.46	838.94
140000	1258.36	1141.71	1085.42	989.50	951.46	940.99	931.43	894.40	870.01
145000	1303.31	1182.48	1124.19	1024.83	985.44	974.59	964.69	926.35	901.08
150000	1348.25	1223.26	1162.95	1060.17	1019.42	1008.20	997.96	958.29	932.15

MONTHLY PAYMENT
NECESSARY TO AMORTIZE A LOAN

AMOUNT	1 YEAR	2 YEARS	3 YEARS	4 YEARS	5 YEARS	7 YEARS	8 YEARS	10 YEARS	12 YEARS
$ 50	4.33	2.25	1.55	1.21	1.00	.76	.69	59	.52
100	8.66	4.49	3.10	2.41	1.99	1.52	1.37	1.17	1.04
200	17.32	8.97	6.19	4.81	3.98	3.04	2.74	2.34	2.08
300	25.98	13.45	9.29	7.21	5.96	4.55	4. *	3.51	3.11
400	34.64	17.94	12.38	9.61	7.95	6.07	5	4.68	4.15
500	43.30	22.42	15.47	12.01	9.94	7.58	6.8	5.84	5.18
600	51.96	26.90	18.57	14.41	11.92	9.10	8.22	7.01	6.22
700	60.61	31.39	21.66	16.81	13.91	10.61	9.59	8.18	7.25
800	69.27	35.87	24.75	19.21	15.89	12.13	10.96	9.35	8.29
900	77.93	40.35	27.85	21.61	17.88	13.64	12.33	10.51	9.32
1000	86.59	44.83	30.94	24.01	19.87	15.16	13.70	11.68	10.36
2000	173.17	89.66	61.87	48.01	39.73	30.31	27.40	23.36	20.71
3000	259.76	134.49	92.81	72.02	59.59	45.47	41.09	35.03	31.06
4000	346.34	179.32	123.74	96.02	79.45	60.62	54.79	46.71	41.41
5000	432.93	224.15	154.68	120.03	99.31	75.77	68.49	58.38	51.76
6000	519.51	268.98	185.61	144.03	119.17	90.93	82.18	70.06	62.11
7000	606.10	313.81	216.54	168.03	139.03	106.08	95.88	81.73	72.46
8000	692.68	358.64	247.48	192.04	158.89	121.24	109.57	93.41	82.81
9000	779.26	403.47	278.41	216.04	178.75	136.39	123.27	105.08	93.16
10000	865.85	448.30	309.35	240.05	198.61	151.54	136.97	116.76	103.51
15000	1298.77	672.44	464.02	360.07	297.91	227.31	205.45	175.14	155.26
20000	1731.69	896.59	618.69	480.09	397.21	303.08	273.93	233.51	207.02
25000	2164.61	1120.74	773.36	600.11	496.51	378.85	342.41	291.89	258.77
30000	2597.54	1344.88	928.03	720.13	595.81	454.62	410.89	350.27	310.52
35000	3030.46	1569.03	1082.70	840.15	695.11	530.39	479.37	408.64	362.27
40000	3463.38	1793.18	1237.38	960.18	794.41	606.16	547.85	467.02	414.03
45000	3896.30	2017.32	1392.05	1080.20	893.72	681.93	616.33	525.40	465.78
46000	3982.89	2062.15	1422.98	1104.20	913.58	697.08	630.02	537.07	476.13
47000	4069.47	2106.98	1453.92	1128.21	933.44	712.24	643.72	548.75	486.48
48000	4156.06	2151.81	1484.85	1152.21	953.30	727.39	657.41	560.42	496.83
49000	4242.64	2196.64	1515.78	1176.21	973.16	742.54	671.11	572.10	507.18
50000	4329.22	2241.47	1546.72	1200.22	993.02	757.70	684.81	583.77	517.53
51000	4415.81	2286.30	1577.65	1224.22	1012.88	772.85	698.50	595.45	527.88
52000	4502.39	2331.13	1608.59	1248.23	1032.74	788.01	712.20	607.12	538.23
53000	4588.98	2375.96	1639.52	1272.23	1052.60	803.16	725.89	618.80	548.58
54000	4675.56	2420.79	1670.46	1296.24	1072.46	818.31	739.59	630.48	558.94
55000	4762.15	2465.61	1701.39	1320.24	1092.32	833.47	753.29	642.15	569.29
56000	4848.73	2510.44	1732.32	1344.24	1112.18	848.62	766.98	653.83	579.64
57000	4935.31	2555.27	1763.26	1368.25	1132.04	863.77	780.68	665.50	589.99
58000	5021.90	2600.10	1794.19	1392.25	1151.90	878.93	794.37	677.18	600.34
59000	5108.48	2644.93	1825.13	1416.26	1171.76	894.08	808.07	688.85	610.69
60000	5195.07	2689.76	1856.06	1440.26	1191.62	909.24	821.77	700.53	621.04
61000	5281.65	2734.59	1887.00	1464.27	1211.48	924.39	835.46	712.20	631.39
62000	5368.24	2779.42	1917.93	1488.27	1231.34	939.54	849.16	723.88	641.74
63000	5454.82	2824.25	1948.86	1512.27	1251.20	954.70	862.85	735.55	652.09
64000	5541.41	2869.08	1979.80	1536.28	1271.06	969.85	876.55	747.23	662.44
65000	5627.99	2913.91	2010.73	1560.28	1290.92	985.01	890.25	758.90	672.79
67500	5844.45	3025.98	2088.07	1620.29	1340.57	1022.89	924.49	788.09	698.67
70000	6060.91	3138.05	2165.40	1680.30	1390.22	1060.78	958.73	817.28	724.54
75000	6493.83	3362.20	2320.08	1800.33	1489.52	1136.54	1027.21	875.66	776.30
80000	6926.76	3586.35	2474.75	1920.35	1588.82	1212.31	1095.69	934.03	828.05
85000	7359.68	3810.49	2629.42	2040.37	1688.12	1288.08	1164.17	992.41	879.80
90000	7792.60	4034.64	2784.09	2160.39	1787.43	1363.85	1232.65	1050.79	931.56
95000	8225.52	4258.79	2938.76	2280.41	1886.73	1439.62	1301.13	1109.17	983.31
100000	8658.44	4482.93	3093.43	2400.43	1986.03	1515.39	1369.61	1167.54	1035.06
105000	9091.37	4707.08	3248.10	2520.45	2085.33	1591.16	1438.09	1225.92	1086.81
110000	9524.29	4931.22	3402.78	2640.48	2184.63	1666.93	1506.57	1284.30	1138.57
115000	9957.21	5155.37	3557.45	2760.50	2283.93	1742.70	1575.05	1342.67	1190.32
120000	10390.13	5379.52	3712.12	2880.52	2383.23	1818.47	1643.53	1401.05	1242.07
125000	10823.05	5603.66	3866.79	3000.54	2482.53	1894.24	1712.01	1459.43	1293.83
130000	11255.97	5827.81	4021.46	3120.56	2581.83	1970.01	1780.49	1517.80	1345.58
135000	11688.90	6051.96	4176.13	3240.58	2681.14	2045.78	1848.97	1576.18	1397.33
140000	12121.82	6276.10	4330.80	3360.60	2780.44	2121.55	1917.45	1634.56	1449.08
145000	12554.74	6500.25	4485.48	3480.63	2879.74	2197.31	1985.93	1692.93	1500.84
150000	12987.66	6724.40	4640.15	3600.65	2979.04	2273.08	2054.41	1751.31	1552.59

MONTHLY PAYMENT 7⅛%
NECESSARY TO AMORTIZE A LOAN

AMOUNT	15 YEARS	18 YEARS	20 YEARS	25 YEARS	28 YEARS	29 YEARS	30 YEARS	35 YEARS	40 YEARS
$ 50	.46	.42	.40	.36	.35	.35	.34	.33	.32
100	.91	.83	.79	.72	.69	.69	.68	.65	.64
200	1.82	1.65	1.57	1.43	1.38	1.37	1.35	1.30	1.27
300	2.72	2.47	2.35	2.15	2.07	2.05	2.03	1.95	1.90
400	3.63	3.30	3.14	2.86	2.76	2.73	2.70	2.60	2.53
500	4.53	4.12	3.92	3.58	3.44	3.41	3.37	3.24	3.16
600	5.44	4.94	4.70	4.29	4.13	4.09	4.05	3.89	3.79
700	6.35	5.76	5.48	5.01	4.82	4.77	4.72	4.54	4.42
800	7.25	6.59	6.27	5.72	5.51	5.45	5.39	5.19	5.05
900	8.16	7.41	7.05	6.44	6.20	6.13	6.07	5.83	5.68
1000	9.06	8.23	7.83	7.15	6.88	6.81	6.74	6.48	6.31
2000	18.12	16.46	15.66	14.30	13.76	13.61	13.48	12.96	12.62
3000	27.18	24.69	23.49	21.45	20.64	20.42	20.22	19.43	18.92
4000	36.24	32.92	31.32	28.60	27.52	27.22	26.95	25.91	25.23
5000	45.30	41.15	39.15	35.74	34.40	34.03	33.69	32.39	31.53
6000	54.35	49.37	46.97	42.89	41.28	40.83	40.43	38.86	37.84
7000	63.41	57.60	54.80	50.04	48.16	47.64	47.17	45.34	44.14
8000	72.47	65.83	62.63	57.19	55.03	54.44	53.90	51.82	50.45
9000	81.53	74.06	70.46	64.33	61.91	61.25	60.64	58.29	56.75
10000	90.59	82.29	78.29	71.48	68.79	68.05	67.38	64.77	63.06
15000	135.88	123.43	117.43	107.22	103.18	102.07	101.06	97.15	94.58
20000	181.17	164.57	156.57	142.96	137.58	136.10	134.75	129.53	126.11
25000	226.46	205.71	195.71	178.70	171.97	170.12	168.43	161.92	157.64
30000	271.75	246.85	234.85	214.44	206.36	204.14	202.12	194.30	189.16
35000	317.05	287.99	273.99	250.18	240.76	238.17	235.81	226.68	220.69
40000	362.34	329.13	313.13	285.91	275.15	272.19	269.49	259.06	252.22
45000	407.63	370.27	352.27	321.65	309.54	306.21	303.18	291.44	283.74
46000	416.69	378.50	360.10	328.80	316.42	313.02	309.92	297.92	290.05
47000	425.75	386.73	367.93	335.95	323.30	319.82	316.65	304.40	296.35
48000	434.80	394.96	375.76	343.10	330.18	326.63	323.39	310.87	302.66
49000	443.86	403.19	383.59	350.24	337.06	333.43	330.13	317.35	308.97
50000	452.92	411.42	391.41	357.39	343.94	340.24	336.86	323.83	315.27
51000	461.98	419.64	399.24	364.54	350.81	347.04	343.60	330.30	321.58
52000	471.04	427.87	407.07	371.69	357.69	353.85	350.34	336.78	327.88
53000	480.10	436.10	414.90	378.83	364.57	360.65	357.08	343.25	334.19
54000	489.15	444.33	422.73	385.98	371.45	367.46	363.81	349.73	340.49
55000	498.21	452.56	430.56	393.13	378.33	374.26	370.55	356.21	346.80
56000	507.27	460.78	438.38	400.28	385.21	381.07	377.29	362.68	353.10
57000	516.33	469.01	446.21	407.43	392.09	387.87	384.02	369.16	359.41
58000	525.39	477.24	454.04	414.57	398.97	394.68	390.76	375.64	365.71
59000	534.45	485.47	461.87	421.72	405.84	401.48	397.50	382.11	372.02
60000	543.50	493.70	469.70	428.87	412.72	408.28	404.24	388.59	378.32
61000	552.56	501.93	477.53	436.02	419.60	415.09	410.97	395.07	384.63
62000	561.62	510.15	485.35	443.16	426.48	421.89	417.71	401.54	390.93
63000	570.68	518.38	493.18	450.31	433.36	428.70	424.45	408.02	397.24
64000	579.74	526.61	501.01	457.46	440.24	435.50	431.18	414.50	403.55
65000	588.80	534.84	508.84	464.61	447.12	442.31	437.92	420.97	409.85
67500	611.44	555.41	528.41	482.48	464.31	459.32	454.77	437.16	425.61
70000	634.09	575.98	547.98	500.35	481.51	476.33	471.61	453.35	441.38
75000	679.38	617.12	587.12	536.08	515.90	510.35	505.29	485.74	472.90
80000	724.67	658.26	626.26	571.82	550.29	544.38	538.98	518.12	504.43
85000	769.96	699.40	665.40	607.56	584.69	578.40	572.67	550.50	535.96
90000	815.25	740.54	704.54	643.30	619.08	612.42	606.35	582.88	567.48
95000	860.54	781.68	743.68	679.04	653.47	646.45	640.04	615.26	599.01
100000	905.84	822.83	782.82	714.78	687.87	680.47	673.72	647.65	630.54
105000	951.13	863.97	821.97	750.52	722.26	714.49	707.41	680.03	662.06
110000	996.42	905.11	861.11	786.26	756.65	748.52	741.10	712.41	693.59
115000	1041.71	946.25	900.25	821.99	791.05	782.54	774.78	744.79	725.12
120000	1087.00	987.39	939.39	857.73	825.44	816.56	808.47	777.17	756.64
125000	1132.29	1028.53	978.53	893.47	859.83	850.59	842.15	809.56	788.17
130000	1177.59	1069.67	1017.67	929.21	894.23	884.61	875.84	841.94	819.70
135000	1222.88	1110.81	1056.81	964.95	928.62	918.63	909.53	874.32	851.22
140000	1268.17	1151.95	1095.95	1000.69	963.01	952.66	943.21	906.70	882.75
145000	1313.46	1193.10	1135.09	1036.43	997.41	986.68	976.90	939.08	914.28
150000	1358.75	1234.24	1174.23	1072.16	1031.80	1020.70	1010.58	971.47	945.80

7

7¼% MONTHLY PAYMENT
NECESSARY TO AMORTIZE A LOAN

AMOUNT	1 YEAR	2 YEARS	3 YEARS	4 YEARS	5 YEARS	7 YEARS	8 YEARS	10 YEARS	12 YEARS
$ 50	4.34	2.25	1.55	1.21	1.00	.77	.69	.59	.53
100	8.67	4.49	3.10	2.41	2.00	1.53	1.38	1.18	1.05
200	17.33	8.98	6.20	4.82	3.99	3.05	2.76	2.35	2.09
300	26.00	13.47	9.30	7.22	5.98	4.57	4.13	3.53	3.13
400	34.66	17.96	12.40	9.63	7.97	6.09	5.51	4.70	4.17
500	43.33	22.45	15.50	12.04	9.96	7.61	6.88	5.88	5.21
600	51.99	26.94	18.60	14.44	11.96	9.13	8.26	7.05	6.26
700	60.65	31.43	21.70	16.85	13.95	10.66	9.64	8.22	7.30
800	69.32	35.91	24.80	19.25	15.94	12.18	11.01	9.40	8.34
900	77.98	40.40	27.90	21.66	17.93	13.70	12.39	10.57	9.38
1000	86.65	44.89	31.00	24.07	19.92	15.22	13.76	11.75	10.42
2000	173.29	89.78	61.99	48.13	39.84	30.44	27.52	23.49	20.84
3000	259.93	134.66	92.98	72.19	59.76	45.65	41.28	35.23	31.26
4000	346.57	179.55	123.97	96.25	79.67	60.87	55.04	46.97	41.68
5000	433.22	224.44	154.96	120.32	99.60	76.08	68.80	58.71	52.09
6000	519.86	269.32	185.95	144.38	119.52	91.30	82.56	70.45	62.51
7000	606.50	314.21	216.95	168.44	139.44	106.51	96.31	82.19	72.93
8000	693.14	359.09	247.94	192.50	159.36	121.73	110.07	93.93	83.35
9000	779.78	403.98	278.93	216.57	179.28	136.94	123.83	105.67	93.76
10000	866.43	448.87	309.92	240.63	199.20	152.16	137.59	117.41	104.18
15000	1299.64	673.30	464.88	360.94	298.80	228.23	206.38	176.11	156.27
20000	1732.85	897.73	619.84	481.25	398.39	304.31	275.17	234.81	208.36
25000	2166.06	1122.16	774.79	601.57	497.99	380.38	343.97	293.51	260.44
30000	2599.27	1346.59	929.75	721.88	597.59	456.46	412.76	352.21	312.53
35000	3032.48	1571.02	1084.71	842.19	697.18	532.54	481.55	410.91	364.62
40000	3465.69	1795.45	1239.67	962.50	796.78	608.61	550.34	469.61	416.71
45000	3898.90	2019.88	1394.62	1082.81	896.38	684.69	619.14	528.31	468.80
46000	3985.54	2064.76	1425.62	1106.88	916.30	699.90	632.89	540.05	479.21
47000	4072.18	2109.65	1456.61	1130.94	936.21	715.12	646.65	551.79	489.63
48000	4158.82	2154.53	1487.60	1155.00	956.13	730.33	660.41	563.53	500.05
49000	4245.46	2199.42	1518.59	1179.06	976.05	745.55	674.17	575.27	510.47
50000	4332.11	2244.31	1549.58	1203.13	995.97	760.76	687.93	587.01	520.88
51000	4418.75	2289.19	1580.57	1227.19	1015.89	775.98	701.69	598.75	531.30
52000	4505.39	2334.08	1611.56	1251.25	1035.81	791.19	715.44	610.49	541.72
53000	4592.03	2378.96	1642.56	1275.31	1055.73	806.41	729.20	622.23	552.14
54000	4678.68	2423.85	1673.55	1299.37	1075.65	821.62	742.96	633.97	562.55
55000	4765.32	2468.74	1704.54	1323.44	1095.57	836.84	756.72	645.71	572.97
56000	4851.96	2513.62	1735.53	1347.50	1115.49	852.06	770.48	657.45	583.39
57000	4938.60	2558.51	1766.52	1371.56	1135.41	867.27	784.24	669.19	593.81
58000	5025.24	2603.39	1797.51	1395.62	1155.33	882.49	798.00	680.93	604.22
59000	5111.89	2648.28	1828.51	1419.69	1175.25	897.70	811.75	692.67	614.64
60000	5198.53	2693.17	1859.50	1443.75	1195.17	912.92	825.51	704.41	625.06
61000	5285.17	2738.05	1890.49	1467.81	1215.09	928.13	839.27	716.15	635.48
62000	5371.81	2782.94	1921.48	1491.87	1235.01	943.35	853.03	727.89	645.89
63000	5458.45	2827.82	1952.47	1515.94	1254.92	958.56	866.79	739.63	656.31
64000	5545.10	2872.71	1983.46	1540.00	1274.84	973.78	880.55	751.37	666.73
65000	5631.74	2917.60	2014.45	1564.06	1294.76	988.99	894.30	763.11	677.15
67500	5848.34	3029.81	2091.93	1624.22	1344.56	1027.03	928.70	792.46	703.19
70000	6064.95	3142.03	2169.41	1684.37	1394.36	1065.07	963.10	821.81	729.23
75000	6498.16	3366.46	2324.37	1804.69	1493.96	1141.14	1031.89	880.51	781.32
80000	6931.37	3590.89	2479.33	1925.00	1593.55	1217.22	1100.68	939.21	833.41
85000	7364.58	3815.32	2634.28	2045.31	1693.15	1293.30	1169.47	997.91	885.50
90000	7797.79	4039.75	2789.24	2165.62	1792.75	1369.37	1238.27	1056.61	937.59
95000	8231.00	4264.18	2944.20	2285.93	1892.34	1445.45	1307.06	1115.31	989.67
100000	8664.21	4488.61	3099.16	2406.25	1991.94	1521.52	1375.85	1174.02	1041.76
105000	9097.42	4713.04	3254.12	2526.56	2091.54	1597.60	1444.64	1232.72	1093.85
110000	9530.63	4937.47	3409.07	2646.87	2191.13	1673.68	1513.44	1291.42	1145.94
115000	9963.84	5161.90	3564.03	2767.18	2290.73	1749.75	1582.23	1350.12	1198.02
120000	10397.05	5386.33	3718.99	2887.49	2390.33	1825.83	1651.02	1408.82	1250.11
125000	10830.26	5610.76	3873.95	3007.81	2489.93	1901.90	1719.81	1467.52	1302.20
130000	11263.47	5835.19	4028.90	3128.12	2589.52	1977.98	1788.60	1526.22	1354.29
135000	11696.68	6059.62	4183.86	3248.43	2689.12	2054.05	1857.40	1584.92	1406.38
140000	12129.89	6284.05	4338.82	3368.74	2788.72	2130.13	1926.19	1643.62	1458.46
145000	12563.10	6508.48	4493.78	3489.05	2888.31	2206.21	1994.98	1702.32	1510.55
150000	12996.31	6732.91	4648.73	3609.37	2987.91	2282.28	2063.77	1761.02	1562.64

MONTHLY PAYMENT 7¼%
NECESSARY TO AMORTIZE A LOAN

AMOUNT	15 YEARS	18 YEARS	20 YEARS	25 YEARS	28 YEARS	29 YEARS	30 YEARS	35 YEARS	40 YEARS
$ 50	.46	.42	.40	.37	.35	.35	.35	.33	.32
100	.92	.84	.80	.73	.70	.69	.69	.66	.64
200	1.83	1.67	1.59	1.45	1.40	1.38	1.37	1.32	1.28
300	2.74	2.50	2.38	2.17	2.09	2.07	2.05	1.97	1.92
400	3.66	3.33	3.17	2.90	2.79	2.76	2.73	2.63	2.56
500	4.57	4.16	3.96	3.62	3.49	3.45	3.42	3.29	3.20
600	5.48	4.99	4.75	4.34	4.18	4.14	4.10	3.94	3.84
700	6.40	5.82	5.54	5.06	4.88	4.83	4.78	4.60	4.48
800	7.31	6.65	6.33	5.79	5.57	5.52	5.46	5.26	5.12
900	8.22	7.48	7.12	6.51	6.27	6.20	6.14	5.91	5.76
1000	9.13	8.31	7.91	7.23	6.97	6.89	6.83	6.57	6.40
2000	18.26	16.61	15.81	14.46	13.93	13.78	13.65	13.13	12.80
3000	27.39	24.91	23.72	21.69	20.89	20.67	20.47	19.70	19.20
4000	36.52	33.21	31.62	28.92	27.85	27.56	27.29	26.26	25.59
5000	45.65	41.51	39.52	36.15	34.81	34.45	34.11	32.83	31.99
6000	54.78	49.82	47.43	43.37	41.77	41.34	40.94	39.39	38.39
7000	63.91	58.12	55.33	50.60	48.74	48.22	47.76	45.96	44.78
8000	73.03	66.42	63.24	57.83	55.70	55.11	54.58	52.52	51.18
9000	82.16	74.72	71.14	65.06	62.66	62.00	61.40	59.09	57.58
10000	91.29	83.02	79.04	72.29	69.62	68.89	68.22	65.65	63.97
15000	136.93	124.53	118.56	108.43	104.43	103.33	102.33	98.48	95.96
20000	182.58	166.04	158.08	144.57	139.24	137.77	136.44	131.30	127.94
25000	228.22	207.55	197.60	180.71	174.04	172.22	170.55	164.12	159.92
30000	273.86	249.06	237.12	216.85	208.85	206.66	204.66	196.95	191.91
35000	319.51	290.57	276.64	252.99	243.66	241.10	238.77	229.77	223.89
40000	365.15	332.07	316.16	289.13	278.47	275.54	272.88	262.59	255.87
45000	410.79	373.58	355.67	325.27	313.28	309.98	306.98	295.42	287.86
46000	419.92	381.88	363.58	332.50	320.24	316.87	313.81	301.98	294.25
47000	429.05	390.19	371.48	339.72	327.20	323.76	320.63	308.54	300.65
48000	438.18	398.49	379.39	346.95	334.16	330.65	327.45	315.11	307.05
49000	447.31	406.79	387.29	354.18	341.12	337.54	334.27	321.67	313.44
50000	456.44	415.09	395.19	361.41	348.08	344.43	341.09	328.24	319.84
51000	465.57	423.39	403.10	368.64	355.05	351.32	347.91	334.80	326.24
52000	474.69	431.69	411.00	375.86	362.01	358.20	354.74	341.37	332.63
53000	483.82	440.00	418.90	383.09	368.97	365.09	361.56	347.93	339.03
54000	492.95	448.30	426.81	390.32	375.93	371.98	368.38	354.50	345.43
55000	502.08	456.60	434.71	397.55	382.89	378.87	375.20	361.06	351.82
56000	511.21	464.90	442.62	404.78	389.85	385.76	382.02	367.63	358.22
57000	520.34	473.20	450.52	412.00	396.81	392.65	388.85	374.19	364.62
58000	529.47	481.50	458.42	419.23	403.78	399.53	395.67	380.76	371.01
59000	538.59	489.81	466.33	426.46	410.74	406.42	402.49	387.32	377.41
60000	547.72	498.11	474.23	433.69	417.70	413.31	409.31	393.89	383.81
61000	556.85	506.41	482.13	440.92	424.66	420.20	416.13	400.45	390.20
62000	565.98	514.71	490.04	448.15	431.62	427.09	422.95	407.01	396.60
63000	575.11	523.01	497.94	455.37	438.58	433.98	429.78	413.58	403.00
64000	584.24	531.32	505.85	462.60	445.55	440.86	436.60	420.14	409.40
65000	593.37	539.62	513.75	469.83	452.51	447.75	443.42	426.71	415.79
67500	616.19	560.37	533.51	487.90	469.91	464.97	460.47	443.12	431.78
70000	639.01	581.13	553.27	505.97	487.31	482.20	477.53	459.53	447.78
75000	684.65	622.63	592.79	542.11	522.12	516.64	511.64	492.36	479.76
80000	730.30	664.14	632.31	578.25	556.93	551.08	545.75	525.18	511.74
85000	775.94	705.65	671.82	614.39	591.74	585.52	579.85	558.00	543.73
90000	821.58	747.16	711.34	650.53	626.55	619.96	613.96	590.83	575.71
95000	867.22	788.67	750.86	686.67	661.35	654.41	648.07	623.65	607.69
100000	912.87	830.18	790.38	722.81	696.16	688.85	682.18	656.47	639.68
105000	958.51	871.69	829.90	758.95	730.97	723.29	716.29	689.30	671.66
110000	1004.15	913.19	869.42	795.09	765.78	757.73	750.40	722.12	703.64
115000	1049.80	954.70	908.94	831.23	800.59	792.17	784.51	754.94	735.63
120000	1095.44	996.21	948.46	867.37	835.39	826.62	818.62	787.77	767.61
125000	1141.08	1037.72	987.97	903.51	870.20	861.06	852.73	820.59	799.59
130000	1186.73	1079.23	1027.49	939.65	905.01	895.50	886.83	853.41	831.58
135000	1232.37	1120.74	1067.01	975.79	939.82	929.94	920.94	886.24	863.56
140000	1278.01	1162.25	1106.53	1011.93	974.62	964.39	955.05	919.06	895.55
145000	1323.66	1203.75	1146.05	1048.07	1009.43	998.83	989.16	951.88	927.53
150000	1369.30	1245.26	1185.57	1084.22	1044.24	1033.27	1023.27	984.71	959.51

9

MONTHLY PAYMENT
NECESSARY TO AMORTIZE A LOAN

AMOUNT	1 YEAR	2 YEARS	3 YEARS	4 YEARS	5 YEARS	7 YEARS	8 YEARS	10 YEARS	12 YEARS
$ 50	4.34	2.25	1.56	1.21	1.00	.77	.70	.60	.53
100	8.67	4.50	3.11	2.42	2.00	1.53	1.39	1.19	1.05
200	17.34	8.99	6.21	4.83	4.00	3.06	2.77	2.37	2.10
300	26.01	13.49	9.32	7.24	6.00	4.59	4.15	3.55	3.15
400	34.68	17.98	12.42	9.65	8.00	6.12	5.53	4.73	4.20
500	43.35	22.48	15.53	12.07	9.99	7.64	6.92	5.91	5.25
600	52.02	26.97	18.63	14.48	11.99	9.17	8.30	7.09	6.30
700	60.69	31.46	21.74	16.89	13.99	10.70	9.68	8.27	7.34
800	69.36	35.96	24.84	19.30	15.99	12.23	11.06	9.45	8.39
900	78.03	40.45	27.95	21.71	17.99	13.75	12.44	10.63	9.44
1000	86.70	44.95	31.05	24.13	19.98	15.28	13.83	11.81	10.49
2000	173.40	89.89	62.10	48.25	39.96	30.56	27.65	23.62	20.97
3000	260.10	134.83	93.15	72.37	59.94	45.83	41.47	35.42	31.46
4000	346.80	179.78	124.20	96.49	79.92	61.11	55.29	47.23	41.94
5000	433.50	224.72	155.25	120.61	99.90	76.39	69.11	59.03	52.43
6000	520.20	269.66	186.30	144.73	119.88	91.66	82.93	70.84	62.91
7000	606.90	314.60	217.35	168.85	139.86	106.94	96.75	82.64	73.40
8000	693.60	359.55	248.40	192.97	159.83	122.22	110.57	94.45	83.88
9000	780.30	404.49	279.44	217.09	179.81	137.49	124.39	106.25	94.37
10000	867.00	449.43	310.49	241.21	199.79	152.77	138.22	118.06	104.85
15000	1300.50	674.15	465.74	361.81	299.68	229.15	207.32	177.08	157.28
20000	1734.00	898.86	620.98	482.42	399.58	305.54	276.43	236.11	209.70
25000	2167.50	1123.57	776.23	603.02	499.47	381.92	345.53	295.13	262.12
30000	2601.00	1348.29	931.47	723.62	599.36	458.30	414.64	354.16	314.55
35000	3034.50	1573.00	1086.71	844.23	699.26	534.69	483.74	413.18	366.97
40000	3467.99	1797.72	1241.96	964.83	799.15	611.07	552.85	472.21	419.40
45000	3901.49	2022.43	1397.20	1085.43	899.04	687.45	621.95	531.23	471.82
46000	3988.19	2067.37	1428.25	1109.55	919.02	702.73	635.77	543.04	482.31
47000	4074.89	2112.32	1459.30	1133.67	939.00	718.01	649.60	554.84	492.79
48000	4161.59	2157.26	1490.35	1157.79	958.98	733.28	663.42	566.65	503.27
49000	4248.29	2202.20	1521.40	1181.91	978.96	748.56	677.24	578.45	513.76
50000	4334.99	2247.14	1552.45	1206.04	998.94	763.84	691.06	590.26	524.24
51000	4421.69	2292.09	1583.50	1230.16	1018.91	779.11	704.88	602.06	534.73
52000	4508.39	2337.03	1614.54	1254.28	1038.89	794.39	718.70	613.87	545.21
53000	4595.09	2381.97	1645.59	1278.40	1058.87	809.67	732.52	625.67	555.70
54000	4681.79	2426.91	1676.64	1302.52	1078.85	824.94	746.34	637.48	566.18
55000	4768.49	2471.86	1707.69	1326.64	1098.83	840.22	760.16	649.28	576.67
56000	4855.19	2516.80	1738.74	1350.76	1118.81	855.50	773.99	661.09	587.15
57000	4941.89	2561.74	1769.79	1374.88	1138.79	870.77	787.81	672.89	597.64
58000	5028.59	2606.69	1800.84	1399.00	1158.76	886.05	801.63	684.70	608.12
59000	5115.29	2651.63	1831.89	1423.12	1178.74	901.33	815.45	696.50	618.61
60000	5201.99	2696.57	1862.94	1447.24	1198.72	916.60	829.27	708.31	629.09
61000	5288.69	2741.51	1893.98	1471.36	1218.70	931.88	843.09	720.11	639.58
62000	5375.39	2786.46	1925.03	1495.48	1238.68	947.16	856.91	731.92	650.06
63000	5462.09	2831.40	1956.08	1519.60	1258.66	962.43	870.73	743.72	660.55
64000	5548.79	2876.34	1987.13	1543.72	1278.64	977.71	884.55	755.53	671.03
65000	5635.49	2921.29	2018.18	1567.84	1298.61	992.99	898.38	767.33	681.52
67500	5852.24	3033.64	2095.80	1628.15	1348.56	1031.18	932.93	796.85	707.73
70000	6068.99	3146.00	2173.42	1688.45	1398.51	1069.37	967.48	826.36	733.94
75000	6502.48	3370.71	2328.67	1809.05	1498.40	1145.75	1036.59	885.38	786.36
80000	6935.98	3595.43	2483.91	1929.65	1598.29	1222.14	1105.69	944.41	838.79
85000	7369.48	3820.14	2639.16	2050.26	1698.19	1298.52	1174.80	1003.43	891.21
90000	7802.98	4044.85	2794.40	2170.86	1798.08	1374.90	1243.90	1062.46	943.64
95000	8236.48	4269.57	2949.64	2291.46	1897.97	1451.29	1313.01	1121.48	996.06
100000	8669.98	4494.28	3104.89	2412.07	1997.87	1527.67	1382.11	1180.51	1048.48
105000	9103.48	4719.00	3260.13	2532.67	2097.76	1604.05	1451.22	1239.53	1100.91
110000	9536.97	4943.71	3415.38	2653.27	2197.65	1680.44	1520.32	1298.56	1153.33
115000	9970.47	5168.42	3570.62	2773.88	2297.54	1756.82	1589.43	1357.58	1205.76
120000	10403.97	5393.14	3725.87	2894.48	2397.44	1833.20	1658.53	1416.61	1258.18
125000	10837.47	5617.85	3881.11	3015.08	2497.33	1909.59	1727.64	1475.63	1310.60
130000	11270.97	5842.57	4036.35	3135.68	2597.22	1985.97	1796.75	1534.66	1363.03
135000	11704.47	6067.28	4191.60	3256.29	2697.12	2062.35	1865.85	1593.69	1415.45
140000	12137.97	6291.99	4346.84	3376.89	2797.01	2138.74	1934.96	1652.71	1467.88
145000	12571.46	6516.71	4502.09	3497.49	2896.90	2215.12	2004.06	1711.74	1520.30
150000	13004.96	6741.42	4657.33	3618.10	2996.80	2291.50	2073.17	1770.76	1572.72

MONTHLY PAYMENT 7⅜%

NECESSARY TO AMORTIZE A LOAN

AMOUNT	15 YEARS	18 YEARS	20 YEARS	25 YEARS	28 YEARS	29 YEARS	30 YEARS	35 YEARS	40 YEARS
$ 50	.46	.42	.40	.37	.36	.35	.35	.34	.33
100	.92	.84	.80	.74	.71	.70	.70	.67	.65
200	1.84	1.68	1.60	1.47	1.41	1.40	1.39	1.34	1.30
300	2.76	2.52	2.40	2.20	2.12	2.10	2.08	2.00	1.95
400	3.68	3.36	3.20	2.93	2.82	2.79	2.77	2.67	2.60
500	4.60	4.19	3.99	3.66	3.53	3.49	3.46	3.33	3.25
600	5.52	5.03	4.79	4.39	4.23	4.19	4.15	4.00	3.90
700	6.44	5.87	5.59	5.12	4.94	4.89	4.84	4.66	4.55
800	7.36	6.71	6.39	5.85	5.64	5.58	5.53	5.33	5.20
900	8.28	7.54	7.19	6.58	6.35	6.28	6.22	5.99	5.84
1000	9.20	8.38	7.98	7.31	7.05	6.98	6.91	6.66	6.49
2000	18.40	16.76	15.96	14.62	14.09	13.95	13.82	13.31	12.98
3000	27.60	25.13	23.94	21.93	21.14	20.92	20.73	19.97	19.47
4000	36.80	33.51	31.92	29.24	28.18	27.90	27.63	26.62	25.96
5000	46.00	41.88	39.90	36.55	35.23	34.87	34.54	33.27	32.45
6000	55.20	50.26	47.88	43.86	42.27	41.84	41.45	39.93	38.94
7000	64.40	58.63	55.86	51.17	49.32	48.81	48.35	46.58	45.42
8000	73.60	67.01	63.84	58.48	56.36	55.79	55.26	53.23	51.91
9000	82.80	75.39	71.82	65.78	63.41	62.76	62.17	59.89	58.40
10000	92.00	83.76	79.80	73.09	70.45	69.73	69.07	66.54	64.89
15000	137.99	125.64	119.70	109.64	105.68	104.59	103.61	99.81	97.33
20000	183.99	167.52	159.60	146.18	140.90	139.46	138.14	133.07	129.78
25000	229.99	209.39	199.50	182.72	176.13	174.32	172.67	166.34	162.22
30000	275.98	251.27	239.40	219.27	211.35	209.18	207.21	199.61	194.66
35000	321.98	293.15	279.29	255.81	246.58	244.05	241.74	232.87	227.10
40000	367.97	335.03	319.19	292.36	281.80	278.91	276.28	266.14	259.55
45000	413.97	376.91	359.09	328.90	317.03	313.77	310.81	299.41	291.99
46000	423.17	385.28	367.07	336.21	324.07	320.75	317.72	306.06	298.48
47000	432.37	393.66	375.05	343.52	331.12	327.72	324.62	312.71	304.97
48000	441.57	402.03	383.03	350.83	338.16	334.69	331.53	319.37	311.45
49000	450.77	410.41	391.01	358.14	345.21	341.66	338.44	326.02	317.94
50000	459.97	418.78	398.99	365.44	352.25	348.64	345.34	332.67	324.43
51000	469.17	427.16	406.97	372.75	359.30	355.61	352.25	339.33	330.92
52000	478.37	435.53	414.95	380.06	366.34	362.58	359.16	345.98	337.41
53000	487.56	443.91	422.93	387.37	373.39	369.55	366.06	352.63	343.90
54000	496.76	452.29	430.91	394.68	380.43	376.53	372.97	359.29	350.39
55000	505.96	460.66	438.89	401.99	387.48	383.50	379.88	365.94	356.87
56000	515.16	469.04	446.87	409.30	394.52	390.47	386.78	372.59	363.36
57000	524.36	477.41	454.85	416.61	401.57	397.44	393.69	379.25	369.85
58000	533.56	485.79	462.83	423.92	408.61	404.42	400.60	385.90	376.34
59000	542.76	494.16	470.81	431.22	415.66	411.39	407.50	392.55	382.83
60000	551.96	502.54	478.79	438.53	422.70	418.36	414.41	399.21	389.32
61000	561.16	510.91	486.76	445.84	429.75	425.33	421.32	405.86	395.80
62000	570.36	519.29	494.74	453.15	436.79	432.31	428.22	412.51	402.29
63000	579.56	527.67	502.72	460.46	443.84	439.28	435.13	419.17	408.78
64000	588.76	536.04	510.70	467.77	450.88	446.25	442.04	425.82	415.27
65000	597.96	544.42	518.68	475.08	457.92	453.22	448.94	432.47	421.76
67500	620.95	565.36	538.63	493.35	475.54	470.66	466.21	449.11	437.98
70000	643.95	586.29	558.58	511.62	493.15	488.09	483.48	465.74	454.20
75000	689.95	628.17	598.48	548.16	528.37	522.95	518.01	499.01	486.64
80000	735.94	670.05	638.38	584.71	563.60	557.81	552.55	532.27	519.09
85000	781.94	711.93	678.28	621.25	598.82	592.68	587.08	565.54	551.53
90000	827.94	753.81	718.18	657.80	634.05	627.54	621.61	598.81	583.97
95000	873.93	795.68	758.07	694.34	669.27	662.40	656.15	632.07	616.41
100000	919.93	837.56	797.97	730.88	704.50	697.27	690.68	665.34	648.86
105000	965.92	879.44	837.87	767.43	739.72	732.13	725.21	698.61	681.30
110000	1011.92	921.32	877.77	803.97	774.95	766.99	759.75	731.87	713.74
115000	1057.92	963.19	917.67	840.52	810.17	801.86	794.28	765.14	746.18
120000	1103.91	1005.07	957.57	877.06	845.40	836.72	828.82	798.41	778.63
125000	1149.91	1046.95	997.46	913.60	880.62	871.58	863.35	831.67	811.07
130000	1195.91	1088.83	1037.36	950.15	915.84	906.44	897.88	864.94	843.51
135000	1241.90	1130.71	1077.26	986.69	951.07	941.31	932.42	898.21	875.96
140000	1287.90	1172.58	1117.16	1023.24	986.29	976.17	966.95	931.47	908.40
145000	1333.89	1214.46	1157.06	1059.78	1021.52	1011.03	1001.48	964.74	940.84
150000	1379.89	1256.34	1196.96	1096.32	1056.74	1045.90	1036.02	998.01	973.28

7½% MONTHLY PAYMENT

NECESSARY TO AMORTIZE A LOAN

AMOUNT	1 YEAR	2 YEARS	3 YEARS	4 YEARS	5 YEARS	7 YEARS	8 YEARS	10 YEARS	12 YEARS
$ 50	4.34	2.25	1.56	1.21	1.01	.77	.70	.60	.53
100	8.68	4.50	3.12	2.42	2.01	1.54	1.39	1.19	1.06
200	17.36	9.00	6.23	4.84	4.01	3.07	2.78	2.38	2.12
300	26.03	13.50	9.34	7.26	6.02	4.61	4.17	3.57	3.17
400	34.71	18.00	12.45	9.68	8.02	6.14	5.56	4.75	4.23
500	43.38	22.50	15.56	12.09	10.02	7.67	6.95	5.94	5.28
600	52.06	27.00	18.67	14.51	12.03	9.21	8.34	7.13	6.34
700	60.74	31.50	21.78	16.93	14.03	10.74	9.72	8.31	7.39
800	69.41	36.00	24.89	19.35	16.04	12.28	11.11	9.50	8.45
900	78.09	40.50	28.00	21.77	18.04	13.81	12.50	10.69	9.50
1000	86.76	45.00	31.11	24.18	20.04	15.34	13.89	11.88	10.56
2000	173.52	90.00	62.22	48.36	40.08	30.68	27.77	23.75	21.11
3000	260.28	135.00	93.32	72.54	60.12	46.02	41.66	35.62	31.66
4000	347.03	180.00	124.43	96.72	80.16	61.36	55.54	47.49	42.21
5000	433.79	225.00	155.54	120.90	100.19	76.70	69.42	59.36	52.77
6000	520.55	270.00	186.64	145.08	120.23	92.03	83.31	71.23	63.32
7000	607.31	315.00	217.75	169.26	140.27	107.37	97.19	83.10	73.87
8000	694.06	360.00	248.85	193.44	160.31	122.71	111.08	94.97	84.42
9000	780.82	405.00	279.96	217.62	180.35	138.05	124.96	106.84	94.98
10000	867.58	450.00	311.07	241.79	200.38	153.39	138.84	118.71	105.53
15000	1301.37	675.00	466.60	362.69	300.57	230.08	208.26	178.06	158.29
20000	1735.15	900.00	622.13	483.58	400.76	306.77	277.68	237.41	211.05
25000	2168.94	1124.99	777.66	604.48	500.95	383.46	347.10	296.76	263.81
30000	2602.73	1349.99	933.19	725.37	601.14	460.15	416.52	356.11	316.57
35000	3036.51	1574.99	1088.72	846.27	701.33	536.84	485.94	415.46	369.33
40000	3470.30	1799.99	1244.25	967.16	801.52	613.54	555.36	474.81	422.10
45000	3904.09	2024.99	1399.78	1088.06	901.71	690.23	624.78	534.16	474.86
46000	3990.85	2069.99	1430.89	1112.23	921.75	705.57	638.66	546.03	485.41
47000	4077.60	2114.99	1462.00	1136.41	941.79	720.90	652.55	557.90	495.96
48000	4164.36	2159.99	1493.10	1160.59	961.83	736.24	666.43	569.77	506.51
49000	4251.12	2204.99	1524.21	1184.77	981.86	751.58	680.31	581.64	517.07
50000	4337.88	2249.98	1555.32	1208.95	1001.90	766.92	694.20	593.51	527.62
51000	4424.63	2294.98	1586.42	1233.13	1021.94	782.26	708.08	605.38	538.17
52000	4511.39	2339.98	1617.53	1257.31	1041.98	797.60	721.97	617.25	548.72
53000	4598.15	2384.98	1648.63	1281.49	1062.02	812.93	735.85	629.12	559.27
54000	4684.91	2429.98	1679.74	1305.67	1082.05	828.27	749.73	640.99	569.83
55000	4771.66	2474.98	1710.85	1329.84	1102.09	843.61	763.62	652.86	580.38
56000	4858.42	2519.98	1741.95	1354.02	1122.13	858.95	777.50	664.73	590.93
57000	4945.18	2564.98	1773.06	1378.20	1142.17	874.29	791.39	676.61	601.48
58000	5031.94	2609.98	1804.17	1402.38	1162.21	889.62	805.27	688.48	612.04
59000	5118.69	2654.98	1835.27	1426.56	1182.24	904.96	819.15	700.35	622.59
60000	5205.45	2699.98	1866.38	1450.74	1202.28	920.30	833.04	712.22	633.14
61000	5292.21	2744.98	1897.48	1474.92	1222.32	935.64	846.92	724.09	643.69
62000	5378.96	2789.98	1928.59	1499.10	1242.36	950.98	860.80	735.96	654.25
63000	5465.72	2834.98	1959.70	1523.28	1262.40	966.32	874.69	747.83	664.80
64000	5552.48	2879.98	1990.80	1547.45	1282.43	981.65	888.57	759.70	675.35
65000	5639.24	2924.98	2021.91	1571.63	1302.47	996.99	902.46	771.57	685.90
67500	5856.13	3037.48	2099.67	1632.08	1352.57	1035.34	937.17	801.24	712.28
70000	6073.02	3149.98	2177.44	1692.53	1402.66	1073.68	971.88	830.92	738.66
75000	6506.81	3374.97	2332.97	1813.42	1502.85	1150.38	1041.30	890.27	791.42
80000	6940.60	3599.97	2488.50	1934.32	1603.04	1227.07	1110.71	949.62	844.19
85000	7374.39	3824.97	2644.03	2055.21	1703.23	1303.76	1180.13	1008.97	896.95
90000	7808.17	4049.97	2799.56	2176.11	1803.42	1380.45	1249.55	1068.32	949.71
95000	8241.96	4274.97	2955.10	2297.00	1903.61	1457.14	1318.97	1127.67	1002.47
100000	8675.75	4499.96	3110.63	2417.90	2003.80	1533.83	1388.39	1187.02	1055.23
105000	9109.53	4724.96	3266.16	2538.79	2103.99	1610.52	1457.81	1246.37	1107.99
110000	9543.32	4949.96	3421.69	2659.68	2204.18	1687.22	1527.23	1305.72	1160.75
115000	9977.11	5174.96	3577.22	2780.58	2304.37	1763.91	1596.65	1365.08	1213.52
120000	10410.90	5399.96	3732.75	2901.47	2404.56	1840.60	1666.07	1424.43	1266.28
125000	10844.68	5624.95	3888.28	3022.37	2504.75	1917.29	1735.49	1483.78	1319.04
130000	11278.47	5849.95	4043.81	3143.26	2604.94	1993.98	1804.91	1543.13	1371.80
135000	11712.26	6074.95	4199.34	3264.16	2705.13	2070.67	1874.33	1602.48	1424.56
140000	12146.04	6299.95	4354.88	3385.05	2805.32	2147.36	1943.75	1661.83	1477.32
145000	12579.83	6524.95	4510.41	3505.95	2905.51	2224.05	2013.17	1721.18	1530.08
150000	13013.62	6749.94	4665.94	3626.84	3005.70	2300.75	2082.59	1780.53	1582.84

MONTHLY PAYMENT 7½%
NECESSARY TO AMORTIZE A LOAN

AMOUNT	15 YEARS	18 YEARS	20 YEARS	25 YEARS	28 YEARS	29 YEARS	30 YEARS	35 YEARS	40 YEARS
$ 50	.47	.43	.41	.37	.36	.36	.35	.34	.33
100	.93	.85	.81	.74	.72	.71	.70	.68	.66
200	1.86	1.69	1.62	1.48	1.43	1.42	1.40	1.35	1.32
300	2.79	2.54	2.42	2.22	2.14	2.12	2.10	2.03	1.98
400	3.71	3.38	3.23	2.96	2.86	2.83	2.80	2.70	2.64
500	4.64	4.23	4.03	3.70	3.57	3.53	3.50	3.38	3.30
600	5.57	5.07	4.84	4.44	4.28	4.24	4.20	4.05	3.95
700	6.49	5.92	5.64	5.18	5.00	4.95	4.90	4.72	4.61
800	7.42	6.76	6.45	5.92	5.71	5.65	5.60	5.40	5.27
900	8.35	7.61	7.26	6.66	6.42	6.36	6.30	6.07	5.93
1000	9.28	8.45	8.06	7.39	7.13	7.06	7.00	6.75	6.59
2000	18.55	16.90	16.12	14.78	14.26	14.12	13.99	13.49	13.17
3000	27.82	25.35	24.17	22.17	21.39	21.18	20.98	20.23	19.75
4000	37.09	33.80	32.23	29.56	28.52	28.23	27.97	26.97	26.33
5000	46.36	42.25	40.28	36.95	35.65	35.29	34.97	33.72	32.91
6000	55.63	50.70	48.34	44.34	42.78	42.35	41.96	40.46	39.49
7000	64.90	59.15	56.40	51.73	49.91	49.41	48.95	47.20	46.07
8000	74.17	67.60	64.45	59.12	57.03	56.46	55.94	53.94	52.65
9000	83.44	76.05	72.51	66.51	64.16	63.52	62.93	60.69	59.23
10000	92.71	84.50	80.56	73.90	71.29	70.58	69.93	67.43	65.81
15000	139.06	126.75	120.84	110.85	106.94	105.86	104.89	101.14	98.72
20000	185.41	169.00	161.12	147.80	142.58	141.15	139.85	134.85	131.62
25000	231.76	211.25	201.40	184.75	178.22	176.44	174.81	168.57	164.52
30000	278.11	253.50	241.68	221.70	213.87	211.72	209.77	202.28	197.43
35000	324.46	295.75	281.96	258.65	249.51	247.01	244.73	235.99	230.33
40000	370.81	337.99	322.24	295.60	285.15	282.29	279.69	269.70	263.23
45000	417.16	380.24	362.52	332.55	320.80	317.58	314.65	303.41	296.14
46000	426.43	388.69	370.58	339.94	327.92	324.64	321.64	310.16	302.72
47000	435.70	397.14	378.63	347.33	335.05	331.69	328.64	316.90	309.30
48000	444.97	405.59	386.69	354.72	342.18	338.75	335.63	323.64	315.88
49000	454.24	414.04	394.75	362.11	349.31	345.81	342.62	330.38	322.46
50000	463.51	422.49	402.80	369.50	356.44	352.87	349.61	337.13	329.04
51000	472.78	430.94	410.86	376.89	363.57	359.92	356.60	343.87	335.62
52000	482.05	439.39	418.91	384.28	370.70	366.98	363.60	350.61	342.20
53000	491.32	447.84	426.97	391.67	377.82	374.04	370.59	357.35	348.78
54000	500.59	456.29	435.03	399.06	384.95	381.09	377.58	364.10	355.36
55000	509.86	464.74	443.08	406.45	392.08	388.15	384.57	370.84	361.94
56000	519.13	473.19	451.14	413.84	399.21	395.21	391.57	377.58	368.52
57000	528.40	481.64	459.19	421.23	406.34	402.27	398.56	384.32	375.11
58000	537.67	490.09	467.25	428.62	413.47	409.32	405.55	391.07	381.69
59000	546.94	498.54	475.30	436.01	420.60	416.38	412.54	397.81	388.27
60000	556.21	506.99	483.36	443.40	427.73	423.44	419.53	404.55	394.85
61000	565.48	515.44	491.42	450.79	434.85	430.49	426.53	411.29	401.43
62000	574.75	523.89	499.47	458.18	441.98	437.55	433.52	418.04	408.01
63000	584.02	532.34	507.53	465.57	449.11	444.61	440.51	424.78	414.59
64000	593.29	540.79	515.58	472.96	456.24	451.67	447.50	431.52	421.17
65000	602.56	549.24	523.64	480.35	463.37	458.72	454.49	438.26	427.75
67500	625.74	570.36	543.78	498.82	481.19	476.37	471.97	455.12	444.20
70000	648.91	591.49	563.92	517.30	499.01	494.01	489.46	471.97	460.65
75000	695.26	633.73	604.20	554.25	534.66	529.30	524.42	505.69	493.56
80000	741.61	675.98	644.48	591.20	570.30	564.58	559.38	539.40	526.46
85000	787.97	718.23	684.76	628.15	605.94	599.87	594.34	573.11	559.37
90000	834.32	760.48	725.04	665.10	641.59	635.15	629.30	606.82	592.27
95000	880.67	802.73	765.32	702.05	677.23	670.44	664.26	640.54	625.17
100000	927.02	844.98	805.60	739.00	712.87	705.73	699.22	674.25	658.08
105000	973.37	887.23	845.88	775.95	748.52	741.01	734.18	707.96	690.98
110000	1019.72	929.48	886.16	812.90	784.16	776.30	769.14	741.67	723.88
115000	1066.07	971.72	926.44	849.84	819.80	811.58	804.10	775.38	756.79
120000	1112.42	1013.97	966.72	886.79	855.45	846.87	839.06	809.10	789.69
125000	1158.77	1056.22	1007.00	923.74	891.09	882.16	874.02	842.81	822.59
130000	1205.12	1098.47	1047.28	960.69	926.73	917.44	908.98	876.52	855.50
135000	1251.47	1140.72	1087.56	997.64	962.38	952.73	943.94	910.23	888.40
140000	1297.82	1182.97	1127.84	1034.59	998.02	988.01	978.91	943.94	921.30
145000	1344.17	1225.22	1168.12	1071.54	1033.66	1023.30	1013.87	977.66	954.21
150000	1390.52	1267.46	1208.39	1108.49	1069.31	1058.59	1048.83	1011.37	987.11

13

7⅝% MONTHLY PAYMENT
NECESSARY TO AMORTIZE A LOAN

AMOUNT	1 YEAR	2 YEARS	3 YEARS	4 YEARS	5 YEARS	7 YEARS	8 YEARS	10 YEARS	12 YEARS
$ 50	4.35	2.26	1.56	1.22	1.01	.78	.70	.60	.54
100	8.69	4.51	3.12	2.43	2.01	1.55	1.40	1.20	1.07
200	17.37	9.02	6.24	4.85	4.02	3.09	2.79	2.39	2.13
300	26.05	13.52	9.35	7.28	6.03	4.63	4.19	3.59	3.19
400	34.73	18.03	12.47	9.70	8.04	6.17	5.58	4.78	4.25
500	43.41	22.53	15.59	12.12	10.05	7.71	6.98	5.97	5.31
600	52.09	27.04	18.70	14.55	12.06	9.25	8.37	7.17	6.38
700	60.78	31.54	21.82	16.97	14.07	10.79	9.77	8.36	7.44
800	69.46	36.05	24.94	19.39	16.08	12.33	11.16	9.55	8.50
900	78.14	40.56	28.05	21.82	18.09	13.87	12.56	10.75	9.56
1000	86.82	45.06	31.17	24.24	20.10	15.41	13.95	11.94	10.62
2000	173.64	90.12	62.33	48.48	40.20	30.81	27.90	23.88	21.24
3000	260.45	135.17	93.50	72.72	60.30	46.21	41.85	35.81	31.86
4000	347.27	180.23	124.66	96.95	80.39	61.61	55.79	47.75	42.48
5000	434.08	225.29	155.82	121.19	100.49	77.01	69.74	59.68	53.10
6000	520.90	270.34	186.99	145.43	120.59	92.41	83.69	71.62	63.72
7000	607.71	315.40	218.15	169.67	140.69	107.81	97.63	83.55	74.34
8000	694.53	360.46	249.31	193.90	160.78	123.21	111.58	95.49	84.96
9000	781.34	405.51	280.48	218.14	180.88	138.61	125.53	107.42	95.58
10000	868.16	450.57	311.64	242.38	200.98	154.01	139.47	119.36	106.20
15000	1302.23	675.85	467.46	363.56	301.47	231.01	209.21	179.04	159.30
20000	1736.31	901.13	623.28	484.75	401.95	308.01	278.94	238.72	212.40
25000	2170.38	1126.42	779.10	605.94	502.44	385.01	348.68	298.39	265.50
30000	2604.46	1351.70	934.91	727.12	602.93	462.01	418.41	358.07	318.60
35000	3038.53	1576.98	1090.73	848.31	703.41	539.01	488.14	417.75	371.70
40000	3472.61	1802.26	1246.55	969.50	803.90	616.01	557.88	477.43	424.80
45000	3906.69	2027.55	1402.37	1090.68	904.39	693.01	627.61	537.10	477.90
46000	3993.50	2072.60	1433.53	1114.92	924.49	708.41	641.56	549.04	488.52
47000	4080.32	2117.66	1464.70	1139.16	944.58	723.81	655.51	560.97	499.14
48000	4167.13	2162.71	1495.86	1163.39	964.68	739.21	669.45	572.91	509.76
49000	4253.95	2207.77	1527.03	1187.63	984.78	754.61	683.40	584.85	520.38
50000	4340.76	2252.83	1558.19	1211.87	1004.88	770.01	697.35	596.78	531.00
51000	4427.58	2297.88	1589.35	1236.11	1024.97	785.41	711.29	608.72	541.62
52000	4514.39	2342.94	1620.52	1260.34	1045.07	800.81	725.24	620.65	552.24
53000	4601.21	2388.00	1651.68	1284.58	1065.17	816.21	739.19	632.59	562.86
54000	4688.02	2433.05	1682.84	1308.82	1085.26	831.61	753.13	644.52	573.48
55000	4774.84	2478.11	1714.01	1333.06	1105.36	847.01	767.08	656.46	584.10
56000	4861.65	2523.17	1745.17	1357.29	1125.46	862.41	781.03	668.39	594.72
57000	4948.47	2568.22	1776.33	1381.53	1145.56	877.81	794.97	680.33	605.34
58000	5035.28	2613.28	1807.50	1405.77	1165.65	893.21	808.92	692.27	615.96
59000	5122.10	2658.34	1838.66	1430.00	1185.75	908.61	822.87	704.20	626.58
60000	5208.91	2703.39	1869.82	1454.24	1205.85	924.01	836.81	716.14	637.20
61000	5295.73	2748.45	1900.99	1478.48	1225.95	939.41	850.76	728.07	647.82
62000	5382.54	2793.51	1932.15	1502.72	1246.04	954.81	864.71	740.01	658.44
63000	5469.36	2838.56	1963.32	1526.95	1266.14	970.21	878.65	751.94	669.06
64000	5556.17	2883.62	1994.48	1551.19	1286.24	985.61	892.60	763.88	679.68
65000	5642.99	2928.67	2025.64	1575.43	1306.34	1001.01	906.55	775.81	690.30
67500	5860.03	3041.32	2103.55	1636.02	1356.58	1039.51	941.42	805.65	716.85
70000	6077.06	3153.96	2181.46	1696.61	1406.82	1078.01	976.28	835.49	743.40
75000	6511.14	3379.24	2337.28	1817.80	1507.31	1155.01	1046.02	895.17	796.50
80000	6945.22	3604.52	2493.10	1938.99	1607.80	1232.01	1115.75	954.85	849.60
85000	7379.29	3829.80	2648.92	2060.17	1708.28	1309.01	1185.49	1014.52	902.70
90000	7813.37	4055.09	2804.73	2181.36	1808.77	1386.01	1255.22	1074.20	955.80
95000	8247.44	4280.37	2960.55	2302.55	1909.26	1463.01	1324.95	1133.88	1008.90
100000	8681.52	4505.65	3116.37	2423.73	2009.75	1540.01	1394.69	1193.56	1062.00
105000	9115.59	4730.93	3272.19	2544.92	2110.23	1617.01	1464.42	1253.23	1115.10
110000	9549.67	4956.21	3428.01	2666.11	2210.72	1694.01	1534.16	1312.91	1168.20
115000	9983.75	5181.50	3583.83	2787.29	2311.21	1771.01	1603.89	1372.59	1221.30
120000	10417.82	5406.78	3739.64	2908.48	2411.69	1848.01	1673.62	1432.27	1274.40
125000	10851.90	5632.06	3895.46	3029.66	2512.18	1925.01	1743.36	1491.94	1327.50
130000	11285.97	5857.34	4051.28	3150.85	2612.67	2002.01	1813.09	1551.62	1380.60
135000	11720.05	6082.63	4207.10	3272.04	2713.15	2079.01	1882.83	1611.30	1433.70
140000	12154.12	6307.91	4362.92	3393.22	2813.64	2156.01	1952.56	1670.98	1486.80
145000	12588.20	6533.19	4518.74	3514.41	2914.13	2233.01	2022.29	1730.66	1539.90
150000	13022.28	6758.47	4674.55	3635.60	3014.62	2310.01	2092.03	1790.33	1593.00

AMOUNT	15 YEARS	18 YEARS	20 YEARS	25 YEARS	28 YEARS	29 YEARS	30 YEARS	35 YEARS	40 YEARS
$ 50	.47	.43	.41	.38	.37	.36	.36	.35	.34
100	.94	.86	.82	.75	.73	.72	.71	.69	.67
200	1.87	1.71	1.63	1.50	1.45	1.43	1.42	1.37	1.34
300	2.81	2.56	2.44	2.25	2.17	2.15	2.13	2.05	2.01
400	3.74	3.41	3.26	2.99	2.89	2.86	2.84	2.74	2.67
500	4.68	4.27	4.07	3.74	3.61	3.58	3.54	3.42	3.34
600	5.61	5.12	4.88	4.49	4.33	4.29	4.25	4.10	4.01
700	6.54	5.97	5.70	5.23	5.05	5.00	4.96	4.79	4.68
800	7.48	6.82	6.51	5.98	5.78	5.72	5.67	5.47	5.34
900	8.41	7.68	7.32	6.73	6.50	6.43	6.38	6.15	6.01
1000	9.35	8.53	8.14	7.48	7.22	7.15	7.08	6.84	6.68
2000	18.69	17.05	16.27	14.95	14.43	14.29	14.16	13.67	13.35
3000	28.03	25.58	24.40	22.42	21.64	21.43	21.24	20.50	20.02
4000	37.37	34.10	32.54	29.89	28.86	28.57	28.32	27.33	26.70
5000	46.71	42.63	40.67	37.36	36.07	35.72	35.39	34.16	33.37
6000	56.05	51.15	48.80	44.83	43.28	42.86	42.47	41.00	40.04
7000	65.39	59.67	56.93	52.30	50.49	50.00	49.55	47.83	46.72
8000	74.74	68.20	65.07	59.78	57.71	57.14	56.63	54.66	53.39
9000	84.08	76.72	73.20	67.25	64.92	64.28	63.71	61.49	60.06
10000	93.42	85.25	81.33	74.72	72.13	71.43	70.78	68.32	66.74
15000	140.12	127.87	121.99	112.08	108.20	107.14	106.17	102.48	100.10
20000	186.83	170.49	162.66	149.43	144.26	142.85	141.56	136.64	133.47
25000	233.54	213.11	203.32	186.79	180.33	178.56	176.95	170.80	166.84
30000	280.24	255.73	243.98	224.15	216.39	214.27	212.34	204.96	200.20
35000	326.95	298.35	284.64	261.50	252.45	249.98	247.73	239.12	233.57
40000	373.66	340.97	325.31	298.86	288.52	285.69	283.12	273.28	266.94
45000	420.36	383.60	365.97	336.22	324.58	321.40	318.51	307.44	300.30
46000	429.70	392.12	374.10	343.69	331.79	328.55	325.59	314.27	306.98
47000	439.05	400.64	382.23	351.16	339.01	335.69	332.67	321.10	313.65
48000	448.39	409.17	390.37	358.63	346.22	342.83	339.75	327.94	320.33
49000	457.73	417.69	398.50	366.10	353.43	349.97	346.82	334.77	327.00
50000	467.07	426.22	406.63	373.58	360.65	357.11	353.90	341.60	333.67
51000	476.41	434.74	414.76	381.05	367.86	364.26	360.98	348.43	340.34
52000	485.75	443.26	422.90	388.52	375.07	371.40	368.06	355.26	347.02
53000	495.09	451.79	431.03	395.99	382.28	378.54	375.14	362.10	353.69
54000	504.44	460.31	439.16	403.46	389.50	385.68	382.21	368.93	360.36
55000	513.78	468.84	447.29	410.93	396.71	392.83	389.29	375.76	367.03
56000	523.12	477.36	455.43	418.40	403.92	399.97	396.37	382.59	373.71
57000	532.46	485.89	463.56	425.88	411.14	407.11	403.45	389.42	380.38
58000	541.80	494.41	471.69	433.35	418.35	414.25	410.53	396.26	387.05
59000	551.14	502.93	479.82	440.82	425.56	421.39	417.60	403.09	393.73
60000	560.48	511.46	487.96	448.29	432.77	428.54	424.68	409.92	400.40
61000	569.82	519.98	496.09	455.76	439.99	435.68	431.76	416.75	407.07
62000	579.17	528.51	504.22	463.23	447.20	442.82	438.84	423.58	413.75
63000	588.51	537.03	512.35	470.70	454.41	449.96	445.92	430.41	420.42
64000	597.85	545.56	520.49	478.18	461.63	457.10	452.99	437.25	427.09
65000	607.19	554.08	528.62	485.65	468.84	464.25	460.07	444.08	433.77
67500	630.54	575.39	548.95	504.33	486.87	482.10	477.77	461.16	450.45
70000	653.90	596.70	569.28	523.00	504.90	499.96	495.46	478.24	467.13
75000	700.60	639.32	609.95	560.36	540.97	535.67	530.85	512.40	500.50
80000	747.31	681.94	650.61	597.72	577.03	571.38	566.24	546.56	533.87
85000	794.02	724.56	691.27	635.07	613.10	607.09	601.63	580.72	567.23
90000	840.72	767.19	731.93	672.43	649.16	642.80	637.02	614.88	600.60
95000	887.43	809.81	772.60	709.79	685.22	678.51	672.41	649.04	633.97
100000	934.13	852.43	813.26	747.15	721.29	714.22	707.80	683.19	667.33
105000	980.84	895.05	853.92	784.50	757.35	749.93	743.19	717.35	700.70
110000	1027.55	937.67	894.58	821.86	793.42	785.65	778.58	751.51	734.06
115000	1074.25	980.29	935.25	859.22	829.48	821.36	813.97	785.67	767.43
120000	1120.96	1022.91	975.91	896.57	865.54	857.07	849.36	819.83	800.80
125000	1167.67	1065.53	1016.57	933.93	901.61	892.78	884.75	853.99	834.16
130000	1214.37	1108.15	1057.23	971.29	937.67	928.49	920.14	888.15	867.53
135000	1261.08	1150.78	1097.90	1008.65	973.74	964.20	955.53	922.31	900.90
140000	1307.79	1193.40	1138.56	1046.00	1009.80	999.91	990.92	956.47	934.26
145000	1354.49	1236.02	1179.22	1083.36	1045.86	1035.62	1026.31	990.63	967.63
150000	1401.20	1278.64	1219.89	1120.72	1081.93	1071.33	1061.70	1024.79	1001.00

MONTHLY PAYMENT
NECESSARY TO AMORTIZE A LOAN

AMOUNT	1 YEAR	2 YEARS	3 YEARS	4 YEARS	5 YEARS	7 YEARS	8 YEARS	10 YEARS	12 YEARS
$ 50	4.35	2.26	1.57	1.22	1.01	.78	.71	.61	54
100	8.69	4.52	3.13	2.43	2.02	1.55	1.41	1.21	1.07
200	17.38	9.03	6.25	4.86	4.04	3.10	2.81	2.41	2.14
300	26.07	13.54	9.37	7.29	6.05	4.64	4.21	3.61	3.21
400	34.75	18.05	12.49	9.72	8.07	6.19	5.61	4.81	4.28
500	43.44	22.56	15.62	12.15	10.08	7.74	7.01	6.01	5.35
600	52.13	27.07	18.74	14.58	12.10	9.28	8.41	7.21	6.42
700	60.82	31.58	21.86	17.01	14.11	10.83	9.81	8.41	7.49
800	69.50	36.10	24.98	19.44	16.13	12.37	11.21	9.61	8.56
900	78.19	40.61	28.10	21.87	18.15	13.92	12.61	10.81	9.62
1000	86.88	45.12	31.23	24.30	20.16	15.47	14.01	12.01	10.69
2000	173.75	90.23	62.45	48.60	40.32	30.93	28.02	24.01	21.38
3000	260.62	135.35	93.67	72.89	60.48	46.39	42.03	36.01	32.07
4000	347.50	180.46	124.89	97.19	80.63	61.85	56.04	48.01	42.76
5000	434.37	225.57	156.11	121.48	100.79	77.31	70.05	60.01	53.44
6000	521.24	270.69	187.33	145.78	120.95	92.78	84.06	72.01	64.13
7000	608.12	315.80	218.55	170.08	141.10	108.24	98.07	84.01	74.82
8000	694.99	360.91	249.77	194.37	161.26	123.70	112.08	96.01	85.51
9000	781.86	406.03	281.00	218.67	181.42	139.16	126.09	108.01	96.20
10000	868.73	451.14	312.22	242.96	201.57	154.62	140.10	120.02	106.88
15000	1303.10	676.71	468.32	364.44	302.36	231.93	210.15	180.02	160.32
20000	1737.46	902.27	624.43	485.92	403.14	309.24	280.20	240.03	213.76
25000	2171.83	1127.84	780.53	607.40	503.93	386.55	350.25	300.03	267.20
30000	2606.19	1353.41	936.64	728.88	604.71	463.86	420.30	360.04	320.64
35000	3040.56	1578.97	1092.75	850.36	705.50	541.17	490.35	420.04	374.08
40000	3474.92	1804.54	1248.85	971.83	806.28	618.48	560.40	480.05	427.52
45000	3909.28	2030.11	1404.96	1093.31	907.07	695.79	630.45	540.05	480.96
46000	3996.16	2075.22	1436.18	1117.61	927.23	711.25	644.46	552.05	491.65
47000	4083.03	2120.33	1467.40	1141.90	947.38	726.72	658.47	564.05	502.34
48000	4169.90	2165.45	1498.62	1166.20	967.54	742.18	672.48	576.06	513.03
49000	4256.78	2210.56	1529.84	1190.50	987.70	757.64	686.49	588.06	523.71
50000	4343.65	2255.67	1561.06	1214.79	1007.85	773.10	700.50	600.06	534.40
51000	4430.52	2300.79	1592.28	1239.09	1028.01	788.56	714.51	612.06	545.09
52000	4517.39	2345.90	1623.51	1263.38	1048.17	804.03	728.52	624.06	555.78
53000	4604.27	2391.01	1654.73	1287.68	1068.32	819.49	742.53	636.06	566.46
54000	4691.14	2436.13	1685.95	1311.98	1088.48	834.95	756.54	648.06	577.15
55000	4778.01	2481.24	1717.17	1336.27	1108.64	850.41	770.55	660.06	587.84
56000	4864.89	2526.35	1748.39	1360.57	1128.79	865.87	784.56	672.06	598.53
57000	4951.76	2571.47	1779.61	1384.86	1148.95	881.34	798.57	684.07	609.22
58000	5038.63	2616.58	1810.83	1409.16	1169.11	896.80	812.58	696.07	619.90
59000	5125.50	2661.69	1842.05	1433.45	1189.27	912.26	826.59	708.07	630.59
60000	5212.38	2706.81	1873.27	1457.75	1209.42	927.72	840.60	720.07	641.28
61000	5299.25	2751.92	1904.50	1482.05	1229.58	943.18	854.61	732.07	651.97
62000	5386.12	2797.03	1935.72	1506.34	1249.74	958.65	868.62	744.07	662.66
63000	5473.00	2842.15	1966.94	1530.64	1269.89	974.11	882.63	756.07	673.34
64000	5559.87	2887.26	1998.16	1554.93	1290.05	989.57	896.64	768.07	684.03
65000	5646.74	2932.37	2029.38	1579.23	1310.21	1005.03	910.65	780.07	694.72
67500	5863.92	3045.16	2107.43	1639.97	1360.60	1043.69	945.68	810.08	721.44
70000	6081.11	3157.94	2185.49	1700.71	1410.99	1082.34	980.70	840.08	748.16
75000	6515.47	3383.51	2341.59	1822.19	1511.78	1159.65	1050.75	900.08	801.60
80000	6949.84	3609.07	2497.70	1943.66	1612.56	1236.96	1120.80	960.09	855.04
85000	7384.20	3834.64	2653.80	2065.14	1713.35	1314.27	1190.85	1020.10	908.48
90000	7818.56	4060.21	2809.91	2186.62	1814.13	1391.58	1260.90	1080.10	961.92
95000	8252.93	4285.77	2966.02	2308.10	1914.92	1468.89	1330.95	1140.11	1015.36
100000	8687.29	4511.34	3122.12	2429.58	2015.70	1546.20	1401.00	1200.11	1068.80
105000	9121.66	4736.91	3278.23	2551.06	2116.49	1623.51	1471.05	1260.12	1122.24
110000	9556.02	4962.47	3434.33	2672.54	2217.27	1700.82	1541.10	1320.12	1175.68
115000	9990.39	5188.04	3590.44	2794.02	2318.06	1778.13	1611.15	1380.13	1229.12
120000	10424.75	5413.61	3746.54	2915.49	2418.84	1855.44	1681.20	1440.13	1282.56
125000	10859.12	5639.17	3902.65	3036.97	2519.62	1932.75	1751.25	1500.14	1336.00
130000	11293.48	5864.74	4058.76	3158.45	2620.41	2010.06	1821.30	1560.14	1389.43
135000	11727.84	6090.31	4214.86	3279.93	2721.19	2087.37	1891.35	1620.15	1442.87
140000	12162.21	6315.87	4370.97	3401.41	2821.98	2164.68	1961.40	1680.15	1496.31
145000	12596.57	6541.44	4527.07	3522.89	2922.76	2241.99	2031.45	1740.16	1549.75
150000	13030.94	6767.01	4683.18	3644.37	3023.55	2319.30	2101.50	1800.16	1603.19

MONTHLY PAYMENT 7¾%

NECESSARY TO AMORTIZE A LOAN

AMOUNT	15 YEARS	18 YEARS	20 YEARS	25 YEARS	28 YEARS	29 YEARS	30 YEARS	35 YEARS	40 YEARS
$ 50	.48	.43	.42	.38	.37	.37	.36	.35	.34
100	.95	.86	.83	.76	.73	.73	.72	.70	.68
200	1.89	1.72	1.65	1.52	1.46	1.45	1.44	1.39	1.36
300	2.83	2.58	2.47	2.27	2.19	2.17	2.15	2.08	2.03
400	3.77	3.44	3.29	3.03	2.92	2.90	2.87	2.77	2.71
500	4.71	4.30	4.11	3.78	3.65	3.62	3.59	3.47	3.39
600	5.65	5.16	4.93	4.54	4.38	4.34	4.30	4.16	4.06
700	6.59	6.02	5.75	5.29	5.11	5.06	5.02	4.85	4.74
800	7.54	6.88	6.57	6.05	5.84	5.79	5.74	5.54	5.42
900	8.48	7.74	7.39	6.80	6.57	6.51	6.45	6.23	6.09
1000	9.42	8.60	8.21	7.56	7.30	7.23	7.17	6.93	6.77
2000	18.83	17.20	16.42	15.11	14.60	14.46	14.33	13.85	13.54
3000	28.24	25.80	24.63	22.66	21.90	21.69	21.50	20.77	20.30
4000	37.66	34.40	32.84	30.22	29.19	28.92	28.66	27.69	27.07
5000	47.07	43.00	41.05	37.77	36.49	36.14	35.83	34.61	33.84
6000	56.48	51.60	49.26	45.32	43.79	43.37	42.99	41.54	40.60
7000	65.89	60.20	57.47	52.88	51.09	50.60	50.15	48.46	47.37
8000	75.31	68.80	65.68	60.43	58.38	57.83	57.32	55.38	54.13
9000	84.72	77.40	73.89	67.98	65.68	65.05	64.48	62.30	60.90
10000	94.13	86.00	82.10	75.54	72.98	72.28	71.65	69.22	67.67
15000	141.20	128.99	123.15	113.30	109.47	108.42	107.47	103.83	101.50
20000	188.26	171.99	164.19	151.07	145.95	144.56	143.29	138.44	135.33
25000	235.32	214.98	205.24	188.84	182.44	180.69	179.11	173.05	169.16
30000	282.39	257.98	246.29	226.60	218.93	216.83	214.93	207.66	202.99
35000	329.45	300.97	287.34	264.37	255.41	252.97	250.75	242.27	236.82
40000	376.52	343.97	328.38	302.14	291.90	289.11	286.57	276.88	270.65
45000	423.58	386.96	369.43	339.90	328.39	325.25	322.39	311.48	304.48
46000	432.99	395.56	377.64	347.46	335.68	332.47	329.55	318.41	311.25
47000	442.40	404.16	385.85	355.01	342.98	339.70	336.72	325.33	318.02
48000	451.82	412.76	394.06	362.56	350.28	346.93	343.88	332.25	324.78
49000	461.23	421.36	402.27	370.12	357.58	354.16	351.05	339.17	331.55
50000	470.64	429.96	410.48	377.67	364.87	361.38	358.21	346.09	338.31
51000	480.06	438.56	418.69	385.22	372.17	368.61	365.38	353.01	345.08
52000	489.47	447.16	426.90	392.78	379.47	375.84	372.54	359.94	351.85
53000	498.88	455.75	435.11	400.33	386.77	383.07	379.70	366.86	358.61
54000	508.29	464.35	443.32	407.88	394.06	390.29	386.87	373.78	365.38
55000	517.71	472.95	451.53	415.44	401.36	397.52	394.03	380.70	372.15
56000	527.12	481.55	459.74	422.99	408.66	404.75	401.20	387.62	378.91
57000	536.53	490.15	467.95	430.54	415.95	411.98	408.36	394.55	385.68
58000	545.94	498.75	476.16	438.10	423.25	419.20	415.52	401.47	392.44
59000	555.36	507.35	484.36	445.65	430.55	426.43	422.69	408.39	399.21
60000	564.77	515.95	492.57	453.20	437.85	433.66	429.85	415.31	405.98
61000	574.18	524.55	500.78	460.76	445.14	440.89	437.02	422.23	412.74
62000	583.60	533.15	508.99	468.31	452.44	448.11	444.18	429.15	419.51
63000	593.01	541.74	517.20	475.86	459.74	455.34	451.34	436.08	426.28
64000	602.42	550.34	525.41	483.42	467.04	462.57	458.51	443.00	433.04
65000	611.83	558.94	533.62	490.97	474.33	469.80	465.67	449.92	439.81
67500	635.37	580.44	554.15	509.85	492.58	487.87	483.58	467.22	456.72
70000	658.90	601.94	574.67	528.74	510.82	505.93	501.49	484.53	473.64
75000	705.96	644.93	615.72	566.50	547.31	542.07	537.31	519.14	507.47
80000	753.03	687.93	656.76	604.27	583.79	578.21	573.13	553.75	541.30
85000	800.09	730.92	697.81	642.03	620.28	614.35	608.96	588.35	575.13
90000	847.15	773.92	738.86	679.80	656.77	650.49	644.78	622.96	608.96
95000	894.22	816.91	779.91	717.57	693.25	686.62	680.60	657.57	642.79
100000	941.28	859.91	820.95	755.33	729.74	722.76	716.42	692.18	676.62
105000	988.34	902.90	862.00	793.10	766.23	758.90	752.24	726.79	710.46
110000	1035.41	945.90	903.05	830.87	802.71	795.04	788.06	761.40	744.29
115000	1082.47	988.89	944.10	868.63	839.20	831.17	823.88	796.01	778.12
120000	1129.54	1031.89	985.14	906.40	875.69	867.31	859.70	830.62	811.95
125000	1176.60	1074.88	1026.19	944.17	912.18	903.45	895.52	865.22	845.78
130000	1223.66	1117.88	1067.24	981.93	948.66	939.59	931.34	899.83	879.61
135000	1270.73	1160.88	1108.29	1019.70	985.15	975.73	967.16	934.44	913.44
140000	1317.79	1203.87	1149.33	1057.47	1021.64	1011.86	1002.98	969.05	947.27
145000	1364.85	1246.87	1190.38	1095.23	1058.12	1048.00	1038.80	1003.66	981.10
150000	1411.92	1289.86	1231.43	1133.00	1094.61	1084.14	1074.62	1038.27	1014.93

7⅞% MONTHLY PAYMENT
NECESSARY TO AMORTIZE A LOAN

AMOUNT	1 YEAR	2 YEARS	3 YEARS	4 YEARS	5 YEARS	7 YEARS	8 YEARS	10 YEARS	12 YEARS
$ 50	4.35	2.26	1.57	1.22	1.02	.78	.71	.61	.54
100	8.70	4.52	3.13	2.44	2.03	1.56	1.41	1.21	1.08
200	17.39	9.04	6.26	4.88	4.05	3.11	2.82	2.42	2.16
300	26.08	13.56	9.39	7.31	6.07	4.66	4.23	3.63	3.23
400	34.78	18.07	12.52	9.75	8.09	6.21	5.63	4.83	4.31
500	43.47	22.59	15.64	12.18	10.11	7.77	7.04	6.04	5.38
600	52.16	27.11	18.77	14.62	12.13	9.32	8.45	7.25	6.46
700	60.86	31.62	21.90	17.05	14.16	10.87	9.86	8.45	7.53
800	69.55	36.14	25.03	19.49	16.18	12.42	11.26	9.66	8.61
900	78.24	40.66	28.16	21.92	18.20	13.98	12.67	10.87	9.69
1000	86.94	45.18	31.28	24.36	20.22	15.53	14.08	12.07	10.76
2000	173.87	90.35	62.56	48.71	40.44	31.05	28.15	24.14	21.52
3000	260.80	135.52	93.84	73.07	60.65	46.58	42.22	36.21	32.27
4000	347.73	180.69	125.12	97.42	80.87	62.10	56.30	48.27	43.03
5000	434.66	225.86	156.40	121.78	101.09	77.63	70.37	60.34	53.79
6000	521.59	271.03	187.68	146.13	121.30	93.15	84.44	72.41	64.54
7000	608.52	316.20	218.96	170.49	141.52	108.67	98.52	84.47	75.30
8000	695.45	361.37	250.23	194.84	161.74	124.20	112.59	96.54	86.05
9000	782.38	406.54	281.51	219.19	181.95	139.72	126.66	108.61	96.81
10000	869.31	451.71	312.79	243.55	202.17	155.25	140.74	120.67	107.57
15000	1303.96	677.56	469.19	365.32	303.25	232.87	211.10	181.01	161.35
20000	1738.62	903.41	625.58	487.09	404.34	310.49	281.47	241.34	215.13
25000	2173.27	1129.26	781.97	608.86	505.42	388.11	351.84	301.68	268.91
30000	2607.92	1355.11	938.37	730.63	606.50	465.73	422.20	362.01	322.69
35000	3042.58	1580.97	1094.76	852.41	707.59	543.35	492.57	422.34	376.47
40000	3477.23	1806.82	1251.15	974.18	808.67	620.97	562.93	482.68	430.25
45000	3911.88	2032.67	1407.55	1095.95	909.75	698.59	633.30	543.01	484.03
46000	3998.81	2077.84	1438.83	1120.30	929.97	714.11	647.37	555.08	494.79
47000	4085.75	2123.01	1470.11	1144.66	950.19	729.63	661.45	567.15	505.54
48000	4172.68	2168.18	1501.38	1169.01	970.40	745.16	675.52	579.21	516.30
49000	4259.61	2213.35	1532.66	1193.37	990.62	760.68	689.59	591.28	527.05
50000	4346.54	2258.52	1563.94	1217.72	1010.84	776.21	703.67	603.35	537.81
51000	4433.47	2303.69	1595.22	1242.07	1031.05	791.73	717.74	615.41	548.57
52000	4520.40	2348.86	1626.50	1266.43	1051.27	807.25	731.81	627.48	559.32
53000	4607.33	2394.03	1657.78	1290.78	1071.49	822.78	745.89	639.55	570.08
54000	4694.26	2439.20	1689.06	1315.14	1091.70	838.30	759.96	651.61	580.83
55000	4781.19	2484.37	1720.34	1339.49	1111.92	853.83	774.03	663.68	591.59
56000	4868.12	2529.54	1751.61	1363.85	1132.14	869.35	788.11	675.75	602.35
57000	4955.05	2574.71	1782.89	1388.20	1152.35	884.87	802.18	687.81	613.10
58000	5041.98	2619.88	1814.17	1412.55	1172.57	900.40	816.25	699.88	623.86
59000	5128.91	2665.05	1845.45	1436.91	1192.79	915.92	830.33	711.95	634.62
60000	5215.84	2710.22	1876.73	1461.26	1213.00	931.45	844.40	724.01	645.37
61000	5302.77	2755.39	1908.01	1485.62	1233.22	946.97	858.47	736.08	656.13
62000	5389.70	2800.56	1939.29	1509.97	1253.44	962.49	872.55	748.15	666.88
63000	5476.64	2845.73	1970.57	1534.33	1273.65	978.02	886.62	760.21	677.64
64000	5563.57	2890.90	2001.84	1558.68	1293.87	993.54	900.69	772.28	688.40
65000	5650.50	2936.07	2033.12	1583.03	1314.09	1009.07	914.76	784.35	699.15
67500	5867.82	3049.00	2111.32	1643.92	1364.63	1047.88	949.95	814.51	726.04
70000	6085.15	3161.93	2189.52	1704.81	1415.17	1086.69	985.13	844.68	752.93
75000	6519.80	3387.78	2345.91	1826.58	1516.25	1164.31	1055.50	905.02	806.71
80000	6954.46	3613.63	2502.30	1948.35	1617.33	1241.93	1125.86	965.35	860.49
85000	7389.11	3839.48	2658.70	2070.12	1718.42	1319.55	1196.23	1025.68	914.27
90000	7823.76	4065.33	2815.09	2191.89	1819.50	1397.17	1266.60	1086.02	968.05
95000	8258.42	4291.18	2971.48	2313.66	1920.58	1474.79	1336.96	1146.35	1021.83
100000	8693.07	4517.04	3127.88	2435.43	2021.67	1552.41	1407.33	1206.69	1075.62
105000	9127.72	4742.89	3284.27	2557.21	2122.75	1630.03	1477.69	1267.02	1129.40
110000	9562.38	4968.74	3440.67	2678.98	2223.83	1707.65	1548.06	1327.35	1183.18
115000	9997.03	5194.59	3597.06	2800.75	2324.92	1785.27	1618.43	1387.69	1236.96
120000	10431.68	5420.44	3753.45	2922.52	2426.00	1862.89	1688.79	1448.02	1290.74
125000	10866.34	5646.29	3909.85	3044.29	2527.08	1940.51	1759.16	1508.36	1344.52
130000	11300.99	5872.14	4066.24	3166.06	2628.17	2018.13	1829.52	1568.69	1398.30
135000	11735.64	6098.00	4222.63	3287.83	2729.25	2095.75	1899.89	1629.02	1452.08
140000	12170.30	6323.85	4379.03	3409.61	2830.33	2173.37	1970.26	1689.36	1505.86
145000	12604.95	6549.70	4535.42	3531.38	2931.42	2250.99	2040.62	1749.69	1559.64
150000	13039.60	6775.55	4691.81	3653.15	3032.50	2328.61	2110.99	1810.03	1613.42

MONTHLY PAYMENT 7⅞%
NECESSARY TO AMORTIZE A LOAN

AMOUNT	15 YEARS	18 YEARS	20 YEARS	25 YEARS	28 YEARS	29 YEARS	30 YEARS	35 YEARS	40 YEARS
$ 50	.48	.44	.42	.39	.37	.37	.37	.36	.35
100	.95	.87	.83	.77	.74	.74	.73	.71	.69
200	1.90	1.74	1.66	1.53	1.48	1.47	1.46	1.41	1.38
300	2.85	2.61	2.49	2.30	2.22	2.20	2.18	2.11	2.06
400	3.80	3.47	3.32	3.06	2.96	2.93	2.91	2.81	2.75
500	4.75	4.34	4.15	3.82	3.70	3.66	3.63	3.51	3.43
600	5.70	5.21	4.98	4.59	4.43	4.39	4.36	4.21	4.12
700	6.64	6.08	5.81	5.35	5.17	5.12	5.08	4.91	4.81
800	7.59	6.94	6.63	6.11	5.91	5.86	5.81	5.61	5.49
900	8.54	7.81	7.46	6.88	6.65	6.59	6.53	6.32	6.18
1000	9.49	8.68	8.29	7.64	7.39	7.32	7.26	7.02	6.86
2000	18.97	17.35	16.58	15.28	14.77	14.63	14.51	14.03	13.72
3000	28.46	26.03	24.87	22.91	22.15	21.94	21.76	21.04	20.58
4000	37.94	34.70	33.15	30.55	29.53	29.26	29.01	28.05	27.44
5000	47.43	43.38	41.44	38.18	36.92	36.57	36.26	35.06	34.30
6000	56.91	52.05	49.73	45.82	44.30	43.88	43.51	42.08	41.16
7000	66.40	60.72	58.01	53.45	51.68	51.20	50.76	49.09	48.02
8000	75.88	69.40	66.30	61.09	59.06	58.51	58.01	56.10	54.88
9000	85.37	78.07	74.59	68.72	66.45	65.82	65.26	63.11	61.74
10000	94.85	86.75	82.87	76.36	73.83	73.14	72.51	70.12	68.60
15000	142.27	130.12	124.31	114.54	110.74	109.70	108.77	105.18	102.90
20000	189.69	173.49	165.74	152.72	147.65	146.27	145.02	140.24	137.19
25000	237.12	216.86	207.17	190.89	184.56	182.84	181.27	175.30	171.49
30000	284.54	260.23	248.61	229.07	221.47	219.40	217.53	210.36	205.79
35000	331.96	303.60	290.04	267.25	258.38	255.97	253.78	245.42	240.09
40000	379.38	346.97	331.48	305.43	295.30	292.54	290.03	280.48	274.38
45000	426.81	390.34	372.91	343.60	332.21	329.10	326.29	315.54	308.68
46000	436.29	399.02	381.20	351.24	339.59	336.42	333.54	322.56	315.54
47000	445.78	407.69	389.48	358.88	346.97	343.73	340.79	329.57	322.40
48000	455.26	416.37	397.77	366.51	354.35	351.04	348.04	336.58	329.26
49000	464.75	425.04	406.06	374.15	361.74	358.36	355.29	343.59	336.12
50000	474.23	433.71	414.34	381.78	369.12	365.67	362.54	350.60	342.98
51000	483.71	442.39	422.63	389.42	376.50	372.98	369.79	357.62	349.84
52000	493.20	451.06	430.92	397.05	383.88	380.30	377.04	364.63	356.70
53000	502.68	459.74	439.20	404.69	391.27	387.61	384.29	371.64	363.56
54000	512.17	468.41	447.49	412.32	398.65	394.92	391.54	378.65	370.42
55000	521.65	477.08	455.78	419.96	406.03	402.24	398.79	385.66	377.28
56000	531.14	485.76	464.06	427.60	413.41	409.55	406.04	392.68	384.14
57000	540.62	494.43	472.35	435.23	420.80	416.86	413.29	399.69	391.00
58000	550.11	503.11	480.64	442.87	428.18	424.18	420.55	406.70	397.86
59000	559.59	511.78	488.92	450.50	435.56	431.49	427.80	413.71	404.71
60000	569.07	520.46	497.21	458.14	442.94	438.80	435.05	420.72	411.57
61000	578.56	529.13	505.50	465.77	450.32	446.12	442.30	427.74	418.43
62000	588.04	537.80	513.79	473.41	457.71	453.43	449.55	434.75	425.29
63000	597.53	546.48	522.07	481.04	465.09	460.74	456.80	441.76	432.15
64000	607.01	555.15	530.36	488.68	472.47	468.06	464.05	448.77	439.01
65000	616.50	563.83	538.65	496.32	479.85	475.37	471.30	455.78	445.87
67500	640.21	585.51	559.36	515.40	498.31	493.65	489.43	473.31	463.02
70000	663.92	607.20	580.08	534.49	516.78	511.94	507.55	490.84	480.17
75000	711.34	650.57	621.51	572.67	553.68	548.50	543.81	525.90	514.47
80000	758.76	693.94	662.95	610.85	590.59	585.07	580.06	560.96	548.76
85000	806.19	737.31	704.38	649.03	627.50	621.64	616.31	596.02	583.06
90000	853.61	780.68	745.81	687.20	664.41	658.20	652.57	631.08	617.36
95000	901.03	824.05	787.25	725.38	701.32	694.77	688.82	666.14	651.66
100000	948.45	867.42	828.68	763.56	738.23	731.34	725.07	701.20	685.95
105000	995.88	910.79	870.12	801.74	775.14	767.90	761.33	736.26	720.25
110000	1043.30	954.16	911.55	839.91	812.06	804.47	797.58	771.32	754.55
115000	1090.72	997.54	952.98	878.09	848.97	841.04	833.83	806.38	788.85
120000	1138.14	1040.91	994.42	916.27	885.88	877.60	870.09	841.44	823.14
125000	1185.57	1084.28	1035.85	954.45	922.79	914.17	906.34	876.50	857.44
130000	1232.99	1127.65	1077.29	992.63	959.70	950.74	942.60	911.56	891.74
135000	1280.41	1171.02	1118.72	1030.80	996.61	987.30	978.85	946.62	926.04
140000	1327.83	1214.39	1160.15	1068.98	1033.52	1023.87	1015.10	981.68	960.33
145000	1375.26	1257.76	1201.59	1107.16	1070.44	1060.44	1051.36	1016.74	994.63
150000	1422.68	1301.13	1243.02	1145.34	1107.35	1097.00	1087.61	1051.80	1028.93

MONTHLY PAYMENT
NECESSARY TO AMORTIZE A LOAN

AMOUNT	1 YEAR	2 YEARS	3 YEARS	4 YEARS	5 YEARS	7 YEARS	8 YEARS	10 YEARS	12 YEARS
$ 50	4.35	2.27	1.57	1.23	1.02	.78	.71	.61	.55
100	8.70	4.53	3.14	2.45	2.03	1.56	1.42	1.22	1.09
200	17.40	9.05	6.27	4.89	4.06	3.12	2.83	2.43	2.17
300	26.10	13.57	9.41	7.33	6.09	4.68	4.25	3.64	3.25
400	34.80	18.10	12.54	9.77	8.12	6.24	5.66	4.86	4.33
500	43.50	22.62	15.67	12.21	10.14	7.80	7.07	6.07	5.42
600	52.20	27.14	18.81	14.65	12.17	9.36	8.49	7.28	6.50
700	60.90	31.66	21.94	17.09	14.20	10.92	9.90	8.50	7.58
800	69.60	36.19	25.07	19.54	16.23	12.47	11.31	9.71	8.66
900	78.29	40.71	28.21	21.98	18.25	14.03	12.73	10.92	9.75
1000	86.99	45.23	31.34	24.42	20.28	15.59	14.14	12.14	10.83
2000	173.98	90.46	62.68	48.83	40.56	31.18	28.28	24.27	21.65
3000	260.97	135.69	94.01	73.24	60.83	46.76	42.42	36.40	32.48
4000	347.96	180.91	125.35	97.66	81.11	62.35	56.55	48.54	43.30
5000	434.95	226.14	156.69	122.07	101.39	77.94	70.69	60.67	54.13
6000	521.94	271.37	188.02	146.48	121.66	93.52	84.83	72.80	64.95
7000	608.92	316.60	219.36	170.90	141.94	109.11	98.96	84.93	75.78
8000	695.91	361.82	250.70	195.31	162.22	124.69	113.10	97.07	86.60
9000	782.90	407.05	282.03	219.72	182.49	140.28	127.24	109.20	97.43
10000	869.89	452.28	313.37	244.13	202.77	155.87	141.37	121.33	108.25
15000	1304.83	678.41	470.05	366.20	304.15	233.80	212.06	182.00	162.37
20000	1739.77	904.55	626.73	488.26	405.53	311.73	282.74	242.66	216.50
25000	2174.72	1130.69	783.41	610.33	506.91	389.66	353.42	303.32	270.62
30000	2609.66	1356.82	940.10	732.39	608.30	467.59	424.11	363.99	324.74
35000	3044.60	1582.96	1096.78	854.46	709.68	545.52	494.79	424.65	378.86
40000	3479.54	1809.10	1253.46	976.52	811.06	623.45	565.47	485.32	432.99
45000	3914.48	2035.23	1410.14	1098.59	912.44	701.38	636.16	545.98	487.11
46000	4001.47	2080.46	1441.48	1123.00	932.72	716.97	650.29	558.11	497.93
47000	4088.46	2125.69	1472.81	1147.41	953.00	732.56	664.43	570.24	508.76
48000	4175.45	2170.91	1504.15	1171.83	973.27	748.14	678.57	582.38	519.58
49000	4262.44	2216.14	1535.49	1196.24	993.55	763.73	692.70	594.51	530.41
50000	4349.43	2261.37	1566.82	1220.65	1013.82	779.32	706.84	606.64	541.23
51000	4436.41	2306.60	1598.16	1245.06	1034.10	794.90	720.98	618.78	552.06
52000	4523.40	2351.82	1629.50	1269.48	1054.38	810.49	735.11	630.91	562.88
53000	4610.39	2397.05	1660.83	1293.89	1074.65	826.07	749.25	643.04	573.70
54000	4697.38	2442.28	1692.17	1318.30	1094.93	841.66	763.39	655.17	584.53
55000	4784.37	2487.51	1723.51	1342.72	1115.21	857.25	777.52	667.31	595.35
56000	4871.36	2532.73	1754.84	1367.13	1135.48	872.83	791.66	679.44	606.18
57000	4958.35	2577.96	1786.18	1391.54	1155.76	888.42	805.80	691.57	617.00
58000	5045.33	2623.19	1817.51	1415.95	1176.00	904.01	819.93	703.71	627.83
59000	5132.32	2668.42	1848.85	1440.37	1196.31	919.59	834.07	715.84	638.65
60000	5219.31	2713.64	1880.19	1464.78	1216.59	935.18	848.21	727.97	649.48
61000	5306.30	2758.87	1911.52	1489.19	1236.87	950.76	862.34	740.10	660.30
62000	5393.29	2804.10	1942.86	1513.61	1257.14	966.35	876.48	752.24	671.13
63000	5480.28	2849.32	1974.20	1538.02	1277.42	981.94	890.62	764.37	681.95
64000	5567.26	2894.55	2005.53	1562.43	1297.69	997.52	904.75	776.50	692.77
65000	5654.25	2939.78	2036.87	1586.84	1317.97	1013.11	918.89	788.63	703.60
67500	5871.72	3052.85	2115.21	1647.88	1368.66	1052.07	954.23	818.97	730.66
70000	6089.20	3165.92	2193.55	1708.91	1419.35	1091.04	989.57	849.30	757.72
75000	6524.14	3392.05	2350.23	1830.97	1520.73	1168.97	1060.26	909.96	811.84
80000	6959.08	3618.19	2506.91	1953.04	1622.12	1246.90	1130.94	970.63	865.97
85000	7394.02	3844.32	2663.60	2075.10	1723.50	1324.83	1201.62	1031.29	920.09
90000	7828.96	4070.46	2820.28	2197.17	1824.88	1402.76	1272.31	1091.95	974.21
95000	8263.91	4296.60	2976.96	2319.23	1926.26	1480.70	1342.99	1152.62	1028.33
100000	8698.85	4522.73	3133.64	2441.30	2027.64	1558.63	1413.67	1213.28	1082.46
105000	9133.79	4748.87	3290.32	2563.36	2129.03	1636.56	1484.36	1273.94	1136.58
110000	9568.73	4975.01	3447.01	2685.43	2230.41	1714.49	1555.04	1334.61	1190.70
115000	10003.67	5201.14	3603.69	2807.49	2331.79	1792.42	1625.72	1395.27	1244.83
120000	10438.62	5427.28	3760.37	2929.56	2433.17	1870.35	1696.41	1455.94	1298.95
125000	10873.56	5653.42	3917.05	3051.62	2534.55	1948.28	1767.09	1516.60	1353.07
130000	11308.50	5879.55	4073.73	3173.68	2635.94	2026.21	1837.77	1577.26	1407.19
135000	11743.44	6105.69	4230.41	3295.75	2737.32	2104.14	1908.46	1637.93	1461.32
140000	12178.39	6331.83	4387.10	3417.81	2838.70	2182.08	1979.14	1698.59	1515.44
145000	12613.33	6557.96	4543.78	3539.88	2940.08	2260.01	2049.82	1759.26	1569.56
150000	13048.27	6784.10	4700.46	3661.94	3041.46	2337.94	2120.51	1819.92	1623.68

MONTHLY PAYMENT 8%

NECESSARY TO AMORTIZE A LOAN

AMOUNT	15 YEARS	18 YEARS	20 YEARS	25 YEARS	28 YEARS	29 YEARS	30 YEARS	35 YEARS	40 YEARS
$ 50	.48	.44	.42	.39	.38	.37	.37	.36	.35
100	.96	.88	.84	.78	.75	.74	.74	.72	.70
200	1.92	1.75	1.68	1.55	1.50	1.48	1.47	1.43	1.40
300	2.87	2.63	2.51	2.32	2.25	2.22	2.21	2.14	2.09
400	3.83	3.50	3.35	3.09	2.99	2.96	2.94	2.85	2.79
500	4.78	4.38	4.19	3.86	3.74	3.70	3.67	3.56	3.48
600	5.74	5.25	5.02	4.64	4.49	4.44	4.41	4.27	4.18
700	6.69	6.13	5.86	5.41	5.23	5.18	5.14	4.98	4.87
800	7.65	7.00	6.70	6.18	5.98	5.92	5.88	5.69	5.57
900	8.61	7.88	7.53	6.95	6.73	6.66	6.61	6.40	6.26
1000	9.56	8.75	8.37	7.72	7.47	7.40	7.34	7.11	6.96
2000	19.12	17.50	16.73	15.44	14.94	14.80	14.68	14.21	13.91
3000	28.67	26.25	25.10	23.16	22.41	22.20	22.02	21.31	20.86
4000	38.23	35.00	33.46	30.88	29.88	29.60	29.36	28.42	27.82
5000	47.79	43.75	41.83	38.60	37.34	37.00	36.69	35.52	34.77
6000	57.34	52.50	50.19	46.31	44.81	44.40	44.03	42.62	41.72
7000	66.90	61.25	58.56	54.03	52.28	51.80	51.37	49.72	48.68
8000	76.46	70.00	66.92	61.75	59.75	59.20	58.71	56.83	55.63
9000	86.01	78.75	75.28	69.47	67.21	66.60	66.04	63.93	62.58
10000	95.57	87.50	83.65	77.19	74.68	74.00	73.38	71.03	69.54
15000	143.35	131.25	125.47	115.78	112.02	111.00	110.07	106.54	104.30
20000	191.14	175.00	167.29	154.37	149.36	147.99	146.76	142.06	139.07
25000	238.92	218.75	209.12	192.96	186.69	184.99	183.45	177.57	173.83
30000	286.70	262.49	250.94	231.55	224.03	221.99	220.13	213.08	208.60
35000	334.48	306.24	292.76	270.14	261.37	258.99	256.82	248.60	243.36
40000	382.27	349.99	334.58	308.73	298.71	295.98	293.51	284.11	278.13
45000	430.05	393.74	376.40	347.32	336.05	332.98	330.20	319.62	312.90
46000	439.60	402.49	384.77	355.04	343.51	340.38	337.54	326.73	319.85
47000	449.16	411.24	393.13	362.76	350.98	347.78	344.87	333.83	326.80
48000	458.72	419.99	401.50	370.48	358.45	355.18	352.21	340.93	333.75
49000	468.27	428.74	409.86	378.19	365.92	362.58	359.55	348.03	340.71
50000	477.83	437.49	418.23	385.91	373.38	369.98	366.89	355.14	347.66
51000	487.39	446.24	426.59	393.63	380.85	377.38	374.22	362.24	354.61
52000	496.94	454.99	434.95	401.35	388.32	384.78	381.56	369.34	361.57
53000	506.50	463.74	443.32	409.07	395.79	392.18	388.90	376.44	368.52
54000	516.06	472.48	451.68	416.79	403.25	399.58	396.24	383.55	375.47
55000	525.61	481.23	460.05	424.50	410.72	406.98	403.58	390.65	382.43
56000	535.17	489.98	468.41	432.22	418.19	414.37	410.91	397.75	389.38
57000	544.73	498.73	476.78	439.94	425.66	421.77	418.25	404.85	396.33
58000	554.28	507.48	485.14	447.66	433.13	429.17	425.59	411.96	403.29
59000	563.84	516.23	493.50	455.38	440.59	436.57	432.93	419.06	410.24
60000	573.40	524.98	501.87	463.09	448.06	443.97	440.26	426.16	417.19
61000	582.95	533.73	510.23	470.81	455.53	451.37	447.60	433.26	424.15
62000	592.51	542.48	518.60	478.53	463.00	458.77	454.94	440.37	431.10
63000	602.07	551.23	526.96	486.25	470.46	466.17	462.28	447.47	438.05
64000	611.62	559.98	535.33	493.97	477.93	473.57	469.61	454.57	445.00
65000	621.18	568.73	543.69	501.69	485.40	480.97	476.95	461.67	451.96
67500	645.07	590.60	564.60	520.98	504.07	499.47	495.30	479.43	469.34
70000	668.96	612.48	585.51	540.28	522.74	517.97	513.64	497.19	486.72
75000	716.74	656.23	627.34	578.87	560.07	554.96	550.33	532.70	521.49
80000	764.53	699.98	669.16	617.46	597.41	591.96	587.02	568.21	556.25
85000	812.31	743.72	710.98	656.05	634.75	628.96	623.70	603.73	591.02
90000	860.09	787.47	752.80	694.64	672.09	665.96	660.39	639.24	625.79
95000	907.87	831.22	794.62	733.23	709.43	702.95	697.08	674.75	660.55
100000	955.66	874.97	836.45	771.82	746.76	739.95	733.77	710.27	695.32
105000	1003.44	918.72	878.27	810.41	784.10	776.95	770.46	745.78	730.08
110000	1051.22	962.46	920.09	849.00	821.44	813.95	807.15	781.29	764.85
115000	1099.00	1006.21	961.91	887.59	858.78	850.94	843.83	816.81	799.61
120000	1146.79	1049.96	1003.73	926.18	896.12	887.94	880.52	852.32	834.38
125000	1194.57	1093.71	1045.56	964.78	933.45	924.94	917.21	887.83	869.14
130000	1242.35	1137.46	1087.38	1003.37	970.79	961.93	953.90	923.34	903.91
135000	1290.14	1181.20	1129.20	1041.96	1008.13	998.93	990.59	958.86	938.68
140000	1337.92	1224.95	1171.02	1080.55	1045.47	1035.93	1027.28	994.37	973.44
145000	1385.70	1268.70	1212.84	1119.14	1082.81	1072.93	1063.96	1029.88	1008.21
150000	1433.48	1312.45	1254.67	1157.73	1120.14	1109.92	1100.65	1065.40	1042.97

8⅛% MONTHLY PAYMENT
NECESSARY TO AMORTIZE A LOAN

AMOUNT	1 YEAR	2 YEARS	3 YEARS	4 YEARS	5 YEARS	7 YEARS	8 YEARS	10 YEARS	12 YEARS
$ 50	4.36	2.27	1.57	1.23	1.02	.79	.72	.61	.55
100	8.71	4.53	3.14	2.45	2.04	1.57	1.43	1.22	1.09
200	17.41	9.06	6.28	4.90	4.07	3.13	2.85	2.44	2.18
300	26.12	13.59	9.42	7.35	6.11	4.70	4.27	3.66	3.27
400	34.82	18.12	12.56	9.79	8.14	6.26	5.69	4.88	4.36
500	43.53	22.65	15.70	12.24	10.17	7.83	7.11	6.10	5.45
600	52.23	27.18	18.84	14.69	12.21	9.39	8.53	7.32	6.54
700	60.94	31.70	21.98	17.14	14.24	10.96	9.95	8.54	7.63
800	69.64	36.23	25.12	19.58	16.27	12.52	11.37	9.76	8.72
900	78.35	40.76	28.26	22.03	18.31	14.09	12.79	10.98	9.81
1000	87.05	45.29	31.40	24.48	20.34	15.65	14.21	12.20	10.90
2000	174.10	90.57	62.79	48.95	40.68	31.30	28.41	24.40	21.79
3000	261.14	135.86	94.19	73.42	61.01	46.95	42.61	36.60	32.68
4000	348.19	181.14	125.58	97.89	81.35	62.60	56.81	48.80	43.58
5000	435.24	226.43	156.98	122.36	101.69	78.25	71.01	61.00	54.47
6000	522.28	271.71	188.37	146.83	122.02	93.90	85.21	73.20	65.36
7000	609.33	317.00	219.76	171.31	142.36	109.54	99.41	85.40	76.26
8000	696.37	362.28	251.16	195.78	162.70	125.19	113.61	97.60	87.15
9000	783.42	407.56	282.55	220.25	183.03	140.84	127.81	109.80	98.04
10000	870.47	452.85	313.95	244.72	203.37	156.49	142.01	121.99	108.94
15000	1305.70	679.27	470.92	367.08	305.05	234.73	213.01	182.99	163.40
20000	1740.93	905.69	627.89	489.44	406.73	312.98	284.01	243.98	217.87
25000	2176.16	1132.11	784.86	611.80	508.41	391.22	355.01	304.98	272.33
30000	2611.39	1358.53	941.83	734.15	610.09	469.46	426.01	365.97	326.80
35000	3046.62	1584.96	1098.80	856.51	711.77	547.70	497.02	426.97	381.27
40000	3481.85	1811.38	1255.77	978.87	813.46	625.95	568.02	487.96	435.73
45000	3917.09	2037.80	1412.74	1101.23	915.14	704.19	639.02	548.96	490.20
46000	4004.13	2083.08	1444.13	1125.70	935.47	719.84	653.22	561.15	501.09
47000	4091.18	2128.37	1475.53	1150.17	955.81	735.49	667.42	573.35	511.98
48000	4178.22	2173.65	1506.92	1174.64	976.15	751.14	681.62	585.55	522.88
49000	4265.27	2218.94	1538.31	1199.12	996.48	766.78	695.82	597.75	533.77
50000	4352.32	2264.22	1569.71	1223.59	1016.82	782.43	710.02	609.95	544.66
51000	4439.36	2309.51	1601.10	1248.06	1037.15	798.08	724.22	622.15	555.56
52000	4526.41	2354.79	1632.50	1272.53	1057.49	813.73	738.42	634.35	566.45
53000	4613.46	2400.07	1663.89	1297.00	1077.83	829.38	752.62	646.55	577.34
54000	4700.50	2445.36	1695.28	1321.47	1098.16	845.03	766.82	658.75	588.24
55000	4787.55	2490.64	1726.68	1345.95	1118.50	860.68	781.02	670.95	599.13
56000	4874.59	2535.93	1758.07	1370.42	1138.84	876.32	795.22	683.14	610.02
57000	4961.64	2581.21	1789.47	1394.89	1159.17	891.97	809.42	695.34	620.92
58000	5048.69	2626.50	1820.86	1419.36	1179.51	907.62	823.62	707.54	631.81
59000	5135.73	2671.78	1852.25	1443.83	1199.84	923.27	837.82	719.74	642.70
60000	5222.78	2717.06	1883.65	1468.30	1220.18	938.92	852.02	731.94	653.60
61000	5309.83	2762.35	1915.04	1492.78	1240.52	954.57	866.22	744.14	664.49
62000	5396.87	2807.63	1946.44	1517.25	1260.85	970.22	880.42	756.34	675.38
63000	5483.92	2852.92	1977.83	1541.72	1281.19	985.86	894.62	768.54	686.28
64000	5570.96	2898.20	2009.22	1566.19	1301.53	1001.51	908.82	780.74	697.17
65000	5658.01	2943.49	2040.62	1590.66	1321.86	1017.16	923.02	792.93	708.06
67500	5875.63	3056.70	2119.10	1651.84	1372.70	1056.28	958.52	823.43	735.29
70000	6093.24	3169.91	2197.59	1713.02	1423.54	1095.40	994.03	853.93	762.53
75000	6528.47	3396.33	2354.56	1835.38	1525.23	1173.65	1065.03	914.92	816.99
80000	6963.70	3622.75	2511.53	1957.74	1626.91	1251.89	1136.03	975.92	871.46
85000	7398.94	3849.17	2668.50	2080.09	1728.59	1330.13	1207.03	1036.91	925.93
90000	7834.17	4075.59	2825.47	2202.45	1830.27	1408.38	1278.03	1097.91	980.39
95000	8269.40	4302.02	2982.44	2324.81	1931.95	1486.62	1349.03	1158.90	1034.86
100000	8704.63	4528.44	3139.41	2447.17	2033.63	1564.86	1420.03	1219.90	1089.32
105000	9139.86	4754.86	3296.38	2569.53	2135.31	1643.10	1491.04	1280.89	1143.79
110000	9575.09	4981.28	3453.35	2691.89	2236.99	1721.35	1562.04	1341.89	1198.26
115000	10010.32	5207.70	3610.32	2814.24	2338.68	1799.59	1633.04	1402.88	1252.72
120000	10445.55	5434.12	3767.29	2936.60	2440.36	1877.83	1704.04	1463.87	1307.19
125000	10880.78	5660.55	3924.26	3058.96	2542.04	1956.08	1775.04	1524.87	1361.65
130000	11316.02	5886.97	4081.23	3181.32	2643.72	2034.32	1846.04	1585.86	1416.12
135000	11751.25	6113.39	4238.20	3303.68	2745.40	2112.56	1917.04	1646.86	1470.58
140000	12186.48	6339.81	4395.17	3426.03	2847.08	2190.80	1988.05	1707.85	1525.05
145000	12621.71	6566.23	4552.14	3548.39	2948.76	2269.05	2059.05	1768.85	1579.52
150000	13056.94	6792.65	4709.11	3670.75	3050.45	2347.29	2130.05	1829.84	1633.98

MONTHLY PAYMENT

NECESSARY TO AMORTIZE A LOAN

8⅛%

AMOUNT	15 YEARS	18 YEARS	20 YEARS	25 YEARS	28 YEARS	29 YEARS	30 YEARS	35 YEARS	40 YEARS
$ 50	.49	.45	.43	.40	.38	.38	.38	.36	.36
100	.97	.89	.85	.79	.76	.75	.75	.72	.71
200	1.93	1.77	1.69	1.57	1.52	1.50	1.49	1.44	1.41
300	2.89	2.65	2.54	2.35	2.27	2.25	2.23	2.16	2.12
400	3.86	3.54	3.38	3.13	3.03	3.00	2.97	2.88	2.82
500	4.82	4.42	4.23	3.91	3.78	3.75	3.72	3.60	3.53
600	5.78	5.30	5.07	4.69	4.54	4.50	4.46	4.32	4.23
700	6.75	6.18	5.91	5.47	5.29	5.25	5.20	5.04	4.94
800	7.71	7.07	6.76	6.25	6.05	5.99	5.94	5.76	5.64
900	8.67	7.95	7.60	7.03	6.80	6.74	6.69	6.48	6.35
1000	9.63	8.83	8.45	7.81	7.56	7.49	7.43	7.20	7.05
2000	19.26	17.66	16.89	15.61	15.11	14.98	14.85	14.39	14.10
3000	28.89	26.48	25.33	23.41	22.66	22.46	22.28	21.59	21.15
4000	38.52	35.31	33.77	31.21	30.22	29.95	29.70	28.78	28.19
5000	48.15	44.13	42.22	39.01	37.77	37.43	37.13	35.97	35.24
6000	57.78	52.96	50.66	46.81	45.32	44.92	44.55	43.17	42.29
7000	67.41	61.78	59.10	54.61	52.88	52.41	51.98	50.36	49.33
8000	77.04	70.61	67.54	62.41	60.43	59.89	59.40	57.55	56.38
9000	86.66	79.43	75.99	70.22	67.98	67.38	66.83	64.75	63.43
10000	96.29	88.26	84.43	78.02	75.54	74.86	74.25	71.94	70.48
15000	144.44	132.39	126.64	117.02	113.30	112.29	111.38	107.91	105.71
20000	192.58	176.51	168.85	156.03	151.07	149.72	148.50	143.88	140.95
25000	240.73	220.64	211.06	195.03	188.84	187.15	185.63	179.84	176.18
30000	288.87	264.77	253.28	234.04	226.60	224.58	222.75	215.81	211.42
35000	337.01	308.89	295.49	273.05	264.37	262.01	259.88	251.78	246.65
40000	385.16	353.02	337.70	312.05	302.14	299.44	297.00	287.75	281.89
45000	433.30	397.15	379.91	351.06	339.90	336.87	334.13	323.72	317.12
46000	442.93	405.97	388.35	358.86	347.46	344.36	341.55	330.91	324.17
47000	452.56	414.80	396.80	366.66	355.01	351.85	348.98	338.10	331.22
48000	462.19	423.62	405.24	374.46	362.56	359.33	356.40	345.30	338.27
49000	471.82	432.45	413.68	382.26	370.11	366.82	363.83	352.49	345.31
50000	481.45	441.27	422.12	390.06	377.67	374.30	371.25	359.68	352.36
51000	491.07	450.10	430.57	397.86	385.22	381.79	378.68	366.88	359.41
52000	500.70	458.93	439.01	405.66	392.77	389.28	386.10	374.07	366.45
53000	510.33	467.75	447.45	413.47	400.33	396.76	393.53	381.26	373.50
54000	519.96	476.58	455.89	421.27	407.88	404.25	400.95	388.46	380.55
55000	529.59	485.40	464.33	429.07	415.43	411.73	408.38	395.65	387.59
56000	539.22	494.23	472.78	436.87	422.99	419.22	415.80	402.85	394.64
57000	548.85	503.05	481.22	444.67	430.54	426.71	423.23	410.04	401.69
58000	558.48	511.88	489.66	452.47	438.09	434.19	430.65	417.23	408.74
59000	568.11	520.70	498.10	460.27	445.65	441.68	438.08	424.43	415.78
60000	577.73	529.53	506.55	468.07	453.20	449.16	445.50	431.62	422.83
61000	587.36	538.35	514.99	475.88	460.75	456.65	452.93	438.81	429.88
62000	596.99	547.18	523.43	483.68	468.31	464.14	460.35	446.01	436.92
63000	606.62	556.00	531.87	491.48	475.86	471.62	467.78	453.20	443.97
64000	616.25	564.83	540.32	499.28	483.41	479.11	475.20	460.39	451.02
65000	625.88	573.66	548.76	507.08	490.97	486.59	482.63	467.59	458.07
67500	649.95	595.72	569.86	526.58	509.85	505.31	501.19	485.57	475.68
70000	674.02	617.78	590.97	546.09	528.73	524.02	519.75	503.56	493.30
75000	722.17	661.91	633.18	585.09	566.50	561.45	556.88	539.52	528.54
80000	770.31	706.04	675.39	624.10	604.27	598.88	594.00	575.49	563.77
85000	818.45	750.16	717.61	663.10	642.03	636.31	631.13	611.46	599.01
90000	866.60	794.29	759.82	702.11	679.80	673.74	668.25	647.43	634.24
95000	914.74	838.42	802.03	741.11	717.56	711.17	705.38	683.40	669.48
100000	962.89	882.54	844.24	780.12	755.33	748.60	742.50	719.36	704.71
105000	1011.03	926.67	886.45	819.13	793.10	786.03	779.63	755.33	739.95
110000	1059.18	970.80	928.66	858.13	830.86	823.46	816.75	791.30	775.18
115000	1107.32	1014.93	970.88	897.14	868.63	860.89	853.88	827.27	810.42
120000	1155.46	1059.05	1013.09	936.14	906.40	898.32	891.00	863.23	845.66
125000	1203.61	1103.18	1055.30	975.15	944.16	935.75	928.13	899.20	880.89
130000	1251.75	1147.31	1097.51	1014.15	981.93	973.18	965.25	935.17	916.13
135000	1299.90	1191.43	1139.72	1053.16	1019.70	1010.61	1002.38	971.14	951.36
140000	1348.04	1235.56	1181.94	1092.17	1057.46	1048.04	1039.50	1007.11	986.60
145000	1396.18	1279.69	1224.15	1131.17	1095.23	1085.47	1076.63	1043.07	1021.83
150000	1444.33	1323.81	1266.36	1170.18	1132.99	1122.90	1113.75	1079.04	1057.07

23

8¼% MONTHLY PAYMENT
NECESSARY TO AMORTIZE A LOAN

AMOUNT	1 YEAR	2 YEARS	3 YEARS	4 YEARS	5 YEARS	6 YEARS	7 YEARS	8 YEARS	10 YEARS	12 YEARS
$ 50	4.36	2.27	1.58	1.23	1.02	.79	.72	.62	.62	.55
100	8.72	4.54	3.15	2.46	2.04	1.58	1.43	1.23	1.23	1.10
200	17.43	9.07	6.30	4.91	4.08	3.15	2.86	2.46	2.46	2.20
300	26.14	13.61	9.44	7.36	6.12	4.72	4.28	3.68	3.68	3.29
400	34.85	18.14	12.59	9.82	8.16	6.29	5.71	4.91	4.91	4.39
500	43.56	22.68	15.73	12.27	10.20	7.86	7.14	6.14	6.14	5.49
600	52.27	27.21	18.88	14.72	12.24	9.43	8.56	7.36	7.36	6.58
700	60.98	31.74	22.02	17.18	14.28	11.00	9.99	8.59	8.59	7.68
800	69.69	36.28	25.17	19.63	16.32	12.57	11.42	9.82	9.82	8.77
900	78.40	40.81	28.31	22.08	18.36	14.14	12.84	11.04	11.04	9.87
1000	87.11	45.35	31.46	24.54	20.40	15.72	14.27	12.27	12.27	10.97
2000	174.21	90.69	62.91	49.07	40.80	31.43	28.53	24.54	24.54	21.93
3000	261.32	136.03	94.36	73.60	61.19	47.14	42.80	36.80	36.80	32.89
4000	348.42	181.37	125.81	98.13	81.59	62.85	57.06	49.07	49.07	43.85
5000	435.53	226.71	157.26	122.66	101.99	78.56	71.33	61.33	61.33	54.82
6000	522.63	272.05	188.72	147.19	122.38	94.27	85.59	73.60	73.60	65.78
7000	609.73	317.39	220.17	171.72	142.78	109.98	99.85	85.86	85.86	76.74
8000	696.84	362.74	251.62	196.25	163.18	125.69	114.12	98.13	98.13	87.70
9000	783.94	408.08	283.07	220.78	183.57	141.40	128.38	110.39	110.39	98.66
10000	871.05	453.42	314.52	245.31	203.97	157.12	142.65	122.66	122.66	109.63
15000	1306.57	680.13	471.78	367.96	305.95	235.67	213.97	183.98	183.98	164.44
20000	1742.09	906.83	629.04	490.61	407.93	314.23	285.29	245.31	245.31	219.25
25000	2177.61	1133.54	786.30	613.27	509.91	392.78	356.61	306.64	306.64	274.06
30000	2613.13	1360.25	943.56	735.92	611.89	471.34	427.93	367.96	367.96	328.87
35000	3048.65	1586.95	1100.82	858.57	713.87	549.89	499.25	429.29	429.29	383.68
40000	3484.17	1813.66	1258.08	981.22	815.86	628.45	570.57	490.62	490.62	438.49
45000	3919.69	2040.37	1415.34	1103.87	917.84	707.00	641.89	551.94	551.94	493.30
46000	4006.79	2085.71	1446.79	1128.41	938.23	722.71	656.15	564.21	564.21	504.26
47000	4093.90	2131.05	1478.24	1152.94	958.63	738.42	670.42	576.47	576.47	515.22
48000	4181.00	2176.39	1509.69	1177.47	979.03	754.14	684.68	588.74	588.74	526.18
49000	4268.10	2221.73	1541.14	1202.00	999.42	769.85	698.94	601.00	601.00	537.15
50000	4355.21	2267.07	1572.60	1226.53	1019.82	785.56	713.21	613.27	613.27	548.11
51000	4442.31	2312.42	1604.05	1251.06	1040.21	801.27	727.47	625.53	625.53	559.07
52000	4529.42	2357.76	1635.50	1275.59	1060.61	816.98	741.74	637.80	637.80	570.03
53000	4616.52	2403.10	1666.95	1300.12	1081.01	832.69	756.00	650.06	650.06	580.99
54000	4703.62	2448.44	1698.40	1324.65	1101.40	848.40	770.27	662.33	662.33	591.96
55000	4790.73	2493.78	1729.86	1349.18	1121.80	864.11	784.53	674.59	674.59	602.92
56000	4877.83	2539.12	1761.31	1373.71	1142.20	879.82	798.79	686.86	686.86	613.88
57000	4964.94	2584.46	1792.76	1398.24	1162.59	895.54	813.06	699.12	699.12	624.84
58000	5052.04	2629.81	1824.21	1422.77	1182.99	911.25	827.32	711.39	711.39	635.81
59000	5139.14	2675.15	1855.66	1447.30	1203.38	926.96	841.59	723.66	723.66	646.77
60000	5226.25	2720.49	1887.11	1471.83	1223.78	942.67	855.85	735.92	735.92	657.73
61000	5313.35	2765.83	1918.57	1496.36	1244.18	958.38	870.11	748.19	748.19	668.69
62000	5400.46	2811.17	1950.02	1520.89	1264.57	974.09	884.38	760.45	760.45	679.65
63000	5487.56	2856.51	1981.47	1545.42	1284.97	989.80	898.64	772.72	772.72	690.62
64000	5574.67	2901.85	2012.92	1569.95	1305.37	1005.51	912.91	784.98	784.98	701.58
65000	5661.77	2947.20	2044.37	1594.48	1325.76	1021.22	927.17	797.25	797.25	712.54
67500	5879.53	3060.55	2123.00	1655.81	1376.75	1060.50	962.83	827.91	827.91	739.94
70000	6097.29	3173.90	2201.63	1717.14	1427.74	1099.78	998.49	858.57	858.57	767.35
75000	6532.81	3400.61	2358.89	1839.79	1529.72	1178.33	1069.81	919.90	919.90	822.16
80000	6968.33	3627.32	2516.15	1962.44	1631.71	1256.89	1141.13	981.23	981.23	876.97
85000	7403.85	3854.02	2673.41	2085.09	1733.69	1335.45	1212.45	1042.55	1042.55	931.78
90000	7839.37	4080.73	2830.67	2207.74	1835.67	1414.00	1283.77	1103.88	1103.88	986.59
95000	8274.89	4307.44	2987.93	2330.40	1937.65	1492.56	1355.09	1165.20	1165.20	1041.40
100000	8710.41	4534.14	3145.19	2453.05	2039.63	1571.11	1426.41	1226.53	1226.53	1096.21
105000	9145.93	4760.85	3302.45	2575.70	2141.61	1649.67	1497.73	1287.86	1287.86	1151.02
110000	9581.45	4987.56	3459.71	2698.35	2243.59	1728.22	1569.05	1349.18	1349.18	1205.83
115000	10016.97	5214.27	3616.96	2821.01	2345.57	1806.78	1640.37	1410.51	1410.51	1260.64
120000	10452.49	5440.97	3774.22	2943.66	2447.56	1885.33	1711.69	1471.84	1471.84	1315.45
125000	10888.01	5667.68	3931.48	3066.31	2549.54	1963.89	1783.01	1533.16	1533.16	1370.26
130000	11323.53	5894.39	4088.74	3188.96	2651.52	2042.44	1854.33	1594.49	1594.49	1425.07
135000	11759.05	6121.09	4246.00	3311.61	2753.50	2121.00	1925.66	1655.82	1655.82	1479.88
140000	12194.57	6347.80	4403.26	3434.27	2855.48	2199.55	1996.98	1717.14	1717.14	1534.70
145000	12630.09	6574.51	4560.52	3556.92	2957.46	2278.11	2068.30	1778.47	1778.47	1589.51
150000	13065.61	6801.21	4717.78	3679.57	3059.44	2356.66	2139.62	1839.79	1839.79	1644.32

24

MONTHLY PAYMENT 8¼%

NECESSARY TO AMORTIZE A LOAN

AMOUNT	15 YEARS	18 YEARS	20 YEARS	25 YEARS	28 YEARS	29 YEARS	30 YEARS	35 YEARS	40 YEARS
$ 50	.49	.45	.43	.40	.39	.38	.38	.37	.36
100	.98	.90	.86	.79	.77	.76	.76	.73	.72
200	1.95	1.79	1.71	1.58	1.53	1.52	1.51	1.46	1.43
300	2.92	2.68	2.56	2.37	2.30	2.28	2.26	2.19	2.15
400	3.89	3.57	3.41	3.16	3.06	3.03	3.01	2.92	2.86
500	4.86	4.46	4.27	3.95	3.82	3.79	3.76	3.65	3.58
600	5.83	5.35	5.12	4.74	4.59	4.55	4.51	4.38	4.29
700	6.80	6.24	5.97	5.52	5.35	5.31	5.26	5.10	5.00
800	7.77	7.13	6.82	6.31	6.12	6.06	6.02	5.83	5.72
900	8.74	8.02	7.67	7.10	6.88	6.82	6.77	6.56	6.43
1000	9.71	8.91	8.53	7.89	7.64	7.58	7.52	7.29	7.15
2000	19.41	17.81	17.05	15.77	15.28	15.15	15.03	14.57	14.29
3000	29.11	26.71	25.57	23.66	22.92	22.72	22.54	21.86	21.43
4000	38.81	35.61	34.09	31.54	30.56	30.30	30.06	29.14	28.57
5000	48.51	44.51	42.61	39.43	38.20	37.87	37.57	36.43	35.71
6000	58.21	53.41	51.13	47.31	45.84	45.44	45.08	43.71	42.85
7000	67.91	62.32	59.65	55.20	53.48	53.01	52.59	51.00	49.99
8000	77.62	71.22	68.17	63.08	61.12	60.59	60.11	58.28	57.14
9000	87.32	80.12	76.69	70.97	68.76	68.16	67.62	65.57	64.28
10000	97.02	89.02	85.21	78.85	76.40	75.73	75.13	72.85	71.42
15000	145.53	133.53	127.81	118.27	114.59	113.60	112.69	109.28	107.13
20000	194.03	178.03	170.42	157.70	152.79	151.46	150.26	145.70	142.83
25000	242.54	222.54	213.02	197.12	190.99	189.33	187.82	182.13	178.54
30000	291.05	267.05	255.62	236.54	229.18	227.19	225.38	218.55	214.25
35000	339.55	311.56	298.23	275.96	267.38	265.05	262.95	254.98	249.95
40000	388.06	356.06	340.83	315.39	305.58	302.92	300.51	291.40	285.66
45000	436.57	400.57	383.43	354.81	343.77	340.78	338.07	327.83	321.37
46000	446.27	409.47	391.96	362.69	351.41	348.36	345.59	335.11	328.51
47000	455.97	418.37	400.48	370.58	359.05	355.93	353.10	342.40	335.65
48000	465.67	427.28	409.00	378.46	366.69	363.50	360.61	349.68	342.79
49000	475.37	436.18	417.52	386.35	374.33	371.07	368.13	356.97	349.93
50000	485.08	445.08	426.04	394.23	381.97	378.65	375.64	364.25	357.07
51000	494.78	453.98	434.56	402.11	389.61	386.22	383.15	371.54	364.22
52000	504.48	462.88	443.08	410.00	397.25	393.79	390.66	378.82	371.36
53000	514.18	471.78	451.60	417.88	404.89	401.37	398.18	386.11	378.50
54000	523.88	480.68	460.12	425.77	412.53	408.94	405.69	393.39	385.64
55000	533.58	489.59	468.64	433.65	420.17	416.51	413.20	400.68	392.78
56000	543.28	498.49	477.16	441.54	427.81	424.08	420.71	407.96	399.92
57000	552.99	507.39	485.68	449.42	435.45	431.66	428.23	415.24	407.06
58000	562.69	516.29	494.20	457.31	443.08	439.23	435.74	422.53	414.21
59000	572.39	525.19	502.72	465.19	450.72	446.80	443.25	429.81	421.35
60000	582.09	534.09	511.24	473.08	458.36	454.38	450.76	437.10	428.49
61000	591.79	543.00	519.77	480.96	466.00	461.95	458.28	444.38	435.63
62000	601.49	551.90	528.29	488.84	473.64	469.52	465.79	451.67	442.77
63000	611.19	560.80	536.81	496.73	481.28	477.09	473.30	458.95	449.91
64000	620.89	569.70	545.33	504.61	488.92	484.67	480.82	466.24	457.05
65000	630.60	578.60	553.85	512.50	496.56	492.24	488.33	473.52	464.20
67500	654.85	600.85	575.15	532.21	515.66	511.17	507.11	491.74	482.05
70000	679.10	623.11	596.45	551.92	534.76	530.10	525.89	509.95	499.90
75000	727.61	667.62	639.05	591.34	572.95	567.97	563.45	546.37	535.61
80000	776.12	712.12	681.66	630.77	611.15	605.83	601.02	582.80	571.32
85000	824.62	756.63	724.26	670.19	649.35	643.70	638.58	619.22	607.02
90000	873.13	801.14	766.86	709.61	687.54	681.56	676.14	655.65	642.73
95000	921.64	845.65	809.47	749.03	725.74	719.43	713.71	692.07	678.44
100000	970.15	890.15	852.07	788.46	763.94	757.29	751.27	728.50	714.14
105000	1018.65	934.66	894.67	827.88	802.13	795.15	788.83	764.92	749.85
110000	1067.16	979.17	937.28	867.30	840.33	833.02	826.40	801.35	785.56
115000	1115.67	1023.67	979.88	906.72	878.53	870.88	863.96	837.77	821.26
120000	1164.17	1068.18	1022.48	946.15	916.72	908.75	901.52	874.19	856.97
125000	1212.68	1112.69	1065.09	985.57	954.92	946.61	939.09	910.62	892.68
130000	1261.19	1157.20	1107.69	1024.99	993.11	984.48	976.65	947.04	928.39
135000	1309.69	1201.70	1150.29	1064.41	1031.31	1022.34	1014.21	983.47	964.09
140000	1358.20	1246.21	1192.90	1103.84	1069.51	1060.20	1051.78	1019.89	999.80
145000	1406.71	1290.72	1235.50	1143.26	1107.70	1098.07	1089.34	1056.32	1035.51
150000	1455.22	1335.23	1278.10	1182.68	1145.90	1135.93	1126.90	1092.74	1071.21

25

8⅜%

MONTHLY PAYMENT
NECESSARY TO AMORTIZE A LOAN

AMOUNT	1 YEAR	2 YEARS	3 YEARS	4 YEARS	5 YEARS	7 YEARS	8 YEARS	10 YEARS	12 YEARS
$ 50	4.36	2.27	1.58	1.23	1.03	.79	.72	.62	.56
100	8.72	4.54	3.16	2.46	2.05	1.58	1.44	1.24	1.11
200	17.44	9.08	6.31	4.92	4.10	3.16	2.87	2.47	2.21
300	26.15	13.62	9.46	7.38	6.14	4.74	4.30	3.70	3.31
400	34.87	18.16	12.61	9.84	8.19	6.31	5.74	4.94	4.42
500	43.59	22.70	15.76	12.30	10.23	7.89	7.17	6.17	5.52
600	52.30	27.24	18.91	14.76	12.28	9.47	8.60	7.40	6.62
700	61.02	31.78	22.06	17.22	14.32	11.05	10.03	8.64	7.73
800	69.73	36.32	25.21	19.68	16.37	12.62	11.47	9.87	8.83
900	78.45	40.86	28.36	22.14	18.42	14.20	12.90	11.10	9.93
1000	87.17	45.40	31.51	24.59	20.46	15.78	14.33	12.34	11.04
2000	174.33	90.80	63.02	49.18	40.92	31.55	28.66	24.67	22.07
3000	261.49	136.20	94.53	73.77	61.37	47.33	42.99	37.00	33.10
4000	348.65	181.60	126.04	98.36	81.83	63.10	57.32	49.33	44.13
5000	435.81	227.00	157.55	122.95	102.29	78.87	71.65	61.66	55.16
6000	522.98	272.40	189.06	147.54	122.74	94.65	85.97	74.00	66.19
7000	610.14	317.79	220.57	172.13	143.20	110.42	100.30	86.33	77.22
8000	697.30	363.19	252.08	196.72	163.66	126.19	114.63	98.66	88.25
9000	784.46	408.59	283.59	221.31	184.11	141.97	128.96	110.99	99.29
10000	871.62	453.99	315.10	245.90	204.57	157.74	143.29	123.32	110.32
15000	1307.43	680.98	472.65	368.84	306.85	236.61	214.93	184.98	165.47
20000	1743.24	907.98	630.20	491.79	409.13	315.48	286.57	246.64	220.63
25000	2179.05	1134.97	787.75	614.74	511.41	394.35	358.21	308.30	275.78
30000	2614.86	1361.96	945.29	737.68	613.70	473.22	429.85	369.96	330.94
35000	3050.67	1588.95	1102.84	860.63	715.98	552.08	501.49	431.62	386.10
40000	3486.48	1815.95	1260.39	983.58	818.26	630.95	573.13	493.28	441.25
45000	3922.29	2042.94	1417.94	1106.52	920.54	709.82	644.77	554.94	496.41
46000	4009.45	2088.34	1449.45	1131.11	941.00	725.60	659.09	567.27	507.44
47000	4096.61	2133.74	1480.96	1155.70	961.45	741.37	673.42	579.60	518.47
48000	4183.78	2179.13	1512.47	1180.29	981.91	757.14	687.75	591.93	529.50
49000	4270.94	2224.53	1543.98	1204.88	1002.37	772.92	702.08	604.26	540.53
50000	4358.10	2269.93	1575.49	1229.47	1022.82	788.69	716.41	616.60	551.56
51000	4445.26	2315.33	1607.00	1254.06	1043.28	804.46	730.73	628.93	562.60
52000	4532.42	2360.73	1638.51	1278.65	1063.73	820.24	745.06	641.26	573.63
53000	4619.59	2406.13	1670.02	1303.24	1084.19	836.01	759.39	653.59	584.66
54000	4706.75	2451.52	1701.53	1327.83	1104.65	851.78	773.72	665.92	595.69
55000	4793.91	2496.92	1733.04	1352.42	1125.10	867.56	788.05	678.25	606.72
56000	4881.07	2542.32	1764.55	1377.01	1145.56	883.33	802.37	690.59	617.75
57000	4968.23	2587.72	1796.05	1401.60	1166.02	899.11	816.70	702.92	628.78
58000	5055.40	2633.12	1827.56	1426.19	1186.47	914.88	831.03	715.25	639.81
59000	5142.56	2678.52	1859.07	1450.78	1206.93	930.65	845.36	727.58	650.85
60000	5229.72	2723.92	1890.58	1475.36	1227.39	946.43	859.69	739.91	661.88
61000	5316.88	2769.31	1922.09	1499.95	1247.84	962.20	874.01	752.25	672.91
62000	5404.04	2814.71	1953.60	1524.54	1268.30	977.97	888.34	764.58	683.94
63000	5491.21	2860.11	1985.11	1549.13	1288.75	993.75	902.67	776.91	694.97
64000	5578.37	2905.51	2016.62	1573.72	1309.21	1009.52	917.00	789.24	706.00
65000	5665.53	2950.91	2048.13	1598.31	1329.67	1025.30	931.33	801.57	717.03
67500	5883.43	3064.40	2126.91	1659.78	1380.81	1064.73	967.15	832.40	744.61
70000	6101.34	3177.90	2205.68	1721.26	1431.95	1104.16	1002.97	863.23	772.19
75000	6537.15	3404.89	2363.23	1844.20	1534.23	1183.03	1074.61	924.89	827.34
80000	6972.96	3631.89	2520.78	1967.15	1636.51	1261.90	1146.25	986.55	882.50
85000	7408.77	3858.88	2678.33	2090.10	1738.79	1340.77	1217.89	1048.21	937.66
90000	7844.58	4085.87	2835.87	2213.04	1841.08	1419.64	1289.53	1109.87	992.81
95000	8280.39	4312.86	2993.42	2335.99	1943.36	1498.51	1361.17	1171.53	1047.97
100000	8716.20	4539.86	3150.97	2458.94	2045.64	1577.37	1432.81	1233.19	1103.12
105000	9152.01	4766.85	3308.52	2581.88	2147.92	1656.24	1504.45	1294.85	1158.28
110000	9587.82	4993.84	3466.07	2704.83	2250.20	1735.11	1576.09	1356.50	1213.44
115000	10023.62	5220.83	3623.61	2827.78	2352.48	1813.98	1647.73	1418.16	1268.59
120000	10459.43	5447.83	3781.16	2950.72	2454.77	1892.85	1719.37	1479.82	1323.75
125000	10895.24	5674.82	3938.71	3073.67	2557.05	1971.72	1791.01	1541.48	1378.90
130000	11331.05	5901.81	4096.26	3196.62	2659.33	2050.59	1862.65	1603.14	1434.06
135000	11766.86	6128.80	4253.81	3319.56	2761.61	2129.45	1934.29	1664.80	1489.22
140000	12202.67	6355.80	4411.36	3442.51	2863.89	2208.32	2005.93	1726.46	1544.37
145000	12638.48	6582.79	4568.90	3565.46	2966.17	2287.19	2077.57	1788.12	1599.53
150000	13074.29	6809.78	4726.45	3688.40	3068.46	2366.06	2149.21	1849.78	1654.68

26

MONTHLY PAYMENT 8⅜%

NECESSARY TO AMORTIZE A LOAN

AMOUNT	15 YEARS	18 YEARS	20 YEARS	25 YEARS	28 YEARS	29 YEARS	30 YEARS	35 YEARS	40 YEARS
$ 50	.49	.45	.43	.40	.39	.39	.39	.37	.37
100	.98	.90	.86	.80	.78	.77	.77	.74	.73
200	1.96	1.80	1.72	1.60	1.55	1.54	1.53	1.48	1.45
300	2.94	2.70	2.58	2.40	2.32	2.30	2.29	2.22	2.18
400	3.91	3.60	3.44	3.19	3.10	3.07	3.05	2.96	2.90
500	4.89	4.49	4.30	3.99	3.87	3.84	3.81	3.69	3.62
600	5.87	5.39	5.16	4.79	4.64	4.60	4.57	4.43	4.35
700	6.85	6.29	6.02	5.58	5.41	5.37	5.33	5.17	5.07
800	7.82	7.19	6.88	6.38	6.19	6.13	6.09	5.91	5.79
900	8.80	8.09	7.74	7.18	6.96	6.90	6.85	6.64	6.52
1000	9.78	8.98	8.60	7.97	7.73	7.67	7.61	7.38	7.24
2000	19.55	17.96	17.20	15.94	15.46	15.33	15.21	14.76	14.48
3000	29.33	26.94	25.80	23.91	23.18	22.99	22.81	22.13	21.71
4000	39.10	35.92	34.40	31.88	30.91	30.65	30.41	29.51	28.95
5000	48.88	44.89	43.00	39.85	38.63	38.31	38.01	36.89	36.19
6000	58.65	53.87	51.60	47.81	46.36	45.97	45.61	44.26	43.42
7000	68.42	62.85	60.20	55.78	54.08	53.63	53.21	51.64	50.66
8000	78.20	71.83	68.80	63.75	61.81	61.29	60.81	59.02	57.89
9000	87.97	80.81	77.40	71.72	69.54	68.95	68.41	66.39	65.13
10000	97.75	89.78	86.00	79.69	77.26	76.61	76.01	73.77	72.37
15000	146.62	134.67	128.99	119.53	115.89	114.91	114.02	110.65	108.55
20000	195.49	179.56	171.99	159.37	154.52	153.21	152.02	147.54	144.73
25000	244.36	224.45	214.99	199.21	193.15	191.51	190.02	184.42	180.91
30000	293.23	269.34	257.98	239.05	231.78	229.81	228.03	221.30	217.09
35000	342.10	314.23	300.98	278.89	270.40	268.11	266.03	258.19	253.27
40000	390.98	359.12	343.98	318.73	309.03	306.41	304.03	295.07	289.45
45000	439.85	404.01	386.97	358.57	347.66	344.71	342.04	331.95	325.63
46000	449.62	412.99	395.57	366.54	355.39	352.37	349.64	339.33	332.86
47000	459.40	421.96	404.17	374.51	363.11	360.03	357.24	346.70	340.10
48000	469.17	430.94	412.77	382.48	370.84	367.69	364.84	354.08	347.33
49000	478.94	439.92	421.37	390.45	378.56	375.35	372.44	361.46	354.57
50000	488.72	448.90	429.97	398.42	386.29	383.01	380.04	368.83	361.81
51000	498.49	457.88	438.57	406.38	394.02	390.67	387.64	376.21	369.04
52000	508.27	466.85	447.17	414.35	401.74	398.33	395.24	383.59	376.28
53000	518.04	475.83	455.77	422.32	409.47	405.99	402.84	390.96	383.51
54000	527.82	484.81	464.37	430.29	417.19	413.65	410.44	398.34	390.75
55000	537.59	493.79	472.97	438.26	424.92	421.31	418.04	405.72	397.99
56000	547.36	502.77	481.56	446.22	432.64	428.97	425.65	413.09	405.22
57000	557.14	511.74	490.16	454.19	440.37	436.63	433.25	420.47	412.46
58000	566.91	520.72	498.76	462.16	448.10	444.29	440.85	427.85	419.69
59000	576.69	529.70	507.36	470.13	455.82	451.95	448.45	435.22	426.93
60000	586.46	538.68	515.96	478.10	463.55	459.61	456.05	442.60	434.17
61000	596.23	547.66	524.56	486.07	471.27	467.27	463.65	449.98	441.40
62000	606.01	556.63	533.16	494.03	479.00	474.93	471.25	457.35	448.64
63000	615.78	565.61	541.76	502.00	486.72	482.59	478.85	464.73	455.87
64000	625.56	574.59	550.36	509.97	494.45	490.25	486.45	472.11	463.11
65000	635.33	583.57	558.96	517.94	502.18	497.91	494.05	479.48	470.35
67500	659.77	606.01	580.45	537.86	521.49	517.06	513.05	497.92	488.44
70000	684.20	628.46	601.95	557.78	540.80	536.21	532.06	516.37	506.53
75000	733.07	673.35	644.95	597.62	579.43	574.51	570.06	553.25	542.71
80000	781.95	718.23	687.95	637.46	618.06	612.81	608.06	590.13	578.89
85000	830.82	763.12	730.94	677.30	656.69	651.11	646.07	627.02	615.07
90000	879.69	808.01	773.94	717.14	695.32	689.41	684.07	663.90	651.25
95000	928.56	852.90	816.94	756.98	733.95	727.71	722.07	700.78	687.43
100000	977.43	897.79	859.93	796.83	772.58	766.02	760.08	737.66	723.61
105000	1026.30	942.68	902.93	836.67	811.20	804.32	798.08	774.55	759.79
110000	1075.17	987.57	945.93	876.51	849.83	842.62	836.08	811.43	795.97
115000	1124.05	1032.46	988.92	916.35	888.46	880.92	874.09	848.31	832.15
120000	1172.92	1077.35	1031.92	956.19	927.09	919.22	912.09	885.20	868.33
125000	1221.79	1122.24	1074.92	996.03	965.72	957.52	950.10	922.08	904.51
130000	1270.66	1167.13	1117.91	1035.87	1004.35	995.82	988.10	958.96	940.69
135000	1319.53	1212.02	1160.91	1075.71	1042.98	1034.12	1026.10	995.84	976.87
140000	1368.40	1256.91	1203.90	1115.55	1081.60	1072.42	1064.11	1032.73	1013.05
145000	1417.27	1301.80	1246.90	1155.40	1120.23	1110.72	1102.11	1069.61	1049.23
150000	1466.14	1346.69	1289.90	1195.24	1158.86	1149.02	1140.11	1106.49	1085.41

MONTHLY PAYMENT
NECESSARY TO AMORTIZE A LOAN

AMOUNT	1 YEAR	2 YEARS	3 YEARS	4 YEARS	5 YEARS	7 YEARS	8 YEARS	10 YEARS	12 YEARS
$ 50	4.37	2.28	1.58	1.24	1.03	.80	.72	.62	.56
100	8.73	4.55	3.16	2.47	2.06	1.59	1.44	1.24	1.12
200	17.45	9.10	6.32	4.93	4.11	3.17	2.88	2.48	2.23
300	26.17	13.64	9.48	7.40	6.16	4.76	4.32	3.72	3.34
400	34.89	18.19	12.63	9.86	8.21	6.34	5.76	4.96	4.45
500	43.61	22.73	15.79	12.33	10.26	7.92	7.20	6.20	5.56
600	52.34	27.28	18.95	14.79	12.31	9.51	8.64	7.44	6.67
700	61.06	31.82	22.10	17.26	14.37	11.09	10.08	8.68	7.78
800	69.78	36.37	25.26	19.72	16.42	12.67	11.52	9.92	8.89
900	78.50	40.92	28.42	22.19	18.47	14.26	12.96	11.16	10.00
1000	87.22	45.46	31.57	24.65	20.52	15.84	14.40	12.40	11.11
2000	174.44	90.92	63.14	49.30	41.04	31.68	28.79	24.80	22.21
3000	261.66	136.37	94.71	73.95	61.55	47.51	43.18	37.20	33.31
4000	348.88	181.83	126.28	98.60	82.07	63.35	57.57	49.60	44.41
5000	436.10	227.28	157.84	123.25	102.59	79.19	71.97	62.00	55.51
6000	523.32	272.74	189.41	147.89	123.10	95.02	86.36	74.40	66.61
7000	610.54	318.19	220.98	172.54	143.62	110.86	100.75	86.79	77.71
8000	697.76	363.65	252.55	197.19	164.14	126.70	115.14	99.19	88.81
9000	784.98	409.11	284.11	221.84	184.65	142.53	129.53	111.59	99.91
10000	872.20	454.56	315.68	246.49	205.17	158.37	143.93	123.99	111.01
15000	1308.30	681.84	473.52	369.73	307.75	237.55	215.89	185.98	166.51
20000	1744.40	909.12	631.36	492.97	410.34	316.73	287.85	247.98	222.02
25000	2180.50	1136.40	789.19	616.21	512.92	395.92	359.81	309.97	277.52
30000	2616.60	1363.68	947.03	739.45	615.50	475.10	431.77	371.96	333.02
35000	3052.70	1590.95	1104.87	862.70	718.08	554.28	503.73	433.95	388.52
40000	3488.80	1818.23	1262.71	985.94	820.67	633.46	575.69	495.95	444.03
45000	3924.90	2045.51	1420.54	1109.18	923.25	712.65	647.65	557.94	499.53
46000	4012.11	2090.97	1452.11	1133.83	943.77	728.48	662.04	570.34	510.63
47000	4099.33	2136.42	1483.68	1158.48	964.28	744.32	676.44	582.74	521.73
48000	4186.55	2181.88	1515.25	1183.12	984.80	760.16	690.83	595.14	532.83
49000	4273.77	2227.33	1546.81	1207.77	1005.32	775.99	705.22	607.53	543.93
50000	4360.99	2272.79	1578.38	1232.42	1025.83	791.83	719.61	619.93	555.03
51000	4448.21	2318.24	1609.95	1257.07	1046.35	807.67	734.00	632.33	566.13
52000	4535.43	2363.70	1641.52	1281.72	1066.86	823.50	748.40	644.73	577.23
53000	4622.65	2409.16	1673.08	1306.37	1087.38	839.34	762.79	657.13	588.33
54000	4709.87	2454.61	1704.65	1331.01	1107.90	855.18	777.18	669.53	599.44
55000	4797.09	2500.07	1736.22	1355.66	1128.41	871.01	791.57	681.93	610.54
56000	4884.31	2545.52	1767.79	1380.31	1148.93	886.85	805.96	694.32	621.64
57000	4971.53	2590.98	1799.35	1404.96	1169.45	902.68	820.36	706.72	632.74
58000	5058.75	2636.43	1830.92	1429.61	1189.96	918.52	834.75	719.12	643.84
59000	5145.97	2681.89	1862.49	1454.25	1210.48	934.36	849.14	731.52	654.94
60000	5233.19	2727.35	1894.06	1478.90	1231.00	950.19	863.53	743.92	666.04
61000	5320.41	2772.80	1925.62	1503.55	1251.51	966.03	877.92	756.32	677.14
62000	5407.63	2818.26	1957.19	1528.20	1272.03	981.87	892.32	768.72	688.24
63000	5494.85	2863.71	1988.76	1552.85	1292.55	997.70	906.71	781.11	699.34
64000	5582.07	2909.17	2020.33	1577.50	1313.06	1013.54	921.10	793.51	710.44
65000	5669.29	2954.62	2051.89	1602.14	1333.58	1029.38	935.49	805.91	721.54
67500	5887.34	3068.26	2130.81	1663.77	1384.87	1068.97	971.47	836.91	749.29
70000	6105.39	3181.90	2209.73	1725.39	1436.16	1108.56	1007.45	867.90	777.04
75000	6541.49	3409.18	2367.57	1848.63	1538.74	1187.74	1079.41	929.90	832.55
80000	6977.59	3636.46	2525.41	1971.87	1641.33	1266.92	1151.38	991.89	888.05
85000	7413.69	3863.74	2683.25	2095.11	1743.91	1346.11	1223.34	1053.88	943.55
90000	7849.79	4091.02	2841.08	2218.35	1846.49	1425.29	1295.30	1115.88	999.06
95000	8285.88	4318.29	2998.92	2341.59	1949.08	1504.47	1367.26	1177.87	1054.56
100000	8721.98	4545.57	3156.76	2464.84	2051.66	1583.65	1439.22	1239.86	1110.06
105000	9158.08	4772.85	3314.60	2588.08	2154.24	1662.84	1511.18	1301.85	1165.56
110000	9594.18	5000.13	3472.43	2711.32	2256.82	1742.02	1583.14	1363.85	1221.07
115000	10030.28	5227.41	3630.27	2834.56	2359.41	1821.20	1655.10	1425.84	1276.57
120000	10466.38	5454.69	3788.11	2957.80	2461.99	1900.38	1727.06	1487.83	1332.07
125000	10902.48	5681.96	3945.95	3081.04	2564.57	1979.57	1799.02	1549.83	1387.57
130000	11338.58	5909.24	4103.78	3204.28	2667.15	2058.75	1870.98	1611.82	1443.08
135000	11774.68	6136.52	4261.62	3327.53	2769.74	2137.93	1942.94	1673.81	1498.58
140000	12210.77	6363.80	4419.46	3450.77	2872.32	2217.11	2014.90	1735.80	1554.08
145000	12646.87	6591.08	4577.30	3574.01	2974.90	2296.30	2086.86	1797.80	1609.59
150000	13082.97	6818.36	4735.14	3697.25	3077.48	2375.48	2158.82	1859.79	1665.09

MONTHLY PAYMENT 8½%
NECESSARY TO AMORTIZE A LOAN

AMOUNT	15 YEARS	18 YEARS	20 YEARS	25 YEARS	28 YEARS	29 YEARS	30 YEARS	35 YEARS	40 YEARS
$ 50	.50	.46	.44	.41	.40	.39	.39	.38	.37
100	.99	.91	.87	.81	.79	.78	.77	.75	.74
200	1.97	1.82	1.74	1.62	1.57	1.55	1.54	1.50	1.47
300	2.96	2.72	2.61	2.42	2.35	2.33	2.31	2.25	2.20
400	3.94	3.63	3.48	3.23	3.13	3.10	3.08	2.99	2.94
500	4.93	4.53	4.34	4.03	3.91	3.88	3.85	3.74	3.67
600	5.91	5.44	5.21	4.84	4.69	4.65	4.62	4.49	4.40
700	6.90	6.34	6.08	5.64	5.47	5.43	5.39	5.23	5.14
800	7.88	7.25	6.95	6.45	6.25	6.20	6.16	5.98	5.87
900	8.87	8.15	7.82	7.25	7.04	6.98	6.93	6.73	6.60
1000	9.85	9.06	8.68	8.06	7.82	7.75	7.69	7.47	7.34
2000	19.70	18.11	17.36	16.11	15.63	15.50	15.38	14.94	14.67
3000	29.55	27.17	26.04	24.16	23.44	23.25	23.07	22.41	22.00
4000	39.39	36.22	34.72	32.21	31.25	31.00	30.76	29.88	29.33
5000	49.24	45.28	43.40	40.27	39.07	38.74	38.45	37.35	36.66
6000	59.09	54.33	52.07	48.32	46.88	46.49	46.14	44.82	43.99
7000	68.94	63.39	60.75	56.37	54.69	54.24	53.83	52.29	51.32
8000	78.78	72.44	69.43	64.42	62.50	61.99	61.52	59.75	58.65
9000	88.63	81.50	78.11	72.48	70.32	69.73	69.21	67.22	65.98
10000	98.48	90.55	86.79	80.53	78.13	77.48	76.90	74.69	73.31
15000	147.72	135.82	130.18	120.79	117.19	116.22	115.34	112.03	109.97
20000	196.95	181.10	173.57	161.05	156.25	154.96	153.79	149.38	146.62
25000	246.19	226.37	216.96	201.31	195.32	193.70	192.23	186.72	183.28
30000	295.43	271.64	260.35	241.57	234.38	232.44	230.68	224.06	219.93
35000	344.66	316.92	303.74	281.83	273.44	271.17	269.12	261.41	256.59
40000	393.90	362.19	347.13	322.10	312.50	309.91	307.57	298.75	293.24
45000	443.14	407.46	390.53	362.36	351.57	348.65	346.02	336.09	329.90
46000	452.99	416.52	399.20	370.41	359.38	356.40	353.71	343.56	337.23
47000	462.83	425.57	407.88	378.46	367.19	364.15	361.39	351.03	344.56
48000	472.68	434.62	416.56	386.51	375.00	371.89	369.08	358.50	351.89
49000	482.53	443.68	425.24	394.57	382.82	379.64	376.77	365.97	359.22
50000	492.37	452.73	433.92	402.62	390.63	387.39	384.46	373.44	366.55
51000	502.22	461.79	442.59	410.67	398.44	395.14	392.15	380.90	373.88
52000	512.07	470.84	451.27	418.72	406.25	402.89	399.84	388.37	381.21
53000	521.92	479.90	459.95	426.78	414.07	410.63	407.53	395.84	388.54
54000	531.76	488.95	468.63	434.83	421.88	418.38	415.22	403.31	395.88
55000	541.61	498.01	477.31	442.88	429.69	426.13	422.91	410.78	403.21
56000	551.46	507.06	485.99	450.93	437.50	433.88	430.60	418.25	410.54
57000	561.31	516.12	494.66	458.98	445.32	441.62	438.29	425.72	417.87
58000	571.15	525.17	503.34	467.04	453.13	449.37	445.97	433.18	425.20
59000	581.00	534.22	512.02	475.09	460.94	457.12	453.66	440.65	432.53
60000	590.85	543.28	520.70	483.14	468.75	464.87	461.35	448.12	439.86
61000	600.70	552.33	529.38	491.19	476.57	472.61	469.04	455.59	447.19
62000	610.54	561.39	538.06	499.25	484.38	480.36	476.73	463.06	454.52
63000	620.39	570.44	546.73	507.30	492.19	488.11	484.42	470.53	461.85
64000	630.24	579.50	555.41	515.35	500.00	495.86	492.11	478.00	469.19
65000	640.09	588.55	564.09	523.40	507.82	503.61	499.80	485.46	476.52
67500	664.70	611.19	585.79	543.53	527.35	522.98	519.02	504.14	494.84
70000	689.32	633.83	607.48	563.66	546.88	542.34	538.24	522.81	513.17
75000	738.56	679.10	650.87	603.93	585.94	581.08	576.69	560.15	549.83
80000	787.80	724.37	694.26	644.19	625.00	619.82	615.14	597.49	586.48
85000	837.03	769.64	737.65	684.45	664.07	658.56	653.58	634.84	623.13
90000	886.27	814.92	781.05	724.71	703.13	697.30	692.03	672.18	659.79
95000	935.51	860.19	824.44	764.97	742.19	736.04	730.47	709.52	696.44
100000	984.74	905.46	867.83	805.23	781.25	774.78	768.92	746.87	733.10
105000	1033.98	950.74	911.22	845.49	820.31	813.51	807.36	784.21	769.75
110000	1083.22	996.01	954.61	885.75	859.38	852.25	845.81	821.55	806.41
115000	1132.46	1041.28	998.00	926.02	898.44	890.99	884.26	858.89	843.06
120000	1181.69	1086.55	1041.39	966.28	937.50	929.73	922.70	896.24	879.72
125000	1230.93	1131.83	1084.78	1006.54	976.56	968.47	961.15	933.58	916.37
130000	1280.17	1177.10	1128.18	1046.80	1015.63	1007.21	999.59	970.92	953.03
135000	1329.40	1222.37	1171.57	1087.06	1054.69	1045.95	1038.04	1008.27	989.68
140000	1378.64	1267.65	1214.96	1127.32	1093.75	1084.68	1076.48	1045.61	1026.34
145000	1427.88	1312.92	1258.35	1167.58	1132.81	1123.42	1114.93	1082.95	1062.99
150000	1477.11	1358.19	1301.74	1207.85	1171.88	1162.16	1153.38	1120.30	1099.65

29

MONTHLY PAYMENT
NECESSARY TO AMORTIZE A LOAN

AMOUNT	1 YEAR	2 YEARS	3 YEARS	4 YEARS	5 YEARS	7 YEARS	8 YEARS	10 YEARS	12 YEARS
$ 50	4.37	2.28	1.59	1.24	1.03	.80	.73	.63	.56
100	8.73	4.56	3.17	2.48	2.06	1.59	1.45	1.25	1.12
200	17.46	9.11	6.33	4.95	4.12	3.18	2.90	2.50	2.24
300	26.19	13.66	9.49	7.42	6.18	4.77	4.34	3.74	3.36
400	34.92	18.21	12.66	9.89	8.24	6.36	5.79	4.99	4.47
500	43.64	22.76	15.82	12.36	10.29	7.95	7.23	6.24	5.59
600	52.37	27.31	18.98	14.83	12.35	9.54	8.68	7.48	6.71
700	61.10	31.86	22.14	17.30	14.41	11.13	10.12	8.73	7.82
800	69.83	36.42	25.31	19.77	16.47	12.72	11.57	9.98	8.94
900	78.55	40.97	28.47	22.24	18.52	14.31	13.02	11.22	10.06
1000	87.28	45.52	31.63	24.71	20.58	15.90	14.46	12.47	11.18
2000	174.56	91.03	63.26	49.42	41.16	31.80	28.92	24.94	22.35
3000	261.84	136.54	94.88	74.13	61.74	47.70	43.37	37.40	33.52
4000	349.12	182.06	126.51	98.83	82.31	63.60	57.83	49.87	44.69
5000	436.39	227.57	158.13	123.54	102.89	79.50	72.29	62.33	55.86
6000	523.67	273.08	189.76	148.25	123.47	95.40	86.74	74.80	67.03
7000	610.95	318.60	221.38	172.96	144.04	111.30	101.20	87.26	78.20
8000	698.23	364.11	253.01	197.66	164.62	127.20	115.66	99.73	89.37
9000	785.50	409.62	284.63	222.37	185.20	143.10	130.11	112.19	100.54
10000	872.78	455.13	316.26	247.08	205.77	159.00	144.57	124.66	111.71
15000	1309.17	682.70	474.39	370.62	308.66	238.50	216.85	186.99	167.56
20000	1745.56	910.26	632.51	494.15	411.54	317.99	289.13	249.32	223.41
25000	2181.95	1137.83	790.64	617.69	514.43	397.49	361.42	311.64	279.26
30000	2618.34	1365.39	948.77	741.23	617.31	476.99	433.70	373.97	335.11
35000	3054.72	1592.96	1106.90	864.76	720.19	556.48	505.98	436.30	390.96
40000	3491.11	1820.52	1265.02	988.30	823.08	635.98	578.26	498.63	446.81
45000	3927.50	2048.08	1423.15	1111.84	925.96	715.48	650.54	560.95	502.66
46000	4014.78	2093.60	1454.78	1136.54	946.54	731.38	665.00	573.42	513.83
47000	4102.06	2139.11	1486.40	1161.25	967.12	747.28	679.46	585.88	525.00
48000	4189.33	2184.62	1518.03	1185.96	987.69	763.18	693.91	598.35	536.17
49000	4276.61	2230.14	1549.65	1210.67	1008.27	779.08	708.37	610.82	547.34
50000	4363.89	2275.65	1581.28	1235.37	1028.85	794.98	722.83	623.28	558.51
51000	4451.17	2321.16	1612.91	1260.08	1049.42	810.88	737.28	635.75	569.68
52000	4538.44	2366.67	1644.53	1284.79	1070.00	826.77	751.74	648.21	580.85
53000	4625.72	2412.19	1676.16	1309.50	1090.58	842.67	766.19	660.68	592.02
54000	4713.00	2457.70	1707.78	1334.20	1111.15	858.57	780.65	673.14	603.19
55000	4800.29	2503.21	1739.41	1358.91	1131.73	874.47	795.11	685.61	614.36
56000	4887.55	2548.73	1771.03	1383.62	1152.31	890.37	809.56	698.07	625.53
57000	4974.83	2594.24	1802.66	1408.32	1172.88	906.27	824.02	710.54	636.70
58000	5062.11	2639.75	1834.28	1433.03	1193.46	922.17	838.48	723.01	647.87
59000	5149.39	2685.26	1865.91	1457.74	1214.04	938.07	852.93	735.47	659.04
60000	5236.67	2730.78	1897.53	1482.45	1234.61	953.97	867.39	747.94	670.21
61000	5323.94	2776.29	1929.16	1507.15	1255.19	969.87	881.85	760.40	681.38
62000	5411.22	2821.80	1960.79	1531.86	1275.77	985.77	896.30	772.87	692.55
63000	5498.50	2867.32	1992.41	1556.57	1296.35	1001.67	910.76	785.33	703.72
64000	5585.78	2912.83	2024.04	1581.28	1316.92	1017.57	925.21	797.80	714.89
65000	5673.05	2958.34	2055.66	1605.98	1337.50	1033.47	939.67	810.26	726.06
67500	5891.25	3072.12	2134.73	1667.75	1388.94	1073.22	975.81	841.43	753.99
70000	6109.44	3185.91	2213.79	1729.52	1440.38	1112.96	1011.95	872.59	781.92
75000	6545.83	3413.47	2371.92	1853.06	1543.27	1192.46	1084.24	934.92	837.77
80000	6982.22	3641.04	2530.04	1976.59	1646.15	1271.96	1156.52	997.25	893.62
85000	7418.61	3868.60	2688.17	2100.13	1749.04	1351.46	1228.80	1059.57	949.47
90000	7855.00	4096.16	2846.30	2223.67	1851.92	1430.95	1301.08	1121.90	1005.32
95000	8291.38	4323.73	3004.43	2347.20	1954.80	1510.45	1373.36	1184.23	1061.17
100000	8727.77	4551.29	3162.55	2470.74	2057.69	1589.95	1445.65	1246.56	1117.02
105000	9164.16	4778.86	3320.68	2594.28	2160.57	1669.44	1517.93	1308.88	1172.87
110000	9600.55	5006.42	3478.81	2717.81	2263.46	1748.94	1590.21	1371.21	1228.72
115000	10036.94	5233.99	3636.94	2841.35	2366.34	1828.44	1662.49	1433.54	1284.57
120000	10473.33	5461.55	3795.06	2964.89	2469.22	1907.93	1734.77	1495.87	1340.42
125000	10909.71	5689.11	3953.19	3088.43	2572.11	1987.43	1807.06	1558.20	1396.27
130000	11346.10	5916.68	4111.32	3211.96	2674.99	2066.93	1879.34	1620.52	1452.12
135000	11782.49	6144.24	4269.45	3335.50	2777.88	2146.43	1951.62	1682.85	1507.97
140000	12218.88	6371.81	4427.57	3459.04	2880.76	2225.92	2023.90	1745.18	1563.83
145000	12655.27	6599.37	4585.70	3582.57	2983.65	2305.42	2096.18	1807.51	1619.68
150000	13091.66	6826.94	4743.83	3706.11	3086.53	2384.92	2168.47	1869.83	1675.53

AMOUNT	15 YEARS	18 YEARS	20 YEARS	25 YEARS	28 YEARS	29 YEARS	30 YEARS	35 YEARS	40 YEARS
$ 50	.50	.46	.44	.41	.40	.40	.39	.38	.38
100	1.00	.92	.88	.82	.79	.79	.78	.76	.75
200	1.99	1.83	1.76	1.63	1.58	1.57	1.56	1.52	1.49
300	2.98	2.74	2.63	2.45	2.37	2.36	2.34	2.27	2.23
400	3.97	3.66	3.51	3.26	3.16	3.14	3.12	3.03	2.98
500	4.97	4.57	4.38	4.07	3.95	3.92	3.89	3.79	3.72
600	5.96	5.48	5.26	4.89	4.74	4.71	4.67	4.54	4.46
700	6.95	6.40	6.14	5.70	5.53	5.49	5.45	5.30	5.20
800	7.94	7.31	7.01	6.51	6.32	6.27	6.23	6.05	5.95
900	8.93	8.22	7.89	7.33	7.11	7.06	7.01	6.81	6.69
1000	9.93	9.14	8.76	8.14	7.90	7.84	7.78	7.57	7.43
2000	19.85	18.27	17.52	16.28	15.80	15.68	15.56	15.13	14.86
3000	29.77	27.40	26.28	24.42	23.70	23.51	23.34	22.69	22.28
4000	39.69	36.53	35.04	32.55	31.60	31.35	31.12	30.25	29.71
5000	49.61	45.66	43.79	40.69	39.50	39.18	38.89	37.81	37.14
6000	59.53	54.79	52.55	48.83	47.40	47.02	46.67	45.37	44.56
7000	69.45	63.93	61.31	56.96	55.30	54.85	54.45	52.93	51.99
8000	79.37	73.06	70.07	65.10	63.20	62.69	62.23	60.49	59.41
9000	89.29	82.19	78.82	73.24	71.10	70.53	70.01	68.05	66.84
10000	99.21	91.32	87.58	81.37	79.00	78.36	77.78	75.61	74.27
15000	148.82	136.98	131.37	122.06	118.50	117.54	116.67	113.42	111.40
20000	198.42	182.64	175.16	162.74	158.00	156.72	155.56	151.22	148.53
25000	248.03	228.29	218.94	203.42	197.49	195.90	194.45	189.03	185.66
30000	297.63	273.95	262.73	244.11	236.99	235.07	233.34	226.83	222.79
35000	347.23	319.61	306.52	284.79	276.49	274.25	272.23	264.64	259.92
40000	396.84	365.27	350.31	325.47	315.99	313.43	311.12	302.44	297.05
45000	446.44	410.93	394.09	366.16	355.49	352.61	350.01	340.25	334.18
46000	456.36	420.06	402.85	374.29	363.39	360.45	357.79	347.81	341.61
47000	466.28	429.19	411.61	382.43	371.29	368.28	365.57	355.37	349.04
48000	476.20	438.32	420.37	390.57	379.19	376.12	373.34	362.93	356.46
49000	486.12	447.45	429.12	398.70	387.08	383.95	381.12	370.49	363.89
50000	496.05	456.58	437.88	406.84	394.98	391.79	388.90	378.05	371.31
51000	505.97	465.72	446.64	414.98	402.88	399.62	396.68	385.61	378.74
52000	515.89	474.85	455.40	423.11	410.78	407.46	404.46	393.17	386.17
53000	525.81	483.98	464.15	431.25	418.68	415.29	412.23	400.74	393.59
54000	535.73	493.11	472.91	439.39	426.58	423.13	420.01	408.30	401.02
55000	545.65	502.24	481.67	447.52	434.48	430.97	427.79	415.86	408.44
56000	555.57	511.37	490.43	455.66	442.38	438.80	435.57	423.42	415.87
57000	565.49	520.51	499.18	463.80	450.28	446.64	443.35	430.98	423.30
58000	575.41	529.64	507.94	471.93	458.18	454.47	451.12	438.54	430.72
59000	585.33	538.77	516.70	480.07	466.08	462.31	458.90	446.10	438.15
60000	595.25	547.90	525.46	488.21	473.98	470.14	466.68	453.66	445.58
61000	605.17	557.03	534.21	496.34	481.88	477.98	474.46	461.22	453.00
62000	615.09	566.16	542.97	504.48	489.78	485.82	482.23	468.78	460.43
63000	625.02	575.29	551.73	512.62	497.68	493.65	490.01	476.35	467.85
64000	634.94	584.43	560.49	520.75	505.58	501.49	497.79	483.91	475.28
65000	644.86	593.56	569.24	528.89	513.48	509.32	505.57	491.47	482.71
67500	669.66	616.39	591.14	549.23	533.23	528.91	525.01	510.37	501.27
70000	694.46	639.22	613.03	569.57	552.98	548.50	544.46	529.27	519.84
75000	744.07	684.87	656.82	610.26	592.47	587.68	583.35	567.08	556.97
80000	793.67	730.53	700.61	650.94	631.97	626.86	622.24	604.88	594.10
85000	843.27	776.19	744.39	691.62	671.47	666.04	661.13	642.69	631.23
90000	892.88	821.85	788.18	732.31	710.97	705.21	700.02	680.49	668.36
95000	942.48	867.51	831.97	772.99	750.47	744.39	738.91	718.30	705.49
100000	992.09	913.16	875.76	813.67	789.96	783.57	777.79	756.10	742.62
105000	1041.69	958.82	919.54	854.36	829.46	822.75	816.68	793.91	779.75
110000	1091.29	1004.48	963.33	895.04	868.96	861.93	855.57	831.71	816.88
115000	1140.90	1050.14	1007.12	935.72	908.46	901.11	894.46	869.51	854.02
120000	1190.50	1095.80	1050.91	976.41	947.96	940.28	933.35	907.32	891.15
125000	1240.11	1141.45	1094.69	1017.09	987.45	979.46	972.24	945.12	928.28
130000	1289.71	1187.11	1138.48	1057.77	1026.95	1018.64	1011.13	982.93	965.41
135000	1339.31	1232.77	1182.27	1098.46	1066.45	1057.82	1050.02	1020.73	1002.54
140000	1388.92	1278.43	1226.06	1139.14	1105.95	1097.00	1088.91	1058.54	1039.67
145000	1438.52	1324.09	1269.84	1179.82	1145.45	1136.18	1127.80	1096.34	1076.80
150000	1488.13	1369.74	1313.63	1220.51	1184.94	1175.35	1166.69	1134.15	1113.93

MONTHLY PAYMENT
NECESSARY TO AMORTIZE A LOAN

AMOUNT	1 YEAR	2 YEARS	3 YEARS	4 YEARS	5 YEARS	7 YEARS	8 YEARS	10 YEARS	12 YEARS
$ 50	4.37	2.28	1.59	1.24	1.04	.80	.73	.63	.57
100	8.74	4.56	3.17	2.48	2.07	1.60	1.46	1.26	1.13
200	17.47	9.12	6.34	4.96	4.13	3.20	2.91	2.51	2.25
300	26.21	13.68	9.51	7.43	6.20	4.79	4.36	3.76	3.38
400	34.94	18.23	12.68	9.91	8.26	6.39	5.81	5.02	4.50
500	43.67	22.79	15.85	12.39	10.32	7.99	7.27	6.27	5.62
600	52.41	27.35	19.02	14.86	12.39	9.58	8.72	7.52	6.75
700	61.14	31.90	22.18	17.34	14.45	11.18	10.17	8.78	7.87
800	69.87	36.46	25.35	19.82	16.51	12.77	11.62	10.03	9.00
900	78.61	41.02	28.52	22.29	18.58	14.37	13.07	11.28	10.12
1000	87.34	45.58	31.69	24.77	20.64	15.97	14.53	12.54	11.24
2000	174.68	91.15	63.37	49.54	41.28	31.93	29.05	25.07	22.48
3000	262.01	136.72	95.06	74.30	61.92	47.89	43.57	37.60	33.72
4000	349.35	182.29	126.74	99.07	82.55	63.85	58.09	50.14	44.96
5000	436.68	227.86	158.42	123.84	103.19	79.82	72.61	62.67	56.20
6000	524.02	273.43	190.11	148.60	123.83	95.78	87.13	75.20	67.44
7000	611.35	319.00	221.79	173.37	144.47	111.74	101.65	87.73	78.68
8000	698.69	364.57	253.47	198.14	165.10	127.70	116.17	100.27	89.92
9000	786.03	410.14	285.16	222.90	185.74	143.67	130.69	112.80	101.16
10000	873.36	455.71	316.84	247.67	206.38	159.63	145.21	125.33	112.40
15000	1310.04	683.56	475.26	371.50	309.56	239.44	217.82	188.00	168.60
20000	1746.72	911.41	633.68	495.34	412.75	319.25	290.42	250.66	224.80
25000	2183.39	1139.26	792.09	619.17	515.94	399.07	363.03	313.32	281.00
30000	2620.07	1367.11	950.51	743.00	619.12	478.88	435.63	375.99	337.20
35000	3056.75	1594.96	1108.93	866.83	722.31	558.69	508.23	438.65	393.40
40000	3493.43	1822.81	1267.35	990.67	825.49	638.50	580.84	501.31	449.60
45000	3930.11	2050.66	1425.76	1114.50	928.68	718.32	653.44	563.98	505.80
46000	4017.44	2096.23	1457.45	1139.26	949.32	734.28	667.96	576.51	517.04
47000	4104.78	2141.80	1489.13	1164.03	969.95	750.24	682.48	589.04	528.28
48000	4192.11	2187.37	1520.81	1188.80	990.59	766.20	697.01	601.57	539.52
49000	4279.45	2232.94	1552.50	1213.56	1011.23	782.17	711.53	614.11	550.76
50000	4366.78	2278.51	1584.18	1238.33	1031.87	798.13	726.05	626.64	562.00
51000	4454.12	2324.08	1615.86	1263.10	1052.50	814.09	740.57	639.17	573.24
52000	4541.46	2369.65	1647.55	1287.86	1073.14	830.05	755.09	651.70	584.48
53000	4628.79	2415.22	1679.23	1312.63	1093.78	846.02	769.61	664.24	595.72
54000	4716.13	2460.79	1710.91	1337.40	1114.42	861.98	784.13	676.77	606.96
55000	4803.46	2506.36	1742.60	1362.16	1135.05	877.94	798.65	689.30	618.20
56000	4890.80	2551.93	1774.28	1386.93	1155.69	893.90	813.17	701.83	629.44
57000	4978.13	2597.50	1805.96	1411.70	1176.33	909.87	827.69	714.37	640.68
58000	5065.47	2643.07	1837.65	1436.46	1196.96	925.83	842.21	726.90	651.92
59000	5152.80	2688.64	1869.33	1461.23	1217.60	941.79	856.73	739.43	663.16
60000	5240.14	2734.21	1901.02	1486.00	1238.24	957.75	871.26	751.97	674.40
61000	5327.48	2779.78	1932.70	1510.76	1258.88	973.72	885.78	764.50	685.64
62000	5414.81	2825.35	1964.38	1535.53	1279.51	989.68	900.30	777.03	696.88
63000	5502.15	2870.92	1996.07	1560.29	1300.15	1005.64	914.82	789.56	708.12
64000	5589.48	2916.49	2027.75	1585.06	1320.79	1021.60	929.34	802.10	719.36
65000	5676.82	2962.06	2059.43	1609.83	1341.43	1037.57	943.86	814.63	730.60
67500	5895.16	3075.99	2138.64	1671.74	1393.02	1077.47	980.16	845.96	758.70
70000	6113.50	3189.91	2217.85	1733.66	1444.61	1117.38	1016.46	877.29	786.80
75000	6550.17	3417.76	2376.27	1857.49	1547.80	1197.19	1089.07	939.96	843.00
80000	6986.85	3645.61	2534.69	1981.33	1650.98	1277.00	1161.67	1002.62	899.20
85000	7423.53	3873.47	2693.10	2105.16	1754.17	1356.82	1234.28	1065.28	955.40
90000	7860.21	4101.32	2851.52	2228.99	1857.36	1436.63	1306.88	1127.95	1011.60
95000	8296.89	4329.17	3009.94	2352.82	1960.54	1516.44	1379.48	1190.61	1067.80
100000	8733.56	4557.02	3168.36	2476.66	2063.73	1596.25	1452.09	1253.27	1124.00
105000	9170.24	4784.87	3326.77	2600.49	2166.91	1676.07	1524.69	1315.94	1180.20
110000	9606.92	5012.72	3485.19	2724.32	2270.10	1755.88	1597.30	1378.60	1236.40
115000	10043.60	5240.57	3643.61	2848.15	2373.29	1835.69	1669.90	1441.26	1292.60
120000	10480.28	5468.42	3802.03	2971.99	2476.47	1915.50	1742.51	1503.93	1348.80
125000	10916.95	5696.27	3960.44	3095.82	2579.66	1995.32	1815.11	1566.59	1405.00
130000	11353.63	5924.12	4118.86	3219.65	2682.85	2075.13	1887.71	1629.25	1461.20
135000	11790.31	6151.97	4277.28	3343.48	2786.03	2154.94	1960.32	1691.92	1517.40
140000	12226.99	6379.82	4435.70	3467.32	2889.22	2234.75	2032.92	1754.58	1573.60
145000	12663.67	6607.67	4594.11	3591.15	2992.40	2314.57	2105.53	1817.24	1629.80
150000	13100.34	6835.52	4752.53	3714.98	3095.59	2394.38	2178.13	1879.91	1686.00

MONTHLY PAYMENT   8¾%

NECESSARY TO AMORTIZE A LOAN

AMOUNT	15 YEARS	18 YEARS	20 YEARS	25 YEARS	28 YEARS	29 YEARS	30 YEARS	35 YEARS	40 YEARS
$ 50	.50	.47	.45	.42	.40	.40	.40	.39	.38
100	1.00	.93	.89	.83	.80	.80	.79	.77	.76
200	2.00	1.85	1.77	1.65	1.60	1.59	1.58	1.54	1.51
300	3.00	2.77	2.66	2.47	2.40	2.38	2.37	2.30	2.26
400	4.00	3.69	3.54	3.29	3.20	3.17	3.15	3.07	3.01
500	5.00	4.61	4.42	4.12	4.00	3.97	3.94	3.83	3.77
600	6.00	5.53	5.31	4.94	4.80	4.76	4.73	4.60	4.52
700	7.00	6.45	6.19	5.76	5.60	5.55	5.51	5.36	5.27
800	8.00	7.37	7.07	6.58	6.39	6.34	6.30	6.13	6.02
900	8.96	8.29	7.96	7.40	7.19	7.14	7.09	6.89	6.77
1000	10.00	9.21	8.84	8.23	7.99	7.93	7.87	7.66	7.53
2000	19.99	18.42	17.68	16.45	15.98	15.85	15.74	15.31	15.05
3000	29.99	27.63	26.52	24.67	23.97	23.78	23.61	22.97	22.57
4000	39.98	36.84	35.35	32.89	31.95	31.70	31.47	30.62	30.09
5000	49.98	46.05	44.19	41.11	39.94	39.62	39.34	38.27	37.61
6000	59.97	55.26	53.03	49.33	47.93	47.55	47.21	45.93	45.14
7000	69.97	64.47	61.86	57.56	55.91	55.47	55.07	53.58	52.66
8000	79.96	73.68	70.70	65.78	63.90	63.40	62.94	61.23	60.18
9000	89.96	82.89	79.54	74.00	71.89	71.32	70.81	68.89	67.70
10000	99.95	92.09	88.38	82.22	79.88	79.24	78.68	76.54	75.22
15000	149.92	138.14	132.56	123.33	119.81	118.86	118.01	114.81	112.83
20000	199.89	184.18	176.75	164.43	159.75	158.48	157.35	153.08	150.44
25000	249.87	230.23	220.93	205.54	199.69	198.10	196.68	191.35	188.05
30000	299.84	276.27	265.12	246.65	239.62	237.72	236.02	229.61	225.66
35000	349.81	322.32	309.30	287.76	279.55	277.34	275.35	267.88	263.26
40000	399.78	368.36	353.49	328.86	319.49	316.96	314.69	306.15	300.87
45000	449.76	414.41	397.67	369.97	359.42	356.58	354.02	344.42	338.48
46000	459.75	423.61	406.51	378.19	367.41	364.51	361.89	352.07	346.00
47000	469.75	432.82	415.35	386.41	375.40	372.43	369.75	359.73	353.53
48000	479.74	442.03	424.19	394.63	383.38	380.36	377.62	367.38	361.05
49000	489.73	451.24	433.02	402.86	391.37	388.28	385.49	375.03	368.57
50000	499.73	460.45	441.86	411.08	399.36	396.20	393.36	382.69	376.09
51000	509.72	469.66	450.70	419.30	407.34	404.13	401.22	390.34	383.61
52000	519.72	478.87	459.53	427.52	415.33	412.05	409.09	397.99	391.13
53000	529.71	488.08	468.37	435.74	423.32	419.97	416.96	405.65	398.66
54000	539.71	497.29	477.21	443.96	431.31	427.90	424.82	413.30	406.18
55000	549.70	506.49	486.05	452.18	439.29	435.82	432.69	420.95	413.70
56000	559.70	515.70	494.88	460.41	447.28	443.75	440.56	428.61	421.22
57000	569.69	524.91	503.72	468.63	455.27	451.67	448.42	436.26	428.74
58000	579.69	534.12	512.56	476.85	463.25	459.59	456.29	443.92	436.26
59000	589.68	543.33	521.39	485.07	471.24	467.52	464.16	451.57	443.79
60000	599.67	552.54	530.23	493.29	479.23	475.44	472.03	459.22	451.31
61000	609.67	561.75	539.07	501.51	487.22	483.37	479.89	466.88	458.83
62000	619.66	570.96	547.91	509.73	495.20	491.29	487.76	474.53	466.35
63000	629.66	580.17	556.74	517.96	503.19	499.21	495.63	482.18	473.87
64000	639.65	589.37	565.58	526.18	511.18	507.14	503.49	489.84	481.39
65000	649.65	598.58	574.42	534.40	519.16	515.06	511.36	497.49	488.92
67500	674.63	621.61	596.51	554.95	539.13	534.87	531.03	516.63	507.72
70000	699.62	644.63	618.60	575.51	559.10	554.68	550.70	535.76	526.52
75000	749.59	690.67	662.79	616.61	599.03	594.30	590.03	574.03	564.13
80000	799.56	736.72	706.97	657.72	638.97	633.92	629.37	612.30	601.74
85000	849.54	782.76	751.16	698.83	678.90	673.54	668.70	650.56	639.35
90000	899.51	828.81	795.34	739.93	718.84	713.16	708.04	688.83	676.96
95000	949.48	874.85	839.53	781.04	758.77	752.78	747.37	727.10	714.57
100000	999.45	920.90	883.72	822.15	798.71	792.40	786.71	765.37	752.18
105000	1049.43	966.94	927.90	863.26	838.65	832.02	826.04	803.64	789.78
110000	1099.40	1012.98	972.09	904.36	878.58	871.64	865.38	841.90	827.39
115000	1149.37	1059.03	1016.27	945.47	918.52	911.26	904.71	880.17	865.00
120000	1199.34	1105.07	1060.46	986.58	958.45	950.88	944.05	918.44	902.61
125000	1249.32	1151.12	1104.64	1027.68	998.39	990.50	983.38	956.71	940.22
130000	1299.29	1197.16	1148.83	1068.79	1038.32	1030.12	1022.72	994.98	977.83
135000	1349.26	1243.21	1193.01	1109.90	1078.26	1069.74	1062.05	1033.25	1015.44
140000	1399.23	1289.25	1237.20	1151.01	1118.19	1109.36	1101.39	1071.51	1053.04
145000	1449.21	1335.30	1281.39	1192.11	1158.13	1148.98	1140.72	1109.78	1090.65
150000	1499.18	1381.34	1325.57	1233.22	1198.06	1188.60	1180.06	1148.05	1128.26

MONTHLY PAYMENT
NECESSARY TO AMORTIZE A LOAN

AMOUNT	1 YEAR	2 YEARS	3 YEARS	4 YEARS	5 YEARS	7 YEARS	8 YEARS	10 YEARS	12 YEARS
$ 50	4.37	2.29	1.59	1.25	1.04	.81	.73	.64	.57
100	8.74	4.57	3.18	2.49	2.07	1.61	1.46	1.27	1.14
200	17.48	9.13	6.35	4.97	4.14	3.21	2.92	2.53	2.27
300	26.22	13.69	9.53	7.45	6.21	4.81	4.38	3.79	3.40
400	34.96	18.26	12.70	9.94	8.28	6.42	5.84	5.05	4.53
500	43.70	22.82	15.88	12.42	10.35	8.02	7.30	6.31	5.66
600	52.44	27.38	19.05	14.90	12.42	9.62	8.76	7.57	6.79
700	61.18	31.94	22.22	17.38	14.49	11.22	10.21	8.83	7.92
800	69.92	36.51	25.40	19.87	16.56	12.83	11.67	10.09	9.05
900	78.66	41.07	28.57	22.35	18.63	14.43	13.13	11.35	10.18
1000	87.40	45.63	31.75	24.83	20.70	16.03	14.59	12.61	11.32
2000	174.79	91.26	63.49	49.66	41.40	32.06	29.18	25.21	22.63
3000	262.19	136.89	95.23	74.48	62.10	48.08	43.76	37.81	33.94
4000	349.58	182.51	126.97	99.31	82.80	64.11	58.35	50.41	45.25
5000	436.97	228.14	158.71	124.13	103.49	80.13	72.93	63.01	56.56
6000	524.37	273.77	190.45	148.96	124.19	96.16	87.52	75.61	67.87
7000	611.76	319.40	222.20	173.79	144.89	112.18	102.10	88.21	79.18
8000	699.15	365.02	253.94	198.61	165.59	128.21	116.69	100.81	90.49
9000	786.55	410.65	285.68	223.44	186.28	144.24	131.27	113.41	101.80
10000	873.94	456.28	317.42	248.26	206.98	160.26	145.86	126.01	113.11
15000	1310.91	684.42	476.13	372.39	310.47	240.39	218.79	189.01	169.66
20000	1747.88	912.55	634.84	496.52	413.96	320.52	291.71	252.01	226.21
25000	2184.84	1140.69	793.54	620.65	517.45	400.65	364.64	315.01	282.76
30000	2621.81	1368.83	952.25	744.78	620.94	480.78	437.57	378.01	339.31
35000	3058.78	1596.96	1110.96	868.91	724.43	560.90	510.50	441.01	395.86
40000	3495.75	1825.10	1269.67	993.03	827.91	641.03	583.42	504.01	452.41
45000	3932.71	2053.24	1428.38	1117.16	931.40	721.16	656.35	567.01	508.96
46000	4020.11	2098.87	1460.12	1141.99	952.10	737.19	670.94	579.61	520.27
47000	4107.50	2144.49	1491.86	1166.81	972.80	753.21	685.52	592.21	531.58
48000	4194.89	2190.12	1523.60	1191.64	993.50	769.24	700.11	604.81	542.89
49000	4282.29	2235.75	1555.34	1216.47	1014.19	785.26	714.69	617.41	554.20
50000	4369.68	2281.38	1587.08	1241.29	1034.89	801.29	729.28	630.01	565.51
51000	4457.07	2327.00	1618.83	1266.12	1055.59	817.32	743.86	642.61	576.82
52000	4544.47	2372.63	1650.57	1290.94	1076.29	833.34	758.45	655.21	588.13
53000	4631.86	2418.26	1682.31	1315.77	1096.99	849.37	773.03	667.81	599.44
54000	4719.26	2463.89	1714.05	1340.59	1117.68	865.39	787.62	680.41	610.75
55000	4806.65	2509.51	1745.79	1365.42	1138.38	881.42	802.20	693.01	622.06
56000	4894.04	2555.14	1777.53	1390.25	1159.08	897.44	816.79	705.61	633.37
57000	4981.44	2600.77	1809.28	1415.07	1179.78	913.47	831.38	718.21	644.68
58000	5068.83	2646.39	1841.02	1439.90	1200.47	929.50	845.96	730.81	655.99
59000	5156.22	2692.02	1872.76	1464.72	1221.17	945.52	860.55	743.41	667.30
60000	5243.62	2737.65	1904.50	1489.55	1241.87	961.55	875.13	756.01	678.61
61000	5331.01	2783.28	1936.24	1514.37	1262.57	977.57	889.72	768.61	689.92
62000	5418.40	2828.90	1967.98	1539.20	1283.26	993.60	904.30	781.21	701.23
63000	5505.80	2874.53	1999.73	1564.03	1303.96	1009.62	918.89	793.81	712.54
64000	5593.19	2920.16	2031.47	1588.85	1324.66	1025.65	933.47	806.41	723.85
65000	5680.58	2965.79	2063.21	1613.68	1345.36	1041.68	948.06	819.01	735.16
67500	5899.07	3079.86	2142.56	1675.74	1397.10	1081.74	984.52	850.51	763.43
70000	6117.55	3193.92	2221.92	1737.81	1448.85	1121.80	1020.99	882.01	791.71
75000	6554.52	3422.06	2380.62	1861.93	1552.34	1201.93	1093.91	945.01	848.26
80000	6991.49	3650.20	2539.33	1986.06	1655.82	1282.06	1166.84	1008.01	904.81
85000	7428.45	3878.33	2698.04	2110.19	1759.31	1362.19	1239.77	1071.01	961.36
90000	7865.42	4106.47	2856.75	2234.32	1862.80	1442.32	1312.69	1134.01	1017.91
95000	8302.39	4334.61	3015.46	2358.45	1966.29	1522.45	1385.62	1197.01	1074.46
100000	8739.36	4562.75	3174.16	2482.58	2069.78	1602.58	1458.55	1260.01	1131.01
105000	9176.32	4790.88	3332.87	2606.71	2173.27	1682.70	1531.48	1323.01	1187.56
110000	9613.29	5019.02	3491.58	2730.84	2276.76	1762.83	1604.40	1386.01	1244.11
115000	10050.26	5247.16	3650.29	2854.96	2380.25	1842.96	1677.33	1449.01	1300.66
120000	10487.23	5475.29	3809.00	2979.09	2483.73	1923.09	1750.26	1512.01	1357.21
125000	10924.20	5703.43	3967.70	3103.22	2587.22	2003.22	1823.18	1575.01	1413.76
130000	11361.16	5931.57	4126.41	3227.35	2690.71	2083.35	1896.11	1638.01	1470.31
135000	11798.13	6159.71	4285.12	3351.48	2794.20	2163.48	1969.04	1701.01	1526.86
140000	12235.10	6387.84	4443.83	3475.61	2897.69	2243.60	2041.97	1764.01	1583.41
145000	12672.07	6615.98	4602.54	3599.74	3001.18	2323.73	2114.89	1827.01	1639.96
150000	13109.03	6844.12	4761.24	3723.86	3104.67	2403.86	2187.82	1890.01	1696.51

MONTHLY PAYMENT 8⅞%

NECESSARY TO AMORTIZE A LOAN

AMOUNT	15 YEARS	18 YEARS	20 YEARS	25 YEARS	28 YEARS	29 YEARS	30 YEARS	35 YEARS	40 YEARS
$ 50	.51	.47	.45	.42	.41	.41	.40	.39	.39
100	1.01	.93	.90	.84	.81	.81	.80	.78	.77
200	2.02	1.86	1.79	1.67	1.62	1.61	1.60	1.55	1.53
300	3.03	2.79	2.68	2.50	2.43	2.41	2.39	2.33	2.29
400	4.03	3.72	3.57	3.33	3.23	3.21	3.19	3.10	3.05
500	5.04	4.65	4.46	4.16	4.04	4.01	3.98	3.88	3.81
600	6.05	5.58	5.36	4.99	4.85	4.81	4.78	4.65	4.58
700	7.05	6.51	6.25	5.82	5.66	5.61	5.57	5.43	5.34
800	8.06	7.43	7.14	6.65	6.46	6.42	6.37	6.20	6.10
900	9.07	8.36	8.03	7.48	7.27	7.22	7.17	6.98	6.86
1000	10.07	9.29	8.92	8.31	8.08	8.02	7.96	7.75	7.62
2000	20.14	18.58	17.84	16.62	16.15	16.03	15.92	15.50	15.24
3000	30.21	27.86	26.76	24.92	24.23	24.04	23.87	23.24	22.86
4000	40.28	37.15	35.67	33.23	32.30	32.06	31.83	30.99	30.48
5000	50.35	46.44	44.59	41.54	40.38	40.07	39.79	38.74	38.09
6000	60.42	55.72	53.51	49.84	48.45	48.08	47.74	46.48	45.71
7000	70.48	65.01	62.42	58.15	56.53	56.09	55.70	54.23	53.33
8000	80.55	74.30	71.34	66.46	64.60	64.11	63.66	61.98	60.95
9000	90.62	83.58	80.26	74.76	72.68	72.12	71.61	69.72	68.56
10000	100.69	92.87	89.18	83.07	80.75	80.13	79.57	77.47	76.18
15000	151.03	139.30	133.76	124.60	121.13	120.19	119.35	116.20	114.27
20000	201.37	185.74	178.35	166.14	161.50	160.26	159.13	154.94	152.36
25000	251.72	232.17	222.93	207.67	201.88	200.32	198.92	193.67	190.44
30000	302.06	278.60	267.52	249.20	242.25	240.38	238.70	232.40	228.53
35000	352.40	325.03	312.10	290.73	282.62	280.45	278.48	271.14	266.62
40000	402.74	371.47	356.69	332.27	323.00	320.51	318.26	309.87	304.71
45000	453.08	417.90	401.27	373.80	363.37	360.57	358.05	348.60	342.79
46000	463.15	427.19	410.19	382.11	371.45	368.58	366.00	356.35	350.41
47000	473.22	436.47	419.11	390.41	379.52	376.60	373.96	364.10	358.03
48000	483.29	445.76	428.02	398.72	387.60	384.61	381.91	371.84	365.65
49000	493.36	455.04	436.94	407.03	395.67	392.62	389.87	379.59	373.26
50000	503.43	464.33	445.86	415.33	403.75	400.64	397.83	387.34	380.88
51000	513.50	473.62	454.77	423.64	411.82	408.65	405.78	395.08	388.50
52000	523.56	482.90	463.69	431.94	419.90	416.66	413.74	402.83	396.12
53000	533.63	492.19	472.61	440.25	427.97	424.67	421.70	410.58	403.73
54000	543.70	501.48	481.52	448.56	436.05	432.69	429.65	418.32	411.35
55000	553.77	510.76	490.44	456.86	444.12	440.70	437.61	426.07	418.97
56000	563.84	520.05	499.36	465.17	452.20	448.71	445.57	433.82	426.59
57000	573.91	529.34	508.28	473.48	460.27	456.72	453.52	441.56	434.20
58000	583.97	538.62	517.19	481.78	468.35	464.74	461.48	449.31	441.82
59000	594.04	547.91	526.11	490.09	476.42	472.75	469.44	457.06	449.44
60000	604.11	557.20	535.03	498.40	484.50	480.76	477.39	464.80	457.06
61000	614.18	566.48	543.94	506.70	492.57	488.77	485.35	472.55	464.67
62000	624.25	575.77	552.86	515.01	500.65	496.79	493.30	480.30	472.29
63000	634.32	585.06	561.78	523.32	508.72	504.80	501.26	488.04	479.91
64000	644.39	594.34	570.69	531.62	516.80	512.81	509.22	495.79	487.53
65000	654.45	603.63	579.61	539.93	524.87	520.82	517.17	503.54	495.14
67500	679.62	626.85	601.90	560.70	545.06	540.86	537.07	522.90	514.19
70000	704.80	650.06	624.20	581.46	565.24	560.89	556.96	542.27	533.23
75000	755.14	696.49	668.78	622.99	605.62	600.95	596.74	581.00	571.32
80000	805.48	742.93	713.37	664.53	645.99	641.01	636.52	619.74	609.41
85000	855.82	789.36	757.95	706.06	686.37	681.08	676.30	658.47	647.49
90000	906.16	835.79	802.54	747.59	726.74	721.14	716.09	697.20	685.58
95000	956.51	882.22	847.12	789.13	767.12	761.20	755.87	735.93	723.67
100000	1006.85	928.66	891.71	830.66	807.49	801.27	795.65	774.67	761.76
105000	1057.19	975.09	936.29	872.19	847.86	841.33	835.43	813.40	799.84
110000	1107.53	1021.52	980.88	913.72	888.24	881.39	875.21	852.13	837.93
115000	1157.88	1067.96	1025.46	955.26	928.61	921.45	915.00	890.87	876.02
120000	1208.22	1114.39	1070.05	996.79	968.99	961.52	954.78	929.60	914.11
125000	1258.56	1160.82	1114.63	1038.32	1009.36	1001.58	994.56	968.33	952.20
130000	1308.90	1207.25	1159.22	1079.85	1049.74	1041.64	1034.34	1007.07	990.28
135000	1359.24	1253.69	1203.80	1121.39	1090.11	1081.71	1074.13	1045.80	1028.37
140000	1409.59	1300.12	1248.39	1162.92	1130.48	1121.77	1113.91	1084.53	1066.46
145000	1459.93	1346.55	1292.97	1204.45	1170.86	1161.83	1153.69	1123.27	1104.55
150000	1510.27	1392.98	1337.56	1245.98	1211.23	1201.90	1193.47	1162.00	1142.63

35

9% MONTHLY PAYMENT
NECESSARY TO AMORTIZE A LOAN

AMOUNT	1 YEAR	2 YEARS	3 YEARS	4 YEARS	5 YEARS	7 YEARS	8 YEARS	10 YEARS	12 YEARS
$ 50	4.38	2.29	1.59	1.25	1.04	.81	.74	.64	.57
100	8.75	4.57	3.18	2.49	2.08	1.61	1.47	1.27	1.14
200	17.50	9.14	6.36	4.98	4.16	3.22	2.94	2.54	2.28
300	26.24	13.71	9.54	7.47	6.23	4.83	4.40	3.81	3.42
400	34.99	18.28	12.72	9.96	8.31	6.44	5.87	5.07	4.56
500	43.73	22.85	15.90	12.45	10.38	8.05	7.33	6.34	5.70
600	52.48	27.42	19.08	14.94	12.46	9.66	8.80	7.61	6.83
700	61.22	31.98	22.26	17.42	14.54	11.27	10.26	8.87	7.97
800	69.97	36.55	25.44	19.91	16.61	12.88	11.73	10.14	9.11
900	78.71	41.12	28.62	22.40	18.69	14.49	13.19	11.41	10.25
1000	87.46	45.69	31.80	24.89	20.76	16.09	14.66	12.67	11.39
2000	174.91	91.37	63.60	49.78	41.52	32.18	29.31	25.34	22.77
3000	262.36	137.06	95.40	74.66	62.28	48.27	43.96	38.01	34.15
4000	349.81	182.74	127.20	99.55	83.04	64.36	58.61	50.68	45.53
5000	437.26	228.43	159.00	124.43	103.80	80.45	73.26	63.34	56.91
6000	524.71	274.11	190.80	149.32	124.56	96.54	87.91	76.01	68.29
7000	612.17	319.80	222.60	174.20	145.31	112.63	102.56	88.68	79.67
8000	699.62	365.48	254.40	199.09	166.07	128.72	117.21	101.35	91.05
9000	787.07	411.17	286.20	223.97	186.83	144.81	131.86	114.01	102.43
10000	874.52	456.85	318.00	248.86	207.59	160.90	146.51	126.68	113.81
15000	1311.78	685.28	477.00	373.28	311.38	241.34	219.76	190.02	170.71
20000	1749.03	913.70	636.00	497.71	415.17	321.79	293.01	253.36	227.61
25000	2186.29	1142.12	795.00	622.13	518.96	402.23	366.26	316.69	284.51
30000	2623.55	1370.55	954.00	746.56	622.76	482.68	439.51	380.03	341.41
35000	3060.81	1598.97	1113.00	870.98	726.55	563.12	512.76	443.37	398.32
40000	3498.06	1827.39	1271.99	995.41	830.34	643.57	586.01	506.71	455.22
45000	3935.32	2055.82	1430.99	1119.83	934.13	724.01	659.26	570.05	512.12
46000	4022.77	2101.50	1462.79	1144.72	954.89	740.10	673.91	582.71	523.50
47000	4110.22	2147.19	1494.59	1169.60	975.65	756.19	688.56	595.38	534.88
48000	4197.68	2192.87	1526.39	1194.49	996.41	772.28	703.21	608.05	546.26
49000	4285.13	2238.56	1558.19	1219.37	1017.16	788.37	717.86	620.72	557.64
50000	4372.58	2284.24	1589.99	1244.26	1037.92	804.46	732.52	633.38	569.02
51000	4460.03	2329.93	1621.79	1269.14	1058.68	820.55	747.17	646.05	580.40
52000	4547.48	2375.61	1653.59	1294.03	1079.44	836.64	761.82	658.72	591.78
53000	4634.93	2421.30	1685.39	1318.91	1100.20	852.73	776.47	671.39	603.16
54000	4722.38	2466.98	1717.19	1343.80	1120.96	868.82	791.12	684.05	614.54
55000	4809.84	2512.67	1748.99	1368.68	1141.71	884.90	805.77	696.72	625.92
56000	4897.29	2558.35	1780.79	1393.57	1162.47	900.99	820.42	709.39	637.30
57000	4984.74	2604.04	1812.59	1418.45	1183.23	917.08	835.07	722.06	648.68
58000	5072.19	2649.72	1844.39	1443.34	1203.99	933.17	849.72	734.72	660.06
59000	5159.64	2695.40	1876.19	1468.22	1224.75	949.26	864.37	747.39	671.44
60000	5247.09	2741.09	1907.99	1493.11	1245.51	965.35	879.02	760.06	682.82
61000	5334.55	2786.77	1939.79	1517.99	1266.26	981.44	893.67	772.73	694.20
62000	5422.00	2832.46	1971.59	1542.88	1287.02	997.53	908.32	785.39	705.58
63000	5509.45	2878.14	2003.39	1567.76	1307.78	1013.62	922.97	798.06	716.96
64000	5596.90	2923.83	2035.19	1592.65	1328.54	1029.71	937.62	810.73	728.34
65000	5684.35	2969.51	2066.99	1617.53	1349.30	1045.80	952.27	823.40	739.72
67500	5902.98	3083.73	2146.49	1679.75	1401.19	1086.02	988.89	855.07	768.18
70000	6121.61	3197.94	2225.99	1741.96	1453.09	1126.24	1025.52	886.74	796.63
75000	6558.87	3426.36	2384.98	1866.38	1556.88	1206.69	1098.77	950.07	853.53
80000	6996.12	3654.78	2543.98	1990.81	1660.67	1287.13	1172.02	1013.41	910.43
85000	7433.38	3883.21	2702.98	2115.23	1764.47	1367.58	1245.27	1076.75	967.33
90000	7870.64	4111.63	2861.98	2239.66	1868.26	1448.02	1318.52	1140.09	1024.23
95000	8307.90	4340.06	3020.98	2364.08	1972.05	1528.47	1391.77	1203.42	1081.13
100000	8745.15	4568.48	3179.98	2488.51	2075.84	1608.91	1465.03	1266.76	1138.04
105000	9182.41	4796.90	3338.98	2612.93	2179.63	1689.36	1538.28	1330.10	1194.94
110000	9619.67	5025.33	3497.98	2737.36	2283.42	1769.80	1611.53	1393.44	1251.84
115000	10056.92	5253.75	3656.97	2861.78	2387.22	1850.25	1684.78	1456.78	1308.74
120000	10494.18	5482.17	3815.97	2986.21	2491.01	1930.69	1758.03	1520.11	1365.64
125000	10931.44	5710.60	3974.97	3110.64	2594.80	2011.14	1831.28	1583.45	1422.54
130000	11368.70	5939.02	4133.97	3235.06	2698.59	2091.59	1904.53	1646.79	1479.44
135000	11805.95	6167.45	4292.97	3359.49	2802.38	2172.03	1977.78	1710.13	1536.35
140000	12243.21	6395.87	4451.97	3483.91	2906.17	2252.48	2051.03	1773.47	1593.25
145000	12680.47	6624.29	4610.97	3608.34	3009.97	2332.92	2124.28	1836.80	1650.15
150000	13117.73	6852.72	4769.96	3732.76	3113.76	2413.37	2197.54	1900.14	1707.05

MONTHLY PAYMENT 9%

NECESSARY TO AMORTIZE A LOAN

AMOUNT	15 YEARS	18 YEARS	20 YEARS	25 YEARS	28 YEARS	29 YEARS	30 YEARS	35 YEARS	40 YEARS
$ 50	.51	.47	.45	.42	.41	.41	.41	.40	.39
100	1.02	.94	.90	.84	.82	.82	.81	.79	.78
200	2.03	1.88	1.80	1.68	1.64	1.63	1.61	1.57	1.55
300	3.05	2.81	2.70	2.52	2.45	2.44	2.42	2.36	2.32
400	4.06	3.75	3.60	3.36	3.27	3.25	3.22	3.14	3.09
500	5.08	4.69	4.50	4.20	4.09	4.06	4.03	3.92	3.86
600	6.09	5.62	5.40	5.04	4.90	4.87	4.83	4.71	4.63
700	7.10	6.56	6.30	5.88	5.72	5.68	5.64	5.49	5.40
800	8.12	7.50	7.20	6.72	6.54	6.49	6.44	6.28	6.18
900	9.13	8.43	8.10	7.56	7.35	7.30	7.25	7.06	6.95
1000	10.15	9.37	9.00	8.40	8.17	8.11	8.05	7.84	7.72
2000	20.29	18.73	18.00	16.79	16.33	16.21	16.10	15.68	15.43
3000	30.43	28.10	27.00	25.18	24.49	24.31	24.14	23.52	23.15
4000	40.58	37.46	35.99	33.57	32.66	32.41	32.19	31.36	30.86
5000	50.72	46.83	44.99	41.96	40.82	40.51	40.24	39.20	38.57
6000	60.86	56.19	53.99	50.36	48.98	48.61	48.28	47.04	46.29
7000	71.00	65.56	62.99	58.75	57.15	56.72	56.33	54.88	54.00
8000	81.15	74.92	71.98	67.14	65.31	64.82	64.37	62.72	61.71
9000	91.29	84.29	80.98	75.53	73.47	72.92	72.42	70.56	69.43
10000	101.43	93.65	89.98	83.92	81.63	81.02	80.47	78.40	77.14
15000	152.14	140.47	134.96	125.88	122.45	121.53	120.70	117.60	115.71
20000	202.86	187.29	179.95	167.84	163.26	162.04	160.93	156.80	154.28
25000	253.57	234.12	224.94	209.80	204.08	202.54	201.16	196.00	192.85
30000	304.28	280.94	269.92	251.76	244.89	243.05	241.39	235.20	231.41
35000	355.00	327.76	314.91	293.72	285.71	283.56	281.62	274.40	269.98
40000	405.71	374.58	359.90	335.68	326.52	324.07	321.85	313.60	308.55
45000	456.42	421.41	404.88	377.64	367.34	364.58	362.09	352.80	347.12
46000	466.57	430.77	413.88	386.04	375.50	372.68	370.13	360.64	354.83
47000	476.71	440.13	422.88	394.43	383.67	380.78	378.18	368.48	362.54
48000	486.85	449.50	431.87	402.82	391.83	388.88	386.22	376.32	370.26
49000	497.00	458.86	440.87	411.21	399.99	396.98	394.27	384.16	377.97
50000	507.14	468.23	449.87	419.60	408.15	405.08	402.32	392.00	385.69
51000	517.28	477.59	458.87	428.00	416.32	413.19	410.36	399.84	393.40
52000	527.42	486.96	467.86	436.39	424.48	421.29	418.41	407.68	401.11
53000	537.57	496.32	476.86	444.78	432.64	429.39	426.45	415.52	408.83
54000	547.71	505.69	485.86	453.17	440.81	437.49	434.50	423.36	416.54
55000	557.85	515.05	494.85	461.56	448.97	445.59	442.55	431.20	424.25
56000	567.99	524.41	503.85	469.95	457.13	453.69	450.59	439.04	431.97
57000	578.14	533.78	512.85	478.35	465.30	461.79	458.64	446.88	439.68
58000	588.28	543.14	521.85	486.74	473.46	469.90	466.69	454.72	447.39
59000	598.42	552.51	530.84	495.13	481.62	478.00	474.73	462.56	455.11
60000	608.56	561.87	539.84	503.52	489.78	486.10	482.78	470.40	462.82
61000	618.71	571.24	548.84	511.91	497.95	494.20	490.82	478.24	470.54
62000	628.85	580.60	557.84	520.31	506.11	502.30	498.87	486.08	478.25
63000	638.99	589.97	566.83	528.70	514.27	510.40	506.92	493.92	485.96
64000	649.14	599.33	575.83	537.09	522.44	518.51	514.96	501.76	493.68
65000	659.28	608.69	584.83	545.48	530.60	526.61	523.01	509.60	501.39
67500	684.63	632.11	607.32	566.46	551.01	546.86	543.13	529.20	520.67
70000	709.99	655.52	629.81	587.44	571.41	567.12	563.24	548.80	539.96
75000	760.70	702.34	674.80	629.40	612.23	607.62	603.47	588.00	578.53
80000	811.42	749.16	719.79	671.36	653.04	648.13	643.70	627.20	617.09
85000	862.13	795.98	764.77	713.32	693.86	688.64	683.93	666.40	655.66
90000	912.84	842.81	809.76	755.28	734.67	729.15	724.17	705.60	694.23
95000	963.56	889.63	854.74	797.24	775.49	769.65	764.40	744.80	732.80
100000	1014.27	936.45	899.73	839.20	816.30	810.16	804.63	784.00	771.37
105000	1064.98	983.27	944.72	881.16	857.12	850.67	844.86	823.20	809.93
110000	1115.70	1030.09	989.70	923.12	897.93	891.18	885.09	862.40	848.50
115000	1166.41	1076.92	1034.69	965.08	938.75	931.69	925.32	901.60	887.07
120000	1217.12	1123.74	1079.68	1007.04	979.56	972.19	965.55	940.80	925.64
125000	1267.84	1170.56	1124.66	1049.00	1020.38	1012.70	1005.78	980.00	964.21
130000	1318.55	1217.38	1169.65	1090.96	1061.19	1053.21	1046.01	1019.20	1002.77
135000	1369.26	1264.21	1214.64	1132.92	1102.01	1093.72	1086.25	1058.40	1041.34
140000	1419.98	1311.03	1259.62	1174.88	1142.82	1134.23	1126.48	1097.60	1079.91
145000	1470.69	1357.85	1304.61	1216.84	1183.64	1174.73	1166.71	1136.79	1118.48
150000	1521.40	1404.67	1349.59	1258.80	1224.45	1215.24	1206.94	1175.99	1157.05

37

MONTHLY PAYMENT
NECESSARY TO AMORTIZE A LOAN

AMOUNT	1 YEAR	2 YEARS	3 YEARS	4 YEARS	5 YEARS	7 YEARS	8 YEARS	10 YEARS	12 YEARS
$ 50	4.38	2.29	1.60	1.25	1.05	.81	.74	.64	.58
100	8.76	4.58	3.19	2.50	2.09	1.62	1.48	1.28	1.15
200	17.51	9.15	6.38	4.99	4.17	3.24	2.95	2.55	2.30
300	26.26	13.73	9.56	7.49	6.25	4.85	4.42	3.83	3.44
400	35.01	18.30	12.75	9.98	8.33	6.47	5.89	5.10	4.59
500	43.76	22.88	15.93	12.48	10.41	8.08	7.36	6.37	5.73
600	52.51	27.45	19.12	14.97	12.50	9.70	8.83	7.65	6.88
700	61.26	32.02	22.31	17.47	14.58	11.31	10.31	8.92	8.02
800	70.01	36.60	25.49	19.96	16.66	12.93	11.78	10.19	9.17
900	78.76	41.17	28.68	22.45	18.74	14.54	13.25	11.47	10.31
1000	87.51	45.75	31.86	24.95	20.82	16.16	14.72	12.74	11.46
2000	175.02	91.49	63.72	49.89	41.64	32.31	29.44	25.48	22.91
3000	262.53	137.23	95.58	74.84	62.46	48.46	44.15	38.21	34.36
4000	350.04	182.97	127.44	99.78	83.28	64.62	58.87	50.95	45.81
5000	437.55	228.72	159.29	124.73	104.10	80.77	73.58	63.68	57.26
6000	525.06	274.46	191.15	149.67	124.92	96.92	88.30	76.42	68.71
7000	612.57	320.20	223.01	174.62	145.74	113.07	103.01	89.15	80.16
8000	700.08	365.94	254.87	199.56	166.56	129.23	117.73	101.89	91.61
9000	787.59	411.68	286.73	224.50	187.38	145.38	132.44	114.62	103.06
10000	875.10	457.43	318.58	249.45	208.20	161.53	147.16	127.36	114.51
15000	1312.65	686.14	477.87	374.17	312.29	242.29	220.73	191.03	171.77
20000	1750.19	914.85	637.16	498.89	416.39	323.06	294.31	254.71	229.02
25000	2187.74	1143.56	796.45	623.62	520.48	403.82	367.88	318.39	286.28
30000	2625.29	1372.27	955.74	748.34	624.58	484.58	441.46	382.06	343.53
35000	3062.84	1600.98	1115.03	873.06	728.67	565.35	515.03	445.74	400.78
40000	3500.38	1829.69	1274.32	997.78	832.77	646.11	588.61	509.42	458.04
45000	3937.93	2058.40	1433.61	1122.50	936.86	726.87	662.19	573.09	515.29
46000	4025.44	2104.14	1465.47	1147.45	957.68	743.02	676.90	585.83	526.74
47000	4112.95	2149.88	1497.33	1172.39	978.50	759.18	691.62	598.57	538.19
48000	4200.46	2195.63	1529.19	1197.34	999.32	775.33	706.33	611.30	549.64
49000	4287.97	2241.37	1561.04	1222.28	1020.14	791.48	721.05	624.04	561.10
50000	4375.48	2287.11	1592.90	1247.23	1040.96	807.63	735.76	636.77	572.55
51000	4462.99	2332.85	1624.76	1272.17	1061.78	823.79	750.48	649.51	584.00
52000	4550.50	2378.60	1656.62	1297.12	1082.60	839.94	765.19	662.24	595.45
53000	4638.01	2424.34	1688.48	1322.06	1103.42	856.09	779.91	674.98	606.90
54000	4725.52	2470.08	1720.33	1347.00	1124.24	872.25	794.62	687.71	618.35
55000	4813.02	2515.82	1752.19	1371.95	1145.05	888.40	809.34	700.45	629.80
56000	4900.53	2561.56	1784.05	1396.89	1165.87	904.55	824.05	713.18	641.25
57000	4988.04	2607.31	1815.91	1421.84	1186.69	920.70	838.77	725.92	652.70
58000	5075.55	2653.05	1847.77	1446.78	1207.51	936.86	853.48	738.65	664.15
59000	5163.06	2698.79	1879.62	1471.73	1228.33	953.01	868.20	751.39	675.60
60000	5250.57	2744.53	1911.48	1496.67	1249.15	969.16	882.91	764.12	687.05
61000	5338.08	2790.27	1943.34	1521.62	1269.97	985.31	897.63	776.86	698.51
62000	5425.59	2836.02	1975.20	1546.56	1290.79	1001.47	912.34	789.60	709.96
63000	5513.10	2881.76	2007.06	1571.50	1311.61	1017.62	927.06	802.33	721.41
64000	5600.61	2927.50	2038.91	1596.45	1332.43	1033.77	941.77	815.07	732.86
65000	5688.12	2973.24	2070.77	1621.39	1353.24	1049.92	956.49	827.80	744.31
67500	5906.89	3087.60	2150.42	1683.75	1405.29	1090.30	993.28	859.64	772.94
70000	6125.67	3201.95	2230.06	1746.12	1457.34	1130.69	1030.06	891.48	801.56
75000	6563.21	3430.68	2389.35	1870.84	1561.44	1211.45	1103.64	955.15	858.82
80000	7000.76	3659.37	2548.64	1995.56	1665.53	1292.21	1177.22	1018.83	916.07
85000	7438.31	3888.08	2707.93	2120.28	1769.63	1372.97	1250.79	1082.51	973.32
90000	7875.86	4116.80	2867.22	2245.00	1873.72	1453.74	1324.37	1146.18	1030.58
95000	8313.40	4345.51	3026.51	2369.73	1977.82	1534.50	1397.94	1209.86	1087.83
100000	8750.95	4574.22	3185.80	2494.45	2081.91	1615.26	1471.52	1273.54	1145.09
105000	9188.50	4802.93	3345.09	2619.17	2186.01	1696.03	1545.09	1337.21	1202.34
110000	9626.04	5031.64	3504.38	2743.89	2290.10	1776.79	1618.67	1400.89	1259.60
115000	10063.59	5260.35	3663.67	2868.62	2394.20	1857.55	1692.24	1464.57	1316.85
120000	10501.14	5489.06	3822.96	2993.34	2498.29	1938.32	1765.82	1528.24	1374.10
125000	10938.69	5717.77	3982.25	3118.06	2602.39	2019.08	1839.40	1591.92	1431.36
130000	11376.23	5946.48	4141.54	3242.78	2706.48	2099.84	1912.97	1655.60	1488.61
135000	11813.78	6175.19	4300.83	3367.50	2810.58	2180.60	1986.55	1719.27	1545.87
140000	12251.33	6403.90	4460.12	3492.23	2914.68	2261.37	2060.12	1782.95	1603.12
145000	12688.88	6632.61	4619.41	3616.95	3018.77	2342.13	2133.70	1846.63	1660.37
150000	13126.42	6861.32	4778.70	3741.67	3122.87	2422.89	2207.27	1910.30	1717.63

MONTHLY PAYMENT 9⅛%

NECESSARY TO AMORTIZE A LOAN

AMOUNT	15 YEARS	18 YEARS	20 YEARS	25 YEARS	28 YEARS	29 YEARS	30 YEARS	35 YEARS	40 YEARS
$ 50	.52	.48	.46	.43	.42	.41	.41	.40	.40
100	1.03	.95	.91	.85	.83	.82	.82	.80	.79
200	2.05	1.89	1.82	1.70	1.66	1.64	1.63	1.59	1.57
300	3.07	2.84	2.73	2.55	2.48	2.46	2.45	2.39	2.35
400	4.09	3.78	3.64	3.40	3.31	3.28	3.26	3.18	3.13
500	5.11	4.73	4.54	4.24	4.13	4.10	4.07	3.97	3.91
600	6.14	5.67	5.45	5.09	4.96	4.92	4.89	4.77	4.69
700	7.16	6.61	6.36	5.94	5.78	5.74	5.70	5.56	5.47
800	8.18	7.56	7.27	6.79	6.61	6.56	6.51	6.35	6.25
900	9.20	8.50	8.18	7.63	7.43	7.38	7.33	7.15	7.03
1000	10.22	9.45	9.08	8.48	8.26	8.20	8.14	7.94	7.81
2000	20.44	18.89	18.16	16.96	16.51	16.39	16.28	15.87	15.62
3000	30.66	28.33	27.24	25.44	24.76	24.58	24.41	23.81	23.43
4000	40.87	37.78	36.32	33.92	33.01	32.77	32.55	31.74	31.24
5000	51.09	47.22	45.39	42.39	41.26	40.96	40.69	39.67	39.05
6000	61.31	56.66	54.47	50.87	49.51	49.15	48.82	47.61	46.86
7000	71.53	66.10	63.55	59.35	57.77	57.34	56.96	55.54	54.67
8000	81.74	75.55	72.63	67.83	66.02	65.53	65.10	63.47	62.48
9000	91.96	84.99	81.71	76.30	74.27	73.72	73.23	71.41	70.29
10000	102.18	94.43	90.78	84.78	82.52	81.91	81.37	79.34	78.10
15000	153.26	141.65	136.17	127.17	123.78	122.87	122.05	119.01	117.15
20000	204.35	188.86	181.56	169.56	165.03	163.82	162.73	158.68	156.20
25000	255.43	236.07	226.95	211.95	206.29	204.78	203.41	198.34	195.25
30000	306.52	283.29	272.34	254.34	247.55	245.73	244.09	238.01	234.30
35000	357.61	330.50	317.73	296.73	288.81	286.69	284.78	277.68	273.35
40000	408.69	377.71	363.12	339.11	330.06	327.64	325.46	317.35	312.40
45000	459.78	424.93	408.51	381.50	371.32	368.59	366.14	357.01	351.45
46000	469.99	434.37	417.58	389.98	379.57	376.79	374.28	364.95	359.26
47000	480.21	443.81	426.66	398.46	387.82	384.98	382.41	372.88	367.07
48000	490.43	453.25	435.74	406.94	396.08	393.17	390.55	380.81	374.88
49000	500.65	462.70	444.82	415.41	404.33	401.36	398.69	388.75	382.69
50000	510.86	472.14	453.90	423.89	412.58	409.55	406.82	396.68	390.50
51000	521.08	481.58	462.97	432.37	420.83	417.74	414.96	404.62	398.31
52000	531.30	491.02	472.05	440.85	429.08	425.93	423.09	412.55	406.12
53000	541.51	500.47	481.13	449.32	437.33	434.12	431.23	420.48	413.93
54000	551.73	509.91	490.21	457.80	445.58	442.31	439.37	428.42	421.74
55000	561.95	519.35	499.28	466.28	453.84	450.50	447.50	436.35	429.55
56000	572.17	528.79	508.36	474.76	462.09	458.69	455.64	444.28	437.36
57000	582.38	538.24	517.44	483.24	470.34	466.89	463.78	452.22	445.17
58000	592.60	547.68	526.52	491.71	478.59	475.08	471.91	460.15	452.98
59000	602.82	557.12	535.60	500.19	486.84	483.27	480.05	468.08	460.79
60000	613.03	566.57	544.67	508.67	495.09	491.46	488.18	476.02	468.60
61000	623.25	576.01	553.75	517.15	503.34	499.65	496.32	483.95	476.41
62000	633.47	585.45	562.83	525.62	511.60	507.84	504.46	491.88	484.22
63000	643.69	594.89	571.91	534.10	519.85	516.03	512.59	499.82	492.03
64000	653.90	604.34	580.98	542.58	528.10	524.22	520.73	507.75	499.84
65000	664.12	613.78	590.06	551.06	536.35	532.41	528.87	515.68	507.65
67500	689.66	637.39	612.76	572.25	556.98	552.89	549.21	535.52	527.18
70000	715.21	660.99	635.45	593.45	577.61	573.37	569.55	555.35	546.70
75000	766.29	708.21	680.84	635.83	618.87	614.32	610.23	595.02	585.75
80000	817.38	755.42	726.23	678.22	660.12	655.28	650.91	634.69	624.80
85000	868.46	802.63	771.62	720.61	701.38	696.23	691.59	674.36	663.85
90000	919.55	849.85	817.01	763.00	742.64	737.18	732.27	714.02	702.90
95000	970.64	897.06	862.40	805.39	783.89	778.14	772.96	753.69	741.95
100000	1021.72	944.27	907.79	847.78	825.15	819.09	813.64	793.36	781.00
105000	1072.81	991.49	953.17	890.17	866.41	860.05	854.32	833.03	820.05
110000	1123.89	1038.70	998.56	932.55	907.67	901.00	895.00	872.69	859.10
115000	1174.98	1085.91	1043.95	974.94	948.92	941.96	935.68	912.36	898.15
120000	1226.06	1133.13	1089.34	1017.33	990.18	982.91	976.36	952.03	937.20
125000	1277.15	1180.34	1134.73	1059.72	1031.44	1023.87	1017.05	991.70	976.25
130000	1328.24	1227.55	1180.12	1102.11	1072.70	1064.82	1057.73	1031.36	1015.30
135000	1379.32	1274.77	1225.51	1144.50	1113.95	1105.77	1098.41	1071.03	1054.35
140000	1430.41	1321.98	1270.90	1186.89	1155.21	1146.73	1139.09	1110.70	1093.40
145000	1481.49	1369.19	1316.29	1229.28	1196.47	1187.68	1179.77	1150.37	1132.45
150000	1532.58	1416.41	1361.68	1271.66	1237.73	1228.64	1220.45	1190.04	1171.50

MONTHLY PAYMENT
NECESSARY TO AMORTIZE A LOAN

AMOUNT	1 YEAR	2 YEARS	3 YEARS	4 YEARS	5 YEARS	7 YEARS	8 YEARS	10 YEARS	12 YEARS
$ 50	4.38	2.29	1.60	1.26	1.05	.82	.74	65	.58
100	8.76	4.58	3.20	2.51	2.09	1.63	1.48	1.29	1.16
200	17.52	9.16	6.39	5.01	4.18	3.25	2.96	2.57	2.31
300	26.28	13.74	9.58	7.51	6.27	4.87	4.44	3.85	3.46
400	35.03	18.32	12.77	10.01	8.36	6.49	5.92	5.13	4.61
500	43.79	22.90	15.96	12.51	10.44	8.11	7.40	6.41	5.77
600	52.55	27.48	19.15	15.01	12.53	9.73	8.87	7.69	6.92
700	61.30	32.06	22.35	17.51	14.62	11.36	10.35	8.97	8.07
800	70.06	36.64	25.54	20.01	16.71	12.98	11.83	10.25	9.22
900	78.82	41.22	28.73	22.51	18.80	14.60	13.31	11.53	10.37
1000	87.57	45.80	31.92	25.01	20.88	16.22	14.79	12.81	11.53
2000	175.14	91.60	63.84	50.01	41.76	32.44	29.57	25.61	23.05
3000	262.71	137.40	95.75	75.02	62.64	48.65	44.35	38.41	34.57
4000	350.27	183.20	127.67	100.02	83.52	64.87	59.13	51.22	46.09
5000	437.84	229.00	159.59	125.02	104.40	81.09	73.91	64.02	57.61
6000	525.41	274.80	191.50	150.03	125.28	97.30	88.69	76.82	69.13
7000	612.98	320.60	223.42	175.03	146.16	113.52	103.47	89.63	80.66
8000	700.54	366.40	255.33	200.04	167.04	129.73	118.25	102.43	92.18
9000	788.11	412.20	287.25	225.04	187.92	145.95	133.03	115.23	103.70
10000	875.68	458.00	319.17	250.04	208.80	162.17	147.81	128.04	115.22
15000	1313.52	687.00	478.75	375.06	313.20	243.25	221.71	192.05	172.83
20000	1751.35	916.00	638.33	500.08	417.60	324.33	295.61	256.07	230.44
25000	2189.19	1144.99	797.91	625.10	522.00	405.41	369.51	320.09	288.04
30000	2627.03	1373.99	957.49	750.12	626.40	486.49	443.41	384.10	345.65
35000	3064.87	1602.99	1117.07	875.14	730.80	567.57	517.31	448.12	403.26
40000	3502.70	1831.99	1276.65	1000.16	835.20	648.65	591.21	512.14	460.87
45000	3940.54	2060.98	1436.23	1125.18	939.60	729.74	665.11	576.15	518.48
46000	4028.11	2106.78	1468.15	1150.19	960.48	745.95	679.90	588.96	530.00
47000	4115.68	2152.58	1500.07	1175.19	981.36	762.17	694.68	601.76	541.52
48000	4203.24	2198.38	1531.98	1200.19	1002.24	778.38	709.46	614.56	553.04
49000	4290.81	2244.18	1563.90	1225.20	1023.12	794.60	724.24	627.37	564.56
50000	4378.38	2289.98	1595.82	1250.20	1044.00	810.82	739.02	640.17	576.08
51000	4465.95	2335.78	1627.73	1275.20	1064.88	827.03	753.80	652.97	587.60
52000	4553.51	2381.58	1659.65	1300.21	1085.76	843.25	768.58	665.78	599.13
53000	4641.08	2427.38	1691.56	1325.21	1106.64	859.47	783.36	678.58	610.65
54000	4728.65	2473.18	1723.48	1350.22	1127.52	875.68	798.14	691.38	622.17
55000	4816.21	2518.98	1755.40	1375.22	1148.40	891.90	812.92	704.18	633.69
56000	4903.78	2564.78	1787.31	1400.22	1169.28	908.11	827.70	716.99	645.21
57000	4991.35	2610.58	1819.23	1425.23	1190.16	924.33	842.48	729.79	656.73
58000	5078.92	2656.38	1851.15	1450.23	1211.04	940.55	857.26	742.59	668.26
59000	5166.48	2702.18	1883.06	1475.24	1231.92	956.76	872.04	755.40	679.78
60000	5254.05	2747.98	1914.98	1500.24	1252.80	972.98	886.82	768.20	691.30
61000	5341.62	2793.78	1946.89	1525.24	1273.68	989.20	901.60	781.00	702.82
62000	5429.19	2839.58	1978.81	1550.25	1294.56	1005.41	916.38	793.81	714.34
63000	5516.75	2885.38	2010.73	1575.25	1315.44	1021.63	931.16	806.61	725.86
64000	5604.32	2931.18	2042.64	1600.26	1336.32	1037.84	945.94	819.41	737.39
65000	5691.89	2976.97	2074.56	1625.26	1357.20	1054.06	960.72	832.22	748.91
67500	5910.81	3091.47	2154.35	1687.77	1409.40	1094.60	997.67	864.23	777.71
70000	6129.73	3205.97	2234.14	1750.28	1461.60	1135.14	1034.62	896.23	806.51
75000	6567.56	3434.97	2393.72	1875.30	1566.00	1216.22	1108.52	960.25	864.12
80000	7005.40	3663.97	2553.30	2000.32	1670.40	1297.30	1182.42	1024.27	921.73
85000	7443.24	3892.97	2712.88	2125.34	1774.80	1378.39	1256.32	1088.28	979.34
90000	7881.08	4121.96	2872.46	2250.36	1879.20	1459.47	1330.22	1152.30	1036.95
95000	8318.91	4350.96	3032.05	2375.38	1983.60	1540.55	1404.13	1216.32	1094.55
100000	8756.75	4579.96	3191.63	2500.40	2087.99	1621.63	1478.03	1280.33	1152.16
105000	9194.59	4808.96	3351.21	2625.42	2192.39	1702.71	1551.93	1344.35	1209.77
110000	9632.42	5037.95	3510.79	2750.44	2296.79	1783.79	1625.83	1408.36	1267.38
115000	10070.26	5266.95	3670.37	2875.46	2401.19	1864.87	1699.73	1472.38	1324.98
120000	10508.10	5495.95	3829.95	3000.48	2505.59	1945.95	1773.63	1536.40	1382.59
125000	10945.94	5724.95	3989.53	3125.50	2609.99	2027.04	1847.53	1600.41	1440.20
130000	11383.77	5953.94	4149.11	3250.51	2714.39	2108.12	1921.43	1664.43	1497.81
135000	11821.61	6182.94	4308.69	3375.53	2818.79	2189.20	1995.33	1728.45	1555.42
140000	12259.45	6411.94	4468.27	3500.55	2923.19	2270.28	2069.24	1792.46	1613.02
145000	12697.29	6640.94	4627.86	3625.57	3027.59	2351.36	2143.14	1856.48	1670.63
150000	13135.12	6869.93	4787.44	3750.59	3131.99	2432.44	2217.04	1920.50	1728.24

MONTHLY PAYMENT 9¼%
NECESSARY TO AMORTIZE A LOAN

AMOUNT	15 YEARS	18 YEARS	20 YEARS	25 YEARS	28 YEARS	29 YEARS	30 YEARS	35 YEARS	40 YEARS
$ 50	.52	.48	.46	.43	.42	.42	.42	.41	.40
100	1.03	.96	.92	.86	.84	.83	.83	.81	.80
200	2.06	1.91	1.84	1.72	1.67	1.66	1.65	1.61	1.59
300	3.09	2.86	2.75	2.57	2.51	2.49	2.47	2.41	2.38
400	4.12	3.81	3.67	3.43	3.34	3.32	3.30	3.22	3.17
500	5.15	4.77	4.58	4.29	4.18	4.15	4.12	4.02	3.96
600	6.18	5.72	5.50	5.14	5.01	4.97	4.94	4.82	4.75
700	7.21	6.67	6.42	6.00	5.84	5.80	5.76	5.62	5.54
800	8.24	7.62	7.33	6.86	6.68	6.63	6.59	6.43	6.33
900	9.27	8.57	8.25	7.71	7.51	7.46	7.41	7.23	7.12
1000	10.30	9.53	9.16	8.57	8.35	8.29	8.23	8.03	7.91
2000	20.59	19.05	18.32	17.13	16.69	16.57	16.46	16.06	15.82
3000	30.88	28.57	27.48	25.70	25.03	24.85	24.69	24.09	23.72
4000	41.17	38.09	36.64	34.26	33.37	33.13	32.91	32.11	31.63
5000	51.46	47.61	45.80	42.82	41.71	41.41	41.14	40.14	39.54
6000	61.76	57.13	54.96	51.39	50.05	49.69	49.37	48.17	47.44
7000	72.05	66.65	64.12	59.95	58.39	57.97	57.59	56.20	55.35
8000	82.34	76.17	73.27	68.52	66.73	66.25	65.82	64.22	63.26
9000	92.63	85.70	82.43	77.08	75.07	74.53	74.05	72.25	71.16
10000	102.92	95.22	91.59	85.64	83.41	82.81	82.27	80.28	79.07
15000	154.38	142.82	137.39	128.46	125.11	124.21	123.41	120.42	118.60
20000	205.84	190.43	183.18	171.28	166.81	165.62	164.54	160.55	158.14
25000	257.30	238.03	228.97	214.10	208.51	207.02	205.67	200.69	197.67
30000	308.76	285.64	274.77	256.92	250.21	248.42	246.81	240.83	237.20
35000	360.22	333.25	320.56	299.74	291.91	289.82	287.94	280.97	276.74
40000	411.68	380.85	366.35	342.56	333.62	331.23	329.08	321.10	316.27
45000	463.14	428.46	412.15	385.38	375.32	372.63	370.21	361.24	355.80
46000	473.43	437.98	421.30	393.94	383.66	380.91	378.44	369.27	363.71
47000	483.73	447.50	430.46	402.50	392.00	389.19	386.66	377.29	371.62
48000	494.02	457.02	439.62	411.07	400.34	397.47	394.89	385.32	379.52
49000	504.31	466.54	448.78	419.63	408.68	405.75	403.12	393.35	387.43
50000	514.60	476.06	457.94	428.20	417.02	414.03	411.34	401.38	395.34
51000	524.89	485.59	467.10	436.76	425.36	422.31	419.57	409.40	403.24
52000	535.18	495.11	476.26	445.32	433.70	430.59	427.80	417.43	411.15
53000	545.48	504.63	485.41	453.89	442.04	438.87	436.02	425.46	419.06
54000	555.77	514.15	494.57	462.45	450.38	447.15	444.25	433.49	426.96
55000	566.06	523.67	503.73	471.02	458.72	455.43	452.48	441.51	434.87
56000	576.35	533.19	512.89	479.58	467.06	463.71	460.70	449.54	442.77
57000	586.64	542.71	522.05	488.14	475.40	471.99	468.93	457.57	450.68
58000	596.94	552.23	531.21	496.71	483.74	480.27	477.16	465.60	458.59
59000	607.23	561.76	540.37	505.27	492.08	488.56	485.38	473.62	466.49
60000	617.52	571.28	549.53	513.83	500.42	496.84	493.61	481.65	474.40
61000	627.81	580.80	558.68	522.40	508.76	505.12	501.84	489.68	482.31
62000	638.10	590.32	567.84	530.96	517.10	513.40	510.06	497.71	490.21
63000	648.40	599.84	577.00	539.53	525.44	521.68	518.29	505.73	498.12
64000	658.69	609.36	586.16	548.09	533.78	529.96	526.52	513.76	506.03
65000	668.98	618.88	595.32	556.65	542.12	538.24	534.74	521.79	513.93
67500	694.71	642.69	618.22	578.06	562.97	558.94	555.31	541.86	533.70
70000	720.44	666.49	641.11	599.47	583.82	579.64	575.88	561.93	553.47
75000	771.90	714.09	686.91	642.29	625.52	621.04	617.01	602.06	593.00
80000	823.36	761.70	732.70	685.11	667.23	662.45	658.15	642.20	632.53
85000	874.82	809.31	778.49	727.93	708.93	703.85	699.28	682.34	672.07
90000	926.28	856.91	824.29	770.75	750.63	745.25	740.41	722.47	711.60
95000	977.74	904.52	870.08	813.57	792.33	786.65	781.55	762.61	751.13
100000	1029.20	952.12	915.87	856.39	834.03	828.06	822.68	802.75	790.67
105000	1080.66	999.73	961.67	899.21	875.73	869.46	863.81	842.89	830.20
110000	1132.12	1047.34	1007.46	942.03	917.43	910.86	904.95	883.02	869.73
115000	1183.58	1094.94	1053.25	984.84	959.14	952.26	946.08	923.16	909.26
120000	1235.04	1142.55	1099.05	1027.66	1000.84	993.67	987.22	963.30	948.80
125000	1286.50	1190.15	1144.84	1070.48	1042.54	1035.07	1028.35	1003.44	988.33
130000	1337.95	1237.76	1190.63	1113.30	1084.24	1076.47	1069.48	1043.57	1027.86
135000	1389.41	1285.37	1236.43	1156.12	1125.94	1117.87	1110.62	1083.71	1067.40
140000	1440.87	1332.97	1282.22	1198.94	1167.64	1159.28	1151.75	1123.85	1106.93
145000	1492.33	1380.58	1328.01	1241.76	1209.34	1200.68	1192.88	1163.98	1146.46
150000	1543.79	1428.18	1373.81	1284.58	1251.04	1242.08	1234.02	1204.12	1186.00

41

MONTHLY PAYMENT
NECESSARY TO AMORTIZE A LOAN

AMOUNT	1 YEAR	2 YEARS	3 YEARS	4 YEARS	5 YEARS	7 YEARS	8 YEARS	10 YEARS	12 YEARS
$ 50	4.39	2.30	1.60	1.26	1.05	.82	.75	.65	.58
100	8.77	4.59	3.20	2.51	2.10	1.63	1.49	1.29	1.16
200	17.53	9.18	6.40	5.02	4.19	3.26	2.97	2.58	2.32
300	26.29	13.76	9.60	7.52	6.29	4.89	4.46	3.87	3.48
400	35.06	18.35	12.79	10.03	8.38	6.52	5.94	5.15	4.64
500	43.82	22.93	15.99	12.54	10.48	8.15	7.43	6.44	5.80
600	52.58	27.52	19.19	15.04	12.57	9.77	8.91	7.73	6.96
700	61.34	32.10	22.39	17.55	14.66	11.40	10.40	9.01	8.12
800	70.11	36.69	25.58	20.06	16.76	13.03	11.88	10.30	9.28
900	78.87	41.28	28.78	22.56	18.85	14.66	13.37	11.59	10.44
1000	87.63	45.86	31.98	25.07	20.95	16.29	14.85	12.88	11.60
2000	175.26	91.72	63.95	50.13	41.89	32.57	29.70	25.75	23.19
3000	262.88	137.58	95.93	75.20	62.83	48.85	44.54	38.62	34.78
4000	350.51	183.43	127.90	100.26	83.77	65.13	59.39	51.49	46.38
5000	438.13	229.29	159.88	125.32	104.71	81.41	74.23	64.36	57.97
6000	525.76	275.15	191.85	150.39	125.65	97.69	89.08	77.23	69.56
7000	613.38	321.00	223.83	175.45	146.59	113.97	103.92	90.10	81.15
8000	701.01	366.86	255.80	200.51	167.53	130.25	118.77	102.98	92.75
9000	788.63	412.72	287.78	225.58	188.47	146.53	133.61	115.85	104.34
10000	876.26	458.57	319.75	250.64	209.41	162.81	148.46	128.72	115.93
15000	1314.39	687.86	479.62	375.96	314.12	244.21	222.69	193.08	173.89
20000	1752.51	917.14	639.50	501.27	418.82	325.61	296.91	257.43	231.86
25000	2190.64	1146.43	799.37	626.59	523.53	407.01	371.14	321.79	289.82
30000	2628.77	1375.71	959.24	751.91	628.23	488.41	445.37	386.15	347.78
35000	3066.90	1605.00	1119.11	877.23	732.93	569.81	519.60	450.50	405.74
40000	3505.02	1834.28	1278.99	1002.54	837.64	651.21	593.82	514.86	463.71
45000	3943.15	2063.57	1438.86	1127.86	942.34	732.61	668.05	579.22	521.67
46000	4030.78	2109.43	1470.83	1152.93	963.28	748.89	682.90	592.09	533.26
47000	4118.40	2155.28	1502.81	1177.99	984.22	765.17	697.74	604.96	544.85
48000	4206.03	2201.14	1534.78	1203.05	1005.16	781.45	712.59	617.83	556.45
49000	4293.65	2247.00	1566.76	1228.12	1026.11	797.73	727.43	630.70	568.04
50000	4381.28	2292.85	1598.73	1253.18	1047.05	814.01	742.28	643.58	579.63
51000	4468.90	2338.71	1630.71	1278.24	1067.99	830.29	757.12	656.45	591.22
52000	4556.53	2384.57	1662.68	1303.31	1088.93	846.57	771.97	669.32	602.82
53000	4644.15	2430.43	1694.66	1328.37	1109.87	862.85	786.82	682.19	614.41
54000	4731.78	2476.28	1726.63	1353.43	1130.81	879.13	801.66	695.06	626.00
55000	4819.91	2522.14	1758.61	1378.50	1151.75	895.41	816.51	707.93	637.59
56000	4907.03	2568.00	1790.58	1403.56	1172.69	911.69	831.35	720.80	649.19
57000	4994.66	2613.85	1822.55	1428.62	1193.63	927.97	846.20	733.68	660.78
58000	5082.28	2659.71	1854.53	1453.69	1214.57	944.25	861.04	746.55	672.37
59000	5169.91	2705.57	1886.50	1478.75	1235.51	960.53	875.89	759.42	683.96
60000	5257.53	2751.42	1918.44	1503.81	1256.45	976.81	890.73	772.29	695.56
61000	5345.16	2797.28	1950.45	1528.88	1277.40	993.09	905.58	785.16	707.15
62000	5432.78	2843.14	1982.43	1553.94	1298.34	1009.37	920.42	798.03	718.74
63000	5520.41	2889.00	2014.40	1579.00	1319.28	1025.65	935.27	810.90	730.33
64000	5608.04	2934.85	2046.38	1604.07	1340.22	1041.93	950.12	823.78	741.93
65000	5695.66	2980.71	2078.35	1629.13	1361.16	1058.21	964.96	836.65	753.52
67500	5914.72	3095.35	2158.29	1691.79	1413.51	1098.91	1002.07	868.83	782.50
70000	6133.79	3209.99	2238.22	1754.45	1465.86	1139.61	1039.19	901.00	811.48
75000	6571.92	3439.28	2398.10	1879.77	1570.57	1221.01	1113.42	965.36	869.45
80000	7010.04	3668.56	2557.97	2005.08	1675.27	1302.41	1187.64	1029.72	927.41
85000	7448.17	3897.85	2717.84	2130.40	1779.98	1383.81	1261.87	1094.08	985.37
90000	7886.30	4127.13	2877.71	2255.72	1884.68	1465.21	1336.10	1158.43	1043.33
95000	8324.42	4356.42	3037.59	2381.04	1989.38	1546.61	1410.32	1222.79	1101.30
100000	8762.55	4585.70	3197.46	2506.35	2094.09	1628.01	1484.55	1287.15	1159.26
105000	9200.68	4814.99	3357.33	2631.67	2198.79	1709.41	1558.78	1351.50	1217.22
110000	9638.81	5044.27	3517.21	2756.99	2303.50	1790.81	1633.01	1415.86	1275.18
115000	10076.93	5273.56	3677.08	2882.31	2408.20	1872.21	1707.23	1480.22	1333.15
120000	10515.06	5502.84	3836.95	3007.62	2512.90	1953.61	1781.46	1544.57	1391.11
125000	10953.19	5732.13	3996.82	3132.94	2617.61	2035.01	1855.69	1608.93	1449.07
130000	11391.32	5961.41	4156.70	3258.26	2722.31	2116.41	1929.92	1673.29	1507.03
135000	11829.44	6190.70	4316.57	3383.58	2827.02	2197.81	2004.14	1737.65	1565.00
140000	12267.57	6419.98	4476.44	3508.89	2931.72	2279.21	2078.37	1802.00	1622.96
145000	12705.70	6649.27	4636.31	3634.21	3036.42	2360.61	2152.60	1866.36	1680.92
150000	13143.83	6878.55	4796.19	3759.53	3141.13	2442.01	2226.83	1930.72	1738.89

MONTHLY PAYMENT 9⅜%
NECESSARY TO AMORTIZE A LOAN

AMOUNT	15 YEARS	18 YEARS	20 YEARS	25 YEARS	28 YEARS	29 YEARS	30 YEARS	35 YEARS	40 YEARS
$ 50	.52	.49	.47	.44	.43	.42	.42	.41	.41
100	1.04	.97	.93	.87	.85	.84	.84	.82	.81
200	2.08	1.93	1.85	1.74	1.69	1.68	1.67	1.63	1.61
300	3.12	2.89	2.78	2.60	2.53	2.52	2.50	2.44	2.41
400	4.15	3.85	3.70	3.47	3.38	3.35	3.33	3.25	3.21
500	5.19	4.81	4.62	4.33	4.22	4.19	4.16	4.07	4.01
600	6.23	5.77	5.55	5.20	5.06	5.03	5.00	4.88	4.81
700	7.26	6.73	6.47	6.06	5.91	5.86	5.83	5.69	5.61
800	8.30	7.69	7.40	6.93	6.75	6.70	6.66	6.50	6.41
900	9.34	8.65	8.32	7.79	7.59	7.54	7.49	7.31	7.21
1000	10.37	9.61	9.24	8.66	8.43	8.38	8.32	8.13	8.01
2000	20.74	19.21	18.48	17.31	16.86	16.75	16.64	16.25	16.01
3000	31.11	28.81	27.72	25.96	25.29	25.12	24.96	24.37	24.02
4000	41.47	38.41	36.96	34.61	33.72	33.49	33.27	32.49	32.02
5000	51.84	48.01	46.20	43.26	42.15	41.86	41.59	40.61	40.02
6000	62.21	57.61	55.44	51.91	50.58	50.23	49.91	48.73	48.03
7000	72.57	67.21	64.68	60.56	59.01	58.60	58.23	56.86	56.03
8000	82.94	76.81	73.92	69.21	67.44	66.97	66.54	64.98	64.03
9000	93.31	86.41	83.16	77.86	75.87	75.34	74.86	73.10	72.04
10000	103.67	96.01	92.40	86.51	84.30	83.71	83.18	81.22	80.04
15000	155.51	144.01	138.60	129.76	126.45	125.56	124.77	121.83	120.06
20000	207.34	192.01	184.80	173.01	168.59	167.41	166.35	162.44	160.07
25000	259.18	240.01	231.00	216.26	210.74	209.27	207.94	203.05	200.09
30000	311.01	288.01	277.20	259.51	252.89	251.12	249.53	243.65	240.11
35000	362.85	336.01	323.40	302.76	295.03	292.97	291.12	284.26	280.13
40000	414.68	384.01	369.60	346.01	337.18	334.82	332.70	324.87	320.14
45000	466.52	432.01	415.80	389.27	379.33	376.68	374.29	365.48	360.16
46000	476.88	441.61	425.04	397.92	387.76	385.05	382.61	373.60	368.17
47000	487.25	451.21	434.28	406.57	396.19	393.42	390.93	381.72	376.17
48000	497.62	460.81	443.52	415.22	404.62	401.79	399.24	389.84	384.17
49000	507.99	470.41	452.76	423.87	413.04	410.16	407.56	397.97	392.18
50000	518.35	480.01	462.00	432.52	421.47	418.53	415.88	406.09	400.18
51000	528.72	489.61	471.24	441.17	429.90	426.90	424.20	414.21	408.18
52000	539.09	499.21	480.48	449.82	438.33	435.27	432.51	422.33	416.19
53000	549.45	508.81	489.72	458.47	446.76	443.64	440.83	430.45	424.19
54000	559.82	518.41	498.96	467.12	455.19	452.01	449.15	438.57	432.19
55000	570.19	528.01	508.20	475.77	463.62	460.38	457.47	446.70	440.20
56000	580.55	537.61	517.44	484.42	472.05	468.75	465.78	454.82	448.20
57000	590.92	547.21	526.68	493.07	480.48	477.12	474.10	462.94	456.20
58000	601.29	556.81	535.92	501.72	488.91	485.49	482.42	471.06	464.21
59000	611.66	566.41	545.16	510.37	497.34	493.86	490.74	479.18	472.21
60000	622.02	576.01	554.40	519.02	505.77	502.23	499.05	487.30	480.21
61000	632.39	585.61	563.64	527.67	514.20	510.60	507.37	495.42	488.22
62000	642.76	595.21	572.87	536.32	522.63	518.97	515.69	503.55	496.22
63000	653.12	604.81	582.11	544.97	531.06	527.34	524.01	511.67	504.22
64000	663.49	614.41	591.35	553.62	539.49	535.71	532.32	519.79	512.23
65000	673.86	624.01	600.59	562.27	547.91	544.08	540.64	527.91	520.23
67500	699.77	648.01	623.69	583.90	568.99	565.01	561.44	548.22	540.24
70000	725.69	672.01	646.79	605.52	590.06	585.94	582.23	568.52	560.25
75000	777.53	720.01	692.99	648.77	632.21	627.79	623.82	609.13	600.27
80000	829.36	768.01	739.19	692.02	674.36	669.64	665.40	649.74	640.28
85000	881.20	816.01	785.39	735.27	716.50	711.49	706.99	690.34	680.30
90000	933.03	864.01	831.59	778.53	758.65	753.35	748.58	730.95	720.32
95000	984.87	912.01	877.79	821.78	800.80	795.20	790.17	771.56	760.34
100000	1036.70	960.01	923.99	865.03	842.94	837.05	831.75	812.17	800.35
105000	1088.53	1008.01	970.19	908.28	885.09	878.90	873.34	852.78	840.37
110000	1140.37	1056.01	1016.39	951.53	927.24	920.76	914.93	893.39	880.39
115000	1192.20	1104.01	1062.59	994.78	969.38	962.61	956.52	933.99	920.41
120000	1244.04	1152.01	1108.79	1038.03	1011.53	1004.46	998.10	974.60	960.42
125000	1295.87	1200.01	1154.98	1081.28	1053.68	1046.31	1039.69	1015.21	1000.44
130000	1347.71	1248.01	1201.18	1124.54	1095.82	1088.16	1081.28	1055.82	1040.46
135000	1399.54	1296.01	1247.38	1167.79	1137.97	1130.02	1122.87	1096.43	1080.48
140000	1451.38	1344.01	1293.58	1211.04	1180.12	1171.87	1164.45	1137.03	1120.49
145000	1503.21	1392.01	1339.78	1254.29	1222.27	1213.72	1206.04	1177.64	1160.51
150000	1555.05	1440.01	1385.98	1297.54	1264.41	1255.57	1247.63	1218.25	1200.53

43

MONTHLY PAYMENT
NECESSARY TO AMORTIZE A LOAN

AMOUNT	1 YEAR	2 YEARS	3 YEARS	4 YEARS	5 YEARS	7 YEARS	8 YEARS	10 YEARS	12 YEARS
50	4.39	2.30	1.61	1.26	1.06	.82	.75	.65	.59
100	8.77	4.60	3.21	2.52	2.11	1.64	1.50	1.30	1.17
200	17.54	9.19	6.41	5.03	4.21	3.27	2.99	2.59	2.34
300	26.31	13.78	9.61	7.54	6.31	4.91	4.48	3.89	3.50
400	35.08	18.37	12.82	10.05	8.41	6.54	5.97	5.18	4.67
500	43.85	22.96	16.02	12.57	10.51	8.18	7.46	6.47	5.84
600	52.62	27.55	19.22	15.08	12.61	9.81	8.95	7.77	7.00
700	61.38	32.15	22.43	17.59	14.71	11.45	10.44	9.06	8.17
800	70.15	36.74	25.63	20.10	16.81	13.08	11.93	10.36	9.34
900	78.92	41.33	28.83	22.62	18.91	14.71	13.42	11.65	10.50
1000	87.69	45.92	32.04	25.13	21.01	16.35	14.92	12.94	11.67
2000	175.37	91.83	64.07	50.25	42.01	32.69	29.83	25.88	23.33
3000	263.06	137.75	96.10	75.37	63.01	49.04	44.74	38.82	35.00
4000	350.74	183.66	128.14	100.50	84.01	65.38	59.65	51.76	46.66
5000	438.42	229.58	160.17	125.62	105.01	81.72	74.56	64.70	58.32
6000	526.11	275.49	192.20	150.74	126.02	98.07	89.47	77.64	69.99
7000	613.79	321.41	224.24	175.87	147.02	114.41	104.38	90.58	81.65
8000	701.47	367.32	256.27	200.99	168.02	130.76	119.29	103.52	93.31
9000	789.16	413.24	288.30	226.11	189.02	147.10	134.20	116.46	104.98
10000	876.84	459.15	320.33	251.24	210.02	163.44	149.11	129.40	116.64
15000	1315.26	688.72	480.50	376.85	315.03	245.16	223.67	194.10	174.96
20000	1753.68	918.29	640.66	502.47	420.04	326.88	298.22	258.80	233.28
25000	2192.09	1147.87	800.83	628.08	525.05	408.60	372.78	323.50	291.60
30000	2630.51	1377.44	960.99	753.70	630.06	490.32	447.33	388.20	349.92
35000	3068.93	1607.01	1121.16	879.31	735.07	572.04	521.89	452.90	408.24
40000	3507.35	1836.58	1281.32	1004.93	840.08	653.76	596.44	517.60	466.55
45000	3945.76	2066.16	1441.49	1130.55	945.09	735.48	670.99	582.29	524.87
46000	4033.45	2112.07	1473.52	1155.67	966.09	751.83	685.91	595.23	536.54
47000	4121.13	2157.99	1505.55	1180.79	987.09	768.17	700.82	608.17	548.20
48000	4208.81	2203.90	1537.59	1205.92	1008.09	784.52	715.73	621.11	559.86
49000	4296.50	2249.82	1569.62	1231.04	1029.10	800.86	730.64	634.05	571.53
50000	4384.18	2295.73	1601.65	1256.16	1050.10	817.20	745.55	646.99	583.19
51000	4471.86	2341.64	1633.69	1281.28	1071.10	833.55	760.46	659.93	594.86
52000	4559.55	2387.56	1665.72	1306.41	1092.10	849.89	775.37	672.87	606.52
53000	4647.23	2433.47	1697.75	1331.53	1113.10	866.24	790.28	685.81	618.18
54000	4734.91	2479.39	1729.78	1356.65	1134.11	882.58	805.19	698.75	629.85
55000	4822.60	2525.30	1761.82	1381.78	1155.11	898.92	820.10	711.69	641.51
56000	4910.28	2571.22	1793.85	1406.90	1176.11	915.27	835.01	724.63	653.17
57000	4997.97	2617.13	1825.88	1432.02	1197.11	931.61	849.93	737.57	664.84
58000	5085.65	2663.05	1857.92	1457.15	1218.11	947.96	864.84	750.51	676.50
59000	5173.33	2708.96	1889.95	1482.27	1239.11	964.30	879.75	763.45	688.17
60000	5261.02	2754.87	1921.98	1507.39	1260.12	980.64	894.66	776.39	699.83
61000	5348.70	2800.79	1954.01	1532.52	1281.12	996.99	909.57	789.33	711.49
62000	5436.38	2846.70	1986.05	1557.64	1302.12	1013.33	924.48	802.27	723.16
63000	5524.07	2892.62	2018.08	1582.76	1323.12	1029.68	939.39	815.21	734.82
64000	5611.75	2938.53	2050.11	1607.89	1344.12	1046.02	954.30	828.15	746.48
65000	5699.43	2984.45	2082.15	1633.01	1365.13	1062.36	969.21	841.09	758.15
67500	5918.64	3099.23	2162.23	1695.82	1417.63	1103.22	1006.49	873.44	787.31
70000	6137.85	3214.02	2242.31	1758.62	1470.14	1144.08	1043.77	905.79	816.47
75000	6576.27	3443.59	2402.48	1884.24	1575.14	1225.80	1118.32	970.49	874.78
80000	7014.69	3673.16	2562.64	2009.86	1680.15	1307.52	1192.88	1035.19	933.10
85000	7453.10	3902.74	2722.81	2135.47	1785.16	1389.24	1267.43	1099.88	991.42
90000	7891.52	4132.31	2882.97	2261.09	1890.17	1470.96	1341.98	1164.58	1049.74
95000	8329.94	4361.88	3043.14	2386.70	1995.18	1552.68	1416.54	1229.28	1108.06
100000	8768.36	4591.45	3203.30	2512.32	2100.19	1634.40	1491.09	1293.98	1166.38
105000	9206.77	4821.03	3363.46	2637.93	2205.20	1716.12	1565.65	1358.68	1224.70
110000	9645.19	5050.60	3523.63	2763.55	2310.21	1797.84	1640.20	1423.38	1283.02
115000	10083.61	5280.17	3683.79	2889.17	2415.22	1879.56	1714.76	1488.08	1341.33
120000	10522.03	5509.74	3843.96	3014.78	2520.23	1961.28	1789.31	1552.78	1399.65
125000	10960.44	5739.32	4004.12	3140.40	2625.24	2043.00	1863.87	1617.47	1457.97
130000	11398.86	5968.89	4164.29	3266.01	2730.25	2124.72	1938.42	1682.17	1516.29
135000	11837.28	6198.46	4324.45	3391.63	2835.26	2206.44	2012.97	1746.87	1574.61
140000	12275.70	6428.03	4484.62	3517.24	2940.27	2288.16	2087.53	1811.57	1632.93
145000	12714.11	6657.61	4644.78	3642.86	3045.27	2369.88	2162.08	1876.27	1691.25
150000	13152.53	6887.18	4804.95	3768.48	3150.28	2451.60	2236.64	1940.97	1749.56

AMOUNT	15 YEARS	18 YEARS	20 YEARS	25 YEARS	28 YEARS	29 YEARS	30 YEARS	35 YEARS	40 YEARS
$ 50	.53	.49	.47	.44	.43	.43	.43	.42	.41
100	1.05	.97	.94	.88	.86	85	85	.83	.82
200	2.09	1.94	1.87	1.75	1.71	1.70	1.69	1.65	1.63
300	3.14	2.91	2.80	2.63	2.56	2.54	2.53	2.47	2.44
400	4.18	3.88	3.73	3.50	3.41	3.39	3.37	3.29	3.25
500	5.23	4.84	4.67	4.37	4.26	4.24	4.21	4.11	4.06
600	6.27	5.81	5.60	5.25	5.12	5.08	5.05	4.93	4.87
700	7.31	6.78	6.53	6.12	5.97	5.93	5.89	5.76	5.68
800	8.36	7.75	7.46	6.99	6.82	6.77	6.73	6.58	6.49
900	9.40	8.72	8.39	7.87	7.67	7.62	7.57	7.40	7.30
1000	10.45	9.68	9.33	8.74	8.52	8.47	8.41	8.22	8.11
2000	20.89	19.36	18.65	17.48	17.04	16.93	16.82	16.44	16.21
3000	31.33	29.04	27.97	26.22	25.56	25.39	25.23	24.65	24.31
4000	41.77	38.72	37.29	34.95	34.08	33.85	33.64	32.87	32.41
5000	52.22	48.40	46.61	43.69	42.60	42.31	42.05	41.09	40.51
6000	62.66	58.08	55.93	52.43	51.12	50.77	50.46	49.30	48.61
7000	73.10	67.76	65.25	61.16	59.64	59.23	58.86	57.52	56.71
8000	83.54	77.44	74.58	69.90	68.16	67.69	67.27	65.73	64.81
9000	93.99	87.12	83.90	78.64	76.67	76.15	75.68	73.95	72.91
10000	104.43	96.80	93.22	87.37	85.19	84.61	84.09	82.17	81.01
15000	156.64	145.19	139.82	131.06	127.79	126.92	126.13	123.25	121.51
20000	208.85	193.59	186.43	174.74	170.38	169.22	168.18	164.33	162.02
25000	261.06	241.98	233.04	218.43	212.98	211.52	210.22	205.41	202.52
30000	313.27	290.38	279.64	262.11	255.57	253.83	252.26	246.49	243.02
35000	365.48	338.77	326.25	305.80	298.16	296.13	294.30	287.57	283.53
40000	417.69	387.17	372.86	349.48	340.76	338.43	336.35	328.65	324.03
45000	469.91	435.57	419.46	393.17	383.35	380.74	378.39	369.73	364.53
46000	480.35	445.24	428.79	401.91	391.87	389.20	386.80	377.95	372.63
47000	490.79	454.92	438.11	410.64	400.39	397.66	395.21	386.16	380.73
48000	501.23	464.60	447.43	419.38	408.91	406.12	403.62	394.38	388.83
49000	511.68	474.28	456.75	428.12	417.43	414.58	412.02	402.59	396.94
50000	522.12	483.96	466.07	436.85	425.95	423.04	420.43	410.81	405.04
51000	532.56	493.64	475.39	445.59	434.46	431.50	428.84	419.03	413.14
52000	543.00	503.32	484.71	454.33	442.98	439.96	437.25	427.24	421.24
53000	553.44	513.00	494.03	463.06	451.50	448.42	445.66	435.46	429.34
54000	563.89	522.68	503.36	471.80	460.02	456.88	454.07	443.68	437.44
55000	574.33	532.36	512.68	480.54	468.54	465.34	462.47	451.89	445.54
56000	584.77	542.04	522.00	489.28	477.06	473.81	470.88	460.11	453.64
57000	595.21	551.71	531.32	498.01	485.58	482.27	479.29	468.32	461.74
58000	605.66	561.39	540.64	506.75	494.10	490.73	487.70	476.54	469.84
59000	616.10	571.07	549.96	515.49	502.62	499.19	496.11	484.76	477.94
60000	626.54	580.75	559.28	524.22	511.13	507.65	504.52	492.97	486.04
61000	636.98	590.43	568.61	532.96	519.65	516.11	512.93	501.19	494.14
62000	647.42	600.11	577.93	541.70	528.17	524.57	521.33	509.40	502.24
63000	657.87	609.79	587.25	550.43	536.69	533.03	529.74	517.62	510.34
64000	668.31	619.47	596.57	559.17	545.21	541.49	538.15	525.84	518.44
65000	678.75	629.15	605.89	567.91	553.73	549.95	546.56	534.05	526.55
67500	704.86	653.35	629.19	589.75	575.03	571.10	567.58	554.59	546.80
70000	730.96	677.54	652.50	611.59	596.32	592.26	588.60	575.13	567.05
75000	783.17	725.94	699.10	655.28	638.92	634.56	630.65	616.21	607.55
80000	835.38	774.33	745.71	698.96	681.51	676.86	672.69	657.29	648.05
85000	887.60	822.73	792.32	742.65	724.10	719.17	714.73	698.37	688.56
90000	939.81	871.13	838.92	786.33	766.70	761.47	756.77	739.46	729.06
95000	992.02	919.52	885.53	830.02	809.29	803.77	798.82	780.54	769.56
100000	1044.23	967.92	932.14	873.70	851.89	846.08	840.86	821.62	810.07
105000	1096.44	1016.31	978.74	917.39	894.48	888.38	882.90	862.70	850.57
110000	1148.65	1064.71	1025.35	961.07	937.07	930.68	924.94	903.78	891.07
115000	1200.86	1113.10	1071.96	1004.76	979.67	972.99	966.99	944.86	931.58
120000	1253.07	1161.50	1118.56	1048.44	1022.26	1015.29	1009.03	985.94	972.08
125000	1305.29	1209.89	1165.17	1092.13	1064.86	1057.59	1051.07	1027.02	1012.58
130000	1357.50	1258.29	1211.78	1135.81	1107.45	1099.90	1093.12	1068.10	1053.09
135000	1409.71	1306.69	1258.38	1179.50	1150.05	1142.20	1135.16	1109.18	1093.59
140000	1461.92	1355.08	1304.99	1223.18	1192.64	1184.51	1177.20	1150.26	1134.09
145000	1514.13	1403.48	1351.60	1266.87	1235.23	1226.81	1219.24	1191.34	1174.59
150000	1566.34	1451.87	1398.20	1310.55	1277.83	1269.11	1261.29	1232.42	1215.10

45

9⅝% MONTHLY PAYMENT
NECESSARY TO AMORTIZE A LOAN

AMOUNT	1 YEAR	2 YEARS	3 YEARS	4 YEARS	5 YEARS	7 YEARS	8 YEARS	10 YEARS	12 YEARS
$ 50	4.39	2.30	1.61	1.26	1.06	.83	.75	.66	.59
100	8.78	4.60	3.21	2.52	2.11	1.65	1.50	1.31	1.18
200	17.55	9.20	6.42	5.04	4.22	3.29	3.00	2.61	2.35
300	26.33	13.80	9.63	7.56	6.32	4.93	4.50	3.91	3.53
400	35.10	18.39	12.84	10.08	8.43	6.57	6.00	5.21	4.70
500	43.88	22.99	16.05	12.60	10.54	8.21	7.49	6.51	5.87
600	52.65	27.59	19.26	15.11	12.64	9.85	8.99	7.81	7.05
700	61.42	32.19	22.47	17.63	14.75	11.49	10.49	9.11	8.22
800	70.20	36.78	25.68	20.15	16.86	13.13	11.99	10.41	9.39
900	78.97	41.38	28.89	22.67	18.96	14.77	13.48	11.71	10.57
1000	87.75	45.98	32.10	25.19	21.07	16.41	14.98	13.01	11.74
2000	175.49	91.95	64.19	50.37	42.13	32.82	29.96	26.02	23.48
3000	263.23	137.92	96.28	75.55	63.19	49.23	44.93	39.03	35.21
4000	350.97	183.89	128.37	100.74	84.26	65.64	59.91	52.04	46.95
5000	438.71	229.87	160.46	125.92	105.32	82.05	74.89	65.05	58.68
6000	526.45	275.84	192.55	151.10	126.38	98.45	89.86	78.05	70.42
7000	614.20	321.81	224.64	176.29	147.45	114.86	104.84	91.06	82.15
8000	701.94	367.78	256.74	201.47	168.51	131.27	119.82	104.07	93.89
9000	789.68	413.75	288.83	226.65	189.57	147.68	134.79	117.08	105.62
10000	877.42	459.73	320.92	251.83	210.64	164.09	149.77	130.09	117.36
15000	1316.13	689.59	481.38	377.75	315.95	246.13	224.65	195.13	176.03
20000	1754.84	919.45	641.83	503.66	421.27	328.17	299.53	260.17	234.71
25000	2193.54	1149.31	802.29	629.58	526.58	410.21	374.42	325.21	293.38
30000	2632.25	1379.17	962.75	755.49	631.90	492.25	449.30	390.25	352.06
35000	3070.96	1609.03	1123.20	881.41	737.21	574.29	524.18	455.30	410.74
40000	3509.67	1838.89	1283.66	1007.32	842.53	656.33	599.06	520.34	469.41
45000	3948.38	2068.75	1444.12	1133.23	947.84	738.37	673.95	585.38	528.09
46000	4036.12	2114.72	1476.21	1158.42	968.90	754.78	688.92	598.39	539.82
47000	4123.86	2160.69	1508.30	1183.60	989.97	771.18	703.90	611.39	551.56
48000	4211.60	2206.66	1540.39	1208.78	1011.03	787.59	718.88	624.40	563.29
49000	4299.34	2252.63	1572.48	1233.97	1032.09	804.00	733.85	637.41	575.03
50000	4387.08	2298.61	1604.58	1259.15	1053.16	820.41	748.83	650.42	586.76
51000	4474.83	2344.58	1636.67	1284.33	1074.22	836.82	763.80	663.43	598.50
52000	4562.57	2390.55	1668.76	1309.51	1095.28	853.22	778.78	676.44	610.23
53000	4650.31	2436.52	1700.85	1334.70	1116.34	869.63	793.76	689.44	621.97
54000	4738.05	2482.50	1732.94	1359.88	1137.41	886.04	808.73	702.45	633.70
55000	4825.79	2528.47	1765.03	1385.06	1158.47	902.45	823.71	715.46	645.44
56000	4913.53	2574.44	1797.12	1410.25	1179.53	918.86	838.69	728.47	657.17
57000	5001.27	2620.41	1829.22	1435.43	1200.60	935.26	853.66	741.48	668.91
58000	5089.02	2666.38	1861.31	1460.61	1221.66	951.67	868.64	754.49	680.64
59000	5176.76	2712.36	1893.40	1485.79	1242.72	968.08	883.62	767.49	692.38
60000	5264.50	2758.33	1925.49	1510.98	1263.79	984.49	898.59	780.50	704.11
61000	5352.24	2804.30	1957.58	1536.16	1284.85	1000.90	913.57	793.51	715.85
62000	5439.98	2850.27	1989.67	1561.34	1305.91	1017.31	928.55	806.52	727.58
63000	5527.72	2896.24	2021.76	1586.53	1326.97	1033.71	943.52	819.53	739.32
64000	5615.47	2942.22	2053.86	1611.71	1348.04	1050.12	958.50	832.54	751.06
65000	5703.21	2988.19	2085.95	1636.89	1369.10	1066.53	973.48	845.54	762.79
67500	5922.56	3103.12	2166.18	1699.85	1421.76	1107.55	1010.92	878.06	792.13
70000	6141.92	3218.05	2246.40	1762.81	1474.42	1148.57	1048.36	910.59	821.47
75000	6580.63	3447.91	2406.86	1888.72	1579.73	1230.61	1123.24	975.63	880.14
80000	7019.33	3677.77	2567.32	2014.63	1685.05	1312.65	1198.12	1040.67	938.82
85000	7458.04	3907.63	2727.78	2140.55	1790.36	1394.69	1273.00	1105.71	997.49
90000	7896.75	4137.49	2888.23	2266.46	1895.68	1476.73	1347.89	1170.75	1056.17
95000	8335.45	4367.35	3048.69	2392.38	2000.99	1558.77	1422.77	1235.79	1114.84
100000	8774.16	4597.21	3209.15	2518.29	2106.31	1640.81	1497.65	1300.83	1173.52
105000	9212.87	4827.07	3369.60	2644.21	2211.62	1722.85	1572.53	1365.88	1232.20
110000	9651.58	5056.93	3530.06	2770.12	2316.94	1804.89	1647.42	1430.92	1290.87
115000	10090.29	5286.79	3690.52	2896.04	2422.25	1886.93	1722.30	1495.96	1349.55
120000	10528.99	5516.65	3850.97	3021.95	2527.57	1968.97	1797.18	1561.00	1408.22
125000	10967.70	5746.51	4011.43	3147.86	2632.88	2051.01	1872.06	1626.04	1466.90
130000	11406.41	5976.37	4171.89	3273.78	2738.20	2133.05	1946.95	1691.08	1525.58
135000	11845.12	6206.23	4332.35	3399.69	2843.51	2215.09	2021.83	1756.12	1584.25
140000	12283.83	6436.09	4492.80	3525.61	2948.83	2297.13	2096.71	1821.17	1642.93
145000	12722.53	6665.95	4653.26	3651.52	3054.14	2379.17	2171.59	1886.21	1701.60
150000	13161.24	6895.81	4813.72	3777.44	3159.46	2461.22	2246.47	1951.25	1760.28

MONTHLY PAYMENT 9⅝%

NECESSARY TO AMORTIZE A LOAN

AMOUNT	15 YEARS	18 YEARS	20 YEARS	25 YEARS	28 YEARS	29 YEARS	30 YEARS	35 YEARS	40 YEARS
$ 50	.53	.49	.48	.45	.44	.43	.43	.42	.41
100	1.06	.98	.95	.89	.87	.86	.85	.84	.82
200	2.11	1.96	1.89	1.77	1.73	1.72	1.70	1.67	1.64
300	3.16	2.93	2.83	2.65	2.59	2.57	2.55	2.50	2.46
400	4.21	3.91	3.77	3.53	3.45	3.43	3.40	3.33	3.28
500	5.26	4.88	4.71	4.42	4.31	4.28	4.25	4.16	4.10
600	6.32	5.86	5.65	5.30	5.17	5.14	5.10	4.99	4.92
700	7.37	6.84	6.59	6.18	6.03	5.99	5.95	5.82	5.74
800	8.42	7.81	7.53	7.06	6.89	6.85	6.80	6.65	6.56
900	9.47	8.79	8.47	7.95	7.75	7.70	7.65	7.48	7.38
1000	10.52	9.76	9.41	8.83	8.61	8.56	8.50	8.32	8.20
2000	21.04	19.52	18.81	17.65	17.22	17.11	17.00	16.63	16.40
3000	31.56	29.28	28.21	26.48	25.83	25.66	25.50	24.94	24.60
4000	42.08	39.04	37.62	35.30	34.44	34.21	34.00	33.25	32.80
5000	52.59	48.80	47.02	44.13	43.05	42.76	42.50	41.56	40.99
6000	63.11	58.56	56.42	52.95	51.66	51.31	51.00	49.87	49.19
7000	73.63	68.31	65.83	61.77	60.26	59.86	59.50	58.18	57.39
8000	84.15	78.07	75.23	70.60	68.87	68.42	68.00	66.49	65.59
9000	94.67	87.83	84.63	79.42	77.48	76.97	76.50	74.80	73.79
10000	105.18	97.59	94.04	88.25	86.09	85.52	85.00	83.11	81.98
15000	157.77	146.38	141.05	132.37	129.13	128.27	127.50	124.67	122.97
20000	210.36	195.18	188.07	176.49	172.18	171.03	170.00	166.22	163.96
25000	262.95	243.97	235.08	220.61	215.22	213.79	212.50	207.78	204.95
30000	315.54	292.76	282.10	264.73	258.26	256.54	255.00	249.33	245.94
35000	368.13	341.55	329.11	308.85	301.30	299.30	297.50	290.89	286.93
40000	420.72	390.35	376.13	352.97	344.35	342.06	340.00	332.44	327.92
45000	473.31	439.14	423.14	397.09	387.39	384.81	382.50	373.99	368.91
46000	483.82	448.90	432.55	405.91	396.00	393.36	391.00	382.31	377.11
47000	494.34	458.66	441.95	414.73	404.61	401.92	399.50	390.62	385.31
48000	504.86	468.41	451.35	423.56	413.22	410.47	408.00	398.93	393.51
49000	515.38	478.17	460.76	432.38	421.82	419.02	416.50	407.24	401.71
50000	525.90	487.93	470.16	441.21	430.43	427.57	425.00	415.55	409.90
51000	536.41	497.69	479.56	450.03	439.04	436.12	433.50	423.86	418.10
52000	546.93	507.45	488.97	458.85	447.65	444.67	442.00	432.17	426.30
53000	557.45	517.21	498.37	467.68	456.26	453.22	450.50	440.48	434.50
54000	567.97	526.96	507.77	476.50	464.87	461.77	459.00	448.79	442.70
55000	578.48	536.72	517.17	485.33	473.48	470.33	467.50	457.10	450.89
56000	589.00	546.48	526.58	494.15	482.08	478.88	476.00	465.41	459.09
57000	599.52	556.24	535.98	502.97	490.69	487.43	484.50	473.72	467.29
58000	610.04	566.00	545.38	511.80	499.30	495.98	493.00	482.04	475.49
59000	620.56	575.76	554.79	520.62	507.91	504.53	501.50	490.35	483.69
60000	631.07	585.52	564.19	529.45	516.52	513.08	510.00	498.66	491.88
61000	641.59	595.27	573.59	538.27	525.13	521.63	518.50	506.97	500.08
62000	652.11	605.03	583.00	547.09	533.74	530.18	527.00	515.28	508.28
63000	662.63	614.79	592.40	555.92	542.34	538.74	535.50	523.59	516.48
64000	673.14	624.55	601.80	564.74	550.95	547.29	544.00	531.90	524.68
65000	683.66	634.31	611.21	573.57	559.56	555.84	552.50	540.21	532.87
67500	709.96	658.70	634.71	595.63	581.08	577.22	573.75	560.99	553.37
70000	736.25	683.10	658.22	617.69	602.60	598.59	595.00	581.77	573.86
75000	788.84	731.89	705.24	661.81	645.65	641.35	637.50	623.32	614.85
80000	841.43	780.69	752.25	705.93	688.69	684.11	680.00	664.87	655.84
85000	894.02	829.48	799.27	750.05	731.73	726.86	722.50	706.43	696.83
90000	946.61	878.27	846.28	794.17	774.78	769.62	765.00	747.98	737.82
95000	999.20	927.06	893.30	838.29	817.82	812.38	807.49	789.54	778.81
100000	1051.79	975.86	940.31	882.41	860.86	855.13	849.99	831.09	819.80
105000	1104.37	1024.65	987.33	926.53	903.90	897.89	892.49	872.65	860.79
110000	1156.96	1073.44	1034.34	970.65	946.95	940.65	934.99	914.20	901.78
115000	1209.55	1122.23	1081.36	1014.77	989.99	983.40	977.49	955.76	942.77
120000	1262.14	1171.03	1128.38	1058.89	1033.03	1026.16	1019.99	997.31	983.76
125000	1314.73	1219.82	1175.39	1103.01	1076.08	1068.92	1062.49	1038.86	1024.75
130000	1367.32	1268.61	1222.41	1147.13	1119.12	1111.67	1104.99	1080.42	1065.74
135000	1419.91	1317.40	1269.42	1191.25	1162.16	1154.43	1147.49	1121.97	1106.73
140000	1472.50	1366.20	1316.44	1235.37	1205.20	1197.18	1189.99	1163.53	1147.72
145000	1525.09	1414.99	1363.45	1279.49	1248.25	1239.94	1232.49	1205.08	1188.71
150000	1577.68	1463.78	1410.47	1323.61	1291.29	1282.70	1274.99	1246.64	1229.70

9¾% MONTHLY PAYMENT
NECESSARY TO AMORTIZE A LOAN

AMOUNT	1 YEAR	2 YEARS	3 YEARS	4 YEARS	5 YEARS	7 YEARS	8 YEARS	10 YEARS	12 YEARS
$ 50	4.39	2.31	1.61	1.27	1.06	.83	.76	.66	.60
100	8.78	4.61	3.22	2.53	2.12	1.65	1.51	1.31	1.19
200	17.56	9.21	6.43	5.05	4.23	3.30	3.01	2.62	2.37
300	26.34	13.81	9.65	7.58	6.34	4.95	4.52	3.93	3.55
400	35.12	18.42	12.86	10.10	8.45	6.59	6.02	5.24	4.73
500	43.90	23.02	16.08	12.63	10.57	8.24	7.53	6.54	5.91
600	52.68	27.62	19.29	15.15	12.68	9.89	9.03	7.85	7.09
700	61.46	32.23	22.51	17.67	14.79	11.54	10.53	9.16	8.27
800	70.24	36.83	25.72	20.20	16.90	13.18	12.04	10.47	9.45
900	79.02	41.43	28.94	22.72	19.02	14.83	13.54	11.77	10.63
1000	87.80	46.03	32.15	25.25	21.13	16.48	15.05	13.08	11.81
2000	175.60	92.06	64.30	50.49	42.25	32.95	30.09	26.16	23.62
3000	263.40	138.09	96.45	75.73	63.38	49.42	45.13	39.24	35.43
4000	351.20	184.12	128.60	100.98	84.50	65.89	60.17	52.31	47.23
5000	439.00	230.15	160.75	126.22	105.63	82.37	75.22	65.39	59.04
6000	526.80	276.18	192.90	151.46	126.75	98.84	90.26	78.47	70.85
7000	614.60	322.21	225.05	176.70	147.87	115.31	105.30	91.54	82.65
8000	702.40	368.24	257.20	201.95	169.00	131.78	120.34	104.62	94.46
9000	790.20	414.27	289.35	227.19	190.12	148.26	135.38	117.70	106.27
10000	878.00	460.30	321.50	252.43	211.25	164.73	150.43	130.78	118.07
15000	1317.00	690.45	482.25	378.65	316.87	247.09	225.64	196.16	177.11
20000	1756.00	920.60	643.00	504.86	422.49	329.45	300.85	261.55	236.14
25000	2195.00	1150.75	803.75	631.07	528.11	411.81	376.06	326.93	295.18
30000	2633.99	1380.89	964.50	757.29	633.73	494.17	451.27	392.32	354.21
35000	3072.99	1611.04	1125.25	883.50	739.35	576.54	526.48	457.70	413.24
40000	3511.99	1841.19	1286.00	1009.71	844.97	658.90	601.69	523.09	472.28
45000	3950.99	2071.34	1446.75	1135.93	950.60	741.26	676.90	588.47	531.31
46000	4038.79	2117.37	1478.90	1161.17	971.72	757.73	691.95	601.55	543.12
47000	4126.59	2163.40	1511.05	1186.41	992.84	774.20	706.99	614.63	554.92
48000	4214.39	2209.43	1543.20	1211.65	1013.97	790.68	722.03	627.70	566.73
49000	4302.19	2255.46	1575.35	1236.90	1035.09	807.15	737.07	640.78	578.54
50000	4389.99	2301.49	1607.50	1262.14	1056.22	823.62	752.12	653.86	590.35
51000	4477.79	2347.52	1639.65	1287.38	1077.34	840.09	767.16	666.93	602.15
52000	4565.59	2393.55	1671.80	1312.62	1098.47	856.56	782.20	680.01	613.96
53000	4653.39	2439.58	1703.95	1337.87	1119.59	873.04	797.24	693.09	625.77
54000	4741.19	2485.60	1736.10	1363.11	1140.71	889.51	812.28	706.16	637.57
55000	4828.99	2531.63	1768.25	1388.35	1161.84	905.98	827.33	719.24	649.38
56000	4916.79	2577.66	1800.40	1413.60	1182.96	922.45	842.37	732.32	661.19
57000	5004.59	2623.69	1832.55	1438.84	1204.09	938.93	857.41	745.40	672.99
58000	5092.39	2669.72	1864.70	1464.08	1225.21	955.40	872.45	758.47	684.80
59000	5180.18	2715.75	1896.85	1489.32	1246.34	971.87	887.49	771.55	696.61
60000	5267.98	2761.78	1929.00	1514.57	1267.46	988.34	902.54	784.63	708.41
61000	5355.78	2807.81	1961.15	1539.81	1288.58	1004.82	917.58	797.70	720.22
62000	5443.58	2853.84	1993.30	1565.05	1309.71	1021.29	932.62	810.78	732.03
63000	5531.38	2899.87	2025.45	1590.29	1330.83	1037.76	947.66	823.86	743.83
64000	5619.18	2945.90	2057.60	1615.54	1351.96	1054.23	962.71	836.93	755.64
65000	5706.98	2991.93	2089.75	1640.78	1373.08	1070.70	977.75	850.01	767.45
67500	5926.48	3107.00	2170.13	1703.89	1425.89	1111.88	1015.35	882.70	796.96
70000	6145.98	3222.08	2250.50	1766.99	1478.70	1153.07	1052.96	915.40	826.48
75000	6584.98	3452.23	2411.25	1893.21	1584.32	1235.43	1128.17	980.78	885.52
80000	7023.98	3682.37	2572.00	2019.42	1689.94	1317.79	1203.38	1046.17	944.55
85000	7462.98	3912.52	2732.75	2145.63	1795.57	1400.15	1278.59	1111.55	1003.58
90000	7901.97	4142.67	2893.50	2271.85	1901.19	1482.51	1353.80	1176.94	1062.62
95000	8340.97	4372.82	3054.25	2398.06	2006.81	1564.87	1429.01	1242.32	1121.65
100000	8779.97	4602.97	3215.00	2524.27	2112.43	1647.23	1504.23	1307.71	1180.69
105000	9218.97	4833.12	3375.75	2650.49	2218.05	1729.60	1579.44	1373.09	1239.72
110000	9657.97	5063.26	3536.50	2776.70	2323.67	1811.96	1654.65	1438.48	1298.75
115000	10096.97	5293.41	3697.25	2902.91	2429.29	1894.32	1729.86	1503.86	1357.79
120000	10535.96	5523.56	3858.00	3029.13	2534.91	1976.68	1805.07	1569.25	1416.82
125000	10974.96	5753.71	4018.75	3155.34	2640.54	2059.04	1880.28	1634.63	1475.86
130000	11413.96	5983.86	4179.50	3281.55	2746.16	2141.40	1955.49	1700.02	1534.89
135000	11852.96	6214.00	4340.25	3407.77	2851.78	2223.76	2030.70	1765.40	1593.92
140000	12291.96	6444.15	4501.00	3533.98	2957.40	2306.13	2105.91	1830.79	1652.96
145000	12730.96	6674.30	4661.75	3660.20	3063.02	2388.49	2181.12	1896.17	1711.99
150000	13169.95	6904.45	4822.50	3786.41	3168.64	2470.85	2256.34	1961.56	1771.03

MONTHLY PAYMENT 9¾%

NECESSARY TO AMORTIZE A LOAN

AMOUNT	15 YEARS	18 YEARS	20 YEARS	25 YEARS	28 YEARS	29 YEARS	30 YEARS	35 YEARS	40 YEARS
$ 50	.53	.50	.48	.45	.44	.44	.43	.43	.42
100	1.06	.99	.95	.90	.87	.87	.86	.85	.83
200	2.12	1.97	1.90	1.79	1.74	1.73	1.72	1.69	1.66
300	3.18	2.96	2.85	2.68	2.61	2.60	2.58	2.53	2.49
400	4.24	3.94	3.80	3.57	3.48	3.46	3.44	3.37	3.32
500	5.30	4.92	4.75	4.46	4.35	4.33	4.30	4.21	4.15
600	6.36	5.91	5.70	5.35	5.22	5.19	5.16	5.05	4.98
700	7.42	6.89	6.64	6.24	6.09	6.05	6.02	5.89	5.81
800	8.48	7.88	7.59	7.13	6.96	6.92	6.88	6.73	6.64
900	9.54	8.86	8.54	8.03	7.83	7.78	7.74	7.57	7.47
1000	10.60	9.84	9.49	8.92	8.70	8.65	8.60	8.41	8.30
2000	21.19	19.68	18.98	17.83	17.40	17.29	17.19	16.82	16.60
3000	31.79	29.52	28.46	26.74	26.10	25.93	25.78	25.22	24.89
4000	42.38	39.36	37.95	35.65	34.80	34.57	34.37	33.63	33.19
5000	52.97	49.20	47.43	44.56	43.50	43.22	42.96	42.03	41.48
6000	63.57	59.03	56.92	53.47	52.20	51.86	51.55	50.44	49.78
7000	74.16	68.87	66.40	62.38	60.90	60.50	60.15	58.85	58.07
8000	84.75	78.71	75.89	71.30	69.59	69.14	68.74	67.25	66.37
9000	95.35	88.55	85.37	80.21	78.29	77.78	77.33	75.66	74.67
10000	105.94	98.39	94.86	89.12	86.99	86.43	85.92	84.06	82.96
15000	158.91	147.58	142.28	133.68	130.48	129.64	128.88	126.09	124.44
20000	211.88	196.77	189.71	178.23	173.98	172.85	171.84	168.12	165.92
25000	264.85	245.96	237.13	222.79	217.47	216.06	214.79	210.15	207.39
30000	317.81	295.15	284.56	267.35	260.96	259.27	257.75	252.18	248.87
35000	370.78	344.34	331.99	311.90	304.46	302.48	300.71	294.21	290.35
40000	423.75	393.53	379.41	356.46	347.95	345.69	343.67	336.24	331.83
45000	476.72	442.72	426.84	401.02	391.44	388.90	386.62	378.27	373.31
46000	487.31	452.56	436.32	409.93	400.14	397.54	395.22	386.68	381.60
47000	497.91	462.40	445.81	418.84	408.84	406.19	403.81	395.08	389.90
48000	508.50	472.24	455.29	427.75	417.54	414.83	412.40	403.49	398.19
49000	519.09	482.08	464.78	436.66	426.24	423.47	420.99	411.89	406.49
50000	529.69	491.92	474.26	445.57	434.94	432.11	429.58	420.30	414.78
51000	540.28	501.75	483.75	454.49	443.63	440.75	438.17	428.71	423.08
52000	550.87	511.59	493.23	463.40	452.33	449.40	446.77	437.11	431.38
53000	561.47	521.43	502.72	472.31	461.03	458.04	455.36	445.52	439.67
54000	572.06	531.27	512.20	481.22	469.73	466.68	463.95	453.92	447.97
55000	582.65	541.11	521.69	490.13	478.43	475.32	472.54	462.33	456.26
56000	593.25	550.94	531.17	499.04	487.13	483.97	481.13	470.74	464.56
57000	603.84	560.78	540.66	507.95	495.83	492.61	489.72	479.14	472.85
58000	614.44	570.62	550.14	516.86	504.52	501.25	498.31	487.55	481.15
59000	625.03	580.46	559.63	525.78	513.22	509.89	506.91	495.95	489.44
60000	635.62	590.30	569.12	534.69	521.92	518.53	515.50	504.36	497.74
61000	646.22	600.14	578.60	543.60	530.62	527.18	524.09	512.76	506.04
62000	656.81	609.97	588.09	552.51	539.32	535.82	532.68	521.17	514.33
63000	667.40	619.81	597.57	561.42	548.02	544.46	541.27	529.58	522.63
64000	678.00	629.65	607.06	570.33	556.72	553.10	549.86	537.98	530.92
65000	688.59	639.49	616.54	579.24	565.41	561.74	558.46	546.39	539.22
67500	715.07	664.08	640.25	601.52	587.16	583.35	579.93	567.40	559.96
70000	741.56	688.68	663.97	623.80	608.91	604.96	601.41	588.42	580.70
75000	794.53	737.87	711.39	668.36	652.40	648.17	644.37	630.45	622.17
80000	847.50	787.06	758.82	712.91	695.89	691.38	687.33	672.48	663.65
85000	900.46	836.25	806.24	757.47	739.39	734.59	730.29	714.51	705.13
90000	953.43	885.44	853.67	802.03	782.88	777.80	773.24	756.54	746.61
95000	1006.40	934.63	901.10	846.59	826.37	821.01	816.20	798.56	788.09
100000	1059.37	983.83	948.52	891.14	869.87	864.22	859.16	840.59	829.56
105000	1112.34	1033.02	995.95	935.70	913.36	907.43	902.12	882.62	871.04
110000	1165.30	1082.21	1043.37	980.26	956.85	950.64	945.07	924.65	912.52
115000	1218.27	1131.40	1090.80	1024.81	1000.35	993.85	988.03	966.68	954.00
120000	1271.24	1180.59	1138.23	1069.37	1043.84	1037.06	1030.99	1008.71	995.48
125000	1324.21	1229.78	1185.65	1113.93	1087.33	1080.27	1073.95	1050.74	1036.95
130000	1377.18	1278.97	1233.08	1158.48	1130.82	1123.48	1116.91	1092.77	1078.43
135000	1430.14	1328.16	1280.50	1203.04	1174.32	1166.70	1159.86	1134.80	1119.91
140000	1483.11	1377.35	1327.93	1247.60	1217.81	1209.91	1202.82	1176.83	1161.39
145000	1536.08	1426.54	1375.35	1292.15	1261.30	1253.12	1245.78	1218.86	1202.86
150000	1589.05	1475.74	1422.78	1336.71	1304.80	1296.33	1288.74	1260.89	1244.34

9⅞%   MONTHLY PAYMENT
NECESSARY TO AMORTIZE A LOAN

AMOUNT	1 YEAR	2 YEARS	3 YEARS	4 YEARS	5 YEARS	6 YEARS	7 YEARS	8 YEARS	10 YEARS	12 YEARS
$ 50	4.40	2.31	1.62	1.27	1.06	.83	.76	.66	.66	.60
100	8.79	4.61	3.23	2.54	2.12	1.66	1.52	1.32	1.32	1.19
200	17.58	9.22	6.45	5.07	4.24	3.31	3.03	2.63	2.63	2.38
300	26.36	13.83	9.67	7.60	6.36	4.97	4.54	3.95	3.95	3.57
400	35.15	18.44	12.89	10.13	8.48	6.62	6.05	5.26	5.26	4.76
500	43.93	23.05	16.11	12.66	10.60	8.27	7.56	6.58	6.58	5.94
600	52.72	27.66	19.33	15.19	12.72	9.93	9.07	7.89	7.89	7.13
700	61.51	32.27	22.55	17.72	14.83	11.58	10.58	9.21	9.21	8.32
800	70.29	36.87	25.77	20.25	16.95	13.23	12.09	10.52	10.52	9.51
900	79.08	41.48	28.99	22.78	19.07	14.89	13.60	11.84	11.84	10.70
1000	87.86	46.09	32.21	25.31	21.19	16.54	15.11	13.15	13.15	11.88
2000	175.72	92.18	64.42	50.61	42.38	33.08	30.22	26.30	26.30	23.76
3000	263.58	138.27	96.63	75.91	63.56	49.62	45.33	39.44	39.44	35.64
4000	351.44	184.35	128.84	101.22	84.75	66.15	60.44	52.59	52.59	47.52
5000	439.29	230.44	161.05	126.52	105.93	82.69	75.55	65.73	65.73	59.40
6000	527.15	276.53	193.26	151.82	127.12	99.23	90.65	78.88	78.88	71.28
7000	615.01	322.62	225.46	177.12	148.30	115.76	105.76	92.03	92.03	83.16
8000	702.87	368.70	257.67	202.43	169.49	132.30	120.87	105.17	105.17	95.03
9000	790.72	414.79	289.88	227.73	190.68	148.84	135.98	118.32	118.32	106.91
10000	878.58	460.88	322.09	253.03	211.86	165.37	151.09	131.46	131.46	118.79
15000	1317.87	691.31	483.13	379.54	317.79	248.06	226.63	197.19	197.19	178.19
20000	1757.16	921.75	644.18	506.06	423.72	330.74	302.17	262.92	262.92	237.58
25000	2196.45	1152.19	805.22	632.57	529.64	413.42	377.71	328.65	328.65	296.97
30000	2635.74	1382.62	966.26	759.08	635.57	496.11	453.25	394.38	394.38	356.37
35000	3075.03	1613.06	1127.30	885.60	741.50	578.79	528.79	460.11	460.11	415.76
40000	3514.32	1843.50	1288.35	1012.11	847.43	661.47	604.33	525.84	525.84	475.15
45000	3953.60	2073.93	1449.39	1138.62	953.36	744.16	679.87	591.57	591.57	534.55
46000	4041.46	2120.02	1481.60	1163.92	974.54	760.69	694.98	604.72	604.72	546.42
47000	4129.32	2166.11	1513.81	1189.23	995.73	777.23	710.09	617.86	617.86	558.30
48000	4217.18	2212.19	1546.01	1214.53	1016.91	793.77	725.19	631.01	631.01	570.18
49000	4305.04	2258.28	1578.22	1239.83	1038.10	810.30	740.30	644.16	644.16	582.06
50000	4392.89	2304.37	1610.43	1265.13	1059.28	826.84	755.41	657.30	657.30	593.94
51000	4480.75	2350.45	1642.64	1290.44	1080.47	843.38	770.52	670.45	670.45	605.82
52000	4568.61	2396.54	1674.85	1315.74	1101.66	859.91	785.63	683.59	683.59	617.70
53000	4656.47	2442.63	1707.06	1341.04	1122.84	876.45	800.73	696.74	696.74	629.58
54000	4744.32	2488.72	1739.27	1366.35	1144.03	892.99	815.84	709.89	709.89	641.45
55000	4832.18	2534.80	1771.47	1391.65	1165.21	909.52	830.95	723.03	723.03	653.33
56000	4920.04	2580.89	1803.68	1416.95	1186.40	926.06	846.06	736.18	736.18	665.21
57000	5007.90	2626.98	1835.89	1442.25	1207.58	942.60	861.17	749.32	749.32	677.09
58000	5095.76	2673.07	1868.10	1467.56	1228.77	959.13	876.27	762.47	762.47	688.97
59000	5183.61	2719.15	1900.31	1492.86	1249.95	975.67	891.38	775.62	775.62	700.85
60000	5271.47	2765.24	1932.52	1518.16	1271.14	992.21	906.49	788.76	788.76	712.73
61000	5359.33	2811.33	1964.73	1543.46	1292.33	1008.74	921.60	801.91	801.91	724.60
62000	5447.19	2857.41	1996.93	1568.77	1313.51	1025.28	936.71	815.05	815.05	736.48
63000	5535.04	2903.50	2029.14	1594.07	1334.70	1041.82	951.82	828.20	828.20	748.36
64000	5622.90	2949.59	2061.35	1619.37	1355.88	1058.35	966.92	841.35	841.35	760.24
65000	5710.76	2995.68	2093.56	1644.67	1377.07	1074.89	982.03	854.49	854.49	772.12
67500	5930.40	3110.89	2174.08	1707.93	1430.03	1116.23	1019.80	887.36	887.36	801.82
70000	6150.05	3226.11	2254.60	1771.19	1483.00	1157.57	1057.57	920.22	920.22	831.51
75000	6589.34	3456.55	2415.64	1897.70	1588.92	1240.26	1133.11	985.95	985.95	890.91
80000	7028.63	3686.99	2576.69	2024.21	1694.85	1322.94	1208.65	1051.68	1051.68	950.30
85000	7467.91	3917.42	2737.73	2150.73	1800.78	1405.62	1284.19	1117.41	1117.41	1009.69
90000	7907.20	4147.86	2898.77	2277.24	1906.71	1488.31	1359.73	1183.14	1183.14	1069.09
95000	8346.49	4378.29	3059.82	2403.75	2012.64	1570.99	1435.27	1248.87	1248.87	1128.48
100000	8785.78	4608.73	3220.86	2530.26	2118.56	1653.67	1510.82	1314.60	1314.60	1187.87
105000	9225.07	4839.17	3381.90	2656.78	2224.49	1736.36	1586.36	1380.33	1380.33	1247.27
110000	9664.36	5069.60	3542.94	2783.29	2330.42	1819.04	1661.90	1446.06	1446.06	1306.66
115000	10103.65	5300.04	3703.99	2909.80	2436.35	1901.72	1737.44	1511.79	1511.79	1366.05
120000	10542.94	5530.48	3865.03	3036.32	2542.28	1984.41	1812.98	1577.52	1577.52	1425.45
125000	10982.23	5760.91	4026.07	3162.83	2648.20	2067.09	1888.52	1643.25	1643.25	1484.84
130000	11421.51	5991.35	4187.11	3289.34	2754.13	2149.77	1964.06	1708.98	1708.98	1544.23
135000	11860.80	6221.78	4348.16	3415.86	2860.06	2232.46	2039.60	1774.71	1774.71	1603.63
140000	12300.09	6452.22	4509.20	3542.37	2965.99	2315.14	2115.14	1840.44	1840.44	1663.02
145000	12739.38	6682.66	4670.24	3668.88	3071.92	2397.82	2190.68	1906.17	1906.17	1722.41
150000	13178.67	6913.09	4831.28	3795.39	3177.84	2480.51	2266.22	1971.90	1971.90	1781.81

MONTHLY PAYMENT 9⅞%

NECESSARY TO AMORTIZE A LOAN

AMOUNT	15 YEARS	18 YEARS	20 YEARS	25 YEARS	28 YEARS	29 YEARS	30 YEARS	35 YEARS	40 YEARS
$ 50	.54	.50	.48	.45	.44	.44	.44	.43	.42
100	1.07	1.00	.96	.90	.88	.88	.87	.86	.84
200	2.14	1.99	1.92	1.80	1.76	1.75	1.74	1.71	1.68
300	3.21	2.98	2.88	2.70	2.64	2.62	2.61	2.56	2.52
400	4.27	3.97	3.83	3.60	3.52	3.50	3.48	3.41	3.36
500	5.34	4.96	4.79	4.50	4.40	4.37	4.35	4.26	4.20
600	6.41	5.96	5.75	5.40	5.28	5.24	5.22	5.11	5.04
700	7.47	6.95	6.70	6.30	6.16	6.12	6.08	5.96	5.88
800	8.54	7.94	7.66	7.20	7.04	6.99	6.95	6.81	6.72
900	9.61	8.93	8.62	8.10	7.92	7.86	7.82	7.66	7.56
1000	10.67	9.92	9.57	9.00	8.79	8.74	8.69	8.51	8.40
2000	21.34	19.84	19.14	18.00	17.58	17.47	17.37	17.01	16.79
3000	32.01	29.76	28.71	27.00	26.37	26.20	26.06	25.51	25.19
4000	42.68	39.68	38.28	36.00	35.16	34.94	34.74	34.01	33.58
5000	53.35	49.60	47.84	45.00	43.95	43.67	43.42	42.51	41.97
6000	64.02	59.51	57.41	54.00	52.74	52.40	52.11	51.01	50.37
7000	74.69	69.43	66.98	63.00	61.53	61.14	60.79	59.51	58.76
8000	85.36	79.35	76.55	72.00	70.32	69.87	69.47	68.01	67.15
9000	96.03	89.27	86.11	81.00	79.11	78.60	78.16	76.52	75.55
10000	106.70	99.19	95.68	90.00	87.89	87.34	86.84	85.02	83.94
15000	160.05	148.78	143.52	134.99	131.84	131.00	130.26	127.52	125.91
20000	213.40	198.37	191.36	179.99	175.78	174.67	173.67	170.03	167.87
25000	266.75	247.96	239.19	224.98	219.73	218.34	217.09	212.53	209.84
30000	320.10	297.55	287.03	269.98	263.67	262.00	260.51	255.04	251.81
35000	373.44	347.14	334.87	314.97	307.62	305.67	303.93	297.55	293.77
40000	426.79	396.73	382.71	359.97	351.56	349.34	347.34	340.05	335.74
45000	480.14	446.32	430.54	404.96	395.51	393.00	390.76	382.56	377.71
46000	490.81	456.24	440.11	413.96	404.30	401.74	399.45	391.06	386.10
47000	501.48	466.16	449.68	422.96	413.09	410.47	408.13	399.56	394.50
48000	512.15	476.08	459.25	431.96	421.88	419.20	416.81	408.06	402.89
49000	522.82	486.00	468.81	440.96	430.66	427.94	425.50	416.56	411.28
50000	533.49	495.91	478.38	449.96	439.45	436.67	434.18	425.06	419.68
51000	544.16	505.83	487.95	458.96	448.24	445.40	442.86	433.57	428.07
52000	554.83	515.75	497.52	467.96	457.03	454.14	451.55	442.07	436.46
53000	565.50	525.67	507.08	476.95	465.82	462.87	460.23	450.57	444.86
54000	576.17	535.59	516.65	485.95	474.61	471.60	468.91	459.07	453.25
55000	586.84	545.50	526.22	494.95	483.40	480.34	477.60	467.57	461.64
56000	597.51	555.42	535.79	503.95	492.19	489.07	486.28	476.07	470.04
57000	608.18	565.34	545.36	512.95	500.98	497.80	494.96	484.57	478.43
58000	618.85	575.26	554.92	521.95	509.76	506.54	503.65	493.07	486.82
59000	629.52	585.18	564.49	530.95	518.55	515.27	512.33	501.57	495.22
60000	640.19	595.10	574.06	539.95	527.34	524.00	521.01	510.08	503.61
61000	650.86	605.01	583.63	548.95	536.13	532.74	529.70	518.58	512.00
62000	661.53	614.93	593.19	557.95	544.92	541.47	538.38	527.08	520.40
63000	672.20	624.85	602.76	566.94	553.71	550.20	547.06	535.58	528.79
64000	682.87	634.77	612.33	575.94	562.50	558.94	555.75	544.08	537.18
65000	693.54	644.69	621.90	584.94	571.29	567.67	564.43	552.58	545.58
67500	720.21	669.48	645.81	607.44	593.26	589.50	586.14	573.83	566.56
70000	746.88	694.28	669.73	629.94	615.23	611.34	607.85	595.09	587.54
75000	800.23	743.87	717.57	674.93	659.18	655.00	651.27	637.59	629.51
80000	853.58	793.46	765.41	719.93	703.12	698.67	694.68	680.10	671.48
85000	906.93	843.05	813.25	764.92	747.07	742.34	738.10	722.61	713.45
90000	960.28	892.64	861.08	809.92	791.01	786.00	781.52	765.11	755.41
95000	1013.63	942.23	908.92	854.91	834.96	829.67	824.94	807.62	797.38
100000	1066.98	991.82	956.76	899.91	878.90	873.34	868.35	850.12	839.35
105000	1120.32	1041.41	1004.60	944.90	922.85	917.00	911.77	892.63	881.31
110000	1173.67	1091.00	1052.43	989.90	966.79	960.67	955.19	935.13	923.28
115000	1227.02	1140.60	1100.27	1034.89	1010.74	1004.34	998.61	977.64	965.25
120000	1280.37	1190.19	1148.11	1079.89	1054.68	1048.00	1042.02	1020.15	1007.21
125000	1333.72	1239.78	1195.95	1124.88	1098.62	1091.67	1085.44	1062.65	1049.18
130000	1387.07	1289.37	1243.79	1169.88	1142.57	1135.34	1128.86	1105.16	1091.15
135000	1440.42	1338.96	1291.62	1214.88	1186.51	1179.00	1172.28	1147.66	1133.12
140000	1493.76	1388.55	1339.46	1259.87	1230.46	1222.67	1215.69	1190.17	1175.08
145000	1547.11	1438.14	1387.30	1304.87	1274.40	1266.34	1259.11	1232.68	1217.05
150000	1600.46	1487.73	1435.14	1349.86	1318.35	1310.00	1302.53	1275.18	1259.02

10% MONTHLY PAYMENT
NECESSARY TO AMORTIZE A LOAN

AMOUNT	1 YEAR	2 YEARS	3 YEARS	4 YEARS	5 YEARS	7 YEARS	8 YEARS	10 YEARS	12 YEARS
$ 50	4.40	2.31	1.62	1.27	1.07	.84	.76	.67	.60
100	8.80	4.62	3.23	2.54	2.13	1.67	1.52	1.33	1.20
200	17.59	9.23	6.46	5.08	4.25	3.33	3.04	2.65	2.40
300	26.38	13.85	9.69	7.61	6.38	4.99	4.56	3.97	3.59
400	35.17	18.46	12.91	10.15	8.50	6.65	6.07	5.29	4.79
500	43.96	23.08	16.14	12.69	10.63	8.31	7.59	6.61	5.98
600	52.75	27.69	19.37	15.22	12.75	9.97	9.11	7.93	7.18
700	61.55	32.31	22.59	17.76	14.88	11.63	10.63	9.26	8.37
800	70.34	36.92	25.82	20.30	17.00	13.29	12.14	10.58	9.57
900	79.13	41.54	29.05	22.83	19.13	14.95	13.66	11.90	10.76
1000	87.92	46.15	32.27	25.37	21.25	16.61	15.18	13.22	11.96
2000	175.84	92.29	64.54	50.73	42.50	33.21	30.35	26.44	23.91
3000	263.75	138.44	96.81	76.09	63.75	49.81	45.53	39.65	35.86
4000	351.67	184.58	129.07	101.46	84.99	66.41	60.70	52.87	47.81
5000	439.58	230.73	161.34	126.82	106.24	83.01	75.88	66.08	59.76
6000	527.50	276.87	193.61	152.18	127.49	99.61	91.05	79.30	71.71
7000	615.42	323.02	225.88	177.54	148.73	116.21	106.22	92.51	83.66
8000	703.33	369.16	258.14	202.91	169.98	132.81	121.40	105.73	95.61
9000	791.25	415.31	290.41	228.27	191.23	149.42	136.57	118.94	107.56
10000	879.16	461.45	322.68	253.63	212.48	166.02	151.75	132.16	119.51
15000	1318.74	692.18	484.01	380.44	318.71	249.02	227.62	198.23	179.27
20000	1758.32	922.90	645.35	507.26	424.95	332.03	303.49	264.31	239.02
25000	2197.90	1153.63	806.68	634.07	531.18	415.03	379.36	330.38	298.77
30000	2637.48	1384.35	968.02	760.88	637.42	498.04	455.23	396.46	358.53
35000	3077.06	1615.08	1129.36	887.70	743.65	581.05	531.10	462.53	418.28
40000	3516.64	1845.80	1290.69	1014.51	849.89	664.05	606.97	528.61	478.04
45000	3956.22	2076.53	1452.03	1141.32	956.12	747.06	682.84	594.68	537.79
46000	4044.14	2122.67	1484.30	1166.68	977.37	763.66	698.02	607.90	549.74
47000	4132.05	2168.82	1516.56	1192.05	998.62	780.26	713.19	621.11	561.69
48000	4219.97	2214.96	1548.83	1217.41	1019.86	796.86	728.36	634.33	573.64
49000	4307.88	2261.11	1581.10	1242.77	1041.11	813.46	743.54	647.54	585.59
50000	4395.80	2307.25	1613.36	1268.13	1062.36	830.06	758.71	660.76	597.54
51000	4483.72	2353.40	1645.63	1293.50	1083.60	846.67	773.89	673.97	609.49
52000	4571.63	2399.54	1677.90	1318.86	1104.85	863.27	789.06	687.19	621.45
53000	4659.55	2445.69	1710.17	1344.22	1126.10	879.87	804.24	700.40	633.40
54000	4747.46	2491.83	1742.43	1369.58	1147.35	896.47	819.41	713.62	645.35
55000	4835.38	2537.98	1774.70	1394.95	1168.59	913.07	834.58	726.83	657.30
56000	4923.29	2584.12	1806.97	1420.31	1189.84	929.67	849.76	740.05	669.25
57000	5011.21	2630.27	1839.23	1445.67	1211.09	946.27	864.93	753.26	681.20
58000	5099.13	2676.41	1871.50	1471.03	1232.33	962.87	880.11	766.48	693.15
59000	5187.04	2722.56	1903.77	1496.40	1253.58	979.47	895.28	779.69	705.10
60000	5274.96	2768.70	1936.04	1521.76	1274.83	996.08	910.45	792.91	717.05
61000	5362.87	2814.85	1968.30	1547.12	1296.07	1012.68	925.63	806.12	729.00
62000	5450.79	2860.99	2000.57	1572.49	1317.32	1029.28	940.80	819.34	740.95
63000	5538.71	2907.14	2032.84	1597.85	1338.57	1045.88	955.98	832.55	752.90
64000	5626.62	2953.28	2065.10	1623.21	1359.82	1062.48	971.15	845.77	764.86
65000	5714.54	2999.43	2097.37	1648.57	1381.06	1079.08	986.33	858.98	776.81
67500	5934.33	3114.79	2178.04	1711.98	1434.18	1120.58	1024.26	892.02	806.68
70000	6154.12	3230.15	2258.71	1775.39	1487.30	1162.09	1062.20	925.06	836.56
75000	6593.70	3460.87	2420.04	1902.20	1593.53	1245.09	1138.07	991.14	896.31
80000	7033.28	3691.60	2581.38	2029.01	1699.77	1328.10	1213.94	1057.21	956.07
85000	7472.86	3922.32	2742.72	2155.82	1806.00	1411.11	1289.81	1123.29	1015.82
90000	7912.43	4153.05	2904.05	2282.64	1912.24	1494.11	1365.68	1189.36	1075.58
95000	8352.01	4383.77	3065.39	2409.45	2018.47	1577.12	1441.55	1255.44	1135.33
100000	8791.59	4614.50	3226.72	2536.26	2124.71	1660.12	1517.42	1321.51	1195.08
105000	9231.17	4845.22	3388.06	2663.08	2230.94	1743.13	1593.29	1387.59	1254.84
110000	9670.75	5075.95	3549.40	2789.89	2337.18	1826.14	1669.16	1453.66	1314.59
115000	10110.33	5306.67	3710.73	2916.70	2443.42	1909.14	1745.03	1519.74	1374.35
120000	10549.91	5537.40	3872.07	3043.52	2549.65	1992.15	1820.90	1585.81	1434.10
125000	10989.49	5768.12	4033.40	3170.33	2655.89	2075.15	1896.78	1651.89	1493.85
130000	11429.07	5998.85	4194.74	3297.14	2762.12	2158.16	1972.65	1717.96	1553.61
135000	11868.65	6229.57	4356.08	3423.95	2868.36	2241.16	2048.52	1784.04	1613.36
140000	12308.23	6460.29	4517.41	3550.77	2974.59	2324.17	2124.39	1850.12	1673.11
145000	12747.81	6691.02	4678.75	3677.58	3080.83	2407.18	2200.26	1916.19	1732.87
150000	13187.39	6921.74	4840.08	3804.39	3187.06	2490.18	2276.13	1982.27	1792.62

MONTHLY PAYMENT

NECESSARY TO AMORTIZE A LOAN

10%

AMOUNT	15 YEARS	18 YEARS	20 YEARS	25 YEARS	28 YEARS	29 YEARS	30 YEARS	35 YEARS	40 YEARS
$ 50	.54	.50	.49	.46	.45	.45	.44	.43	.43
100	1.08	1.00	.97	.91	.89	.89	.88	.86	.85
200	2.15	2.00	1.94	1.82	1.78	1.77	1.76	1.72	1.70
300	3.23	3.00	2.90	2.73	2.67	2.65	2.64	2.58	2.55
400	4.30	4.00	3.87	3.64	3.56	3.53	3.52	3.44	3.40
500	5.38	5.00	4.83	4.55	4.44	4.42	4.39	4.30	4.25
600	6.45	6.00	5.80	5.46	5.33	5.30	5.27	5.16	5.10
700	7.53	7.00	6.76	6.37	6.22	6.18	6.15	6.02	5.95
800	8.60	8.00	7.73	7.27	7.11	7.06	7.03	6.88	6.80
900	9.68	9.00	8.69	8.18	8.00	7.95	7.90	7.74	7.65
1000	10.75	10.00	9.66	9.09	8.88	8.83	8.78	8.60	8.50
2000	21.50	20.00	19.31	18.18	17.76	17.65	17.56	17.20	16.99
3000	32.24	30.00	28.96	27.27	26.64	26.48	26.33	25.80	25.48
4000	42.99	40.00	38.61	36.35	35.52	35.30	35.11	34.39	33.97
5000	53.74	50.00	48.26	45.44	44.40	44.13	43.88	42.99	42.46
6000	64.48	60.00	57.91	54.53	53.28	52.95	52.66	51.59	50.95
7000	75.23	69.99	67.56	63.61	62.16	61.78	61.44	60.18	59.45
8000	85.97	79.99	77.21	72.70	71.04	70.60	70.21	68.78	67.94
9000	96.72	89.99	86.86	81.79	79.92	79.43	78.99	77.38	76.43
10000	107.47	99.99	96.51	90.88	88.80	88.25	87.76	85.97	84.92
15000	161.20	149.98	144.76	136.31	133.20	132.38	131.64	128.96	127.38
20000	214.93	199.97	193.01	181.75	177.60	176.50	175.52	171.94	169.83
25000	268.66	249.97	241.26	227.18	222.00	220.62	219.40	214.92	212.29
30000	322.39	299.96	289.51	272.62	266.39	264.75	263.28	257.91	254.75
35000	376.12	349.95	337.76	318.05	310.79	308.87	307.16	300.89	297.21
40000	429.85	399.94	386.01	363.49	355.19	353.00	351.03	343.87	339.66
45000	483.58	449.93	434.26	408.92	399.59	397.12	394.91	386.86	382.12
46000	494.32	459.93	443.91	418.01	408.47	405.94	403.69	395.45	390.61
47000	505.07	469.93	453.57	427.09	417.35	414.77	412.46	404.05	399.10
48000	515.82	479.93	463.22	436.18	426.23	423.59	421.24	412.65	407.60
49000	526.56	489.93	472.87	445.27	435.11	432.42	430.02	421.24	416.09
50000	537.31	499.93	482.52	454.36	443.99	441.24	438.79	429.84	424.58
51000	548.05	509.93	492.17	463.44	452.86	450.07	447.57	438.44	433.07
52000	558.80	519.92	501.82	472.53	461.74	458.89	456.34	447.03	441.56
53000	569.55	529.92	511.47	481.62	470.62	467.72	465.12	455.63	450.05
54000	580.29	539.92	521.12	490.70	479.50	476.54	473.89	464.23	458.54
55000	591.04	549.92	530.77	499.79	488.38	485.37	482.67	472.82	467.04
56000	601.78	559.92	540.42	508.88	497.26	494.19	491.45	481.42	475.53
57000	612.53	569.92	550.07	517.96	506.14	503.02	500.22	490.02	484.02
58000	623.28	579.91	559.72	527.05	515.02	511.84	509.00	498.62	492.51
59000	634.02	589.91	569.37	536.14	523.90	520.67	517.77	507.21	501.00
60000	644.77	599.91	579.02	545.23	532.78	529.49	526.55	515.81	509.49
61000	655.51	609.91	588.67	554.31	541.66	538.32	535.32	524.41	517.98
62000	666.26	619.91	598.32	563.40	550.54	547.14	544.10	533.00	526.48
63000	677.01	629.91	607.97	572.49	559.42	555.97	552.88	541.60	534.97
64000	687.75	639.90	617.62	581.57	568.30	564.79	561.65	550.20	543.46
65000	698.50	649.90	627.27	590.66	577.18	573.62	570.43	558.79	551.95
67500	725.36	674.90	651.39	613.38	599.38	595.68	592.37	580.28	573.18
70000	752.23	699.90	675.52	636.10	621.58	617.74	614.31	601.78	594.41
75000	805.96	749.89	723.77	681.53	665.98	661.86	658.18	644.76	636.86
80000	859.69	799.88	772.02	726.97	710.37	705.99	702.06	687.74	679.32
85000	913.42	849.87	820.27	772.40	754.77	750.11	745.94	730.73	721.78
90000	967.15	899.86	868.52	817.84	799.17	794.23	789.82	773.71	764.24
95000	1020.88	949.86	916.78	863.27	843.57	838.36	833.70	816.69	806.69
100000	1074.61	999.85	965.03	908.71	887.97	882.48	877.58	859.68	849.15
105000	1128.34	1049.84	1013.28	954.14	932.36	926.61	921.46	902.66	891.61
110000	1182.07	1099.83	1061.53	999.58	976.76	970.73	965.33	945.64	934.07
115000	1235.80	1149.83	1109.78	1045.01	1021.16	1014.85	1009.21	988.63	976.52
120000	1289.53	1199.82	1158.03	1090.45	1065.56	1058.98	1053.09	1031.61	1018.98
125000	1343.26	1249.81	1206.28	1135.88	1109.96	1103.10	1096.97	1074.60	1061.44
130000	1396.99	1299.80	1254.53	1181.32	1154.35	1147.23	1140.85	1117.58	1103.89
135000	1450.72	1349.79	1302.78	1226.75	1198.75	1191.35	1184.73	1160.56	1146.35
140000	1504.45	1399.79	1351.04	1272.19	1243.15	1235.47	1228.61	1203.55	1188.81
145000	1558.18	1449.78	1399.29	1317.62	1287.55	1279.60	1272.48	1246.53	1231.27
150000	1611.91	1499.77	1447.54	1363.06	1331.95	1323.72	1316.36	1289.51	1273.72

10⅛ %　MONTHLY PAYMENT
NECESSARY TO AMORTIZE A LOAN

AMOUNT	1 YEAR	2 YEARS	3 YEARS	4 YEARS	5 YEARS	7 YEARS	8 YEARS	10 YEARS	12 YEARS
$ 50	4.40	2.32	1.62	1.28	1.07	.84	.77	.67	.61
100	8.80	4.63	3.24	2.55	2.14	1.67	1.53	1.33	1.21
200	17.60	9.25	6.47	5.09	4.27	3.34	3.05	2.66	2.41
300	26.40	13.87	9.70	7.63	6.40	5.00	4.58	3.99	3.61
400	35.19	18.49	12.94	10.17	8.53	6.67	6.10	5.32	4.81
500	43.99	23.11	16.17	12.72	10.66	8.34	7.63	6.65	6.02
600	52.79	27.73	19.40	15.26	12.79	10.00	9.15	7.98	7.22
700	61.59	32.35	22.63	17.80	14.92	11.67	10.67	9.30	8.42
800	70.38	36.97	25.87	20.34	17.05	13.34	12.20	10.63	9.62
900	79.18	41.59	29.10	22.89	19.18	15.00	13.72	11.96	10.83
1000	87.98	46.21	32.33	25.43	21.31	16.67	15.25	13.29	12.03
2000	175.95	92.41	64.66	50.85	42.62	33.34	30.49	26.57	24.05
3000	263.93	138.61	96.98	76.27	63.93	50.00	45.73	39.86	36.07
4000	351.90	184.82	129.31	101.70	85.24	66.67	60.97	53.14	48.10
5000	439.88	231.02	161.63	127.12	106.55	83.33	76.21	66.43	60.12
6000	527.85	277.22	193.96	152.54	127.86	100.00	91.45	79.71	72.14
7000	615.82	323.42	226.29	177.96	149.17	116.67	106.69	93.00	84.17
8000	703.80	369.63	258.61	203.39	170.47	133.33	121.93	106.28	96.19
9000	791.77	415.83	290.94	228.81	191.78	150.00	137.17	119.56	108.21
10000	879.75	462.03	323.26	254.23	213.09	166.66	152.41	132.85	120.24
15000	1319.62	693.04	484.89	381.34	319.63	249.99	228.61	199.27	180.35
20000	1759.49	924.06	646.52	508.46	426.18	333.32	304.81	265.69	240.47
25000	2199.36	1155.07	808.15	635.57	532.72	416.65	381.01	332.11	300.58
30000	2639.23	1386.08	969.78	762.68	639.26	499.98	457.22	398.54	360.70
35000	3079.10	1617.10	1131.41	889.80	745.81	583.31	533.42	464.96	420.81
40000	3518.97	1848.11	1293.04	1016.91	852.35	666.64	609.62	531.38	480.93
45000	3958.84	2079.12	1454.67	1144.02	958.89	749.97	685.82	597.80	541.04
46000	4046.81	2125.33	1487.00	1169.45	980.20	766.63	701.06	611.09	553.07
47000	4134.78	2171.53	1519.32	1194.87	1001.51	783.30	716.30	624.37	565.09
48000	4222.76	2217.73	1551.65	1220.29	1022.82	799.97	731.54	637.66	577.11
49000	4310.73	2263.93	1583.97	1245.72	1044.13	816.63	746.78	650.94	589.14
50000	4398.71	2310.14	1616.30	1271.14	1065.44	833.30	762.02	664.22	601.16
51000	4486.68	2356.34	1648.63	1296.56	1086.74	849.96	777.26	677.51	613.18
52000	4574.65	2402.54	1680.95	1321.98	1108.05	866.63	792.51	690.79	625.21
53000	4662.63	2448.74	1713.28	1347.41	1129.36	883.29	807.75	704.08	637.23
54000	4750.60	2494.95	1745.60	1372.83	1150.67	899.96	822.99	717.36	649.25
55000	4838.58	2541.15	1777.93	1398.25	1171.98	916.63	838.23	730.65	661.28
56000	4926.55	2587.35	1810.26	1423.67	1193.29	933.29	853.47	743.93	673.30
57000	5014.52	2633.56	1842.58	1449.10	1214.60	949.96	868.71	757.22	685.32
58000	5102.50	2679.76	1874.91	1474.52	1235.90	966.62	883.95	770.50	697.35
59000	5190.47	2725.96	1907.23	1499.94	1257.21	983.29	899.19	783.78	709.37
60000	5278.45	2772.16	1939.56	1525.36	1278.52	999.96	914.43	797.07	721.39
61000	5366.42	2818.37	1971.89	1550.79	1299.83	1016.62	929.67	810.35	733.41
62000	5454.40	2864.57	2004.21	1576.21	1321.14	1033.29	944.91	823.64	745.44
63000	5542.37	2910.77	2036.54	1601.63	1342.45	1049.95	960.15	836.92	757.46
64000	5630.34	2956.97	2068.86	1627.05	1363.76	1066.62	975.39	850.21	769.48
65000	5718.32	3003.18	2101.19	1652.48	1385.06	1083.28	990.63	863.49	781.51
67500	5938.25	3118.68	2182.00	1716.03	1438.34	1124.95	1028.73	896.70	811.56
70000	6158.19	3234.19	2262.82	1779.59	1491.61	1166.61	1066.83	929.91	841.62
75000	6598.06	3465.20	2424.45	1906.70	1598.15	1249.94	1143.03	996.33	901.74
80000	7037.93	3696.22	2586.08	2033.82	1704.69	1333.27	1219.24	1062.76	961.85
85000	7477.80	3927.23	2747.71	2160.93	1811.24	1416.60	1295.44	1129.18	1021.97
90000	7917.67	4158.24	2909.34	2288.04	1917.78	1499.93	1371.64	1195.60	1082.08
95000	8357.54	4389.26	3070.97	2415.16	2024.32	1583.26	1447.84	1262.02	1142.20
100000	8797.41	4620.27	3232.60	2542.27	2130.87	1666.59	1524.04	1328.44	1202.32
105000	9237.28	4851.28	3394.23	2669.38	2237.41	1749.92	1600.25	1394.87	1262.43
110000	9677.15	5082.30	3555.85	2796.50	2343.95	1833.25	1676.45	1461.29	1322.55
115000	10117.02	5313.31	3717.48	2923.61	2450.49	1916.58	1752.65	1527.71	1382.66
120000	10556.89	5544.32	3879.11	3050.72	2557.04	1999.91	1828.85	1594.13	1442.78
125000	10996.76	5775.34	4040.74	3177.84	2663.58	2083.24	1905.05	1660.55	1502.89
130000	11436.63	6006.35	4202.37	3304.95	2770.12	2166.56	1981.26	1726.98	1563.01
135000	11876.50	6237.36	4364.00	3432.06	2876.67	2249.89	2057.46	1793.40	1623.12
140000	12316.37	6468.37	4525.63	3559.18	2983.21	2333.22	2133.66	1859.82	1683.24
145000	12756.24	6699.39	4687.26	3686.29	3089.75	2416.55	2209.86	1926.24	1743.36
150000	13196.11	6930.40	4848.89	3813.40	3196.30	2499.88	2286.06	1992.66	1803.47

MONTHLY PAYMENT 10⅛ %

NECESSARY TO AMORTIZE A LOAN

AMOUNT	15 YEARS	18 YEARS	20 YEARS	25 YEARS	28 YEARS	29 YEARS	30 YEARS	35 YEARS	40 YEARS
$ 50	.55	.51	.49	.46	.45	.45	.45	.44	.43
100	1.09	1.01	.98	.92	.90	.90	.89	.87	.86
200	2.17	2.02	1.95	1.84	1.80	1.79	1.78	1.74	1.72
300	3.25	3.03	2.92	2.76	2.70	2.68	2.67	2.61	2.58
400	4.33	4.04	3.90	3.68	3.59	3.57	3.55	3.48	3.44
500	5.42	5.04	4.87	4.59	4.49	4.46	4.44	4.35	4.30
600	6.50	6.05	5.84	5.51	5.39	5.35	5.33	5.22	5.16
700	7.58	7.06	6.82	6.43	6.28	6.25	6.21	6.09	6.02
800	8.66	8.07	7.79	7.35	7.18	7.14	7.10	6.96	6.88
900	9.75	9.08	8.76	8.26	8.08	8.03	7.99	7.83	7.74
1000	10.83	10.08	9.74	9.18	8.98	8.92	8.87	8.70	8.59
2000	21.65	20.16	19.47	18.36	17.95	17.84	17.74	17.39	17.18
3000	32.47	30.24	29.20	27.53	26.92	26.75	26.61	26.08	25.77
4000	43.30	40.32	38.94	36.71	35.89	35.67	35.48	34.78	34.36
5000	54.12	50.40	48.67	45.88	44.86	44.59	44.35	43.47	42.95
6000	64.94	60.48	58.40	55.06	53.83	53.50	53.21	52.16	51.54
7000	75.76	70.56	68.14	64.23	62.80	62.42	62.08	60.85	60.13
8000	86.59	80.64	77.87	73.41	71.77	71.34	70.95	69.55	68.72
9000	97.41	90.72	87.60	82.58	80.74	80.25	79.82	78.24	77.31
10000	108.23	100.79	97.34	91.76	89.71	89.17	88.69	86.93	85.90
15000	162.34	151.19	146.00	137.63	134.56	133.75	133.03	130.39	128.85
20000	216.46	201.58	194.67	183.51	179.42	178.34	177.37	173.86	171.80
25000	270.57	251.98	243.33	229.39	224.27	222.92	221.71	217.32	214.75
30000	324.68	302.37	292.00	275.26	269.12	267.50	266.05	260.78	257.70
35000	378.80	352.77	340.67	321.14	313.97	312.08	310.39	304.24	300.65
40000	432.91	403.16	389.33	367.02	358.83	356.67	354.73	347.71	343.59
45000	487.02	453.56	438.00	412.89	403.68	401.25	399.08	391.17	386.54
46000	497.85	463.64	447.73	422.07	412.65	410.16	407.94	399.86	395.13
47000	508.67	473.72	457.46	431.24	421.62	419.08	416.81	408.55	403.72
48000	519.49	483.80	467.20	440.42	430.59	428.00	425.68	417.25	412.31
49000	530.31	493.87	476.93	449.59	439.56	436.91	434.55	425.94	420.90
50000	541.14	503.95	486.66	458.77	448.53	445.83	443.42	434.63	429.49
51000	551.96	514.03	496.40	467.94	457.50	454.75	452.28	443.32	438.08
52000	562.78	524.11	506.13	477.12	466.47	463.66	461.15	452.02	446.67
53000	573.61	534.19	515.86	486.29	475.44	472.58	470.02	460.71	455.26
54000	584.43	544.27	525.60	495.47	484.41	481.50	478.89	469.40	463.85
55000	595.25	554.35	535.33	504.65	493.38	490.41	487.76	478.09	472.44
56000	606.07	564.43	545.06	513.82	502.36	499.33	496.63	486.79	481.03
57000	616.90	574.51	554.80	523.00	511.33	508.25	505.49	495.48	489.62
58000	627.72	584.59	564.53	532.17	520.30	517.16	514.36	504.17	498.21
59000	638.54	594.66	574.26	541.35	529.27	526.08	523.23	512.86	506.80
60000	649.36	604.74	584.00	550.52	538.24	535.00	532.10	521.56	515.39
61000	660.19	614.82	593.73	559.70	547.21	543.91	540.97	530.25	523.98
62000	671.01	624.90	603.46	568.87	556.18	552.83	549.84	538.94	532.57
63000	681.83	634.98	613.20	578.05	565.15	561.75	558.70	547.63	541.16
64000	692.65	645.06	622.93	587.22	574.12	570.66	567.57	556.33	549.75
65000	703.48	655.14	632.66	596.40	583.09	579.58	576.44	565.02	558.34
67500	730.53	680.34	656.99	619.34	605.52	601.87	598.61	586.75	579.81
70000	757.59	705.53	681.33	642.27	627.94	624.16	620.78	608.48	601.29
75000	811.70	755.93	729.99	688.15	672.80	668.74	665.12	651.94	644.23
80000	865.82	806.32	778.66	734.03	717.65	713.33	709.46	695.41	687.18
85000	919.93	856.72	827.33	779.90	762.50	757.91	753.80	738.87	730.13
90000	974.04	907.11	875.99	825.78	807.35	802.49	798.15	782.33	773.08
95000	1028.16	957.51	924.66	871.66	852.21	847.07	842.49	825.79	816.03
100000	1082.27	1007.90	973.32	917.53	897.06	891.66	886.83	869.26	858.98
105000	1136.38	1058.30	1021.99	963.41	941.91	936.24	931.17	912.72	901.93
110000	1190.50	1108.69	1070.65	1009.29	986.76	980.82	975.51	956.18	944.87
115000	1244.61	1159.09	1119.32	1055.16	1031.62	1025.40	1019.85	999.64	987.82
120000	1298.72	1209.48	1167.99	1101.04	1076.47	1069.99	1064.19	1043.11	1030.77
125000	1352.84	1259.88	1216.65	1146.91	1121.32	1114.57	1108.53	1086.57	1073.72
130000	1406.95	1310.27	1265.32	1192.79	1166.18	1159.15	1152.87	1130.03	1116.67
135000	1461.06	1360.67	1313.98	1238.67	1211.03	1203.73	1197.22	1173.49	1159.62
140000	1515.18	1411.06	1362.65	1284.54	1255.88	1248.32	1241.56	1216.96	1202.57
145000	1569.29	1461.46	1411.32	1330.42	1300.73	1292.90	1285.90	1260.42	1245.51
150000	1623.40	1511.85	1459.98	1376.30	1345.59	1337.48	1330.24	1303.88	1288.46

10¼%   MONTHLY PAYMENT
NECESSARY TO AMORTIZE A LOAN

AMOUNT	1 YEAR	2 YEARS	3 YEARS	4 YEARS	5 YEARS	7 YEARS	8 YEARS	10 YEARS	12 YEARS
$ 50	4.41	2.32	1.62	1.28	1.07	.84	.77	.67	61
100	8.81	4.63	3.24	2.55	2.14	1.68	1.54	1.34	1.21
200	17.61	9.26	6.48	5.10	4.28	3.35	3.07	2.68	2.42
300	26.41	13.88	9.72	7.65	6.42	5.02	4.60	4.01	3.63
400	35.22	18.51	12.96	10.20	8.55	6.70	6.13	5.35	4.84
500	44.02	23.14	16.20	12.75	10.69	8.37	7.66	6.68	6.05
600	52.82	27.76	19.44	15.29	12.83	10.04	9.19	8.02	7.26
700	61.63	32.39	22.67	17.84	14.96	11.72	10.72	9.35	8.47
800	70.43	37.01	25.91	20.39	17.10	13.39	12.25	10.69	9.68
900	79.23	41.64	29.15	22.94	19.24	15.06	13.78	12.02	10.89
1000	88.04	46.27	32.39	25.49	21.38	16.74	15.31	13.36	12.10
2000	176.07	92.53	64.77	50.97	42.75	33.47	30.62	26.71	24.20
3000	264.10	138.79	97.16	76.45	64.12	50.20	45.93	40.07	36.29
4000	352.13	185.05	129.54	101.94	85.49	66.93	61.23	53.42	48.39
5000	440.17	231.31	161.93	127.42	106.86	83.66	76.54	66.77	60.48
6000	528.20	277.57	194.31	152.90	128.23	100.39	91.85	80.13	72.58
7000	616.23	323.83	226.70	178.38	149.60	117.12	107.15	93.48	84.67
8000	704.26	370.09	259.08	203.87	170.97	133.85	122.46	106.84	96.77
9000	792.29	416.35	291.47	229.35	192.34	150.58	137.77	120.19	108.87
10000	880.33	462.61	323.85	254.83	213.71	167.31	153.07	133.54	120.96
15000	1320.49	693.91	485.78	382.25	320.56	250.96	229.61	200.31	181.44
20000	1760.65	925.21	647.70	509.66	427.41	334.62	306.14	267.08	241.92
25000	2200.81	1156.51	809.62	637.08	534.26	418.27	382.67	333.85	302.40
30000	2640.97	1387.82	971.55	764.49	641.11	501.92	459.21	400.62	362.87
35000	3081.13	1619.12	1133.47	891.90	747.96	585.58	535.74	467.39	423.35
40000	3521.29	1850.42	1295.39	1019.32	854.82	669.23	612.28	534.16	483.83
45000	3961.45	2081.72	1457.32	1146.73	961.67	752.88	688.81	600.93	544.31
46000	4049.49	2127.98	1489.70	1172.21	983.04	769.61	704.12	614.28	556.40
47000	4137.52	2174.24	1522.09	1197.70	1004.41	786.35	719.42	627.64	568.50
48000	4225.55	2220.50	1554.47	1223.18	1025.78	803.08	734.73	640.99	580.60
49000	4313.58	2266.76	1586.85	1248.66	1047.15	819.81	750.04	654.35	592.69
50000	4401.62	2313.02	1619.24	1274.15	1068.52	836.54	765.34	667.70	604.79
51000	4489.65	2359.29	1651.62	1299.63	1089.89	853.27	780.65	681.05	616.88
52000	4577.68	2405.55	1684.01	1325.11	1111.26	870.00	795.96	694.41	628.98
53000	4665.71	2451.81	1716.39	1350.59	1132.63	886.73	811.26	707.76	641.07
54000	4753.74	2498.07	1748.78	1376.08	1154.00	903.46	826.57	721.12	653.17
55000	4841.78	2544.33	1781.16	1401.56	1175.37	920.19	841.88	734.47	665.27
56000	4929.81	2590.59	1813.55	1427.04	1196.74	936.92	857.18	747.82	677.36
57000	5017.84	2636.85	1845.93	1452.53	1218.11	953.65	872.49	761.18	689.46
58000	5105.87	2683.11	1878.32	1478.01	1239.48	970.38	887.80	774.53	701.55
59000	5193.90	2729.37	1910.70	1503.49	1260.85	987.11	903.10	787.89	713.65
60000	5281.94	2775.63	1943.09	1528.97	1282.22	1003.84	918.41	801.24	725.74
61000	5369.97	2821.89	1975.47	1554.46	1303.59	1020.57	933.72	814.59	737.84
62000	5458.00	2868.15	2007.86	1579.94	1324.96	1037.30	949.02	827.95	749.94
63000	5546.03	2914.41	2040.24	1605.42	1346.33	1054.04	964.33	841.30	762.03
64000	5634.07	2960.67	2072.63	1630.91	1367.70	1070.77	979.64	854.65	774.13
65000	5722.10	3006.93	2105.01	1656.39	1389.07	1087.50	994.95	868.01	786.22
67500	5942.18	3122.58	2185.97	1720.09	1442.50	1129.32	1033.21	901.39	816.46
70000	6162.26	3238.23	2266.93	1783.80	1495.92	1171.15	1071.48	934.78	846.70
75000	6602.42	3469.53	2428.86	1911.22	1602.77	1254.80	1148.01	1001.55	907.18
80000	7042.58	3700.84	2590.78	2038.63	1709.63	1338.46	1224.55	1068.32	967.66
85000	7482.74	3932.14	2752.70	2166.04	1816.48	1422.11	1301.08	1135.09	1028.14
90000	7922.90	4163.45	2914.63	2293.46	1923.33	1505.76	1377.61	1201.86	1088.61
95000	8363.06	4394.74	3076.55	2420.87	2030.18	1589.42	1454.15	1268.63	1149.09
100000	8803.23	4626.04	3238.47	2548.29	2137.03	1673.07	1530.68	1335.40	1209.57
105000	9243.39	4857.35	3400.40	2675.70	2243.88	1756.72	1607.22	1402.16	1270.05
110000	9683.55	5088.65	3562.32	2803.11	2350.73	1840.38	1683.75	1468.93	1330.53
115000	10123.71	5319.95	3724.24	2930.53	2457.59	1924.03	1760.28	1535.70	1391.00
120000	10563.87	5551.25	3886.17	3057.94	2564.44	2007.68	1836.82	1602.47	1451.48
125000	11004.03	5782.55	4048.09	3185.36	2671.29	2091.34	1913.35	1669.24	1511.96
130000	11444.19	6013.86	4210.01	3312.77	2778.14	2174.99	1989.89	1736.01	1572.44
135000	11884.35	6245.16	4371.94	3440.18	2884.99	2258.64	2066.42	1802.78	1632.92
140000	12324.51	6476.46	4533.86	3567.60	2991.84	2342.30	2142.95	1869.55	1693.40
145000	12764.67	6707.76	4695.78	3695.01	3098.69	2425.95	2219.49	1936.32	1753.87
150000	13204.84	6939.06	4857.71	3822.43	3205.54	2509.60	2296.02	2003.09	1814.35

MONTHLY PAYMENT 10¼%

NECESSARY TO AMORTIZE A LOAN

AMOUNT	15 YEARS	18 YEARS	20 YEARS	25 YEARS	28 YEARS	29 YEARS	30 YEARS	35 YEARS	40 YEARS
$ 50	.55	.51	.50	.47	.46	.46	.45	.44	.44
100	1.09	1.02	.99	.93	.91	.91	.90	.88	.87
200	2.18	2.04	1.97	1.86	1.82	1.81	1.80	1.76	1.74
300	3.27	3.05	2.95	2.78	2.72	2.71	2.69	2.64	2.61
400	4.36	4.07	3.93	3.71	3.63	3.61	3.59	3.52	3.48
500	5.45	5.08	4.91	4.64	4.54	4.51	4.49	4.40	4.35
600	6.54	6.10	5.89	5.56	5.44	5.41	5.38	5.28	5.22
700	7.63	7.12	6.88	6.49	6.35	6.31	6.28	6.16	6.09
800	8.72	8.13	7.86	7.42	7.25	7.21	7.17	7.04	6.96
900	9.81	9.15	8.84	8.34	8.16	8.11	8.07	7.91	7.82
1000	10.90	10.16	9.82	9.27	9.07	9.01	8.97	8.79	8.69
2000	21.80	20.32	19.64	18.53	18.13	18.02	17.93	17.58	17.38
3000	32.70	30.48	29.45	27.80	27.19	27.03	26.89	26.37	26.07
4000	43.60	40.64	39.27	37.06	36.25	36.04	35.85	35.16	34.76
5000	54.50	50.80	49.09	46.32	45.31	45.05	44.81	43.95	43.45
6000	65.40	60.96	58.90	55.59	54.38	54.06	53.77	52.74	52.13
7000	76.30	71.12	68.72	64.85	63.44	63.06	62.73	61.52	60.82
8000	87.20	81.28	78.54	74.12	72.50	72.07	71.69	70.31	69.51
9000	98.10	91.44	88.35	83.38	81.56	81.08	80.65	79.10	78.20
10000	109.00	101.60	98.17	92.64	90.62	90.09	89.62	87.89	86.89
15000	163.50	152.40	147.25	138.96	135.93	135.13	134.42	131.83	130.33
20000	218.00	203.20	196.33	185.28	181.24	180.18	179.23	175.78	173.77
25000	272.49	254.00	245.42	231.60	226.55	225.22	224.03	219.72	217.21
30000	326.99	304.80	294.50	277.92	271.86	270.26	268.84	263.66	260.65
35000	381.49	355.60	343.58	324.24	317.17	315.30	313.64	307.60	304.09
40000	435.99	406.40	392.66	370.56	362.48	360.35	358.45	351.55	347.53
45000	490.48	457.20	441.74	416.88	407.78	405.39	403.25	395.49	390.97
46000	501.38	467.36	451.56	426.14	416.85	414.40	412.21	404.28	399.66
47000	512.28	477.52	461.38	435.41	425.91	423.41	421.17	413.07	408.35
48000	523.18	487.68	471.19	444.67	434.97	432.41	430.13	421.86	417.04
49000	534.08	497.84	481.01	453.93	444.03	441.42	439.09	430.64	425.73
50000	544.98	508.00	490.83	463.20	453.09	450.43	448.06	439.43	434.41
51000	555.88	518.15	500.64	472.46	462.15	459.44	457.02	448.22	443.10
52000	566.78	528.31	510.46	481.72	471.22	468.45	465.98	457.01	451.79
53000	577.68	538.47	520.28	490.99	480.28	477.46	474.94	465.80	460.48
54000	588.58	548.63	530.09	500.25	489.34	486.47	483.90	474.59	469.17
55000	599.48	558.79	539.91	509.52	498.40	495.47	492.86	483.38	477.86
56000	610.38	568.95	549.73	518.78	507.46	504.48	501.82	492.16	486.54
57000	621.28	579.11	559.54	528.04	516.53	513.49	510.78	500.95	495.23
58000	632.18	589.27	569.36	537.31	525.59	522.50	519.74	509.74	503.92
59000	643.08	599.43	579.17	546.57	534.65	531.51	528.70	518.53	512.61
60000	653.98	609.59	588.99	555.83	543.71	540.52	537.67	527.32	521.30
61000	664.88	619.75	598.81	565.10	552.77	549.53	546.63	536.11	529.98
62000	675.77	629.91	608.62	574.36	561.83	558.53	555.59	544.90	538.67
63000	686.67	640.07	618.44	583.63	570.90	567.54	564.55	553.68	547.36
64000	697.57	650.23	628.26	592.89	579.96	576.55	573.51	562.47	556.05
65000	708.47	660.39	638.07	602.15	589.02	585.56	582.47	571.26	564.74
67500	735.72	685.79	662.61	625.31	611.67	608.08	604.87	593.23	586.46
70000	762.97	711.19	687.16	648.47	634.33	630.60	627.28	615.20	608.18
75000	817.47	761.99	736.24	694.79	679.64	675.65	672.08	659.15	651.62
80000	871.97	812.79	785.32	741.11	724.95	720.69	716.89	703.09	695.06
85000	926.46	863.59	834.40	787.43	770.25	765.73	761.69	747.03	738.50
90000	980.96	914.39	883.48	833.75	815.56	810.77	806.50	790.98	781.94
95000	1035.46	965.19	932.57	880.07	860.87	855.82	851.30	834.92	825.38
100000	1089.96	1015.99	981.65	926.39	906.18	900.86	896.11	878.86	868.82
105000	1144.45	1066.78	1030.73	972.71	951.49	945.90	940.91	922.80	912.26
110000	1198.95	1117.58	1079.81	1019.03	996.80	990.94	985.72	966.75	955.71
115000	1253.45	1168.38	1128.89	1065.35	1042.11	1035.99	1030.52	1010.69	999.15
120000	1307.95	1219.18	1177.98	1111.66	1087.42	1081.03	1075.33	1054.63	1042.59
125000	1362.44	1269.98	1227.06	1157.98	1132.72	1126.07	1120.13	1098.57	1086.03
130000	1416.94	1320.78	1276.14	1204.30	1178.03	1171.11	1164.94	1142.52	1129.47
135000	1471.44	1371.58	1325.22	1250.62	1223.34	1216.16	1209.74	1186.46	1172.91
140000	1525.94	1422.38	1374.31	1296.94	1268.65	1261.20	1254.55	1230.40	1216.35
145000	1580.43	1473.18	1423.39	1343.26	1313.96	1306.24	1299.35	1274.35	1259.79
150000	1634.93	1523.98	1472.47	1389.58	1359.27	1351.29	1344.16	1318.29	1303.23

10⅜% MONTHLY PAYMENT
NECESSARY TO AMORTIZE A LOAN

AMOUNT	1 YEAR	2 YEARS	3 YEARS	4 YEARS	5 YEARS	7 YEARS	8 YEARS	10 YEARS	12 YEARS
$ 50	4.41	2.32	1.63	1.28	1.08	.84	.77	.68	.61
100	8.81	4.64	3.25	2.56	2.15	1.68	1.54	1.35	1.22
200	17.62	9.27	6.49	5.11	4.29	3.36	3.08	2.69	2.44
300	26.43	13.90	9.74	7.67	6.43	5.04	4.62	4.03	3.66
400	35.24	18.53	12.98	10.22	8.58	6.72	6.15	5.37	4.87
500	44.05	23.16	16.23	12.78	10.72	8.40	7.69	6.72	6.09
600	52.86	27.80	19.47	15.33	12.86	10.08	9.23	8.06	7.31
700	61.67	32.43	22.72	17.89	15.01	11.76	10.77	9.40	8.52
800	70.48	37.06	25.96	20.44	17.15	13.44	12.30	10.74	9.74
900	79.29	41.69	29.20	22.99	19.29	15.12	13.84	12.09	10.96
1000	88.10	46.32	32.45	25.55	21.44	16.80	15.38	13.43	12.17
2000	176.19	92.64	64.89	51.09	42.87	33.60	30.75	26.85	24.34
3000	264.28	138.96	97.34	76.63	64.30	50.39	46.12	40.28	36.51
4000	352.37	185.28	129.78	102.18	85.73	67.19	61.50	53.70	48.68
5000	440.46	231.60	162.22	127.72	107.17	83.98	76.87	67.12	60.85
6000	528.55	277.91	194.67	153.26	128.60	100.78	92.24	80.55	73.02
7000	616.64	324.23	227.11	178.81	150.03	117.57	107.62	93.97	85.18
8000	704.73	370.55	259.55	204.35	171.46	134.37	122.99	107.39	97.35
9000	792.82	416.87	292.00	229.89	192.89	151.17	138.36	120.82	109.52
10000	880.91	463.19	324.44	255.44	214.33	167.96	153.74	134.24	121.69
15000	1321.36	694.78	486.66	383.15	321.49	251.94	230.60	201.36	182.53
20000	1761.81	926.37	648.88	510.87	428.65	335.92	307.47	268.48	243.37
25000	2202.26	1157.96	811.09	638.58	535.81	419.89	384.34	335.60	304.22
30000	2642.72	1389.55	973.31	766.30	642.97	503.87	461.20	402.71	365.06
35000	3083.17	1621.14	1135.53	894.01	750.13	587.85	538.07	469.83	425.90
40000	3523.62	1852.73	1297.75	1021.73	857.29	671.83	614.94	536.95	486.74
45000	3964.07	2084.32	1459.96	1149.44	964.45	755.81	691.80	604.07	547.58
46000	4052.16	2130.64	1492.41	1174.99	985.88	772.60	707.18	617.49	559.75
47000	4140.25	2176.96	1524.85	1200.53	1007.31	789.40	722.55	630.91	571.92
48000	4228.34	2223.28	1557.29	1226.07	1028.74	806.19	737.92	644.34	584.09
49000	4316.43	2269.60	1589.74	1251.61	1050.17	822.99	753.30	657.76	596.26
50000	4404.52	2315.91	1622.18	1277.16	1071.61	839.78	768.67	671.19	608.43
51000	4492.61	2362.23	1654.63	1302.70	1093.04	856.56	784.04	684.61	620.59
52000	4580.71	2408.55	1687.07	1328.24	1114.47	873.38	799.42	698.03	632.76
53000	4668.80	2454.87	1719.51	1353.79	1135.90	890.17	814.79	711.46	644.93
54000	4756.89	2501.19	1751.96	1379.33	1157.33	906.97	830.16	724.88	657.10
55000	4844.98	2547.51	1784.40	1404.87	1178.77	923.76	845.54	738.30	669.27
56000	4933.07	2593.82	1816.84	1430.42	1200.20	940.56	860.91	751.73	681.44
57000	5021.16	2640.14	1849.29	1455.96	1221.63	957.35	876.28	765.15	693.60
58000	5109.25	2686.46	1881.73	1481.50	1243.06	974.15	891.66	778.57	705.77
59000	5197.34	2732.78	1914.17	1507.05	1264.49	990.94	907.03	792.00	717.94
60000	5285.43	2779.10	1946.62	1532.59	1285.93	1007.74	922.40	805.42	730.11
61000	5373.52	2825.42	1979.06	1558.13	1307.36	1024.54	937.78	818.84	742.28
62000	5461.61	2871.73	2011.50	1583.67	1328.79	1041.33	953.15	832.27	754.45
63000	5549.70	2918.05	2043.95	1609.22	1350.22	1058.13	968.52	845.69	766.62
64000	5637.79	2964.37	2076.39	1634.76	1371.65	1074.92	983.90	859.12	778.78
65000	5725.88	3010.69	2108.83	1660.30	1393.09	1091.72	999.27	872.54	790.95
67500	5946.11	3126.48	2189.94	1724.16	1446.67	1133.71	1037.70	906.10	821.37
70000	6166.33	3242.28	2271.05	1788.02	1500.25	1175.70	1076.14	939.66	851.79
75000	6606.78	3473.87	2433.27	1915.73	1607.41	1259.67	1153.00	1006.78	912.64
80000	7047.24	3705.46	2595.49	2043.45	1714.57	1343.65	1229.87	1073.89	973.48
85000	7487.69	3937.05	2757.71	2171.16	1821.73	1427.63	1306.74	1141.01	1034.32
90000	7928.14	4168.64	2919.92	2298.88	1928.89	1511.61	1383.60	1208.13	1095.16
95000	8368.59	4400.23	3082.14	2426.60	2036.05	1595.59	1460.47	1275.25	1156.00
100000	8809.04	4631.82	3244.36	2554.31	2143.21	1679.56	1537.34	1342.37	1216.85
105000	9249.50	4863.42	3406.58	2682.03	2250.37	1763.54	1614.20	1409.48	1277.69
110000	9689.95	5095.01	3568.79	2809.74	2357.53	1847.52	1691.07	1476.60	1338.53
115000	10130.40	5326.60	3731.01	2937.46	2464.69	1931.50	1767.94	1543.72	1399.37
120000	10570.85	5558.19	3893.23	3065.17	2571.85	2015.48	1844.80	1610.84	1460.22
125000	11011.30	5789.78	4055.45	3192.89	2679.01	2099.45	1921.67	1677.96	1521.06
130000	11451.76	6021.37	4217.66	3320.60	2786.17	2183.43	1998.54	1745.07	1581.90
135000	11892.21	6252.96	4379.88	3448.32	2893.33	2267.41	2075.40	1812.19	1642.74
140000	12332.66	6484.55	4542.10	3576.03	3000.49	2351.39	2152.27	1879.31	1703.58
145000	12773.11	6716.14	4704.32	3703.75	3107.65	2435.37	2229.14	1946.43	1764.43
150000	13213.56	6947.73	4866.54	3831.46	3214.81	2519.34	2306.00	2013.55	1825.27

MONTHLY PAYMENT 10⅜%

NECESSARY TO AMORTIZE A LOAN

AMOUNT	15 YEARS	18 YEARS	20 YEARS	25 YEARS	28 YEARS	29 YEARS	30 YEARS	35 YEARS	40 YEARS
$ 50	.55	.52	.50	.47	.46	.46	.46	.45	.44
100	1.10	1.03	.99	.94	.92	.92	.91	.89	.88
200	2.20	2.05	1.98	1.88	1.84	1.83	1.82	1.78	1.76
300	3.30	3.08	2.97	2.81	2.75	2.74	2.72	2.67	2.64
400	4.40	4.10	3.96	3.75	3.67	3.65	3.63	3.56	3.52
500	5.49	5.13	4.95	4.68	4.58	4.56	4.53	4.45	4.40
600	6.59	6.15	5.94	5.62	5.50	5.47	5.44	5.34	5.28
700	7.69	7.17	6.93	6.55	6.41	6.38	6.34	6.22	6.16
800	8.79	8.20	7.92	7.49	7.33	7.29	7.25	7.11	7.03
900	9.88	9.22	8.91	8.42	8.24	8.20	8.15	8.00	7.91
1000	10.98	10.25	9.90	9.36	9.16	9.11	9.06	8.89	8.79
2000	21.96	20.49	19.80	18.71	18.31	18.21	18.11	17.77	17.58
3000	32.93	30.73	29.70	28.06	27.46	27.31	27.17	26.66	26.37
4000	43.91	40.97	39.60	37.42	36.62	36.41	36.22	35.54	35.15
5000	54.89	51.21	49.50	46.77	45.77	45.51	45.28	44.43	43.94
6000	65.86	61.45	59.40	56.12	54.92	54.61	54.33	53.31	52.73
7000	76.84	71.69	69.30	65.47	64.08	63.71	63.38	62.20	61.51
8000	87.82	81.93	79.20	74.83	73.23	72.81	72.44	71.08	70.30
9000	98.79	92.17	89.10	84.18	82.38	81.91	81.49	79.97	79.09
10000	109.77	102.41	99.00	93.53	91.54	91.01	90.55	88.85	87.87
15000	164.65	153.62	148.50	140.30	137.30	136.52	135.82	133.28	131.81
20000	219.54	204.82	198.00	187.06	183.07	182.02	181.09	177.70	175.74
25000	274.42	256.03	247.50	233.82	228.84	227.53	226.36	222.13	219.68
30000	329.30	307.23	297.00	280.59	274.60	273.03	271.63	266.55	263.61
35000	384.19	358.44	346.50	327.35	320.37	318.53	316.90	310.97	307.54
40000	439.07	409.64	396.00	374.11	366.14	364.04	362.17	355.40	351.48
45000	493.95	460.85	445.50	420.88	411.90	409.54	407.44	399.82	395.41
46000	504.93	471.09	455.40	430.23	421.05	418.64	416.49	408.71	404.20
47000	515.91	481.33	465.30	439.58	430.21	427.74	425.55	417.59	412.99
48000	526.88	491.57	475.20	448.93	439.36	436.85	434.60	426.48	421.77
49000	537.86	501.81	485.10	458.29	448.51	445.95	443.65	435.36	430.56
50000	548.84	512.05	495.00	467.64	457.67	455.05	452.71	444.25	439.35
51000	559.81	522.29	504.90	476.99	466.82	464.15	461.76	453.13	448.13
52000	570.79	532.53	514.80	486.34	475.97	473.25	470.82	462.02	456.92
53000	581.77	542.77	524.70	495.70	485.13	482.35	479.87	470.90	465.71
54000	592.74	553.01	534.60	505.05	494.28	491.45	488.92	479.79	474.49
55000	603.72	563.25	544.50	514.40	503.43	500.55	497.98	488.67	483.28
56000	614.70	573.50	554.40	523.76	512.59	509.65	507.03	497.56	492.07
57000	625.67	583.74	564.30	533.11	521.74	518.75	516.09	506.44	500.86
58000	636.65	593.98	574.20	542.46	530.89	527.85	525.14	515.33	509.64
59000	647.63	604.22	584.10	551.81	540.05	536.95	534.20	524.21	518.43
60000	658.60	614.46	594.00	561.17	549.20	546.06	543.25	533.09	527.22
61000	669.58	624.70	603.90	570.52	558.35	555.16	552.30	541.98	536.00
62000	680.56	634.94	613.80	579.87	567.51	564.26	561.36	550.86	544.79
63000	691.53	645.18	623.70	589.22	576.66	573.36	570.41	559.75	553.58
64000	702.51	655.42	633.60	598.58	585.81	582.46	579.47	568.63	562.36
65000	713.49	665.66	643.50	607.93	594.97	591.56	588.52	577.52	571.15
67500	740.93	691.27	668.25	631.31	617.85	614.31	611.15	599.73	593.12
70000	768.37	716.87	693.00	654.69	640.73	637.06	633.79	621.94	615.08
75000	823.25	768.07	742.50	701.46	686.50	682.57	679.06	666.37	659.02
80000	878.13	819.28	792.00	748.22	732.27	728.07	724.33	710.79	702.95
85000	933.02	870.48	841.50	794.98	778.03	773.58	769.60	755.22	746.89
90000	987.90	921.69	891.00	841.75	823.80	819.08	814.87	799.64	790.82
95000	1042.78	972.89	940.50	888.51	869.56	864.58	860.14	844.06	834.76
100000	1097.67	1024.10	990.00	935.27	915.33	910.09	905.41	888.49	878.69
105000	1152.55	1075.30	1039.50	982.04	961.10	955.59	950.68	932.91	922.62
110000	1207.43	1126.50	1089.00	1028.80	1006.86	1001.10	995.95	977.34	966.56
115000	1262.32	1177.71	1138.50	1075.56	1052.63	1046.60	1041.22	1021.76	1010.49
120000	1317.20	1228.91	1188.00	1122.33	1098.40	1092.11	1086.49	1066.18	1054.43
125000	1372.08	1280.12	1237.50	1169.09	1144.16	1137.61	1131.76	1110.61	1098.36
130000	1426.97	1331.32	1287.00	1215.85	1189.93	1183.11	1177.03	1155.03	1142.29
135000	1481.85	1382.53	1336.50	1262.62	1235.70	1228.62	1222.30	1199.46	1186.23
140000	1536.73	1433.73	1386.00	1309.38	1281.46	1274.12	1267.57	1243.88	1230.16
145000	1591.62	1484.94	1435.50	1356.14	1327.23	1319.63	1312.85	1288.31	1274.10
150000	1646.50	1536.14	1485.00	1402.91	1372.99	1365.13	1358.12	1332.73	1318.03

10½% MONTHLY PAYMENT
NECESSARY TO AMORTIZE A LOAN

AMOUNT	1 YEAR	2 YEARS	3 YEARS	4 YEARS	5 YEARS	7 YEARS	8 YEARS	10 YEARS	12 YEARS
$ 50	4.41	2.32	1.63	1.29	1.08	.85	.78	.68	.62
100	8.82	4.64	3.26	2.57	2.15	1.69	1.55	1.35	1.23
200	17.63	9.28	6.51	5.13	4.30	3.38	3.09	2.70	2.45
300	26.45	13.92	9.76	7.69	6.45	5.06	4.64	4.05	3.68
400	35.26	18.56	13.01	10.25	8.60	6.75	6.18	5.40	4.90
500	44.08	23.19	16.26	12.81	10.75	8.44	7.73	6.75	6.13
600	52.89	27.83	19.51	15.37	12.90	10.12	9.27	8.10	7.35
700	61.71	32.47	22.76	17.93	15.05	11.81	10.81	9.45	8.57
800	70.52	37.11	26.01	20.49	17.20	13.49	12.36	10.80	9.80
900	79.34	41.74	29.26	23.05	19.35	15.18	13.90	12.15	11.02
1000	88.15	46.38	32.51	25.61	21.50	16.87	15.45	13.50	12.25
2000	176.30	92.76	65.01	51.21	42.99	33.73	30.89	26.99	24.49
3000	264.45	139.13	97.51	76.82	64.49	50.59	46.33	40.49	36.73
4000	352.60	185.51	130.01	102.42	85.98	67.45	61.77	53.98	48.97
5000	440.75	231.89	162.52	128.02	107.47	84.31	77.21	67.47	61.21
6000	528.90	278.26	195.02	153.63	128.97	101.17	92.65	80.97	73.45
7000	617.05	324.64	227.52	179.23	150.46	118.03	108.09	94.46	85.69
8000	705.19	371.01	260.02	204.83	171.96	134.89	123.53	107.95	97.94
9000	793.34	417.39	292.53	230.44	193.45	151.75	138.97	121.45	110.18
10000	881.49	463.77	325.03	256.04	214.94	168.61	154.41	134.94	122.42
15000	1322.23	695.65	487.54	384.06	322.41	252.92	231.61	202.41	183.63
20000	1762.98	927.53	650.05	512.07	429.88	337.22	308.81	269.87	244.83
25000	2203.72	1159.41	812.57	640.09	537.35	421.52	386.01	337.34	306.04
30000	2644.46	1391.29	975.08	768.11	644.82	505.83	463.21	404.81	367.25
35000	3085.21	1623.17	1137.59	896.12	752.29	590.13	540.41	472.28	428.45
40000	3525.95	1855.05	1300.10	1024.14	859.76	674.43	617.61	539.74	489.66
45000	3966.69	2086.93	1462.61	1152.16	967.23	758.74	694.81	607.21	550.87
46000	4054.84	2133.30	1495.12	1177.76	988.72	775.60	710.25	620.71	563.11
47000	4142.99	2179.68	1527.62	1203.36	1010.22	792.46	725.69	634.20	575.35
48000	4231.14	2226.05	1560.12	1228.97	1031.71	809.32	741.13	647.69	587.59
49000	4319.29	2272.43	1592.62	1254.57	1053.21	826.18	756.57	661.19	599.83
50000	4407.44	2318.81	1625.13	1280.17	1074.70	843.04	772.01	674.68	612.08
51000	4495.58	2365.18	1657.63	1305.78	1096.19	859.90	787.45	688.17	624.32
52000	4583.73	2411.56	1690.13	1331.38	1117.69	876.76	802.89	701.67	636.56
53000	4671.88	2457.94	1722.63	1356.98	1139.18	893.62	818.33	715.16	648.80
54000	4760.03	2504.31	1755.14	1382.59	1160.68	910.48	833.77	728.65	661.04
55000	4848.18	2550.69	1787.64	1408.19	1182.17	927.34	849.21	742.15	673.28
56000	4936.33	2597.06	1820.14	1433.79	1203.66	944.20	864.65	755.64	685.52
57000	5024.48	2643.44	1852.64	1459.40	1225.16	961.06	880.09	769.13	697.77
58000	5112.62	2689.82	1885.15	1485.00	1246.65	977.92	895.53	782.63	710.01
59000	5200.77	2736.19	1917.65	1510.60	1268.15	994.78	910.97	796.12	722.25
60000	5288.92	2782.57	1950.15	1536.21	1289.64	1011.65	926.41	809.61	734.49
61000	5377.07	2828.94	1982.65	1561.81	1311.13	1028.51	941.85	823.11	746.73
62000	5465.22	2875.32	2015.16	1587.41	1332.63	1045.37	957.29	836.60	758.97
63000	5553.37	2921.70	2047.66	1613.02	1354.12	1062.23	972.73	850.10	771.21
64000	5641.52	2968.07	2080.16	1638.62	1375.61	1079.09	988.17	863.59	783.46
65000	5729.66	3014.45	2112.66	1664.22	1397.11	1095.95	1003.61	877.08	795.70
67500	5950.04	3130.39	2193.92	1728.23	1450.84	1138.10	1042.21	910.82	826.30
70000	6170.41	3246.33	2275.18	1792.24	1504.58	1180.25	1080.81	944.55	856.90
75000	6611.15	3478.21	2437.69	1920.26	1612.05	1264.56	1158.01	1012.01	918.11
80000	7051.89	3710.09	2600.20	2048.28	1719.52	1348.86	1235.21	1079.48	979.32
85000	7492.64	3941.97	2762.71	2176.29	1826.99	1433.16	1312.41	1146.95	1040.52
90000	7933.38	4173.85	2925.22	2304.31	1934.46	1517.47	1389.61	1214.42	1101.73
95000	8374.12	4405.73	3087.74	2432.33	2041.93	1601.77	1466.81	1281.89	1162.94
100000	8814.83	4637.61	3250.25	2560.34	2149.40	1686.07	1544.01	1349.35	1224.15
105000	9255.61	4869.49	3412.76	2688.36	2256.86	1770.38	1621.21	1416.82	1285.35
110000	9696.35	5101.37	3575.27	2816.38	2364.33	1854.68	1698.41	1484.29	1346.56
115000	10137.09	5333.25	3737.79	2944.39	2471.80	1938.98	1775.61	1551.76	1407.77
120000	10577.84	5565.13	3900.30	3072.41	2579.27	2023.29	1852.81	1619.22	1468.97
125000	11018.58	5797.01	4062.81	3200.43	2686.74	2107.59	1930.01	1686.69	1530.18
130000	11459.32	6028.89	4225.32	3328.44	2794.21	2191.89	2007.21	1754.16	1591.39
135000	11900.07	6260.77	4387.83	3456.46	2901.68	2276.20	2084.41	1821.63	1652.59
140000	12340.81	6492.65	4550.35	3584.48	3009.15	2360.50	2161.61	1889.09	1713.80
145000	12781.55	6724.53	4712.86	3712.50	3116.62	2444.80	2238.81	1956.56	1775.01
150000	13222.30	6956.41	4875.37	3840.51	3224.09	2529.11	2316.01	2024.03	1836.22

AMOUNT	15 YEARS	18 YEARS	20 YEARS	25 YEARS	28 YEARS	29 YEARS	30 YEARS	35 YEARS	40 YEARS
$ 50	.56	.52	.50	.48	.47	.46	.46	.45	.45
100	1.11	1.04	1.00	.95	.93	.92	.92	.90	.89
200	2.22	2.07	2.00	1.89	1.85	1.84	1.83	1.80	1.78
300	3.32	3.10	3.00	2.84	2.78	2.76	2.75	2.70	2.67
400	4.43	4.13	4.00	3.78	3.70	3.68	3.66	3.60	3.56
500	5.53	5.17	5.00	4.73	4.63	4.60	4.58	4.50	4.45
600	6.64	6.20	6.00	5.67	5.55	5.52	5.49	5.39	5.34
700	7.74	7.23	6.99	6.61	6.48	6.44	6.41	6.29	6.22
800	8.85	8.26	7.99	7.56	7.40	7.36	7.32	7.19	7.11
900	9.95	9.30	8.99	8.50	8.33	8.28	8.24	8.09	8.00
1000	11.06	10.33	9.99	9.45	9.25	9.20	9.15	8.99	8.89
2000	22.11	20.65	19.97	18.89	18.50	18.39	18.30	17.97	17.78
3000	33.17	30.97	29.96	28.33	27.74	27.59	27.45	26.95	26.66
4000	44.22	41.29	39.94	37.77	36.99	36.78	36.59	35.93	35.55
5000	55.27	51.62	49.92	47.21	46.23	45.97	45.74	44.91	44.43
6000	66.33	61.94	59.91	56.66	55.48	55.17	54.89	53.89	53.32
7000	77.38	72.26	69.89	66.10	64.72	64.36	64.04	62.87	62.20
8000	88.44	82.58	79.88	75.54	73.97	73.55	73.18	71.86	71.09
9000	99.49	92.91	89.86	84.98	83.21	82.75	82.33	80.84	79.98
10000	110.54	103.23	99.84	94.42	92.46	91.94	91.48	89.82	88.86
15000	165.81	154.84	149.76	141.63	138.68	137.91	137.22	134.73	133.29
20000	221.08	206.45	199.68	188.84	184.91	183.87	182.95	179.63	177.72
25000	276.35	258.06	249.60	236.05	231.13	229.84	228.69	224.54	222.15
30000	331.62	309.67	299.52	283.26	277.36	275.81	274.43	269.45	266.58
35000	386.89	361.28	349.44	330.47	323.58	321.77	320.16	314.35	311.00
40000	442.16	412.90	399.36	377.68	369.81	367.74	365.90	359.26	355.43
45000	497.43	464.51	449.28	424.89	416.03	413.71	411.64	404.17	399.86
46000	508.49	474.83	459.26	434.33	425.28	422.90	420.79	413.15	408.75
47000	519.54	485.15	469.24	443.77	434.52	432.10	429.93	422.13	417.63
48000	530.60	495.47	479.23	453.21	443.77	441.29	439.08	431.11	426.52
49000	541.65	505.80	489.21	462.65	453.01	450.48	448.23	440.09	435.40
50000	552.70	516.12	499.19	472.10	462.26	459.68	457.37	449.07	444.29
51000	563.76	526.44	509.18	481.54	471.50	468.87	466.52	458.05	453.18
52000	574.81	536.76	519.16	490.98	480.75	478.06	475.67	467.03	462.06
53000	585.87	547.09	529.15	500.42	489.99	487.26	484.82	476.02	470.95
54000	596.92	557.41	539.13	509.86	499.24	496.45	493.96	485.00	479.83
55000	607.97	567.73	549.11	519.30	508.48	505.64	503.11	493.98	488.72
56000	619.03	578.05	559.10	528.75	517.73	514.84	512.26	502.96	497.60
57000	630.08	588.37	569.08	538.19	526.97	524.03	521.41	511.94	506.49
58000	641.14	598.70	579.07	547.63	536.22	533.22	530.55	520.92	515.38
59000	652.19	609.02	589.05	557.07	545.46	542.42	539.70	529.90	524.26
60000	663.24	619.34	599.03	566.51	554.71	551.61	548.85	538.89	533.15
61000	674.30	629.66	609.02	575.96	563.95	560.80	558.00	547.87	542.03
62000	685.35	639.99	619.00	585.40	573.20	570.00	567.14	556.85	550.92
63000	696.41	650.31	628.98	594.84	582.44	579.19	576.29	565.83	559.80
64000	707.46	660.63	638.97	604.28	591.69	588.38	585.44	574.81	568.69
65000	718.51	670.95	648.95	613.72	600.93	597.58	594.59	583.79	577.58
67500	746.15	696.76	673.91	637.33	624.04	620.56	617.45	606.25	599.79
70000	773.78	722.56	698.87	660.93	647.16	643.54	640.32	628.70	622.00
75000	829.05	774.18	748.79	708.14	693.38	689.51	686.06	673.61	666.43
80000	884.32	825.79	798.71	755.35	739.61	735.48	731.80	718.51	710.86
85000	939.59	877.40	848.63	802.56	785.83	781.44	777.53	763.42	755.29
90000	994.86	929.01	898.55	849.77	832.06	827.41	823.27	808.33	799.72
95000	1050.13	980.62	948.47	896.98	878.28	873.38	869.01	853.23	844.15
100000	1105.40	1032.23	998.38	944.19	924.51	919.35	914.74	898.14	888.58
105000	1160.67	1083.84	1048.30	991.40	970.73	965.31	960.48	943.05	933.00
110000	1215.94	1135.46	1098.22	1038.60	1016.96	1011.28	1006.22	987.95	977.43
115000	1271.21	1187.07	1148.14	1085.81	1063.18	1057.25	1051.96	1032.86	1021.86
120000	1326.48	1238.68	1198.06	1133.02	1109.41	1103.21	1097.69	1077.77	1066.29
125000	1381.75	1290.29	1247.98	1180.23	1155.63	1149.18	1143.43	1122.67	1110.72
130000	1437.02	1341.90	1297.90	1227.44	1201.86	1195.15	1189.17	1167.58	1155.15
135000	1492.29	1393.51	1347.82	1274.65	1248.08	1241.11	1234.90	1212.49	1199.57
140000	1547.56	1445.12	1397.74	1321.86	1294.31	1287.08	1280.64	1257.39	1244.00
145000	1602.83	1496.74	1447.66	1369.07	1340.54	1333.05	1326.38	1302.30	1288.43
150000	1658.10	1548.35	1497.57	1416.28	1386.76	1379.02	1372.11	1347.21	1332.86

10⅝% MONTHLY PAYMENT
NECESSARY TO AMORTIZE A LOAN

AMOUNT	1 YEAR	2 YEARS	3 YEARS	4 YEARS	5 YEARS	7 YEARS	8 YEARS	10 YEARS	12 YEARS
$ 50	4.42	2.33	1.63	1.29	1.08	.85	.78	.68	.62
100	8.83	4.65	3.26	2.57	2.16	1.70	1.56	1.36	1.24
200	17.65	9.29	6.52	5.14	4.32	3.39	3.11	2.72	2.47
300	26.47	13.94	9.77	7.70	6.47	5.08	4.66	4.07	3.70
400	35.29	18.58	13.03	10.27	8.63	6.78	6.21	5.43	4.93
500	44.11	23.22	16.29	12.84	10.78	8.47	7.76	6.79	6.16
600	52.93	27.87	19.54	15.40	12.94	10.16	9.31	8.14	7.39
700	61.75	32.51	22.80	17.97	15.09	11.85	10.86	9.50	8.63
800	70.57	37.15	26.05	20.54	17.25	13.55	12.41	10.86	9.86
900	79.39	41.80	29.31	23.10	19.41	15.24	13.96	12.21	11.09
1000	88.21	46.44	32.57	25.67	21.56	16.93	15.51	13.57	12.32
2000	176.42	92.87	65.13	51.33	43.12	33.86	31.02	27.13	24.63
3000	264.63	139.31	97.69	77.00	64.67	50.78	46.53	40.70	36.95
4000	352.83	185.74	130.25	102.66	86.23	67.71	62.03	54.26	49.26
5000	441.04	232.17	162.81	128.32	107.78	84.63	77.54	67.82	61.58
6000	529.25	278.61	195.37	153.99	129.34	101.56	93.05	81.39	73.89
7000	617.45	325.04	227.93	179.65	150.90	118.49	108.55	94.95	86.21
8000	705.66	371.48	260.50	205.32	172.45	135.41	124.06	108.51	98.52
9000	793.87	417.91	293.06	230.98	194.01	152.34	139.57	122.08	110.84
10000	882.07	464.34	325.62	256.64	215.56	169.26	155.07	135.64	123.15
15000	1323.11	696.51	488.43	384.96	323.34	253.89	232.61	203.46	184.72
20000	1764.14	928.68	651.23	513.28	431.12	338.52	310.14	271.28	246.30
25000	2205.18	1160.85	814.04	641.60	538.90	423.15	387.68	339.09	307.87
30000	2646.21	1393.02	976.85	769.92	646.68	507.78	465.21	406.91	369.44
35000	3087.24	1625.19	1139.65	898.24	754.46	592.41	542.75	474.73	431.02
40000	3528.28	1857.36	1302.46	1026.56	862.24	677.04	620.28	542.55	492.59
45000	3969.31	2089.53	1465.27	1154.88	970.02	761.67	697.81	610.37	554.16
46000	4057.52	2135.97	1497.83	1180.54	991.58	778.60	713.32	623.93	566.48
47000	4145.73	2182.40	1530.39	1206.20	1013.13	795.52	728.83	637.49	578.79
48000	4233.93	2228.83	1562.95	1231.87	1034.69	812.45	744.34	651.06	591.11
49000	4322.14	2275.27	1595.51	1257.53	1056.24	829.37	759.84	664.62	603.42
50000	4410.15	2321.70	1628.08	1283.19	1077.80	846.30	775.35	678.18	615.74
51000	4498.55	2368.14	1660.64	1308.86	1099.35	863.23	790.86	691.75	628.05
52000	4586.76	2414.57	1693.20	1334.52	1120.91	880.15	806.36	705.31	640.36
53000	4674.97	2461.00	1725.76	1360.19	1142.47	897.08	821.87	718.88	652.68
54000	4763.17	2507.44	1758.32	1385.85	1164.02	914.00	837.38	732.44	664.99
55000	4851.38	2553.87	1790.88	1411.51	1185.58	930.93	852.88	746.00	677.31
56000	4939.59	2600.30	1823.44	1437.18	1207.13	947.86	868.39	759.57	689.62
57000	5027.79	2646.74	1856.01	1462.84	1228.69	964.78	883.90	773.13	701.94
58000	5116.00	2693.17	1888.57	1488.50	1250.25	981.71	899.40	786.69	714.25
59000	5204.21	2739.61	1921.13	1514.17	1271.80	998.63	914.91	800.26	726.57
60000	5292.42	2786.04	1953.69	1539.83	1293.36	1015.56	930.42	813.82	738.88
61000	5380.62	2832.47	1986.25	1565.50	1314.91	1032.48	945.92	827.38	751.20
62000	5468.83	2878.91	2018.81	1591.16	1336.47	1049.41	961.43	840.95	763.51
63000	5557.04	2925.34	2051.37	1616.82	1358.03	1066.34	976.94	854.51	775.83
64000	5645.24	2971.78	2083.94	1642.49	1379.58	1083.26	992.45	868.07	788.14
65000	5733.45	3018.21	2116.50	1668.15	1401.14	1100.19	1007.95	881.64	800.45
67500	5953.97	3134.30	2197.90	1732.31	1455.03	1142.50	1046.72	915.55	831.24
70000	6174.48	3250.38	2279.30	1796.47	1508.92	1184.82	1085.49	949.46	862.03
75000	6615.52	3482.55	2442.11	1924.79	1616.70	1269.45	1163.02	1017.27	923.60
80000	7056.55	3714.72	2604.92	2053.11	1724.47	1354.08	1240.56	1085.09	985.17
85000	7497.59	3946.89	2767.73	2181.43	1832.25	1438.71	1318.09	1152.91	1046.75
90000	7938.62	4179.06	2930.53	2309.75	1940.03	1523.34	1395.62	1220.73	1108.32
95000	8379.65	4411.23	3093.34	2438.06	2047.81	1607.97	1473.16	1288.55	1169.89
100000	8820.69	4643.40	3256.15	2566.38	2155.59	1692.60	1550.69	1356.36	1231.47
105000	9261.72	4875.57	3418.95	2694.70	2263.37	1777.22	1628.23	1424.18	1293.04
110000	9702.76	5107.74	3581.76	2823.02	2371.15	1861.85	1705.76	1492.00	1354.61
115000	10143.79	5339.91	3744.57	2951.34	2478.93	1946.48	1783.30	1559.82	1416.19
120000	10584.83	5572.08	3907.37	3079.66	2586.71	2031.11	1860.83	1627.64	1477.76
125000	11025.86	5804.25	4070.18	3207.98	2694.49	2115.74	1938.36	1695.45	1539.33
130000	11466.89	6036.42	4232.99	3336.30	2802.27	2200.37	2015.90	1763.27	1600.90
135000	11907.93	6268.59	4395.80	3464.62	2910.05	2285.00	2093.43	1831.09	1662.48
140000	12348.96	6500.75	4558.60	3592.94	3017.83	2369.63	2170.97	1898.91	1724.05
145000	12790.00	6732.92	4721.41	3721.25	3125.61	2454.26	2248.50	1966.73	1785.62
150000	13231.03	6965.09	4884.22	3849.57	3233.39	2538.89	2326.04	2034.54	1847.20

MONTHLY PAYMENT 10⅝%

NECESSARY TO AMORTIZE A LOAN

AMOUNT	15 YEARS	18 YEARS	20 YEARS	25 YEARS	28 YEARS	29 YEARS	30 YEARS	35 YEARS	40 YEARS
$ 50	.56	.53	.51	.48	.47	.47	.47	.46	.45
100	1.12	1.05	1.01	.96	.94	.93	.93	.91	.90
200	2.23	2.09	2.02	1.91	1.87	1.86	1.85	1.82	1.80
300	3.34	3.13	3.03	2.86	2.81	2.79	2.78	2.73	2.70
400	4.46	4.17	4.03	3.82	3.74	3.72	3.70	3.64	3.60
500	5.57	5.21	5.04	4.77	4.67	4.65	4.63	4.54	4.50
600	6.68	6.25	6.05	5.72	5.61	5.58	5.55	5.45	5.40
700	7.80	7.29	7.05	6.68	6.54	6.51	6.47	6.36	6.29
800	8.91	8.33	8.06	7.63	7.47	7.43	7.40	7.27	7.19
900	10.02	9.37	9.07	8.58	8.41	8.36	8.32	8.18	8.09
1000	11.14	10.41	10.07	9.54	9.34	9.29	9.25	9.08	8.99
2000	22.27	20.81	20.14	19.07	18.68	18.58	18.49	18.16	17.97
3000	33.40	31.22	30.21	28.60	28.02	27.86	27.73	27.24	26.96
4000	44.53	41.62	40.28	38.13	37.35	37.15	36.97	36.32	35.94
5000	55.66	52.02	50.34	47.66	46.69	46.44	46.21	45.40	44.93
6000	66.79	62.43	60.41	57.19	56.03	55.72	55.45	54.47	53.91
7000	77.93	72.83	70.48	66.72	65.36	65.01	64.69	63.55	62.90
8000	89.06	83.24	80.55	76.25	74.70	74.29	73.93	72.63	71.88
9000	100.19	93.64	90.62	85.79	84.04	83.58	83.17	81.71	80.87
10000	111.32	104.04	100.68	95.32	93.38	92.87	92.41	90.79	89.85
15000	166.98	156.06	151.02	142.97	140.06	139.30	138.62	136.18	134.78
20000	222.64	208.08	201.36	190.63	186.75	185.73	184.82	181.57	179.70
25000	278.30	260.10	251.70	238.29	233.43	232.16	231.03	226.96	224.62
30000	333.95	312.12	302.04	285.94	280.12	278.59	277.23	272.35	269.55
35000	389.61	364.14	352.38	333.60	326.80	325.02	323.44	317.74	314.47
40000	445.27	416.16	402.72	381.25	373.49	371.45	369.64	363.13	359.39
45000	500.93	468.18	453.06	428.91	420.17	417.89	415.85	408.52	404.32
46000	512.06	478.59	463.13	438.44	429.51	427.17	425.09	417.60	413.30
47000	523.19	488.99	473.20	447.97	438.85	436.46	434.33	426.67	422.29
48000	534.32	499.39	483.26	457.50	448.18	445.74	443.57	435.75	431.27
49000	545.45	509.80	493.33	467.04	457.52	455.03	452.81	444.83	440.26
50000	556.59	520.20	503.40	476.57	466.86	464.32	462.05	453.91	449.24
51000	567.72	530.61	513.47	486.10	476.20	473.60	471.29	462.99	458.23
52000	578.85	541.01	523.54	495.63	485.53	482.89	480.54	472.06	467.21
53000	589.98	551.41	533.60	505.16	494.87	492.18	489.78	481.14	476.20
54000	601.11	561.82	543.67	514.69	504.21	501.46	499.02	490.22	485.18
55000	612.24	572.22	553.74	524.22	513.54	510.75	508.26	499.30	494.17
56000	623.38	582.62	563.81	533.75	522.88	520.03	517.50	508.38	503.15
57000	634.51	593.03	573.88	543.29	532.22	529.32	526.74	517.46	512.14
58000	645.64	603.43	583.94	552.82	541.56	538.61	535.98	526.53	521.12
59000	656.77	613.84	594.01	562.35	550.89	547.89	545.22	535.61	530.11
60000	667.90	624.24	604.08	571.88	560.23	557.18	554.46	544.69	539.09
61000	679.03	634.64	614.15	581.41	569.57	566.47	563.70	553.77	548.07
62000	690.16	645.05	624.22	590.94	578.90	575.75	572.95	562.85	557.06
63000	701.30	655.45	634.28	600.47	588.24	585.04	582.19	571.92	566.04
64000	712.43	665.86	644.35	610.00	597.58	594.32	591.43	581.00	575.03
65000	723.56	676.26	654.42	619.54	606.92	603.61	600.67	590.08	584.01
67500	751.39	702.27	679.59	643.36	630.26	626.83	623.77	612.78	606.48
70000	779.22	728.28	704.76	667.19	653.60	650.04	646.87	635.47	628.94
75000	834.88	780.30	755.10	714.85	700.29	696.47	693.08	680.86	673.86
80000	890.53	832.32	805.44	762.50	746.97	742.90	739.28	726.25	718.78
85000	946.19	884.34	855.78	810.16	793.66	789.34	785.49	771.64	763.71
90000	1001.85	936.36	906.12	857.82	840.34	835.77	831.69	817.03	808.63
95000	1057.51	988.38	956.46	905.47	887.03	882.20	877.90	862.42	853.56
100000	1113.17	1040.40	1006.80	953.13	933.71	928.63	924.10	907.81	898.48
105000	1168.82	1092.42	1057.14	1000.78	980.40	975.06	970.31	953.20	943.40
110000	1224.48	1144.44	1107.47	1048.44	1027.08	1021.49	1016.51	998.59	988.33
115000	1280.14	1196.46	1157.81	1096.10	1073.77	1067.92	1062.72	1043.98	1033.25
120000	1335.80	1248.48	1208.15	1143.75	1120.45	1114.35	1108.92	1089.37	1078.17
125000	1391.46	1300.50	1258.49	1191.41	1167.14	1160.79	1155.13	1134.76	1123.10
130000	1447.11	1352.52	1308.83	1239.07	1213.83	1207.22	1201.33	1180.15	1168.02
135000	1502.77	1404.54	1359.17	1286.72	1260.51	1253.65	1247.54	1225.55	1212.95
140000	1558.43	1456.55	1409.51	1334.38	1307.20	1300.08	1293.74	1270.94	1257.87
145000	1614.09	1508.57	1459.85	1382.03	1353.88	1346.51	1339.95	1316.33	1302.79
150000	1669.75	1560.59	1510.19	1429.69	1400.57	1392.94	1386.15	1361.72	1347.72

AMOUNT	1 YEAR	2 YEARS	3 YEARS	4 YEARS	5 YEARS	7 YEARS	8 YEARS	10 YEARS	12 YEARS
$ 50	4.42	2.33	1.64	1.29	1.09	.85	.78	69	.62
100	8.83	4.65	3.27	2.58	2.17	1.70	1.56	1.37	1.24
200	17.66	9.30	6.53	5.15	4.33	3.40	3.12	2.73	2.48
300	26.48	13.95	9.79	7.72	6.49	5.10	4.68	4.10	3.72
400	35.31	18.60	13.05	10.29	8.65	6.80	6.23	5.46	4.96
500	44.14	23.25	16.32	12.87	10.81	8.50	7.79	6.82	6.20
600	52.96	27.90	19.58	15.44	12.98	10.20	9.35	8.19	7.44
700	61.79	32.55	22.84	18.01	15.14	11.90	10.91	9.55	8.68
800	70.62	37.20	26.10	20.58	17.30	13.60	12.46	10.91	9.92
900	79.44	41.85	29.36	23.16	19.46	15.30	14.02	12.28	11.15
1000	88.27	46.50	32.63	25.73	21.62	17.00	15.58	13.64	12.39
2000	176.54	92.99	65.25	51.45	43.24	33.99	31.15	27.27	24.78
3000	264.80	139.48	97.87	77.18	64.86	50.98	46.73	40.91	37.17
4000	353.07	185.97	130.49	102.90	86.48	67.97	62.30	54.54	49.56
5000	441.33	232.46	163.11	128.63	108.09	84.96	77.87	68.17	61.95
6000	529.60	278.96	195.73	154.35	129.71	101.95	93.45	81.81	74.33
7000	617.86	325.45	228.35	180.07	151.33	118.94	109.02	95.44	86.72
8000	706.13	371.94	260.97	205.80	172.95	135.94	124.60	109.08	99.11
9000	794.39	418.43	293.59	231.52	194.57	152.93	140.17	122.71	111.50
10000	882.66	464.92	326.21	257.25	216.18	169.92	155.74	136.34	123.89
15000	1323.98	697.38	489.31	385.87	324.27	254.87	233.61	204.51	185.83
20000	1765.31	929.84	652.41	514.49	432.36	339.83	311.48	272.68	247.77
25000	2206.63	1162.30	815.52	643.11	540.45	424.79	389.35	340.85	309.71
30000	2647.96	1394.76	978.62	771.73	648.54	509.74	467.22	409.02	371.65
35000	3089.28	1627.22	1141.72	900.35	756.63	594.70	545.09	477.19	433.59
40000	3530.61	1859.68	1304.82	1028.98	864.72	679.66	622.96	545.36	495.53
45000	3971.93	2092.14	1467.93	1157.60	972.81	764.61	700.83	613.53	557.47
46000	4060.20	2138.63	1500.55	1183.32	994.43	781.60	716.40	627.16	569.85
47000	4148.46	2185.12	1533.17	1209.05	1016.05	798.59	731.98	640.80	582.24
48000	4236.73	2231.61	1565.79	1234.77	1037.67	815.59	747.55	654.43	594.63
49000	4324.99	2278.11	1598.41	1260.49	1059.28	832.58	763.13	668.06	607.02
50000	4413.26	2324.60	1631.03	1286.22	1080.90	849.57	778.70	681.70	619.41
51000	4501.52	2371.09	1663.65	1311.94	1102.52	866.56	794.27	695.33	631.80
52000	4589.79	2417.58	1696.27	1337.67	1124.14	883.55	809.85	708.97	644.18
53000	4678.05	2464.07	1728.89	1363.39	1145.76	900.54	825.42	722.60	656.57
54000	4766.32	2510.57	1761.51	1389.12	1167.37	917.53	841.00	736.23	668.96
55000	4854.58	2557.06	1794.13	1414.84	1188.99	934.52	856.57	749.87	681.35
56000	4942.85	2603.55	1826.75	1440.56	1210.61	951.52	872.14	763.50	693.74
57000	5031.12	2650.04	1859.37	1466.29	1232.23	968.51	887.72	777.14	706.12
58000	5119.38	2696.53	1891.99	1492.01	1253.85	985.50	903.29	790.77	718.51
59000	5207.65	2743.02	1924.61	1517.74	1275.46	1002.49	918.87	804.40	730.90
60000	5295.91	2789.52	1957.23	1543.46	1297.08	1019.48	934.44	818.04	743.29
61000	5384.18	2836.01	1989.85	1569.19	1318.70	1036.47	950.01	831.67	755.68
62000	5472.44	2882.50	2022.47	1594.91	1340.32	1053.46	965.59	845.30	768.06
63000	5560.71	2928.99	2055.09	1620.63	1361.94	1070.46	981.16	858.94	780.45
64000	5648.97	2975.48	2087.71	1646.36	1383.55	1087.45	996.73	872.57	792.84
65000	5737.24	3021.98	2120.33	1672.08	1405.17	1104.44	1012.31	886.21	805.23
67500	5957.90	3138.21	2201.89	1736.39	1459.22	1146.92	1051.24	920.29	836.20
70000	6178.56	3254.43	2283.44	1800.70	1513.26	1189.39	1090.18	954.38	867.17
75000	6619.89	3486.89	2446.54	1929.33	1621.35	1274.35	1168.05	1022.55	929.11
80000	7061.21	3719.35	2609.64	2057.95	1729.44	1359.31	1245.92	1090.71	991.05
85000	7502.54	3951.81	2772.74	2186.57	1837.53	1444.26	1323.79	1158.88	1052.99
90000	7943.86	4184.27	2935.85	2315.19	1945.62	1529.22	1401.66	1227.05	1114.93
95000	8385.19	4416.73	3098.95	2443.81	2053.71	1614.18	1479.53	1295.22	1176.87
100000	8826.51	4649.19	3262.05	2572.43	2161.80	1699.13	1557.40	1363.39	1238.81
105000	9267.84	4881.65	3425.15	2701.05	2269.89	1784.09	1635.26	1431.56	1300.75
110000	9709.16	5114.11	3588.25	2829.68	2377.98	1869.04	1713.13	1499.73	1362.69
115000	10150.49	5346.57	3751.36	2958.30	2486.07	1954.00	1791.00	1567.90	1424.63
120000	10591.82	5579.03	3914.46	3086.92	2594.16	2038.96	1868.87	1636.07	1486.57
125000	11033.14	5811.49	4077.56	3215.54	2702.25	2123.91	1946.74	1704.24	1548.51
130000	11474.47	6043.95	4240.66	3344.16	2810.34	2208.87	2024.61	1772.41	1610.45
135000	11915.79	6276.41	4403.77	3472.78	2918.43	2293.83	2102.48	1840.58	1672.39
140000	12357.12	6508.86	4566.87	3601.40	3026.52	2378.78	2180.35	1908.75	1734.33
145000	12798.44	6741.32	4729.97	3730.03	3134.61	2463.74	2258.22	1976.92	1796.27
150000	13239.77	6973.78	4893.07	3858.65	3242.70	2548.70	2336.09	2045.09	1858.21

MONTHLY PAYMENT 10¾%

NECESSARY TO AMORTIZE A LOAN

AMOUNT	15 YEARS	18 YEARS	20 YEARS	25 YEARS	28 YEARS	29 YEARS	30 YEARS	35 YEARS	40 YEARS
$ 50	.57	.53	.51	.49	.48	.47	.47	.46	.46
100	1.13	1.05	1.02	.97	.95	.94	.94	.92	.91
200	2.25	2.10	2.04	1.93	1.89	1.88	1.87	1.84	1.82
300	3.37	3.15	3.05	2.89	2.83	2.82	2.81	2.76	2.73
400	4.49	4.20	4.07	3.85	3.78	3.76	3.74	3.68	3.64
500	5.61	5.25	5.08	4.82	4.72	4.69	4.67	4.59	4.55
600	6.73	6.30	6.10	5.78	5.66	5.63	5.61	5.51	5.46
700	7.85	7.35	7.11	6.74	6.61	6.57	6.54	6.43	6.36
800	8.97	8.39	8.13	7.70	7.55	7.51	7.47	7.35	7.27
900	10.09	9.44	9.14	8.66	8.49	8.45	8.41	8.26	8.18
1000	11.21	10.49	10.16	9.63	9.43	9.38	9.34	9.18	9.09
2000	22.42	20.98	20.31	19.25	18.86	18.76	18.67	18.36	18.17
3000	33.63	31.46	30.46	28.87	28.29	28.14	28.01	27.53	27.26
4000	44.84	41.95	40.61	38.49	37.72	37.52	37.34	36.71	36.34
5000	56.05	52.43	50.77	48.11	47.15	46.90	46.68	45.88	45.42
6000	67.26	62.92	60.92	57.73	56.58	56.28	56.01	55.06	54.51
7000	78.47	73.41	71.07	67.35	66.01	65.66	65.35	64.23	63.59
8000	89.68	83.89	81.22	76.97	75.44	75.04	74.68	73.41	72.68
9000	100.89	94.38	91.38	86.59	84.87	84.42	84.02	82.58	81.76
10000	112.10	104.86	101.53	96.21	94.30	93.80	93.35	91.76	90.84
15000	168.15	157.29	152.29	144.32	141.45	140.70	140.03	137.63	136.26
20000	224.19	209.72	203.05	192.42	188.59	187.59	186.70	183.51	181.68
25000	280.24	262.15	253.81	240.53	235.74	234.49	233.38	229.38	227.10
30000	336.29	314.58	304.57	288.63	282.89	281.39	280.05	275.26	272.52
35000	392.34	367.01	355.34	336.74	330.03	328.28	326.72	321.13	317.94
40000	448.38	419.44	406.10	384.84	377.18	375.18	373.40	367.01	363.36
45000	504.43	471.87	456.86	432.95	424.33	422.08	420.07	412.88	408.78
46000	515.64	482.35	467.01	442.57	433.76	431.45	429.41	422.06	417.87
47000	526.85	492.84	477.16	452.19	443.19	440.83	438.74	431.23	426.95
48000	538.06	503.33	487.31	461.81	452.62	450.21	448.08	440.41	436.04
49000	549.27	513.81	497.47	471.43	462.05	459.59	457.41	449.58	445.12
50000	560.48	524.30	507.62	481.05	471.47	468.97	466.75	458.76	454.20
51000	571.69	534.78	517.77	490.67	480.90	478.35	476.08	467.93	463.29
52000	582.90	545.27	527.92	500.29	490.33	487.73	485.42	477.11	472.37
53000	594.11	555.75	538.08	509.91	499.76	497.11	494.75	486.28	481.46
54000	605.32	566.24	548.23	519.54	509.19	506.49	504.08	495.46	490.54
55000	616.53	576.73	558.38	529.16	518.62	515.87	513.42	504.63	499.62
56000	627.74	587.21	568.53	538.78	528.05	525.25	522.75	513.81	508.71
57000	638.95	597.70	578.69	548.40	537.48	534.63	532.09	522.98	517.79
58000	650.15	608.18	588.84	558.02	546.91	544.01	541.42	532.16	526.88
59000	661.36	618.67	598.99	567.64	556.34	553.39	550.76	541.33	535.96
60000	672.57	629.16	609.14	577.26	565.77	562.77	560.09	550.51	545.04
61000	683.78	639.64	619.29	586.88	575.20	572.14	569.43	559.68	554.13
62000	694.99	650.13	629.45	596.50	584.63	581.52	578.76	568.86	563.21
63000	706.20	660.61	639.60	606.12	594.06	590.90	588.10	578.03	572.30
64000	717.41	671.10	649.75	615.74	603.49	600.28	597.43	587.21	581.38
65000	728.62	681.59	659.90	625.37	612.92	609.66	606.77	596.38	590.46
67500	756.64	707.80	685.28	649.42	636.49	633.11	630.10	619.32	613.17
70000	784.67	734.01	710.67	673.47	660.06	656.56	653.44	642.26	635.88
75000	840.72	786.44	761.43	721.57	707.21	703.46	700.12	688.13	681.30
80000	896.76	838.87	812.19	769.68	754.36	750.35	746.79	734.01	726.72
85000	952.81	891.30	862.95	817.78	801.50	797.25	793.46	779.88	772.14
90000	1008.86	943.73	913.71	865.89	848.65	844.15	840.14	825.76	817.56
95000	1064.91	996.16	964.47	913.99	895.80	891.04	886.81	871.63	862.98
100000	1120.95	1048.59	1015.23	962.10	942.94	937.94	933.49	917.51	908.40
105000	1177.00	1101.02	1066.00	1010.20	990.09	984.84	980.16	963.38	953.82
110000	1233.05	1153.45	1116.76	1058.31	1037.24	1031.73	1026.83	1009.26	999.24
115000	1289.10	1205.88	1167.52	1106.41	1084.39	1078.63	1073.51	1055.13	1044.66
120000	1345.14	1258.31	1218.28	1154.52	1131.53	1125.53	1120.18	1101.01	1090.08
125000	1401.19	1310.74	1269.04	1202.62	1178.68	1172.42	1166.86	1146.88	1135.50
130000	1457.24	1363.17	1319.80	1250.73	1225.83	1219.32	1213.53	1192.76	1180.92
135000	1513.28	1415.59	1370.56	1298.83	1272.97	1266.22	1260.20	1238.63	1226.34
140000	1569.33	1468.02	1421.33	1346.93	1320.12	1313.11	1306.88	1284.51	1271.76
145000	1625.38	1520.45	1472.09	1395.04	1367.27	1360.01	1353.55	1330.38	1317.18
150000	1681.43	1572.88	1522.85	1443.14	1414.41	1406.91	1400.23	1376.26	1362.60

MONTHLY PAYMENT
NECESSARY TO AMORTIZE A LOAN

AMOUNT	1 YEAR	2 YEARS	3 YEARS	4 YEARS	5 YEARS	7 YEARS	8 YEARS	10 YEARS	12 YEARS
$ 50	4.42	2.33	1.64	1.29	1.09	.86	.79	.69	.63
100	8.84	4.66	3.27	2.58	2.17	1.71	1.57	1.38	1.25
200	17.67	9.31	6.54	5.16	4.34	3.42	3.13	2.75	2.50
300	26.50	13.97	9.81	7.74	6.51	5.12	4.70	4.12	3.74
400	35.33	18.62	13.08	10.32	8.68	6.83	6.26	5.49	4.99
500	44.17	23.28	16.34	12.90	10.85	8.53	7.83	6.86	6.24
600	53.00	27.93	19.61	15.48	13.01	10.24	9.39	8.23	7.48
700	61.83	32.59	22.88	18.05	15.18	11.94	10.95	9.60	8.73
800	70.66	37.24	26.15	20.63	17.35	13.65	12.52	10.97	9.97
900	79.50	41.90	29.42	23.21	19.52	15.36	14.08	12.34	11.22
1000	88.33	46.55	32.68	25.79	21.69	17.06	15.65	13.71	12.47
2000	176.65	93.10	65.36	51.57	43.37	34.12	31.29	27.41	24.93
3000	264.98	139.65	98.04	77.36	65.05	51.18	46.93	41.12	37.39
4000	353.30	186.20	130.72	103.14	86.73	68.23	62.57	54.82	49.85
5000	441.62	232.75	163.40	128.93	108.41	85.29	78.21	68.53	62.31
6000	529.95	279.30	196.08	154.71	130.09	102.35	93.85	82.23	74.78
7000	618.27	325.85	228.76	180.50	151.77	119.40	109.49	95.94	87.24
8000	706.59	372.40	261.44	206.28	173.45	136.46	125.13	109.64	99.70
9000	794.92	418.95	294.12	232.07	195.13	153.52	140.77	123.34	112.16
10000	883.24	465.50	326.80	257.85	216.81	170.57	156.42	137.05	124.62
15000	1324.86	698.25	490.20	386.78	325.21	255.86	234.62	205.57	186.93
20000	1766.47	931.00	653.60	515.70	433.61	341.14	312.83	274.09	249.24
25000	2208.09	1163.75	816.99	644.63	542.01	426.42	391.03	342.61	311.55
30000	2649.71	1396.50	980.39	773.55	650.41	511.71	469.24	411.14	373.86
35000	3091.32	1629.25	1143.79	902.48	758.81	596.99	547.44	479.66	436.16
40000	3532.94	1862.00	1307.19	1031.40	867.21	682.28	625.65	548.18	498.47
45000	3974.56	2094.75	1470.58	1160.32	975.61	767.56	703.85	616.70	560.78
46000	4062.88	2141.30	1503.26	1186.11	997.29	784.62	719.49	630.40	573.24
47000	4151.20	2187.85	1535.94	1211.89	1018.97	801.67	735.14	644.11	585.70
48000	4239.53	2234.40	1568.62	1237.68	1040.65	818.73	750.78	657.81	598.17
49000	4327.85	2280.95	1601.30	1263.46	1062.33	835.79	766.42	671.52	610.63
50000	4416.17	2327.50	1633.98	1289.25	1084.01	852.84	782.06	685.22	623.09
51000	4504.50	2374.05	1666.66	1315.03	1105.69	869.90	797.70	698.93	635.55
52000	4592.82	2420.60	1699.34	1340.82	1127.37	886.96	813.34	712.63	648.01
53000	4681.14	2467.15	1732.02	1366.60	1149.05	904.01	828.98	726.33	660.47
54000	4769.47	2513.70	1764.70	1392.39	1170.73	921.07	844.62	740.04	672.94
55000	4857.79	2560.25	1797.38	1418.17	1192.41	938.13	860.26	753.74	685.40
56000	4946.11	2606.80	1830.06	1443.96	1214.09	955.18	875.91	767.45	697.86
57000	5034.44	2653.35	1862.74	1469.74	1235.77	972.24	891.55	781.15	710.32
58000	5122.76	2699.89	1895.42	1495.53	1257.45	989.30	907.19	794.86	722.78
59000	5211.08	2746.44	1928.10	1521.31	1279.13	1006.36	922.83	808.56	735.24
60000	5299.41	2792.99	1960.78	1547.10	1300.81	1023.41	938.47	822.27	747.71
61000	5387.73	2839.54	1993.46	1572.88	1322.49	1040.47	954.11	835.97	760.17
62000	5476.05	2886.09	2026.14	1598.67	1344.17	1057.53	969.75	849.67	772.63
63000	5564.38	2932.64	2058.82	1624.45	1365.85	1074.58	985.39	863.38	785.09
64000	5652.70	2979.19	2091.50	1650.24	1387.53	1091.64	1001.03	877.08	797.55
65000	5741.02	3025.74	2124.18	1676.02	1409.21	1108.70	1016.68	890.79	810.01
67500	5961.83	3142.12	2205.87	1740.48	1463.41	1151.34	1055.78	925.05	841.17
70000	6182.64	3258.49	2287.57	1804.95	1517.61	1193.98	1094.88	959.31	872.32
75000	6624.26	3491.24	2450.97	1933.87	1626.02	1279.26	1173.09	1027.83	934.63
80000	7065.87	3723.99	2614.37	2062.79	1734.42	1364.55	1251.29	1096.35	996.94
85000	7507.49	3956.74	2777.77	2191.72	1842.82	1449.83	1329.50	1164.87	1059.25
90000	7949.11	4189.49	2941.16	2320.64	1951.22	1535.12	1407.70	1233.40	1121.56
95000	8390.72	4422.24	3104.56	2449.57	2059.62	1620.40	1485.91	1301.92	1183.87
100000	8832.34	4654.99	3267.96	2578.49	2168.02	1705.68	1564.11	1370.44	1246.17
105000	9273.96	4887.74	3431.36	2707.42	2276.42	1790.97	1642.32	1438.96	1308.48
110000	9715.57	5120.49	3594.76	2836.34	2384.82	1876.25	1720.52	1507.48	1370.79
115000	10157.19	5353.23	3758.15	2965.26	2493.22	1961.54	1798.73	1576.00	1433.10
120000	10598.81	5585.98	3921.55	3094.19	2601.62	2046.82	1876.94	1644.53	1495.41
125000	11040.43	5818.73	4084.95	3223.11	2710.02	2132.10	1955.14	1713.05	1557.72
130000	11482.04	6051.48	4248.35	3352.04	2818.42	2217.39	2033.35	1781.57	1620.02
135000	11923.66	6284.23	4411.74	3480.96	2926.82	2302.67	2111.55	1850.09	1682.33
140000	12365.28	6516.98	4575.14	3609.89	3035.22	2387.95	2189.76	1918.61	1744.64
145000	12806.89	6749.73	4738.54	3738.81	3143.62	2473.24	2267.96	1987.13	1806.95
150000	13248.51	6982.48	4901.94	3867.73	3252.03	2558.52	2346.17	2055.66	1869.26

MONTHLY PAYMENT 10⅞%
NECESSARY TO AMORTIZE A LOAN

AMOUNT	15 YEARS	18 YEARS	20 YEARS	25 YEARS	28 YEARS	29 YEARS	30 YEARS	35 YEARS	40 YEARS
$ 50	.57	.53	.52	.49	48	.48	.48	.47	.46
100	1.13	1.06	1.03	.98	.96	.95	.95	.93	.92
200	2.26	2.12	2.05	1.95	1.91	1.90	1.89	1.86	1.84
300	3.39	3.18	3.08	2.92	2.86	2.85	2.83	2.79	2.76
400	4.52	4.23	4.10	3.89	3.81	3.79	3.78	3.71	3.68
500	5.65	5.29	5.12	4.86	4.77	4.74	4.72	4.64	4.60
600	6.78	6.35	6.15	5.83	5.72	5.69	5.66	5.57	5.52
700	7.91	7.40	7.17	6.80	6.67	6.64	6.61	6.50	6.43
800	9.04	8.46	8.19	7.77	7.62	7.58	7.55	7.42	7.35
900	10.16	9.52	9.22	8.74	8.57	8.53	8.49	8.35	8.27
1000	11.29	10.57	10.24	9.72	9.53	9.48	9.43	9.28	9.19
2000	22.58	21.14	20.48	19.43	19.05	18.95	18.86	18.55	18.37
3000	33.87	31.71	30.72	29.14	28.57	28.42	28.29	27.82	27.56
4000	45.16	42.28	40.95	38.85	38.09	37.90	37.72	37.09	36.74
5000	56.44	52.85	51.19	48.56	47.61	47.37	47.15	46.37	45.92
6000	67.73	63.41	61.43	58.27	57.14	56.84	56.58	55.64	55.11
7000	79.02	73.98	71.66	67.98	66.66	66.31	66.01	64.91	64.29
8000	90.31	84.55	81.90	77.69	76.18	75.79	75.44	74.18	73.47
9000	101.59	95.12	92.14	87.40	85.70	85.26	84.87	83.45	82.66
10000	112.88	105.69	102.37	97.11	95.22	94.73	94.29	92.73	91.84
15000	169.32	158.53	153.56	145.67	142.83	142.10	141.44	139.09	137.76
20000	225.76	211.37	204.74	194.22	190.44	189.46	188.58	185.45	183.67
25000	282.20	264.21	255.93	242.78	238.05	236.82	235.73	231.81	229.59
30000	338.63	317.05	307.11	291.33	285.66	284.19	282.87	278.17	275.51
35000	395.07	369.89	358.30	339.89	333.27	331.55	330.02	324.53	321.42
40000	451.51	422.73	409.48	388.44	380.88	378.91	377.16	370.89	367.34
45000	507.95	475.57	460.67	437.00	428.49	426.28	424.31	417.25	413.26
46000	519.23	486.13	470.90	446.71	438.02	435.75	433.73	426.53	422.44
47000	530.52	496.70	481.14	456.42	447.54	445.22	443.16	435.80	431.62
48000	541.81	507.27	491.38	466.13	457.06	454.69	452.59	445.07	440.81
49000	553.10	517.84	501.62	475.84	466.58	464.17	462.02	454.34	449.99
50000	564.39	528.41	511.85	485.55	476.10	473.64	471.45	463.61	459.17
51000	575.67	538.97	522.09	495.26	485.63	483.11	480.88	472.89	468.36
52000	586.96	549.54	532.33	504.97	495.15	492.58	490.31	482.16	477.54
53000	598.25	560.11	542.56	514.68	504.67	502.06	499.74	491.43	486.72
54000	609.54	570.68	552.80	524.39	514.19	511.53	509.17	500.70	495.91
55000	620.82	581.25	563.04	534.10	523.71	521.00	518.59	509.98	505.09
56000	632.11	591.82	573.27	543.82	533.24	530.48	528.02	519.25	514.27
57000	643.40	602.38	583.51	553.53	542.76	539.95	537.45	528.52	523.46
58000	654.69	612.95	593.75	563.24	552.28	549.42	546.88	537.79	532.64
59000	665.97	623.52	603.99	572.95	561.80	558.89	556.31	547.06	541.82
60000	677.26	634.09	614.22	582.66	571.32	568.37	565.74	556.34	551.01
61000	688.55	644.66	624.46	592.37	580.85	577.84	575.17	565.61	560.19
62000	699.84	655.22	634.70	602.08	590.37	587.31	584.60	574.88	569.37
63000	711.12	665.79	644.93	611.79	599.89	596.78	594.03	584.15	578.56
64000	722.41	676.36	655.17	621.50	609.41	606.26	603.45	593.43	587.74
65000	733.70	686.93	665.41	631.21	618.93	615.73	612.88	602.70	596.92
67500	761.92	713.35	691.00	655.49	642.74	639.41	636.46	625.88	619.88
70000	790.14	739.77	716.59	679.77	666.54	663.09	660.03	649.06	642.84
75000	846.58	792.61	767.78	728.32	714.15	710.46	707.17	695.42	688.76
80000	903.01	845.45	818.96	776.88	761.76	757.82	754.32	741.78	734.67
85000	959.45	898.29	870.15	825.43	809.37	805.18	801.46	788.14	780.59
90000	1015.89	951.13	921.33	873.99	856.98	852.55	848.61	834.50	826.51
95000	1072.33	1003.97	972.52	922.54	904.59	899.91	895.75	880.86	872.43
100000	1128.77	1056.81	1023.70	971.09	952.20	947.27	942.90	927.22	918.34
105000	1185.20	1109.65	1074.88	1019.65	999.81	994.64	990.04	973.59	964.26
110000	1241.64	1162.49	1126.07	1068.20	1047.42	1042.00	1037.18	1019.95	1010.18
115000	1298.08	1215.33	1177.25	1116.76	1095.03	1089.36	1084.33	1066.31	1056.09
120000	1354.52	1268.17	1228.44	1165.31	1142.64	1136.73	1131.47	1112.67	1102.01
125000	1410.96	1321.01	1279.62	1213.87	1190.25	1184.09	1178.62	1159.03	1147.93
130000	1467.39	1373.85	1330.81	1262.42	1237.86	1231.45	1225.76	1205.39	1193.84
135000	1523.83	1426.69	1381.99	1310.98	1285.47	1278.82	1272.91	1251.75	1239.76
140000	1580.27	1479.53	1433.18	1359.53	1333.08	1326.18	1320.05	1298.11	1285.68
145000	1636.71	1532.37	1484.36	1408.08	1380.69	1373.55	1367.20	1344.47	1331.59
150000	1693.15	1585.21	1535.55	1456.64	1428.30	1420.91	1414.34	1390.83	1377.51

11%

MONTHLY PAYMENT
NECESSARY TO AMORTIZE A LOAN

AMOUNT	1 YEAR	2 YEARS	3 YEARS	4 YEARS	5 YEARS	7 YEARS	8 YEARS	10 YEARS	12 YEARS
$ 50	4.42	2.34	1.64	1.30	1.09	.86	.79	.69	.63
100	8.84	4.67	3.28	2.59	2.18	1.72	1.58	1.38	1.26
200	17.68	9.33	6.55	5.17	4.35	3.43	3.15	2.76	2.51
300	26.52	13.99	9.83	7.76	6.53	5.14	4.72	4.14	3.77
400	35.36	18.65	13.10	10.34	8.70	6.85	6.29	5.52	5.02
500	44.20	23.31	16.37	12.93	10.88	8.57	7.86	6.89	6.27
600	53.03	27.97	19.65	15.51	13.05	10.28	9.43	8.27	7.53
700	61.87	32.63	22.92	18.10	15.22	11.99	11.00	9.65	8.78
800	70.71	37.29	26.20	20.68	17.40	13.70	12.57	11.03	10.03
900	79.55	41.95	29.47	23.27	19.57	15.42	14.14	12.40	11.29
1000	88.39	46.61	32.74	25.85	21.75	17.13	15.71	13.78	12.54
2000	176.77	93.22	65.48	51.70	43.49	34.25	31.42	27.56	25.08
3000	265.15	139.83	98.22	77.54	65.23	51.37	47.13	41.33	37.61
4000	353.53	186.44	130.96	103.39	86.97	68.49	62.84	55.11	50.15
5000	441.91	233.04	163.70	129.23	108.72	85.62	78.55	68.88	62.68
6000	530.29	279.65	196.44	155.08	130.46	102.74	94.26	82.66	75.22
7000	618.68	326.26	229.18	180.92	152.20	119.86	109.96	96.43	87.75
8000	707.06	372.87	261.91	206.77	173.94	136.98	125.67	110.21	100.29
9000	795.44	419.48	294.65	232.61	195.69	154.11	141.38	123.98	112.82
10000	883.82	466.08	327.39	258.46	217.43	171.23	157.09	137.76	125.36
15000	1325.73	699.12	491.09	387.69	326.14	256.84	235.63	206.63	188.04
20000	1767.64	932.16	654.78	516.92	434.85	342.45	314.17	275.51	250.72
25000	2209.55	1165.20	818.47	646.14	543.57	428.07	392.72	344.38	313.39
30000	2651.45	1398.24	982.17	775.37	652.28	513.68	471.26	413.26	376.07
35000	3093.36	1631.28	1145.86	904.60	760.99	599.29	549.80	482.13	438.75
40000	3535.27	1864.32	1309.55	1033.83	869.70	684.90	628.34	551.01	501.43
45000	3977.18	2097.36	1473.25	1163.05	978.41	770.51	706.88	619.88	564.10
46000	4065.65	2143.97	1505.99	1188.90	1000.16	787.64	722.59	633.66	576.64
47000	4153.94	2190.57	1538.72	1214.74	1021.90	804.76	738.30	647.43	589.18
48000	4242.32	2237.18	1571.46	1240.59	1043.64	821.88	754.01	661.21	601.71
49000	4330.71	2283.79	1604.20	1266.44	1065.38	839.00	769.72	674.98	614.25
50000	4419.09	2330.40	1636.94	1292.28	1087.13	856.13	785.43	688.76	626.78
51000	4507.47	2377.00	1669.68	1318.13	1108.87	873.25	801.13	702.53	639.32
52000	4595.85	2423.61	1702.42	1343.97	1130.61	890.37	816.84	716.31	651.85
53000	4684.23	2470.22	1735.16	1369.82	1152.35	907.49	832.55	730.08	664.39
54000	4772.61	2516.83	1767.90	1395.66	1174.10	924.62	848.26	743.86	676.92
55000	4861.00	2563.44	1800.63	1421.51	1195.84	941.74	863.97	757.63	689.46
56000	4949.38	2610.04	1833.37	1447.35	1217.58	958.86	879.68	771.41	702.00
57000	5037.76	2656.65	1866.11	1473.20	1239.32	975.98	895.39	785.18	714.53
58000	5126.14	2703.26	1898.85	1499.05	1261.07	993.11	911.09	798.96	727.07
59000	5214.52	2749.87	1931.59	1524.89	1282.81	1010.23	926.80	812.73	739.60
60000	5302.90	2796.48	1964.33	1550.74	1304.55	1027.35	942.51	826.51	752.14
61000	5391.29	2843.08	1997.07	1576.58	1326.29	1044.47	958.22	840.28	764.67
62000	5479.67	2889.69	2029.81	1602.43	1348.04	1061.60	973.93	854.06	777.21
63000	5568.05	2936.30	2062.54	1628.27	1369.78	1078.72	989.64	867.83	789.74
64000	5656.43	2982.91	2095.28	1654.12	1391.52	1095.84	1005.34	881.61	802.28
65000	5744.81	3029.51	2128.02	1679.96	1413.26	1112.96	1021.05	895.38	814.82
67500	5965.77	3146.03	2209.87	1744.58	1467.62	1155.77	1060.32	929.82	846.15
70000	6186.72	3262.55	2291.72	1809.19	1521.97	1198.58	1099.59	964.26	877.49
75000	6628.63	3495.59	2455.41	1938.42	1630.69	1284.19	1178.14	1033.13	940.17
80000	7070.54	3728.63	2619.10	2067.65	1739.40	1369.80	1256.68	1102.01	1002.85
85000	7512.45	3961.67	2782.80	2196.87	1848.11	1455.41	1335.22	1170.88	1065.53
90000	7954.35	4194.71	2946.49	2326.10	1956.82	1541.02	1413.76	1239.76	1128.20
95000	8396.26	4427.75	3110.18	2455.33	2065.54	1626.64	1492.31	1308.63	1190.88
100000	8838.17	4660.79	3273.88	2584.56	2174.25	1712.25	1570.85	1377.51	1253.56
105000	9280.08	4893.83	3437.57	2713.78	2282.96	1797.86	1649.39	1446.38	1316.24
110000	9721.99	5126.87	3601.26	2843.01	2391.67	1883.47	1727.93	1515.26	1378.92
115000	10163.90	5359.91	3764.96	2972.24	2500.38	1969.09	1806.47	1584.13	1441.59
120000	10605.80	5592.95	3928.65	3101.47	2609.10	2054.70	1885.02	1653.01	1504.27
125000	11047.71	5825.98	4092.34	3230.70	2717.81	2140.31	1963.56	1721.88	1566.95
130000	11489.62	6059.02	4256.04	3359.92	2826.52	2225.92	2042.10	1790.76	1629.63
135000	11931.53	6292.06	4419.73	3489.15	2935.23	2311.53	2120.64	1859.63	1692.30
140000	12373.44	6525.10	4583.43	3618.38	3043.94	2397.15	2199.18	1928.51	1754.98
145000	12815.35	6758.14	4747.12	3747.61	3152.66	2482.76	2277.73	1997.38	1817.66
150000	13257.25	6991.18	4910.81	3876.83	3261.37	2568.37	2356.27	2066.26	1880.34

MONTHLY PAYMENT 11%
NECESSARY TO AMORTIZE A LOAN

AMOUNT	15 YEARS	18 YEARS	20 YEARS	25 YEARS	28 YEARS	29 YEARS	30 YEARS	35 YEARS	40 YEARS
$ 50	.57	.54	.52	.50	.49	.48	.48	.47	.47
100	1.14	1.07	1.04	.99	.97	.96	.96	.94	.93
200	2.28	2.14	2.07	1.97	1.93	1.92	1.91	1.88	1.86
300	3.41	3.20	3.10	2.95	2.89	2.87	2.86	2.82	2.79
400	4.55	4.27	4.13	3.93	3.85	3.83	3.81	3.75	3.72
500	5.69	5.33	5.17	4.91	4.81	4.79	4.77	4.69	4.65
600	6.82	6.40	6.20	5.89	5.77	5.74	5.72	5.63	5.57
700	7.96	7.46	7.23	6.87	6.74	6.70	6.67	6.56	6.50
800	9.10	8.53	8.26	7.85	7.70	7.66	7.62	7.50	7.43
900	10.23	9.59	9.29	8.83	8.66	8.61	8.58	8.44	8.36
1000	11.37	10.66	10.33	9.81	9.62	9.57	9.53	9.37	9.29
2000	22.74	21.31	20.65	19.61	19.23	19.14	19.05	18.74	18.57
3000	34.10	31.96	30.97	29.41	28.85	28.70	28.57	28.11	27.85
4000	45.47	42.61	41.29	39.21	38.46	38.27	38.10	37.48	37.14
5000	56.83	53.26	51.61	49.01	48.08	47.84	47.62	46.85	46.42
6000	68.20	63.91	61.94	58.81	57.69	57.40	57.14	56.22	55.70
7000	79.57	74.56	72.26	68.61	67.31	66.97	66.67	65.59	64.99
8000	90.93	85.21	82.58	78.41	76.92	76.54	76.19	74.96	74.27
9000	102.30	95.86	92.90	88.22	86.54	86.10	85.71	84.33	83.55
10000	113.66	106.51	103.22	98.02	96.15	95.67	95.24	93.70	92.83
15000	170.49	159.76	154.83	147.02	144.23	143.50	142.85	140.55	139.25
20000	227.32	213.01	206.44	196.03	192.30	191.33	190.47	187.40	185.66
25000	284.15	266.27	258.05	245.03	240.37	239.16	238.09	234.24	232.08
30000	340.98	319.52	309.66	294.04	288.45	286.99	285.70	281.09	278.49
35000	397.81	372.77	361.27	343.04	336.52	334.83	333.32	327.94	324.91
40000	454.64	426.02	412.88	392.05	384.60	382.66	380.93	374.79	371.32
45000	511.47	479.28	464.49	441.06	432.67	430.49	428.55	421.64	417.74
46000	522.84	489.93	474.81	450.86	442.29	440.05	438.07	431.01	427.02
47000	534.21	500.58	485.13	460.66	451.90	449.62	447.60	440.38	436.30
48000	545.57	511.23	495.46	470.46	461.52	459.19	457.12	449.74	445.59
49000	556.94	521.88	505.78	480.26	471.13	468.75	466.64	459.11	454.87
50000	568.30	532.53	516.10	490.06	480.74	478.32	476.17	468.48	464.15
51000	579.67	543.18	526.42	499.86	490.36	487.89	485.69	477.85	473.44
52000	591.04	553.83	536.74	509.66	499.97	497.45	495.21	487.22	482.72
53000	602.40	564.48	547.06	519.46	509.59	507.02	504.74	496.59	492.00
54000	613.77	575.13	557.39	529.27	519.20	516.58	514.26	505.96	501.28
55000	625.13	585.78	567.71	539.07	528.82	526.15	523.78	515.33	510.57
56000	636.50	596.43	578.03	548.87	538.43	535.72	533.31	524.70	519.85
57000	647.87	607.08	588.35	558.67	548.05	545.28	542.83	534.07	529.13
58000	659.23	617.73	598.67	568.47	557.66	554.85	552.35	543.44	538.42
59000	670.60	628.38	609.00	578.27	567.28	564.42	561.88	552.81	547.70
60000	681.96	639.03	619.32	588.07	576.89	573.98	571.40	562.18	556.98
61000	693.33	649.69	629.64	597.87	586.51	583.55	580.92	571.55	566.26
62000	704.70	660.34	639.96	607.68	596.12	593.12	590.45	580.92	575.55
63000	716.06	670.99	650.28	617.48	605.74	602.68	599.97	590.29	584.83
64000	727.43	681.64	660.61	627.28	615.35	612.25	609.49	599.66	594.11
65000	738.79	692.29	670.93	637.08	624.97	621.81	619.02	609.03	603.40
67500	767.21	718.91	696.73	661.58	649.00	645.73	642.82	632.45	626.60
70000	795.62	745.54	722.54	686.08	673.04	669.65	666.63	655.88	649.81
75000	852.45	798.79	774.15	735.09	721.11	717.48	714.25	702.72	696.23
80000	909.28	852.04	825.76	784.10	769.19	765.31	761.86	749.57	742.64
85000	966.11	905.30	877.37	833.10	817.26	813.14	809.48	796.42	789.06
90000	1022.94	958.55	928.97	882.11	865.34	860.97	857.10	843.27	835.47
95000	1079.77	1011.80	980.58	931.11	913.41	908.80	904.71	890.11	881.88
100000	1136.60	1065.05	1032.19	980.12	961.48	956.63	952.33	936.96	928.30
105000	1193.43	1118.31	1083.80	1029.12	1009.56	1004.47	999.94	983.81	974.71
110000	1250.26	1171.56	1135.41	1078.13	1057.63	1052.30	1047.56	1030.66	1021.13
115000	1307.09	1224.81	1187.02	1127.14	1105.71	1100.13	1095.18	1077.51	1067.54
120000	1363.92	1278.06	1238.63	1176.14	1153.78	1147.96	1142.79	1124.35	1113.96
125000	1420.75	1331.32	1290.24	1225.15	1201.85	1195.79	1190.41	1171.20	1160.37
130000	1477.58	1384.57	1341.85	1274.15	1249.93	1243.62	1238.03	1218.05	1206.79
135000	1534.41	1437.82	1393.46	1323.16	1298.00	1291.45	1285.64	1264.90	1253.20
140000	1591.24	1491.07	1445.07	1372.16	1346.08	1339.29	1333.26	1311.75	1299.62
145000	1648.07	1544.33	1496.68	1421.17	1394.15	1387.12	1380.87	1358.59	1346.03
150000	1704.90	1597.58	1548.29	1470.17	1442.22	1434.95	1428.49	1405.44	1392.45

11⅛%

MONTHLY PAYMENT
NECESSARY TO AMORTIZE A LOAN

AMOUNT	1 YEAR	2 YEARS	3 YEARS	4 YEARS	5 YEARS	7 YEARS	8 YEARS	10 YEARS	12 YEARS
$ 50	4.43	2.34	1.64	1.30	1.10	.86	.79	.70	.64
100	8.85	4.67	3.28	2.60	2.19	1.72	1.58	1.39	1.27
200	17.69	9.34	6.56	5.19	4.37	3.44	3.16	2.77	2.53
300	26.54	14.00	9.84	7.78	6.55	5.16	4.74	4.16	3.79
400	35.38	18.67	13.12	10.37	8.73	6.88	6.32	5.54	5.05
500	44.22	23.34	16.40	12.96	10.91	8.60	7.89	6.93	6.31
600	53.07	28.00	19.68	15.55	13.09	10.32	9.47	8.31	7.57
700	61.91	32.67	22.96	18.14	15.27	12.04	11.05	9.70	8.83
800	70.76	37.34	26.24	20.73	17.45	13.76	12.63	11.08	10.09
900	79.60	42.00	29.52	23.32	19.63	15.47	14.20	12.47	11.35
1000	88.44	46.67	32.80	25.91	21.81	17.19	15.78	13.85	12.61
2000	176.88	93.34	65.60	51.82	43.61	34.38	31.56	27.70	25.22
3000	265.32	140.00	98.40	77.72	65.42	51.57	47.33	41.54	37.83
4000	353.76	186.67	131.20	103.63	87.22	68.76	63.11	55.39	50.44
5000	442.20	233.33	163.99	129.54	109.03	85.95	78.88	69.23	63.05
6000	530.64	280.00	196.79	155.44	130.83	103.13	94.66	83.08	75.66
7000	619.08	326.67	229.59	181.35	152.64	120.32	110.44	96.93	88.27
8000	707.52	373.33	262.39	207.26	174.44	137.51	126.21	110.77	100.88
9000	795.96	420.00	295.19	233.16	196.25	154.70	141.99	124.62	113.49
10000	884.40	466.66	327.98	259.07	218.05	171.89	157.76	138.46	126.10
15000	1326.60	699.99	491.97	388.60	327.08	257.83	236.64	207.69	189.15
20000	1768.80	933.32	655.96	518.13	436.10	343.77	315.52	276.92	252.20
25000	2211.00	1166.65	819.95	647.66	545.13	429.71	394.40	346.15	315.25
30000	2653.20	1399.98	983.94	777.19	654.15	515.65	473.28	415.38	378.29
35000	3095.40	1633.31	1147.93	906.72	763.17	601.59	552.16	484.61	441.34
40000	3537.60	1866.64	1311.92	1036.26	872.20	687.53	631.04	553.84	504.39
45000	3979.80	2099.97	1475.91	1165.79	981.22	773.48	709.92	623.07	567.44
46000	4068.24	2146.64	1508.71	1191.69	1003.03	790.66	725.70	636.91	580.05
47000	4156.68	2193.30	1541.51	1217.60	1024.83	807.85	741.47	650.76	592.66
48000	4245.12	2239.97	1574.31	1243.51	1046.64	825.04	757.25	664.61	605.27
49000	4333.56	2286.63	1607.10	1269.41	1068.44	842.23	773.03	678.45	617.88
50000	4422.00	2333.30	1639.90	1295.32	1090.25	859.42	788.80	692.30	630.49
51000	4510.44	2379.97	1672.70	1321.22	1112.05	876.60	804.58	706.14	643.10
52000	4598.88	2426.63	1705.50	1347.13	1133.86	893.79	820.35	719.99	655.71
53000	4687.32	2473.30	1738.30	1373.04	1155.66	910.98	836.13	733.84	668.32
54000	4775.76	2519.96	1771.09	1398.94	1177.46	928.17	851.90	747.68	680.93
55000	4864.20	2566.63	1803.89	1424.85	1199.27	945.36	867.68	761.53	693.53
56000	4952.64	2613.30	1836.69	1450.76	1221.07	962.55	883.46	775.37	706.14
57000	5041.08	2659.96	1869.49	1476.66	1242.88	979.73	899.23	789.22	718.75
58000	5129.52	2706.63	1902.29	1502.57	1264.68	996.92	915.01	803.06	731.36
59000	5217.96	2753.29	1935.08	1528.47	1286.49	1014.11	930.78	816.91	743.97
60000	5306.40	2799.96	1967.88	1554.38	1308.29	1031.30	946.56	830.76	756.58
61000	5394.84	2846.62	2000.68	1580.29	1330.10	1048.49	962.34	844.60	769.19
62000	5483.28	2893.29	2033.48	1606.19	1351.90	1065.68	978.11	858.45	781.80
63000	5571.72	2939.96	2066.28	1632.10	1373.71	1082.86	993.89	872.29	794.41
64000	5660.16	2986.62	2099.07	1658.01	1395.51	1100.05	1009.66	886.14	807.02
65000	5748.60	3033.29	2131.87	1683.91	1417.32	1117.24	1025.44	899.99	819.63
67500	5969.70	3149.95	2213.87	1748.68	1471.83	1160.21	1064.88	934.60	851.16
70000	6190.80	3266.62	2295.86	1813.44	1526.34	1203.18	1104.32	969.21	882.68
75000	6633.00	3499.95	2459.85	1942.98	1635.37	1289.12	1183.20	1038.44	945.73
80000	7075.20	3733.28	2623.84	2072.51	1744.39	1375.06	1262.08	1107.67	1008.78
85000	7517.40	3966.61	2787.83	2202.04	1853.41	1461.00	1340.96	1176.90	1071.82
90000	7959.60	4199.94	2951.82	2331.57	1962.44	1546.95	1419.84	1246.13	1134.87
95000	8401.80	4433.26	3115.81	2461.10	2071.46	1632.89	1498.72	1315.36	1197.92
100000	8844.00	4666.59	3279.80	2590.63	2180.49	1718.83	1577.60	1384.59	1260.97
105000	9286.20	4899.92	3443.79	2720.16	2289.51	1804.77	1656.48	1453.82	1324.02
110000	9728.40	5133.25	3607.78	2849.69	2398.53	1890.71	1735.36	1523.05	1387.06
115000	10170.60	5366.58	3771.77	2979.23	2507.56	1976.65	1814.24	1592.28	1450.11
120000	10612.80	5599.91	3935.76	3108.76	2616.58	2062.59	1893.12	1661.51	1513.16
125000	11055.00	5833.24	4099.75	3238.29	2725.61	2148.53	1972.00	1730.74	1576.21
130000	11497.20	6066.57	4263.74	3367.82	2834.63	2234.48	2050.88	1799.97	1639.26
135000	11939.40	6299.90	4427.73	3497.35	2943.65	2320.42	2129.75	1869.20	1702.31
140000	12381.60	6533.23	4591.72	3626.88	3052.68	2406.36	2208.63	1938.42	1765.35
145000	12823.80	6766.56	4755.71	3756.41	3161.70	2492.30	2287.51	2007.65	1828.40
150000	13266.00	6999.89	4919.70	3885.95	3270.73	2578.24	2366.39	2076.88	1891.45

70

MONTHLY PAYMENT 11⅛%

NECESSARY TO AMORTIZE A LOAN

AMOUNT	15 YEARS	18 YEARS	20 YEARS	25 YEARS	28 YEARS	29 YEARS	30 YEARS	35 YEARS	40 YEARS
$ 50	.58	.54	.53	.50	.49	.49	.49	.48	.47
100	1.15	1.08	1.05	.99	.98	.97	.97	.95	.94
200	2.29	2.15	2.09	1.98	1.95	1.94	1.93	1.90	1.88
300	3.44	3.22	3.13	2.97	2.92	2.90	2.89	2.85	2.82
400	4.58	4.30	4.17	3.96	3.89	3.87	3.85	3.79	3.76
500	5.73	5.37	5.21	4.95	4.86	4.84	4.81	4.74	4.70
600	6.87	6.44	6.25	5.94	5.83	5.80	5.78	5.69	5.63
700	8.02	7.52	7.29	6.93	6.80	6.77	6.74	6.63	6.57
800	9.16	8.59	8.33	7.92	7.77	7.73	7.70	7.58	7.51
900	10.31	9.66	9.37	8.91	8.74	8.70	8.66	8.53	8.45
1000	11.45	10.74	10.41	9.90	9.71	9.67	9.62	9.47	9.39
2000	22.89	21.47	20.82	19.79	19.42	19.33	19.24	18.94	18.77
3000	34.34	32.20	31.23	29.68	29.13	28.99	28.86	28.41	28.15
4000	45.78	42.94	41.63	39.57	38.84	38.65	38.48	37.87	37.54
5000	57.23	53.67	52.04	49.46	48.54	48.31	48.09	47.34	46.92
6000	68.67	64.40	62.45	59.35	58.25	57.97	57.71	56.81	56.30
7000	80.12	75.14	72.85	69.25	67.96	67.63	67.33	66.28	65.68
8000	91.56	85.87	83.26	79.14	77.67	77.29	76.95	75.74	75.07
9000	103.01	96.60	93.67	89.03	87.38	86.95	86.57	85.21	84.45
10000	114.45	107.34	104.08	98.92	97.08	96.61	96.18	94.68	93.83
15000	171.67	161.00	156.11	148.38	145.62	144.91	144.27	142.01	140.75
20000	228.90	214.67	208.15	197.84	194.16	193.21	192.36	189.35	187.66
25000	286.12	268.34	260.18	247.30	242.70	241.51	240.45	236.68	234.57
30000	343.34	322.00	312.22	296.75	291.24	289.81	288.54	284.02	281.49
35000	400.57	375.67	364.25	346.21	339.78	338.11	336.63	331.36	328.40
40000	457.79	429.33	416.29	395.67	388.32	386.41	384.72	378.69	375.31
45000	515.01	483.00	468.32	445.13	436.86	434.71	432.81	426.03	422.23
46000	526.46	493.73	478.73	455.02	446.57	444.37	442.42	435.49	431.61
47000	537.90	504.47	489.14	464.91	456.28	454.03	452.04	444.96	440.99
48000	549.35	515.20	499.55	474.80	465.98	463.69	461.66	454.43	450.37
49000	560.79	525.93	509.95	484.69	475.69	473.35	471.28	463.90	459.76
50000	572.23	536.67	520.36	494.59	485.40	483.01	480.90	473.36	469.14
51000	583.68	547.40	530.77	504.48	495.11	492.67	490.51	482.83	478.52
52000	595.12	558.13	541.17	514.37	504.81	502.33	500.13	492.30	487.90
53000	606.57	568.87	551.58	524.26	514.52	511.99	509.75	501.76	497.29
54000	618.01	579.60	561.99	534.15	524.23	521.65	519.37	511.23	506.67
55000	629.46	590.33	572.39	544.04	533.94	531.31	528.98	520.70	516.05
56000	640.90	601.07	582.80	553.94	543.65	540.97	538.60	530.17	525.44
57000	652.35	611.80	593.21	563.83	553.35	550.63	548.22	539.63	534.82
58000	663.79	622.53	603.62	573.72	563.06	560.29	557.84	549.10	544.20
59000	675.24	633.26	614.02	583.61	572.77	569.95	567.46	558.57	553.58
60000	686.68	644.00	624.43	593.50	582.48	579.61	577.07	568.03	562.97
61000	698.12	654.73	634.84	603.39	592.19	589.27	586.69	577.50	572.35
62000	709.57	665.46	645.24	613.29	601.89	598.93	596.31	586.97	581.73
63000	721.01	676.20	655.65	623.18	611.60	608.59	605.93	596.44	591.11
64000	732.46	686.93	666.06	633.07	621.31	618.25	615.54	605.90	600.50
65000	743.90	697.66	676.47	642.96	631.02	627.91	625.16	615.37	609.88
67500	772.51	724.50	702.48	667.69	655.29	652.06	649.21	639.04	633.34
70000	801.13	751.33	728.50	692.42	679.56	676.22	673.25	662.71	656.79
75000	858.35	805.00	780.54	741.88	728.10	724.52	721.34	710.04	703.71
80000	915.57	858.66	832.57	791.34	776.64	772.82	769.43	757.38	750.62
85000	972.79	912.33	884.61	840.79	825.17	821.12	817.52	804.71	797.53
90000	1030.02	965.99	936.64	890.25	873.71	869.42	865.61	852.05	844.45
95000	1087.24	1019.66	988.68	939.71	922.25	917.72	913.70	899.39	891.36
100000	1144.46	1073.33	1040.71	989.17	970.79	966.02	961.79	946.72	938.27
105000	1201.69	1126.99	1092.75	1038.63	1019.33	1014.32	1009.87	994.06	985.19
110000	1258.91	1180.66	1144.78	1088.08	1067.87	1062.62	1057.96	1041.39	1032.10
115000	1316.13	1234.33	1196.82	1137.54	1116.41	1110.92	1106.05	1088.73	1079.01
120000	1373.36	1287.99	1248.86	1187.00	1164.95	1159.22	1154.14	1136.06	1125.93
125000	1430.58	1341.66	1300.89	1236.46	1213.49	1207.52	1202.23	1183.40	1172.84
130000	1487.80	1395.32	1352.93	1285.92	1262.03	1255.82	1250.32	1230.74	1219.75
135000	1545.02	1448.99	1404.96	1335.38	1310.57	1304.12	1298.41	1278.07	1266.67
140000	1602.25	1502.66	1457.00	1384.83	1359.11	1352.43	1346.50	1325.41	1313.58
145000	1659.47	1556.32	1509.03	1434.29	1407.65	1400.73	1394.59	1372.74	1360.49
150000	1716.69	1609.99	1561.07	1483.75	1456.19	1449.03	1442.68	1420.08	1407.41

MONTHLY PAYMENT
NECESSARY TO AMORTIZE A LOAN

AMOUNT	1 YEAR	2 YEARS	3 YEARS	4 YEARS	5 YEARS	7 YEARS	8 YEARS	10 YEARS	12 YEARS
$ 50	4.43	2.34	1.65	1.30	1.10	.87	.80	.70	.64
100	8.85	4.68	3.29	2.60	2.19	1.73	1.59	1.40	1.27
200	17.70	9.35	6.58	5.20	4.38	3.46	3.17	2.79	2.54
300	26.55	14.02	9.86	7.80	6.57	5.18	4.76	4.18	3.81
400	35.40	18.69	13.15	10.39	8.75	6.91	6.34	5.57	5.08
500	44.25	23.37	16.43	12.99	10.94	8.63	7.93	6.96	6.35
600	53.10	28.04	19.72	15.59	13.13	10.36	9.51	8.36	7.62
700	61.95	32.71	23.01	18.18	15.31	12.08	11.10	9.75	8.88
800	70.80	37.38	26.29	20.78	17.50	13.81	12.68	11.14	10.15
900	79.65	42.06	29.58	23.38	19.69	15.53	14.26	12.53	11.42
1000	88.50	46.73	32.86	25.97	21.87	17.26	15.85	13.92	12.69
2000	177.00	93.45	65.72	51.94	43.74	34.51	31.69	27.84	25.37
3000	265.50	140.18	98.58	77.91	65.61	51.77	47.54	41.76	38.06
4000	354.00	186.90	131.43	103.87	87.47	69.02	63.38	55.67	50.74
5000	442.50	233.62	164.29	129.84	109.34	86.28	79.22	69.59	63.42
6000	530.99	280.35	197.15	155.81	131.21	103.53	95.07	83.51	76.11
7000	619.49	327.07	230.01	181.77	153.08	120.78	110.91	97.42	88.79
8000	707.99	373.80	262.86	207.74	174.94	138.04	126.75	111.34	101.48
9000	796.49	420.52	295.72	233.71	196.81	155.29	142.60	125.26	114.16
10000	884.99	467.24	328.58	259.68	218.68	172.55	158.44	139.17	126.84
15000	1327.48	700.86	492.86	389.51	328.01	258.82	237.66	208.76	190.26
20000	1769.97	934.48	657.15	519.35	437.35	345.09	316.88	278.34	253.68
25000	2212.46	1168.10	821.44	649.18	546.69	431.36	396.09	347.93	317.10
30000	2654.95	1401.72	985.72	779.02	656.02	517.63	475.31	417.51	380.52
35000	3097.45	1635.34	1150.01	908.85	765.36	603.90	554.53	487.10	443.94
40000	3539.94	1868.96	1314.29	1038.69	874.70	690.17	633.75	556.68	507.36
45000	3982.43	2102.58	1478.58	1168.52	984.03	776.44	712.97	626.27	570.78
46000	4070.93	2149.31	1511.44	1194.49	1005.90	793.70	728.81	640.18	583.47
47000	4159.43	2196.03	1544.30	1220.46	1027.77	810.95	744.65	654.10	596.15
48000	4247.92	2242.76	1577.15	1246.43	1049.64	828.21	760.50	668.02	608.83
49000	4336.42	2289.48	1610.01	1272.39	1071.50	845.46	776.34	681.93	621.52
50000	4424.92	2336.20	1642.87	1298.36	1093.37	862.71	792.18	695.85	634.20
51000	4513.42	2382.93	1675.72	1324.33	1115.24	879.97	808.03	709.77	646.89
52000	4601.92	2429.65	1708.58	1350.29	1137.11	897.22	823.87	723.68	659.57
53000	4690.42	2476.38	1741.44	1376.26	1158.97	914.48	839.71	737.60	672.25
54000	4778.91	2523.10	1774.30	1402.23	1180.84	931.73	855.56	751.52	684.94
55000	4867.41	2569.82	1807.15	1428.20	1202.71	948.98	871.40	765.43	697.62
56000	4955.91	2616.55	1840.01	1454.16	1224.57	966.24	887.25	779.35	710.31
57000	5044.41	2663.27	1872.87	1480.13	1246.44	983.49	903.09	793.27	722.99
58000	5132.91	2710.00	1905.72	1506.10	1268.31	1000.75	918.93	807.18	735.67
59000	5221.41	2756.72	1938.58	1532.06	1290.18	1018.00	934.78	821.10	748.36
60000	5309.90	2803.44	1971.44	1558.03	1312.04	1035.26	950.62	835.02	761.04
61000	5398.40	2850.17	2004.30	1584.00	1333.91	1052.51	966.46	848.94	773.72
62000	5486.90	2896.89	2037.15	1609.97	1355.78	1069.76	982.31	862.85	786.41
63000	5575.40	2943.62	2070.01	1635.93	1377.65	1087.02	998.15	876.77	799.09
64000	5663.90	2990.34	2102.87	1661.90	1399.51	1104.27	1013.99	890.69	811.78
65000	5752.40	3037.06	2135.73	1687.87	1421.38	1121.53	1029.84	904.60	824.46
67500	5973.64	3153.87	2217.87	1752.78	1476.05	1164.66	1069.45	939.40	856.17
70000	6194.89	3270.68	2300.01	1817.70	1530.72	1207.80	1109.06	974.19	887.88
75000	6637.38	3504.30	2464.30	1947.54	1640.05	1294.07	1188.27	1043.77	951.30
80000	7079.87	3737.92	2628.58	2077.37	1749.39	1380.34	1267.49	1113.36	1014.72
85000	7522.36	3971.54	2792.87	2207.21	1858.73	1466.61	1346.71	1182.94	1078.14
90000	7964.85	4205.16	2957.16	2337.04	1968.06	1552.88	1425.93	1252.53	1141.56
95000	8407.34	4438.78	3121.44	2466.88	2077.40	1639.15	1505.15	1322.11	1204.98
100000	8849.84	4672.40	3285.73	2596.71	2186.74	1725.42	1584.36	1391.69	1268.40
105000	9292.33	4906.02	3450.01	2726.55	2296.07	1811.69	1663.58	1461.28	1331.82
110000	9734.82	5139.64	3614.30	2856.39	2405.41	1897.96	1742.80	1530.86	1395.24
115000	10177.31	5373.26	3778.59	2986.22	2514.75	1984.23	1822.02	1600.45	1458.66
120000	10619.80	5606.88	3942.87	3116.06	2624.08	2070.51	1901.24	1670.03	1522.08
125000	11062.29	5840.50	4107.16	3245.89	2733.42	2156.78	1980.45	1739.62	1585.50
130000	11504.79	6074.12	4271.45	3375.73	2842.76	2243.05	2059.67	1809.20	1648.92
135000	11947.28	6307.74	4435.73	3505.56	2952.09	2329.32	2138.89	1878.79	1712.34
140000	12389.77	6541.36	4600.02	3635.40	3061.43	2415.59	2218.11	1948.37	1775.76
145000	12832.26	6774.98	4764.30	3765.23	3170.76	2501.86	2297.32	2017.95	1839.17
150000	13274.75	7008.60	4928.59	3895.07	3280.10	2588.13	2376.54	2087.54	1902.59

MONTHLY PAYMENT 11¼%
NECESSARY TO AMORTIZE A LOAN

AMOUNT	15 YEARS	18 YEARS	20 YEARS	25 YEARS	28 YEARS	29 YEARS	30 YEARS	35 YEARS	40 YEARS
$ 50	.58	.55	.53	.50	.50	.49	.49	.48	.48
100	1.16	1.09	1.05	1.00	.99	.98	.98	.96	.95
200	2.31	2.17	2.10	2.00	1.97	1.96	1.95	1.92	1.90
300	3.46	3.25	3.15	3.00	2.95	2.93	2.92	2.87	2.85
400	4.61	4.33	4.20	4.00	3.93	3.91	3.89	3.83	3.80
500	5.77	5.41	5.25	5.00	4.91	4.88	4.86	4.79	4.75
600	6.92	6.49	6.30	5.99	5.89	5.86	5.83	5.74	5.69
700	8.07	7.58	7.35	6.99	6.87	6.83	6.80	6.70	6.64
800	9.22	8.66	8.40	7.99	7.85	7.81	7.78	7.66	7.59
900	10.38	9.74	9.45	8.99	8.83	8.78	8.75	8.61	8.54
1000	11.53	10.82	10.50	9.99	9.81	9.76	9.72	9.57	9.49
2000	23.05	21.64	20.99	19.97	19.61	19.51	19.43	19.13	18.97
3000	34.58	32.45	31.48	29.95	29.41	29.27	29.14	28.70	28.45
4000	46.10	43.27	41.98	39.93	39.21	39.02	38.86	38.26	37.94
5000	57.62	54.09	52.47	49.92	49.01	48.78	48.57	47.83	47.42
6000	69.15	64.90	62.96	59.90	58.81	58.53	58.28	57.39	56.90
7000	80.67	75.72	73.45	69.88	68.61	68.28	67.99	66.96	66.38
8000	92.19	86.53	83.95	79.86	78.41	78.04	77.71	76.52	75.87
9000	103.72	97.35	94.44	89.85	88.22	87.79	87.42	86.09	85.35
10000	115.24	108.17	104.93	99.83	98.02	97.55	97.13	95.65	94.83
15000	172.86	162.25	157.39	149.74	147.02	146.32	145.69	143.48	142.24
20000	230.47	216.33	209.86	199.65	196.03	195.09	194.26	191.30	189.66
25000	288.09	270.41	262.32	249.56	245.04	243.86	242.82	239.13	237.07
30000	345.71	324.49	314.78	299.48	294.04	292.63	291.38	286.95	284.48
35000	403.33	378.57	367.24	349.39	343.05	341.40	339.95	334.78	331.90
40000	460.94	432.65	419.71	399.30	392.05	390.17	388.51	382.60	379.31
45000	518.56	486.73	472.17	449.21	441.06	438.95	437.07	430.43	426.72
46000	530.08	497.55	482.66	459.20	450.86	448.70	446.79	439.99	436.20
47000	541.61	508.37	493.16	469.18	460.66	458.45	456.50	449.56	445.69
48000	553.13	519.18	503.65	479.16	470.46	468.21	466.21	459.12	455.17
49000	564.65	530.00	514.14	489.14	480.26	477.96	475.92	468.69	464.65
50000	576.18	540.82	524.63	499.12	490.07	487.72	485.64	478.25	474.13
51000	587.70	551.63	535.13	509.11	499.87	497.47	495.35	487.82	483.62
52000	599.22	562.45	545.62	519.09	509.67	507.23	505.06	497.38	493.10
53000	610.75	573.26	556.11	529.07	519.47	516.98	514.77	506.95	502.58
54000	622.27	584.08	566.60	539.05	529.27	526.73	524.49	516.51	512.06
55000	633.79	594.90	577.10	549.04	539.07	536.49	534.20	526.08	521.55
56000	645.32	605.71	587.59	559.02	548.87	546.24	543.91	535.64	531.03
57000	656.84	616.53	598.08	569.00	558.67	556.00	553.62	545.21	540.51
58000	668.36	627.34	608.57	578.98	568.48	565.75	563.34	554.77	549.99
59000	679.89	638.16	619.07	588.97	578.28	575.50	573.05	564.34	559.48
60000	691.41	648.98	629.56	598.95	588.08	585.26	582.76	573.90	568.96
61000	702.94	659.79	640.05	608.93	597.88	595.01	592.47	583.47	578.44
62000	714.46	670.61	650.54	618.91	607.68	604.77	602.19	593.03	587.92
63000	725.98	681.43	661.04	628.90	617.48	614.52	611.90	602.60	597.41
64000	737.51	692.24	671.53	638.88	627.28	624.28	621.61	612.16	606.89
65000	749.03	703.06	682.02	648.86	637.08	634.03	631.32	621.73	616.37
67500	777.84	730.10	708.25	673.82	661.59	658.42	655.61	645.64	640.08
70000	806.65	757.14	734.48	698.77	686.09	682.80	679.89	669.55	663.79
75000	864.26	811.22	786.95	748.68	735.10	731.57	728.45	717.38	711.20
80000	921.88	865.30	839.41	798.60	784.10	780.34	777.01	765.20	758.61
85000	979.50	919.38	891.87	848.51	833.11	829.11	825.58	813.02	806.02
90000	1037.12	973.46	944.34	898.42	882.11	877.89	874.14	860.85	853.44
95000	1094.73	1027.54	996.80	948.33	931.12	926.66	922.70	908.67	900.85
100000	1152.35	1081.63	1049.26	998.24	980.13	975.43	971.27	956.50	948.26
105000	1209.97	1135.71	1101.72	1048.16	1029.13	1024.20	1019.83	1004.32	995.68
110000	1267.58	1189.79	1154.19	1098.07	1078.14	1072.97	1068.39	1052.15	1043.09
115000	1325.20	1243.87	1206.65	1147.98	1127.14	1121.74	1116.96	1099.97	1090.50
120000	1382.82	1297.95	1259.11	1197.89	1176.15	1170.51	1165.52	1147.80	1137.91
125000	1440.44	1352.03	1311.58	1247.80	1225.16	1219.28	1214.08	1195.62	1185.33
130000	1498.05	1406.11	1364.04	1297.72	1274.16	1268.06	1262.64	1243.45	1232.74
135000	1555.67	1460.19	1416.50	1347.63	1323.17	1316.83	1311.21	1291.27	1280.15
140000	1613.29	1514.27	1468.96	1397.54	1372.17	1365.60	1359.77	1339.10	1327.57
145000	1670.90	1568.35	1521.43	1447.45	1421.18	1414.37	1408.33	1386.92	1374.98
150000	1728.52	1622.44	1573.89	1497.36	1470.19	1463.14	1456.90	1434.75	1422.39

11⅜% MONTHLY PAYMENT
NECESSARY TO AMORTIZE A LOAN

AMOUNT	1 YEAR	2 YEARS	3 YEARS	4 YEARS	5 YEARS	7 YEARS	8 YEARS	10 YEARS	12 YEARS
$ 50	4.43	2.34	1.65	1.31	1.10	.87	.80	.70	.64
100	8.86	4.68	3.30	2.61	2.20	1.74	1.60	1.40	1.28
200	17.72	9.36	6.59	5.21	4.39	3.47	3.19	2.80	2.56
300	26.57	14.04	9.88	7.81	6.58	5.20	4.78	4.20	3.83
400	35.43	18.72	13.17	10.42	8.78	6.93	6.37	5.60	5.11
500	44.28	23.40	16.46	13.02	10.97	8.67	7.96	7.00	6.38
600	53.14	28.07	19.75	15.62	13.16	10.40	9.55	8.40	7.66
700	61.99	32.75	23.05	18.22	15.36	12.13	11.14	9.80	8.94
800	70.85	37.43	26.34	20.83	17.55	13.86	12.73	11.20	10.21
900	79.71	42.11	29.63	23.43	19.74	15.59	14.33	12.59	11.49
1000	88.56	46.79	32.92	26.03	21.93	17.33	15.92	13.99	12.76
2000	177.12	93.57	65.84	52.06	43.86	34.65	31.83	27.98	25.52
3000	265.68	140.35	98.75	78.09	65.79	51.97	47.74	41.97	38.28
4000	354.23	187.13	131.67	104.12	87.72	69.29	63.65	55.96	51.04
5000	442.79	233.92	164.59	130.15	109.65	86.61	79.56	69.95	63.80
6000	531.35	280.70	197.50	156.17	131.58	103.93	95.47	83.93	76.56
7000	619.90	327.48	230.42	182.20	153.51	121.25	111.38	97.92	89.31
8000	708.46	374.26	263.34	208.23	175.44	138.57	127.30	111.91	102.07
9000	797.02	421.04	296.25	234.26	197.37	155.89	143.21	125.90	114.83
10000	885.57	467.83	329.17	260.29	219.30	173.21	159.12	139.89	127.59
15000	1328.36	701.74	493.75	390.43	328.95	259.81	238.68	209.83	191.38
20000	1771.14	935.65	658.34	520.57	438.60	346.41	318.23	279.77	255.17
25000	2213.92	1169.56	822.92	650.71	548.25	433.01	397.79	349.71	318.97
30000	2656.71	1403.47	987.50	780.85	657.90	519.61	477.35	419.65	382.76
35000	3099.49	1637.38	1152.09	910.99	767.55	606.21	556.90	489.59	446.55
40000	3542.27	1871.29	1316.67	1041.13	877.20	692.81	636.46	559.53	510.34
45000	3985.06	2105.20	1481.25	1171.27	986.85	779.42	716.02	629.47	574.13
46000	4073.61	2151.98	1514.17	1197.29	1008.78	796.74	731.93	643.46	586.89
47000	4162.17	2198.77	1547.08	1223.32	1030.71	814.06	747.84	657.45	599.65
48000	4250.73	2245.55	1580.00	1249.35	1052.64	831.38	763.75	671.44	612.41
49000	4339.28	2292.33	1612.92	1275.38	1074.57	848.70	779.66	685.42	625.17
50000	4427.84	2339.11	1645.83	1301.41	1096.50	866.02	795.57	699.41	637.93
51000	4516.40	2385.89	1678.75	1327.43	1118.43	883.34	811.49	713.40	650.69
52000	4604.95	2432.68	1711.67	1353.46	1140.36	900.66	827.40	727.39	663.44
53000	4693.51	2479.46	1744.58	1379.49	1162.29	917.98	843.31	741.38	676.20
54000	4782.07	2526.24	1777.50	1405.52	1184.22	935.30	859.22	755.36	688.96
55000	4870.62	2573.02	1810.42	1431.55	1206.15	952.62	875.13	769.35	701.72
56000	4959.18	2619.80	1843.33	1457.57	1228.08	969.94	891.04	783.34	714.48
57000	5047.74	2666.59	1876.25	1483.60	1250.01	987.26	906.95	797.33	727.24
58000	5136.29	2713.37	1909.17	1509.63	1271.94	1004.58	922.87	811.32	739.99
59000	5224.85	2760.15	1942.08	1535.66	1293.87	1021.90	938.78	825.30	752.75
60000	5313.41	2806.93	1975.00	1561.69	1315.80	1039.22	954.69	839.29	765.51
61000	5401.96	2853.72	2007.92	1587.71	1337.73	1056.54	970.60	853.28	778.27
62000	5490.52	2900.50	2040.83	1613.74	1359.66	1073.86	986.51	867.27	791.03
63000	5579.08	2947.28	2073.75	1639.77	1381.59	1091.18	1002.42	881.26	803.79
64000	5667.63	2994.06	2106.67	1665.80	1403.52	1108.50	1018.33	895.25	816.55
65000	5756.19	3040.84	2139.58	1691.83	1425.45	1125.82	1034.25	909.23	829.30
67500	5977.58	3157.80	2221.87	1756.90	1480.27	1169.12	1074.02	944.20	861.20
70000	6198.97	3274.75	2304.17	1821.97	1535.10	1212.42	1113.80	979.17	893.10
75000	6641.76	3508.66	2468.75	1952.11	1644.75	1299.02	1193.36	1049.11	956.89
80000	7084.54	3742.58	2633.33	2082.25	1754.40	1385.62	1272.92	1119.06	1020.68
85000	7527.32	3976.49	2797.92	2212.39	1864.05	1472.23	1352.47	1189.00	1084.47
90000	7970.11	4210.40	2962.50	2342.53	1973.70	1558.83	1432.03	1258.94	1148.26
95000	8412.89	4444.31	3127.08	2472.67	2083.35	1645.43	1511.59	1328.88	1212.06
100000	8855.67	4678.22	3291.66	2602.81	2193.00	1732.03	1591.14	1398.82	1275.85
105000	9298.46	4912.13	3456.25	2732.95	2302.65	1818.63	1670.70	1468.76	1339.64
110000	9741.24	5146.04	3620.83	2863.09	2412.29	1905.23	1750.26	1538.70	1403.43
115000	10184.02	5379.95	3785.41	2993.23	2521.94	1991.83	1829.82	1608.64	1467.23
120000	10626.81	5613.86	3950.00	3123.37	2631.59	2078.43	1909.37	1678.58	1531.02
125000	11069.59	5847.77	4114.58	3253.51	2741.24	2165.04	1988.93	1748.52	1594.81
130000	11512.37	6081.68	4279.16	3383.65	2850.89	2251.64	2068.49	1818.46	1658.60
135000	11955.16	6315.59	4443.74	3513.79	2960.54	2338.24	2148.04	1888.40	1722.39
140000	12397.94	6549.50	4608.33	3643.93	3070.19	2424.84	2227.60	1958.34	1786.19
145000	12840.72	6783.41	4772.91	3774.07	3179.84	2511.44	2307.16	2028.28	1849.98
150000	13283.51	7017.32	4937.49	3904.21	3289.49	2598.04	2386.71	2098.22	1913.77

MONTHLY PAYMENT 11⅜%
NECESSARY TO AMORTIZE A LOAN

AMOUNT	15 YEARS	18 YEARS	20 YEARS	25 YEARS	28 YEARS	29 YEARS	30 YEARS	35 YEARS	40 YEARS
$ 50	.59	.55	.53	.51	.50	.50	.50	.49	.48
100	1.17	1.09	1.06	1.01	.99	.99	.99	.97	.96
200	2.33	2.18	2.12	2.02	1.98	1.97	1.97	1.94	1.92
300	3.49	3.27	3.18	3.03	2.97	2.96	2.95	2.90	2.88
400	4.65	4.36	4.24	4.03	3.96	3.94	3.93	3.87	3.84
500	5.81	5.45	5.29	5.04	4.95	4.93	4.91	4.84	4.80
600	6.97	6.54	6.35	6.05	5.94	5.91	5.89	5.80	5.75
700	8.13	7.63	7.41	7.06	6.93	6.90	6.87	6.77	6.71
800	9.29	8.72	8.47	8.06	7.92	7.88	7.85	7.74	7.67
900	10.45	9.81	9.53	9.07	8.91	8.87	8.83	8.70	8.63
1000	11.61	10.90	10.58	10.08	9.90	9.85	9.81	9.67	9.59
2000	23.21	21.80	21.16	20.15	19.79	19.70	19.62	19.33	19.17
3000	34.81	32.70	31.74	30.23	29.69	29.55	29.43	28.99	28.75
4000	46.42	43.60	42.32	40.30	39.58	39.40	39.24	38.66	38.34
5000	58.02	54.50	52.90	50.37	49.48	49.25	49.04	48.32	47.92
6000	69.62	65.40	63.47	60.45	59.37	59.10	58.85	57.98	57.50
7000	81.22	76.30	74.05	70.52	69.27	68.94	68.66	67.65	67.08
8000	92.83	87.20	84.63	80.59	79.16	78.79	78.47	77.31	76.67
9000	104.43	98.10	95.21	90.67	89.06	88.64	88.27	86.97	86.25
10000	116.03	109.00	105.79	100.74	98.95	98.49	98.08	96.63	95.83
15000	174.04	163.50	158.68	151.11	148.43	147.73	147.12	144.95	143.74
20000	232.06	217.99	211.57	201.47	197.90	196.98	196.16	193.26	191.66
25000	290.07	272.49	264.46	251.84	247.37	246.22	245.20	241.58	239.57
30000	348.08	326.99	317.35	302.21	296.85	295.46	294.23	289.89	287.48
35000	406.09	381.49	370.25	352.57	346.32	344.70	343.27	338.21	335.40
40000	464.11	435.98	423.14	402.94	395.80	393.95	392.31	386.52	383.31
45000	522.12	490.48	476.03	453.31	445.27	443.19	441.35	434.84	431.22
46000	533.72	501.38	486.61	463.38	455.17	453.04	451.16	444.50	440.81
47000	545.32	512.28	497.18	473.46	465.06	462.89	460.96	454.16	450.39
48000	556.93	523.18	507.76	483.53	474.95	472.74	470.77	463.82	459.97
49000	568.53	534.08	518.34	493.60	484.85	482.58	480.58	473.49	469.55
50000	580.13	544.98	528.92	503.68	494.74	492.43	490.39	483.15	479.14
51000	591.74	555.88	539.50	513.75	504.64	502.28	500.20	492.81	488.72
52000	603.34	566.78	550.08	523.82	514.53	512.13	510.00	502.48	498.30
53000	614.94	577.68	560.65	533.90	524.43	521.98	519.81	512.14	507.88
54000	626.54	588.58	571.23	543.97	534.32	531.83	529.62	521.80	517.47
55000	638.15	599.47	581.81	554.04	544.22	541.68	539.43	531.47	527.05
56000	649.75	610.37	592.39	564.12	554.11	551.52	549.23	541.13	536.63
57000	661.35	621.27	602.97	574.19	564.01	561.37	559.04	550.79	546.21
58000	672.95	632.17	613.55	584.26	573.90	571.22	568.85	560.45	555.80
59000	684.56	643.07	624.12	594.34	583.80	581.07	578.66	570.12	565.38
60000	696.16	653.97	634.70	604.41	593.69	590.92	588.46	579.78	574.96
61000	707.76	664.87	645.28	614.48	603.59	600.77	598.27	589.44	584.54
62000	719.36	675.77	655.86	624.56	613.48	610.62	608.08	599.11	594.13
63000	730.97	686.67	666.44	634.63	623.38	620.46	617.89	608.77	603.71
64000	742.57	697.57	677.02	644.70	633.27	630.31	627.69	618.43	613.29
65000	754.17	708.47	687.59	654.78	643.17	640.16	637.50	628.09	622.88
67500	783.18	735.72	714.04	679.96	667.90	664.78	662.02	652.25	646.83
70000	812.18	762.97	740.49	705.14	692.64	689.40	686.54	676.41	670.79
75000	870.20	817.46	793.38	755.51	742.11	738.65	735.58	724.72	718.70
80000	928.21	871.96	846.27	805.88	791.59	787.89	784.62	773.04	766.61
85000	986.22	926.46	899.16	856.25	841.06	837.13	833.66	821.35	814.53
90000	1044.23	980.96	952.05	906.61	890.54	886.38	882.69	869.67	862.44
95000	1102.25	1035.45	1004.94	956.98	940.01	935.62	931.73	917.98	910.35
100000	1160.26	1089.95	1057.83	1007.35	989.48	984.86	980.77	966.30	958.27
105000	1218.27	1144.45	1110.73	1057.71	1038.96	1034.10	1029.81	1014.61	1006.18
110000	1276.29	1198.94	1163.62	1108.08	1088.43	1083.35	1078.85	1062.93	1054.09
115000	1334.30	1253.44	1216.51	1158.45	1137.91	1132.59	1127.88	1111.24	1102.01
120000	1392.31	1307.94	1269.40	1208.81	1187.38	1181.83	1176.92	1159.55	1149.92
125000	1450.32	1362.44	1322.29	1259.18	1236.85	1231.08	1225.96	1207.87	1197.83
130000	1508.34	1416.93	1375.18	1309.55	1286.33	1280.32	1275.00	1256.18	1245.75
135000	1566.35	1471.43	1428.08	1359.92	1335.80	1329.56	1324.04	1304.50	1293.66
140000	1624.36	1525.93	1480.97	1410.28	1385.27	1378.80	1373.08	1352.81	1341.57
145000	1682.37	1580.43	1533.86	1460.65	1434.75	1428.05	1422.11	1401.13	1389.49
150000	1740.39	1634.92	1586.75	1511.02	1484.22	1477.29	1471.15	1449.44	1437.40

11½% MONTHLY PAYMENT
NECESSARY TO AMORTIZE A LOAN

AMOUNT	1 YEAR	2 YEARS	3 YEARS	4 YEARS	5 YEARS	7 YEARS	8 YEARS	10 YEARS	12 YEARS
$ 50	4.44	2.35	1.65	1.31	1.10	.87	.80	.71	.65
100	8.87	4.69	3.30	2.61	2.20	1.74	1.60	1.41	1.29
200	17.73	9.37	6.60	5.22	4.40	3.48	3.20	2.82	2.57
300	26.59	14.06	9.90	7.83	6.60	5.22	4.80	4.22	3.85
400	35.45	18.74	13.20	10.44	8.80	6.96	6.40	5.63	5.14
500	44.31	23.43	16.49	13.05	11.00	8.70	7.99	7.03	6.42
600	53.17	28.11	19.79	15.66	13.20	10.44	9.59	8.44	7.70
700	62.04	32.79	23.09	18.27	15.40	12.18	11.19	9.85	8.99
800	70.90	37.48	26.39	20.88	17.60	13.91	12.79	11.25	10.27
900	79.76	42.16	29.68	23.49	19.80	15.65	14.39	12.66	11.55
1000	88.62	46.85	32.98	26.09	22.00	17.39	15.98	14.06	12.84
2000	177.24	93.69	65.96	52.18	43.99	34.78	31.96	28.12	25.67
3000	265.85	140.53	98.93	78.27	65.98	52.16	47.94	42.18	38.50
4000	354.47	187.37	131.91	104.36	87.98	69.55	63.92	56.24	51.34
5000	443.08	234.21	164.89	130.45	109.97	86.94	79.90	70.30	64.17
6000	531.70	281.05	197.86	156.54	131.96	104.32	95.88	84.36	77.00
7000	620.31	327.89	230.84	182.63	153.95	121.71	111.86	98.42	89.84
8000	708.93	374.73	263.81	208.72	175.95	139.10	127.84	112.48	102.67
9000	797.54	421.57	296.79	234.81	197.94	156.48	143.82	126.54	115.50
10000	886.16	468.41	329.77	260.90	219.93	173.87	159.80	140.60	128.34
15000	1329.23	702.61	494.65	391.34	329.89	260.80	239.70	210.90	192.50
20000	1772.31	936.81	659.53	521.79	439.86	347.73	319.59	281.20	256.67
25000	2215.38	1171.01	824.41	652.23	549.82	434.67	399.49	351.49	320.83
30000	2658.46	1405.21	989.29	782.68	659.78	521.60	479.39	421.79	385.00
35000	3101.53	1639.42	1154.17	913.12	769.75	608.53	559.28	492.09	449.17
40000	3544.61	1873.62	1319.05	1043.57	879.71	695.46	639.18	562.39	513.33
45000	3987.68	2107.82	1483.93	1174.01	989.67	782.40	719.08	632.68	577.50
46000	4076.30	2154.66	1516.90	1200.10	1011.66	799.78	735.06	646.74	590.33
47000	4164.91	2201.50	1549.88	1226.19	1033.66	817.17	751.04	660.80	603.16
48000	4253.53	2248.34	1582.85	1252.28	1055.65	834.56	767.01	674.86	616.00
49000	4342.14	2295.18	1615.83	1278.37	1077.64	851.94	782.99	688.92	628.83
50000	4430.76	2342.02	1648.81	1304.46	1099.64	869.33	798.97	702.98	641.66
51000	4519.37	2388.86	1681.78	1330.54	1121.63	886.71	814.95	717.04	654.50
52000	4607.99	2435.70	1714.76	1356.63	1143.62	904.10	830.93	731.10	667.33
53000	4696.60	2482.54	1747.73	1382.72	1165.61	921.49	846.91	745.16	680.16
54000	4785.22	2529.38	1780.71	1408.81	1187.61	938.87	862.89	759.22	693.00
55000	4873.83	2576.22	1813.69	1434.90	1209.60	956.26	878.87	773.28	705.83
56000	4962.45	2623.06	1846.66	1460.99	1231.59	973.65	894.85	787.34	718.66
57000	5051.06	2669.90	1879.64	1487.08	1253.58	991.03	910.83	801.40	731.50
58000	5139.68	2716.74	1912.61	1513.17	1275.58	1008.42	926.81	815.46	744.33
59000	5228.29	2763.58	1945.59	1539.26	1297.57	1025.81	942.79	829.52	757.16
60000	5316.91	2810.42	1978.57	1565.35	1319.56	1043.19	958.77	843.58	769.99
61000	5405.52	2857.26	2011.54	1591.43	1341.55	1060.58	974.75	857.64	782.83
62000	5494.14	2904.10	2044.52	1617.52	1363.55	1077.97	990.73	871.70	795.66
63000	5582.75	2950.94	2077.49	1643.61	1385.54	1095.35	1006.71	885.76	808.49
64000	5671.37	2997.79	2110.47	1669.70	1407.53	1112.74	1022.68	899.82	821.33
65000	5759.98	3044.63	2143.45	1695.79	1429.52	1130.12	1038.66	913.88	834.16
67500	5981.52	3161.73	2225.89	1761.01	1484.51	1173.59	1078.61	949.02	866.24
70000	6203.06	3278.83	2308.33	1826.24	1539.49	1217.06	1118.56	984.17	898.33
75000	6646.13	3513.03	2473.21	1956.68	1649.45	1303.99	1198.46	1054.47	962.49
80000	7089.21	3747.23	2638.09	2087.13	1759.41	1390.92	1278.35	1124.77	1026.66
85000	7532.28	3981.43	2802.97	2217.57	1869.38	1477.85	1358.25	1195.07	1090.82
90000	7975.36	4215.63	2967.85	2348.02	1979.34	1564.79	1438.15	1265.36	1154.99
95000	8418.44	4449.83	3132.73	2478.46	2089.30	1651.72	1518.05	1335.66	1219.16
100000	8861.51	4684.04	3297.61	2608.91	2199.27	1738.65	1597.94	1405.96	1283.32
105000	9304.59	4918.24	3462.49	2739.35	2309.23	1825.58	1677.84	1476.26	1347.49
110000	9747.66	5152.44	3627.37	2869.80	2419.19	1912.52	1757.74	1546.55	1411.65
115000	10190.74	5386.64	3792.25	3000.24	2529.15	1999.45	1837.63	1616.85	1475.82
120000	10633.81	5620.84	3957.13	3130.69	2639.12	2086.38	1917.53	1687.15	1539.98
125000	11076.89	5855.04	4122.01	3261.13	2749.08	2173.31	1997.43	1757.45	1604.15
130000	11519.96	6089.25	4286.89	3391.58	2859.04	2260.24	2077.32	1827.75	1668.32
135000	11963.04	6323.45	4451.77	3522.02	2969.01	2347.18	2157.22	1898.04	1732.48
140000	12406.11	6557.65	4616.65	3652.47	3078.97	2434.11	2237.12	1968.34	1796.65
145000	12849.19	6791.85	4781.53	3782.91	3188.93	2521.04	2317.01	2038.64	1860.81
150000	13292.26	7026.05	4946.41	3913.36	3298.90	2607.97	2396.91	2108.94	1924.98

MONTHLY PAYMENT 11½%
NECESSARY TO AMORTIZE A LOAN

AMOUNT	15 YEARS	18 YEARS	20 YEARS	25 YEARS	28 YEARS	29 YEARS	30 YEARS	35 YEARS	40 YEARS
$ 50	.59	.55	.54	.51	.50	.50	.50	.49	.49
100	1.17	1.10	1.07	1.02	1.00	1.00	1.00	.98	.97
200	2.34	2.20	2.14	2.04	2.00	1.99	1.99	1.96	1.94
300	3.51	3.30	3.20	3.05	3.00	2.99	2.98	2.93	2.91
400	4.68	4.40	4.27	4.07	4.00	3.98	3.97	3.91	3.88
500	5.85	5.50	5.34	5.09	5.00	4.98	4.96	4.89	4.85
600	7.01	6.59	6.40	6.10	6.00	5.97	5.95	5.86	5.81
700	8.18	7.69	7.47	7.12	7.00	6.97	6.94	6.84	6.78
800	9.35	8.79	8.54	8.14	8.00	7.96	7.93	7.81	7.75
900	10.52	9.89	9.60	9.15	8.99	8.95	8.92	8.79	8.72
1000	11.69	10.99	10.67	10.17	9.99	9.95	9.91	9.77	9.69
2000	23.37	21.97	21.33	20.33	19.98	19.89	19.81	19.53	19.37
3000	35.05	32.95	32.00	30.50	29.97	29.83	29.71	29.29	29.05
4000	46.73	43.94	42.66	40.66	39.96	39.78	39.62	39.05	38.74
5000	58.41	54.92	53.33	50.83	49.95	49.72	49.52	48.81	48.42
6000	70.10	65.90	63.99	60.99	59.94	59.66	59.42	58.57	58.10
7000	81.78	76.89	74.66	71.16	69.93	69.61	69.33	68.33	67.78
8000	93.46	87.87	85.32	81.32	79.91	79.55	79.23	78.09	77.47
9000	105.14	98.85	95.98	91.49	89.90	89.49	89.13	87.85	87.15
10000	116.82	109.83	106.65	101.65	99.89	99.44	99.03	97.62	96.83
15000	175.23	164.75	159.97	152.48	149.83	149.15	148.55	146.42	145.25
20000	233.64	219.66	213.29	203.30	199.78	198.87	198.06	195.23	193.66
25000	292.05	274.58	266.61	254.12	249.72	248.58	247.58	244.03	242.08
30000	350.46	329.49	319.93	304.95	299.66	298.30	297.09	292.84	290.49
35000	408.87	384.41	373.26	355.77	349.61	348.01	346.61	341.64	338.90
40000	467.28	439.32	426.58	406.59	399.55	397.73	396.12	390.45	387.32
45000	525.69	494.24	479.90	457.42	449.49	447.45	445.64	439.25	435.73
46000	537.37	505.22	490.56	467.58	459.48	457.39	455.54	449.01	445.41
47000	549.05	516.20	501.23	477.75	469.47	467.33	465.44	458.78	455.10
48000	560.74	527.19	511.89	487.91	479.46	477.27	475.34	468.54	464.78
49000	572.42	538.17	522.56	498.07	489.45	487.22	485.25	478.30	474.46
50000	584.10	549.15	533.22	508.24	499.43	497.16	495.15	488.06	484.15
51000	595.78	560.14	543.88	518.40	509.42	507.10	505.05	497.82	493.83
52000	607.46	571.12	554.55	528.57	519.41	517.05	514.96	507.58	503.51
53000	619.15	582.10	565.21	538.73	529.40	526.99	524.86	517.34	513.19
54000	630.83	593.08	575.88	548.90	539.39	536.93	534.76	527.10	522.88
55000	642.51	604.07	586.54	559.06	549.38	546.88	544.67	536.86	532.56
56000	654.19	615.05	597.21	569.23	559.37	556.82	554.57	546.63	542.24
57000	665.87	626.03	607.87	579.39	569.35	566.76	564.47	556.39	551.93
58000	677.56	637.02	618.53	589.56	579.34	576.71	574.37	566.15	561.61
59000	689.24	648.00	629.20	599.72	589.33	586.65	584.28	575.91	571.29
60000	700.92	658.98	639.86	609.89	599.32	596.59	594.18	585.67	580.97
61000	712.60	669.97	650.53	620.05	609.31	606.54	604.08	595.43	590.66
62000	724.28	680.95	661.19	630.22	619.30	616.48	613.99	605.19	600.34
63000	735.96	691.93	671.86	640.38	629.29	626.42	623.89	614.95	610.02
64000	747.65	702.91	682.52	650.55	639.28	636.36	633.79	624.71	619.71
65000	759.33	713.90	693.18	660.71	649.26	646.31	643.69	634.47	629.39
67500	788.53	741.35	719.85	686.12	674.24	671.17	668.45	658.88	653.60
70000	817.74	768.81	746.51	711.53	699.21	696.02	693.21	683.28	677.80
75000	876.15	823.73	799.83	762.36	749.15	745.74	742.72	732.09	726.22
80000	934.56	878.64	853.15	813.18	799.09	795.45	792.24	780.89	774.63
85000	992.97	933.56	906.47	864.00	849.04	845.17	841.75	829.70	823.04
90000	1051.38	988.47	959.79	914.83	898.98	894.89	891.27	878.50	871.46
95000	1109.79	1043.39	1013.11	965.65	948.92	944.60	940.78	927.31	919.87
100000	1168.19	1098.30	1066.43	1016.47	998.86	994.32	990.30	976.11	968.29
105000	1226.60	1153.22	1119.76	1067.30	1048.81	1044.03	1039.81	1024.92	1016.70
110000	1285.01	1208.13	1173.08	1118.12	1098.75	1093.75	1089.33	1073.72	1065.12
115000	1343.42	1263.04	1226.40	1168.94	1148.69	1143.46	1138.84	1122.53	1113.53
120000	1401.83	1317.96	1279.72	1219.77	1198.64	1193.18	1188.35	1171.33	1161.94
125000	1460.24	1372.87	1333.04	1270.59	1248.58	1242.90	1237.87	1220.14	1210.36
130000	1518.65	1427.79	1386.36	1321.41	1298.52	1292.61	1287.38	1268.94	1258.77
135000	1577.06	1482.70	1439.69	1372.24	1348.47	1342.33	1336.90	1317.75	1307.19
140000	1635.47	1537.62	1493.01	1423.06	1398.41	1392.04	1386.41	1366.56	1355.60
145000	1693.88	1592.53	1546.33	1473.88	1448.35	1441.76	1435.93	1415.36	1404.01
150000	1752.29	1647.45	1599.65	1524.71	1498.29	1491.47	1485.44	1464.17	1452.43

11⅝ % MONTHLY PAYMENT
NECESSARY TO AMORTIZE A LOAN

AMOUNT	1 YEAR	2 YEARS	3 YEARS	4 YEARS	5 YEARS	7 YEARS	8 YEARS	10 YEARS	12 YEARS
$ 50	4.44	2.35	1.66	1.31	1.11	.88	.81	.71	.65
100	8.87	4.69	3.31	2.62	2.21	1.75	1.61	1.42	1.30
200	17.74	9.38	6.61	5.24	4.42	3.50	3.21	2.83	2.59
300	26.61	14.07	9.92	7.85	6.62	5.24	4.82	4.24	3.88
400	35.47	18.76	13.22	10.47	8.83	6.99	6.42	5.66	5.17
500	44.34	23.45	16.52	13.08	11.03	8.73	8.03	7.07	6.46
600	53.21	28.14	19.83	15.70	13.24	10.48	9.63	8.48	7.75
700	62.08	32.83	23.13	18.31	15.44	12.22	11.24	9.90	9.04
800	70.94	37.52	26.43	20.93	17.65	13.97	12.84	11.31	10.33
900	79.81	42.21	29.74	23.54	19.85	15.71	14.45	12.72	11.62
1000	88.68	46.90	33.04	26.16	22.06	17.46	16.05	14.14	12.91
2000	177.35	93.80	66.08	52.31	44.12	34.91	32.10	28.27	25.82
3000	266.03	140.70	99.11	78.46	66.17	52.36	48.15	42.40	38.73
4000	354.70	187.60	132.15	104.61	88.23	69.82	64.20	56.53	51.64
5000	443.37	234.50	165.18	130.76	110.28	87.27	80.24	70.66	64.55
6000	532.05	281.40	198.22	156.91	132.34	104.72	96.29	84.79	77.45
7000	620.72	328.29	231.25	183.06	154.39	122.17	112.34	98.92	90.36
8000	709.39	375.19	264.29	209.21	176.45	139.63	128.39	113.05	103.27
9000	798.07	422.09	297.32	235.36	198.50	157.08	144.43	127.19	116.18
10000	886.74	468.99	330.36	261.51	220.56	174.53	160.48	141.32	129.09
15000	1330.11	703.48	495.54	392.26	330.84	261.80	240.72	211.97	193.63
20000	1773.47	937.98	660.71	523.01	441.11	349.06	320.96	282.63	258.17
25000	2216.84	1172.47	825.89	653.76	551.39	436.33	401.19	353.28	322.71
30000	2660.21	1406.96	991.07	784.51	661.67	523.59	481.43	423.94	387.25
35000	3103.58	1641.45	1156.25	915.26	771.94	610.85	561.67	494.60	451.79
40000	3546.94	1875.95	1321.42	1046.01	882.22	698.12	641.91	565.25	516.33
45000	3990.31	2110.44	1486.60	1176.76	992.50	785.38	722.14	635.91	580.87
46000	4078.98	2157.34	1519.64	1202.91	1014.55	802.83	738.19	650.04	593.78
47000	4167.66	2204.24	1552.67	1229.06	1036.61	820.29	754.24	664.17	606.69
48000	4256.33	2251.13	1585.71	1255.21	1058.66	837.74	770.29	678.30	619.59
49000	4345.00	2298.03	1618.74	1281.36	1080.72	855.19	786.33	692.43	632.50
50000	4433.68	2344.93	1651.78	1307.51	1102.78	872.65	802.38	706.56	645.41
51000	4522.35	2391.83	1684.81	1333.66	1124.83	890.10	818.43	720.69	658.32
52000	4611.02	2438.73	1717.85	1359.81	1146.89	907.55	834.48	734.82	671.23
53000	4699.70	2485.63	1750.89	1385.96	1168.94	925.00	850.52	748.96	684.13
54000	4788.37	2532.53	1783.92	1412.11	1191.00	942.46	866.57	763.09	697.04
55000	4877.05	2579.42	1816.96	1438.26	1213.05	959.91	882.62	777.22	709.95
56000	4965.72	2626.32	1849.99	1464.41	1235.11	977.36	898.67	791.35	722.86
57000	5054.39	2673.22	1883.03	1490.56	1257.16	994.82	914.71	805.48	735.77
58000	5143.07	2720.12	1916.06	1516.71	1279.22	1012.27	930.76	819.61	748.68
59000	5231.74	2767.02	1949.10	1542.86	1301.27	1029.72	946.81	833.74	761.58
60000	5320.41	2813.92	1982.13	1569.01	1323.33	1047.17	962.86	847.87	774.49
61000	5409.09	2860.82	2015.17	1595.16	1345.39	1064.63	978.90	862.01	787.40
62000	5497.76	2907.71	2048.21	1621.31	1367.44	1082.08	994.95	876.14	800.31
63000	5586.43	2954.61	2081.24	1647.46	1389.50	1099.53	1011.00	890.27	813.22
64000	5675.11	3001.51	2114.28	1673.61	1411.55	1116.99	1027.05	904.40	826.12
65000	5763.78	3048.41	2147.31	1699.76	1433.61	1134.44	1043.09	918.53	839.03
67500	5985.46	3165.66	2229.90	1765.14	1488.75	1178.07	1083.21	953.86	871.30
70000	6207.15	3282.90	2312.49	1830.51	1543.88	1221.70	1123.33	989.19	903.57
75000	6650.51	3517.40	2477.67	1961.26	1654.16	1308.97	1203.57	1059.84	968.11
80000	7093.88	3751.89	2642.84	2092.01	1764.44	1396.23	1283.81	1130.50	1032.65
85000	7537.25	3986.38	2808.02	2222.76	1874.72	1483.49	1364.04	1201.15	1097.19
90000	7980.62	4220.87	2973.20	2353.51	1984.99	1570.76	1444.28	1271.81	1161.73
95000	8423.98	4455.37	3138.38	2484.26	2095.27	1658.02	1524.52	1342.46	1226.27
100000	8867.35	4689.86	3303.55	2615.01	2205.55	1745.29	1604.76	1413.12	1290.82
105000	9310.72	4924.35	3468.73	2745.76	2315.82	1832.55	1684.99	1483.78	1355.36
110000	9754.09	5158.84	3633.91	2876.51	2426.10	1919.82	1765.23	1554.43	1419.90
115000	10197.45	5393.34	3799.09	3007.27	2536.38	2007.08	1845.47	1625.09	1484.44
120000	10640.82	5627.83	3964.26	3138.02	2646.65	2094.34	1925.71	1695.74	1548.98
125000	11084.19	5862.32	4129.44	3268.77	2756.93	2181.61	2005.94	1766.40	1613.52
130000	11527.55	6096.82	4294.62	3399.52	2867.21	2268.87	2086.18	1837.05	1678.06
135000	11970.92	6331.31	4459.80	3530.27	2977.49	2356.14	2166.42	1907.71	1742.60
140000	12414.29	6565.80	4624.97	3661.02	3087.76	2443.40	2246.66	1978.37	1807.14
145000	12857.66	6800.29	4790.15	3791.77	3198.04	2530.66	2326.89	2049.02	1871.68
150000	13301.02	7034.79	4955.33	3922.52	3308.32	2617.93	2407.13	2119.68	1936.22

MONTHLY PAYMENT 11⅝%

NECESSARY TO AMORTIZE A LOAN

AMOUNT	15 YEARS	18 YEARS	20 YEARS	25 YEARS	28 YEARS	29 YEARS	30 YEARS	35 YEARS	40 YEARS
$ 50	.59	.56	.54	.52	.51	.51	.50	.50	.49
100	1.18	1.11	1.08	1.03	1.01	1.01	1.00	.99	.98
200	2.36	2.22	2.16	2.06	2.02	2.01	2.00	1.98	1.96
300	3.53	3.33	3.23	3.08	3.03	3.02	3.00	2.96	2.94
400	4.71	4.43	4.31	4.11	4.04	4.02	4.00	3.95	3.92
500	5.89	5.54	5.38	5.13	5.05	5.02	5.00	4.93	4.90
600	7.06	6.65	6.46	6.16	6.05	6.03	6.00	5.92	5.87
700	8.24	7.75	7.53	7.18	7.06	7.03	7.00	6.91	6.85
800	9.41	8.86	8.61	8.21	8.07	8.04	8.00	7.89	7.83
900	10.59	9.97	9.68	9.24	9.08	9.04	9.00	8.88	8.81
1000	11.77	11.07	10.76	10.26	10.09	10.04	10.00	9.86	9.79
2000	23.53	22.14	21.51	20.52	20.17	20.08	20.00	19.72	19.57
3000	35.29	33.21	32.26	30.77	30.25	30.12	30.00	29.58	29.35
4000	47.05	44.27	43.01	41.03	40.34	40.16	40.00	39.44	39.14
5000	58.81	55.34	53.76	51.29	50.42	50.19	50.00	49.30	48.92
6000	70.57	66.41	64.51	61.54	60.50	60.23	60.00	59.16	58.70
7000	82.34	77.47	75.26	71.80	70.58	70.27	69.99	69.02	68.49
8000	94.10	88.54	86.01	82.05	80.67	80.31	79.99	78.88	78.27
9000	105.86	99.61	96.76	92.31	90.75	90.35	89.99	88.74	88.05
10000	117.62	110.67	107.51	102.57	100.83	100.38	99.99	98.60	97.84
15000	176.43	166.01	161.26	153.85	151.24	150.57	149.98	147.90	146.75
20000	235.23	221.34	215.02	205.13	201.66	200.76	199.97	197.19	195.67
25000	294.04	276.67	268.77	256.41	252.07	250.95	249.96	246.49	244.58
30000	352.85	332.01	322.52	307.69	302.48	301.14	299.96	295.79	293.50
35000	411.66	387.34	376.27	358.97	352.90	351.33	349.95	345.08	342.42
40000	470.46	442.67	430.03	410.25	403.31	401.52	399.94	394.38	391.33
45000	529.27	498.01	483.78	461.53	453.72	451.71	449.93	443.68	440.25
46000	541.03	509.07	494.53	471.79	463.81	461.75	459.93	453.54	450.03
47000	552.79	520.14	505.28	482.05	473.89	471.79	469.93	463.40	459.81
48000	564.56	531.21	516.03	492.30	483.97	481.82	479.93	473.26	469.60
49000	576.32	542.27	526.78	502.56	494.05	491.86	489.93	483.12	479.38
50000	588.08	553.34	537.53	512.82	504.14	501.90	499.92	492.98	489.16
51000	599.84	564.41	548.28	523.07	514.22	511.94	509.92	502.84	498.95
52000	611.60	575.47	559.03	533.33	524.30	521.98	519.92	512.69	508.73
53000	623.36	586.54	569.78	543.58	534.38	532.01	529.92	522.55	518.51
54000	635.13	597.61	580.53	553.84	544.47	542.05	539.92	532.41	528.30
55000	646.89	608.67	591.29	564.10	554.55	552.09	549.92	542.27	538.08
56000	658.65	619.74	602.04	574.35	564.63	562.13	559.92	552.13	547.86
57000	670.41	630.81	612.79	584.61	574.72	572.17	569.91	561.99	557.65
58000	682.17	641.87	623.54	594.87	584.80	582.20	579.91	571.85	567.43
59000	693.93	652.94	634.29	605.12	594.88	592.24	589.91	581.71	577.21
60000	705.69	664.01	645.04	615.38	604.96	602.28	599.91	591.57	586.99
61000	717.46	675.07	655.79	625.63	615.05	612.32	609.91	601.43	596.78
62000	729.22	686.14	666.54	635.89	625.13	622.36	619.91	611.29	606.56
63000	740.98	697.21	677.29	646.15	635.21	632.39	629.90	621.15	616.34
64000	752.74	708.27	688.04	656.40	645.29	642.43	639.90	631.01	626.13
65000	764.50	719.34	698.79	666.66	655.38	652.47	649.90	640.87	635.91
67500	793.91	747.01	725.67	692.30	680.58	677.56	674.90	665.52	660.37
70000	823.31	774.67	752.54	717.94	705.79	702.66	699.89	690.16	684.83
75000	882.12	830.01	806.30	769.22	756.20	752.85	749.88	739.46	733.74
80000	940.92	885.34	860.05	820.50	806.62	803.04	799.88	788.76	782.66
85000	999.73	940.68	913.80	871.78	857.03	853.23	849.87	838.06	831.57
90000	1058.54	996.01	967.55	923.06	907.44	903.42	899.86	887.35	880.49
95000	1117.35	1051.34	1021.31	974.35	957.86	953.61	949.85	936.65	929.41
100000	1176.15	1106.68	1075.06	1025.63	1008.27	1003.80	999.84	985.95	978.32
105000	1234.96	1162.01	1128.81	1076.91	1058.68	1053.99	1049.84	1035.24	1027.24
110000	1293.77	1217.34	1182.57	1128.19	1109.10	1104.17	1099.83	1084.54	1076.15
115000	1352.58	1272.68	1236.32	1179.47	1159.51	1154.36	1149.82	1133.84	1125.07
120000	1411.38	1328.01	1290.07	1230.75	1209.92	1204.55	1199.81	1183.14	1173.98
125000	1470.19	1383.34	1343.82	1282.03	1260.33	1254.74	1249.80	1232.43	1222.90
130000	1529.00	1438.68	1397.58	1333.31	1310.75	1304.93	1299.80	1281.73	1271.82
135000	1587.81	1494.01	1451.33	1384.59	1361.16	1355.12	1349.79	1331.03	1320.73
140000	1646.61	1549.34	1505.08	1435.87	1411.57	1405.31	1399.78	1380.32	1369.65
145000	1705.42	1604.68	1558.84	1487.16	1461.99	1455.50	1449.77	1429.62	1418.56
150000	1764.23	1660.01	1612.59	1538.44	1512.40	1505.69	1499.76	1478.92	1467.48

11¾% MONTHLY PAYMENT
NECESSARY TO AMORTIZE A LOAN

AMOUNT	1 YEAR	2 YEARS	3 YEARS	4 YEARS	5 YEARS	7 YEARS	8 YEARS	10 YEARS	12 YEARS
$ 50	4.44	2.35	1.66	1.32	1.11	.88	.81	.72	.65
100	8.88	4.70	3.31	2.63	2.22	1.76	1.62	1.43	1.30
200	17.75	9.40	6.62	5.25	4.43	3.51	3.23	2.85	2.60
300	26.62	14.09	9.93	7.87	6.64	5.26	4.84	4.27	3.90
400	35.50	18.79	13.24	10.49	8.85	7.01	6.45	5.69	5.20
500	44.37	23.48	16.55	13.11	11.06	8.76	8.06	7.11	6.50
600	53.24	28.18	19.86	15.73	13.28	10.52	9.67	8.53	7.79
700	62.12	32.87	23.17	18.35	15.49	12.27	11.29	9.95	9.09
800	70.99	37.57	26.48	20.97	17.70	14.02	12.90	11.37	10.39
900	79.86	42.27	29.79	23.60	19.91	15.77	14.51	12.79	11.69
1000	88.74	46.96	33.10	26.22	22.12	17.52	16.12	14.21	12.99
2000	177.47	93.92	66.20	52.43	44.24	35.04	32.24	28.41	25.97
3000	266.20	140.88	99.29	78.64	66.36	52.56	48.35	42.61	38.95
4000	354.93	187.83	132.39	104.85	88.48	70.08	64.47	56.82	51.94
5000	443.66	234.79	165.48	131.06	110.60	87.60	80.58	71.02	64.92
6000	532.40	281.75	198.58	157.27	132.71	105.12	96.70	85.22	77.90
7000	621.13	328.70	231.67	183.48	154.83	122.64	112.82	99.43	90.89
8000	709.86	375.66	264.77	209.70	176.95	140.16	128.93	113.63	103.87
9000	798.59	422.62	297.86	235.91	199.07	157.68	145.05	127.83	116.85
10000	887.32	469.57	330.96	262.12	221.19	175.20	161.16	142.03	129.84
15000	1330.98	704.36	496.43	393.17	331.78	262.79	241.74	213.05	194.75
20000	1774.64	939.14	661.91	524.23	442.37	350.39	322.32	284.06	259.67
25000	2218.30	1173.93	827.38	655.29	552.96	437.99	402.90	355.08	324.59
30000	2661.96	1408.71	992.86	786.34	663.55	525.58	483.48	426.09	389.50
35000	3105.62	1643.49	1158.33	917.40	774.15	613.18	564.06	497.11	454.42
40000	3549.28	1878.28	1323.81	1048.46	884.74	700.78	644.64	568.12	519.34
45000	3992.94	2113.06	1489.28	1179.51	995.33	788.37	725.22	639.14	584.25
46000	4081.67	2160.02	1522.38	1205.72	1017.45	805.89	741.33	653.34	597.23
47000	4170.40	2206.98	1555.47	1231.93	1039.57	823.41	757.45	667.54	610.22
48000	4259.14	2253.93	1588.57	1258.15	1061.68	840.93	773.56	681.75	623.20
49000	4347.87	2300.89	1621.66	1284.36	1083.80	858.45	789.68	695.95	636.18
50000	4436.60	2347.85	1654.76	1310.57	1105.92	875.97	805.79	710.15	649.17
51000	4525.33	2394.80	1687.85	1336.78	1128.04	893.49	821.91	724.36	662.15
52000	4614.06	2441.76	1720.95	1362.99	1150.16	911.01	838.03	738.56	675.13
53000	4702.79	2488.72	1754.04	1389.20	1172.28	928.53	854.14	752.76	688.12
54000	4791.53	2535.67	1787.14	1415.41	1194.39	946.05	870.26	766.96	701.10
55000	4880.26	2582.63	1820.23	1441.62	1216.51	963.57	886.37	781.17	714.08
56000	4968.99	2629.59	1853.33	1467.84	1238.63	981.09	902.49	795.37	727.07
57000	5057.72	2676.54	1886.42	1494.05	1260.75	998.61	918.61	809.57	740.05
58000	5146.45	2723.50	1919.52	1520.26	1282.87	1016.13	934.72	823.78	753.03
59000	5235.19	2770.46	1952.61	1546.47	1304.99	1033.64	950.84	837.98	766.02
60000	5323.92	2817.41	1985.71	1572.68	1327.10	1051.16	966.95	852.18	779.00
61000	5412.65	2864.37	2018.80	1598.89	1349.22	1068.68	983.07	866.38	791.98
62000	5501.38	2911.33	2051.90	1625.10	1371.34	1086.20	999.18	880.59	804.97
63000	5590.11	2958.28	2084.99	1651.31	1393.46	1103.72	1015.30	894.79	817.95
64000	5678.85	3005.24	2118.09	1677.53	1415.58	1121.24	1031.42	908.99	830.93
65000	5767.58	3052.20	2151.18	1703.74	1437.70	1138.76	1047.53	923.20	843.92
67500	5989.41	3169.59	2233.92	1769.26	1492.99	1182.56	1087.82	958.70	876.37
70000	6211.24	3286.98	2316.66	1834.79	1548.29	1226.36	1128.11	994.21	908.83
75000	6654.90	3521.77	2482.13	1965.85	1658.88	1313.95	1208.69	1065.23	973.75
80000	7098.56	3756.55	2647.61	2096.91	1769.47	1401.55	1289.27	1136.24	1038.67
85000	7542.21	3991.33	2813.08	2227.96	1880.06	1489.15	1369.85	1207.26	1103.58
90000	7985.87	4226.12	2978.56	2359.02	1990.65	1576.74	1450.43	1278.27	1168.50
95000	8429.53	4460.90	3144.03	2490.07	2101.25	1664.34	1531.01	1349.28	1233.41
100000	8873.19	4695.69	3309.51	2621.13	2211.84	1751.94	1611.58	1420.30	1298.33
105000	9316.85	4930.47	3474.98	2752.19	2322.43	1839.53	1692.16	1491.31	1363.25
110000	9760.51	5165.25	3640.46	2883.24	2433.02	1927.13	1772.74	1562.33	1428.16
115000	10204.17	5400.04	3805.93	3014.30	2543.61	2014.73	1853.32	1633.34	1493.08
120000	10647.83	5634.82	3971.41	3145.36	2654.20	2102.32	1933.90	1704.36	1558.00
125000	11091.49	5869.61	4136.88	3276.41	2764.80	2189.92	2014.48	1775.37	1622.91
130000	11535.15	6104.39	4302.36	3407.47	2875.39	2277.52	2095.06	1846.39	1687.83
135000	11978.81	6339.17	4467.83	3538.52	2985.98	2365.11	2175.64	1917.40	1752.74
140000	12422.47	6573.96	4633.31	3669.58	3096.57	2452.71	2256.22	1988.42	1817.66
145000	12866.13	6808.74	4798.78	3800.64	3207.16	2540.31	2336.80	2059.43	1882.58
150000	13309.79	7043.53	4964.26	3931.69	3317.75	2627.90	2417.37	2130.45	1947.49

MONTHLY PAYMENT 11¾%
NECESSARY TO AMORTIZE A LOAN

AMOUNT	15 YEARS	18 YEARS	20 YEARS	25 YEARS	28 YEARS	29 YEARS	30 YEARS	35 YEARS	40 YEARS
$ 50	.60	.56	.55	.52	.51	.51	.51	.50	.50
100	1.19	1.12	1.09	1.04	1.02	1.02	1.01	1.00	.99
200	2.37	2.24	2.17	2.07	2.04	2.03	2.02	2.00	1.98
300	3.56	3.35	3.26	3.11	3.06	3.04	3.03	2.99	2.97
400	4.74	4.47	4.34	4.14	4.08	4.06	4.04	3.99	3.96
500	5.93	5.58	5.42	5.18	5.09	5.07	5.05	4.98	4.95
600	7.11	6.70	6.51	6.21	6.11	6.08	6.06	5.98	5.94
700	8.29	7.81	7.59	7.25	7.13	7.10	7.07	6.98	6.92
800	9.48	8.93	8.67	8.28	8.15	8.11	8.08	7.97	7.91
900	10.66	10.04	9.76	9.32	9.16	9.12	9.09	8.97	8.90
1000	11.85	11.16	10.84	10.35	10.18	10.14	10.10	9.96	9.89
2000	23.69	22.31	21.68	20.70	20.36	20.27	20.19	19.92	19.77
3000	35.53	33.46	32.52	31.05	30.54	30.40	30.29	29.88	29.66
4000	47.37	44.61	43.35	41.40	40.71	40.54	40.38	39.84	39.54
5000	59.21	55.76	54.19	51.74	50.89	50.67	50.48	49.79	49.42
6000	71.05	66.91	65.03	62.09	61.07	60.80	60.57	59.75	59.31
7000	82.89	78.06	75.86	72.44	71.24	70.94	70.66	69.71	69.19
8000	94.74	89.21	86.70	82.79	81.42	81.07	80.76	79.67	79.07
9000	106.58	100.36	97.54	93.14	91.60	91.20	90.85	89.63	88.96
10000	118.42	111.51	108.38	103.48	101.77	101.33	100.95	99.58	98.84
15000	177.62	167.27	162.56	155.22	152.66	152.00	151.42	149.37	148.26
20000	236.83	223.02	216.75	206.96	203.54	202.66	201.89	199.16	197.68
25000	296.04	278.77	270.93	258.70	254.43	253.33	252.36	248.95	247.10
30000	355.24	334.53	325.12	310.44	305.31	303.99	302.83	298.74	296.51
35000	414.45	390.28	379.30	362.18	356.20	354.66	353.30	348.53	345.93
40000	473.66	446.03	433.49	413.92	407.08	405.32	403.77	398.32	395.35
45000	532.86	501.79	487.67	465.66	457.97	455.99	454.24	448.11	444.77
46000	544.71	512.94	498.51	476.01	468.14	466.12	464.33	458.07	454.65
47000	556.55	524.09	509.35	486.36	478.32	476.25	474.43	468.03	464.54
48000	568.39	535.24	520.18	496.71	488.50	486.39	484.52	477.99	474.42
49000	580.23	546.39	531.02	507.06	498.67	496.52	494.62	487.94	484.30
50000	592.07	557.54	541.86	517.40	508.85	506.65	504.71	497.90	494.19
51000	603.91	568.69	552.70	527.75	519.03	516.78	514.80	507.86	504.07
52000	615.75	579.84	563.53	538.10	529.20	526.92	524.90	517.82	513.95
53000	627.59	590.99	574.37	548.45	539.38	537.05	534.99	527.78	523.84
54000	639.44	602.14	585.21	558.80	549.56	547.18	545.09	537.73	533.72
55000	651.28	613.29	596.04	569.14	559.74	557.32	555.18	547.69	543.61
56000	663.12	624.45	606.88	579.49	569.91	567.45	565.27	557.65	553.49
57000	674.96	635.60	617.72	589.84	580.09	577.58	575.37	567.61	563.37
58000	686.80	646.75	628.56	600.19	590.27	587.71	585.46	577.57	573.26
59000	698.64	657.90	639.39	610.54	600.44	597.85	595.56	587.52	583.14
60000	710.48	669.05	650.23	620.88	610.62	607.98	605.65	597.48	593.02
61000	722.33	680.20	661.07	631.23	620.80	618.11	615.74	607.44	602.91
62000	734.17	691.35	671.90	641.58	630.97	628.25	625.84	617.40	612.79
63000	746.01	702.50	682.74	651.93	641.15	638.38	635.93	627.36	622.67
64000	757.85	713.65	693.58	662.28	651.33	648.51	646.03	637.31	632.56
65000	769.69	724.80	704.41	672.62	661.50	658.64	656.12	647.27	642.44
67500	799.29	752.68	731.51	698.49	686.95	683.98	681.36	672.17	667.15
70000	828.90	780.56	758.60	724.36	712.39	709.31	706.59	697.06	691.86
75000	888.10	836.31	812.79	776.10	763.27	759.97	757.06	746.85	741.28
80000	947.31	892.06	866.97	827.84	814.16	810.64	807.53	796.64	790.70
85000	1006.52	947.82	921.16	879.58	865.04	861.30	858.00	846.43	840.11
90000	1065.72	1003.57	975.34	931.32	915.93	911.97	908.47	896.22	889.53
95000	1124.93	1059.32	1029.53	983.06	966.81	962.63	958.94	946.01	938.95
100000	1184.14	1115.08	1083.71	1034.80	1017.70	1013.30	1009.41	995.80	988.37
105000	1243.34	1170.83	1137.90	1086.54	1068.58	1063.96	1059.89	1045.59	1037.79
110000	1302.55	1226.58	1192.08	1138.28	1119.47	1114.63	1110.36	1095.38	1087.21
115000	1361.76	1282.34	1246.27	1190.02	1170.35	1165.29	1160.83	1145.17	1136.62
120000	1420.96	1338.09	1300.45	1241.76	1221.23	1215.96	1211.30	1194.96	1186.04
125000	1480.17	1393.85	1354.64	1293.50	1272.12	1266.62	1261.77	1244.75	1235.46
130000	1539.38	1449.60	1408.82	1345.24	1323.00	1317.28	1312.24	1294.54	1284.88
135000	1598.58	1505.35	1463.01	1396.98	1373.89	1367.95	1362.71	1344.33	1334.30
140000	1657.79	1561.11	1517.19	1448.72	1424.77	1418.61	1413.18	1394.12	1383.71
145000	1717.00	1616.86	1571.38	1500.46	1475.66	1469.28	1463.65	1443.91	1433.13
150000	1776.20	1672.61	1625.57	1552.20	1526.54	1519.94	1514.12	1493.70	1482.55

11⅞% MONTHLY PAYMENT
NECESSARY TO AMORTIZE A LOAN

AMOUNT	1 YEAR	2 YEARS	3 YEARS	4 YEARS	5 YEARS	7 YEARS	8 YEARS	10 YEARS	12 YEARS
$ 50	4.44	2.36	1.66	1.32	1.11	.88	.81	.72	.66
100	8.88	4.71	3.32	2.63	2.22	1.76	1.62	1.43	1.31
200	17.76	9.41	6.64	5.26	4.44	3.52	3.24	2.86	2.62
300	26.64	14.11	9.95	7.89	6.66	5.28	4.86	4.29	3.92
400	35.52	18.81	13.27	10.51	8.88	7.04	6.48	5.71	5.23
500	44.40	23.51	16.58	13.14	11.10	8.80	8.10	7.14	6.53
600	53.28	28.21	19.90	15.77	13.31	10.56	9.72	8.57	7.84
700	62.16	32.92	23.21	18.40	15.53	12.32	11.33	10.00	9.15
800	71.04	37.62	26.53	21.02	17.75	14.07	12.95	11.42	10.45
900	79.92	42.32	29.84	23.65	19.97	15.83	14.57	12.85	11.76
1000	88.80	47.02	33.16	26.28	22.19	17.59	16.19	14.28	13.06
2000	177.59	94.04	66.31	52.55	44.37	35.18	32.37	28.55	26.12
3000	266.38	141.05	99.47	78.82	66.55	52.76	48.56	42.83	39.18
4000	355.17	188.07	132.62	105.10	88.73	70.35	64.74	57.10	52.24
5000	443.96	235.08	165.78	131.37	110.91	87.93	80.93	71.38	65.30
6000	532.75	282.10	198.93	157.64	133.09	105.52	97.11	85.65	78.36
7000	621.54	329.11	232.09	183.91	155.27	123.11	113.29	99.93	91.42
8000	710.33	376.13	265.24	210.19	177.46	140.69	129.48	114.20	104.47
9000	799.12	423.14	298.40	236.46	199.64	158.28	145.66	128.48	117.53
10000	887.91	470.16	331.55	262.73	221.82	175.86	161.85	142.75	130.59
15000	1331.86	705.23	497.32	394.09	332.72	263.79	242.77	214.13	195.88
20000	1775.81	940.31	663.10	525.46	443.63	351.72	323.69	285.50	261.18
25000	2219.76	1175.38	828.87	656.82	554.54	439.65	404.61	356.88	326.47
30000	2663.71	1410.46	994.64	788.18	665.44	527.58	485.53	428.25	391.76
35000	3107.67	1645.53	1160.42	919.54	776.35	615.51	566.45	499.63	457.06
40000	3551.62	1880.61	1326.19	1050.91	887.26	703.44	647.37	571.00	522.35
45000	3995.57	2115.69	1491.96	1182.27	998.16	791.37	728.30	642.38	587.64
46000	4084.36	2162.70	1525.12	1208.54	1020.35	808.96	744.48	656.65	600.70
47000	4173.15	2209.72	1558.27	1234.81	1042.53	826.54	760.66	670.93	613.76
48000	4261.94	2256.73	1591.43	1261.09	1064.71	844.13	776.85	685.20	626.82
49000	4350.73	2303.75	1624.58	1287.36	1086.89	861.72	793.03	699.48	639.88
50000	4439.52	2350.76	1657.74	1313.63	1109.07	879.30	809.22	713.75	652.94
51000	4528.31	2397.78	1690.89	1339.90	1131.25	896.89	825.40	728.03	665.99
52000	4617.10	2444.79	1724.05	1366.18	1153.43	914.47	841.59	742.30	679.05
53000	4705.89	2491.81	1757.20	1392.45	1175.62	932.06	857.77	756.58	692.11
54000	4794.68	2538.82	1790.36	1418.72	1197.80	949.65	873.95	770.85	705.17
55000	4883.47	2585.84	1823.51	1444.99	1219.98	967.23	890.14	785.13	718.23
56000	4972.26	2632.85	1856.66	1471.27	1242.16	984.82	906.32	799.40	731.29
57000	5061.05	2679.87	1889.82	1497.54	1264.34	1002.40	922.51	813.68	744.35
58000	5149.84	2726.88	1922.97	1523.81	1286.52	1019.99	938.69	827.95	757.40
59000	5238.63	2773.90	1956.13	1550.08	1308.70	1037.58	954.88	842.23	770.46
60000	5327.42	2820.91	1989.28	1576.36	1330.88	1055.16	971.06	856.50	783.52
61000	5416.21	2867.93	2022.44	1602.63	1353.07	1072.75	987.24	870.78	796.58
62000	5505.01	2914.94	2055.59	1628.90	1375.25	1090.33	1003.43	885.05	809.64
63000	5593.80	2961.96	2088.75	1655.17	1397.43	1107.92	1019.61	899.33	822.70
64000	5682.59	3008.97	2121.90	1681.45	1419.61	1125.51	1035.80	913.60	835.76
65000	5771.38	3055.99	2155.06	1707.72	1441.79	1143.09	1051.98	927.88	848.82
67500	5993.35	3173.53	2237.94	1773.40	1497.24	1187.06	1092.44	963.56	881.46
70000	6215.33	3291.06	2320.83	1839.08	1552.70	1231.02	1132.90	999.25	914.11
75000	6659.28	3526.14	2486.60	1970.44	1663.60	1318.95	1213.82	1070.62	979.40
80000	7103.23	3761.21	2652.38	2101.81	1774.51	1406.88	1294.74	1142.00	1044.69
85000	7547.18	3996.29	2818.15	2233.17	1885.42	1494.81	1375.67	1213.37	1109.99
90000	7991.13	4231.37	2983.92	2364.53	1996.32	1582.74	1456.59	1284.75	1175.28
95000	8435.09	4466.44	3149.70	2495.89	2107.23	1670.67	1537.51	1356.12	1240.57
100000	8879.04	4701.52	3315.47	2627.26	2218.14	1758.60	1618.43	1427.50	1305.87
105000	9322.99	4936.59	3481.24	2758.62	2329.04	1846.53	1699.35	1498.87	1371.16
110000	9766.94	5171.67	3647.02	2889.98	2439.95	1934.46	1780.27	1570.25	1436.45
115000	10210.89	5406.74	3812.79	3021.34	2550.86	2022.39	1861.19	1641.62	1501.75
120000	10654.84	5641.82	3978.56	3152.71	2661.76	2110.32	1942.11	1713.00	1567.04
125000	11098.80	5876.89	4144.33	3284.07	2772.67	2198.25	2023.03	1784.37	1632.33
130000	11542.75	6111.97	4310.11	3415.43	2883.58	2286.18	2103.96	1855.75	1697.63
135000	11986.70	6347.05	4475.88	3546.79	2994.48	2374.11	2184.88	1927.12	1762.92
140000	12430.65	6582.12	4641.65	3678.16	3105.39	2462.04	2265.80	1998.49	1828.21
145000	12874.60	6817.20	4807.43	3809.52	3216.30	2549.97	2346.72	2069.87	1893.50
150000	13318.55	7052.27	4973.20	3940.88	3327.20	2637.90	2427.64	2141.24	1958.80

MONTHLY PAYMENT 11⅞%
NECESSARY TO AMORTIZE A LOAN

AMOUNT	15 YEARS	18 YEARS	20 YEARS	25 YEARS	28 YEARS	29 YEARS	30 YEARS	35 YEARS	40 YEARS
$ 50	.60	.57	.55	.53	.52	.52	.51	.51	.50
100	1.20	1.13	1.10	1.05	1.03	1.03	1.02	1.01	1.00
200	2.39	2.25	2.19	2.09	2.06	2.05	2.04	2.02	2.00
300	3.58	3.38	3.28	3.14	3.09	3.07	3.06	3.02	3.00
400	4.77	4.50	4.37	4.18	4.11	4.10	4.08	4.03	4.00
500	5.97	5.62	5.47	5.22	5.14	5.12	5.10	5.03	5.00
600	7.16	6.75	6.56	6.27	6.17	6.14	6.12	6.04	6.00
700	8.35	7.87	7.65	7.31	7.19	7.16	7.14	7.04	6.99
800	9.54	8.99	8.74	8.36	8.22	8.19	8.16	8.05	7.99
900	10.73	10.12	9.84	9.40	9.25	9.21	9.18	9.06	8.99
1000	11.93	11.24	10.93	10.44	10.28	10.23	10.20	10.06	9.99
2000	23.85	22.47	21.85	20.88	20.55	20.46	20.39	20.12	19.97
3000	35.77	33.71	32.78	31.32	30.82	30.69	30.58	30.17	29.96
4000	47.69	44.94	43.70	41.76	41.09	40.92	40.77	40.23	39.94
5000	59.61	56.18	54.62	52.20	51.36	51.15	50.96	50.29	49.93
6000	71.53	67.41	65.55	62.64	61.63	61.37	61.15	60.34	59.91
7000	83.45	78.65	76.47	73.08	71.90	71.60	71.34	70.40	69.89
8000	95.38	89.88	87.40	83.52	82.18	81.83	81.53	80.46	79.88
9000	107.30	101.12	98.32	93.96	92.45	92.06	91.72	90.51	89.86
10000	119.22	112.35	109.24	104.40	102.72	102.29	101.91	100.57	99.85
15000	178.83	168.53	163.86	156.60	154.08	153.43	152.86	150.85	149.77
20000	238.43	224.70	218.48	208.80	205.43	204.57	203.81	201.14	199.69
25000	298.04	280.88	273.10	261.00	256.79	255.71	254.76	251.42	249.61
30000	357.65	337.05	327.72	313.20	308.15	306.85	305.71	301.70	299.53
35000	417.25	393.23	382.34	365.40	359.50	357.99	356.66	351.99	349.45
40000	476.86	449.40	436.96	417.60	410.86	409.13	407.61	402.27	399.38
45000	536.47	505.58	491.58	469.80	462.22	460.27	458.56	452.55	449.30
46000	548.39	516.81	502.50	480.24	472.49	470.50	468.75	462.61	459.28
47000	560.31	528.05	513.43	490.68	482.76	480.73	478.94	472.67	469.26
48000	572.23	539.28	524.35	501.12	493.03	490.96	489.13	482.72	479.25
49000	584.15	550.52	535.27	511.56	503.30	501.18	499.32	492.78	489.23
50000	596.07	561.75	546.20	522.00	513.58	511.41	509.51	502.84	499.22
51000	608.00	572.99	557.12	532.44	523.85	521.64	519.70	512.89	509.20
52000	619.92	584.22	568.04	542.88	534.12	531.87	529.89	522.95	519.19
53000	631.84	595.46	578.97	553.32	544.39	542.10	540.08	533.01	529.17
54000	643.76	606.69	589.89	563.76	554.66	552.32	550.27	543.06	539.15
55000	655.68	617.93	600.82	574.20	564.93	562.55	560.46	553.12	549.14
56000	667.60	629.16	611.74	584.64	575.20	572.78	570.65	563.18	559.12
57000	679.52	640.40	622.66	595.08	585.48	583.01	580.84	573.23	569.11
58000	691.44	651.63	633.59	605.52	595.75	593.24	591.03	583.29	579.09
59000	703.37	662.87	644.51	615.96	606.02	603.47	601.22	593.35	589.08
60000	715.29	674.10	655.44	626.40	616.29	613.69	611.41	603.40	599.06
61000	727.21	685.34	666.36	636.84	626.56	623.92	621.60	613.46	609.04
62000	739.13	696.57	677.28	647.28	636.83	634.15	631.79	623.52	619.03
63000	751.05	707.81	688.21	657.72	647.10	644.38	641.98	633.57	629.01
64000	762.97	719.04	699.13	668.16	657.38	654.61	652.17	643.63	639.00
65000	774.89	730.28	710.05	678.60	667.65	664.83	662.36	653.69	648.98
67500	804.70	758.37	737.36	704.70	693.33	690.40	687.83	678.83	673.94
70000	834.50	786.45	764.67	730.80	719.00	715.98	713.31	703.97	698.90
75000	894.11	842.63	819.29	783.00	770.36	767.12	764.26	754.25	748.82
80000	953.72	898.80	873.91	835.20	821.72	818.26	815.21	804.54	798.75
85000	1013.32	954.98	928.53	887.40	873.07	869.40	866.16	854.82	848.67
90000	1072.93	1011.15	983.15	939.60	924.43	920.54	917.11	905.10	898.59
95000	1132.54	1067.33	1037.77	991.80	975.79	971.68	968.06	955.39	948.51
100000	1192.14	1123.50	1092.39	1044.00	1027.15	1022.82	1019.01	1005.67	998.43
105000	1251.75	1179.68	1147.01	1096.20	1078.50	1073.96	1069.96	1055.95	1048.35
110000	1311.36	1235.85	1201.63	1148.40	1129.86	1125.10	1120.91	1106.23	1098.27
115000	1370.96	1292.03	1256.25	1200.60	1181.22	1176.24	1171.86	1156.52	1148.19
120000	1430.57	1348.20	1310.87	1252.80	1232.57	1227.38	1222.81	1206.80	1198.12
125000	1490.18	1404.38	1365.49	1305.00	1283.93	1278.52	1273.76	1257.08	1248.04
130000	1549.78	1460.55	1420.10	1357.20	1335.29	1329.66	1324.71	1307.37	1297.96
135000	1609.39	1516.73	1474.72	1409.40	1386.65	1380.80	1375.66	1357.65	1347.88
140000	1669.00	1572.90	1529.34	1461.60	1438.00	1431.95	1426.61	1407.93	1397.80
145000	1728.60	1629.08	1583.96	1513.80	1489.36	1483.09	1477.56	1458.22	1447.72
150000	1788.21	1685.25	1638.58	1566.00	1540.72	1534.23	1528.51	1508.50	1497.64

12% MONTHLY PAYMENT
NECESSARY TO AMORTIZE A LOAN

AMOUNT	1 YEAR	2 YEARS	3 YEARS	4 YEARS	5 YEARS	7 YEARS	8 YEARS	10 YEARS	12 YEARS
$ 50	4.45	2.36	1.67	1.32	1.12	.89	.82	.72	.66
100	8.89	4.71	3.33	2.64	2.23	1.77	1.63	1.44	1.32
200	17.77	9.42	6.65	5.27	4.45	3.54	3.26	2.87	2.63
300	26.66	14.13	9.97	7.91	6.68	5.30	4.88	4.31	3.95
400	35.54	18.83	13.29	10.54	8.90	7.07	6.51	5.74	5.26
500	44.43	23.54	16.61	13.17	11.13	8.83	8.13	7.18	6.57
600	53.31	28.25	19.93	15.81	13.35	10.60	9.76	8.61	7.89
700	62.20	32.96	23.26	18.44	15.58	12.36	11.38	10.05	9.20
800	71.08	37.66	26.58	21.07	17.80	14.13	13.01	11.48	10.51
900	79.97	42.37	29.90	23.71	20.03	15.89	14.63	12.92	11.83
1000	88.85	47.08	33.22	26.34	22.25	17.66	16.26	14.35	13.14
2000	177.70	94.15	66.43	52.67	44.49	35.31	32.51	28.70	26.27
3000	266.55	141.23	99.65	79.01	66.74	52.96	48.76	43.05	39.41
4000	355.40	188.30	132.86	105.34	88.98	70.62	65.02	57.39	52.54
5000	444.25	235.37	166.08	131.67	111.23	88.27	81.27	71.74	65.68
6000	533.10	282.45	199.29	158.01	133.47	105.92	97.52	86.09	78.81
7000	621.95	329.52	232.51	184.34	155.72	123.57	113.77	100.43	91.94
8000	710.80	376.59	265.72	210.68	177.96	141.23	130.03	114.78	105.08
9000	799.64	423.67	298.93	237.01	200.21	158.88	146.28	129.13	118.21
10000	888.49	470.74	332.15	263.34	222.45	176.53	162.53	143.48	131.35
15000	1332.74	706.11	498.22	395.01	333.67	264.80	243.80	215.21	197.02
20000	1776.98	941.47	664.29	526.68	444.89	353.06	325.06	286.95	262.69
25000	2221.22	1176.84	830.36	658.35	556.12	441.32	406.33	358.68	328.36
30000	2665.47	1412.21	996.43	790.02	667.34	529.59	487.59	430.42	394.03
35000	3109.71	1647.58	1162.51	921.69	778.56	617.85	568.85	502.15	459.70
40000	3553.96	1882.94	1328.58	1053.36	889.78	706.11	650.12	573.89	525.37
45000	3998.20	2118.31	1494.65	1185.03	1001.01	794.38	731.38	645.62	591.04
46000	4087.05	2165.38	1527.86	1211.36	1023.25	812.03	747.64	659.97	604.18
47000	4175.90	2212.46	1561.08	1237.70	1045.49	829.68	763.89	674.32	617.31
48000	4264.75	2259.53	1594.29	1264.03	1067.74	847.34	780.14	688.67	630.45
49000	4353.60	2306.61	1627.51	1290.36	1089.98	864.99	796.39	703.01	643.58
50000	4442.84	2353.68	1660.72	1316.70	1112.23	882.64	812.65	717.36	656.71
51000	4531.29	2400.75	1693.93	1343.03	1134.47	900.29	828.90	731.71	669.85
52000	4620.14	2447.83	1727.15	1369.36	1156.72	917.95	845.15	746.05	682.98
53000	4708.99	2494.90	1760.36	1395.70	1178.96	935.60	861.41	760.40	696.12
54000	4797.84	2541.97	1793.58	1422.03	1201.21	953.25	877.66	774.75	709.25
55000	4886.69	2589.05	1826.79	1448.37	1223.45	970.91	893.91	789.10	722.39
56000	4975.54	2636.12	1860.01	1474.70	1245.69	988.56	910.16	803.44	735.52
57000	5064.39	2683.19	1893.22	1501.03	1267.94	1006.21	926.42	817.79	748.65
58000	5153.23	2730.27	1926.43	1527.37	1290.18	1023.86	942.67	832.14	761.79
59000	5242.08	2777.34	1959.65	1553.70	1312.43	1041.52	958.92	846.48	774.92
60000	5330.93	2824.41	1992.86	1580.04	1334.67	1059.17	975.18	860.83	788.06
61000	5419.78	2871.49	2026.08	1606.37	1356.92	1076.82	991.43	875.18	801.19
62000	5508.63	2918.56	2059.29	1632.70	1379.16	1094.47	1007.68	889.52	814.32
63000	5597.48	2965.63	2092.51	1659.04	1401.41	1112.13	1023.93	903.87	827.46
64000	5686.33	3012.71	2125.72	1685.37	1423.65	1129.78	1040.19	918.22	840.59
65000	5775.18	3059.78	2158.94	1711.70	1445.89	1147.43	1056.44	932.57	853.73
67500	5997.30	3177.46	2241.97	1777.54	1501.51	1191.56	1097.07	968.43	886.56
70000	6219.42	3295.15	2325.01	1843.37	1557.12	1235.70	1137.70	1004.30	919.40
75000	6663.66	3530.52	2491.08	1975.04	1668.34	1323.96	1218.97	1076.04	985.07
80000	7107.91	3765.88	2657.15	2106.71	1779.56	1412.22	1300.23	1147.77	1050.74
85000	7552.15	4001.25	2823.22	2238.38	1890.78	1500.49	1381.50	1219.51	1116.41
90000	7996.40	4236.62	2989.29	2370.05	2002.01	1588.75	1462.76	1291.24	1182.08
95000	8440.64	4471.98	3155.36	2501.72	2113.23	1677.01	1544.02	1362.98	1247.75
100000	8884.88	4707.35	3321.44	2633.39	2224.45	1765.28	1625.29	1434.71	1313.42
105000	9329.13	4942.72	3487.51	2765.06	2335.67	1853.54	1706.55	1506.45	1379.09
110000	9773.37	5178.09	3653.58	2896.73	2446.89	1941.81	1787.82	1578.19	1444.77
115000	10217.62	5413.45	3819.65	3028.40	2558.12	2030.07	1869.08	1649.92	1510.44
120000	10661.86	5648.82	3985.72	3160.07	2669.34	2118.33	1950.35	1721.66	1576.11
125000	11106.10	5884.19	4151.79	3291.73	2780.56	2206.60	2031.61	1793.39	1641.78
130000	11550.35	6119.56	4317.87	3423.40	2891.78	2294.86	2112.87	1865.13	1707.45
135000	11994.59	6354.92	4483.94	3555.07	3003.01	2383.12	2194.14	1936.86	1773.12
140000	12438.84	6590.29	4650.01	3686.74	3114.23	2471.39	2275.40	2008.60	1838.79
145000	12883.08	6825.66	4816.08	3818.41	3225.45	2559.65	2356.67	2080.33	1904.46
150000	13327.32	7061.03	4982.15	3950.08	3336.67	2647.91	2437.93	2152.07	1970.13

MONTHLY PAYMENT 12%

NECESSARY TO AMORTIZE A LOAN

AMOUNT	15 YEARS	18 YEARS	20 YEARS	25 YEARS	28 YEARS	29 YEARS	30 YEARS	35 YEARS	40 YEARS
$ 50	.61	.57	.56	.53	.52	.52	.52	.51	.51
100	1.21	1.14	1.11	1.06	1.04	1.04	1.03	1.02	1.01
200	2.41	2.27	2.21	2.11	2.08	2.07	2.06	2.04	2.02
300	3.61	3.40	3.31	3.16	3.11	3.10	3.09	3.05	3.03
400	4.81	4.53	4.41	4.22	4.15	4.13	4.12	4.07	4.04
500	6.01	5.66	5.51	5.27	5.19	5.17	5.15	5.08	5.05
600	7.21	6.80	6.61	6.32	6.22	6.20	6.18	6.10	6.06
700	8.41	7.93	7.71	7.38	7.26	7.23	7.21	7.11	7.06
800	9.61	9.06	8.81	8.43	8.30	8.26	8.23	8.13	8.07
900	10.81	10.19	9.91	9.48	9.33	9.30	9.26	9.14	9.08
1000	12.01	11.32	11.02	10.54	10.37	10.33	10.29	10.16	10.09
2000	24.01	22.64	22.03	21.07	20.74	20.65	20.58	20.32	20.17
3000	36.01	33.96	33.04	31.60	31.10	30.98	30.86	30.47	30.26
4000	48.01	45.28	44.05	42.13	41.47	41.30	41.15	40.63	40.34
5000	60.01	56.60	55.06	52.67	51.84	51.62	51.44	50.78	50.43
6000	72.02	67.92	66.07	63.20	62.20	61.95	61.72	60.94	60.51
7000	84.02	79.24	77.08	73.73	72.57	72.27	72.01	71.09	70.60
8000	96.02	90.56	88.09	84.26	82.93	82.59	82.29	81.25	80.68
9000	108.02	101.88	99.10	94.80	93.30	92.92	92.58	91.40	90.77
10000	120.02	113.20	110.11	105.33	103.67	103.24	102.87	101.56	100.85
15000	180.03	169.80	165.17	157.99	155.50	154.86	154.30	152.34	151.28
20000	240.04	226.40	220.22	210.65	207.33	206.48	205.73	203.11	201.70
25000	300.05	282.99	275.28	263.31	259.16	258.09	257.16	253.89	252.13
30000	360.06	339.59	330.33	315.97	310.99	309.71	308.59	304.67	302.55
35000	420.06	396.19	385.39	368.63	362.82	361.33	360.02	355.45	352.98
40000	480.07	452.79	440.44	421.29	414.65	412.95	411.45	406.22	403.40
45000	540.08	509.38	495.49	473.96	466.48	464.57	462.88	457.00	453.83
46000	552.08	520.70	506.50	484.49	476.85	474.89	473.17	467.16	463.91
47000	564.08	532.02	517.52	495.02	487.21	485.21	483.45	477.31	474.00
48000	576.09	543.34	528.53	505.55	497.58	495.54	493.74	487.47	484.08
49000	588.09	554.66	539.54	516.08	507.95	505.86	504.03	497.62	494.17
50000	600.09	565.98	550.55	526.62	518.31	516.18	514.31	507.78	504.25
51000	612.09	577.30	561.56	537.15	528.68	526.51	524.60	517.94	514.34
52000	624.09	588.62	572.57	547.68	539.04	536.83	534.88	528.09	524.42
53000	636.09	599.94	583.58	558.21	549.41	547.16	545.17	538.25	534.51
54000	648.10	611.26	594.59	568.75	559.78	557.48	555.46	548.40	544.59
55000	660.10	622.58	605.60	579.28	570.14	567.80	565.74	558.56	554.68
56000	672.10	633.90	616.61	589.81	580.51	578.13	576.03	568.71	564.76
57000	684.10	645.22	627.62	600.34	590.87	588.45	586.31	578.87	574.85
58000	696.10	656.54	638.63	610.88	601.24	598.77	596.60	589.02	584.93
59000	708.10	667.86	649.65	621.41	611.61	609.10	606.89	599.18	595.02
60000	720.11	679.18	660.66	631.94	621.97	619.42	617.17	609.33	605.10
61000	732.11	690.49	671.67	642.47	632.34	629.74	627.46	619.49	615.19
62000	744.11	701.81	682.68	653.00	642.71	640.07	637.74	629.65	625.27
63000	756.11	713.13	693.69	663.54	653.07	650.39	648.03	639.80	635.36
64000	768.11	724.45	704.70	674.07	663.44	660.71	658.32	649.96	645.44
65000	780.11	735.77	715.71	684.60	673.80	671.04	668.60	660.11	655.53
67500	810.12	764.07	743.24	710.93	699.72	696.85	694.32	685.50	680.74
70000	840.12	792.37	770.77	737.26	725.63	722.66	720.03	710.89	705.95
75000	900.13	848.97	825.82	789.92	777.46	774.27	771.46	761.67	756.38
80000	960.14	905.57	880.87	842.58	829.30	825.89	822.90	812.44	806.80
85000	1020.15	962.16	935.93	895.25	881.13	877.51	874.33	863.22	857.23
90000	1080.16	1018.76	990.98	947.91	932.96	929.13	925.76	914.00	907.65
95000	1140.16	1075.36	1046.04	1000.57	984.79	980.75	977.19	964.78	958.08
100000	1200.17	1131.96	1101.09	1053.23	1036.62	1032.36	1028.62	1015.55	1008.50
105000	1260.18	1188.55	1156.15	1105.89	1088.45	1083.98	1080.05	1066.33	1058.93
110000	1320.19	1245.15	1211.20	1158.55	1140.28	1135.60	1131.48	1117.11	1109.35
115000	1380.20	1301.75	1266.25	1211.21	1192.11	1187.22	1182.91	1167.89	1159.78
120000	1440.21	1358.35	1321.31	1263.87	1243.94	1238.84	1234.34	1218.66	1210.20
125000	1500.22	1414.94	1376.36	1316.54	1295.77	1290.45	1285.77	1269.44	1260.63
130000	1560.22	1471.54	1431.42	1369.20	1347.60	1342.07	1337.20	1320.22	1311.05
135000	1620.23	1528.14	1486.47	1421.86	1399.43	1393.69	1388.63	1371.00	1361.48
140000	1680.24	1584.74	1541.53	1474.52	1451.26	1445.31	1440.06	1421.77	1411.90
145000	1740.25	1641.33	1596.58	1527.18	1503.09	1496.93	1491.49	1472.55	1462.33
150000	1800.26	1697.93	1651.63	1579.84	1554.92	1548.54	1542.92	1523.33	1512.75

12⅛% MONTHLY PAYMENT
NECESSARY TO AMORTIZE A LOAN

AMOUNT	1 YEAR	2 YEARS	3 YEARS	4 YEARS	5 YEARS	7 YEARS	8 YEARS	10 YEARS	12 YEARS
$ 50	4.45	2.36	1.67	1.32	1.12	.89	.82	.73	.67
100	8.90	4.72	3.33	2.64	2.24	1.78	1.64	1.45	1.33
200	17.79	9.43	6.66	5.28	4.47	3.55	3.27	2.89	2.65
300	26.68	14.14	9.99	7.92	6.70	5.32	4.90	4.33	3.97
400	35.57	18.86	13.31	10.56	8.93	7.09	6.53	5.77	5.29
500	44.46	23.57	16.64	13.20	11.16	8.86	8.17	7.21	6.61
600	53.35	28.28	19.97	15.84	13.39	10.64	9.80	8.66	7.93
700	62.24	33.00	23.30	18.48	15.62	12.41	11.43	10.10	9.25
800	71.13	37.71	26.62	21.11	17.85	14.18	13.06	11.54	10.57
900	80.02	42.42	29.95	23.76	20.08	15.95	14.69	12.98	11.89
1000	88.91	47.14	33.28	26.40	22.31	17.72	16.33	14.42	13.21
2000	177.82	94.27	66.55	52.80	44.62	35.44	32.65	28.84	26.42
3000	266.73	141.40	99.83	79.19	66.93	53.16	48.97	43.26	39.63
4000	355.63	188.53	133.10	105.59	89.24	70.88	65.29	57.68	52.84
5000	444.54	235.66	166.38	131.98	111.54	88.60	81.61	72.10	66.05
6000	533.45	282.80	199.65	158.38	133.85	106.32	97.93	86.52	79.26
7000	622.36	329.93	232.92	184.77	156.16	124.04	114.26	100.94	92.47
8000	711.26	377.06	266.20	211.17	178.47	141.76	130.58	115.36	105.68
9000	800.17	424.19	299.47	237.56	200.77	159.48	146.90	129.78	118.89
10000	889.08	471.32	332.75	263.96	223.08	177.20	163.22	144.20	132.10
15000	1333.61	706.98	499.12	395.93	334.62	265.80	244.83	216.30	198.15
20000	1778.15	942.64	665.49	527.91	446.16	354.40	326.44	288.39	264.20
25000	2222.69	1178.30	831.86	659.89	557.70	443.00	408.04	360.49	330.25
30000	2667.22	1413.96	998.23	791.86	669.23	531.59	489.65	432.59	396.30
35000	3111.76	1649.62	1164.60	923.84	780.77	620.19	571.26	504.69	462.35
40000	3556.30	1885.28	1330.97	1055.82	892.31	708.79	652.87	576.78	528.40
45000	4000.83	2120.94	1497.34	1187.79	1003.85	797.39	734.48	648.88	594.45
46000	4089.74	2168.07	1530.61	1214.19	1026.16	815.11	750.80	663.30	607.66
47000	4178.65	2215.20	1563.89	1240.58	1048.47	832.83	767.12	677.72	620.87
48000	4267.55	2262.33	1597.16	1266.98	1070.77	850.55	783.44	692.14	634.08
49000	4356.46	2309.47	1630.43	1293.37	1093.08	868.27	799.76	706.56	647.29
50000	4445.37	2356.60	1663.71	1319.77	1115.39	885.99	816.08	720.98	660.50
51000	4534.28	2403.73	1696.98	1346.16	1137.70	903.71	832.41	735.40	673.71
52000	4623.18	2450.86	1730.26	1372.56	1160.00	921.43	848.73	749.82	686.92
53000	4712.09	2497.99	1763.53	1398.95	1182.31	939.15	865.05	764.24	700.13
54000	4801.00	2545.13	1796.80	1425.35	1204.62	956.87	881.37	778.66	713.34
55000	4889.91	2592.26	1830.08	1451.74	1226.93	974.59	897.69	793.07	726.55
56000	4978.81	2639.39	1863.35	1478.14	1249.23	992.31	914.01	807.49	739.76
57000	5067.72	2686.52	1896.63	1504.53	1271.54	1010.03	930.34	821.91	752.97
58000	5156.63	2733.65	1929.90	1530.93	1293.85	1027.74	946.66	836.33	766.18
59000	5245.53	2780.79	1963.17	1557.32	1316.16	1045.46	962.98	850.75	779.39
60000	5334.44	2827.92	1996.45	1583.72	1338.46	1063.18	979.30	865.17	792.60
61000	5423.35	2875.05	2029.72	1610.12	1360.77	1080.90	995.62	879.59	805.81
62000	5512.26	2922.18	2063.00	1636.51	1383.08	1098.62	1011.94	894.01	819.02
63000	5601.16	2969.31	2096.27	1662.91	1405.39	1116.34	1028.27	908.43	832.23
64000	5690.07	3016.44	2129.54	1689.30	1427.70	1134.06	1044.59	922.85	845.44
65000	5778.98	3063.58	2162.82	1715.70	1450.00	1151.78	1060.91	937.27	858.65
67500	6001.25	3181.41	2246.00	1781.68	1505.77	1196.08	1101.71	973.32	891.68
70000	6223.51	3299.24	2329.19	1847.67	1561.54	1240.38	1142.52	1009.37	924.70
75000	6668.05	3534.90	2495.56	1979.65	1673.08	1328.98	1224.12	1081.46	990.75
80000	7112.59	3770.56	2661.93	2111.63	1784.62	1417.58	1305.73	1153.56	1056.80
85000	7557.12	4006.21	2828.30	2243.60	1896.16	1506.18	1387.34	1225.66	1122.85
90000	8001.66	4241.87	2994.67	2375.58	2007.69	1594.77	1468.95	1297.76	1188.90
95000	8446.20	4477.53	3161.04	2507.55	2119.23	1683.37	1550.56	1369.85	1254.95
100000	8890.73	4713.19	3327.41	2639.53	2230.77	1771.97	1632.16	1441.95	1321.00
105000	9335.27	4948.85	3493.78	2771.51	2342.31	1860.57	1713.77	1514.05	1387.05
110000	9779.81	5184.51	3660.15	2903.48	2453.85	1949.17	1795.38	1586.14	1453.10
115000	10224.34	5420.17	3826.52	3035.46	2565.39	2037.76	1876.99	1658.24	1519.15
120000	10668.88	5655.83	3992.89	3167.44	2676.92	2126.36	1958.60	1730.34	1585.20
125000	11113.41	5891.49	4159.26	3299.41	2788.46	2214.96	2040.20	1802.44	1651.25
130000	11557.95	6127.15	4325.63	3431.39	2900.00	2303.56	2121.81	1874.53	1717.30
135000	12002.49	6362.81	4492.00	3563.36	3011.54	2392.16	2203.42	1946.63	1783.35
140000	12447.02	6598.47	4658.37	3695.34	3123.08	2480.76	2285.03	2018.73	1849.40
145000	12891.56	6834.13	4824.74	3827.32	3234.62	2569.35	2366.64	2090.82	1915.45
150000	13336.10	7069.79	4991.11	3959.29	3346.15	2657.95	2448.24	2162.92	1981.50

MONTHLY PAYMENT 12⅛%

NECESSARY TO AMORTIZE A LOAN

AMOUNT	15 YEARS	18 YEARS	20 YEARS	25 YEARS	28 YEARS	29 YEARS	30 YEARS	35 YEARS	40 YEARS
$ 50	.61	.58	.56	.54	.53	.53	.52	.52	.51
100	1.21	1.15	1.11	1.07	1.05	1.05	1.04	1.03	1.02
200	2.42	2.29	2.22	2.13	2.10	2.09	2.08	2.06	2.04
300	3.63	3.43	3.33	3.19	3.14	3.13	3.12	3.08	3.06
400	4.84	4.57	4.44	4.25	4.19	4.17	4.16	4.11	4.08
500	6.05	5.71	5.55	5.32	5.24	5.21	5.20	5.13	5.10
600	7.25	6.85	6.66	6.38	6.28	6.26	6.23	6.16	6.12
700	8.46	7.99	7.77	7.44	7.33	7.30	7.27	7.18	7.14
800	9.67	9.13	8.88	8.50	8.37	8.34	8.31	8.21	8.15
900	10.88	10.27	9.99	9.57	9.42	9.38	9.35	9.23	9.17
1000	12.09	11.41	11.10	10.63	10.47	10.42	10.39	10.26	10.19
2000	24.17	22.81	22.20	21.25	20.93	20.84	20.77	20.51	20.38
3000	36.25	34.22	33.30	31.88	31.39	31.26	31.15	30.77	30.56
4000	48.33	45.62	44.40	42.50	41.85	41.68	41.53	41.02	40.75
5000	60.42	57.03	55.50	53.13	52.31	52.10	51.92	51.28	50.93
6000	72.50	68.43	66.59	63.75	62.77	62.52	62.30	61.53	61.12
7000	84.58	79.83	77.69	74.38	73.23	72.94	72.68	71.79	71.31
8000	96.66	91.24	88.79	85.00	83.69	83.36	83.06	82.04	81.49
9000	108.74	102.64	99.89	95.63	94.15	93.78	93.45	92.30	91.68
10000	120.83	114.05	110.99	106.25	104.62	104.20	103.83	102.55	101.86
15000	181.24	171.07	166.48	159.38	156.92	156.29	155.74	153.82	152.79
20000	241.65	228.09	221.97	212.50	209.23	208.39	207.65	205.10	203.72
25000	302.06	285.11	277.46	265.62	261.53	260.49	259.57	256.37	254.65
30000	362.47	342.13	332.95	318.75	313.84	312.58	311.48	307.64	305.58
35000	422.88	399.15	388.44	371.87	366.14	364.68	363.39	358.91	356.51
40000	483.29	456.18	443.93	424.99	418.45	416.77	415.30	410.19	407.44
45000	543.70	513.20	499.42	478.12	470.75	468.87	467.22	461.46	458.37
46000	555.79	524.60	510.52	488.74	481.21	479.29	477.60	471.71	468.56
47000	567.87	536.01	521.62	499.37	491.68	489.71	487.98	481.97	478.74
48000	579.95	547.41	532.72	509.99	502.14	500.13	498.36	492.22	488.93
49000	592.03	558.81	543.81	520.62	512.60	510.55	508.74	502.48	499.11
50000	604.12	570.22	554.91	531.24	523.06	520.97	519.13	512.73	509.30
51000	616.20	581.62	566.01	541.87	533.52	531.39	529.51	522.99	519.48
52000	628.28	593.03	577.11	552.49	543.98	541.81	539.89	533.24	529.67
53000	640.36	604.43	588.21	563.12	554.44	552.22	550.27	543.49	539.86
54000	652.44	615.84	599.30	573.74	564.90	562.64	560.66	553.75	550.04
55000	664.53	627.24	610.40	584.36	575.36	573.06	571.04	564.00	560.23
56000	676.61	638.64	621.50	594.99	585.82	583.48	581.42	574.26	570.41
57000	688.69	650.05	632.60	605.61	596.29	593.90	591.80	584.51	580.60
58000	700.77	661.45	643.70	616.24	606.75	604.32	602.19	594.77	590.79
59000	712.86	672.86	654.79	626.86	617.21	614.74	612.57	605.02	600.97
60000	724.94	684.26	665.89	637.49	627.67	625.16	622.95	615.28	611.16
61000	737.02	695.67	676.99	648.11	638.13	635.58	633.33	625.53	621.34
62000	749.10	707.07	688.09	658.74	648.59	646.00	643.72	635.79	631.53
63000	761.18	718.47	699.19	669.36	659.05	656.42	654.10	646.04	641.71
64000	773.27	729.88	710.29	679.99	669.51	666.84	664.48	656.29	651.90
65000	785.35	741.28	721.38	690.61	679.97	677.26	674.86	666.55	662.09
67500	815.55	769.79	749.13	717.17	706.13	703.30	700.82	692.19	687.55
70000	845.76	798.30	776.87	743.74	732.28	729.35	726.78	717.82	713.02
75000	906.17	855.32	832.36	796.86	784.58	781.45	778.69	769.09	763.95
80000	966.58	912.35	887.86	849.98	836.89	833.54	830.60	820.37	814.87
85000	1026.99	969.37	943.35	903.11	889.20	885.64	882.51	871.64	865.80
90000	1087.40	1026.39	998.84	956.23	941.50	937.74	934.43	922.91	916.73
95000	1147.82	1083.41	1054.33	1009.35	993.81	989.83	986.34	974.18	967.66
100000	1208.23	1140.43	1109.82	1062.48	1046.11	1041.93	1038.25	1025.46	1018.59
105000	1268.64	1197.45	1165.31	1115.60	1098.42	1094.03	1090.16	1076.73	1069.52
110000	1329.05	1254.47	1220.80	1168.72	1150.72	1146.12	1142.07	1128.00	1120.45
115000	1389.46	1311.50	1276.29	1221.85	1203.03	1198.22	1193.99	1179.28	1171.38
120000	1449.87	1368.52	1331.78	1274.97	1255.33	1250.31	1245.90	1230.55	1222.31
125000	1510.28	1425.54	1387.27	1328.10	1307.64	1302.41	1297.81	1281.82	1273.24
130000	1570.69	1482.56	1442.76	1381.22	1359.94	1354.51	1349.72	1333.09	1324.17
135000	1631.10	1539.58	1498.25	1434.34	1412.25	1406.60	1401.64	1384.37	1375.10
140000	1691.52	1596.60	1553.74	1487.47	1464.55	1458.70	1453.55	1435.64	1426.03
145000	1751.93	1653.62	1609.23	1540.59	1516.86	1510.79	1505.46	1486.91	1476.96
150000	1812.34	1710.64	1664.72	1593.71	1569.16	1562.89	1557.37	1538.18	1527.89

12¼% MONTHLY PAYMENT
NECESSARY TO AMORTIZE A LOAN

AMOUNT	1 YEAR	2 YEARS	3 YEARS	4 YEARS	5 YEARS	7 YEARS	8 YEARS	10 YEARS	12 YEARS
$ 50	4.45	2.36	1.67	1.33	1.12	.89	.82	.73	.67
100	8.90	4.72	3.34	2.65	2.24	1.78	1.64	1.45	1.33
200	17.80	9.44	6.67	5.30	4.48	3.56	3.28	2.90	2.66
300	26.69	14.16	10.01	7.94	6.72	5.34	4.92	4.35	3.99
400	35.59	18.88	13.34	10.59	8.95	7.12	6.56	5.80	5.32
500	44.49	23.60	16.67	13.23	11.19	8.90	8.20	7.25	6.65
600	53.38	28.32	20.01	15.88	13.43	10.68	9.84	8.70	7.98
700	62.28	33.04	23.34	18.52	15.66	12.46	11.48	10.15	9.31
800	71.18	37.76	26.67	21.17	17.90	14.23	13.12	11.60	10.63
900	80.07	42.48	30.01	23.82	20.14	16.01	14.76	13.05	11.96
1000	88.97	47.20	33.34	26.46	22.38	17.79	16.40	14.50	13.29
2000	177.94	94.39	66.67	52.92	44.75	35.58	32.79	28.99	26.58
3000	266.90	141.58	100.01	79.38	67.12	53.37	49.18	43.48	39.86
4000	355.87	188.77	133.34	105.83	89.49	71.15	65.57	57.97	53.15
5000	444.83	235.96	166.67	132.29	111.86	88.94	81.96	72.46	66.43
6000	533.80	283.15	200.01	158.75	134.23	106.73	98.35	86.96	79.72
7000	622.77	330.34	233.34	185.20	156.60	124.51	114.74	101.45	93.01
8000	711.73	377.53	266.68	211.66	178.97	142.30	131.13	115.94	106.29
9000	800.70	424.72	300.01	238.12	201.34	160.09	147.52	130.43	119.58
10000	889.66	471.91	333.34	264.57	223.71	177.87	163.91	144.92	132.86
15000	1334.49	707.86	500.01	396.86	335.57	266.81	245.86	217.38	199.29
20000	1779.32	943.81	666.68	529.14	447.42	355.74	327.82	289.84	265.72
25000	2224.15	1179.76	833.35	661.42	559.28	444.67	409.77	362.30	332.15
30000	2668.98	1415.71	1000.02	793.71	671.13	533.61	491.72	434.76	398.58
35000	3113.81	1651.67	1166.69	925.99	782.99	622.54	573.67	507.22	465.01
40000	3558.64	1887.62	1333.36	1058.28	894.84	711.47	655.63	579.68	531.44
45000	4003.47	2123.57	1500.03	1190.56	1006.70	800.41	737.58	652.14	597.87
46000	4092.43	2170.76	1533.36	1217.02	1029.07	818.19	753.97	666.64	611.16
47000	4181.40	2217.95	1566.70	1243.47	1051.44	835.98	770.36	681.13	624.45
48000	4270.36	2265.14	1600.03	1269.93	1073.81	853.77	786.75	695.62	637.73
49000	4359.33	2312.33	1633.36	1296.39	1096.18	871.55	803.14	710.11	651.02
50000	4448.29	2359.52	1666.70	1322.84	1118.55	889.34	819.53	724.60	664.30
51000	4537.26	2406.71	1700.03	1349.30	1140.93	907.13	835.92	739.10	677.59
52000	4626.23	2453.90	1733.36	1375.76	1163.30	924.91	852.31	753.59	690.88
53000	4715.19	2501.09	1766.70	1402.21	1185.67	942.70	868.70	768.08	704.16
54000	4804.16	2548.28	1800.03	1428.67	1208.04	960.49	885.09	782.57	717.45
55000	4893.12	2595.47	1833.37	1455.13	1230.41	978.27	901.48	797.06	730.73
56000	4982.09	2642.66	1866.70	1481.58	1252.78	996.06	917.87	811.56	744.02
57000	5071.05	2689.85	1900.03	1508.04	1275.15	1013.85	934.26	826.05	757.31
58000	5160.02	2737.04	1933.37	1534.50	1297.52	1031.63	950.65	840.54	770.59
59000	5248.99	2784.23	1966.70	1560.95	1319.89	1049.42	967.05	855.03	783.88
60000	5337.95	2831.42	2000.04	1587.41	1342.26	1067.21	983.44	869.52	797.16
61000	5426.92	2878.61	2033.37	1613.87	1364.64	1084.99	999.83	884.02	810.45
62000	5515.88	2925.80	2066.70	1640.32	1387.01	1102.78	1016.22	898.51	823.73
63000	5604.85	2972.99	2100.04	1666.78	1409.38	1120.57	1032.61	913.00	837.02
64000	5693.82	3020.18	2133.37	1693.24	1431.75	1138.35	1049.00	927.49	850.31
65000	5782.78	3067.37	2166.70	1719.69	1454.12	1156.14	1065.39	941.98	863.59
67500	6005.20	3185.35	2250.04	1785.84	1510.05	1200.61	1106.36	978.21	896.81
70000	6227.61	3303.33	2333.37	1851.98	1565.97	1245.07	1147.34	1014.44	930.02
75000	6672.44	3539.28	2500.04	1984.26	1677.83	1334.01	1229.29	1086.90	996.45
80000	7117.27	3775.23	2666.71	2116.55	1789.68	1422.94	1311.25	1159.36	1062.88
85000	7562.10	4011.18	2833.38	2248.83	1901.54	1511.88	1393.20	1231.82	1129.31
90000	8006.93	4247.13	3000.05	2381.11	2013.39	1600.81	1475.15	1304.28	1195.74
95000	8451.75	4483.08	3166.72	2513.40	2125.25	1689.74	1557.10	1376.74	1262.17
100000	8896.58	4719.04	3333.39	2645.68	2237.10	1778.68	1639.06	1449.20	1328.60
105000	9341.41	4954.99	3500.06	2777.96	2348.96	1867.61	1721.01	1521.66	1395.03
110000	9786.24	5190.94	3666.73	2910.25	2460.81	1956.54	1802.96	1594.12	1461.46
115000	10231.07	5426.89	3833.40	3042.53	2572.67	2045.48	1884.91	1666.58	1527.89
120000	10675.90	5662.84	4000.07	3174.82	2684.52	2134.41	1966.87	1739.04	1594.32
125000	11120.73	5898.79	4166.74	3307.10	2796.38	2223.34	2048.82	1811.50	1660.75
130000	11565.56	6134.74	4333.40	3439.38	2908.23	2312.28	2130.77	1883.96	1727.18
135000	12010.39	6370.70	4500.07	3571.67	3020.09	2401.21	2212.72	1956.42	1793.61
140000	12455.21	6606.65	4666.74	3703.95	3131.94	2490.14	2294.68	2028.88	1860.04
145000	12900.04	6842.60	4833.41	3836.23	3243.80	2579.08	2376.63	2101.34	1926.47
150000	13344.87	7078.55	5000.08	3968.52	3355.65	2668.01	2458.58	2173.80	1992.90

MONTHLY PAYMENT 12¼%
NECESSARY TO AMORTIZE A LOAN

AMOUNT	15 YEARS	18 YEARS	20 YEARS	25 YEARS	28 YEARS	29 YEARS	30 YEARS	35 YEARS	40 YEARS
$ 50	.61	.58	.56	.54	.53	.53	.53	.52	.52
100	1.22	1.15	1.12	1.08	1.06	1.06	1.05	1.04	1.03
200	2.44	2.30	2.24	2.15	2.12	2.11	2.10	2.08	2.06
300	3.65	3.45	3.36	3.22	3.17	3.16	3.15	3.11	3.09
400	4.87	4.60	4.48	4.29	4.23	4.21	4.20	4.15	4.12
500	6.09	5.75	5.60	5.36	5.28	5.26	5.24	5.18	5.15
600	7.30	6.90	6.72	6.44	6.34	6.31	6.29	6.22	6.18
700	8.52	8.05	7.83	7.51	7.39	7.37	7.34	7.25	7.21
800	9.74	9.20	8.95	8.58	8.45	8.42	8.39	8.29	8.23
900	10.95	10.35	10.07	9.65	9.51	9.47	9.44	9.32	9.26
1000	12.17	11.49	11.19	10.72	10.56	10.52	10.48	10.36	10.29
2000	24.33	22.98	22.38	21.44	21.12	21.04	20.96	20.71	20.58
3000	36.49	34.47	33.56	32.16	31.67	31.55	31.44	31.07	30.87
4000	48.66	45.96	44.75	42.87	42.23	42.07	41.92	41.42	41.15
5000	60.82	57.45	55.93	53.59	52.79	52.58	52.40	51.77	51.44
6000	72.98	68.94	67.12	64.31	63.34	63.10	62.88	62.13	61.73
7000	85.15	80.43	78.30	75.03	73.90	73.61	73.36	72.48	72.01
8000	97.31	91.92	89.49	85.74	84.45	84.13	83.84	82.83	82.30
9000	109.47	103.41	100.68	96.46	95.01	94.64	94.32	93.19	92.59
10000	121.63	114.90	111.86	107.18	105.57	105.16	104.79	103.54	102.87
15000	182.45	172.34	167.79	160.77	158.35	157.73	157.19	155.31	154.31
20000	243.26	229.79	223.72	214.35	211.13	210.31	209.58	207.08	205.74
25000	304.08	287.24	279.65	267.94	263.91	262.88	261.98	258.85	257.18
30000	364.89	344.68	335.57	321.53	316.69	315.46	314.37	310.62	308.61
35000	425.71	402.13	391.50	375.12	369.47	368.03	366.77	362.38	360.05
40000	486.52	459.58	447.43	428.70	422.25	420.61	419.16	414.15	411.48
45000	547.34	517.02	503.36	482.29	475.03	473.18	471.56	465.92	462.91
46000	559.50	528.51	514.54	493.01	485.59	483.70	482.04	476.28	473.20
47000	571.67	540.00	525.73	503.72	496.15	494.21	492.52	486.63	483.49
48000	583.83	551.49	536.92	514.44	506.70	504.73	503.00	496.98	493.77
49000	595.99	562.98	548.10	525.16	517.26	515.24	513.47	507.34	504.06
50000	608.15	574.47	559.29	535.88	527.82	525.76	523.95	517.69	514.35
51000	620.32	585.96	570.47	546.59	538.37	536.27	534.43	528.04	524.63
52000	632.48	597.45	581.66	557.31	548.93	546.79	544.91	538.40	534.92
53000	644.64	608.94	592.84	568.03	559.48	557.31	555.39	548.75	545.21
54000	656.81	620.43	604.03	578.75	570.04	567.82	565.87	559.11	555.50
55000	668.97	631.91	615.22	589.46	580.60	578.34	576.35	569.46	565.78
56000	681.13	643.40	626.40	600.18	591.15	588.85	586.83	579.81	576.07
57000	693.30	654.89	637.59	610.90	601.71	599.37	597.31	590.17	586.36
58000	705.46	666.38	648.77	621.62	612.27	609.88	607.78	600.52	596.64
59000	717.62	677.87	659.96	632.33	622.82	620.40	618.26	610.87	606.93
60000	729.78	689.36	671.14	643.05	633.38	630.91	628.74	621.23	617.22
61000	741.95	700.85	682.33	653.77	643.93	641.43	639.22	631.58	627.50
62000	754.11	712.34	693.52	664.49	654.49	651.94	649.70	641.94	637.79
63000	766.27	723.83	704.70	675.20	665.05	662.46	660.18	652.29	648.08
64000	778.44	735.32	715.89	685.92	675.60	672.97	670.66	662.64	658.36
65000	790.60	746.81	727.07	696.64	686.16	683.49	681.14	673.00	668.65
67500	821.01	775.53	755.04	723.43	712.55	709.77	707.34	698.88	694.37
70000	851.41	804.25	783.00	750.23	738.94	736.06	733.53	724.76	720.09
75000	912.23	861.70	838.93	803.81	791.72	788.64	785.93	776.53	771.52
80000	973.04	919.15	894.86	857.40	844.50	841.21	838.32	828.30	822.95
85000	1033.86	976.59	950.78	910.99	897.28	893.79	890.72	880.07	874.39
90000	1094.67	1034.04	1006.71	964.57	950.06	946.36	943.11	931.84	925.82
95000	1155.49	1091.49	1062.64	1018.16	1002.85	998.94	995.51	983.61	977.26
100000	1216.30	1148.93	1118.57	1071.75	1055.63	1051.51	1047.90	1035.38	1028.69
105000	1277.12	1206.38	1174.50	1125.34	1108.41	1104.09	1100.30	1087.14	1080.13
110000	1337.93	1263.82	1230.43	1178.92	1161.19	1156.67	1152.69	1138.91	1131.56
115000	1398.75	1321.27	1286.35	1232.51	1213.97	1209.24	1205.09	1190.68	1182.99
120000	1459.56	1378.72	1342.28	1286.10	1266.75	1261.82	1257.48	1242.45	1234.43
125000	1520.38	1436.16	1398.21	1339.68	1319.53	1314.39	1309.88	1294.22	1285.86
130000	1581.19	1493.61	1454.14	1393.27	1372.31	1366.97	1362.27	1345.99	1337.30
135000	1642.01	1551.06	1510.07	1446.86	1425.09	1419.54	1414.67	1397.76	1388.73
140000	1702.82	1608.50	1566.00	1500.45	1477.87	1472.12	1467.06	1449.52	1440.17
145000	1763.64	1665.95	1621.92	1554.03	1530.66	1524.69	1519.45	1501.29	1491.60
150000	1824.45	1723.40	1677.85	1607.62	1583.44	1577.27	1571.85	1553.06	1543.03

MONTHLY PAYMENT
NECESSARY TO AMORTIZE A LOAN

AMOUNT	1 YEAR	2 YEARS	3 YEARS	4 YEARS	5 YEARS	7 YEARS	8 YEARS	10 YEARS	12 YEARS
$ 50	4.46	2.37	1.67	1.33	1.13	.90	.83	.73	.67
100	8.91	4.73	3.34	2.66	2.25	1.79	1.65	1.46	1.34
200	17.81	9.45	6.68	5.31	4.49	3.58	3.30	2.92	2.68
300	26.71	14.18	10.02	7.96	6.74	5.36	4.94	4.37	4.01
400	35.61	18.90	13.36	10.61	8.98	7.15	6.59	5.83	5.35
500	44.52	23.63	16.70	13.26	11.22	8.93	8.23	7.29	6.69
600	53.42	28.35	20.04	15.92	13.47	10.72	9.88	8.74	8.02
700	62.32	33.08	23.38	18.57	15.71	12.50	11.53	10.20	9.36
800	71.22	37.80	26.72	21.22	17.95	14.29	13.17	11.66	10.69
900	80.13	42.53	30.06	23.87	20.20	16.07	14.82	13.11	12.03
1000	89.03	47.25	33.40	26.52	22.44	17.86	16.46	14.57	13.37
2000	178.05	94.50	66.79	53.04	44.87	35.71	32.92	29.13	26.73
3000	267.08	141.75	100.19	79.56	67.31	53.57	49.38	43.70	40.09
4000	356.10	189.00	133.58	106.08	89.74	71.42	65.84	58.26	53.45
5000	445.13	236.25	166.97	132.60	112.18	89.27	82.30	72.83	66.82
6000	534.15	283.50	200.37	159.11	134.61	107.13	98.76	87.39	80.18
7000	623.18	330.75	233.76	185.63	157.05	124.98	115.22	101.96	93.54
8000	712.20	378.00	267.15	212.15	179.48	142.84	131.68	116.52	106.90
9000	801.22	425.24	300.55	238.67	201.91	160.69	148.14	131.09	120.26
10000	890.25	472.49	333.94	265.19	224.35	178.54	164.60	145.65	133.63
15000	1335.37	708.74	500.91	397.78	336.52	267.81	246.90	218.48	200.44
20000	1780.49	944.98	667.88	530.37	448.69	357.08	329.20	291.30	267.25
25000	2225.61	1181.22	834.85	662.96	560.87	446.35	411.49	364.12	334.06
30000	2670.73	1417.47	1001.82	795.55	673.04	535.62	493.79	436.95	400.87
35000	3115.86	1653.71	1168.78	928.15	785.21	624.89	576.09	509.77	467.68
40000	3560.98	1889.96	1335.75	1060.74	897.38	714.16	658.39	582.59	534.49
45000	4006.10	2126.20	1502.72	1193.33	1009.55	803.43	740.69	655.42	601.30
46000	4095.12	2173.45	1536.12	1219.85	1031.99	821.28	757.15	669.98	614.66
47000	4184.15	2220.70	1569.51	1246.37	1054.42	839.14	773.61	684.55	628.03
48000	4273.17	2267.95	1602.90	1272.88	1076.86	856.99	790.07	699.11	641.39
49000	4362.20	2315.20	1636.30	1299.40	1099.29	874.85	806.52	713.68	654.75
50000	4451.22	2362.44	1669.69	1325.92	1121.73	892.70	822.98	728.24	668.11
51000	4540.24	2409.69	1703.08	1352.44	1144.16	910.55	839.44	742.81	681.48
52000	4629.27	2456.94	1736.48	1378.96	1166.59	928.41	855.90	757.37	694.84
53000	4718.29	2504.19	1769.87	1405.48	1189.03	946.26	872.36	771.93	708.20
54000	4807.32	2551.44	1803.26	1431.99	1211.46	964.12	888.82	786.50	721.56
55000	4896.34	2598.69	1836.66	1458.51	1233.90	981.97	905.28	801.06	734.92
56000	4985.37	2645.94	1870.05	1485.03	1256.33	999.82	921.74	815.63	748.29
57000	5074.39	2693.19	1903.45	1511.55	1278.77	1017.68	938.20	830.19	761.65
58000	5163.42	2740.43	1936.84	1538.07	1301.20	1035.53	954.66	844.76	775.01
59000	5252.44	2787.68	1970.23	1564.59	1323.64	1053.39	971.12	859.32	788.37
60000	5341.46	2834.93	2003.63	1591.10	1346.07	1071.24	987.58	873.89	801.73
61000	5430.49	2882.18	2037.02	1617.62	1368.50	1089.09	1004.04	888.45	815.10
62000	5519.51	2929.43	2070.41	1644.14	1390.94	1106.95	1020.50	903.02	828.46
63000	5608.54	2976.68	2103.81	1670.66	1413.37	1124.80	1036.96	917.58	841.82
64000	5697.56	3023.93	2137.20	1697.18	1435.81	1142.65	1053.42	932.15	855.18
65000	5786.59	3071.18	2170.60	1723.70	1458.24	1160.51	1069.88	946.71	868.55
67500	6009.15	3189.30	2254.08	1789.99	1514.33	1205.14	1111.03	983.12	901.95
70000	6231.71	3307.42	2337.56	1856.29	1570.41	1249.78	1152.18	1019.53	935.36
75000	6676.83	3543.66	2504.53	1988.88	1682.59	1339.05	1234.47	1092.36	1002.17
80000	7121.95	3779.91	2671.50	2121.47	1794.76	1428.32	1316.77	1165.18	1068.98
85000	7567.07	4016.15	2838.47	2254.06	1906.93	1517.59	1399.07	1238.01	1135.79
90000	8012.19	4252.40	3005.44	2386.65	2019.10	1606.86	1481.37	1310.83	1202.60
95000	8457.31	4488.64	3172.41	2519.25	2131.27	1696.13	1563.67	1383.65	1269.41
100000	8902.44	4724.88	3339.38	2651.84	2243.45	1785.40	1645.96	1456.48	1336.22
105000	9347.56	4961.13	3506.34	2784.43	2355.62	1874.66	1728.26	1529.30	1403.03
110000	9792.68	5197.37	3673.31	2917.02	2467.79	1963.93	1810.56	1602.12	1469.84
115000	10237.80	5433.62	3840.28	3049.61	2579.96	2053.20	1892.86	1674.95	1536.65
120000	10682.92	5669.86	4007.25	3182.20	2692.13	2142.47	1975.16	1747.77	1603.46
125000	11128.04	5906.10	4174.22	3314.80	2804.31	2231.74	2057.45	1820.59	1670.28
130000	11573.17	6142.35	4341.19	3447.39	2916.48	2321.01	2139.75	1893.42	1737.09
135000	12018.29	6378.59	4508.15	3579.98	3028.65	2410.28	2222.05	1966.24	1803.90
140000	12463.41	6614.83	4675.12	3712.57	3140.82	2499.55	2304.35	2039.06	1870.71
145000	12908.53	6851.08	4842.09	3845.16	3252.99	2588.82	2386.64	2111.89	1937.52
150000	13353.65	7087.32	5009.06	3977.75	3365.17	2678.09	2468.94	2184.71	2004.33

MONTHLY PAYMENT 12⅜%
NECESSARY TO AMORTIZE A LOAN

AMOUNT	15 YEARS	18 YEARS	20 YEARS	25 YEARS	28 YEARS	29 YEARS	30 YEARS	35 YEARS	40 YEARS
$ 50	.62	.58	.57	.55	.54	.54	.53	.53	.52
100	1.23	1.16	1.13	1.09	1.07	1.07	1.06	1.05	1.04
200	2.45	2.32	2.26	2.17	2.14	2.13	2.12	2.10	2.08
300	3.68	3.48	3.39	3.25	3.20	3.19	3.18	3.14	3.12
400	4.90	4.63	4.51	4.33	4.27	4.25	4.24	4.19	4.16
500	6.13	5.79	5.64	5.41	5.33	5.31	5.29	5.23	5.20
600	7.35	6.95	6.77	6.49	6.40	6.37	6.35	6.28	6.24
700	8.58	8.11	7.90	7.57	7.46	7.43	7.41	7.32	7.28
800	9.80	9.26	9.02	8.65	8.53	8.49	8.47	8.37	8.32
900	11.02	10.42	10.15	9.73	9.59	9.56	9.52	9.41	9.35
1000	12.25	11.58	11.28	10.82	10.66	10.62	10.58	10.46	10.39
2000	24.49	23.15	22.55	21.63	21.31	21.23	21.16	20.91	20.78
3000	36.74	34.73	33.83	32.44	31.96	31.84	31.73	31.36	31.17
4000	48.98	46.30	45.10	43.25	42.61	42.45	42.31	41.82	41.56
5000	61.22	57.88	56.37	54.06	53.26	53.06	52.88	52.27	51.94
6000	73.47	69.45	67.65	64.87	63.91	63.67	63.46	62.72	62.33
7000	85.71	81.03	78.92	75.68	74.57	74.28	74.03	73.18	72.72
8000	97.96	92.60	90.19	86.49	85.22	84.89	84.61	83.63	83.11
9000	110.20	104.18	101.47	97.30	95.87	95.51	95.19	94.08	93.50
10000	122.44	115.75	112.74	108.11	106.52	106.12	105.76	104.54	103.88
15000	183.66	173.62	169.11	162.16	159.78	159.17	158.64	156.80	155.82
20000	244.88	231.50	225.47	216.21	213.04	212.23	211.52	209.07	207.76
25000	306.10	289.37	281.84	270.26	266.29	265.28	264.40	261.33	259.70
30000	367.32	347.24	338.21	324.32	319.55	318.34	317.28	313.60	311.64
35000	428.54	405.11	394.57	378.37	372.81	371.40	370.15	365.86	363.58
40000	489.76	462.99	450.94	432.42	426.07	424.45	423.03	418.13	415.52
45000	550.98	520.86	507.31	486.47	479.33	477.51	475.91	470.39	467.46
46000	563.23	532.43	518.58	497.28	489.98	488.12	486.49	480.85	477.85
47000	575.47	544.01	529.86	508.09	500.63	498.73	497.06	491.30	488.24
48000	587.72	555.58	541.13	518.90	511.28	509.34	507.64	501.75	498.63
49000	599.96	567.16	552.40	529.71	521.93	519.95	518.21	512.20	509.02
50000	612.20	578.73	563.68	540.52	532.58	530.56	528.79	522.66	519.40
51000	624.45	590.31	574.95	551.33	543.24	541.17	539.36	533.11	529.79
52000	636.69	601.88	586.22	562.14	553.89	551.79	549.94	543.56	540.18
53000	648.94	613.45	597.50	572.96	564.54	562.40	560.52	554.02	550.57
54000	661.18	625.03	608.77	583.77	575.19	573.01	571.09	564.47	560.96
55000	673.42	636.60	620.04	594.58	585.84	583.62	581.67	574.92	571.34
56000	685.67	648.18	631.32	605.39	596.49	594.23	592.24	585.38	581.73
57000	697.91	659.75	642.59	616.20	607.14	604.84	602.82	595.83	592.12
58000	710.16	671.33	653.86	627.01	617.80	615.45	613.39	606.28	602.51
59000	722.40	682.90	665.14	637.82	628.45	626.06	623.97	616.74	612.90
60000	734.64	694.48	676.41	648.63	639.10	636.67	634.55	627.19	623.28
61000	746.89	706.05	687.68	659.44	649.75	647.29	645.12	637.64	633.67
62000	759.13	717.63	698.96	670.25	660.40	657.90	655.70	648.09	644.06
63000	771.38	729.20	710.23	681.06	671.05	668.51	666.27	658.55	654.45
64000	783.62	740.77	721.50	691.88	681.71	679.12	676.85	669.00	664.84
65000	795.86	752.35	732.78	702.68	692.36	689.73	687.42	679.45	675.22
67500	826.47	781.29	760.96	729.71	718.99	716.26	713.86	705.59	701.19
70000	857.08	810.23	789.14	756.73	745.61	742.79	740.30	731.72	727.16
75000	918.30	868.09	845.51	810.78	798.87	795.84	793.18	783.98	779.10
80000	979.52	925.97	901.88	864.84	852.13	848.90	846.06	836.25	831.04
85000	1040.74	983.84	958.24	918.89	905.39	901.95	898.94	888.51	882.98
90000	1101.96	1041.71	1014.61	972.94	958.65	955.01	951.82	940.78	934.92
95000	1163.18	1099.58	1070.98	1026.99	1011.90	1008.06	1004.69	993.04	986.86
100000	1224.40	1157.46	1127.35	1081.04	1065.16	1061.12	1057.57	1045.31	1038.80
105000	1285.62	1215.33	1183.71	1135.09	1118.42	1114.18	1110.45	1097.58	1090.74
110000	1346.84	1273.20	1240.08	1189.15	1171.68	1167.23	1163.33	1149.84	1142.68
115000	1408.06	1331.07	1296.45	1243.20	1224.94	1220.29	1216.21	1202.11	1194.62
120000	1469.28	1388.95	1352.81	1297.25	1278.19	1273.34	1269.09	1254.37	1246.56
125000	1530.50	1446.82	1409.18	1351.30	1331.45	1326.40	1321.96	1306.64	1298.50
130000	1591.72	1504.69	1465.55	1405.35	1384.71	1379.46	1374.84	1358.90	1350.44
135000	1652.94	1562.57	1521.91	1459.41	1437.97	1432.51	1427.72	1411.17	1402.38
140000	1714.16	1620.44	1578.28	1513.46	1491.22	1485.57	1480.60	1463.43	1454.32
145000	1775.38	1678.31	1634.65	1567.51	1544.48	1538.62	1533.48	1515.70	1506.26
150000	1836.60	1736.18	1691.02	1621.56	1597.74	1591.68	1586.36	1567.96	1558.20

12½% MONTHLY PAYMENT
NECESSARY TO AMORTIZE A LOAN

AMOUNT	1 YEAR	2 YEARS	3 YEARS	4 YEARS	5 YEARS	7 YEARS	8 YEARS	10 YEARS	12 YEARS
$ 50	4.46	2.37	1.68	1.33	1.13	.90	.83	.74	.68
100	8.91	4.74	3.35	2.66	2.25	1.80	1.66	1.47	1.35
200	17.82	9.47	6.70	5.32	4.50	3.59	3.31	2.93	2.69
300	26.73	14.20	10.04	7.98	6.75	5.38	4.96	4.40	4.04
400	35.64	18.93	13.39	10.64	9.00	7.17	6.62	5.86	5.38
500	44.55	23.66	16.73	13.29	11.25	8.97	8.27	7.32	6.72
600	53.45	28.39	20.08	15.95	13.50	10.76	9.92	8.79	8.07
700	62.36	33.12	23.42	18.61	15.75	12.55	11.58	10.25	9.41
800	71.27	37.85	26.77	21.27	18.00	14.34	13.23	11.72	10.76
900	80.18	42.58	30.11	23.93	20.25	16.13	14.88	13.18	12.10
1000	89.09	47.31	33.46	26.58	22.50	17.93	16.53	14.64	13.44
2000	178.17	94.62	66.91	53.16	45.00	35.85	33.06	29.28	26.88
3000	267.25	141.93	100.37	79.74	67.50	53.77	49.59	43.92	40.32
4000	356.34	189.23	133.82	106.32	90.00	71.69	66.12	58.56	53.76
5000	445.42	236.54	167.27	132.90	112.49	89.61	82.65	73.19	67.20
6000	534.50	283.85	200.73	159.48	134.99	107.53	99.18	87.83	80.64
7000	623.59	331.16	234.18	186.06	157.49	125.45	115.71	102.47	94.08
8000	712.67	378.46	267.63	212.64	179.99	143.37	132.24	117.11	107.51
9000	801.75	425.77	301.09	239.22	202.49	161.30	148.76	131.74	120.95
10000	890.83	473.08	334.54	265.80	224.98	179.22	165.29	146.38	134.39
15000	1336.25	709.61	501.81	398.70	337.47	268.82	247.94	219.57	201.58
20000	1781.66	946.15	669.08	531.60	449.96	358.43	330.58	292.76	268.78
25000	2227.08	1182.69	836.35	664.50	562.45	448.04	413.23	365.95	335.97
30000	2672.49	1419.22	1003.61	797.40	674.94	537.64	495.87	439.13	403.16
35000	3117.91	1655.76	1170.88	930.30	787.43	627.25	578.51	512.32	470.36
40000	3563.32	1892.30	1338.15	1063.20	899.92	716.85	661.16	585.51	537.55
45000	4008.73	2128.83	1505.42	1196.10	1012.41	806.46	743.80	658.70	604.74
46000	4097.82	2176.14	1538.87	1222.68	1034.91	824.38	760.33	673.34	618.18
47000	4186.90	2223.45	1572.33	1249.26	1057.41	842.30	776.86	687.97	631.62
48000	4275.98	2270.76	1605.78	1275.84	1079.91	860.22	793.39	702.61	645.06
49000	4365.07	2318.06	1639.23	1302.42	1102.40	878.15	809.92	717.25	658.50
50000	4454.15	2365.37	1672.69	1329.00	1124.90	896.07	826.45	731.89	671.93
51000	4543.23	2412.68	1706.14	1355.58	1147.40	913.99	842.37	746.52	685.37
52000	4632.31	2459.99	1739.59	1382.16	1169.90	931.91	859.50	761.16	698.81
53000	4721.40	2507.29	1773.05	1408.74	1192.40	949.83	876.03	775.80	712.25
54000	4810.48	2554.60	1806.50	1435.32	1214.89	967.75	892.56	790.44	725.69
55000	4899.56	2601.91	1839.95	1461.90	1237.39	985.67	909.09	805.07	739.13
56000	4988.65	2649.21	1873.41	1488.48	1259.89	1003.59	925.62	819.71	752.57
57000	5077.73	2696.52	1906.86	1515.06	1282.39	1021.52	942.15	834.35	766.00
58000	5166.81	2743.83	1940.32	1541.64	1304.89	1039.44	958.68	848.99	779.44
59000	5255.89	2791.14	1973.77	1568.22	1327.38	1057.36	975.20	863.62	792.88
60000	5344.98	2838.44	2007.22	1594.80	1349.88	1075.28	991.73	878.26	806.32
61000	5434.06	2885.75	2040.68	1621.38	1372.38	1093.20	1008.26	892.90	819.76
62000	5523.14	2933.06	2074.13	1647.96	1394.88	1111.12	1024.79	907.54	833.20
63000	5612.23	2980.37	2107.58	1674.54	1417.38	1129.04	1041.32	922.17	846.64
64000	5701.31	3027.67	2141.04	1701.12	1439.87	1146.96	1057.85	936.81	860.07
65000	5790.39	3074.98	2174.49	1727.70	1462.37	1164.89	1074.38	951.45	873.51
67500	6013.10	3193.25	2258.12	1794.15	1518.62	1209.69	1115.70	988.04	907.11
70000	6235.81	3311.52	2341.76	1860.60	1574.86	1254.49	1157.02	1024.64	940.71
75000	6681.22	3548.05	2509.03	1993.50	1687.35	1344.10	1239.67	1097.83	1007.90
80000	7126.63	3784.59	2676.30	2126.40	1799.84	1433.70	1322.31	1171.01	1075.09
85000	7572.05	4021.13	2843.56	2259.30	1912.33	1523.31	1404.95	1244.20	1142.28
90000	8017.46	4257.66	3010.83	2392.20	2024.82	1612.92	1487.60	1317.39	1209.48
95000	8462.88	4494.20	3178.10	2525.10	2137.31	1702.52	1570.24	1390.58	1276.67
100000	8908.29	4730.74	3345.37	2658.00	2249.80	1792.13	1652.89	1463.77	1343.86
105000	9353.71	4967.27	3512.64	2790.90	2362.29	1881.74	1735.53	1536.95	1411.06
110000	9799.12	5203.81	3679.90	2923.80	2474.78	1971.34	1818.17	1610.14	1478.25
115000	10244.53	5440.35	3847.17	3056.70	2587.27	2060.95	1900.82	1683.33	1545.44
120000	10689.95	5676.88	4014.44	3189.60	2699.76	2150.55	1983.46	1756.52	1612.63
125000	11135.36	5913.42	4181.71	3322.50	2812.25	2240.16	2066.11	1829.71	1679.83
130000	11580.78	6149.96	4348.98	3455.40	2924.74	2329.77	2148.75	1902.90	1747.02
135000	12026.19	6386.49	4516.24	3588.30	3037.23	2419.37	2231.39	1976.08	1814.21
140000	12471.61	6623.03	4683.51	3721.20	3149.72	2508.98	2314.04	2049.27	1881.41
145000	12917.02	6859.56	4850.78	3854.10	3262.21	2598.58	2396.68	2122.46	1948.60
150000	13362.43	7096.10	5018.05	3987.00	3374.70	2688.19	2479.33	2195.65	2015.79

MONTHLY PAYMENT 12½%
NECESSARY TO AMORTIZE A LOAN

AMOUNT	15 YEARS	18 YEARS	20 YEARS	25 YEARS	28 YEARS	29 YEARS	30 YEARS	35 YEARS	40 YEARS
$ 50	.62	.59	.57	.55	.54	.54	.54	.53	.53
100	1.24	1.17	1.14	1.10	1.08	1.08	1.07	1.06	1.05
200	2.47	2.34	2.28	2.19	2.15	2.15	2.14	2.12	2.10
300	3.70	3.50	3.41	3.28	3.23	3.22	3.21	3.17	3.15
400	4.94	4.67	4.55	4.37	4.30	4.29	4.27	4.23	4.20
500	6.17	5.84	5.69	5.46	5.38	5.36	5.34	5.28	5.25
600	7.40	7.00	6.82	6.55	6.45	6.43	6.41	6.34	6.30
700	8.63	8.17	7.96	7.64	7.53	7.50	7.48	7.39	7.35
800	9.87	9.33	9.09	8.73	8.60	8.57	8.54	8.45	8.40
900	11.10	10.50	10.23	9.82	9.68	9.64	9.61	9.50	9.45
1000	12.33	11.67	11.37	10.91	10.75	10.71	10.68	10.56	10.49
2000	24.66	23.33	22.73	21.81	21.50	21.42	21.35	21.11	20.98
3000	36.98	34.99	34.09	32.72	32.25	32.13	32.02	31.66	31.47
4000	49.31	46.65	45.45	43.62	42.99	42.83	42.70	42.22	41.96
5000	61.63	58.31	56.81	54.52	53.74	53.54	53.37	52.77	52.45
6000	73.96	69.97	68.17	65.43	64.49	64.25	64.04	63.32	62.94
7000	86.28	81.63	79.53	76.33	75.23	74.96	74.71	73.87	73.43
8000	98.61	93.29	90.90	87.23	85.98	85.66	85.39	84.43	83.92
9000	110.93	104.95	102.26	98.14	96.73	96.37	96.06	94.98	94.41
10000	123.26	116.61	113.62	109.04	107.48	107.08	106.73	105.53	104.90
15000	184.88	174.91	170.43	163.56	161.21	160.62	160.09	158.29	157.34
20000	246.51	233.21	227.23	218.08	214.95	214.15	213.46	211.06	209.79
25000	308.14	291.51	284.04	272.59	268.68	267.69	266.82	263.82	262.23
30000	369.76	349.81	340.85	327.11	322.42	321.23	320.18	316.58	314.68
35000	431.39	408.11	397.65	381.63	376.15	374.76	373.55	369.34	367.13
40000	493.01	466.41	454.46	436.15	429.89	428.30	426.91	422.11	419.57
45000	554.64	524.71	511.27	490.66	483.63	481.84	480.27	474.87	472.02
46000	566.97	536.37	522.63	501.57	494.37	492.55	490.94	485.42	482.51
47000	579.29	548.03	533.99	512.47	505.12	503.25	501.62	495.97	493.00
48000	591.62	559.69	545.35	523.37	515.87	513.96	512.29	506.53	503.49
49000	603.94	571.35	556.71	534.28	526.61	524.67	522.96	517.08	513.98
50000	616.27	583.01	568.08	545.18	537.36	535.38	533.63	527.63	524.46
51000	628.59	594.67	579.44	556.09	548.11	546.08	544.31	538.18	534.95
52000	640.92	606.33	590.80	566.99	558.86	556.79	554.98	548.74	545.44
53000	653.24	617.99	602.16	577.89	569.60	567.50	565.65	559.29	555.93
54000	665.57	629.65	613.52	588.80	580.35	578.21	576.32	569.84	566.42
55000	677.89	641.31	624.88	599.70	591.10	588.91	587.00	580.39	576.91
56000	690.22	652.97	636.24	610.60	601.84	599.62	597.67	590.95	587.40
57000	702.54	664.63	647.61	621.51	612.59	610.33	608.34	601.50	597.89
58000	714.87	676.29	658.97	632.41	623.34	621.03	619.01	612.05	608.38
59000	727.19	687.95	670.33	643.31	634.09	631.74	629.69	622.61	618.87
60000	739.52	699.61	681.69	654.22	644.83	642.45	640.36	633.16	629.36
61000	751.84	711.27	693.05	665.12	655.58	653.16	651.03	643.71	639.85
62000	764.17	722.93	704.41	676.02	666.33	663.86	661.70	654.26	650.34
63000	776.49	734.59	715.77	686.93	677.07	674.57	672.38	664.82	660.82
64000	788.82	746.25	727.13	697.83	687.82	685.28	683.05	675.37	671.31
65000	801.14	757.91	738.50	708.74	698.57	695.99	693.72	685.92	681.80
67500	831.96	787.06	766.90	735.99	725.44	722.76	720.40	712.30	708.03
70000	862.77	816.21	795.30	763.25	752.30	749.52	747.09	738.68	734.25
75000	924.40	874.51	852.11	817.77	806.04	803.06	800.45	791.45	786.69
80000	986.02	932.81	908.92	872.29	859.78	856.60	853.81	844.21	839.14
85000	1047.65	991.11	965.72	926.81	913.51	910.13	907.17	896.97	891.59
90000	1109.27	1049.41	1022.53	981.32	967.25	963.67	960.54	949.73	944.03
95000	1170.90	1107.71	1079.34	1035.84	1020.98	1017.21	1013.90	1002.50	996.48
100000	1232.53	1166.01	1136.15	1090.36	1074.72	1070.75	1067.26	1055.26	1048.92
105000	1294.15	1224.31	1192.95	1144.88	1128.45	1124.28	1120.63	1108.02	1101.37
110000	1355.78	1282.61	1249.76	1199.39	1182.19	1177.82	1173.99	1160.78	1153.82
115000	1417.41	1340.91	1306.57	1253.91	1235.93	1231.36	1227.35	1213.55	1206.26
120000	1479.03	1399.21	1363.37	1308.43	1289.66	1284.89	1280.71	1266.31	1258.71
125000	1540.66	1457.51	1420.18	1362.95	1343.40	1338.43	1334.08	1319.07	1311.15
130000	1602.28	1515.81	1476.99	1417.47	1397.13	1391.97	1387.44	1371.84	1363.60
135000	1663.91	1574.11	1533.79	1471.98	1450.87	1445.51	1440.80	1424.60	1416.05
140000	1725.54	1632.41	1590.60	1526.50	1504.60	1499.04	1494.17	1477.36	1468.49
145000	1787.16	1690.71	1647.41	1581.02	1558.34	1552.58	1547.53	1530.12	1520.94
150000	1848.79	1749.01	1704.22	1635.54	1612.07	1606.12	1600.89	1582.89	1573.38

MONTHLY PAYMENT
NECESSARY TO AMORTIZE A LOAN

AMOUNT	1 YEAR	2 YEARS	3 YEARS	4 YEARS	5 YEARS	7 YEARS	8 YEARS	10 YEARS	12 YEARS
$ 50	4.46	2.37	1.68	1.34	1.13	.90	.83	.74	.68
100	8.92	4.74	3.36	2.67	2.26	1.80	1.66	1.48	1.36
200	17.83	9.48	6.71	5.33	4.52	3.60	3.32	2.95	2.71
300	26.75	14.21	10.06	8.00	6.77	5.40	4.98	4.42	4.06
400	35.66	18.95	13.41	10.66	9.03	7.20	6.64	5.89	5.41
500	44.58	23.69	16.76	13.33	11.29	9.00	8.30	7.36	6.76
600	53.49	28.42	20.11	15.99	13.54	10.80	9.96	8.83	8.11
700	62.40	33.16	23.46	18.65	15.80	12.60	11.62	10.30	9.47
800	71.32	37.90	26.82	21.32	18.05	14.40	13.28	11.77	10.82
900	80.23	42.63	30.17	23.98	20.31	16.19	14.94	13.24	12.17
1000	89.15	47.37	33.52	26.65	22.57	17.99	16.60	14.72	13.52
2000	178.29	94.74	67.03	53.29	45.13	35.98	33.20	29.43	27.04
3000	267.43	142.10	100.55	79.93	67.69	53.97	49.80	44.14	40.55
4000	356.57	189.47	134.06	106.57	90.25	71.96	66.40	58.85	54.07
5000	445.71	236.83	167.57	133.21	112.81	89.95	83.00	73.56	67.58
6000	534.85	284.20	201.09	159.86	135.37	107.94	99.59	88.27	81.10
7000	624.00	331.57	234.60	186.50	157.94	125.93	116.19	102.98	94.61
8000	713.14	378.93	268.11	213.14	180.50	143.91	132.79	117.69	108.13
9000	802.28	426.30	301.63	239.78	203.06	161.90	149.39	132.40	121.64
10000	891.42	473.66	335.14	266.42	225.62	179.89	165.99	147.11	135.16
15000	1337.13	710.49	502.71	399.63	338.43	269.84	248.98	220.67	202.73
20000	1782.83	947.32	670.28	532.84	451.24	359.78	331.97	294.22	270.31
25000	2228.54	1184.15	837.85	666.05	564.04	449.72	414.96	367.77	337.88
30000	2674.25	1420.98	1005.41	799.26	676.85	539.67	497.95	441.33	405.46
35000	3119.96	1657.81	1172.98	932.47	789.66	629.61	580.94	514.88	473.04
40000	3565.66	1894.64	1340.55	1065.67	902.47	719.55	663.93	588.43	540.61
45000	4011.37	2131.47	1508.12	1198.88	1015.28	809.50	746.92	661.99	608.19
46000	4100.51	2178.84	1541.63	1225.53	1037.84	827.49	763.52	676.70	621.70
47000	4189.65	2226.20	1575.14	1252.17	1060.40	845.47	780.12	691.41	635.22
48000	4278.79	2273.57	1608.66	1278.81	1082.96	863.46	796.72	706.12	648.73
49000	4367.94	2320.93	1642.17	1305.45	1105.52	881.45	813.32	720.83	662.25
50000	4457.08	2368.30	1675.69	1332.09	1128.08	899.44	829.91	735.54	675.76
51000	4546.22	2415.66	1709.20	1358.73	1150.64	917.42	846.51	750.25	689.28
52000	4635.36	2463.03	1742.71	1385.38	1173.21	935.42	863.11	764.96	702.79
53000	4724.50	2510.40	1776.23	1412.02	1195.77	953.41	879.71	779.67	716.31
54000	4813.64	2557.76	1809.74	1438.66	1218.33	971.40	896.31	794.38	729.83
55000	4902.78	2605.13	1843.25	1465.30	1240.89	989.38	912.91	809.09	743.34
56000	4991.93	2652.49	1876.77	1491.94	1263.45	1007.37	929.50	823.80	756.86
57000	5081.07	2699.86	1910.28	1518.58	1286.01	1025.36	946.10	838.52	770.37
58000	5170.21	2747.23	1943.79	1545.23	1308.58	1043.35	962.70	853.23	783.89
59000	5259.35	2794.59	1977.31	1571.87	1331.14	1061.34	979.30	867.94	797.40
60000	5348.49	2841.96	2010.82	1598.51	1353.70	1079.33	995.90	882.65	810.92
61000	5437.63	2889.32	2044.34	1625.15	1376.26	1097.32	1012.49	897.36	824.43
62000	5526.77	2936.69	2077.85	1651.79	1398.82	1115.31	1029.09	912.07	837.95
63000	5615.92	2984.06	2111.36	1678.44	1421.38	1133.29	1045.69	926.78	851.46
64000	5705.06	3031.42	2144.88	1705.08	1443.95	1151.28	1062.29	941.49	864.98
65000	5794.20	3078.79	2178.39	1731.72	1466.51	1169.27	1078.89	956.20	878.49
67500	6017.05	3197.20	2262.17	1798.32	1522.91	1214.24	1120.38	992.98	912.28
70000	6239.91	3315.62	2345.96	1864.93	1579.31	1259.21	1161.88	1029.75	946.07
75000	6685.61	3552.45	2513.53	1998.14	1692.12	1349.16	1244.87	1103.31	1013.64
80000	7131.32	3789.27	2681.09	2131.34	1804.93	1439.10	1327.86	1176.86	1081.22
85000	7577.03	4026.10	2848.66	2264.55	1917.74	1529.05	1410.85	1250.42	1148.80
90000	8022.73	4262.93	3016.23	2397.76	2030.55	1618.99	1493.84	1323.97	1216.37
95000	8468.44	4499.76	3183.80	2530.97	2143.35	1708.93	1576.83	1323.97	1283.95
100000	8914.15	4736.59	3351.37	2664.18	2256.16	1798.88	1659.82	1471.08	1351.52
105000	9359.86	4973.42	3518.93	2797.39	2368.97	1888.82	1742.81	1544.63	1419.10
110000	9805.56	5210.25	3686.50	2930.60	2481.78	1978.76	1825.81	1618.18	1486.68
115000	10251.27	5447.08	3854.07	3063.81	2594.59	2068.71	1908.80	1691.74	1554.25
120000	10696.98	5683.91	4021.64	3197.01	2707.39	2158.65	1991.79	1765.29	1621.83
125000	11142.68	5920.74	4189.21	3330.22	2820.20	2248.59	2074.78	1838.84	1689.40
130000	11588.39	6157.57	4356.77	3463.43	2933.01	2338.54	2157.77	1912.40	1756.98
135000	12034.10	6394.40	4524.34	3596.64	3045.82	2428.48	2240.76	1985.95	1824.56
140000	12479.81	6631.23	4691.91	3729.85	3158.62	2518.42	2323.75	2059.50	1892.13
145000	12925.51	6868.06	4859.48	3863.06	3271.43	2608.37	2406.74	2133.06	1959.71
150000	13371.22	7104.89	5027.05	3996.27	3384.24	2698.31	2489.73	2206.61	2027.28

MONTHLY PAYMENT 12⅝%

NECESSARY TO AMORTIZE A LOAN

AMOUNT	15 YEARS	18 YEARS	20 YEARS	25 YEARS	28 YEARS	29 YEARS	30 YEARS	35 YEARS	40 YEARS
$ 50	.63	.59	.58	.55	.55	.55	.54	.54	.53
100	1.25	1.18	1.15	1.10	1.09	1.09	1.08	1.07	1.06
200	2.49	2.35	2.29	2.20	2.17	2.17	2.16	2.14	2.12
300	3.73	3.53	3.44	3.30	3.26	3.25	3.24	3.20	3.18
400	4.97	4.70	4.58	4.40	4.34	4.33	4.31	4.27	4.24
500	6.21	5.88	5.73	5.50	5.43	5.41	5.39	5.33	5.30
600	7.45	7.05	6.87	6.60	6.51	6.49	6.47	6.40	6.36
700	8.69	8.23	8.02	7.70	7.60	7.57	7.54	7.46	7.42
800	9.93	9.40	9.16	8.80	8.68	8.65	8.62	8.53	8.48
900	11.17	10.58	10.31	9.90	9.76	9.73	9.70	9.59	9.54
1000	12.41	11.75	11.45	11.00	10.85	10.81	10.77	10.66	10.60
2000	24.82	23.50	22.90	22.00	21.69	21.61	21.54	21.31	21.19
3000	37.23	35.24	34.35	33.00	32.53	32.42	32.31	31.96	31.78
4000	49.63	46.99	45.80	43.99	43.38	43.22	43.08	42.61	42.37
5000	62.04	58.73	57.25	54.99	54.22	54.02	53.85	53.27	52.96
6000	74.45	70.48	68.70	65.99	65.06	64.83	64.62	63.92	63.55
7000	86.85	82.23	80.15	76.98	75.91	75.63	75.39	74.57	74.14
8000	99.26	93.97	91.60	87.98	86.75	86.44	86.16	85.22	84.73
9000	111.67	105.72	103.05	98.98	97.59	97.24	96.93	95.87	95.32
10000	124.07	117.46	114.50	109.97	108.43	108.04	107.70	106.53	105.91
15000	186.11	176.19	171.75	164.96	162.65	162.06	161.55	159.79	158.86
20000	248.14	234.92	229.00	219.94	216.86	216.08	215.40	213.05	211.82
25000	310.17	293.65	286.25	274.93	271.08	270.10	269.25	266.31	264.77
30000	372.21	352.38	343.49	329.91	325.29	324.12	323.09	319.57	317.72
35000	434.24	411.11	400.74	384.90	379.51	378.14	376.94	372.83	370.67
40000	496.27	469.83	457.99	439.88	433.72	432.16	430.79	426.09	423.63
45000	558.31	528.56	515.24	494.87	487.94	486.18	484.64	479.35	476.58
46000	570.71	540.31	526.69	505.86	498.78	496.98	495.41	490.01	487.17
47000	583.12	552.05	538.14	516.86	509.62	507.79	506.18	500.66	497.76
48000	595.53	563.80	549.59	527.86	520.46	518.59	516.95	511.31	508.35
49000	607.93	575.55	561.04	538.85	531.31	529.39	527.72	521.96	518.94
50000	620.34	587.29	572.49	549.85	542.15	540.20	538.49	532.61	529.53
51000	632.75	599.04	583.94	560.85	552.99	551.00	549.26	543.27	540.12
52000	645.15	610.78	595.39	571.85	563.84	561.81	560.03	553.92	550.71
53000	657.56	622.53	606.84	582.84	574.68	572.61	570.80	564.57	561.30
54000	669.97	634.27	618.29	593.84	585.52	583.41	581.57	575.22	571.89
55000	682.37	646.02	629.74	604.84	596.36	594.22	592.34	585.87	582.48
56000	694.78	657.77	641.19	615.83	607.21	605.02	603.11	596.53	593.07
57000	707.19	669.51	652.63	626.83	618.05	615.82	613.88	607.18	603.66
58000	719.59	681.26	664.08	637.83	628.89	626.63	624.65	617.83	614.26
59000	732.00	693.00	675.53	648.82	639.74	637.43	635.42	628.48	624.85
60000	744.41	704.75	686.98	659.82	650.58	648.24	646.18	639.14	635.44
61000	756.81	716.49	698.43	670.82	661.42	659.04	656.95	649.79	646.03
62000	769.22	728.24	709.88	681.81	672.26	669.84	667.72	660.44	656.62
63000	781.63	739.99	721.33	692.81	683.11	680.65	678.49	671.09	667.21
64000	794.03	751.73	732.78	703.81	693.95	691.45	689.26	681.74	677.80
65000	806.44	763.48	744.23	714.81	704.79	702.26	700.03	692.40	688.39
67500	837.46	792.84	772.86	742.30	731.90	729.27	726.96	719.03	714.87
70000	868.47	822.21	801.48	769.79	759.01	756.28	753.88	745.66	741.34
75000	930.51	880.94	858.73	824.77	813.22	810.29	807.73	798.92	794.29
80000	992.54	939.66	915.98	879.76	867.44	864.31	861.58	852.18	847.25
85000	1054.57	998.39	973.22	934.74	921.65	918.33	915.43	905.44	900.20
90000	1116.61	1057.12	1030.47	989.73	975.87	972.35	969.27	958.70	953.15
95000	1178.64	1115.85	1087.72	1044.71	1030.08	1026.37	1023.12	1011.96	1006.10
100000	1240.67	1174.58	1144.97	1099.70	1084.29	1080.39	1076.97	1065.22	1059.06
105000	1302.71	1233.31	1202.22	1154.68	1138.51	1134.41	1130.82	1118.48	1112.01
110000	1364.74	1292.04	1259.47	1209.67	1192.72	1188.43	1184.67	1171.74	1164.96
115000	1426.77	1350.76	1316.71	1264.65	1246.94	1242.45	1238.52	1225.01	1217.92
120000	1488.81	1409.49	1373.96	1319.64	1301.15	1296.47	1292.36	1278.27	1270.87
125000	1550.84	1468.22	1431.21	1374.62	1355.37	1350.49	1346.21	1331.53	1323.82
130000	1612.87	1526.95	1488.46	1429.61	1409.58	1404.51	1400.06	1384.79	1376.77
135000	1674.91	1585.68	1545.71	1484.59	1463.80	1458.53	1453.91	1438.05	1429.73
140000	1736.94	1644.41	1602.96	1539.57	1518.01	1512.55	1507.76	1491.31	1482.68
145000	1798.97	1703.14	1660.20	1594.56	1572.22	1566.56	1561.61	1544.57	1535.63
150000	1861.01	1761.87	1717.45	1649.54	1626.44	1620.58	1615.45	1597.83	1588.58

12¾% MONTHLY PAYMENT
NECESSARY TO AMORTIZE A LOAN

AMOUNT	1 YEAR	2 YEARS	3 YEARS	4 YEARS	5 YEARS	7 YEARS	8 YEARS	10 YEARS	12 YEARS
$ 50	4.47	2.38	1.68	1.34	1.14	.91	.84	.74	.68
100	8.93	4.75	3.36	2.68	2.27	1.81	1.67	1.48	1.36
200	17.85	9.49	6.72	5.35	4.53	3.62	3.34	2.96	2.72
300	26.77	14.23	10.08	8.02	6.79	5.42	5.01	4.44	4.08
400	35.69	18.97	13.43	10.69	9.06	7.23	6.67	5.92	5.44
500	44.61	23.72	16.79	13.36	11.32	9.03	8.34	7.40	6.80
600	53.53	28.46	20.15	16.03	13.58	10.84	10.01	8.88	8.16
700	62.45	33.20	23.51	18.70	15.84	12.64	11.67	10.35	9.52
800	71.37	37.94	26.86	21.37	18.11	14.45	13.34	11.83	10.88
900	80.29	42.69	30.22	24.04	20.37	16.26	15.01	13.31	12.24
1000	89.21	47.43	33.58	26.71	22.63	18.06	16.67	14.79	13.60
2000	178.41	94.85	67.15	53.41	45.26	36.12	33.34	29.57	27.19
3000	267.61	142.28	100.73	80.12	67.88	54.17	50.01	44.36	40.78
4000	356.81	189.70	134.30	106.82	90.51	72.23	66.68	59.14	54.37
5000	446.01	237.13	167.87	133.52	113.13	90.29	83.34	73.92	67.97
6000	535.21	284.55	201.45	160.23	135.76	108.34	100.01	88.71	81.56
7000	624.41	331.98	235.02	186.93	158.38	126.40	116.68	103.49	95.15
8000	713.61	379.40	268.59	213.63	181.01	144.46	133.35	118.28	108.74
9000	802.81	426.83	302.17	240.34	203.63	162.51	150.01	133.06	122.33
10000	892.01	474.25	335.74	267.04	226.26	180.57	166.68	147.84	135.93
15000	1338.01	711.37	503.61	400.56	339.38	270.85	250.02	221.76	203.89
20000	1784.01	948.49	671.48	534.08	452.51	361.13	333.36	295.68	271.85
25000	2230.01	1185.62	839.35	667.59	565.64	451.41	416.70	369.60	339.81
30000	2676.01	1422.74	1007.21	801.11	678.76	541.69	500.04	443.52	407.77
35000	3122.01	1659.86	1175.08	934.63	791.89	631.98	583.38	517.44	475.73
40000	3568.01	1896.98	1342.95	1068.15	905.02	722.26	666.71	591.36	543.69
45000	4014.01	2134.11	1510.82	1201.67	1018.14	812.54	750.05	665.28	611.65
46000	4103.21	2181.53	1544.39	1228.37	1040.77	830.60	766.72	680.07	625.24
47000	4192.41	2228.96	1577.97	1255.07	1063.39	848.65	783.39	694.85	638.83
48000	4281.61	2276.38	1611.54	1281.78	1086.02	866.71	800.06	709.64	652.42
49000	4370.81	2323.80	1645.11	1308.48	1108.64	884.76	816.72	724.42	666.01
50000	4460.01	2371.23	1678.69	1335.18	1131.27	902.82	833.39	739.20	679.61
51000	4549.21	2418.65	1712.26	1361.89	1153.90	920.88	850.06	753.99	693.20
52000	4638.41	2466.08	1745.84	1388.59	1176.52	938.93	866.73	768.77	706.79
53000	4727.61	2513.50	1779.41	1415.29	1199.15	956.99	883.39	783.56	720.38
54000	4816.81	2560.93	1812.98	1442.00	1221.77	975.05	900.06	798.34	733.97
55000	4906.01	2608.35	1846.56	1468.70	1244.40	993.10	916.73	813.12	747.57
56000	4995.21	2655.78	1880.13	1495.41	1267.02	1011.16	933.40	827.91	761.16
57000	5084.41	2703.20	1913.70	1522.11	1289.65	1029.22	950.07	842.69	774.75
58000	5173.61	2750.62	1947.28	1548.81	1312.27	1047.27	966.73	857.48	788.34
59000	5262.81	2798.05	1980.85	1575.52	1334.90	1065.33	983.40	872.26	801.93
60000	5352.01	2845.47	2014.42	1602.22	1357.52	1083.38	1000.07	887.04	815.53
61000	5441.21	2892.90	2048.00	1628.92	1380.15	1101.44	1016.74	901.83	829.12
62000	5530.41	2940.32	2081.57	1655.63	1402.77	1119.50	1033.40	916.61	842.71
63000	5619.61	2987.75	2115.15	1682.33	1425.40	1137.55	1050.07	931.40	856.30
64000	5708.81	3035.17	2148.72	1709.03	1448.02	1155.61	1066.74	946.18	869.89
65000	5798.01	3082.60	2182.29	1735.74	1470.65	1173.67	1083.41	960.96	883.49
67500	6021.01	3201.16	2266.23	1802.50	1527.21	1218.81	1125.08	997.92	917.47
70000	6244.01	3319.72	2350.16	1869.26	1583.78	1263.95	1166.75	1034.88	951.45
75000	6690.01	3556.84	2518.03	2002.77	1696.90	1354.23	1250.08	1108.80	1019.41
80000	7136.01	3793.96	2685.90	2136.29	1810.03	1444.51	1333.42	1182.72	1087.37
85000	7582.01	4031.09	2853.77	2269.81	1923.16	1534.79	1416.76	1256.64	1155.33
90000	8028.01	4268.21	3021.63	2403.33	2036.28	1625.07	1500.10	1330.56	1223.29
95000	8474.01	4505.33	3189.50	2536.85	2149.41	1715.36	1583.44	1404.48	1291.25
100000	8920.01	4742.45	3357.37	2670.36	2262.54	1805.64	1666.78	1478.40	1359.21
105000	9366.01	4979.58	3525.24	2803.88	2375.66	1895.92	1750.12	1552.32	1427.17
110000	9812.01	5216.70	3693.11	2937.40	2488.79	1986.20	1833.45	1626.24	1495.13
115000	10258.01	5453.82	3860.98	3070.92	2601.91	2076.48	1916.79	1700.16	1563.09
120000	10704.01	5690.94	4028.84	3204.43	2715.04	2166.76	2000.13	1774.08	1631.05
125000	11150.01	5928.07	4196.71	3337.95	2828.17	2257.05	2083.47	1848.00	1699.01
130000	11596.01	6165.19	4364.58	3471.47	2941.29	2347.33	2166.81	1921.92	1766.97
135000	12042.01	6402.31	4532.45	3604.99	3054.42	2437.61	2250.15	1995.84	1834.93
140000	12488.01	6639.43	4700.32	3738.51	3167.55	2527.89	2333.49	2069.76	1902.89
145000	12934.01	6876.55	4868.19	3872.02	3280.67	2618.17	2416.82	2143.68	1970.85
150000	13380.01	7113.68	5036.05	4005.54	3393.80	2708.45	2500.16	2217.60	2038.81

AMOUNT	15 YEARS	18 YEARS	20 YEARS	25 YEARS	28 YEARS	29 YEARS	30 YEARS	35 YEARS	40 YEARS
$ 50	.63	.60	.58	.56	.55	.55	.55	.54	.54
100	1.25	1.19	1.16	1.11	1.10	1.10	1.09	1.08	1.07
200	2.50	2.37	2.31	2.22	2.19	2.19	2.18	2.16	2.14
300	3.75	3.55	3.47	3.33	3.29	3.28	3.27	3.23	3.21
400	5.00	4.74	4.62	4.44	4.38	4.37	4.35	4.31	4.28
500	6.25	5.92	5.77	5.55	5.47	5.46	5.44	5.38	5.35
600	7.50	7.10	6.93	6.66	6.57	6.55	6.53	6.46	6.42
700	8.75	8.29	8.08	7.77	7.66	7.64	7.61	7.53	7.49
800	10.00	9.47	9.24	8.88	8.76	8.73	8.70	8.61	8.56
900	11.24	10.65	10.39	9.99	9.85	9.82	9.79	9.68	9.63
1000	12.49	11.84	11.54	11.10	10.94	10.91	10.87	10.76	10.70
2000	24.98	23.67	23.08	22.19	21.88	21.81	21.74	21.51	21.39
3000	37.47	35.50	34.62	33.28	32.82	32.71	32.61	32.26	32.08
4000	49.96	47.33	46.16	44.37	43.76	43.61	43.47	43.01	42.77
5000	62.45	59.16	57.70	55.46	54.70	54.51	54.34	53.76	53.46
6000	74.94	71.00	69.23	66.55	65.64	65.41	65.21	64.52	64.16
7000	87.42	82.83	80.77	77.64	76.58	76.31	76.07	75.27	74.85
8000	99.91	94.66	92.31	88.73	87.52	87.21	86.94	86.02	85.54
9000	112.40	106.49	103.85	99.82	98.45	98.11	97.81	96.77	96.23
10000	124.89	118.32	115.39	110.91	109.39	109.01	108.67	107.52	106.92
15000	187.33	177.48	173.08	166.36	164.09	163.51	163.01	161.28	160.38
20000	249.77	236.64	230.77	221.82	218.78	218.01	217.34	215.04	213.84
25000	312.21	295.80	288.46	277.27	273.48	272.52	271.68	268.80	267.30
30000	374.66	354.96	346.15	332.72	328.17	327.02	326.01	322.56	320.76
35000	437.10	414.11	403.84	388.17	382.86	381.52	380.35	376.32	374.22
40000	499.54	473.27	461.53	443.63	437.56	436.02	434.68	430.08	427.68
45000	561.98	532.43	519.22	499.08	492.25	490.53	489.02	483.84	481.14
46000	574.47	544.26	530.76	510.17	503.19	501.43	499.88	494.60	491.84
47000	586.96	556.09	542.30	521.26	514.13	512.33	510.75	505.35	502.53
48000	599.45	567.93	553.83	532.35	525.07	523.23	521.62	516.10	513.22
49000	611.94	579.76	565.37	543.44	536.01	534.13	532.48	526.85	523.91
50000	624.42	591.59	576.91	554.53	546.95	545.03	543.35	537.60	534.60
51000	636.91	603.42	588.45	565.62	557.89	555.93	554.22	548.36	545.30
52000	649.40	615.25	599.99	576.71	568.83	566.83	565.09	559.11	555.99
53000	661.89	627.09	611.53	587.80	579.76	577.73	575.95	569.86	566.68
54000	674.38	638.92	623.06	598.89	590.70	588.63	586.82	580.61	577.37
55000	686.87	650.75	634.60	609.98	601.64	599.53	597.69	591.36	588.06
56000	699.35	662.58	646.14	621.07	612.58	610.43	608.55	602.11	598.75
57000	711.84	674.41	657.68	632.16	623.52	621.33	619.42	612.87	609.45
58000	724.33	686.24	669.22	643.26	634.46	632.23	630.29	623.62	620.14
59000	736.82	698.08	680.75	654.35	645.40	643.13	641.15	634.37	630.83
60000	749.31	709.91	692.29	665.44	656.34	654.03	652.02	645.12	641.52
61000	761.80	721.74	703.83	676.53	667.27	664.94	662.89	655.87	652.21
62000	774.28	733.57	715.37	687.62	678.21	675.84	673.75	666.63	662.91
63000	786.77	745.40	726.91	698.71	689.15	686.74	684.62	677.38	673.60
64000	799.26	757.23	738.44	709.80	700.09	697.64	695.49	688.13	684.29
65000	811.75	769.07	749.98	720.89	711.03	708.54	706.36	698.88	694.98
67500	842.97	798.64	778.83	748.62	738.38	735.79	733.52	725.76	721.71
70000	874.19	828.22	807.67	776.34	765.72	763.04	760.69	752.64	748.44
75000	936.63	887.38	865.36	831.79	820.42	817.54	815.02	806.40	801.90
80000	999.07	946.54	923.05	887.25	875.11	872.04	869.36	860.16	855.36
85000	1061.52	1005.70	980.74	942.70	929.81	926.55	923.69	913.92	908.82
90000	1123.96	1064.86	1038.44	998.15	984.50	981.05	978.03	967.68	962.28
95000	1186.40	1124.02	1096.13	1053.60	1039.20	1035.55	1032.36	1021.44	1015.74
100000	1248.84	1183.17	1153.82	1109.06	1093.89	1090.05	1086.70	1075.20	1069.20
105000	1311.28	1242.33	1211.51	1164.51	1148.58	1144.56	1141.03	1128.96	1122.66
110000	1373.73	1301.49	1269.20	1219.96	1203.28	1199.06	1195.37	1182.72	1176.12
115000	1436.17	1360.65	1326.89	1275.42	1257.97	1253.56	1249.70	1236.48	1229.58
120000	1498.61	1419.81	1384.58	1330.87	1312.67	1308.06	1304.04	1290.24	1283.04
125000	1561.05	1478.97	1442.27	1386.32	1367.36	1362.57	1358.37	1344.00	1336.50
130000	1623.49	1538.13	1499.96	1441.77	1422.06	1417.07	1412.71	1397.76	1389.96
135000	1685.93	1597.28	1557.65	1497.23	1476.75	1471.57	1467.04	1451.52	1443.42
140000	1748.38	1656.44	1615.34	1552.68	1531.44	1526.07	1521.38	1505.28	1496.88
145000	1810.82	1715.60	1673.03	1608.13	1586.14	1580.58	1575.71	1559.04	1550.34
150000	1873.26	1774.76	1730.72	1663.58	1640.83	1635.08	1630.04	1612.80	1603.80

12⅞%   MONTHLY PAYMENT
NECESSARY TO AMORTIZE A LOAN

AMOUNT	1 YEAR	2 YEARS	3 YEARS	4 YEARS	5 YEARS	7 YEARS	8 YEARS	10 YEARS	12 YEARS
$ 50	4.47	2.38	1.69	1.34	1.14	.91	.84	.75	.69
100	8.93	4.75	3.37	2.68	2.27	1.82	1.68	1.49	1.37
200	17.86	9.50	6.73	5.36	4.54	3.63	3.35	2.98	2.74
300	26.78	14.25	10.10	8.03	6.81	5.44	5.03	4.46	4.11
400	35.71	19.00	13.46	10.71	9.08	7.25	6.70	5.95	5.47
500	44.63	23.75	16.82	13.39	11.35	9.07	8.37	7.43	6.84
600	53.56	28.49	20.19	16.06	13.62	10.88	10.05	8.92	8.21
700	62.49	33.24	23.55	18.74	15.89	12.69	11.72	10.41	9.57
800	71.41	37.99	26.91	21.42	18.16	14.50	13.39	11.89	10.94
900	80.34	42.74	30.28	24.09	20.43	16.32	15.07	13.38	12.31
1000	89.26	47.49	33.64	26.77	22.69	18.13	16.74	14.86	13.67
2000	178.52	94.97	67.27	53.54	45.38	36.25	33.48	29.72	27.34
3000	267.78	142.45	100.91	80.30	68.07	54.38	50.22	44.58	41.01
4000	357.04	189.94	134.54	107.07	90.76	72.50	66.95	59.43	54.68
5000	446.30	237.42	168.17	133.83	113.45	90.63	83.69	74.29	68.35
6000	535.56	284.90	201.81	160.60	136.14	108.75	100.43	89.15	82.02
7000	624.82	332.39	235.44	187.36	158.83	126.87	117.17	104.01	95.69
8000	714.07	379.87	269.08	214.13	181.52	145.00	133.90	118.86	109.36
9000	803.33	427.35	302.71	240.89	204.21	163.12	150.64	133.72	123.03
10000	892.59	474.84	336.34	267.66	226.90	181.25	167.38	148.58	136.70
15000	1338.88	712.25	504.51	401.49	340.34	271.87	251.07	222.87	205.04
20000	1785.18	949.67	672.68	535.31	453.79	362.49	334.75	297.15	273.39
25000	2231.47	1187.08	840.85	669.14	567.23	453.11	418.44	371.44	341.73
30000	2677.76	1424.50	1009.02	802.97	680.68	543.73	502.13	445.73	410.08
35000	3124.06	1661.91	1177.19	936.80	794.12	634.35	585.81	520.02	478.42
40000	3570.35	1899.33	1345.36	1070.62	907.57	724.97	669.50	594.30	546.77
45000	4016.64	2136.75	1513.52	1204.45	1021.02	815.59	753.19	668.59	615.11
46000	4105.90	2184.23	1547.16	1231.22	1043.71	833.71	769.93	683.45	628.78
47000	4195.16	2231.71	1580.79	1257.98	1066.39	851.84	786.66	698.30	642.45
48000	4284.42	2279.20	1614.43	1284.75	1089.08	869.96	803.40	713.16	656.12
49000	4373.68	2326.68	1648.06	1311.51	1111.77	888.08	820.14	728.02	669.79
50000	4462.94	2374.16	1681.69	1338.28	1134.46	906.21	836.88	742.88	683.46
51000	4552.20	2421.64	1715.33	1365.05	1157.15	924.33	853.61	757.73	697.13
52000	4641.45	2469.13	1748.96	1391.81	1179.84	942.46	870.35	772.59	710.79
53000	4730.71	2516.61	1782.60	1418.58	1202.53	960.58	887.09	787.45	724.46
54000	4819.97	2564.09	1816.23	1445.34	1225.22	978.71	903.83	802.31	738.13
55000	4909.23	2611.58	1849.86	1472.11	1247.91	996.83	920.56	817.16	751.80
56000	4998.49	2659.06	1883.50	1498.87	1270.60	1014.95	937.30	832.02	765.47
57000	5087.75	2706.54	1917.13	1525.64	1293.29	1033.08	954.04	846.88	779.14
58000	5177.01	2754.03	1950.76	1552.40	1315.97	1051.20	970.77	861.74	792.81
59000	5266.26	2801.51	1984.40	1579.17	1338.66	1069.33	987.51	876.59	806.48
60000	5355.52	2848.99	2018.03	1605.93	1361.35	1087.45	1004.25	891.45	820.15
61000	5444.78	2896.48	2051.67	1632.70	1384.04	1105.57	1020.99	906.31	833.82
62000	5534.04	2943.96	2085.30	1659.47	1406.73	1123.70	1037.72	921.17	847.48
63000	5623.30	2991.44	2118.93	1686.23	1429.42	1141.82	1054.46	936.02	861.15
64000	5712.56	3038.93	2152.57	1713.00	1452.11	1159.95	1071.20	950.88	874.82
65000	5801.82	3086.41	2186.20	1739.76	1474.80	1178.07	1087.94	965.74	888.49
67500	6024.96	3205.12	2270.28	1806.68	1531.52	1223.38	1129.78	1002.88	922.66
70000	6248.11	3323.82	2354.37	1873.59	1588.24	1268.69	1171.62	1040.03	956.84
75000	6694.40	3561.24	2522.54	2007.42	1701.69	1359.31	1255.31	1114.31	1025.18
80000	7140.70	3798.66	2690.71	2141.24	1815.14	1449.93	1339.00	1188.60	1093.53
85000	7586.99	4036.07	2858.88	2275.07	1928.58	1540.55	1422.69	1262.89	1161.87
90000	8033.28	4273.49	3027.04	2408.90	2042.03	1631.17	1506.37	1337.17	1230.22
95000	8479.58	4510.90	3195.21	2542.73	2155.47	1721.79	1590.06	1411.46	1298.56
100000	8925.87	4748.32	3363.38	2676.55	2268.92	1812.41	1673.75	1485.75	1366.91
105000	9372.16	4985.73	3531.55	2810.38	2382.36	1903.03	1757.43	1560.04	1435.25
110000	9818.46	5223.15	3699.72	2944.21	2495.81	1993.65	1841.12	1634.32	1503.60
115000	10264.75	5460.57	3867.89	3078.04	2609.26	2084.27	1924.81	1708.61	1571.94
120000	10711.04	5697.98	4036.06	3211.86	2722.70	2174.89	2008.49	1782.90	1640.29
125000	11157.34	5935.40	4204.23	3345.69	2836.15	2265.51	2092.18	1857.18	1708.63
130000	11603.63	6172.81	4372.40	3479.52	2949.59	2356.13	2175.87	1931.47	1776.98
135000	12049.92	6410.23	4540.56	3613.35	3063.04	2446.76	2259.56	2005.76	1845.32
140000	12496.21	6647.64	4708.73	3747.17	3176.48	2537.38	2343.24	2080.05	1913.67
145000	12942.51	6885.06	4876.90	3881.00	3289.93	2628.00	2426.93	2154.33	1982.01
150000	13388.80	7122.47	5045.07	4014.83	3403.38	2718.62	2510.62	2228.62	2050.36

98

MONTHLY PAYMENT 12⅞%
NECESSARY TO AMORTIZE A LOAN

AMOUNT	15 YEARS	18 YEARS	20 YEARS	25 YEARS	28 YEARS	29 YEARS	30 YEARS	35 YEARS	40 YEARS
$ 50	.63	.60	.59	.56	.56	.55	.55	.55	.54
100	1.26	1.20	1.17	1.12	1.11	1.10	1.10	1.09	1.08
200	2.52	2.39	2.33	2.24	2.21	2.20	2.20	2.18	2.16
300	3.78	3.58	3.49	3.36	3.32	3.30	3.29	3.26	3.24
400	5.03	4.77	4.66	4.48	4.42	4.40	4.39	4.35	4.32
500	6.29	5.96	5.82	5.60	5.52	5.50	5.49	5.43	5.40
600	7.55	7.16	6.98	6.72	6.63	6.60	6.58	6.52	6.48
700	8.80	8.35	8.14	7.83	7.73	7.70	7.68	7.60	7.56
800	10.06	9.54	9.31	8.95	8.83	8.80	8.78	8.69	8.64
900	11.32	10.73	10.47	10.07	9.94	9.90	9.87	9.77	9.72
1000	12.58	11.92	11.63	11.19	11.04	11.00	10.97	10.86	10.80
2000	25.15	23.84	23.26	22.37	22.07	22.00	21.93	21.71	21.59
3000	37.72	35.76	34.89	33.56	33.11	33.00	32.90	32.56	32.39
4000	50.29	47.68	46.51	44.74	44.14	43.99	43.86	43.41	43.18
5000	62.86	59.59	58.14	55.93	55.18	54.99	54.83	54.26	53.97
6000	75.43	71.51	69.77	67.11	66.21	65.99	65.79	65.12	64.77
7000	88.00	83.43	81.39	78.30	77.25	76.99	76.76	75.97	75.56
8000	100.57	95.35	93.02	89.48	88.28	87.98	87.72	86.82	86.35
9000	113.14	107.27	104.65	100.66	99.32	98.98	98.68	97.67	97.15
10000	125.71	119.18	116.27	111.85	110.35	109.98	109.65	108.52	107.94
15000	188.56	178.77	174.41	167.77	165.53	164.96	164.47	162.78	161.91
20000	251.41	238.36	232.54	223.69	220.70	219.95	219.29	217.04	215.88
25000	314.26	297.95	290.68	279.61	275.88	274.94	274.11	271.30	269.84
30000	377.11	357.54	348.81	335.54	331.05	329.92	328.94	325.56	323.81
35000	439.96	417.13	406.94	391.46	386.23	384.91	383.76	379.82	377.78
40000	502.82	476.72	465.08	447.38	441.40	439.90	438.58	434.08	431.75
45000	565.67	536.31	523.21	503.30	496.58	494.88	493.40	488.34	485.71
46000	578.24	548.23	534.84	514.48	507.61	505.88	504.37	499.19	496.51
47000	590.81	560.15	546.47	525.67	518.65	516.88	515.33	510.04	507.30
48000	603.38	572.06	558.09	536.85	529.68	527.88	526.30	520.90	518.09
49000	615.95	583.98	569.72	548.04	540.72	538.87	537.26	531.75	528.89
50000	628.52	595.90	581.35	559.22	551.75	549.87	548.22	542.60	539.68
51000	641.09	607.82	592.97	570.41	562.79	560.87	559.19	553.45	550.47
52000	653.66	619.74	604.60	581.59	573.82	571.87	570.15	564.30	561.27
53000	666.23	631.65	616.23	592.77	584.86	582.86	581.12	575.15	572.06
54000	678.80	643.57	627.85	603.96	595.89	593.86	592.08	586.01	582.85
55000	691.37	655.49	639.48	615.14	606.93	604.86	603.05	596.86	593.65
56000	703.94	667.41	651.11	626.33	617.96	615.85	614.01	607.71	604.44
57000	716.51	679.33	662.73	637.51	629.00	626.85	624.97	618.56	615.23
58000	729.08	691.24	674.36	648.70	640.03	637.85	635.94	629.41	626.03
59000	741.65	703.16	685.99	659.88	651.07	648.85	646.90	640.27	636.82
60000	754.22	715.08	697.61	671.07	662.10	659.84	657.87	651.12	647.62
61000	766.79	727.00	709.24	682.25	673.14	670.84	668.83	661.97	658.41
62000	779.36	738.91	720.87	693.43	684.17	681.84	679.80	672.82	669.20
63000	791.93	750.83	732.49	704.62	695.21	692.84	690.76	683.67	680.00
64000	804.50	762.75	744.12	715.80	706.24	703.83	701.73	694.53	690.79
65000	817.07	774.67	755.75	726.99	717.28	714.83	712.69	705.38	701.58
67500	848.50	804.46	784.82	754.95	744.87	742.32	740.10	732.51	728.57
70000	879.92	834.26	813.88	782.91	772.45	769.82	767.51	759.64	755.55
75000	942.78	893.85	872.02	838.83	827.63	824.80	822.33	813.90	809.52
80000	1005.63	953.44	930.15	894.75	882.80	879.79	877.16	868.16	863.49
85000	1068.48	1013.03	988.28	950.67	937.98	934.78	931.98	922.41	917.45
90000	1131.33	1072.62	1046.42	1006.60	993.15	989.76	986.80	976.67	971.42
95000	1194.18	1132.21	1104.55	1062.52	1048.33	1044.75	1041.62	1030.93	1025.39
100000	1257.03	1191.79	1162.69	1118.44	1103.50	1099.74	1096.44	1085.19	1079.36
105000	1319.88	1251.38	1220.82	1174.36	1158.68	1154.72	1151.26	1139.45	1133.32
110000	1382.74	1310.97	1278.96	1230.28	1213.85	1209.71	1206.09	1193.71	1187.29
115000	1445.59	1370.56	1337.09	1286.20	1269.03	1264.70	1260.91	1247.97	1241.26
120000	1508.44	1430.15	1395.22	1342.13	1324.20	1319.68	1315.73	1302.23	1295.23
125000	1571.29	1489.74	1453.36	1398.05	1379.38	1374.67	1370.55	1356.49	1349.19
130000	1634.14	1549.33	1511.49	1453.97	1434.55	1429.66	1425.37	1410.75	1403.16
135000	1696.99	1608.92	1569.63	1509.89	1489.73	1484.64	1480.20	1465.01	1457.13
140000	1759.84	1668.51	1627.76	1565.81	1544.90	1539.63	1535.02	1519.27	1511.10
145000	1822.70	1728.10	1685.89	1621.73	1600.08	1594.62	1589.84	1573.53	1565.06
150000	1885.55	1787.69	1744.03	1677.66	1655.25	1649.60	1644.66	1627.79	1619.03

13% MONTHLY PAYMENT
NECESSARY TO AMORTIZE A LOAN

AMOUNT	1 YEAR	2 YEARS	3 YEARS	4 YEARS	5 YEARS	7 YEARS	8 YEARS	10 YEARS	12 YEARS
$ 50	4.47	2.38	1.69	1.35	1.14	.91	.85	.75	.69
100	8.94	4.76	3.37	2.69	2.28	1.82	1.69	1.50	1.38
200	17.87	9.51	6.74	5.37	4.56	3.64	3.37	2.99	2.75
300	26.80	14.27	10.11	8.05	6.83	5.46	5.05	4.48	4.13
400	35.73	19.02	13.48	10.74	9.11	7.28	6.73	5.98	5.50
500	44.66	23.78	16.85	13.42	11.38	9.10	8.41	7.47	6.88
600	53.60	28.53	20.22	16.10	13.66	10.92	10.09	8.96	8.25
700	62.53	33.28	23.59	18.78	15.93	12.74	11.77	10.46	9.63
800	71.46	38.04	26.96	21.47	18.21	14.56	13.45	11.95	11.00
900	80.39	42.79	30.33	24.15	20.48	16.38	15.13	13.44	12.38
1000	89.32	47.55	33.70	26.83	22.76	18.20	16.81	14.94	13.75
2000	178.64	95.09	67.39	53.66	45.51	36.39	33.62	29.87	27.50
3000	267.96	142.63	101.09	80.49	68.26	54.58	50.43	44.80	41.24
4000	357.27	190.17	134.78	107.31	91.02	72.77	67.23	59.73	54.99
5000	446.59	237.71	168.47	134.14	113.77	90.96	84.04	74.66	68.74
6000	535.91	285.26	202.17	160.97	136.52	109.16	100.85	89.59	82.48
7000	625.23	332.80	235.86	187.80	159.28	127.35	117.66	104.52	96.23
8000	714.54	380.34	269.56	214.62	182.03	145.54	134.46	119.45	109.98
9000	803.86	427.88	303.25	241.45	204.78	163.73	151.27	134.38	123.72
10000	893.18	475.42	336.94	268.28	227.54	181.92	168.08	149.32	137.47
15000	1339.76	713.13	505.41	402.42	341.30	272.88	252.11	223.97	206.20
20000	1786.35	950.84	673.88	536.55	455.07	363.84	336.15	298.63	274.93
25000	2232.94	1188.55	842.35	670.69	568.83	454.80	420.19	373.28	343.66
30000	2679.52	1426.26	1010.82	804.83	682.60	545.76	504.22	447.94	412.39
35000	3126.11	1663.97	1179.29	938.97	796.36	636.72	588.26	522.59	481.12
40000	3572.70	1901.68	1347.76	1073.10	910.13	727.68	672.30	597.25	549.86
45000	4019.28	2139.39	1516.23	1207.24	1023.89	818.64	756.33	671.90	618.59
46000	4108.60	2186.93	1549.93	1234.07	1046.65	836.84	773.14	686.83	632.33
47000	4197.92	2234.47	1583.62	1260.90	1069.40	855.03	789.95	701.77	646.08
48000	4287.23	2282.01	1617.31	1287.72	1092.15	873.22	806.75	716.70	659.83
49000	4376.55	2329.55	1651.01	1314.55	1114.91	891.41	823.56	731.63	673.57
50000	4465.87	2377.10	1684.70	1341.38	1137.66	909.60	840.37	746.56	687.32
51000	4555.19	2424.64	1718.40	1368.21	1160.41	927.80	857.18	761.49	701.06
52000	4644.50	2472.18	1752.09	1395.03	1183.16	945.99	873.98	776.42	714.81
53000	4733.82	2519.72	1785.78	1421.86	1205.92	964.18	890.79	791.35	728.56
54000	4823.14	2567.26	1819.48	1448.69	1228.67	982.37	907.60	806.28	742.30
55000	4912.46	2614.81	1853.17	1475.52	1251.42	1000.56	924.40	821.21	756.05
56000	5001.77	2662.35	1886.87	1502.34	1274.18	1018.75	941.21	836.15	769.80
57000	5091.09	2709.89	1920.56	1529.17	1296.93	1036.95	958.02	851.08	783.54
58000	5180.41	2757.43	1954.25	1556.00	1319.68	1055.14	974.83	866.01	797.29
59000	5269.72	2804.97	1987.95	1582.83	1342.44	1073.33	991.63	880.94	811.03
60000	5359.04	2852.51	2021.64	1609.65	1365.19	1091.52	1008.44	895.87	824.78
61000	5448.36	2900.06	2055.34	1636.48	1387.94	1109.71	1025.25	910.80	838.53
62000	5537.68	2947.60	2089.03	1663.31	1410.70	1127.91	1042.05	925.73	852.27
63000	5626.99	2995.14	2122.72	1690.14	1433.45	1146.10	1058.86	940.66	866.02
64000	5716.31	3042.68	2156.42	1716.96	1456.20	1164.29	1075.67	955.59	879.77
65000	5805.63	3090.22	2190.11	1743.79	1478.95	1182.48	1092.48	970.52	893.51
67500	6028.92	3209.08	2274.35	1810.86	1535.84	1227.96	1134.49	1007.85	927.88
70000	6252.21	3327.93	2358.58	1877.93	1592.72	1273.44	1176.51	1045.18	962.24
75000	6698.80	3565.64	2527.05	2012.07	1706.49	1364.40	1260.55	1119.84	1030.97
80000	7145.39	3803.35	2695.52	2146.20	1820.25	1455.36	1344.59	1194.49	1099.71
85000	7591.97	4041.06	2863.99	2280.34	1934.02	1546.32	1428.62	1269.15	1168.44
90000	8038.56	4278.77	3032.46	2414.48	2047.78	1637.28	1512.66	1343.80	1237.17
95000	8485.15	4516.48	3200.93	2548.62	2161.55	1728.24	1596.69	1418.46	1305.90
100000	8931.73	4754.19	3369.40	2682.75	2275.31	1819.20	1680.73	1493.11	1374.63
105000	9378.32	4991.90	3537.87	2816.89	2389.08	1910.16	1764.77	1567.77	1443.36
110000	9824.91	5229.61	3706.34	2951.03	2502.84	2001.12	1848.80	1642.42	1512.09
115000	10271.49	5467.31	3874.81	3085.17	2616.61	2092.08	1932.84	1717.08	1580.82
120000	10718.08	5705.02	4043.28	3219.30	2730.37	2183.04	2016.88	1791.73	1649.56
125000	11164.66	5942.73	4211.75	3353.44	2844.14	2274.00	2100.91	1866.39	1718.29
130000	11611.25	6180.44	4380.22	3487.58	2957.90	2364.96	2184.95	1941.04	1787.02
135000	12057.84	6418.15	4548.69	3621.72	3071.67	2455.92	2268.98	2015.70	1855.75
140000	12504.42	6655.86	4717.16	3755.85	3185.44	2546.88	2353.02	2090.36	1924.48
145000	12951.01	6893.57	4885.63	3889.99	3299.20	2637.84	2437.06	2165.01	1993.21
150000	13397.60	7131.28	5054.10	4024.13	3412.97	2728.80	2521.09	2239.67	2061.94

AMOUNT	15 YEARS	18 YEARS	20 YEARS	25 YEARS	28 YEARS	29 YEARS	30 YEARS	35 YEARS	40 YEARS
$ 50	.64	.61	.59	.57	.56	.56	.56	.55	.55
100	1.27	1.21	1.18	1.13	1.12	1.11	1.11	1.10	1.09
200	2.54	2.41	2.35	2.26	2.23	2.22	2.22	2.20	2.18
300	3.80	3.61	3.52	3.39	3.34	3.33	3.32	3.29	3.27
400	5.07	4.81	4.69	4.52	4.46	4.44	4.43	4.39	4.36
500	6.33	6.01	5.86	5.64	5.57	5.55	5.54	5.48	5.45
600	7.60	7.21	7.03	6.77	6.68	6.66	6.64	6.58	6.54
700	8.86	8.41	8.21	7.90	7.80	7.77	7.75	7.67	7.63
800	10.13	9.61	9.38	9.03	8.91	8.88	8.85	8.77	8.72
900	11.39	10.81	10.55	10.16	10.02	9.99	9.96	9.86	9.81
1000	12.66	12.01	11.72	11.28	11.14	11.10	11.07	10.96	10.90
2000	25.31	24.01	23.44	22.56	22.27	22.19	22.13	21.91	21.80
3000	37.96	36.02	35.15	33.84	33.40	33.29	33.19	32.86	32.69
4000	50.61	48.02	46.87	45.12	44.53	44.38	44.25	43.81	43.59
5000	63.27	60.03	58.58	56.40	55.66	55.48	55.31	54.76	54.48
6000	75.92	72.03	70.30	67.68	66.79	66.57	66.38	65.72	65.38
7000	88.57	84.04	82.02	78.95	77.92	77.67	77.44	76.67	76.27
8000	101.22	96.04	93.73	90.23	89.06	88.76	88.50	87.62	87.17
9000	113.88	108.04	105.45	101.51	100.19	99.85	99.56	98.57	98.06
10000	126.53	120.05	117.16	112.79	111.32	110.95	110.62	109.52	108.96
15000	189.79	180.07	175.74	169.18	166.98	166.42	165.93	164.28	163.43
20000	253.05	240.09	234.32	225.57	222.63	221.89	221.24	219.04	217.91
25000	316.32	300.11	292.90	281.96	278.29	277.36	276.55	273.80	272.38
30000	379.58	360.13	351.48	338.36	333.95	332.83	331.86	328.56	326.86
35000	442.84	420.16	410.06	394.75	389.60	388.31	387.17	383.32	381.33
40000	506.10	480.18	468.64	451.14	445.26	443.78	442.48	438.08	435.81
45000	569.36	540.20	527.21	507.53	500.92	499.25	497.79	492.84	490.29
46000	582.02	552.20	538.93	518.81	512.05	510.34	508.86	503.79	501.18
47000	594.67	564.21	550.65	530.09	523.18	521.44	519.92	514.75	512.08
48000	607.32	576.21	562.36	541.37	534.31	532.53	530.98	525.70	522.97
49000	619.97	588.22	574.08	552.64	545.44	543.63	542.04	536.65	533.87
50000	632.63	600.22	585.79	563.92	556.57	554.72	553.10	547.60	544.76
51000	645.28	612.23	597.51	575.20	567.70	565.82	564.17	558.55	555.66
52000	657.93	624.23	609.22	586.48	578.83	576.91	575.23	569.51	566.55
53000	670.58	636.23	620.94	597.76	589.97	588.00	586.29	580.46	577.45
54000	683.24	648.24	632.66	609.04	601.10	599.10	597.35	591.41	588.34
55000	695.89	660.24	644.37	620.31	612.23	610.19	608.41	602.36	599.24
56000	708.54	672.25	656.09	631.59	623.36	621.29	619.48	613.31	610.13
57000	721.19	684.25	667.80	642.87	634.49	632.38	630.54	624.27	621.03
58000	733.85	696.26	679.52	654.15	645.62	643.48	641.60	635.22	631.92
59000	746.50	708.26	691.23	665.43	656.75	654.57	652.66	646.17	642.82
60000	759.15	720.26	702.95	676.71	667.89	665.66	663.72	657.12	653.71
61000	771.80	732.27	714.67	687.98	679.02	676.76	674.79	668.07	664.61
62000	784.46	744.27	726.38	699.26	690.15	687.85	685.85	679.02	675.50
63000	797.11	756.28	738.10	710.54	701.28	698.95	696.91	689.98	686.40
64000	809.76	768.28	749.81	721.82	712.41	710.04	707.97	700.93	697.29
65000	822.41	780.29	761.53	733.10	723.54	721.14	719.03	711.88	708.19
67500	854.04	810.30	790.82	761.29	751.37	748.87	746.69	739.26	735.43
70000	885.67	840.31	820.11	789.49	779.20	776.61	774.34	766.64	762.66
75000	948.94	900.33	878.69	845.88	834.86	832.08	829.65	821.40	817.14
80000	1012.20	960.35	937.27	902.27	890.51	887.55	884.96	876.16	871.62
85000	1075.46	1020.37	995.84	958.67	946.17	943.02	940.27	930.92	926.09
90000	1138.72	1080.39	1054.42	1015.06	1001.83	998.49	995.58	985.68	980.57
95000	1201.99	1140.42	1113.00	1071.45	1057.48	1053.97	1050.89	1040.44	1035.04
100000	1265.25	1200.44	1171.58	1127.84	1113.14	1109.44	1106.20	1095.20	1089.52
105000	1328.51	1260.46	1230.16	1184.23	1168.80	1164.91	1161.51	1149.96	1143.99
110000	1391.77	1320.48	1288.74	1240.62	1224.45	1220.38	1216.82	1204.72	1198.47
115000	1455.03	1380.50	1347.32	1297.02	1280.11	1275.85	1272.13	1259.48	1252.95
120000	1518.30	1440.52	1405.90	1353.41	1335.77	1331.32	1327.44	1314.24	1307.42
125000	1581.56	1500.55	1464.47	1409.80	1391.42	1386.79	1382.75	1369.00	1361.90
130000	1644.82	1560.57	1523.05	1466.19	1447.08	1442.27	1438.06	1423.76	1416.37
135000	1708.08	1620.59	1581.63	1522.58	1502.74	1497.74	1493.37	1478.52	1470.85
140000	1771.34	1680.61	1640.21	1578.97	1558.39	1553.21	1548.68	1533.28	1525.32
145000	1834.61	1740.63	1698.79	1635.37	1614.05	1608.68	1603.99	1588.04	1579.80
150000	1897.87	1800.65	1757.37	1691.76	1669.71	1664.15	1659.30	1642.79	1634.28

13⅛%   MONTHLY PAYMENT
NECESSARY TO AMORTIZE A LOAN

AMOUNT	1 YEAR	2 YEARS	3 YEARS	4 YEARS	5 YEARS	7 YEARS	8 YEARS	10 YEARS	12 YEARS
$ 50	4.47	2.39	1.69	1.35	1.15	.92	.85	.76	.70
100	8.94	4.77	3.38	2.69	2.29	1.83	1.69	1.51	1.39
200	17.88	9.53	6.76	5.38	4.57	3.66	3.38	3.01	2.77
300	26.82	14.29	10.13	8.07	6.85	5.48	5.07	4.51	4.15
400	35.76	19.05	13.51	10.76	9.13	7.31	6.76	6.01	5.53
500	44.69	23.81	16.88	13.45	11.41	9.13	8.44	7.51	6.92
600	53.63	28.57	20.26	16.14	13.70	10.96	10.13	9.01	8.30
700	62.57	33.33	23.63	18.83	15.98	12.79	11.82	10.51	9.68
800	71.51	38.09	27.01	21.52	18.26	14.61	13.51	12.01	11.06
900	80.44	42.85	30.38	24.21	20.54	16.44	15.19	13.51	12.45
1000	89.38	47.61	33.76	26.89	22.82	18.26	16.88	15.01	13.83
2000	178.76	95.21	67.51	53.78	45.64	36.52	33.76	30.01	27.65
3000	268.13	142.81	101.27	80.67	68.46	54.78	50.64	45.02	41.48
4000	357.51	190.41	135.02	107.56	91.27	73.04	67.51	60.02	55.30
5000	446.88	238.01	168.78	134.45	114.09	91.30	84.39	75.03	69.12
6000	536.26	285.61	202.53	161.34	136.91	109.56	101.27	90.03	82.95
7000	625.64	333.21	236.28	188.23	159.72	127.82	118.15	105.04	96.77
8000	715.01	380.81	270.04	215.12	182.54	146.08	135.02	120.04	110.59
9000	804.39	428.41	303.79	242.01	205.36	164.34	151.90	135.05	124.42
10000	893.76	476.01	337.55	268.90	228.18	182.60	168.78	150.05	138.24
15000	1340.64	714.01	506.32	403.35	342.26	273.90	253.16	225.08	207.36
20000	1787.52	952.02	675.09	537.80	456.35	365.20	337.55	300.10	276.48
25000	2234.40	1190.02	843.86	672.24	570.43	456.50	421.94	375.13	345.60
30000	2681.28	1428.02	1012.63	806.69	684.52	547.80	506.32	450.15	414.72
35000	3128.16	1666.02	1181.40	941.14	798.60	639.10	590.71	525.18	483.83
40000	3575.04	1904.03	1350.17	1075.59	912.69	730.40	675.10	600.20	552.95
45000	4021.92	2142.03	1518.94	1210.04	1026.78	821.70	759.48	675.23	622.07
46000	4111.30	2189.63	1552.70	1236.93	1049.59	839.96	776.36	690.23	635.89
47000	4200.67	2237.23	1586.45	1263.82	1072.41	858.22	793.24	705.23	649.72
48000	4290.05	2284.83	1620.21	1290.70	1095.23	876.48	810.11	720.24	663.54
49000	4379.43	2332.43	1653.96	1317.59	1118.04	894.74	826.99	735.24	677.37
50000	4468.80	2380.03	1687.71	1344.48	1140.86	913.00	843.87	750.25	691.19
51000	4558.18	2427.63	1721.47	1371.37	1163.68	931.26	860.74	765.25	705.01
52000	4647.55	2475.23	1755.22	1398.26	1186.49	949.52	877.62	780.26	718.84
53000	4736.93	2522.83	1788.98	1425.15	1209.31	967.78	894.50	795.26	732.66
54000	4826.31	2570.44	1822.73	1452.04	1232.13	986.04	911.38	810.27	746.48
55000	4915.68	2618.04	1856.49	1478.93	1254.95	1004.30	928.25	825.27	760.31
56000	5005.06	2665.64	1890.24	1505.82	1277.76	1022.56	945.13	840.28	774.13
57000	5094.43	2713.24	1923.99	1532.71	1300.58	1040.82	962.01	855.28	787.95
58000	5183.81	2760.84	1957.75	1559.60	1323.40	1059.08	978.89	870.29	801.78
59000	5273.18	2808.44	1991.50	1586.49	1346.21	1077.34	995.76	885.29	815.60
60000	5362.56	2856.04	2025.26	1613.38	1369.03	1095.60	1012.64	900.30	829.43
61000	5451.94	2903.64	2059.01	1640.27	1391.85	1113.86	1029.52	915.30	843.25
62000	5541.31	2951.24	2092.76	1667.16	1414.67	1132.12	1046.39	930.31	857.07
63000	5630.69	2998.84	2126.52	1694.05	1437.48	1150.38	1063.27	945.31	870.90
64000	5720.06	3046.44	2160.27	1720.94	1460.30	1168.64	1080.15	960.32	884.72
65000	5809.44	3094.04	2194.03	1747.83	1483.12	1186.90	1097.03	975.32	898.54
67500	6032.88	3213.04	2278.41	1815.05	1540.16	1232.55	1139.22	1012.84	933.10
70000	6256.32	3332.04	2362.80	1882.28	1597.20	1278.20	1181.41	1050.35	967.66
75000	6703.20	3570.05	2531.57	2016.72	1711.29	1369.50	1265.80	1125.37	1036.78
80000	7150.08	3808.05	2700.34	2151.17	1825.37	1460.80	1350.19	1200.40	1105.90
85000	7596.96	4046.05	2869.11	2285.62	1939.46	1552.10	1434.57	1275.42	1175.02
90000	8043.84	4284.06	3037.88	2420.07	2053.55	1643.40	1518.96	1350.45	1244.14
95000	8490.72	4522.06	3206.65	2554.51	2167.63	1734.70	1603.34	1425.47	1313.25
100000	8937.60	4760.06	3375.42	2688.96	2281.72	1826.00	1687.73	1500.49	1382.37
105000	9384.48	4998.06	3544.20	2823.41	2395.80	1917.30	1772.12	1575.52	1451.49
110000	9831.36	5236.07	3712.97	2957.86	2509.89	2008.60	1856.50	1650.54	1520.61
115000	10278.24	5474.07	3881.74	3092.31	2623.97	2099.90	1940.89	1725.57	1589.73
120000	10725.12	5712.07	4050.51	3226.75	2738.06	2191.20	2025.28	1800.59	1658.85
125000	11172.00	5950.07	4219.28	3361.20	2852.14	2282.50	2109.66	1875.62	1727.97
130000	11618.88	6188.08	4388.05	3495.65	2966.23	2373.80	2194.05	1950.64	1797.08
135000	12065.76	6426.08	4556.82	3630.10	3080.32	2465.10	2278.43	2025.67	1866.20
140000	12512.64	6664.08	4725.59	3764.55	3194.40	2556.40	2362.82	2100.69	1935.32
145000	12959.52	6902.09	4894.36	3898.99	3308.49	2647.70	2447.21	2175.71	2004.44
150000	13406.39	7140.09	5063.13	4033.44	3422.57	2739.00	2531.59	2250.74	2073.56

MONTHLY PAYMENT 13⅛ %

NECESSARY TO AMORTIZE A LOAN

AMOUNT	15 YEARS	18 YEARS	20 YEARS	25 YEARS	28 YEARS	29 YEARS	30 YEARS	35 YEARS	40 YEARS
$ 50	.64	.61	.60	.57	.57	.56	.56	.56	.55
100	1.28	1.21	1.19	1.14	1.13	1.12	1.12	1.11	1.10
200	2.55	2.42	2.37	2.28	2.25	2.24	2.24	2.22	2.20
300	3.83	3.63	3.55	3.42	3.37	3.36	3.35	3.32	3.30
400	5.10	4.84	4.73	4.55	4.50	4.48	4.47	4.43	4.40
500	6.37	6.05	5.91	5.69	5.62	5.60	5.58	5.53	5.50
600	7.65	7.26	7.09	6.83	6.74	6.72	6.70	6.64	6.60
700	8.92	8.47	8.27	7.97	7.86	7.84	7.82	7.74	7.70
800	10.19	9.68	9.45	9.10	8.99	8.96	8.93	8.85	8.80
900	11.47	10.89	10.63	10.24	10.11	10.08	10.05	9.95	9.90
1000	12.74	12.10	11.81	11.38	11.23	11.20	11.16	11.06	11.00
2000	25.47	24.19	23.61	22.75	22.46	22.39	22.32	22.11	22.00
3000	38.21	36.28	35.42	34.12	33.69	33.58	33.48	33.16	33.00
4000	50.94	48.37	47.22	45.50	44.92	44.77	44.64	44.21	43.99
5000	63.68	60.46	59.03	56.87	56.14	55.96	55.80	55.27	54.99
6000	76.41	72.55	70.83	68.24	67.37	67.15	66.96	66.32	65.99
7000	89.15	84.64	82.64	79.61	78.60	78.35	78.12	77.37	76.98
8000	101.88	96.73	94.44	90.99	89.83	89.54	89.28	88.42	87.98
9000	114.62	108.82	106.25	102.36	101.06	100.73	100.44	99.47	98.98
10000	127.35	120.91	118.05	113.73	112.28	111.92	111.60	110.53	109.97
15000	191.03	181.37	177.08	170.59	168.42	167.88	167.40	165.79	164.96
20000	254.70	241.82	236.10	227.46	224.56	223.83	223.20	221.05	219.94
25000	318.37	302.28	295.13	284.32	280.70	279.79	279.00	276.31	274.93
30000	382.05	362.73	354.15	341.18	336.84	335.75	334.80	331.57	329.91
35000	445.72	423.19	413.18	398.05	392.98	391.71	390.60	386.83	384.90
40000	509.40	483.64	472.20	454.91	449.12	447.66	446.40	442.09	439.88
45000	573.07	544.10	531.23	511.77	505.26	503.62	502.20	497.35	494.86
46000	585.80	556.19	543.03	523.14	516.49	514.81	513.35	508.40	505.86
47000	598.54	568.28	554.84	534.52	527.71	526.01	524.51	519.45	516.86
48000	611.27	580.37	566.64	545.89	538.94	537.20	535.67	530.51	527.85
49000	624.01	592.46	578.45	557.26	550.17	548.39	546.83	541.56	538.85
50000	636.74	604.55	590.25	568.63	561.40	559.58	557.99	552.61	549.85
51000	649.48	616.65	602.06	580.01	572.63	570.77	569.15	563.66	560.85
52000	662.21	628.74	613.86	591.38	583.85	581.96	580.31	574.71	571.84
53000	674.95	640.83	625.67	602.75	595.08	593.15	591.47	585.77	582.84
54000	687.68	652.92	637.47	614.12	606.31	604.35	602.63	596.82	593.84
55000	700.42	665.01	649.28	625.50	617.54	615.54	613.79	607.87	604.83
56000	713.15	677.10	661.08	636.87	628.76	626.73	624.95	618.92	615.83
57000	725.89	689.19	672.89	648.24	639.99	637.92	636.11	629.98	626.83
58000	738.62	701.28	684.69	659.61	651.22	649.11	647.27	641.03	637.82
59000	751.36	713.37	696.50	670.99	662.45	660.30	658.43	652.08	648.82
60000	764.09	725.46	708.30	682.36	673.68	671.49	669.59	663.13	659.82
61000	776.83	737.55	720.11	693.73	684.90	682.69	680.75	674.18	670.81
62000	789.56	749.65	731.91	705.10	696.13	693.88	691.91	685.24	681.81
63000	802.30	761.74	743.71	716.48	707.36	705.07	703.07	696.29	692.81
64000	815.03	773.83	755.52	727.85	718.59	716.26	714.23	707.34	703.80
65000	827.77	785.92	767.32	739.22	729.82	727.45	725.39	718.39	714.80
67500	859.60	816.15	796.84	767.65	757.89	755.43	753.29	746.02	742.29
70000	891.44	846.37	826.35	796.09	785.95	783.41	781.19	773.65	769.79
75000	955.11	906.83	885.37	852.95	842.09	839.37	836.99	828.91	824.77
80000	1018.79	967.28	944.40	909.81	898.23	895.32	892.79	884.17	879.75
85000	1082.46	1027.74	1003.42	966.67	954.37	951.28	948.59	939.43	934.74
90000	1146.14	1088.19	1062.45	1023.54	1010.51	1007.24	1004.39	994.70	989.72
95000	1209.81	1148.65	1121.47	1080.40	1066.65	1063.20	1060.18	1049.96	1044.71
100000	1273.48	1209.10	1180.50	1137.26	1122.79	1119.15	1115.98	1105.22	1099.69
105000	1337.16	1269.56	1239.52	1194.13	1178.93	1175.11	1171.78	1160.48	1154.68
110000	1400.83	1330.01	1298.55	1250.99	1235.07	1231.07	1227.58	1215.74	1209.66
115000	1464.50	1390.47	1357.57	1307.85	1291.21	1287.03	1283.38	1271.00	1264.65
120000	1528.18	1450.92	1416.60	1364.71	1347.35	1342.98	1339.18	1326.26	1319.63
125000	1591.85	1511.38	1475.62	1421.58	1403.49	1398.94	1394.98	1381.52	1374.61
130000	1655.53	1571.83	1534.64	1478.44	1459.63	1454.90	1450.78	1436.78	1429.60
135000	1719.20	1632.29	1593.67	1535.30	1515.77	1510.86	1506.58	1492.04	1484.58
140000	1782.87	1692.74	1652.69	1592.17	1571.90	1566.81	1562.37	1547.30	1539.57
145000	1846.55	1753.20	1711.72	1649.03	1628.04	1622.77	1618.17	1602.56	1594.55
150000	1910.22	1813.65	1770.74	1705.89	1684.18	1678.73	1673.97	1657.82	1649.54

13¼% MONTHLY PAYMENT
NECESSARY TO AMORTIZE A LOAN

AMOUNT	1 YEAR	2 YEARS	3 YEARS	4 YEARS	5 YEARS	7 YEARS	8 YEARS	10 YEARS	12 YEARS
$ 50	4.48	2.39	1.70	1.35	1.15	.92	.85	.76	.70
100	8.95	4.77	3.39	2.70	2.29	1.84	1.70	1.51	1.40
200	17.89	9.54	6.77	5.40	4.58	3.67	3.39	3.02	2.79
300	26.84	14.30	10.15	8.09	6.87	5.50	5.09	4.53	4.18
400	35.78	19.07	13.53	10.79	9.16	7.34	6.78	6.04	5.57
500	44.72	23.83	16.91	13.48	11.45	9.17	8.48	7.54	6.96
600	53.67	28.60	20.29	16.18	13.73	11.00	10.17	9.05	8.35
700	62.61	33.37	23.68	18.87	16.02	12.83	11.87	10.56	9.74
800	71.55	38.13	27.06	21.57	18.31	14.67	13.56	12.07	11.13
900	80.50	42.90	30.44	24.26	20.60	16.50	15.26	13.58	12.52
1000	89.44	47.66	33.82	26.96	22.89	18.33	16.95	15.08	13.91
2000	178.87	95.32	67.63	53.91	45.77	36.66	33.90	30.16	27.81
3000	268.31	142.98	101.45	80.86	68.65	54.99	50.85	45.24	41.71
4000	357.74	190.64	135.26	107.81	91.53	73.32	67.79	60.32	55.61
5000	447.18	238.30	169.08	134.76	114.41	91.65	84.74	75.40	69.51
6000	536.61	285.96	202.89	161.72	137.29	109.97	101.69	90.48	83.41
7000	626.05	333.62	236.71	188.67	160.17	128.30	118.64	105.56	97.31
8000	715.48	381.28	270.52	215.62	183.06	146.63	135.58	120.64	111.22
9000	804.92	428.94	304.34	242.57	205.94	164.96	152.53	135.72	125.12
10000	894.35	476.60	338.15	269.52	228.82	183.29	169.48	150.79	139.02
15000	1341.52	714.90	507.22	404.28	343.22	274.93	254.22	226.19	208.52
20000	1788.70	953.19	676.29	539.04	457.63	366.57	338.95	301.58	278.03
25000	2235.87	1191.49	845.37	673.80	572.04	458.21	423.69	376.98	347.54
30000	2683.04	1429.79	1014.44	808.56	686.44	549.85	508.43	452.37	417.04
35000	3130.22	1668.08	1183.51	943.32	800.85	641.49	593.16	527.77	486.55
40000	3577.39	1906.38	1352.58	1078.07	915.26	733.13	677.90	603.16	556.06
45000	4024.56	2144.68	1521.66	1212.83	1029.66	824.77	762.64	678.56	625.56
46000	4114.00	2192.33	1555.47	1239.79	1052.54	843.10	779.59	693.63	639.47
47000	4203.43	2239.99	1589.29	1266.74	1075.42	861.43	796.53	708.71	653.37
48000	4292.87	2287.65	1623.10	1293.69	1098.31	879.76	813.48	723.79	667.27
49000	4382.30	2335.31	1656.92	1320.64	1121.19	898.08	830.43	738.87	681.17
50000	4471.74	2382.97	1690.73	1347.59	1144.07	916.41	847.38	753.95	695.07
51000	4561.17	2430.63	1724.54	1374.54	1166.95	934.74	864.32	769.03	708.97
52000	4650.60	2478.29	1758.36	1401.50	1189.83	953.07	881.27	784.11	722.87
53000	4740.04	2525.95	1792.17	1428.45	1212.71	971.40	898.22	799.19	736.77
54000	4829.47	2573.61	1825.99	1455.40	1235.59	989.73	915.16	814.27	750.68
55000	4918.91	2621.27	1859.80	1482.35	1258.47	1008.05	932.11	829.34	764.58
56000	5008.34	2668.93	1893.62	1509.30	1281.36	1026.38	949.06	844.42	778.48
57000	5097.78	2716.59	1927.43	1536.25	1304.24	1044.71	966.01	859.50	792.38
58000	5187.21	2764.25	1961.25	1563.21	1327.12	1063.04	982.95	874.58	806.28
59000	5276.65	2811.91	1995.06	1590.16	1350.00	1081.37	999.90	889.66	820.18
60000	5366.08	2859.57	2028.87	1617.11	1372.88	1099.69	1016.85	904.74	834.08
61000	5455.52	2907.22	2062.69	1644.06	1395.76	1118.02	1033.80	919.82	847.98
62000	5544.95	2954.88	2096.50	1671.01	1418.64	1136.35	1050.74	934.90	861.89
63000	5634.39	3002.54	2130.32	1697.96	1441.52	1154.68	1067.69	949.98	875.79
64000	5723.82	3050.20	2164.13	1724.92	1464.41	1173.01	1084.64	965.05	889.69
65000	5813.25	3097.86	2197.95	1751.87	1487.29	1191.33	1101.59	980.13	903.59
67500	6036.84	3217.01	2282.48	1819.25	1544.49	1237.16	1143.95	1017.83	938.34
70000	6260.43	3336.16	2367.02	1886.63	1601.69	1282.98	1186.32	1055.53	973.10
75000	6707.60	3574.46	2536.09	2021.39	1716.10	1374.62	1271.06	1130.92	1042.60
80000	7154.77	3812.75	2705.16	2156.14	1830.51	1466.26	1355.80	1206.32	1112.11
85000	7601.95	4051.05	2874.24	2290.90	1944.91	1557.90	1440.53	1281.71	1181.62
90000	8049.12	4289.35	3043.31	2425.66	2059.32	1649.54	1525.27	1357.11	1251.12
95000	8496.29	4527.64	3212.38	2560.42	2173.72	1741.18	1610.01	1432.50	1320.63
100000	8943.47	4765.94	3381.45	2695.18	2288.13	1832.82	1694.75	1507.89	1390.14
105000	9390.64	5004.24	3550.53	2829.94	2402.54	1924.46	1779.48	1583.29	1459.64
110000	9837.81	5242.53	3719.60	2964.70	2516.94	2016.10	1864.22	1658.68	1529.15
115000	10284.99	5480.83	3888.67	3099.46	2631.35	2107.74	1948.96	1734.08	1598.66
120000	10732.16	5719.13	4057.74	3234.21	2745.76	2199.38	2033.69	1809.47	1668.16
125000	11179.33	5957.42	4226.82	3368.97	2860.16	2291.02	2118.43	1884.87	1737.67
130000	11626.50	6195.72	4395.89	3503.73	2974.57	2382.66	2203.17	1960.26	1807.18
135000	12073.68	6434.02	4564.96	3638.49	3088.97	2474.31	2287.90	2035.66	1876.68
140000	12520.85	6672.31	4734.03	3773.25	3203.38	2565.95	2372.64	2111.05	1946.19
145000	12968.02	6910.61	4903.11	3908.01	3317.79	2657.59	2457.38	2186.44	2015.70
150000	13415.20	7148.91	5072.18	4042.77	3432.19	2749.23	2542.12	2261.84	2085.20

MONTHLY PAYMENT 13¼%

NECESSARY TO AMORTIZE A LOAN

AMOUNT	15 YEARS	18 YEARS	20 YEARS	25 YEARS	28 YEARS	29 YEARS	30 YEARS	35 YEARS	40 YEARS
$ 50	.65	.61	.60	.58	.57	.57	.57	.56	.56
100	1.29	1.22	1.19	1.15	1.14	1.13	1.13	1.12	1.11
200	2.57	2.44	2.38	2.30	2.27	2.26	2.26	2.24	2.22
300	3.85	3.66	3.57	3.45	3.40	3.39	3.38	3.35	3.33
400	5.13	4.88	4.76	4.59	4.53	4.52	4.51	4.47	4.44
500	6.41	6.09	5.95	5.74	5.67	5.65	5.63	5.58	5.55
600	7.70	7.31	7.14	6.89	6.80	6.78	6.76	6.70	6.66
700	8.98	8.53	8.33	8.03	7.93	7.91	7.89	7.81	7.77
800	10.26	9.75	9.52	9.18	9.06	9.04	9.01	8.93	8.88
900	11.54	10.97	10.71	10.33	10.20	10.16	10.14	10.04	9.99
1000	12.82	12.18	11.90	11.47	11.33	11.29	11.26	11.16	11.10
2000	25.64	24.36	23.79	22.94	22.65	22.58	22.52	22.31	22.20
3000	38.46	36.54	35.69	34.41	33.98	33.87	33.78	33.46	33.30
4000	51.27	48.72	47.58	45.87	45.30	45.16	45.04	44.61	44.40
5000	64.09	60.89	59.48	57.34	56.63	56.45	56.29	55.77	55.50
6000	76.91	73.07	71.37	68.81	67.95	67.74	67.55	66.92	66.60
7000	89.73	85.25	83.27	80.27	79.28	79.03	78.81	78.07	77.70
8000	102.54	97.43	95.16	91.74	90.60	90.32	90.07	89.22	88.79
9000	115.36	109.61	107.05	103.21	101.93	101.60	101.32	100.38	99.89
10000	128.18	121.78	118.95	114.68	113.25	112.89	112.58	111.53	110.99
15000	192.27	182.67	178.42	172.01	169.87	169.34	168.87	167.29	166.49
20000	256.35	243.56	237.89	229.35	226.50	225.78	225.16	223.05	221.98
25000	320.44	304.45	297.36	286.68	283.12	282.23	281.45	278.82	277.47
30000	384.53	365.34	356.83	344.02	339.74	338.67	337.74	334.58	332.97
35000	448.61	426.23	416.31	401.35	396.36	395.11	394.03	390.34	388.46
40000	512.70	487.12	475.78	458.69	452.99	451.56	450.31	446.10	443.95
45000	576.79	548.01	535.25	516.02	509.61	508.00	506.60	501.86	499.45
46000	589.60	560.19	547.14	527.49	520.93	519.29	517.86	513.02	510.55
47000	602.42	572.36	559.04	538.95	532.26	530.58	529.12	524.17	521.64
48000	615.24	584.54	570.93	550.42	543.58	541.87	540.38	535.32	532.74
49000	628.06	596.72	582.83	561.89	554.91	553.16	551.63	546.47	543.84
50000	640.87	608.90	594.72	573.36	566.23	564.45	562.89	557.63	554.94
51000	653.69	621.08	606.61	584.82	577.56	575.74	574.15	568.78	566.04
52000	666.51	633.25	618.51	596.29	588.88	587.03	585.41	579.93	577.14
53000	679.33	645.43	630.40	607.76	600.21	598.31	596.66	591.09	588.24
54000	692.14	657.61	642.30	619.22	611.53	609.60	607.92	602.24	599.33
55000	704.96	669.79	654.19	630.69	622.86	620.89	619.18	613.39	610.43
56000	717.78	681.97	666.09	642.16	634.18	632.18	630.44	624.54	621.53
57000	730.59	694.14	677.98	653.62	645.50	643.47	641.70	635.69	632.63
58000	743.41	706.32	689.87	665.09	656.83	654.76	652.95	646.85	643.73
59000	756.23	718.50	701.77	676.56	668.15	666.05	664.21	658.00	654.83
60000	769.05	730.68	713.66	688.03	679.48	677.34	675.47	669.15	665.93
61000	781.86	742.86	725.56	699.49	690.80	688.62	686.73	680.30	677.03
62000	794.68	755.03	737.45	710.96	702.13	699.91	697.98	691.46	688.12
63000	807.50	767.21	749.35	722.43	713.45	711.20	709.24	702.61	699.22
64000	820.32	779.39	761.24	733.89	724.78	722.49	720.50	713.76	710.32
65000	833.13	791.57	773.13	745.36	736.10	733.78	731.76	724.91	721.42
67500	865.18	822.01	802.87	774.03	764.41	762.00	759.90	752.79	749.17
70000	897.22	852.46	832.61	802.70	792.72	790.22	788.05	780.67	776.91
75000	961.31	913.35	892.08	860.03	849.35	846.67	844.34	836.44	832.41
80000	1025.39	974.23	951.55	917.37	905.97	903.11	900.62	892.20	887.90
85000	1089.48	1035.12	1011.02	974.70	962.59	959.56	956.91	947.96	943.39
90000	1153.57	1096.01	1070.49	1032.04	1019.22	1016.00	1013.20	1003.72	998.89
95000	1217.65	1156.90	1129.96	1089.37	1075.84	1072.45	1069.49	1059.49	1054.38
100000	1281.74	1217.79	1189.44	1146.71	1132.46	1128.89	1125.78	1115.25	1109.87
105000	1345.83	1278.68	1248.91	1204.04	1189.08	1185.33	1182.07	1171.01	1165.37
110000	1409.92	1339.57	1308.38	1261.38	1245.71	1241.78	1238.36	1226.77	1220.86
115000	1474.00	1400.46	1367.85	1318.71	1302.33	1298.22	1294.64	1282.53	1276.36
120000	1538.09	1461.35	1427.32	1376.05	1358.95	1354.67	1350.93	1338.30	1331.85
125000	1602.18	1522.24	1486.79	1433.38	1415.57	1411.11	1407.22	1394.06	1387.34
130000	1666.26	1583.13	1546.26	1490.72	1472.20	1467.56	1463.51	1449.82	1442.84
135000	1730.35	1644.02	1605.74	1548.05	1528.82	1524.00	1519.80	1505.58	1498.33
140000	1794.44	1704.91	1665.21	1605.39	1585.44	1580.44	1576.09	1561.34	1553.82
145000	1858.52	1765.80	1724.68	1662.72	1642.07	1636.89	1632.38	1617.11	1609.32
150000	1922.61	1826.69	1784.15	1720.06	1698.69	1693.33	1688.67	1672.87	1664.81

MONTHLY PAYMENT

NECESSARY TO AMORTIZE A LOAN

AMOUNT	1 YEAR	2 YEARS	3 YEARS	4 YEARS	5 YEARS	7 YEARS	8 YEARS	10 YEARS	12 YEARS
$ 50	4.48	2.39	1.70	1.36	1.15	.92	.86	.76	.70
100	8.95	4.78	3.39	2.71	2.30	1.84	1.71	1.52	1.40
200	17.90	9.55	6.78	5.41	4.59	3.68	3.41	3.04	2.80
300	26.85	14.32	10.17	8.11	6.89	5.52	5.11	4.55	4.20
400	35.80	19.09	13.55	10.81	9.18	7.36	6.81	6.07	5.60
500	44.75	23.86	16.94	13.51	11.48	9.20	8.51	7.58	6.99
600	53.70	28.64	20.33	16.21	13.77	11.04	10.22	9.10	8.39
700	62.65	33.41	23.72	18.91	16.07	12.88	11.92	10.61	9.79
800	71.60	38.18	27.10	21.62	18.36	14.72	13.62	12.13	11.19
900	80.55	42.95	30.49	24.32	20.66	16.56	15.32	13.64	12.59
1000	89.50	47.72	33.88	27.02	22.95	18.40	17.02	15.16	13.98
2000	178.99	95.44	67.75	54.03	45.90	36.80	34.04	30.31	27.96
3000	268.48	143.16	101.63	81.05	68.84	55.19	51.06	45.46	41.94
4000	357.98	190.88	135.50	108.06	91.79	73.59	68.08	60.62	55.92
5000	447.47	238.60	169.38	135.07	114.73	91.99	85.09	75.77	69.90
6000	536.96	286.31	203.25	162.09	137.68	110.38	102.11	90.92	83.88
7000	626.46	334.03	237.13	189.10	160.62	128.78	119.13	106.08	97.86
8000	715.95	381.75	271.00	216.12	183.57	147.18	136.15	121.23	111.84
9000	805.44	429.47	304.88	243.13	206.51	165.57	153.16	136.38	125.82
10000	894.94	477.19	338.75	270.14	229.46	183.97	170.18	151.54	139.80
15000	1342.40	715.78	508.13	405.21	344.19	275.95	255.27	227.30	209.69
20000	1789.87	954.37	677.50	540.28	458.91	367.93	340.36	303.07	279.59
25000	2237.34	1192.96	846.88	675.35	573.64	459.92	425.45	378.83	349.48
30000	2684.80	1431.55	1016.25	810.42	688.37	551.90	510.54	454.60	419.38
35000	3132.27	1670.14	1185.63	945.49	803.10	643.88	595.62	530.36	489.27
40000	3579.74	1908.73	1355.00	1080.56	917.82	735.86	680.71	606.13	559.17
45000	4027.20	2147.32	1524.37	1215.63	1032.55	827.85	765.80	681.89	629.07
46000	4116.70	2195.04	1558.25	1242.65	1055.50	846.24	782.82	697.05	643.05
47000	4206.19	2242.76	1592.12	1269.66	1078.44	864.64	799.84	712.20	657.02
48000	4295.68	2290.48	1626.00	1296.68	1101.39	883.03	816.85	727.35	671.00
49000	4385.18	2338.19	1659.87	1323.69	1124.33	901.43	833.87	742.51	684.98
50000	4474.67	2385.91	1693.75	1350.70	1147.28	919.83	850.89	757.66	698.96
51000	4564.16	2433.63	1727.62	1377.72	1170.23	938.22	867.91	772.81	712.94
52000	4653.66	2481.35	1761.50	1404.73	1193.17	956.62	884.93	787.96	726.92
53000	4743.15	2529.07	1795.37	1431.75	1216.12	975.02	901.94	803.12	740.90
54000	4832.64	2576.79	1829.25	1458.76	1239.06	993.41	918.96	818.27	754.88
55000	4922.14	2624.50	1863.12	1485.77	1262.01	1011.81	935.98	833.42	768.86
56000	5011.63	2672.22	1897.00	1512.79	1284.95	1030.21	953.00	848.58	782.84
57000	5101.12	2719.94	1930.87	1539.80	1307.90	1048.60	970.01	863.73	796.82
58000	5190.62	2767.66	1964.75	1566.82	1330.84	1067.00	987.03	878.88	810.80
59000	5280.11	2815.38	1998.62	1593.83	1353.79	1085.40	1004.05	894.04	824.77
60000	5369.60	2863.09	2032.50	1620.84	1376.73	1103.79	1021.07	909.19	838.75
61000	5459.10	2910.81	2066.37	1647.86	1399.68	1122.19	1038.08	924.34	852.73
62000	5548.59	2958.53	2100.25	1674.87	1422.63	1140.59	1055.10	939.50	866.71
63000	5638.08	3006.25	2134.12	1701.89	1445.57	1158.98	1072.12	954.65	880.69
64000	5727.58	3053.97	2168.00	1728.90	1468.52	1177.38	1089.14	969.80	894.67
65000	5817.07	3101.68	2201.87	1755.91	1491.46	1195.77	1106.16	984.95	908.65
67500	6040.80	3220.98	2286.56	1823.45	1548.83	1241.77	1148.70	1022.84	943.60
70000	6264.54	3340.28	2371.25	1890.98	1606.19	1287.76	1191.24	1060.72	978.54
75000	6712.00	3578.87	2540.62	2026.05	1720.92	1379.74	1276.33	1136.49	1048.44
80000	7159.47	3817.46	2709.99	2161.12	1835.64	1471.72	1361.42	1212.25	1118.34
85000	7606.94	4056.05	2879.37	2296.19	1950.37	1563.70	1446.51	1288.02	1188.23
90000	8054.40	4294.64	3048.74	2431.26	2065.10	1655.69	1531.60	1363.78	1258.13
95000	8501.87	4533.23	3218.12	2566.33	2179.83	1747.67	1616.69	1439.55	1328.02
100000	8949.34	4771.82	3387.49	2701.40	2294.55	1839.65	1701.78	1515.31	1397.92
105000	9396.80	5010.41	3556.87	2836.47	2409.28	1931.63	1786.86	1591.08	1467.81
110000	9844.27	5249.00	3726.24	2971.54	2524.01	2023.62	1871.95	1666.84	1537.71
115000	10291.74	5487.59	3895.61	3106.61	2638.74	2115.60	1957.04	1742.61	1607.61
120000	10739.20	5726.18	4064.99	3241.68	2753.46	2207.58	2042.13	1818.37	1677.50
125000	11186.67	5964.77	4234.36	3376.75	2868.19	2299.56	2127.22	1894.14	1747.40
130000	11634.14	6203.36	4403.74	3511.82	2982.92	2391.54	2212.31	1969.90	1817.29
135000	12081.60	6441.96	4573.11	3646.89	3097.65	2483.53	2297.40	2045.67	1887.19
140000	12529.07	6680.55	4742.49	3781.96	3212.37	2575.51	2382.48	2121.43	1957.09
145000	12976.53	6919.14	4911.86	3917.03	3327.10	2667.49	2467.57	2197.20	2026.98
150000	13424.00	7157.73	5081.23	4052.10	3441.83	2759.47	2552.66	2272.97	2096.88

MONTHLY PAYMENT 13⅜%
NECESSARY TO AMORTIZE A LOAN

AMOUNT	15 YEARS	18 YEARS	20 YEARS	25 YEARS	28 YEARS	29 YEARS	30 YEARS	35 YEARS	40 YEARS
$ 50	.65	.62	.60	.58	.58	.57	.57	.57	.57
100	1.30	1.23	1.20	1.16	1.15	1.14	1.14	1.13	1.13
200	2.59	2.46	2.40	2.32	2.29	2.28	2.28	2.26	2.25
300	3.88	3.68	3.60	3.47	3.43	3.42	3.41	3.38	3.37
400	5.17	4.91	4.80	4.63	4.57	4.56	4.55	4.51	4.49
500	6.46	6.14	6.00	5.79	5.72	5.70	5.68	5.63	5.61
600	7.75	7.36	7.20	6.94	6.86	6.84	6.82	6.76	6.73
700	9.04	8.59	8.39	8.10	8.00	7.98	7.95	7.88	7.85
800	10.33	9.82	9.59	9.25	9.14	9.11	9.09	9.01	8.97
900	11.62	11.04	10.79	10.41	10.28	10.25	10.23	10.13	10.09
1000	12.91	12.27	11.99	11.57	11.43	11.39	11.36	11.26	11.21
2000	25.81	24.53	23.97	23.13	22.85	22.78	22.72	22.51	22.41
3000	38.71	36.80	35.96	34.69	34.27	34.16	34.07	33.76	33.61
4000	51.61	49.06	47.94	46.25	45.69	45.55	45.43	45.02	44.81
5000	64.51	61.33	59.92	57.81	57.11	56.94	56.78	56.27	56.01
6000	77.41	73.59	71.91	69.37	68.53	68.32	68.14	67.52	67.21
7000	90.31	85.86	83.89	80.94	79.96	79.71	79.50	78.77	78.41
8000	103.21	98.12	95.88	92.50	91.38	91.10	90.85	90.03	89.61
9000	116.11	110.39	107.86	104.06	102.80	102.48	102.21	101.28	100.81
10000	129.01	122.65	119.84	115.62	114.22	113.87	113.56	112.53	112.01
15000	193.51	183.98	179.76	173.43	171.33	170.80	170.34	168.80	168.01
20000	258.01	245.30	239.68	231.24	228.43	227.73	227.12	225.06	224.02
25000	322.51	306.63	299.60	289.05	285.54	284.66	283.90	281.33	280.02
30000	387.01	367.95	359.52	346.85	342.65	341.60	340.68	337.59	336.02
35000	451.51	429.28	419.44	404.66	399.76	398.53	397.46	393.85	392.03
40000	516.01	490.60	479.36	462.47	456.86	455.46	454.24	450.12	448.03
45000	580.51	551.93	539.28	520.28	513.97	512.39	511.02	506.38	504.03
46000	593.41	564.19	551.27	531.84	525.39	523.78	522.37	517.64	515.23
47000	606.31	576.46	563.25	543.40	536.81	535.16	533.73	528.89	526.43
48000	619.21	588.72	575.23	554.96	548.23	546.55	545.09	540.14	537.63
49000	632.11	600.99	587.22	566.52	559.66	557.94	556.44	551.39	548.84
50000	645.01	613.25	599.20	578.09	571.08	569.32	567.80	562.65	560.04
51000	657.91	625.52	611.18	589.65	582.50	580.71	579.15	573.90	571.24
52000	670.81	637.78	623.17	601.21	593.92	592.10	590.51	585.15	582.44
53000	683.71	650.05	635.15	612.77	605.34	603.48	601.87	596.41	593.64
54000	696.61	662.31	647.14	624.33	616.76	614.87	613.22	607.66	604.84
55000	709.51	674.58	659.12	635.89	628.18	626.26	624.58	618.91	616.04
56000	722.41	686.84	671.10	647.46	639.61	637.64	635.93	630.16	627.24
57000	735.31	699.11	683.09	659.02	651.03	649.03	647.29	641.42	638.44
58000	748.21	711.37	695.07	670.58	662.45	660.41	658.64	652.67	649.64
59000	761.11	723.64	707.06	682.14	673.87	671.80	670.00	663.92	660.84
60000	774.01	735.90	719.04	693.70	685.29	683.19	681.36	675.18	672.04
61000	786.92	748.17	731.02	705.26	696.71	694.57	692.71	686.43	683.24
62000	799.82	760.43	743.01	716.83	708.13	705.96	704.07	697.68	694.44
63000	812.72	772.70	754.99	728.39	719.56	717.35	715.42	708.93	705.64
64000	825.62	784.96	766.98	739.95	730.98	728.73	726.78	720.19	716.84
65000	838.52	797.23	778.96	751.51	742.40	740.12	738.14	731.44	728.04
67500	870.77	827.89	808.92	780.41	770.95	768.59	766.52	759.57	756.05
70000	903.02	858.55	838.88	809.32	799.51	797.05	794.91	787.70	784.05
75000	967.52	919.88	898.80	867.13	856.61	853.98	851.69	843.97	840.05
80000	1032.02	981.20	958.72	924.94	913.72	910.91	908.47	900.23	896.05
85000	1096.52	1042.53	1018.64	982.74	970.83	967.85	965.25	956.50	952.06
90000	1161.02	1103.85	1078.56	1040.55	1027.93	1024.78	1022.03	1012.76	1008.06
95000	1225.52	1165.18	1138.48	1098.36	1085.04	1081.71	1078.81	1069.03	1064.06
100000	1290.02	1226.50	1198.40	1156.17	1142.15	1138.64	1135.59	1125.29	1120.07
105000	1354.52	1287.83	1258.32	1213.98	1199.26	1195.57	1192.37	1181.55	1176.07
110000	1419.02	1349.15	1318.24	1271.78	1256.36	1252.51	1249.15	1237.82	1232.07
115000	1483.52	1410.48	1378.16	1329.59	1313.47	1309.44	1305.93	1294.08	1288.08
120000	1548.02	1471.80	1438.08	1387.40	1370.58	1366.37	1362.71	1350.35	1344.08
125000	1612.53	1533.13	1497.99	1445.21	1427.68	1423.30	1419.49	1406.61	1400.08
130000	1677.03	1594.45	1557.91	1503.02	1484.79	1480.23	1476.27	1462.88	1456.08
135000	1741.53	1655.78	1617.83	1560.82	1541.90	1537.17	1533.04	1519.14	1512.09
140000	1806.03	1717.10	1677.75	1618.63	1599.01	1594.10	1589.82	1575.40	1568.09
145000	1870.53	1778.43	1737.67	1676.44	1656.11	1651.03	1646.60	1631.67	1624.09
150000	1935.03	1839.75	1797.59	1734.25	1713.22	1707.96	1703.38	1687.93	1680.10

13½% MONTHLY PAYMENT
NECESSARY TO AMORTIZE A LOAN

AMOUNT	1 YEAR	2 YEARS	3 YEARS	4 YEARS	5 YEARS	7 YEARS	8 YEARS	10 YEARS	12 YEARS
$ 50	4.48	2.39	1.70	1.36	1.16	.93	.86	.77	.71
100	8.96	4.78	3.40	2.71	2.31	1.85	1.71	1.53	1.41
200	17.92	9.56	6.79	5.42	4.61	3.70	3.42	3.05	2.82
300	26.87	14.34	10.19	8.13	6.91	5.54	5.13	4.57	4.22
400	35.83	19.12	13.58	10.84	9.21	7.39	6.84	6.10	5.63
500	44.78	23.89	16.97	13.54	11.51	9.24	8.55	7.62	7.03
600	53.74	28.67	20.37	16.25	13.81	11.08	10.26	9.14	8.44
700	62.69	33.45	23.76	18.96	16.11	12.93	11.97	10.66	9.85
800	71.65	38.23	27.15	21.67	18.41	14.78	13.68	12.19	11.25
900	80.60	43.00	30.55	24.37	20.71	16.62	15.38	13.71	12.66
1000	89.56	47.78	33.94	27.08	23.01	18.47	17.09	15.23	14.06
2000	179.11	95.56	67.88	54.16	46.02	36.93	34.18	30.46	28.12
3000	268.66	143.34	101.81	81.23	69.03	55.40	51.27	45.69	42.18
4000	358.21	191.11	135.75	108.31	92.04	73.86	68.36	60.91	56.23
5000	447.77	238.89	169.68	135.39	115.05	92.33	85.45	76.14	70.29
6000	537.32	286.67	203.62	162.46	138.06	110.79	102.53	91.37	84.35
7000	626.87	334.44	237.55	189.54	161.07	129.26	119.62	106.60	98.41
8000	716.42	382.22	271.49	216.62	184.08	147.72	136.71	121.82	112.46
9000	805.97	430.00	305.42	243.69	207.09	166.19	153.80	137.05	126.52
10000	895.53	477.78	339.36	270.77	230.10	184.65	170.89	152.28	140.58
15000	1343.29	716.66	509.03	406.15	345.15	276.98	256.33	228.42	210.86
20000	1791.05	955.55	678.71	541.53	460.20	369.30	341.77	304.55	281.15
25000	2238.81	1194.43	848.39	676.91	575.25	461.63	427.21	380.69	351.43
30000	2686.57	1433.32	1018.06	812.29	690.30	553.95	512.65	456.83	421.72
35000	3134.33	1672.20	1187.74	947.68	805.35	646.28	598.09	532.97	492.01
40000	3582.09	1911.09	1357.42	1083.06	920.40	738.60	683.53	609.10	562.29
45000	4029.85	2149.97	1527.09	1218.44	1035.45	830.93	768.97	685.24	632.58
46000	4119.40	2197.75	1561.03	1245.52	1058.46	849.39	786.06	700.47	646.63
47000	4208.95	2245.52	1594.96	1272.59	1081.47	867.85	803.15	715.69	660.69
48000	4298.50	2293.30	1628.90	1299.67	1104.48	886.32	820.24	730.92	674.75
49000	4388.05	2341.08	1662.83	1326.74	1127.49	904.78	837.32	746.15	688.81
50000	4477.61	2388.86	1696.77	1353.82	1150.50	923.25	854.41	761.38	702.86
51000	4567.16	2436.63	1730.70	1380.90	1173.51	941.71	871.50	776.60	716.92
52000	4656.71	2484.41	1764.64	1407.97	1196.52	960.18	888.59	791.83	730.98
53000	4746.26	2532.19	1798.58	1435.05	1219.53	978.64	905.68	807.06	745.04
54000	4835.81	2579.96	1832.51	1462.13	1242.54	997.11	922.77	822.29	759.09
55000	4925.37	2627.74	1866.45	1489.20	1265.55	1015.57	939.85	837.51	773.15
56000	5014.92	2675.52	1900.38	1516.28	1288.56	1034.04	956.94	852.74	787.21
57000	5104.47	2723.29	1934.32	1543.36	1311.57	1052.50	974.03	867.97	801.26
58000	5194.02	2771.07	1968.25	1570.43	1334.58	1070.97	991.12	883.20	815.32
59000	5283.57	2818.85	2002.19	1597.51	1357.59	1089.43	1008.21	898.42	829.38
60000	5373.13	2866.63	2036.12	1624.58	1380.60	1107.90	1025.29	913.65	843.44
61000	5462.68	2914.40	2070.06	1651.66	1403.61	1126.36	1042.38	928.88	857.49
62000	5552.23	2962.18	2103.99	1678.74	1426.62	1144.83	1059.47	944.11	871.55
63000	5641.78	3009.96	2137.93	1705.81	1449.63	1163.29	1076.56	959.33	885.61
64000	5731.33	3057.73	2171.86	1732.89	1472.64	1181.76	1093.65	974.56	899.66
65000	5820.89	3105.51	2205.80	1759.97	1495.64	1200.22	1110.74	989.79	913.72
67500	6044.77	3224.95	2290.64	1827.66	1553.17	1246.39	1153.46	1027.86	948.86
70000	6268.65	3344.40	2375.48	1895.35	1610.69	1292.55	1196.18	1065.93	984.01
75000	6716.41	3583.28	2545.15	2030.73	1725.74	1384.87	1281.62	1142.06	1054.29
80000	7164.17	3822.17	2714.83	2166.11	1840.79	1477.20	1367.06	1218.20	1124.58
85000	7611.93	4061.05	2884.50	2301.49	1955.84	1569.52	1452.50	1294.34	1194.86
90000	8059.69	4299.94	3054.18	2436.87	2070.89	1661.85	1537.94	1370.47	1265.15
95000	8507.45	4538.82	3223.86	2572.26	2185.94	1754.17	1623.38	1446.61	1335.44
100000	8955.21	4777.71	3393.53	2707.64	2300.99	1846.49	1708.82	1522.75	1405.72
105000	9402.97	5016.59	3563.21	2843.02	2416.04	1938.82	1794.26	1598.89	1476.01
110000	9850.73	5255.48	3732.89	2978.40	2531.09	2031.14	1879.70	1675.02	1546.29
115000	10298.49	5494.36	3902.56	3113.78	2646.14	2123.47	1965.14	1751.16	1616.58
120000	10746.25	5733.25	4072.24	3249.16	2761.19	2215.79	2050.58	1827.30	1686.87
125000	11194.01	5972.13	4241.92	3384.55	2876.24	2308.12	2136.02	1903.43	1757.15
130000	11641.77	6211.02	4411.59	3519.93	2991.28	2400.44	2221.47	1979.57	1827.44
135000	12089.53	6449.90	4581.27	3655.31	3106.33	2492.77	2306.91	2055.71	1897.72
140000	12537.29	6688.79	4750.95	3790.69	3221.38	2585.09	2392.35	2131.85	1968.01
145000	12985.05	6927.67	4920.62	3926.07	3336.43	2677.41	2477.79	2207.98	2038.29
150000	13432.81	7166.56	5090.30	4061.45	3451.48	2769.74	2563.23	2284.12	2108.58

MONTHLY PAYMENT 13½%

NECESSARY TO AMORTIZE A LOAN

AMOUNT	15 YEARS	18 YEARS	20 YEARS	25 YEARS	28 YEARS	29 YEARS	30 YEARS	35 YEARS	40 YEARS
$ 50	.65	.62	.61	.59	.58	.58	.58	.57	.57
100	1.30	1.24	1.21	1.17	1.16	1.15	1.15	1.14	1.14
200	2.60	2.48	2.42	2.34	2.31	2.30	2.30	2.28	2.27
300	3.90	3.71	3.63	3.50	3.46	3.45	3.44	3.41	3.40
400	5.20	4.95	4.83	4.67	4.61	4.60	4.59	4.55	4.53
500	6.50	6.18	6.04	5.83	5.76	5.75	5.73	5.68	5.66
600	7.79	7.42	7.25	7.00	6.92	6.90	6.88	6.82	6.79
700	9.09	8.65	8.46	8.16	8.07	8.04	8.02	7.95	7.92
800	10.39	9.89	9.66	9.33	9.22	9.19	9.17	9.09	9.05
900	11.69	11.12	10.87	10.50	10.37	10.34	10.31	10.22	10.18
1000	12.99	12.36	12.08	11.66	11.52	11.49	11.46	11.36	11.31
2000	25.97	24.71	24.15	23.32	23.04	22.97	22.91	22.71	22.61
3000	38.95	37.06	36.23	34.97	34.56	34.46	34.37	34.07	33.91
4000	51.94	49.41	48.30	46.63	46.08	45.94	45.82	45.42	45.22
5000	64.92	61.77	60.37	58.29	57.60	57.43	57.28	56.77	56.52
6000	77.90	74.12	72.45	69.94	69.12	68.91	68.73	68.13	67.82
7000	90.89	86.47	84.52	81.60	80.63	80.39	80.18	79.48	79.12
8000	103.87	98.82	96.59	93.26	92.15	91.88	91.64	90.83	90.43
9000	116.85	111.18	108.67	104.91	103.67	103.36	103.09	102.19	101.73
10000	129.84	123.53	120.74	116.57	115.19	114.85	114.55	113.54	113.03
15000	194.75	185.29	181.11	174.85	172.78	172.27	171.82	170.31	169.54
20000	259.67	247.05	241.48	233.13	230.37	229.69	229.09	227.07	226.06
25000	324.58	308.81	301.85	291.42	287.97	287.11	286.36	283.84	282.57
30000	389.50	370.57	362.22	349.70	345.56	344.53	343.63	340.61	339.08
35000	454.42	432.34	422.59	407.98	403.15	401.95	400.90	397.37	395.60
40000	519.33	494.10	482.95	466.26	460.74	459.37	458.17	454.14	452.11
45000	584.25	555.86	543.32	524.55	518.34	516.79	515.44	510.91	508.62
46000	597.23	568.21	555.40	536.20	529.86	528.27	526.89	522.26	519.93
47000	610.21	580.56	567.47	547.86	541.37	539.76	538.35	533.62	531.23
48000	623.20	592.92	579.54	559.51	552.89	551.24	549.80	544.97	542.53
49000	636.18	605.27	591.62	571.17	564.41	562.72	561.26	556.32	553.83
50000	649.16	617.62	603.69	582.83	575.93	574.21	572.71	567.68	565.14
51000	662.15	629.97	615.77	594.48	587.45	585.69	584.17	579.03	576.44
52000	675.13	642.33	627.84	606.14	598.97	597.18	595.62	590.38	587.74
53000	688.11	654.68	639.91	617.80	610.48	608.66	607.07	601.74	599.04
54000	701.10	667.03	651.99	629.45	622.00	620.14	618.53	613.09	610.35
55000	714.08	679.38	664.06	641.11	633.52	631.63	629.98	624.44	621.65
56000	727.06	691.73	676.13	652.77	645.04	643.11	641.44	635.80	632.95
57000	740.05	704.09	688.21	664.42	656.56	654.60	652.89	647.15	644.25
58000	753.03	716.44	700.28	676.08	668.08	666.08	664.34	658.50	655.56
59000	766.01	728.79	712.36	687.74	679.60	677.56	675.80	669.86	666.86
60000	779.00	741.14	724.43	699.39	691.11	689.05	687.25	681.21	678.16
61000	791.98	753.50	736.50	711.05	702.63	700.53	698.71	692.56	689.46
62000	804.96	765.85	748.58	722.70	714.15	712.02	710.16	703.92	700.77
63000	817.95	778.20	760.65	734.36	725.67	723.50	721.61	715.27	712.07
64000	830.93	790.55	772.72	746.02	737.19	734.98	733.07	726.62	723.37
65000	843.91	802.91	784.80	757.67	748.71	746.47	744.52	737.98	734.67
67500	876.37	833.79	814.98	786.82	777.50	775.18	773.16	766.36	762.93
70000	908.83	864.67	845.17	815.96	806.30	803.89	801.79	794.74	791.19
75000	973.74	926.43	905.54	874.24	863.89	861.31	859.06	851.51	847.70
80000	1038.66	988.19	965.90	932.52	921.48	918.73	916.33	908.28	904.21
85000	1103.58	1049.95	1026.27	990.80	979.08	976.15	973.61	965.04	960.73
90000	1168.49	1111.71	1086.64	1049.09	1036.67	1033.57	1030.88	1021.81	1017.24
95000	1233.41	1173.47	1147.01	1107.37	1094.26	1090.99	1088.15	1078.58	1073.75
100000	1298.32	1235.24	1207.38	1165.65	1151.85	1148.41	1145.42	1135.35	1130.27
105000	1363.24	1297.00	1267.75	1223.93	1209.45	1205.83	1202.69	1192.11	1186.78
110000	1428.16	1358.76	1328.12	1282.21	1267.04	1263.25	1259.96	1248.88	1243.29
115000	1493.07	1420.52	1388.49	1340.50	1324.63	1320.67	1317.23	1305.65	1299.81
120000	1557.99	1482.28	1448.85	1398.78	1382.22	1378.09	1374.50	1362.41	1356.32
125000	1622.90	1544.04	1509.22	1457.06	1439.82	1435.51	1431.77	1419.18	1412.83
130000	1687.82	1605.81	1569.59	1515.34	1497.41	1492.93	1489.04	1475.95	1469.34
135000	1752.74	1667.57	1629.96	1573.63	1555.00	1550.35	1546.31	1532.71	1525.86
140000	1817.65	1729.33	1690.33	1631.91	1612.59	1607.77	1603.58	1589.48	1582.37
145000	1882.57	1791.09	1750.70	1690.19	1670.19	1665.19	1660.85	1646.25	1638.88
150000	1947.48	1852.85	1811.07	1748.47	1727.78	1722.61	1718.12	1703.02	1695.40

MONTHLY PAYMENT
NECESSARY TO AMORTIZE A LOAN

AMOUNT	1 YEAR	2 YEARS	3 YEARS	4 YEARS	5 YEARS	7 YEARS	8 YEARS	10 YEARS	12 YEARS
$ 50	4.49	2.40	1.70	1.36	1.16	.93	.86	.77	.71
100	8.97	4.79	3.40	2.72	2.31	1.86	1.72	1.54	1.42
200	17.93	9.57	6.80	5.43	4.62	3.71	3.44	3.07	2.83
300	26.89	14.36	10.20	8.15	6.93	5.57	5.15	4.60	4.25
400	35.85	19.14	13.60	10.86	9.23	7.42	6.87	6.13	5.66
500	44.81	23.92	17.00	13.57	11.54	9.27	8.58	7.66	7.07
600	53.77	28.71	20.40	16.29	13.85	11.13	10.30	9.19	8.49
700	62.73	33.49	23.80	19.00	16.16	12.98	12.02	10.72	9.90
800	71.69	38.27	27.20	21.72	18.46	14.83	13.73	12.25	11.31
900	80.65	43.06	30.60	24.43	20.77	16.69	15.45	13.78	12.73
1000	89.62	47.84	34.00	27.14	23.08	18.54	17.16	15.31	14.14
2000	179.23	95.68	68.00	54.28	46.15	37.07	34.32	30.61	28.28
3000	268.84	143.51	101.99	81.42	69.23	55.61	51.48	45.91	42.41
4000	358.45	191.35	135.99	108.56	92.30	74.14	68.64	61.21	56.55
5000	448.06	239.18	169.98	135.70	115.38	92.67	85.80	76.51	70.68
6000	537.67	287.02	203.98	162.84	138.45	111.21	102.96	91.82	84.82
7000	627.28	334.86	237.98	189.98	161.53	129.74	120.12	107.12	98.95
8000	716.89	382.69	271.97	217.11	184.60	148.27	137.28	122.42	113.09
9000	806.50	430.53	305.97	244.25	207.67	166.81	154.43	137.72	127.22
10000	896.11	478.36	339.96	271.39	230.75	185.34	171.59	153.02	141.36
15000	1344.17	717.54	509.94	407.09	346.12	278.01	257.39	229.53	212.04
20000	1792.22	956.72	679.92	542.78	461.49	370.67	343.18	306.04	282.71
25000	2240.27	1195.90	849.90	678.47	576.86	463.34	428.97	382.55	353.39
30000	2688.33	1435.08	1019.88	814.17	692.23	556.01	514.77	459.06	424.07
35000	3136.38	1674.26	1189.86	949.86	807.61	648.68	600.56	535.57	494.74
40000	3584.44	1913.44	1359.84	1085.55	922.98	741.34	686.36	612.08	565.42
45000	4032.49	2152.62	1529.82	1221.25	1038.35	834.01	772.15	688.59	636.10
46000	4122.10	2200.46	1563.81	1248.39	1061.42	852.54	789.31	703.90	650.23
47000	4211.71	2248.29	1597.81	1275.53	1084.50	871.08	806.47	719.20	664.37
48000	4301.32	2296.13	1631.80	1302.66	1107.57	889.61	823.63	734.50	678.50
49000	4390.93	2343.96	1665.80	1329.80	1130.65	908.14	840.78	749.80	692.64
50000	4480.54	2391.80	1699.79	1356.94	1153.72	926.68	857.94	765.10	706.78
51000	4570.15	2439.64	1733.79	1384.08	1176.79	945.21	875.10	780.41	720.91
52000	4659.76	2487.47	1767.79	1411.22	1199.87	963.75	892.26	795.71	735.05
53000	4749.38	2535.31	1801.78	1438.36	1222.94	982.28	909.42	811.01	749.18
54000	4838.99	2583.14	1835.78	1465.50	1246.02	1000.81	926.58	826.31	763.32
55000	4928.60	2630.98	1869.77	1492.64	1269.09	1019.35	943.74	841.61	777.45
56000	5018.21	2678.82	1903.77	1519.77	1292.17	1037.88	960.90	856.92	791.59
57000	5107.82	2726.65	1937.76	1546.91	1315.24	1056.41	978.05	872.22	805.72
58000	5197.43	2774.49	1971.76	1574.05	1338.31	1074.95	995.21	887.52	819.86
59000	5287.04	2822.32	2005.76	1601.19	1361.39	1093.48	1012.37	902.82	833.99
60000	5376.65	2870.16	2039.75	1628.33	1384.46	1112.01	1029.53	918.12	848.13
61000	5466.26	2918.00	2073.75	1655.47	1407.54	1130.55	1046.69	933.42	862.26
62000	5555.87	2965.83	2107.74	1682.61	1430.61	1149.08	1063.85	948.73	876.40
63000	5645.48	3013.67	2141.74	1709.75	1453.69	1167.61	1081.01	964.03	890.54
64000	5735.09	3061.50	2175.73	1736.88	1476.76	1186.15	1098.17	979.33	904.67
65000	5824.70	3109.34	2209.73	1764.02	1499.83	1204.68	1115.32	994.63	918.81
67500	6048.73	3228.93	2294.72	1831.87	1557.52	1251.01	1158.22	1032.89	954.14
70000	6272.76	3348.52	2379.71	1899.72	1615.21	1297.35	1201.12	1071.14	989.48
75000	6720.81	3587.70	2549.69	2035.41	1730.58	1390.02	1286.91	1147.65	1060.16
80000	7168.87	3826.88	2719.67	2171.10	1845.95	1482.68	1372.71	1224.16	1130.84
85000	7616.92	4066.06	2889.65	2306.80	1961.32	1575.35	1458.50	1300.67	1201.51
90000	8064.97	4305.24	3059.63	2442.49	2076.69	1668.02	1544.29	1377.18	1272.19
95000	8513.03	4544.42	3229.60	2578.19	2192.06	1760.68	1630.09	1453.69	1342.87
100000	8961.08	4783.60	3399.58	2713.88	2307.43	1853.35	1715.88	1530.20	1413.55
105000	9409.14	5022.78	3569.56	2849.57	2422.81	1946.02	1801.68	1606.71	1484.22
110000	9857.19	5261.96	3739.54	2985.27	2538.18	2038.69	1887.47	1683.22	1554.90
115000	10305.24	5501.14	3909.52	3120.96	2653.55	2131.35	1973.26	1759.73	1625.58
120000	10753.30	5740.32	4079.50	3256.65	2768.92	2224.02	2059.06	1836.24	1696.25
125000	11201.35	5979.49	4249.48	3392.35	2884.29	2316.69	2144.85	1912.75	1766.93
130000	11649.40	6218.67	4419.46	3528.04	2999.66	2409.36	2230.64	1989.26	1837.61
135000	12097.46	6457.85	4589.44	3663.73	3115.03	2502.02	2316.44	2065.77	1908.28
140000	12545.51	6697.03	4759.41	3799.43	3230.41	2594.69	2402.23	2142.28	1978.96
145000	12993.57	6936.21	4929.39	3935.12	3345.78	2687.36	2488.03	2218.79	2049.64
150000	13441.62	7175.39	5099.37	4070.82	3461.15	2780.03	2573.82	2295.30	2120.32

MONTHLY PAYMENT 13⅝%
NECESSARY TO AMORTIZE A LOAN

AMOUNT	15 YEARS	18 YEARS	20 YEARS	25 YEARS	28 YEARS	29 YEARS	30 YEARS	35 YEARS	40 YEARS
$ 50	.66	.63	.61	.59	.59	.58	.58	.58	.58
100	1.31	1.25	1.22	1.18	1.17	1.16	1.16	1.15	1.15
200	2.62	2.49	2.44	2.36	2.33	2.32	2.32	2.30	2.29
300	3.92	3.74	3.65	3.53	3.49	3.48	3.47	3.44	3.43
400	5.23	4.98	4.87	4.71	4.65	4.64	4.63	4.59	4.57
500	6.54	6.22	6.09	5.88	5.81	5.80	5.78	5.73	5.71
600	7.84	7.47	7.30	7.06	6.97	6.95	6.94	6.88	6.85
700	9.15	8.71	8.52	8.23	8.14	8.11	8.09	8.02	7.99
800	10.46	9.96	9.74	9.41	9.30	9.27	9.25	9.17	9.13
900	11.76	11.20	10.95	10.58	10.46	10.43	10.40	10.31	10.27
1000	13.07	12.44	12.17	11.76	11.62	11.59	11.56	11.46	11.41
2000	26.14	24.88	24.33	23.51	23.24	23.17	23.11	22.91	22.81
3000	39.20	37.32	36.50	35.26	34.85	34.75	34.66	34.37	34.22
4000	52.27	49.76	48.66	47.01	46.47	46.33	46.22	45.82	45.62
5000	65.34	62.20	60.82	58.76	58.08	57.91	57.77	57.28	57.03
6000	78.40	74.64	72.99	70.51	69.70	69.50	69.32	68.73	68.43
7000	91.47	87.08	85.15	82.27	81.31	81.08	80.87	80.18	79.84
8000	104.54	99.52	97.32	94.02	92.93	92.66	92.43	91.64	91.24
9000	117.60	111.96	109.48	105.77	104.55	104.24	103.98	103.09	102.65
10000	130.67	124.40	121.64	117.52	116.16	115.82	115.53	114.55	114.05
15000	196.00	186.60	182.46	176.28	174.24	173.73	173.29	171.82	171.08
20000	261.33	248.80	243.28	235.03	232.32	231.64	231.06	229.09	228.10
25000	326.67	311.00	304.10	293.79	290.40	289.55	288.82	286.36	285.12
30000	392.00	373.20	364.92	352.55	348.48	347.46	346.58	343.63	342.15
35000	457.33	435.40	425.74	411.31	406.55	405.37	404.34	400.90	399.17
40000	522.66	497.60	486.56	470.06	464.63	463.28	462.11	458.17	456.19
45000	587.99	559.80	547.38	528.82	522.71	521.19	519.87	515.44	513.22
46000	601.06	572.24	559.54	540.57	534.33	532.77	531.42	526.89	524.62
47000	614.13	584.68	571.70	552.32	545.94	544.35	542.97	538.35	536.03
48000	627.19	597.12	583.87	564.08	557.56	555.94	554.53	549.80	547.43
49000	640.26	609.56	596.03	575.83	569.17	567.52	566.08	561.25	558.83
50000	653.33	622.00	608.19	587.58	580.79	579.10	577.63	572.71	570.24
51000	666.39	634.44	620.36	599.33	592.41	590.68	589.18	584.16	581.64
52000	679.46	646.88	632.52	611.08	604.02	602.26	600.74	595.62	593.05
53000	692.53	659.32	644.69	622.83	615.64	613.85	612.29	607.07	604.45
54000	705.59	671.76	656.85	634.58	627.25	625.43	623.84	618.52	615.86
55000	718.66	684.20	669.01	646.34	638.87	637.01	635.40	629.98	627.26
56000	731.72	696.64	681.18	658.09	650.48	648.59	646.95	641.43	638.67
57000	744.79	709.08	693.34	669.84	662.10	660.17	658.50	652.89	650.07
58000	757.86	721.52	705.51	681.59	673.72	671.76	670.05	664.34	661.48
59000	770.92	733.96	717.67	693.34	685.33	683.34	681.61	675.80	672.88
60000	783.99	746.40	729.83	705.09	696.95	694.92	693.16	687.25	684.29
61000	797.06	758.84	742.00	716.84	708.56	706.50	704.71	698.70	695.69
62000	810.12	771.28	754.16	728.60	720.18	718.09	716.26	710.16	707.10
63000	823.19	783.72	766.32	740.35	731.79	729.67	727.82	721.61	718.50
64000	836.26	796.16	778.49	752.10	743.41	741.25	739.37	733.07	729.91
65000	849.32	808.60	790.65	763.85	755.03	752.83	750.92	744.52	741.31
67500	881.99	839.70	821.06	793.23	784.07	781.78	779.80	773.15	769.82
70000	914.65	870.80	851.47	822.61	813.10	810.74	808.68	801.79	798.33
75000	979.99	932.99	912.29	881.36	871.18	868.65	866.45	859.06	855.36
80000	1045.32	995.19	973.11	940.12	929.26	926.56	924.21	916.33	912.38
85000	1110.65	1057.39	1033.93	998.88	987.34	984.47	981.97	973.60	969.40
90000	1175.98	1119.59	1094.75	1057.64	1045.42	1042.38	1039.73	1030.87	1026.43
95000	1241.32	1181.79	1155.57	1116.39	1103.50	1100.29	1097.50	1088.14	1083.45
100000	1306.65	1243.99	1216.38	1175.15	1161.58	1158.20	1155.26	1145.41	1140.47
105000	1371.98	1306.19	1277.20	1233.91	1219.65	1216.11	1213.02	1202.68	1197.50
110000	1437.31	1368.39	1338.02	1292.67	1277.73	1274.01	1270.79	1259.95	1254.52
115000	1502.64	1430.59	1398.84	1351.42	1335.81	1331.92	1328.55	1317.22	1311.54
120000	1567.98	1492.79	1459.66	1410.18	1393.89	1389.83	1386.31	1374.49	1368.57
125000	1633.31	1554.99	1520.48	1468.94	1451.97	1447.74	1444.07	1431.76	1425.59
130000	1698.64	1617.19	1581.30	1527.69	1510.05	1505.65	1501.84	1489.03	1482.62
135000	1763.97	1679.39	1642.12	1586.45	1568.13	1563.56	1559.60	1546.30	1539.64
140000	1829.30	1741.59	1702.94	1645.21	1626.20	1621.47	1617.36	1603.58	1596.66
145000	1894.64	1803.79	1763.76	1703.97	1684.28	1679.38	1675.12	1660.85	1653.69
150000	1959.97	1865.98	1824.57	1762.72	1742.36	1737.29	1732.89	1718.12	1710.71

13¾% MONTHLY PAYMENT
NECESSARY TO AMORTIZE A LOAN

AMOUNT	1 YEAR	2 YEARS	3 YEARS	4 YEARS	5 YEARS	7 YEARS	8 YEARS	10 YEARS	12 YEARS
$ 50	4.49	2.40	1.71	1.37	1.16	.94	.87	.77	.72
100	8.97	4.79	3.41	2.73	2.32	1.87	1.73	1.54	1.43
200	17.94	9.58	6.82	5.45	4.63	3.73	3.45	3.08	2.85
300	26.91	14.37	10.22	8.17	6.95	5.59	5.17	4.62	4.27
400	35.87	19.16	13.63	10.89	9.26	7.45	6.90	6.16	5.69
500	44.84	23.95	17.03	13.61	11.57	9.31	8.62	7.69	7.11
600	53.81	28.74	20.44	16.33	13.89	11.17	10.34	9.23	8.53
700	62.77	33.53	23.84	19.05	16.20	13.03	12.07	10.77	9.95
800	71.74	38.32	27.25	21.77	18.52	14.89	13.79	12.31	11.38
900	80.71	43.11	30.66	24.49	20.83	16.75	15.51	13.84	12.80
1000	89.67	47.90	34.06	27.21	23.14	18.61	17.23	15.38	14.22
2000	179.34	95.79	68.12	54.41	46.28	37.21	34.46	30.76	28.43
3000	269.01	143.69	102.17	81.61	69.42	55.81	51.69	46.14	42.65
4000	358.68	191.58	136.23	108.81	92.56	74.41	68.92	61.51	56.86
5000	448.35	239.48	170.29	136.01	115.70	93.02	86.15	76.89	71.07
6000	538.02	287.37	204.34	163.21	138.84	111.62	103.38	92.27	85.29
7000	627.69	335.27	238.40	190.41	161.98	130.22	120.61	107.64	99.50
8000	717.36	383.16	272.46	217.61	185.12	148.82	137.84	123.02	113.72
9000	807.03	431.06	306.51	244.82	208.25	167.42	155.07	138.40	127.93
10000	896.70	478.95	340.57	272.02	231.39	186.03	172.30	153.77	142.14
15000	1345.05	718.43	510.85	408.02	347.09	279.04	258.45	230.66	213.21
20000	1793.40	957.90	681.13	544.03	462.78	372.05	344.60	307.54	284.28
25000	2241.74	1197.38	851.41	680.04	578.48	465.06	430.74	384.42	355.35
30000	2690.09	1436.85	1021.69	816.04	694.17	558.07	516.89	461.31	426.42
35000	3138.44	1676.33	1191.98	952.05	809.86	651.08	603.04	538.19	497.49
40000	3586.79	1915.80	1362.26	1088.05	925.56	744.09	689.19	615.07	568.56
45000	4035.13	2155.27	1532.54	1224.06	1041.25	837.10	775.33	691.96	639.63
46000	4124.80	2203.17	1566.60	1251.26	1064.39	855.71	792.56	707.33	653.84
47000	4214.47	2251.06	1600.65	1278.46	1087.53	874.31	809.79	722.71	668.05
48000	4304.14	2298.96	1634.71	1305.66	1110.67	892.91	827.02	738.09	682.27
49000	4393.81	2346.85	1668.77	1332.87	1133.81	911.51	844.25	753.46	696.48
50000	4483.48	2394.75	1702.82	1360.07	1156.95	930.11	861.48	768.84	710.70
51000	4573.15	2442.64	1736.88	1387.27	1180.09	948.72	878.71	784.22	724.91
52000	4662.82	2490.54	1770.93	1414.47	1203.22	967.32	895.94	799.59	739.12
53000	4752.49	2538.43	1804.99	1441.67	1226.36	985.92	913.17	814.97	753.34
54000	4842.16	2586.33	1839.05	1468.87	1249.50	1004.52	930.40	830.35	767.55
55000	4931.83	2634.22	1873.10	1496.07	1272.64	1023.12	947.63	845.72	781.77
56000	5021.50	2682.12	1907.16	1523.27	1295.78	1041.73	964.86	861.10	795.98
57000	5111.17	2730.01	1941.22	1550.48	1318.92	1060.33	982.09	876.48	810.19
58000	5200.84	2777.91	1975.27	1577.68	1342.06	1078.93	999.32	891.85	824.41
59000	5290.51	2825.80	2009.33	1604.88	1365.20	1097.53	1016.55	907.23	838.62
60000	5380.18	2873.70	2043.38	1632.08	1388.34	1116.14	1033.78	922.61	852.83
61000	5469.85	2921.59	2077.44	1659.28	1411.47	1134.74	1051.01	937.98	867.05
62000	5559.52	2969.49	2111.50	1686.48	1434.61	1153.34	1068.24	953.36	881.26
63000	5649.19	3017.38	2145.55	1713.68	1457.75	1171.94	1085.47	968.74	895.48
64000	5738.85	3065.28	2179.61	1740.88	1480.89	1190.54	1102.69	984.11	909.69
65000	5828.52	3113.17	2213.67	1768.09	1504.03	1209.15	1119.92	999.49	923.90
67500	6052.70	3232.91	2298.81	1836.09	1561.88	1255.65	1163.00	1037.93	959.44
70000	6276.87	3352.65	2383.95	1904.09	1619.72	1302.16	1206.07	1076.37	994.97
75000	6725.22	3592.12	2554.23	2040.10	1735.42	1395.17	1292.22	1153.26	1066.04
80000	7173.57	3831.59	2724.51	2176.10	1851.11	1488.18	1378.37	1230.14	1137.11
85000	7621.92	4071.07	2894.79	2312.11	1966.81	1581.19	1464.51	1307.02	1208.18
90000	8070.26	4310.54	3065.07	2448.12	2082.50	1674.20	1550.66	1383.91	1279.25
95000	8518.61	4550.02	3235.36	2584.12	2198.20	1767.21	1636.81	1460.79	1350.32
100000	8966.96	4789.49	3405.64	2720.13	2313.89	1860.22	1722.96	1537.67	1421.39
105000	9415.31	5028.97	3575.92	2856.13	2429.58	1953.23	1809.11	1614.56	1492.46
110000	9863.65	5268.44	3746.20	2992.14	2545.28	2046.24	1895.25	1691.44	1563.53
115000	10312.00	5507.91	3916.48	3128.15	2660.97	2139.26	1981.40	1768.32	1634.60
120000	10760.35	5747.39	4086.76	3264.15	2776.67	2232.27	2067.55	1845.21	1705.66
125000	11208.70	5986.86	4257.05	3400.16	2892.36	2325.28	2153.70	1922.09	1776.73
130000	11657.04	6226.34	4427.33	3536.17	3008.05	2418.29	2239.84	1998.97	1847.80
135000	12105.39	6465.81	4597.61	3672.17	3123.75	2511.30	2325.99	2075.86	1918.87
140000	12553.74	6705.29	4767.89	3808.18	3239.44	2604.31	2412.14	2152.74	1989.94
145000	13002.09	6944.76	4938.17	3944.18	3355.14	2697.32	2498.29	2229.62	2061.01
150000	13450.43	7184.23	5108.45	4080.19	3470.83	2790.33	2584.43	2306.51	2132.08

112

MONTHLY PAYMENT 13¾%
NECESSARY TO AMORTIZE A LOAN

AMOUNT	15 YEARS	18 YEARS	20 YEARS	25 YEARS	28 YEARS	29 YEARS	30 YEARS	35 YEARS	40 YEARS
$ 50	.66	.63	.62	.60	.59	.59	.59	.58	.58
100	1.32	1.26	1.23	1.19	1.18	1.17	1.17	1.16	1.16
200	2.63	2.51	2.46	2.37	2.35	2.34	2.34	2.32	2.31
300	3.95	3.76	3.68	3.56	3.52	3.51	3.50	3.47	3.46
400	5.26	5.02	4.91	4.74	4.69	4.68	4.67	4.63	4.61
500	6.58	6.27	6.13	5.93	5.86	5.84	5.83	5.78	5.76
600	7.89	7.52	7.36	7.11	7.03	7.01	7.00	6.94	6.91
700	9.21	8.77	8.58	8.30	8.20	8.18	8.16	8.09	8.06
800	10.52	10.03	9.81	9.48	9.38	9.35	9.33	9.25	9.21
900	11.84	11.28	11.03	10.67	10.55	10.52	10.49	10.40	10.36
1000	13.15	12.53	12.26	11.85	11.72	11.68	11.66	11.56	11.51
2000	26.30	25.06	24.51	23.70	23.43	23.36	23.31	23.11	23.02
3000	39.45	37.59	36.77	35.54	35.14	35.04	34.96	34.67	34.53
4000	52.60	50.12	49.02	47.39	46.86	46.72	46.61	46.22	46.03
5000	65.75	62.64	61.28	59.24	58.57	58.40	58.26	57.78	57.54
6000	78.90	75.17	73.53	71.08	70.28	70.08	69.91	69.33	69.05
7000	92.05	87.70	85.78	82.93	82.00	81.76	81.56	80.89	80.55
8000	105.20	100.23	98.04	94.78	93.71	93.44	93.21	92.44	92.06
9000	118.35	112.75	110.29	106.62	105.42	105.12	104.87	104.00	103.57
10000	131.50	125.28	122.55	118.47	117.14	116.80	116.52	115.55	115.07
15000	197.25	187.92	183.82	177.70	175.70	175.20	174.77	173.33	172.61
20000	263.00	250.56	245.09	236.94	234.27	233.60	233.03	231.10	230.14
25000	328.75	313.20	306.36	296.17	292.83	292.00	291.28	288.88	287.68
30000	394.50	375.83	367.63	355.40	351.40	350.40	349.54	346.65	345.21
35000	460.25	438.47	428.90	414.64	409.96	408.80	407.79	404.42	402.74
40000	526.00	501.11	490.17	473.87	468.53	467.20	466.05	462.20	460.28
45000	591.75	563.75	551.44	533.10	527.09	525.60	524.31	519.97	517.81
46000	604.90	576.28	563.69	544.95	538.81	537.28	535.96	531.53	529.32
47000	618.05	588.80	575.95	556.80	550.52	548.96	547.61	543.08	540.83
48000	631.20	601.33	588.20	568.64	562.23	560.64	559.26	554.64	552.33
49000	644.35	613.86	600.45	580.49	573.95	572.32	570.91	566.19	563.84
50000	657.50	626.39	612.71	592.34	585.66	584.00	582.56	577.75	575.35
51000	670.65	638.91	624.96	604.18	597.37	595.68	594.21	589.30	586.85
52000	683.80	651.44	637.22	616.03	609.09	607.36	605.86	600.86	598.36
53000	696.95	663.97	649.47	627.88	620.80	619.04	617.51	612.41	609.87
54000	710.10	676.50	661.72	639.72	632.51	630.72	629.17	623.97	621.38
55000	723.25	689.03	673.98	651.57	644.23	642.40	640.82	635.52	632.88
56000	736.40	701.55	686.23	663.42	655.94	654.08	652.47	647.08	644.39
57000	749.55	714.08	698.49	675.26	667.65	665.76	664.12	658.63	655.90
58000	762.70	726.61	710.74	687.11	679.36	677.44	675.77	670.19	667.40
59000	775.85	739.14	722.99	698.96	691.08	689.12	687.42	681.74	678.91
60000	789.00	751.66	735.25	710.80	702.79	700.80	699.07	693.30	690.42
61000	802.15	764.19	747.50	722.65	714.50	712.48	710.72	704.85	701.92
62000	815.30	776.72	759.76	734.50	726.22	724.16	722.37	716.41	713.43
63000	828.45	789.25	772.01	746.34	737.93	735.84	734.03	727.96	724.94
64000	841.60	801.77	784.26	758.19	749.64	747.52	745.68	739.52	736.44
65000	854.75	814.30	796.52	770.04	761.36	759.20	757.33	751.07	747.95
67500	887.62	845.62	827.15	799.65	790.64	788.40	786.46	779.96	776.72
70000	920.50	876.94	857.79	829.27	819.92	817.60	815.58	808.84	805.48
75000	986.25	939.58	919.06	888.50	878.49	876.00	873.84	866.62	863.02
80000	1051.99	1002.22	980.33	947.74	937.05	934.40	932.10	924.39	920.55
85000	1117.74	1064.85	1041.60	1006.97	995.62	992.80	990.35	982.17	978.09
90000	1183.49	1127.49	1102.87	1066.20	1054.18	1051.20	1048.61	1039.94	1035.62
95000	1249.24	1190.13	1164.14	1125.44	1112.75	1109.60	1106.86	1097.72	1093.16
100000	1314.99	1252.77	1225.41	1184.67	1171.32	1168.00	1165.12	1155.49	1150.69
105000	1380.74	1315.41	1286.68	1243.90	1229.88	1226.40	1223.37	1213.26	1208.22
110000	1446.49	1378.05	1347.95	1303.14	1288.45	1284.80	1281.63	1271.04	1265.76
115000	1512.24	1440.68	1409.22	1362.37	1347.01	1343.20	1339.88	1328.81	1323.29
120000	1577.99	1503.32	1470.49	1421.60	1405.58	1401.59	1398.14	1386.59	1380.83
125000	1643.74	1565.96	1531.76	1480.84	1464.14	1459.99	1456.40	1444.36	1438.36
130000	1709.49	1628.60	1593.03	1540.07	1522.71	1518.39	1514.65	1502.14	1495.90
135000	1775.24	1691.24	1654.30	1599.30	1581.27	1576.79	1572.91	1559.91	1553.43
140000	1840.99	1753.87	1715.57	1658.54	1639.84	1635.19	1631.16	1617.68	1610.96
145000	1906.74	1816.51	1776.84	1717.77	1698.40	1693.59	1689.42	1675.46	1668.50
150000	1972.49	1879.15	1838.11	1777.00	1756.97	1751.99	1747.67	1733.23	1726.03

13⅞% MONTHLY PAYMENT
NECESSARY TO AMORTIZE A LOAN

AMOUNT	1 YEAR	2 YEARS	3 YEARS	4 YEARS	5 YEARS	7 YEARS	8 YEARS	10 YEARS	12 YEARS
$ 50	4.49	2.40	1.71	1.37	1.17	.94	.87	.78	.72
100	8.98	4.80	3.42	2.73	2.33	1.87	1.74	1.55	1.43
200	17.95	9.60	6.83	5.46	4.65	3.74	3.47	3.10	2.86
300	26.92	14.39	10.24	8.18	6.97	5.61	5.20	4.64	4.29
400	35.90	19.19	13.65	10.91	9.29	7.47	6.93	6.19	5.72
500	44.87	23.98	17.06	13.64	11.61	9.34	8.66	7.73	7.15
600	53.84	28.78	20.48	16.36	13.93	11.21	10.39	9.28	8.58
700	62.81	33.57	23.89	19.09	16.25	13.07	12.12	10.82	10.01
800	71.79	38.37	27.30	21.82	18.57	14.94	13.85	12.37	11.44
900	80.76	43.16	30.71	24.54	20.89	16.81	15.58	13.91	12.87
1000	89.73	47.96	34.12	27.27	23.21	18.68	17.31	15.46	14.30
2000	179.46	95.91	68.24	54.53	46.41	37.35	34.61	30.91	28.59
3000	269.19	143.87	102.36	81.80	69.62	56.02	51.91	46.36	42.88
4000	358.92	191.82	136.47	109.06	92.82	74.69	69.21	61.81	57.17
5000	448.65	239.77	170.59	136.32	116.02	93.36	86.51	77.26	71.47
6000	538.37	287.73	204.71	163.59	139.23	112.03	103.81	92.71	85.76
7000	628.10	335.68	238.82	190.85	162.43	130.70	121.11	108.17	100.05
8000	717.83	383.64	272.94	218.12	185.63	149.37	138.41	123.62	114.34
9000	807.56	431.59	307.06	245.38	208.84	168.04	155.71	139.07	128.64
10000	897.29	479.54	341.17	272.64	232.04	186.72	173.01	154.52	142.93
15000	1345.93	719.31	511.76	408.96	348.06	280.07	259.51	231.78	214.39
20000	1794.57	959.08	682.34	545.28	464.07	373.43	346.01	309.04	285.85
25000	2243.21	1198.85	852.93	681.60	580.09	466.78	432.52	386.29	357.32
30000	2691.85	1438.62	1023.51	817.92	696.11	560.14	519.02	463.55	428.78
35000	3140.50	1678.39	1194.10	954.24	812.13	653.49	605.52	540.81	500.24
40000	3589.14	1918.16	1364.68	1090.56	928.14	746.85	692.00	618.07	571.70
45000	4037.78	2157.93	1535.27	1226.88	1044.16	840.20	778.52	695.33	643.17
46000	4127.51	2205.88	1569.38	1254.14	1067.37	858.87	795.83	710.78	657.46
47000	4217.24	2253.84	1603.50	1281.40	1090.57	877.54	813.13	726.23	671.75
48000	4306.96	2301.79	1637.62	1308.67	1113.77	896.21	830.43	741.68	686.04
49000	4396.69	2349.74	1671.74	1335.93	1136.98	914.89	847.73	757.13	700.34
50000	4486.42	2397.70	1705.85	1363.20	1160.18	933.56	865.03	772.58	714.63
51000	4576.15	2445.65	1739.97	1390.46	1183.38	952.23	882.33	788.04	728.92
52000	4665.88	2493.61	1774.09	1417.72	1206.59	970.90	899.63	803.49	743.21
53000	4755.61	2541.56	1808.20	1444.99	1229.79	989.57	916.93	818.94	757.50
54000	4845.33	2589.51	1842.32	1472.25	1252.99	1008.24	934.23	834.39	771.80
55000	4935.06	2637.47	1876.44	1499.51	1276.20	1026.91	951.53	849.84	786.09
56000	5024.79	2685.42	1910.55	1526.78	1299.40	1045.58	968.83	865.29	800.38
57000	5114.52	2733.37	1944.67	1554.04	1322.60	1064.25	986.13	880.74	814.67
58000	5204.25	2781.33	1978.79	1581.31	1345.81	1082.92	1003.43	896.20	828.97
59000	5293.98	2829.28	2012.91	1608.57	1369.01	1101.60	1020.73	911.65	843.26
60000	5383.70	2877.24	2047.02	1635.83	1392.21	1120.27	1038.03	927.10	857.55
61000	5473.43	2925.19	2081.14	1663.10	1415.42	1138.94	1055.33	942.55	871.84
62000	5563.16	2973.14	2115.26	1690.36	1438.62	1157.61	1072.63	958.00	886.14
63000	5652.89	3021.10	2149.37	1717.63	1461.83	1176.28	1089.93	973.45	900.43
64000	5742.62	3069.05	2183.49	1744.89	1485.03	1194.95	1107.23	988.91	914.72
65000	5832.35	3117.01	2217.61	1772.15	1508.23	1213.62	1124.53	1004.36	929.01
67500	6056.67	3236.89	2302.90	1840.31	1566.24	1260.30	1167.78	1042.99	964.75
70000	6280.99	3356.77	2388.19	1908.47	1624.25	1306.98	1211.04	1081.62	1000.48
75000	6729.63	3596.54	2558.78	2044.79	1740.27	1400.33	1297.54	1158.87	1071.94
80000	7178.27	3836.31	2729.36	2181.11	1856.28	1493.69	1384.04	1236.13	1143.40
85000	7626.91	4076.08	2899.95	2317.43	1972.30	1587.04	1470.54	1313.39	1214.86
90000	8075.55	4315.85	3070.53	2453.75	2088.32	1680.40	1557.05	1390.65	1286.33
95000	8524.19	4555.62	3241.12	2590.07	2204.34	1773.75	1643.55	1467.90	1357.79
100000	8972.84	4795.39	3411.70	2726.39	2320.35	1867.11	1730.05	1545.16	1429.25
105000	9421.48	5035.16	3582.28	2862.71	2436.37	1960.46	1816.55	1622.42	1500.71
110000	9870.12	5274.93	3752.87	2999.02	2552.39	2053.82	1903.05	1699.68	1572.17
115000	10318.76	5514.70	3923.45	3135.34	2668.41	2147.17	1989.56	1776.94	1643.64
120000	10767.40	5754.47	4094.04	3271.66	2784.42	2240.53	2076.06	1854.19	1715.10
125000	11216.04	5994.24	4264.62	3407.98	2900.44	2333.88	2162.56	1931.45	1786.56
130000	11664.69	6234.01	4435.21	3544.30	3016.46	2427.24	2249.06	2008.71	1858.02
135000	12113.33	6473.78	4605.79	3680.62	3132.48	2520.59	2335.56	2085.97	1929.49
140000	12561.97	6713.54	4776.38	3816.94	3248.49	2613.95	2422.07	2163.23	2000.95
145000	13010.61	6953.31	4946.96	3953.26	3364.51	2707.30	2508.57	2240.48	2072.41
150000	13459.25	7193.08	5117.55	4089.58	3480.53	2800.66	2595.07	2317.74	2143.87

AMOUNT	15 YEARS	18 YEARS	20 YEARS	25 YEARS	28 YEARS	29 YEARS	30 YEARS	35 YEARS	40 YEARS
$ 50	.67	.64	.62	.60	.60	.59	.59	.59	.59
100	1.33	1.27	1.24	1.20	1.19	1.18	1.18	1.17	1.17
200	2.65	2.53	2.47	2.39	2.37	2.36	2.35	2.34	2.33
300	3.98	3.79	3.71	3.59	3.55	3.54	3.53	3.50	3.49
400	5.30	5.05	4.94	4.78	4.73	4.72	4.70	4.67	4.65
500	6.62	6.31	6.18	5.98	5.91	5.89	5.88	5.83	5.81
600	7.95	7.57	7.41	7.17	7.09	7.07	7.05	7.00	6.97
700	9.27	8.84	8.65	8.36	8.27	8.25	8.23	8.16	8.13
800	10.59	10.10	9.88	9.56	9.45	9.43	9.40	9.33	9.29
900	11.92	11.36	11.12	10.75	10.63	10.61	10.58	10.50	10.45
1000	13.24	12.62	12.35	11.95	11.82	11.78	11.75	11.66	11.61
2000	26.47	25.24	24.69	23.89	23.63	23.56	23.50	23.32	23.22
3000	39.71	37.85	37.04	35.83	35.44	35.34	35.25	34.97	34.83
4000	52.94	50.47	49.38	47.77	47.25	47.12	47.00	46.63	46.44
5000	66.17	63.08	61.73	59.72	59.06	58.90	58.75	58.28	58.05
6000	79.41	75.70	74.07	71.66	70.87	70.67	70.50	69.94	69.66
7000	92.64	88.31	86.42	83.60	82.68	82.45	82.25	81.60	81.27
8000	105.87	100.93	98.76	95.54	94.49	94.23	94.00	93.25	92.88
9000	119.11	113.55	111.11	107.48	106.30	106.01	105.75	104.91	104.49
10000	132.34	126.16	123.45	119.43	118.11	117.79	117.50	116.56	116.10
15000	198.51	189.24	185.17	179.14	177.16	176.68	176.25	174.84	174.14
20000	264.68	252.32	246.90	238.85	236.22	235.57	235.00	233.12	232.19
25000	330.84	315.40	308.62	298.56	295.27	294.46	293.75	291.40	290.23
30000	397.01	378.47	370.34	358.27	354.32	353.35	352.50	349.68	348.28
35000	463.18	441.55	432.06	417.98	413.38	412.24	411.25	407.96	406.32
40000	529.35	504.63	493.79	477.69	472.43	471.13	470.00	466.23	464.37
45000	595.51	567.71	555.51	537.40	531.48	530.02	528.75	524.51	522.41
46000	608.75	580.32	567.85	549.34	543.30	541.80	540.50	536.17	534.02
47000	621.98	592.94	580.20	561.28	555.11	553.57	552.25	547.82	545.63
48000	635.21	605.56	592.54	573.22	566.92	565.35	564.00	559.48	557.24
49000	648.45	618.17	604.89	585.17	578.73	577.13	575.75	571.14	568.85
50000	661.68	630.79	617.23	597.11	590.54	588.91	587.50	582.79	580.46
51000	674.92	643.40	629.58	609.05	602.35	600.69	599.25	594.45	592.07
52000	688.15	656.02	641.92	620.99	614.16	612.47	611.00	606.10	603.68
53000	701.38	668.63	654.26	632.93	625.97	624.24	622.75	617.76	615.29
54000	714.62	681.25	666.61	644.88	637.78	636.02	634.50	629.41	626.90
55000	727.85	693.86	678.95	656.82	649.59	647.80	646.25	641.07	638.50
56000	741.08	706.48	691.30	668.76	661.40	659.58	658.00	652.73	650.11
57000	754.32	719.10	703.64	680.70	673.21	671.36	669.75	664.38	661.72
58000	767.55	731.71	715.99	692.64	685.02	683.13	681.50	676.04	673.33
59000	780.78	744.33	728.33	704.59	696.83	694.91	693.25	687.69	684.94
60000	794.02	756.94	740.68	716.53	708.64	706.69	705.00	699.35	696.55
61000	807.25	769.56	753.02	728.47	720.45	718.47	716.75	711.01	708.16
62000	820.48	782.17	765.37	740.41	732.27	730.25	728.50	722.66	719.77
63000	833.72	794.79	777.71	752.35	744.08	742.02	740.25	734.32	731.38
64000	846.95	807.41	790.05	764.30	755.89	753.80	752.00	745.97	742.99
65000	860.18	820.02	802.40	776.24	767.70	765.58	763.75	757.63	754.60
67500	893.27	851.56	833.26	806.09	797.22	795.03	793.12	786.77	783.62
70000	926.35	883.10	864.12	835.95	826.75	824.47	822.49	815.91	812.64
75000	992.52	946.18	925.84	895.66	885.80	883.36	881.24	874.19	870.69
80000	1058.69	1009.26	987.57	955.37	944.86	942.25	939.99	932.46	928.73
85000	1124.86	1072.33	1049.29	1015.08	1003.91	1001.14	998.74	990.74	986.78
90000	1191.02	1135.41	1111.01	1074.79	1062.96	1060.03	1057.49	1049.02	1044.82
95000	1257.19	1198.49	1172.74	1134.50	1122.02	1118.92	1116.24	1107.30	1102.87
100000	1323.36	1261.57	1234.46	1194.21	1181.07	1177.81	1174.99	1165.58	1160.91
105000	1389.53	1324.65	1296.18	1253.92	1240.12	1236.70	1233.74	1223.86	1218.96
110000	1455.69	1387.72	1357.90	1313.63	1299.18	1295.59	1292.49	1282.14	1277.00
115000	1521.86	1450.80	1419.63	1373.34	1358.23	1354.48	1351.24	1340.41	1335.05
120000	1588.03	1513.88	1481.35	1433.05	1417.28	1413.37	1409.99	1398.69	1393.10
125000	1654.20	1576.96	1543.07	1492.76	1476.34	1472.26	1468.74	1456.97	1451.14
130000	1720.36	1640.04	1604.79	1552.47	1535.39	1531.16	1527.49	1515.25	1509.19
135000	1786.53	1703.11	1666.52	1612.18	1594.44	1590.05	1586.23	1573.53	1567.23
140000	1852.70	1766.19	1728.24	1671.89	1653.50	1648.94	1644.98	1631.81	1625.28
145000	1918.87	1829.27	1789.96	1731.60	1712.55	1707.83	1703.73	1690.09	1683.32
150000	1985.04	1892.35	1851.68	1791.31	1771.60	1766.72	1762.48	1748.37	1741.37

14% MONTHLY PAYMENT
NECESSARY TO AMORTIZE A LOAN

AMOUNT	1 YEAR	2 YEARS	3 YEARS	4 YEARS	5 YEARS	7 YEARS	8 YEARS	10 YEARS	12 YEARS
$ 50	4.49	2.41	1.71	1.37	1.17	.94	.87	.78	.72
100	8.98	4.81	3.42	2.74	2.33	1.88	1.74	1.56	1.44
200	17.96	9.61	6.84	5.47	4.66	3.75	3.48	3.11	2.88
300	26.94	14.41	10.26	8.20	6.99	5.63	5.22	4.66	4.32
400	35.92	19.21	13.68	10.94	9.31	7.50	6.95	6.22	5.75
500	44.90	24.01	17.09	13.67	11.64	9.38	8.69	7.77	7.19
600	53.88	28.81	20.51	16.40	13.97	11.25	10.43	9.32	8.63
700	62.86	33.61	23.93	19.13	16.29	13.12	12.17	10.87	10.06
800	71.83	38.42	27.35	21.87	18.62	15.00	13.90	12.43	11.50
900	80.81	43.22	30.76	24.60	20.95	16.87	15.64	13.98	12.94
1000	89.79	48.02	34.18	27.33	23.27	18.75	17.38	15.53	14.38
2000	179.58	96.03	68.36	54.66	46.54	37.49	34.75	31.06	28.75
3000	269.37	144.04	102.54	81.98	69.81	56.23	52.12	46.58	43.12
4000	359.15	192.06	136.72	109.31	93.08	74.97	69.49	62.11	57.49
5000	448.94	240.07	170.89	136.64	116.35	93.71	86.86	77.64	71.86
6000	538.73	288.08	205.07	163.96	139.61	112.45	104.23	93.16	86.23
7000	628.51	336.10	239.25	191.29	162.88	131.19	121.61	108.69	100.60
8000	718.30	384.11	273.43	218.62	186.15	149.93	138.98	124.22	114.98
9000	808.09	432.12	307.60	245.94	209.42	168.67	156.35	139.74	129.35
10000	897.88	480.13	341.78	273.27	232.69	187.41	173.72	155.27	143.72
15000	1346.81	720.20	512.67	409.90	349.03	281.11	260.58	232.90	215.57
20000	1795.75	960.26	683.56	546.53	465.37	374.81	347.44	310.54	287.43
25000	2244.68	1200.33	854.45	683.17	581.71	468.51	434.29	388.17	359.29
30000	2693.62	1440.39	1025.33	819.80	698.05	562.21	521.15	465.80	431.14
35000	3142.55	1680.46	1196.22	956.43	814.39	655.91	608.01	543.44	503.00
40000	3591.49	1920.52	1367.11	1093.06	930.74	749.61	694.87	621.07	574.86
45000	4040.43	2160.58	1538.00	1229.70	1047.08	843.31	781.72	698.70	646.71
46000	4130.21	2208.60	1572.18	1257.02	1070.34	862.05	799.09	714.23	661.08
47000	4220.00	2256.61	1606.35	1284.35	1093.61	880.79	816.47	729.76	675.45
48000	4309.79	2304.62	1640.53	1311.68	1116.88	899.53	833.84	745.28	689.83
49000	4399.57	2352.64	1674.71	1339.00	1140.15	918.27	851.21	760.81	704.20
50000	4489.36	2400.65	1708.89	1366.33	1163.42	937.01	868.58	776.34	718.57
51000	4579.15	2448.66	1743.06	1393.66	1186.69	955.75	885.95	791.86	732.94
52000	4668.94	2496.67	1777.24	1420.98	1209.95	974.49	903.32	807.39	747.31
53000	4758.72	2544.69	1811.42	1448.31	1233.22	993.23	920.69	822.92	761.68
54000	4848.51	2592.70	1845.60	1475.63	1256.49	1011.97	938.07	838.44	776.05
55000	4938.30	2640.71	1879.77	1502.96	1279.76	1030.71	955.44	853.97	790.42
56000	5028.08	2688.72	1913.95	1530.29	1303.03	1049.45	972.81	869.50	804.80
57000	5117.87	2736.74	1948.13	1557.61	1326.30	1068.19	990.18	885.02	819.17
58000	5207.66	2784.75	1982.31	1584.94	1349.56	1086.93	1007.55	900.55	833.54
59000	5297.44	2832.77	2016.49	1612.27	1372.83	1105.67	1024.92	916.08	847.91
60000	5387.23	2880.78	2050.66	1639.59	1396.10	1124.41	1042.30	931.60	862.28
61000	5477.02	2928.79	2084.84	1666.92	1419.37	1143.15	1059.67	947.13	876.65
62000	5566.81	2976.80	2119.02	1694.25	1442.64	1161.89	1077.04	962.66	891.02
63000	5656.59	3024.82	2153.20	1721.57	1465.90	1180.63	1094.41	978.18	905.40
64000	5746.38	3072.83	2187.37	1748.90	1489.17	1199.37	1111.78	993.71	919.77
65000	5836.17	3120.84	2221.55	1776.23	1512.44	1218.11	1129.15	1009.24	934.14
67500	6060.64	3240.87	2307.00	1844.54	1570.61	1264.96	1172.58	1048.05	970.07
70000	6285.10	3360.91	2392.44	1912.86	1628.78	1311.81	1216.01	1086.87	1005.99
75000	6734.04	3600.97	2563.33	2049.49	1745.12	1405.51	1302.87	1164.50	1077.85
80000	7182.97	3841.04	2734.22	2186.12	1861.47	1499.21	1389.73	1242.14	1149.71
85000	7631.91	4081.10	2905.10	2322.76	1977.81	1592.91	1476.58	1319.77	1221.56
90000	8080.85	4321.16	3075.99	2459.39	2094.15	1686.61	1563.44	1397.40	1293.42
95000	8529.78	4561.23	3246.88	2596.02	2210.49	1780.31	1650.30	1475.04	1365.28
100000	8978.72	4801.29	3417.77	2732.65	2326.83	1874.01	1737.16	1552.67	1437.13
105000	9427.65	5041.36	3588.66	2869.29	2443.17	1967.71	1824.01	1630.30	1508.99
110000	9876.59	5281.42	3759.54	3005.92	2559.51	2061.41	1910.87	1707.94	1580.84
115000	10325.53	5521.49	3930.43	3142.55	2675.85	2155.11	1997.73	1785.57	1652.70
120000	10774.46	5761.55	4101.32	3279.18	2792.20	2248.81	2084.59	1863.20	1724.56
125000	11223.39	6001.62	4272.21	3415.81	2908.54	2342.51	2171.44	1940.84	1796.41
130000	11672.33	6241.68	4443.10	3552.45	3024.88	2436.21	2258.30	2018.47	1868.27
135000	12121.27	6481.74	4613.99	3689.08	3141.22	2529.91	2345.16	2096.10	1940.13
140000	12570.20	6721.81	4784.87	3825.71	3257.56	2623.61	2432.02	2173.74	2011.98
145000	13019.14	6961.87	4955.76	3962.34	3373.90	2717.31	2518.87	2251.37	2083.84
150000	13468.07	7201.94	5126.65	4098.98	3490.24	2811.01	2605.73	2329.00	2155.70

AMOUNT	15 YEARS	18 YEARS	20 YEARS	25 YEARS	28 YEARS	29 YEARS	30 YEARS	35 YEARS	40 YEARS
$ 50	.67	.64	.63	.61	.60	.60	.60	.59	.59
100	1.34	1.28	1.25	1.21	1.20	1.19	1.19	1.18	1.18
200	2.67	2.55	2.49	2.41	2.39	2.38	2.37	2.36	2.35
300	4.00	3.82	3.74	3.62	3.58	3.57	3.56	3.53	3.52
400	5.33	5.09	4.98	4.82	4.77	4.76	4.74	4.71	4.69
500	6.66	6.36	6.22	6.02	5.96	5.94	5.93	5.88	5.86
600	8.00	7.63	7.47	7.23	7.15	7.13	7.11	7.06	7.03
700	9.33	8.90	8.71	8.43	8.34	8.32	8.30	8.23	8.20
800	10.66	10.17	9.95	9.64	9.53	9.51	9.48	9.41	9.37
900	11.99	11.44	11.20	10.84	10.72	10.69	10.67	10.59	10.55
1000	13.32	12.71	12.44	12.04	11.91	11.88	11.85	11.76	11.72
2000	26.64	25.41	24.88	24.08	23.82	23.76	23.70	23.52	23.43
3000	39.96	38.12	37.31	36.12	35.73	35.63	35.55	35.28	35.14
4000	53.27	50.82	49.75	48.16	47.64	47.51	47.40	47.03	46.85
5000	66.59	63.52	62.18	60.19	59.55	59.39	59.25	58.79	58.56
6000	79.91	76.23	74.62	72.23	71.46	71.26	71.10	70.55	70.27
7000	93.23	88.93	87.05	84.27	83.36	83.14	82.95	82.30	81.98
8000	106.54	101.64	99.49	96.31	95.27	95.02	94.79	94.06	93.70
9000	119.86	114.34	111.92	108.34	107.18	106.89	106.64	105.82	105.41
10000	133.18	127.04	124.36	120.38	119.09	118.77	118.49	117.57	117.12
15000	199.77	190.56	186.53	180.57	178.63	178.15	177.74	176.36	175.68
20000	266.35	254.08	248.71	240.76	238.17	237.53	236.98	235.14	234.23
25000	332.94	317.60	310.89	300.95	297.71	296.91	296.22	293.92	292.79
30000	399.53	381.12	373.06	361.13	357.26	356.30	355.47	352.71	351.35
35000	466.11	444.64	435.24	421.32	416.80	415.68	414.71	411.49	409.90
40000	532.70	508.16	497.41	481.51	476.34	475.06	473.95	470.27	468.46
45000	599.29	571.68	559.59	541.70	535.88	534.44	533.20	529.06	527.02
46000	612.61	584.38	572.02	553.74	547.79	546.32	545.05	540.81	538.73
47000	625.92	597.09	584.46	565.77	559.70	558.20	556.89	552.57	550.44
48000	639.24	609.79	596.89	577.81	571.61	570.07	568.74	564.33	562.15
49000	652.56	622.49	609.33	589.85	583.51	581.95	580.59	576.08	573.86
50000	665.88	635.20	621.77	601.89	595.42	593.82	592.44	587.84	585.58
51000	679.19	647.90	634.20	613.92	607.33	605.70	604.29	599.60	597.29
52000	692.51	660.60	646.64	625.96	619.24	617.58	616.14	611.36	609.00
53000	705.83	673.31	659.07	638.00	631.15	629.45	627.99	623.11	620.71
54000	719.15	686.01	671.51	650.04	643.06	641.33	639.84	634.87	632.42
55000	732.46	698.72	683.94	662.07	654.97	653.21	651.68	646.63	644.13
56000	745.78	711.42	696.38	674.11	666.87	665.08	663.53	658.38	655.84
57000	759.10	724.12	708.81	686.15	678.78	676.96	675.38	670.14	667.55
58000	772.42	736.83	721.25	698.19	690.69	688.84	687.23	681.90	679.27
59000	785.73	749.53	733.68	710.22	702.60	700.71	699.08	693.65	690.98
60000	799.05	762.23	746.12	722.26	714.51	712.59	710.93	705.41	702.69
61000	812.37	774.94	758.55	734.30	726.42	724.47	722.78	717.17	714.40
62000	825.68	787.64	770.99	746.34	738.32	736.34	734.63	728.92	726.11
63000	839.00	800.35	783.42	758.37	750.23	748.22	746.47	740.68	737.82
64000	852.32	813.05	795.86	770.41	762.14	760.09	758.32	752.44	749.53
65000	865.64	825.75	808.29	782.45	774.05	771.97	770.17	764.19	761.25
67500	898.93	857.51	839.38	812.54	803.82	801.66	799.79	793.58	790.52
70000	932.22	889.27	870.47	842.64	833.59	831.35	829.42	822.98	819.80
75000	998.81	952.79	932.65	902.83	893.13	890.73	888.66	881.76	878.36
80000	1065.40	1016.31	994.82	963.01	952.67	950.12	947.90	940.54	936.92
85000	1131.99	1079.83	1057.00	1023.20	1012.22	1009.50	1007.15	999.33	995.47
90000	1198.57	1143.35	1119.17	1083.39	1071.76	1068.88	1066.39	1058.11	1054.03
95000	1265.16	1206.87	1181.35	1143.58	1131.30	1128.26	1125.63	1116.89	1112.59
100000	1331.75	1270.39	1243.53	1203.77	1190.84	1187.64	1184.88	1175.68	1171.15
105000	1398.33	1333.91	1305.70	1263.95	1250.38	1247.03	1244.12	1234.46	1229.70
110000	1464.92	1397.43	1367.88	1324.14	1309.93	1306.41	1303.36	1293.25	1288.26
115000	1531.51	1460.95	1430.05	1384.33	1369.47	1365.79	1362.61	1352.03	1346.82
120000	1598.09	1524.46	1492.23	1444.52	1429.01	1425.17	1421.85	1410.81	1405.37
125000	1664.68	1587.98	1554.41	1504.71	1488.55	1484.55	1481.09	1469.60	1463.93
130000	1731.27	1651.50	1616.58	1564.89	1548.09	1543.94	1540.34	1528.38	1522.49
135000	1797.86	1715.02	1678.76	1625.08	1607.63	1603.32	1599.58	1587.16	1581.04
140000	1864.44	1778.54	1740.93	1685.27	1667.18	1662.70	1658.83	1645.95	1639.60
145000	1931.03	1842.06	1803.11	1745.46	1726.72	1722.08	1718.07	1704.73	1698.16
150000	1997.62	1905.58	1865.29	1805.65	1786.26	1781.46	1777.31	1763.51	1756.72

14⅛%   MONTHLY PAYMENT
NECESSARY TO AMORTIZE A LOAN

AMOUNT	1 YEAR	2 YEARS	3 YEARS	4 YEARS	5 YEARS	7 YEARS	8 YEARS	10 YEARS	12 YEARS
$ 50	4.50	2.41	1.72	1.37	1.17	.95	.88	.79	.73
100	8.99	4.81	3.43	2.74	2.34	1.89	1.75	1.57	1.45
200	17.97	9.62	6.85	5.48	4.67	3.77	3.49	3.13	2.90
300	26.96	14.43	10.28	8.22	7.00	5.65	5.24	4.69	4.34
400	35.94	19.23	13.70	10.96	9.34	7.53	6.98	6.25	5.79
500	44.93	24.04	17.12	13.70	11.67	9.41	8.73	7.81	7.23
600	53.91	28.85	20.55	16.44	14.00	11.29	10.47	9.37	8.68
700	62.90	33.66	23.97	19.18	16.34	13.17	12.21	10.93	10.12
800	71.88	38.46	27.40	21.92	18.67	15.05	13.96	12.49	11.57
900	80.87	43.27	30.82	24.66	21.00	16.93	15.70	14.05	13.01
1000	89.85	48.08	34.24	27.39	23.34	18.81	17.45	15.61	14.46
2000	179.70	96.15	68.48	54.78	46.67	37.62	34.89	31.21	28.91
3000	269.54	144.22	102.72	82.17	70.00	56.43	52.33	46.81	43.36
4000	359.39	192.29	136.96	109.56	93.34	75.24	69.78	62.41	57.81
5000	449.23	240.36	171.20	136.95	116.67	94.05	87.22	78.01	72.26
6000	539.08	288.44	205.44	164.34	140.00	112.86	104.66	93.62	86.71
7000	628.93	336.51	239.67	191.73	163.34	131.67	122.10	109.22	101.16
8000	718.77	384.58	273.91	219.12	186.67	150.48	139.55	124.82	115.61
9000	808.62	432.65	308.15	246.51	210.00	169.29	156.99	140.42	130.06
10000	898.46	480.72	342.39	273.90	233.34	188.10	174.43	156.02	144.51
15000	1347.69	721.08	513.58	410.84	350.00	282.14	261.65	234.03	216.76
20000	1796.92	961.44	684.77	547.79	466.67	376.19	348.86	312.04	289.01
25000	2246.15	1201.80	855.96	684.74	583.33	470.23	436.07	390.05	361.26
30000	2695.38	1442.16	1027.16	821.68	700.00	564.28	523.29	468.06	433.51
35000	3144.61	1682.52	1198.35	958.63	816.66	658.32	610.50	546.07	505.76
40000	3593.84	1922.88	1369.54	1095.57	933.33	752.37	697.71	624.08	578.02
45000	4043.07	2163.24	1540.73	1232.52	1049.99	846.42	784.93	702.09	650.27
46000	4132.92	2211.31	1574.97	1259.91	1073.33	865.23	802.37	717.69	664.72
47000	4222.76	2259.39	1609.21	1287.30	1096.66	884.03	819.81	733.29	679.17
48000	4312.61	2307.46	1643.45	1314.69	1119.99	902.84	837.26	748.90	693.62
49000	4402.46	2355.53	1677.69	1342.08	1143.33	921.65	854.70	764.50	708.07
50000	4492.30	2403.60	1711.92	1369.47	1166.66	940.46	872.14	780.10	722.52
51000	4582.15	2451.67	1746.16	1396.86	1189.99	959.27	889.58	795.70	736.97
52000	4671.99	2499.75	1780.40	1424.24	1213.33	978.08	907.03	811.30	751.42
53000	4761.84	2547.82	1814.64	1451.63	1236.66	996.89	924.47	826.91	765.87
54000	4851.69	2595.89	1848.88	1479.02	1259.99	1015.70	941.91	842.51	780.32
55000	4941.53	2643.96	1883.12	1506.41	1283.33	1034.51	959.35	858.11	794.77
56000	5031.38	2692.03	1917.35	1533.80	1306.66	1053.32	976.80	873.71	809.22
57000	5121.22	2740.11	1951.59	1561.19	1329.99	1072.13	994.24	889.31	823.67
58000	5211.07	2788.18	1985.83	1588.58	1353.33	1090.93	1011.68	904.91	838.12
59000	5300.92	2836.25	2020.07	1615.97	1376.66	1109.74	1029.13	920.52	852.57
60000	5390.76	2884.32	2054.31	1643.36	1399.99	1128.55	1046.57	936.12	867.02
61000	5480.61	2932.39	2088.55	1670.75	1423.32	1147.36	1064.01	951.72	881.47
62000	5570.45	2980.47	2122.78	1698.14	1446.66	1166.17	1081.45	967.32	895.92
63000	5660.30	3028.54	2157.02	1725.53	1469.99	1184.98	1098.90	982.92	910.37
64000	5750.15	3076.61	2191.26	1752.92	1493.32	1203.79	1116.34	998.53	924.82
65000	5839.99	3124.68	2225.50	1780.30	1516.66	1222.60	1133.78	1014.13	939.27
67500	6064.61	3244.86	2311.10	1848.78	1574.99	1269.62	1177.39	1053.15	975.40
70000	6289.22	3365.04	2396.69	1917.25	1633.32	1316.64	1221.00	1092.14	1011.52
75000	6738.45	3605.40	2567.88	2054.20	1749.99	1410.69	1308.21	1170.15	1083.78
80000	7187.68	3845.76	2739.07	2191.14	1866.65	1504.74	1395.42	1248.16	1156.03
85000	7636.91	4086.12	2910.27	2328.09	1983.32	1598.78	1482.64	1326.17	1228.28
90000	8086.14	4326.48	3081.46	2465.03	2099.98	1692.83	1569.85	1404.18	1300.53
95000	8535.37	4566.84	3252.65	2601.98	2216.65	1786.87	1657.06	1482.18	1372.78
100000	8984.60	4807.20	3423.84	2738.93	2333.32	1880.92	1744.28	1560.19	1445.03
105000	9433.83	5047.56	3595.03	2875.87	2449.98	1974.96	1831.49	1638.20	1517.28
110000	9883.06	5287.92	3766.23	3012.82	2566.65	2069.01	1918.70	1716.21	1589.54
115000	10332.29	5528.28	3937.42	3149.77	2683.31	2163.06	2005.92	1794.22	1661.79
120000	10781.52	5768.64	4108.61	3286.71	2799.98	2257.10	2093.13	1872.23	1734.04
125000	11230.75	6009.00	4279.80	3423.66	2916.64	2351.15	2180.34	1950.24	1806.29
130000	11679.98	6249.36	4450.99	3560.60	3033.31	2445.19	2267.56	2028.25	1878.54
135000	12129.21	6489.72	4622.19	3697.55	3149.97	2539.24	2354.77	2106.26	1950.79
140000	12578.44	6730.08	4793.38	3834.50	3266.64	2633.28	2441.99	2184.27	2023.04
145000	13027.67	6970.44	4964.57	3971.44	3383.31	2727.33	2529.20	2262.28	2095.30
150000	13476.90	7210.80	5135.76	4108.39	3499.97	2821.37	2616.41	2340.29	2167.55

AMOUNT	15 YEARS	18 YEARS	20 YEARS	25 YEARS	28 YEARS	29 YEARS	30 YEARS	35 YEARS	40 YEARS
$ 50	.68	.64	.63	.61	.61	.60	.60	.60	.60
100	1.35	1.28	1.26	1.22	1.21	1.20	1.20	1.19	1.19
200	2.69	2.56	2.51	2.43	2.41	2.40	2.39	2.38	2.37
300	4.03	3.84	3.76	3.65	3.61	3.60	3.59	3.56	3.55
400	5.37	5.12	5.02	4.86	4.81	4.79	4.78	4.75	4.73
500	6.71	6.40	6.27	6.07	6.01	5.99	5.98	5.93	5.91
600	8.05	7.68	7.52	7.29	7.21	7.19	7.17	7.12	7.09
700	9.39	8.96	8.77	8.50	8.41	8.39	8.37	8.31	8.27
800	10.73	10.24	10.03	9.71	9.61	9.58	9.56	9.49	9.46
900	12.07	11.52	11.28	10.93	10.81	10.78	10.76	10.68	10.64
1000	13.41	12.80	12.53	12.14	12.01	11.98	11.95	11.86	11.82
2000	26.81	25.59	25.06	24.27	24.02	23.95	23.90	23.72	23.63
3000	40.21	38.38	37.58	36.41	36.02	35.93	35.85	35.58	35.45
4000	53.61	51.17	50.11	48.54	48.03	47.90	47.80	47.44	47.26
5000	67.01	63.97	62.64	60.67	60.04	59.88	59.74	59.29	59.07
6000	80.41	76.76	75.16	72.81	72.04	71.85	71.69	71.15	70.89
7000	93.82	89.55	87.69	84.94	84.05	83.83	83.64	83.01	82.70
8000	107.22	102.34	100.21	97.07	96.05	95.80	95.59	94.87	94.52
9000	120.62	115.14	112.74	109.21	108.06	107.78	107.53	106.73	106.33
10000	134.02	127.93	125.27	121.34	120.07	119.75	119.48	118.58	118.14
15000	201.03	191.89	187.90	182.01	180.10	179.63	179.22	177.87	177.21
20000	268.04	255.85	250.53	242.67	240.13	239.50	238.96	237.16	236.28
25000	335.04	319.81	313.16	303.34	300.16	299.38	298.70	296.45	295.35
30000	402.05	383.77	375.79	364.01	360.19	359.25	358.44	355.74	354.42
35000	469.06	447.73	438.42	424.67	420.22	419.12	418.18	415.03	413.49
40000	536.07	511.69	501.05	485.34	480.25	479.00	477.91	474.32	472.56
45000	603.07	575.66	563.68	546.01	540.29	538.87	537.65	533.61	531.63
46000	616.47	588.45	576.21	558.14	552.29	550.85	549.60	545.47	543.44
47000	629.88	601.24	588.73	570.27	564.30	562.82	561.55	557.32	555.25
48000	643.28	614.03	601.26	582.41	576.30	574.80	573.50	569.18	567.07
49000	656.68	626.83	613.78	594.54	588.31	586.77	585.44	581.04	578.88
50000	670.08	639.62	626.31	606.67	600.32	598.75	597.39	592.90	590.69
51000	683.48	652.41	638.84	618.81	612.32	610.72	609.34	604.75	602.51
52000	696.88	665.20	651.36	630.94	624.33	622.70	621.29	616.61	614.32
53000	710.28	677.99	663.89	643.07	636.34	634.67	633.23	628.47	626.14
54000	723.69	690.79	676.41	655.21	648.34	646.65	645.18	640.33	637.95
55000	737.09	703.58	688.94	667.34	660.35	658.62	657.13	652.19	649.76
56000	750.49	716.37	701.47	679.47	672.35	670.60	669.08	664.04	661.58
57000	763.89	729.16	713.99	691.61	684.36	682.57	681.03	675.90	673.39
58000	777.29	741.96	726.52	703.74	696.37	694.55	692.97	687.76	685.20
59000	790.69	754.75	739.04	715.87	708.37	706.52	704.92	699.62	697.02
60000	804.10	767.54	751.57	728.01	720.38	718.50	716.87	711.47	708.83
61000	817.50	780.33	764.10	740.14	732.39	730.47	728.82	723.33	720.65
62000	830.90	793.12	776.62	752.27	744.39	742.45	740.76	735.19	732.46
63000	844.30	805.92	789.15	764.41	756.40	754.42	752.71	747.05	744.27
64000	857.70	818.71	801.68	776.54	768.40	766.40	764.66	758.91	756.09
65000	871.10	831.50	814.20	788.67	780.41	778.37	776.61	770.76	767.90
67500	904.61	863.48	845.52	819.01	810.43	808.31	806.48	800.41	797.44
70000	938.11	895.46	876.83	849.34	840.44	838.24	836.35	830.05	826.97
75000	1005.12	959.42	939.46	910.01	900.47	898.12	896.08	889.34	886.04
80000	1072.13	1023.38	1002.09	970.67	960.50	957.99	955.82	948.63	945.11
85000	1139.13	1087.35	1064.72	1031.34	1020.53	1017.87	1015.56	1007.92	1004.18
90000	1206.14	1151.31	1127.35	1092.01	1080.57	1077.74	1075.30	1067.21	1063.25
95000	1273.15	1215.27	1189.98	1152.67	1140.60	1137.62	1135.04	1126.50	1122.31
100000	1340.16	1279.23	1252.61	1213.34	1200.63	1197.49	1194.78	1185.79	1181.38
105000	1407.16	1343.19	1315.25	1274.01	1260.66	1257.36	1254.52	1245.08	1240.45
110000	1474.17	1407.15	1377.88	1334.67	1320.69	1317.24	1314.25	1304.37	1299.52
115000	1541.18	1471.11	1440.51	1395.34	1380.72	1377.11	1373.99	1363.66	1358.59
120000	1608.19	1535.07	1503.14	1456.01	1440.75	1436.99	1433.73	1422.94	1417.66
125000	1675.19	1599.04	1565.77	1516.67	1500.78	1496.86	1493.47	1482.23	1476.73
130000	1742.20	1663.00	1628.40	1577.34	1560.82	1556.74	1553.21	1541.52	1535.80
135000	1809.21	1726.96	1691.03	1638.01	1620.85	1616.61	1612.95	1600.81	1594.87
140000	1876.22	1790.92	1753.66	1698.67	1680.88	1676.48	1672.69	1660.10	1653.93
145000	1943.22	1854.88	1816.29	1759.34	1740.91	1736.36	1732.43	1719.39	1713.00
150000	2010.23	1918.84	1878.92	1820.01	1800.94	1796.23	1792.16	1778.68	1772.07

14¼% MONTHLY PAYMENT
NECESSARY TO AMORTIZE A LOAN

AMOUNT	1 YEAR	2 YEARS	3 YEARS	4 YEARS	5 YEARS	7 YEARS	8 YEARS	10 YEARS	12 YEARS
$ 50	4.50	2.41	1.72	1.38	1.17	.95	.88	.79	.73
100	9.00	4.82	3.43	2.75	2.34	1.89	1.76	1.57	1.46
200	17.99	9.63	6.86	5.50	4.68	3.78	3.51	3.14	2.91
300	26.98	14.44	10.29	8.24	7.02	5.67	5.26	4.71	4.36
400	35.97	19.26	13.72	10.99	9.36	7.56	7.01	6.28	5.82
500	44.96	24.07	17.15	13.73	11.70	9.44	8.76	7.84	7.27
600	53.95	28.88	20.58	16.48	14.04	11.33	10.51	9.41	8.72
700	62.94	33.70	24.01	19.22	16.38	13.22	12.26	10.98	10.18
800	71.93	38.51	27.44	21.97	18.72	15.11	14.02	12.55	11.63
900	80.92	43.32	30.87	24.71	21.06	17.00	15.77	14.11	13.08
1000	89.91	48.14	34.30	27.46	23.40	18.88	17.52	15.68	14.53
2000	179.81	96.27	68.60	54.91	46.80	37.76	35.03	31.36	29.06
3000	269.72	144.40	102.90	82.36	70.20	56.64	52.55	47.04	43.59
4000	359.62	192.53	137.20	109.81	93.60	75.52	70.06	62.71	58.12
5000	449.53	240.66	171.50	137.27	117.00	94.40	87.58	78.39	72.65
6000	539.43	288.79	205.80	164.72	140.39	113.28	105.09	94.07	87.18
7000	629.34	336.92	240.10	192.17	163.79	132.15	122.60	109.75	101.71
8000	719.24	385.05	274.40	219.62	187.19	151.03	140.12	125.42	116.24
9000	809.15	433.18	308.70	247.07	210.59	169.91	157.63	141.10	130.77
10000	899.05	481.32	343.00	274.53	233.99	188.79	175.15	156.78	145.30
15000	1348.58	721.97	514.49	411.79	350.98	283.18	262.72	235.16	217.95
20000	1798.10	962.63	685.99	549.05	467.97	377.57	350.29	313.55	290.59
25000	2247.62	1203.28	857.48	686.31	584.96	471.96	437.86	391.94	363.24
30000	2697.15	1443.94	1028.98	823.57	701.95	566.36	525.43	470.32	435.89
35000	3146.67	1684.59	1200.48	960.83	818.94	660.75	613.00	548.71	508.54
40000	3596.20	1925.25	1371.97	1098.09	935.93	755.14	700.57	627.10	581.18
45000	4045.72	2165.90	1543.47	1235.35	1052.92	849.53	788.14	705.48	653.83
46000	4135.63	2214.03	1577.77	1262.80	1076.32	868.41	805.65	721.16	668.36
47000	4225.53	2262.17	1612.07	1290.25	1099.71	887.29	823.17	736.84	682.89
48000	4315.43	2310.30	1646.37	1317.70	1123.11	906.17	840.68	752.52	697.42
49000	4405.34	2358.43	1680.66	1345.16	1146.51	925.05	858.19	768.19	711.95
50000	4495.24	2406.56	1714.96	1372.61	1169.91	943.92	875.71	783.87	726.48
51000	4585.15	2454.69	1749.26	1400.06	1193.31	962.80	893.22	799.55	741.01
52000	4675.05	2502.82	1783.56	1427.51	1216.70	981.68	910.74	815.23	755.54
53000	4764.96	2550.95	1817.86	1454.96	1240.10	1000.56	928.25	830.90	770.07
54000	4854.86	2599.08	1852.16	1482.42	1263.50	1019.44	945.77	846.58	784.60
55000	4944.77	2647.21	1886.46	1509.87	1286.90	1038.32	963.28	862.26	799.13
56000	5034.67	2695.34	1920.76	1537.32	1310.30	1057.19	980.79	877.93	813.66
57000	5124.58	2743.48	1955.06	1564.77	1333.69	1076.07	998.31	893.61	828.19
58000	5214.48	2791.61	1989.36	1592.22	1357.09	1094.95	1015.82	909.29	842.72
59000	5304.39	2839.74	2023.66	1619.68	1380.49	1113.83	1033.34	924.97	857.25
60000	5394.29	2887.87	2057.96	1647.13	1403.89	1132.71	1050.85	940.64	871.77
61000	5484.20	2936.00	2092.25	1674.58	1427.29	1151.59	1068.36	956.32	886.30
62000	5574.10	2984.13	2126.55	1702.03	1450.68	1170.47	1085.88	972.00	900.83
63000	5664.01	3032.26	2160.85	1729.48	1474.08	1189.34	1103.39	987.68	915.36
64000	5753.91	3080.39	2195.15	1756.94	1497.48	1208.22	1120.91	1003.35	929.89
65000	5843.82	3128.52	2229.45	1784.39	1520.88	1227.10	1138.42	1019.03	944.42
67500	6068.58	3248.85	2315.20	1853.02	1579.37	1274.30	1182.21	1058.22	980.75
70000	6293.34	3369.18	2400.95	1921.65	1637.87	1321.49	1225.99	1097.42	1017.07
75000	6742.86	3609.84	2572.44	2058.91	1754.86	1415.88	1313.56	1175.80	1089.72
80000	7192.39	3850.49	2743.94	2196.17	1871.85	1510.28	1401.13	1254.19	1162.36
85000	7641.91	4091.15	2915.44	2333.43	1988.84	1604.67	1488.70	1332.58	1235.01
90000	8091.44	4331.80	3086.93	2470.69	2105.83	1699.06	1576.27	1410.96	1307.66
95000	8540.96	4572.46	3258.43	2607.95	2222.82	1793.45	1663.84	1489.35	1380.31
100000	8990.48	4813.11	3429.92	2745.21	2339.81	1887.84	1751.41	1567.74	1452.95
105000	9440.01	5053.77	3601.42	2882.47	2456.80	1982.24	1838.98	1646.12	1525.60
110000	9889.53	5294.42	3772.91	3019.73	2573.79	2076.63	1926.55	1724.51	1598.25
115000	10339.06	5535.08	3944.41	3156.99	2690.78	2171.02	2014.12	1802.90	1670.90
120000	10788.58	5775.73	4115.91	3294.25	2807.77	2265.41	2101.69	1881.28	1743.54
125000	11238.10	6016.39	4287.40	3431.51	2924.76	2359.80	2189.26	1959.67	1816.19
130000	11687.63	6257.04	4458.90	3568.77	3041.75	2454.20	2276.84	2038.06	1888.84
135000	12137.15	6497.70	4630.39	3706.03	3158.74	2548.59	2364.41	2116.44	1961.49
140000	12586.68	6738.35	4801.89	3843.29	3275.73	2642.98	2451.98	2194.83	2034.13
145000	13036.20	6979.01	4973.39	3980.55	3392.72	2737.37	2539.55	2273.22	2106.78
150000	13485.72	7219.67	5144.88	4117.81	3509.71	2831.76	2627.12	2351.60	2179.43

120

MONTHLY PAYMENT 14¼%

NECESSARY TO AMORTIZE A LOAN

AMOUNT	15 YEARS	18 YEARS	20 YEARS	25 YEARS	28 YEARS	29 YEARS	30 YEARS	35 YEARS	40 YEARS
$ 50	.68	.65	.64	.62	.61	.61	.61	.60	.60
100	1.35	1.29	1.27	1.23	1.22	1.21	1.21	1.20	1.20
200	2.70	2.58	2.53	2.45	2.43	2.42	2.41	2.40	2.39
300	4.05	3.87	3.79	3.67	3.64	3.63	3.62	3.59	3.58
400	5.40	5.16	5.05	4.90	4.85	4.83	4.82	4.79	4.77
500	6.75	6.45	6.31	6.12	6.06	6.04	6.03	5.98	5.96
600	8.10	7.73	7.58	7.34	7.27	7.25	7.23	7.18	7.15
700	9.45	9.02	8.84	8.57	8.48	8.46	8.44	8.38	8.35
800	10.79	10.31	10.10	9.79	9.69	9.66	9.64	9.57	9.54
900	12.14	11.60	11.36	11.01	10.90	10.87	10.85	10.77	10.73
1000	13.49	12.89	12.62	12.23	12.11	12.08	12.05	11.96	11.92
2000	26.98	25.77	25.24	24.46	24.21	24.15	24.10	23.92	23.84
3000	40.46	38.65	37.86	36.69	36.32	36.23	36.15	35.88	35.75
4000	53.95	51.53	50.47	48.92	48.42	48.30	48.19	47.84	47.67
5000	67.43	64.41	63.09	61.15	60.53	60.37	60.24	59.80	59.59
6000	80.92	77.29	75.71	73.38	72.63	72.45	72.29	71.76	71.50
7000	94.41	90.17	88.33	85.61	84.73	84.52	84.33	83.72	83.42
8000	107.89	103.05	100.94	97.84	96.84	96.59	96.38	95.68	95.33
9000	121.38	115.93	113.56	110.07	108.94	108.67	108.43	107.64	107.25
10000	134.86	128.81	126.18	122.30	121.05	120.74	120.47	119.60	119.17
15000	202.29	193.22	189.26	183.44	181.57	181.11	180.71	179.39	178.75
20000	269.72	257.62	252.35	244.59	242.09	241.47	240.94	239.19	238.33
25000	337.15	322.03	315.43	305.74	302.61	301.84	301.18	298.98	297.91
30000	404.58	386.43	378.52	366.88	363.13	362.21	361.41	358.78	357.49
35000	472.01	450.84	441.61	428.03	423.65	422.58	421.65	418.57	417.07
40000	539.44	515.24	504.69	489.18	484.18	482.94	481.88	478.37	476.65
45000	606.87	579.64	567.78	550.32	544.70	543.31	542.11	538.16	536.24
46000	620.35	592.53	580.40	562.55	556.80	555.38	554.16	550.12	548.15
47000	633.84	605.41	593.01	574.78	568.90	567.46	566.21	562.08	560.07
48000	647.32	618.29	605.63	587.01	581.01	579.53	578.25	574.04	571.98
49000	660.81	631.17	618.25	599.24	593.11	591.60	590.30	586.00	583.90
50000	674.29	644.05	630.86	611.47	605.22	603.68	602.35	597.96	595.82
51000	687.78	656.93	643.48	623.70	617.32	615.75	614.40	609.92	607.73
52000	701.27	669.81	656.10	635.93	629.43	627.83	626.44	621.87	619.65
53000	714.75	682.69	668.72	648.16	641.53	639.90	638.49	633.83	631.57
54000	728.24	695.57	681.33	660.39	653.63	651.97	650.54	645.79	643.48
55000	741.72	708.45	693.95	672.62	665.74	664.05	662.58	657.75	655.40
56000	755.21	721.33	706.57	684.84	677.84	676.12	674.63	669.71	667.31
57000	768.70	734.21	719.18	697.07	689.95	688.19	686.68	681.67	679.23
58000	782.18	747.10	731.80	709.30	702.05	700.27	698.72	693.63	691.15
59000	795.67	759.98	744.42	721.53	714.16	712.34	710.77	705.59	703.06
60000	809.15	772.86	757.04	733.76	726.26	724.41	722.82	717.55	714.98
61000	822.64	785.74	769.65	745.99	738.36	736.49	734.86	729.51	726.90
62000	836.12	798.62	782.27	758.22	750.47	748.56	746.91	741.46	738.81
63000	849.61	811.50	794.89	770.45	762.57	760.63	758.96	753.42	750.73
64000	863.10	824.38	807.51	782.68	774.68	772.71	771.00	765.38	762.64
65000	876.58	837.26	820.12	794.91	786.78	784.78	783.05	777.34	774.56
67500	910.30	869.46	851.67	825.48	817.04	814.96	813.17	807.24	804.35
70000	944.01	901.67	883.21	856.05	847.30	845.15	843.29	837.14	834.14
75000	1011.44	966.07	946.29	917.20	907.82	905.51	903.52	896.93	893.72
80000	1078.87	1030.47	1009.38	978.35	968.35	965.88	963.75	956.73	953.30
85000	1146.30	1094.88	1072.47	1039.49	1028.87	1026.25	1023.99	1016.52	1012.88
90000	1213.73	1159.28	1135.55	1100.64	1089.39	1086.62	1084.22	1076.32	1072.47
95000	1281.16	1223.69	1198.64	1161.79	1149.91	1146.98	1144.46	1136.11	1132.05
100000	1348.58	1288.09	1261.72	1222.93	1210.43	1207.35	1204.69	1195.91	1191.63
105000	1416.01	1352.50	1324.81	1284.08	1270.95	1267.72	1264.93	1255.70	1251.21
110000	1483.44	1416.90	1387.90	1345.23	1331.47	1328.09	1325.16	1315.50	1310.79
115000	1550.87	1481.31	1450.98	1406.37	1391.99	1388.45	1385.40	1375.29	1370.37
120000	1618.30	1545.71	1514.07	1467.52	1452.52	1448.82	1445.63	1435.09	1429.95
125000	1685.73	1610.11	1577.15	1528.66	1513.04	1509.19	1505.86	1494.88	1489.53
130000	1753.16	1674.52	1640.24	1589.81	1573.56	1569.56	1566.10	1554.68	1549.12
135000	1820.59	1738.92	1703.33	1650.96	1634.08	1629.92	1626.33	1614.47	1608.70
140000	1888.02	1803.33	1766.41	1712.10	1694.60	1690.29	1686.57	1674.27	1668.28
145000	1955.45	1867.73	1829.50	1773.25	1755.12	1750.66	1746.80	1734.06	1727.86
150000	2022.87	1932.14	1892.58	1834.40	1815.64	1811.02	1807.04	1793.86	1787.44

14⅜% MONTHLY PAYMENT
NECESSARY TO AMORTIZE A LOAN

AMOUNT	1 YEAR	2 YEARS	3 YEARS	4 YEARS	5 YEARS	7 YEARS	8 YEARS	10 YEARS	12 YEARS
$ 50	4.50	2.41	1.72	1.38	1.18	.95	.88	.79	.74
100	9.00	4.82	3.44	2.76	2.35	1.90	1.76	1.58	1.47
200	18.00	9.64	6.88	5.51	4.70	3.79	3.52	3.16	2.93
300	26.99	14.46	10.31	8.26	7.04	5.69	5.28	4.73	4.39
400	35.99	19.28	13.75	11.01	9.39	7.58	7.04	6.31	5.85
500	44.99	24.10	17.19	13.76	11.74	9.48	8.80	7.88	7.31
600	53.98	28.92	20.62	16.51	14.08	11.37	10.56	9.46	8.77
700	62.98	33.74	24.06	19.27	16.43	13.27	12.31	11.03	10.23
800	71.98	38.56	27.49	22.02	18.78	15.16	14.07	12.61	11.69
900	80.97	43.38	30.93	24.77	21.12	17.06	15.83	14.18	13.15
1000	89.97	48.20	34.37	27.52	23.47	18.95	17.59	15.76	14.61
2000	179.93	96.39	68.73	55.03	46.93	37.90	35.18	31.51	29.22
3000	269.90	144.58	103.09	82.55	70.39	56.85	52.76	47.26	43.83
4000	359.86	192.77	137.45	110.06	93.86	75.80	70.35	63.02	58.44
5000	449.82	240.96	171.81	137.58	117.32	94.74	87.93	78.77	73.05
6000	539.79	289.15	206.17	165.09	140.78	113.69	105.52	94.52	87.66
7000	629.75	337.34	240.53	192.61	164.25	132.64	123.10	110.28	102.27
8000	719.71	385.53	274.89	220.12	187.71	151.59	140.69	126.03	116.88
9000	809.68	433.72	309.25	247.64	211.17	170.54	158.28	141.78	131.49
10000	899.64	481.91	343.61	275.15	234.64	189.48	175.86	157.53	146.09
15000	1349.46	722.86	515.41	412.73	351.95	284.22	263.79	236.30	219.14
20000	1799.28	963.81	687.21	550.30	469.27	378.96	351.72	315.06	292.18
25000	2249.10	1204.76	859.01	687.88	586.58	473.70	439.64	393.83	365.23
30000	2698.91	1445.71	1030.81	825.45	703.90	568.44	527.57	472.59	438.27
35000	3148.73	1686.66	1202.61	963.03	821.21	663.18	615.50	551.36	511.32
40000	3598.55	1927.61	1374.41	1100.60	938.53	757.92	703.43	630.12	584.36
45000	4048.37	2168.57	1546.21	1238.18	1055.85	852.66	791.36	708.89	657.41
46000	4138.33	2216.76	1580.57	1265.69	1079.31	871.60	808.94	724.64	672.01
47000	4228.30	2264.95	1614.93	1293.21	1102.77	890.55	826.53	740.39	686.62
48000	4318.26	2313.14	1649.29	1320.72	1126.23	909.50	844.11	756.14	701.23
49000	4408.22	2361.33	1683.65	1348.24	1149.70	928.45	861.70	771.90	715.84
50000	4498.19	2409.52	1718.01	1375.75	1173.16	947.39	879.28	787.65	730.45
51000	4588.15	2457.71	1752.37	1403.27	1196.62	966.34	896.87	803.40	745.06
52000	4678.12	2505.90	1786.73	1430.78	1220.09	985.29	914.46	819.16	759.67
53000	4768.08	2554.05	1821.09	1458.30	1243.55	1004.24	932.04	834.91	774.28
54000	4858.04	2602.28	1855.45	1485.81	1267.01	1023.19	949.63	850.66	788.89
55000	4948.01	2650.47	1889.81	1513.33	1290.48	1042.13	967.21	866.41	803.49
56000	5037.97	2698.66	1924.17	1540.84	1313.94	1061.08	984.80	882.17	818.10
57000	5127.93	2746.85	1958.53	1568.36	1337.40	1080.03	1002.38	897.92	832.71
58000	5217.90	2795.04	1992.89	1595.87	1360.87	1098.98	1019.97	913.67	847.32
59000	5307.86	2843.23	2027.25	1623.39	1384.33	1117.92	1037.55	929.43	861.93
60000	5397.82	2891.42	2061.61	1650.90	1407.79	1136.87	1055.14	945.18	876.54
61000	5487.79	2939.61	2095.97	1678.42	1431.26	1155.82	1072.73	960.93	891.15
62000	5577.75	2987.80	2130.33	1705.93	1454.72	1174.77	1090.31	976.69	905.76
63000	5667.72	3035.99	2164.69	1733.45	1478.18	1193.72	1107.90	992.44	920.37
64000	5757.68	3084.18	2199.05	1760.96	1501.64	1212.66	1125.48	1008.19	934.97
65000	5847.64	3132.37	2233.41	1788.48	1525.11	1231.61	1143.07	1023.94	949.58
67500	6072.55	3252.85	2319.31	1857.26	1583.77	1278.98	1187.03	1063.33	986.11
70000	6297.46	3373.32	2405.21	1926.05	1642.42	1326.35	1231.00	1102.71	1022.63
75000	6747.28	3614.27	2577.01	2063.63	1759.74	1421.09	1318.92	1181.47	1095.67
80000	7197.10	3855.22	2748.81	2201.20	1877.05	1515.83	1406.85	1260.24	1168.72
85000	7646.92	4096.17	2920.61	2338.78	1994.37	1610.57	1494.78	1339.00	1241.76
90000	8096.73	4337.13	3092.41	2476.35	2111.69	1705.31	1582.71	1417.77	1314.81
95000	8546.55	4578.08	3264.21	2613.93	2229.00	1800.04	1670.64	1496.53	1387.85
100000	8996.37	4819.03	3436.01	2751.50	2346.32	1894.78	1758.56	1575.30	1460.89
105000	9446.19	5059.98	3607.81	2889.08	2463.63	1989.52	1846.49	1654.06	1533.94
110000	9896.01	5300.93	3779.61	3026.65	2680.95	2084.26	1934.42	1732.82	1606.98
115000	10345.83	5541.88	3951.41	3164.23	2698.26	2179.00	2022.35	1811.59	1680.03
120000	10795.64	5782.83	4123.21	3301.80	2815.58	2273.74	2110.28	1890.35	1753.07
125000	11245.46	6023.78	4295.01	3439.37	2932.90	2368.48	2198.20	1969.12	1826.12
130000	11695.28	6264.73	4466.81	3576.95	3050.21	2463.22	2286.13	2047.88	1899.16
135000	12145.10	6505.69	4638.61	3714.52	3167.53	2557.96	2374.06	2126.65	1972.21
140000	12594.92	6746.64	4810.41	3852.10	3284.84	2652.69	2461.99	2205.41	2045.25
145000	13044.74	6987.59	4982.21	3989.67	3402.16	2747.43	2549.92	2284.18	2118.29
150000	13494.55	7228.54	5154.01	4127.25	3519.47	2842.17	2637.84	2362.94	2191.34

MONTHLY PAYMENT 14⅜%
NECESSARY TO AMORTIZE A LOAN

AMOUNT	15 YEARS	18 YEARS	20 YEARS	25 YEARS	28 YEARS	29 YEARS	30 YEARS	35 YEARS	40 YEARS
$ 50	.68	.65	.64	.62	.62	.61	.61	.61	.61
100	1.36	1.30	1.28	1.24	1.23	1.22	1.22	1.21	1.21
200	2.72	2.60	2.55	2.47	2.45	2.44	2.43	2.42	2.41
300	4.08	3.90	3.82	3.70	3.67	3.66	3.65	3.62	3.61
400	5.43	5.19	5.09	4.94	4.89	4.87	4.86	4.83	4.81
500	6.79	6.49	6.36	6.17	6.11	6.09	6.08	6.04	6.01
600	8.15	7.79	7.63	7.40	7.33	7.31	7.29	7.24	7.22
700	9.50	9.08	8.90	8.63	8.55	8.53	8.51	8.45	8.42
800	10.86	10.38	10.17	9.87	9.77	9.74	9.72	9.65	9.62
900	12.22	11.68	11.44	11.10	10.99	10.96	10.94	10.86	10.82
1000	13.58	12.97	12.71	12.33	12.21	12.18	12.15	12.07	12.02
2000	27.15	25.94	25.42	24.66	24.41	24.35	24.30	24.13	24.04
3000	40.72	38.91	38.13	36.98	36.61	36.52	36.44	36.19	36.06
4000	54.29	51.88	50.84	49.31	48.81	48.69	48.59	48.25	48.08
5000	67.86	64.85	63.55	61.63	61.02	60.87	60.74	60.31	60.10
6000	81.43	77.82	76.26	73.96	73.22	73.04	72.88	72.37	72.12
7000	95.00	90.79	88.96	86.28	85.42	85.21	85.03	84.43	84.14
8000	108.57	103.76	101.67	98.61	97.62	97.38	97.17	96.49	96.15
9000	122.14	116.73	114.38	110.93	109.83	109.55	109.32	108.55	108.17
10000	135.71	129.70	127.09	123.26	122.03	121.73	121.47	120.61	120.19
15000	203.56	194.55	190.63	184.89	183.04	182.59	182.20	180.91	180.28
20000	271.41	259.40	254.17	246.51	244.05	243.45	242.93	241.21	240.38
25000	339.26	324.25	317.72	308.14	305.07	304.31	303.66	301.51	300.47
30000	407.11	389.10	381.26	369.77	366.08	365.17	364.39	361.81	360.57
35000	474.97	453.94	444.80	431.39	427.09	426.03	425.12	422.12	420.66
40000	542.82	518.79	508.34	493.02	488.10	486.89	485.85	482.42	480.75
45000	610.67	583.64	571.89	554.65	549.11	547.75	546.58	542.72	540.85
46000	624.24	596.61	584.60	566.97	561.32	559.93	558.73	554.78	552.87
47000	637.81	609.58	597.30	579.30	573.52	572.10	570.87	566.84	564.89
48000	651.38	622.55	610.01	591.62	585.72	584.27	583.02	578.90	576.90
49000	664.95	635.52	622.72	603.95	597.92	596.44	595.17	590.96	588.92
50000	678.52	648.49	635.43	616.27	610.13	608.62	607.31	603.02	600.94
51000	692.09	661.46	648.14	628.60	622.33	620.79	619.46	615.08	612.96
52000	705.66	674.43	660.85	640.92	634.53	632.96	631.60	627.14	624.98
53000	719.23	687.40	673.55	653.25	646.73	645.13	643.75	639.20	637.00
54000	732.80	700.37	686.26	665.57	658.94	657.30	655.90	651.26	649.02
55000	746.37	713.34	698.97	677.90	671.14	669.48	668.04	663.32	661.04
56000	759.94	726.31	711.68	690.23	683.34	681.65	680.19	675.38	673.05
57000	773.51	739.28	724.39	702.55	695.54	693.82	692.34	687.44	685.07
58000	787.08	752.25	737.10	714.88	707.75	705.99	704.48	699.50	697.09
59000	800.65	765.22	749.81	727.20	719.95	718.17	716.63	711.56	709.11
60000	814.22	778.19	762.51	739.53	732.15	730.34	728.77	723.62	721.13
61000	827.79	791.16	775.22	751.85	744.35	742.51	740.92	735.68	733.15
62000	841.36	804.13	787.93	764.18	756.56	754.68	753.07	747.74	745.17
63000	854.93	817.10	800.64	776.50	768.76	766.85	765.21	759.81	757.19
64000	868.50	830.07	813.35	788.83	780.96	779.03	777.36	771.87	769.20
65000	882.07	843.04	826.06	801.15	793.16	791.20	789.50	783.93	781.22
67500	916.00	875.46	857.83	831.97	823.67	821.63	819.87	814.08	811.27
70000	949.93	907.88	889.60	862.78	854.17	852.06	850.24	844.23	841.32
75000	1017.78	972.73	953.14	924.41	915.19	912.92	910.97	904.53	901.41
80000	1085.63	1037.58	1016.68	986.03	976.20	973.78	971.70	964.83	961.50
85000	1153.48	1102.43	1080.23	1047.66	1037.21	1034.64	1032.43	1025.13	1021.60
90000	1221.33	1167.28	1143.77	1109.29	1098.22	1095.50	1093.16	1085.43	1081.69
95000	1289.18	1232.13	1207.31	1170.91	1159.23	1156.37	1153.89	1145.74	1141.79
100000	1357.03	1296.98	1270.85	1232.54	1220.25	1217.23	1214.62	1206.04	1201.88
105000	1424.89	1361.82	1334.40	1294.17	1281.26	1278.09	1275.35	1266.34	1261.97
110000	1492.74	1426.67	1397.94	1355.80	1342.27	1338.95	1336.08	1326.64	1322.07
115000	1560.59	1491.52	1461.48	1417.42	1403.28	1399.81	1396.81	1386.94	1382.16
120000	1628.44	1556.37	1525.02	1479.05	1464.30	1460.67	1457.54	1447.24	1442.25
125000	1696.29	1621.22	1588.57	1540.68	1525.31	1521.53	1518.27	1507.54	1502.35
130000	1764.14	1686.07	1652.11	1602.30	1586.32	1582.39	1579.00	1567.85	1562.44
135000	1832.00	1750.91	1715.65	1663.93	1647.33	1643.25	1639.74	1628.15	1622.54
140000	1899.85	1815.76	1779.19	1725.56	1708.34	1704.11	1700.47	1688.45	1682.63
145000	1967.70	1880.61	1842.74	1787.18	1769.36	1764.98	1761.20	1748.75	1742.72
150000	2035.55	1945.46	1906.28	1848.81	1830.37	1825.84	1821.93	1809.05	1802.82

MONTHLY PAYMENT
NECESSARY TO AMORTIZE A LOAN

AMOUNT	1 YEAR	2 YEARS	3 YEARS	4 YEARS	5 YEARS	7 YEARS	8 YEARS	10 YEARS	12 YEARS
$ 50	4.51	2.42	1.73	1.38	1.18	.96	.89	.80	.74
100	9.01	4.83	3.45	2.76	2.36	1.91	1.77	1.59	1.47
200	18.01	9.65	6.89	5.52	4.71	3.81	3.54	3.17	2.94
300	27.01	14.48	10.33	8.28	7.06	5.71	5.30	4.75	4.41
400	36.01	19.30	13.77	11.04	9.42	7.61	7.07	6.34	5.88
500	45.02	24.13	17.22	13.79	11.77	9.51	8.83	7.92	7.35
600	54.02	28.95	20.66	16.55	14.12	11.42	10.60	9.50	8.82
700	63.02	33.78	24.10	19.31	16.47	13.32	12.37	11.09	10.29
800	72.02	38.60	27.54	22.07	18.83	15.22	14.13	12.67	11.76
900	81.03	43.43	30.98	24.83	21.18	17.12	15.90	14.25	13.22
1000	90.03	48.25	34.43	27.58	23.53	19.02	17.66	15.83	14.69
2000	180.05	96.50	68.85	55.16	47.06	38.04	35.32	31.66	29.38
3000	270.07	144.75	103.27	82.74	70.59	57.06	52.98	47.49	44.07
4000	360.10	193.00	137.69	110.32	94.12	76.07	70.63	63.32	58.76
5000	450.12	241.25	172.11	137.89	117.65	95.09	88.29	79.15	73.45
6000	540.14	289.50	206.53	165.47	141.17	114.11	105.95	94.98	88.14
7000	630.16	337.75	240.95	193.05	164.70	133.13	123.61	110.81	102.82
8000	720.19	386.00	275.37	220.63	188.23	152.14	141.26	126.63	117.51
9000	810.21	434.25	309.79	248.21	211.76	171.16	158.92	142.46	132.20
10000	900.23	482.50	344.21	275.78	235.29	190.18	176.58	158.29	146.89
15000	1350.34	723.75	516.32	413.67	352.93	285.26	264.86	237.44	220.33
20000	1800.46	964.99	688.42	551.56	470.57	380.35	353.15	316.58	293.77
25000	2250.57	1206.24	860.53	689.45	588.21	475.44	441.44	395.72	367.22
30000	2700.68	1447.49	1032.63	827.34	705.85	570.52	529.72	474.87	440.66
35000	3150.79	1688.73	1204.74	965.23	823.49	665.61	618.01	554.01	514.10
40000	3600.91	1929.98	1376.84	1103.12	941.14	760.70	706.30	633.15	587.54
45000	4051.02	2171.23	1548.95	1241.01	1058.78	855.78	794.58	712.30	660.99
46000	4141.04	2219.48	1583.37	1268.59	1082.31	874.80	812.24	728.12	675.68
47000	4231.06	2267.73	1617.79	1296.17	1105.83	893.82	829.90	743.95	690.36
48000	4321.09	2315.98	1652.21	1323.75	1129.36	912.84	847.55	759.78	705.05
49000	4411.11	2364.23	1686.63	1351.32	1152.89	931.85	865.21	775.61	719.74
50000	4501.13	2412.48	1721.05	1378.90	1176.42	950.87	882.87	791.44	734.43
51000	4591.15	2460.73	1755.47	1406.48	1199.95	969.89	900.53	807.27	749.12
52000	4681.18	2508.98	1789.90	1434.06	1223.48	988.90	918.18	823.10	763.81
53000	4771.20	2557.22	1824.32	1461.64	1247.00	1007.92	935.84	838.92	778.49
54000	4861.22	2605.47	1858.74	1489.21	1270.53	1026.94	953.50	854.75	793.18
55000	4951.25	2653.72	1893.16	1516.79	1294.06	1045.96	971.15	870.58	807.87
56000	5041.27	2701.97	1927.58	1544.37	1317.59	1064.97	988.81	886.41	822.56
57000	5131.29	2750.22	1962.00	1571.95	1341.12	1083.99	1006.47	902.24	837.25
58000	5221.31	2798.47	1996.42	1599.53	1364.65	1103.01	1024.13	918.07	851.94
59000	5311.34	2846.72	2030.84	1627.10	1388.17	1122.03	1041.78	933.90	866.63
60000	5401.36	2894.97	2065.26	1654.68	1411.70	1141.04	1059.44	949.73	881.31
61000	5491.38	2943.22	2099.68	1682.26	1435.23	1160.06	1077.10	965.55	896.00
62000	5581.40	2991.47	2134.11	1709.84	1458.76	1179.08	1094.75	981.38	910.69
63000	5671.43	3039.72	2168.53	1737.42	1482.29	1198.10	1112.41	997.21	925.38
64000	5761.45	3087.97	2202.95	1764.99	1505.81	1217.11	1130.07	1013.04	940.07
65000	5851.47	3136.22	2237.37	1792.57	1529.34	1236.13	1147.73	1028.87	954.76
67500	6076.53	3256.84	2323.42	1861.52	1588.16	1283.67	1191.87	1068.44	991.48
70000	6301.58	3377.46	2409.47	1930.46	1646.98	1331.22	1236.01	1108.01	1028.20
75000	6751.70	3618.71	2581.58	2068.35	1764.63	1426.30	1324.30	1187.16	1101.64
80000	7201.81	3859.96	2753.68	2206.24	1882.27	1521.39	1412.59	1266.30	1175.08
85000	7651.92	4101.21	2925.79	2344.13	1999.91	1616.48	1500.87	1345.44	1248.53
90000	8102.03	4342.45	3097.89	2482.02	2117.55	1711.56	1589.16	1424.59	1321.97
95000	8552.15	4583.70	3270.00	2619.91	2235.19	1806.65	1677.44	1503.73	1395.41
100000	9002.26	4824.95	3442.10	2757.80	2352.83	1901.74	1765.73	1582.87	1468.85
105000	9452.37	5066.19	3614.21	2895.69	2470.47	1996.82	1854.02	1662.02	1542.30
110000	9902.49	5307.44	3786.31	3033.58	2588.12	2091.91	1942.30	1741.16	1615.74
115000	10352.60	5548.69	3958.42	3171.47	2705.76	2186.99	2030.59	1820.30	1689.18
120000	10802.71	5789.94	4130.53	3309.36	2823.40	2282.08	2118.88	1899.45	1762.62
125000	11252.82	6031.18	4302.63	3447.25	2941.04	2377.17	2207.16	1978.59	1836.07
130000	11702.94	6272.43	4474.73	3585.14	3058.68	2472.25	2295.45	2057.73	1909.51
135000	12153.05	6513.68	4646.84	3723.03	3176.32	2567.34	2383.73	2136.88	1982.95
140000	12603.16	6754.92	4818.94	3860.92	3293.96	2662.43	2472.02	2216.02	2056.39
145000	13053.27	6996.17	4991.05	3998.81	3411.61	2757.51	2560.31	2295.16	2129.84
150000	13503.39	7237.42	5163.15	4136.70	3529.25	2852.60	2648.59	2374.31	2203.28

MONTHLY PAYMENT 14½%
NECESSARY TO AMORTIZE A LOAN

AMOUNT	15 YEARS	18 YEARS	20 YEARS	25 YEARS	28 YEARS	29 YEARS	30 YEARS	35 YEARS	40 YEARS
$ 50	.69	.66	.64	.63	.62	.62	.62	.61	.61
100	1.37	1.31	1.28	1.25	1.24	1.23	1.23	1.22	1.22
200	2.74	2.62	2.56	2.49	2.47	2.46	2.45	2.44	2.43
300	4.10	3.92	3.84	3.73	3.70	3.69	3.68	3.65	3.64
400	5.47	5.23	5.12	4.97	4.93	4.91	4.90	4.87	4.85
500	6.83	6.53	6.40	6.22	6.16	6.14	6.13	6.09	6.07
600	8.20	7.84	7.68	7.46	7.39	7.37	7.35	7.30	7.28
700	9.56	9.15	8.96	8.70	8.62	8.59	8.58	8.52	8.49
800	10.93	10.45	10.24	9.94	9.85	9.82	9.80	9.73	9.70
900	12.29	11.76	11.52	11.18	11.08	11.05	11.03	10.95	10.91
1000	13.66	13.06	12.80	12.43	12.31	12.28	12.25	12.17	12.13
2000	27.32	26.12	25.60	24.85	24.61	24.55	24.50	24.33	24.25
3000	40.97	39.18	38.40	37.27	36.91	36.82	36.74	36.49	36.37
4000	54.63	52.24	51.20	49.69	49.21	49.09	48.99	48.65	48.49
5000	68.28	65.30	64.00	62.11	61.51	61.36	61.23	60.81	60.61
6000	81.94	78.36	76.80	74.53	73.81	73.63	73.48	72.98	72.73
7000	95.59	91.42	89.60	86.96	86.11	85.90	85.72	85.14	84.85
8000	109.25	104.47	102.40	99.38	98.41	98.17	97.97	97.30	96.98
9000	122.90	117.53	115.20	111.80	110.71	110.44	110.22	109.46	109.10
10000	136.56	130.59	128.00	124.22	123.01	122.72	122.46	121.62	121.22
15000	204.83	195.89	192.00	186.33	184.52	184.07	183.69	182.43	181.82
20000	273.11	261.18	256.00	248.44	246.02	245.43	244.92	243.24	242.43
25000	341.38	326.47	320.00	310.55	307.52	306.78	306.14	304.05	303.04
30000	409.66	391.77	384.00	372.65	369.03	368.14	367.37	364.86	363.64
35000	477.93	457.06	448.00	434.76	430.53	429.49	428.60	425.66	424.25
40000	546.21	522.35	512.00	496.87	492.03	490.85	489.83	486.47	484.86
45000	614.48	587.65	576.00	558.98	553.54	552.20	551.06	547.28	545.46
46000	628.14	600.71	588.80	571.40	565.84	564.48	563.30	559.44	557.59
47000	641.79	613.77	601.60	583.82	578.14	576.75	575.55	571.61	569.71
48000	655.45	626.82	614.40	596.24	590.44	589.02	587.79	583.77	581.83
49000	669.10	639.88	627.20	608.66	602.74	601.29	600.04	595.93	593.95
50000	682.76	652.94	640.00	621.09	615.04	613.56	612.28	608.09	606.07
51000	696.41	666.00	652.80	633.51	627.34	625.83	624.53	620.25	618.19
52000	710.07	679.06	665.60	645.93	639.64	638.10	636.77	632.41	630.31
53000	723.72	692.12	678.40	658.35	651.94	650.37	649.02	644.58	642.44
54000	737.38	705.18	691.20	670.77	664.24	662.64	661.27	656.74	654.56
55000	751.03	718.24	704.00	683.19	676.55	674.92	673.51	668.90	666.68
56000	764.69	731.29	716.80	695.62	688.85	687.19	685.76	681.06	678.80
57000	778.34	744.35	729.60	708.04	701.15	699.46	698.00	693.22	690.92
58000	792.00	757.41	742.40	720.46	713.45	711.73	710.25	705.38	703.04
59000	805.65	770.47	755.20	732.88	725.75	724.00	722.49	717.55	715.16
60000	819.31	783.53	768.00	745.30	738.05	736.27	734.74	729.71	727.28
61000	832.96	796.59	780.80	757.72	750.35	748.54	746.98	741.87	739.41
62000	846.62	809.65	793.60	770.15	762.65	760.81	759.23	754.03	751.53
63000	860.27	822.71	806.40	782.57	774.95	773.08	771.48	766.19	763.65
64000	873.93	835.76	819.20	794.99	787.25	785.36	783.72	778.35	775.77
65000	887.58	848.82	832.00	807.41	799.55	797.63	795.97	790.52	787.89
67500	921.72	881.47	864.00	838.46	830.30	828.30	826.58	820.92	818.19
70000	955.86	914.12	896.00	869.52	861.06	858.98	857.19	851.32	848.50
75000	1024.13	979.41	960.00	931.63	922.56	920.34	918.42	912.13	909.10
80000	1092.41	1044.70	1024.00	993.74	984.06	981.69	979.65	972.94	969.71
85000	1160.68	1110.00	1088.00	1055.84	1045.57	1043.05	1040.88	1033.75	1030.32
90000	1228.96	1175.29	1152.00	1117.95	1107.07	1104.40	1102.11	1094.56	1090.92
95000	1297.23	1240.59	1216.00	1180.06	1168.57	1165.76	1163.33	1155.37	1151.53
100000	1365.51	1305.88	1280.00	1242.17	1230.08	1227.12	1224.56	1216.18	1212.14
105000	1433.78	1371.17	1344.00	1304.28	1291.58	1288.47	1285.79	1276.98	1272.74
110000	1502.06	1436.47	1408.00	1366.38	1353.09	1349.83	1347.02	1337.79	1333.35
115000	1570.33	1501.76	1472.00	1428.49	1414.59	1411.18	1408.24	1398.60	1393.96
120000	1638.61	1567.05	1536.00	1490.60	1476.09	1472.54	1469.47	1459.41	1454.56
125000	1706.88	1632.35	1600.00	1552.71	1537.60	1533.89	1530.70	1520.22	1515.17
130000	1775.16	1697.64	1664.00	1614.82	1599.10	1595.25	1591.93	1581.03	1575.78
135000	1843.43	1762.94	1728.00	1676.92	1660.60	1656.60	1653.16	1641.84	1636.38
140000	1911.71	1828.23	1792.00	1739.03	1722.11	1717.96	1714.38	1702.64	1696.99
145000	1979.98	1893.52	1856.00	1801.14	1783.61	1779.31	1775.61	1763.45	1757.60
150000	2048.26	1958.82	1920.00	1863.25	1845.12	1840.67	1836.84	1824.26	1818.20

14⅝% MONTHLY PAYMENT
NECESSARY TO AMORTIZE A LOAN

AMOUNT	1 YEAR	2 YEARS	3 YEARS	4 YEARS	5 YEARS	7 YEARS	8 YEARS	10 YEARS	12 YEARS
$ 50	4.51	2.42	1.73	1.39	1.18	.96	.89	.80	.74
100	9.01	4.84	3.45	2.77	2.36	1.91	1.78	1.60	1.48
200	18.02	9.67	6.90	5.53	4.72	3.82	3.55	3.19	2.96
300	27.03	14.50	10.35	8.30	7.08	5.73	5.32	4.78	4.44
400	36.04	19.33	13.80	11.06	9.44	7.64	7.10	6.37	5.91
500	45.05	24.16	17.25	13.83	11.80	9.55	8.87	7.96	7.39
600	54.05	28.99	20.69	16.59	14.16	11.46	10.64	9.55	8.87
700	63.06	33.82	24.14	19.35	16.52	13.37	12.42	11.14	10.34
800	72.07	38.65	27.59	22.12	18.88	15.27	14.19	12.73	11.82
900	81.08	43.48	31.04	24.88	21.24	17.18	15.96	14.32	13.30
1000	90.09	48.31	34.49	27.65	23.60	19.09	17.73	15.91	14.77
2000	180.17	96.62	68.97	55.29	47.19	38.18	35.46	31.81	29.54
3000	270.25	144.93	103.45	82.93	70.79	57.27	53.19	47.72	44.31
4000	360.33	193.24	137.93	110.57	94.38	76.35	70.92	63.62	59.08
5000	450.41	241.55	172.41	138.21	117.97	95.44	88.65	79.53	73.85
6000	540.49	289.86	206.90	165.85	141.57	114.53	106.38	95.43	88.61
7000	630.58	338.17	241.38	193.49	165.16	133.61	124.11	111.34	103.38
8000	720.66	386.47	275.86	221.13	188.75	152.70	141.84	127.24	118.15
9000	810.74	434.78	310.34	248.77	212.35	171.79	159.57	143.15	132.92
10000	900.82	483.09	344.82	276.42	235.94	190.87	177.30	159.05	147.69
15000	1351.23	724.64	517.23	414.62	353.91	286.31	265.94	238.57	221.53
20000	1801.63	966.18	689.64	552.83	471.88	381.74	354.59	318.10	295.37
25000	2252.04	1207.72	862.05	691.03	589.84	477.18	443.23	397.62	369.21
30000	2702.45	1449.27	1034.46	829.24	707.81	572.61	531.88	477.14	443.05
35000	3152.86	1690.81	1206.87	967.44	825.78	668.05	620.52	556.67	516.89
40000	3603.26	1932.35	1379.28	1105.65	943.75	763.48	709.17	636.19	590.74
45000	4053.67	2173.90	1551.69	1243.85	1061.71	858.92	797.81	715.71	664.58
46000	4143.75	2222.20	1586.18	1271.49	1085.31	878.01	815.54	731.62	679.35
47000	4233.83	2270.51	1620.66	1299.13	1108.90	897.09	833.27	747.52	694.11
48000	4323.91	2318.82	1655.14	1326.77	1132.50	916.18	851.00	763.43	708.88
49000	4414.00	2367.13	1689.62	1354.42	1156.09	935.27	868.73	779.33	723.65
50000	4504.08	2415.44	1724.10	1382.06	1179.68	954.35	886.46	795.24	738.42
51000	4594.16	2463.75	1758.59	1409.70	1203.28	973.44	904.19	811.14	753.19
52000	4684.24	2512.06	1793.07	1437.34	1226.87	992.53	921.92	827.05	767.96
53000	4774.32	2560.36	1827.55	1464.98	1250.46	1011.61	939.65	842.95	782.72
54000	4864.40	2608.67	1862.03	1492.62	1274.06	1030.70	957.37	858.85	797.49
55000	4954.49	2656.98	1896.51	1520.26	1297.65	1049.79	975.10	874.76	812.26
56000	5044.57	2705.29	1931.00	1547.90	1321.24	1068.88	992.83	890.66	827.03
57000	5134.65	2753.60	1965.48	1575.54	1344.84	1087.96	1010.56	906.57	841.80
58000	5224.73	2801.91	1999.96	1603.18	1368.43	1107.05	1028.29	922.47	856.56
59000	5314.81	2850.22	2034.44	1630.83	1392.02	1126.14	1046.02	938.38	871.33
60000	5404.89	2898.53	2068.92	1658.47	1415.62	1145.22	1063.75	954.28	886.10
61000	5494.97	2946.83	2103.41	1686.11	1439.21	1164.31	1081.48	970.19	900.87
62000	5585.06	2995.14	2137.89	1713.75	1462.80	1183.40	1099.21	986.09	915.64
63000	5675.14	3043.45	2172.37	1741.39	1486.40	1202.48	1116.94	1002.00	930.41
64000	5765.22	3091.76	2206.85	1769.03	1509.99	1221.57	1134.67	1017.90	945.17
65000	5855.30	3140.07	2241.33	1796.67	1533.59	1240.66	1152.39	1033.81	959.94
67500	6080.50	3260.84	2327.54	1865.77	1592.57	1288.38	1196.72	1073.57	996.86
70000	6305.71	3381.61	2413.74	1934.88	1651.55	1336.09	1241.04	1113.33	1033.78
75000	6756.11	3623.16	2586.15	2073.08	1769.52	1431.53	1329.69	1192.85	1107.63
80000	7206.52	3864.70	2758.56	2211.29	1887.49	1526.96	1418.33	1272.37	1181.47
85000	7656.93	4106.24	2930.97	2349.49	2005.46	1622.40	1506.98	1351.90	1255.31
90000	8107.34	4347.79	3103.38	2487.70	2123.42	1717.83	1595.62	1431.42	1329.15
95000	8557.74	4589.33	3275.79	2625.90	2241.39	1813.27	1684.27	1510.94	1402.99
100000	9008.15	4830.87	3448.20	2764.11	2359.36	1908.70	1772.91	1590.47	1476.83
105000	9458.56	5072.42	3620.61	2902.31	2477.33	2004.14	1861.56	1669.99	1550.67
110000	9908.97	5313.96	3793.02	3040.52	2595.29	2099.57	1950.20	1749.51	1624.52
115000	10359.37	5555.50	3965.43	3178.72	2713.26	2195.01	2038.85	1829.04	1698.36
120000	10809.78	5797.05	4137.84	3316.93	2831.23	2290.44	2127.49	1908.56	1772.20
125000	11260.19	6038.59	4310.25	3455.13	2949.20	2385.88	2216.14	1988.08	1846.04
130000	11710.59	6280.13	4482.66	3593.34	3067.17	2481.31	2304.78	2067.61	1919.88
135000	12161.00	6521.68	4655.07	3731.54	3185.13	2576.75	2393.43	2147.13	1993.72
140000	12611.41	6763.22	4827.48	3869.75	3303.10	2672.18	2482.07	2226.65	2067.56
145000	13061.82	7004.76	4999.89	4007.95	3421.07	2767.61	2570.72	2306.18	2141.40
150000	13512.22	7246.31	5172.30	4146.16	3539.04	2863.05	2659.37	2385.70	2215.25

MONTHLY PAYMENT 14⅝%

NECESSARY TO AMORTIZE A LOAN

AMOUNT	15 YEARS	18 YEARS	20 YEARS	25 YEARS	28 YEARS	29 YEARS	30 YEARS	35 YEARS	40 YEARS
$ 50	.69	.66	.65	.63	.62	.62	.62	.62	.62
100	1.38	1.32	1.29	1.26	1.24	1.24	1.24	1.23	1.23
200	2.75	2.63	2.58	2.51	2.48	2.48	2.47	2.46	2.45
300	4.13	3.95	3.87	3.76	3.72	3.72	3.71	3.68	3.67
400	5.50	5.26	5.16	5.01	4.96	4.95	4.94	4.91	4.89
500	6.87	6.58	6.45	6.26	6.20	6.19	6.18	6.14	6.12
600	8.25	7.89	7.74	7.52	7.44	7.43	7.41	7.36	7.34
700	9.62	9.21	9.03	8.77	8.68	8.66	8.65	8.59	8.56
800	11.00	10.52	10.32	10.02	9.92	9.90	9.88	9.82	9.78
900	12.37	11.84	11.61	11.27	11.16	11.14	11.12	11.04	11.01
1000	13.74	13.15	12.90	12.52	12.40	12.38	12.35	12.27	12.23
2000	27.48	26.30	25.79	25.04	24.80	24.75	24.70	24.53	24.45
3000	41.22	39.45	38.68	37.56	37.20	37.12	37.04	36.79	36.68
4000	54.96	52.60	51.57	50.08	49.60	49.49	49.39	49.06	48.90
5000	68.70	65.74	64.46	62.60	62.00	61.86	61.73	61.32	61.12
6000	82.44	78.89	77.36	75.11	74.40	74.23	74.08	73.58	73.35
7000	96.18	92.04	90.25	87.63	86.80	86.60	86.42	85.85	85.57
8000	109.92	105.19	103.14	100.15	99.20	98.97	98.77	98.11	97.80
9000	123.66	118.34	116.03	112.67	111.60	111.34	111.11	110.37	110.02
10000	137.40	131.48	128.92	125.19	124.00	123.71	123.46	122.64	122.24
15000	206.10	197.22	193.38	187.78	185.99	185.56	185.18	183.95	183.36
20000	274.80	262.96	257.84	250.37	247.99	247.41	246.91	245.27	244.48
25000	343.50	328.70	322.30	312.96	309.98	309.26	308.63	306.58	305.60
30000	412.20	394.44	386.76	375.55	371.98	371.11	370.36	367.90	366.72
35000	480.90	460.18	451.21	438.14	433.98	432.96	432.08	429.22	427.84
40000	549.60	525.92	515.67	500.73	495.97	494.81	493.81	490.53	488.96
45000	618.30	591.66	580.13	563.32	557.97	556.66	555.53	551.85	550.08
46000	632.04	604.81	593.02	575.84	570.37	569.03	567.88	564.11	562.31
47000	645.78	617.96	605.91	588.35	582.77	581.40	580.22	576.37	574.53
48000	659.52	631.11	618.81	600.87	595.17	593.77	592.57	588.64	586.76
49000	673.26	644.26	631.70	613.39	607.57	606.14	604.91	600.90	598.98
50000	687.00	657.40	644.59	625.91	619.96	618.51	617.26	613.16	611.20
51000	700.74	670.55	657.48	638.43	632.36	630.88	629.60	625.43	623.43
52000	714.48	683.70	670.37	650.94	644.76	643.25	641.95	637.69	635.65
53000	728.22	696.85	683.26	663.46	657.16	655.62	654.30	649.95	647.88
54000	741.96	710.00	696.16	675.98	669.56	667.99	666.64	662.22	660.10
55000	755.70	723.14	709.05	688.50	681.96	680.36	678.99	674.48	672.32
56000	769.44	736.29	721.94	701.02	694.36	692.73	691.33	686.74	684.55
57000	783.18	749.44	734.83	713.53	706.76	705.10	703.68	699.01	696.77
58000	796.92	762.59	747.72	726.05	719.16	717.47	716.02	711.27	709.00
59000	810.66	775.74	760.61	738.57	731.56	729.84	728.37	723.53	721.22
60000	824.40	788.88	773.51	751.09	743.96	742.21	740.71	735.80	733.44
61000	838.14	802.03	786.40	763.61	756.36	754.58	753.06	748.06	745.67
62000	851.88	815.18	799.29	776.12	768.76	766.95	765.40	760.32	757.89
63000	865.62	828.33	812.18	788.64	781.15	779.32	777.75	772.59	770.12
64000	879.36	841.48	825.07	801.16	793.55	791.69	790.09	784.85	782.34
65000	893.10	854.62	837.96	813.68	805.95	804.06	802.44	797.11	794.56
67500	927.45	887.49	870.19	844.97	836.95	834.99	833.30	827.77	825.12
70000	961.80	920.36	902.42	876.27	867.95	865.91	864.16	858.43	855.68
75000	1030.50	986.10	966.88	938.86	929.94	927.76	925.89	919.74	916.80
80000	1099.20	1051.84	1031.34	1001.45	991.94	989.61	987.61	981.06	977.92
85000	1167.90	1117.58	1095.80	1064.04	1053.94	1051.47	1049.34	1042.38	1039.04
90000	1236.60	1183.32	1160.26	1126.63	1115.93	1113.32	1111.06	1103.69	1100.16
95000	1305.30	1249.06	1224.71	1189.22	1177.93	1175.17	1172.79	1165.01	1161.28
100000	1374.00	1314.80	1289.17	1251.81	1239.92	1237.02	1234.51	1226.32	1222.40
105000	1442.70	1380.54	1353.63	1314.40	1301.92	1298.87	1296.24	1287.64	1283.52
110000	1511.40	1446.28	1418.09	1376.99	1363.92	1360.72	1357.97	1348.96	1344.64
115000	1580.10	1512.02	1482.55	1439.58	1425.91	1422.57	1419.69	1410.27	1405.76
120000	1648.80	1577.76	1547.01	1502.17	1487.91	1484.42	1481.42	1471.59	1466.88
125000	1717.50	1643.50	1611.46	1564.76	1549.90	1546.27	1543.14	1532.90	1528.00
130000	1786.19	1709.24	1675.92	1627.35	1611.90	1608.12	1604.87	1594.22	1589.12
135000	1854.89	1774.98	1740.38	1689.94	1673.90	1669.97	1666.59	1655.53	1650.24
140000	1923.59	1840.72	1804.84	1752.53	1735.89	1731.82	1728.32	1716.85	1711.36
145000	1992.29	1906.46	1869.30	1815.12	1797.89	1793.67	1790.04	1778.17	1772.48
150000	2060.99	1972.20	1933.76	1877.71	1859.88	1855.52	1851.77	1839.48	1833.60

14¾% MONTHLY PAYMENT
NECESSARY TO AMORTIZE A LOAN

AMOUNT	1 YEAR	2 YEARS	3 YEARS	4 YEARS	5 YEARS	7 YEARS	8 YEARS	10 YEARS	12 YEARS
$ 50	4.51	2.42	1.73	1.39	1.19	.96	.90	.80	.75
100	9.02	4.84	3.46	2.78	2.37	1.92	1.79	1.60	1.49
200	18.03	9.68	6.91	5.55	4.74	3.84	3.57	3.20	2.97
300	27.05	14.52	10.37	8.32	7.10	5.75	5.35	4.80	4.46
400	36.06	19.35	13.82	11.09	9.47	7.67	7.13	6.40	5.94
500	45.08	24.19	17.28	13.86	11.83	9.58	8.91	8.00	7.43
600	54.09	29.03	20.73	16.63	14.20	11.50	10.69	9.59	8.91
700	63.10	33.86	24.19	19.40	16.57	13.41	12.47	11.19	10.40
800	72.12	38.70	27.64	22.17	18.93	15.33	14.25	12.79	11.88
900	81.13	43.54	31.09	24.94	21.30	17.25	16.03	14.39	13.37
1000	90.15	48.37	34.55	27.71	23.66	19.16	17.81	15.99	14.85
2000	180.29	96.74	69.09	55.41	47.32	38.32	35.61	31.97	29.70
3000	270.43	145.11	103.63	83.12	70.98	57.48	53.41	47.95	44.55
4000	360.57	193.48	138.18	110.82	94.64	76.63	71.21	63.93	59.40
5000	450.71	241.84	172.72	138.53	118.30	95.79	89.01	79.91	74.25
6000	540.85	290.21	207.26	166.23	141.96	114.95	106.81	95.89	89.09
7000	630.99	338.58	241.81	193.93	165.62	134.10	124.61	111.87	103.94
8000	721.13	386.95	276.35	221.64	189.28	153.26	142.41	127.85	118.79
9000	811.27	435.32	310.89	249.34	212.94	172.42	160.21	143.83	133.64
10000	901.41	483.68	345.44	277.05	236.59	191.57	178.02	159.81	148.49
15000	1352.11	725.52	518.15	415.57	354.89	287.36	267.02	239.72	222.73
20000	1802.81	967.36	690.87	554.09	473.18	383.14	356.03	319.62	296.97
25000	2253.51	1209.20	863.58	692.61	591.48	478.92	445.03	399.52	371.21
30000	2704.22	1451.04	1036.30	831.13	709.77	574.71	534.04	479.43	445.45
35000	3154.92	1692.88	1209.01	969.65	828.07	670.49	623.04	559.33	519.69
40000	3605.62	1934.72	1381.73	1108.17	946.36	766.28	712.05	639.23	593.94
45000	4056.32	2176.56	1554.44	1246.69	1064.66	862.06	801.05	719.14	668.18
46000	4146.46	2224.93	1588.98	1274.40	1088.31	881.22	818.85	735.12	683.02
47000	4236.60	2273.30	1623.53	1302.10	1111.97	900.37	836.65	751.10	697.87
48000	4326.74	2321.67	1658.07	1329.81	1135.63	919.53	854.45	767.08	712.72
49000	4416.88	2370.03	1692.61	1357.51	1159.29	938.69	872.26	783.06	727.57
50000	4507.02	2418.40	1727.16	1385.21	1182.95	957.84	890.06	799.04	742.42
51000	4597.16	2466.77	1761.70	1412.92	1206.61	977.00	907.86	815.02	757.27
52000	4687.31	2515.14	1796.24	1440.62	1230.27	996.16	925.66	831.00	772.11
53000	4777.45	2563.51	1830.79	1468.33	1253.93	1015.31	943.46	846.98	786.96
54000	4867.59	2611.87	1865.33	1496.03	1277.59	1034.47	961.26	862.97	801.81
55000	4957.73	2660.24	1899.87	1523.74	1301.24	1053.63	979.06	878.95	816.66
56000	5047.87	2708.61	1934.41	1551.44	1324.90	1072.78	996.86	894.93	831.51
57000	5138.01	2756.98	1968.96	1579.14	1348.56	1091.94	1014.66	910.91	846.36
58000	5228.15	2805.35	2003.50	1606.85	1372.22	1111.10	1032.46	926.89	861.20
59000	5318.29	2853.71	2038.04	1634.55	1395.88	1130.25	1050.27	942.87	876.05
60000	5408.43	2902.08	2072.59	1662.26	1419.54	1149.41	1068.07	958.85	890.90
61000	5498.57	2950.45	2107.13	1689.96	1443.20	1168.57	1085.87	974.83	905.75
62000	5588.71	2998.82	2141.67	1717.66	1466.86	1187.72	1103.67	990.81	920.60
63000	5678.85	3047.19	2176.22	1745.37	1490.52	1206.88	1121.47	1006.79	935.44
64000	5768.99	3095.55	2210.76	1773.07	1514.17	1226.04	1139.27	1022.77	950.29
65000	5859.13	3143.92	2245.30	1800.78	1537.83	1245.19	1157.07	1038.75	965.14
67500	6084.48	3264.84	2331.66	1870.04	1596.98	1293.09	1201.57	1078.71	1002.26
70000	6309.83	3385.76	2418.02	1939.30	1656.13	1340.98	1246.08	1118.66	1039.38
75000	6760.53	3627.60	2590.73	2077.82	1774.42	1436.76	1335.08	1198.56	1113.62
80000	7211.24	3869.44	2763.45	2216.34	1892.72	1532.55	1424.09	1278.46	1187.87
85000	7661.94	4111.28	2936.16	2354.86	2011.01	1628.33	1513.09	1358.37	1262.11
90000	8112.64	4353.12	3108.88	2493.38	2129.31	1724.11	1602.10	1438.27	1336.35
95000	8563.34	4594.96	3281.59	2631.90	2247.60	1819.90	1691.10	1518.18	1410.59
100000	9014.04	4836.80	3454.31	2770.42	2365.90	1915.68	1780.11	1598.08	1484.83
105000	9464.75	5078.64	3627.02	2908.94	2484.19	2011.46	1869.11	1677.98	1559.07
110000	9915.45	5320.48	3799.74	3047.47	2602.48	2107.25	1958.12	1757.89	1633.31
115000	10366.15	5562.32	3972.45	3185.99	2720.78	2203.03	2047.12	1837.79	1707.55
120000	10816.85	5804.16	4145.17	3324.51	2839.07	2298.82	2136.13	1917.69	1781.80
125000	11267.55	6046.00	4317.88	3463.03	2957.37	2394.60	2225.13	1997.60	1856.04
130000	11718.26	6287.84	4490.60	3601.55	3075.66	2490.38	2314.14	2077.50	1930.28
135000	12168.96	6529.68	4663.31	3740.07	3193.96	2586.17	2403.14	2157.41	2004.52
140000	12619.66	6771.52	4836.03	3878.59	3312.25	2681.95	2492.15	2237.31	2078.76
145000	13070.36	7013.36	5008.74	4017.11	3430.55	2777.74	2581.15	2317.21	2153.00
150000	13521.06	7255.20	5181.46	4155.63	3548.84	2873.52	2670.16	2397.12	2227.24

128

MONTHLY PAYMENT 14¾%
NECESSARY TO AMORTIZE A LOAN

AMOUNT	15 YEARS	18 YEARS	20 YEARS	25 YEARS	28 YEARS	29 YEARS	30 YEARS	35 YEARS	40 YEARS
$ 50	.70	.67	.65	.64	63	63	63	62	62
100	1.39	1.33	1.30	1.27	1.25	1.25	1.25	1.24	1.24
200	2.77	2.65	2.60	2.53	2.50	2.50	2.49	2.48	2.47
300	4.15	3.98	3.90	3.79	3.75	3.75	3.74	3.71	3.70
400	5.54	5.30	5.20	5.05	5.00	4.99	4.98	4.95	4.94
500	6.92	6.62	6.50	6.31	6.25	6.24	6.23	6.19	6.17
600	8.30	7.95	7.80	7.57	7.50	7.49	7.47	7.42	7.40
700	9.68	9.27	9.09	8.84	8.75	8.73	8.72	8.66	8.63
800	11.07	10.59	10.39	10.10	10.00	9.98	9.96	9.90	9.87
900	12.45	11.92	11.69	11.36	11.25	11.23	11.21	11.13	11.10
1000	13.83	13.24	12.99	12.62	12.50	12.47	12.45	12.37	12.33
2000	27.66	26.48	25.97	25.23	25.00	24.94	24.89	24.73	24.66
3000	41.48	39.72	38.96	37.85	37.50	37.41	37.34	37.10	36.99
4000	55.31	52.95	51.94	50.46	50.00	49.88	49.78	49.46	49.31
5000	69.13	66.19	64.92	63.08	62.49	62.35	62.23	61.83	61.64
6000	82.96	79.43	77.91	75.69	74.99	74.82	74.67	74.19	73.97
7000	96.78	92.67	90.89	88.31	87.49	87.29	87.12	86.56	86.29
8000	110.61	105.90	103.87	100.92	99.99	99.76	99.56	98.92	98.62
9000	124.43	119.14	116.86	113.54	112.49	112.23	112.01	111.29	110.95
10000	138.26	132.38	129.84	126.15	124.98	124.70	124.45	123.65	123.27
15000	207.38	198.57	194.76	189.22	187.47	187.04	186.68	185.48	184.91
20000	276.51	264.75	259.68	252.30	249.96	249.39	248.90	247.30	246.54
25000	345.63	330.94	324.59	315.37	312.45	311.74	311.12	309.12	308.17
30000	414.76	397.13	389.51	378.44	374.94	374.08	373.35	370.95	369.81
35000	483.88	463.31	454.43	441.52	437.43	436.43	435.57	432.77	431.44
40000	553.01	529.50	519.35	504.59	499.92	498.78	497.80	494.59	493.07
45000	622.13	595.69	584.26	567.66	562.41	561.12	560.02	556.42	554.71
46000	635.96	608.93	597.25	580.28	574.90	573.59	572.46	568.78	567.03
47000	649.78	622.16	610.23	592.89	587.40	586.06	584.91	581.15	579.36
48000	663.61	635.40	623.22	605.51	599.90	598.53	597.35	593.51	591.69
49000	677.43	648.64	636.20	618.12	612.40	611.00	609.80	605.88	604.01
50000	691.26	661.88	649.18	630.74	624.89	623.47	622.24	618.24	616.34
51000	705.08	675.11	662.17	643.35	637.39	635.94	634.69	630.61	628.67
52000	718.91	688.35	675.15	655.97	649.89	648.41	647.13	642.97	640.99
53000	732.73	701.59	688.13	668.58	662.39	660.88	659.58	655.34	653.32
54000	746.56	714.83	701.12	681.20	674.89	673.35	672.02	667.70	665.65
55000	760.38	728.06	714.10	693.81	687.38	685.82	684.47	680.07	677.97
56000	774.21	741.30	727.08	706.43	699.88	698.28	696.91	692.43	690.30
57000	788.03	754.54	740.07	719.04	712.38	710.75	709.36	704.80	702.63
58000	801.86	767.78	753.05	731.65	724.88	723.22	721.80	717.16	714.95
59000	815.68	781.01	766.03	744.27	737.37	735.69	734.25	729.53	727.28
60000	829.51	794.25	779.02	756.88	749.87	748.16	746.69	741.89	739.61
61000	843.33	807.49	792.00	769.50	762.37	760.63	759.14	754.25	751.93
62000	857.16	820.73	804.99	782.11	774.87	773.10	771.58	766.62	764.26
63000	870.98	833.96	817.97	794.73	787.37	785.57	784.02	778.98	776.59
64000	884.81	847.20	830.95	807.34	799.86	798.04	796.47	791.35	788.91
65000	898.63	860.44	843.94	819.96	812.36	810.51	808.91	803.71	801.24
67500	933.20	893.53	876.39	851.49	843.61	841.68	840.03	834.63	832.06
70000	967.76	926.62	908.85	883.03	874.85	872.85	871.14	865.54	862.87
75000	1036.88	992.81	973.77	946.10	937.34	935.20	933.36	927.36	924.51
80000	1106.01	1059.00	1038.69	1009.18	999.83	997.55	995.59	939.18	986.14
85000	1175.13	1125.19	1103.61	1072.25	1062.32	1059.89	1057.81	1051.01	1047.77
90000	1244.26	1191.37	1168.52	1135.32	1124.81	1122.24	1120.03	1112.83	1109.41
95000	1313.38	1257.56	1233.44	1198.40	1187.30	1184.59	1182.26	1174.66	1171.04
100000	1382.51	1323.75	1298.36	1261.47	1249.78	1246.93	1244.48	1236.48	1232.67
105000	1451.63	1389.93	1363.28	1324.54	1312.27	1309.28	1306.70	1298.30	1294.31
110000	1520.76	1456.12	1428.20	1387.62	1374.76	1371.63	1368.93	1360.13	1355.94
115000	1589.88	1522.31	1493.11	1450.69	1437.25	1433.97	1431.15	1421.95	1417.57
120000	1659.01	1588.50	1558.03	1513.76	1499.74	1496.32	1493.38	1483.77	1479.21
125000	1728.13	1654.68	1622.95	1576.84	1562.23	1558.66	1555.60	1545.60	1540.84
130000	1797.26	1720.87	1687.87	1639.91	1624.72	1621.01	1617.82	1607.42	1602.47
135000	1866.39	1787.06	1752.78	1702.98	1687.21	1683.36	1680.05	1669.25	1664.11
140000	1935.51	1853.24	1817.70	1766.06	1749.70	1745.70	1742.27	1731.07	1725.74
145000	2004.64	1919.43	1882.62	1829.13	1812.18	1808.05	1804.49	1792.89	1787.37
150000	2073.76	1985.62	1947.54	1892.20	1874.67	1870.40	1866.72	1854.72	1849.01

14⅞% MONTHLY PAYMENT
NECESSARY TO AMORTIZE A LOAN

AMOUNT	1 YEAR	2 YEARS	3 YEARS	4 YEARS	5 YEARS	7 YEARS	8 YEARS	10 YEARS	12 YEARS
$ 50	4.51	2.43	1.74	1.39	1.19	.97	.90	.81	.75
100	9.02	4.85	3.47	2.78	2.38	1.93	1.79	1.61	1.50
200	18.04	9.69	6.93	5.56	4.75	3.85	3.58	3.22	2.99
300	27.06	14.53	10.39	8.34	7.12	5.77	5.37	4.82	4.48
400	36.08	19.38	13.85	11.11	9.49	7.70	7.15	6.43	5.98
500	45.10	24.22	17.31	13.89	11.87	9.62	8.94	8.03	7.47
600	54.12	29.06	20.77	16.67	14.24	11.54	10.73	9.64	8.96
700	63.14	33.90	24.23	19.44	16.61	13.46	12.52	11.24	10.45
800	72.16	38.75	27.69	22.22	18.98	15.39	14.30	12.85	11.95
900	81.18	43.59	31.15	25.00	21.36	17.31	16.09	14.46	13.44
1000	90.20	48.43	34.61	27.77	23.73	19.23	17.88	16.06	14.93
2000	180.40	96.86	69.21	55.54	47.45	38.46	35.75	32.12	29.86
3000	270.60	145.29	103.82	83.31	71.18	57.69	53.62	48.18	44.79
4000	360.80	193.71	138.42	111.07	94.90	76.91	71.50	64.23	59.72
5000	451.00	242.14	173.03	138.84	118.63	96.14	89.37	80.29	74.65
6000	541.20	290.57	207.63	166.61	142.35	115.37	107.24	96.35	89.58
7000	631.40	339.00	242.23	194.38	166.08	134.59	125.12	112.40	104.50
8000	721.60	387.42	276.84	222.14	189.80	153.82	142.99	128.46	119.43
9000	811.80	435.85	311.44	249.91	213.52	173.05	160.86	144.52	134.36
10000	902.00	484.28	346.05	277.68	237.25	192.27	178.74	160.58	149.29
15000	1353.00	726.41	519.07	416.52	355.87	288.41	268.10	240.86	223.93
20000	1803.99	968.55	692.09	555.35	474.49	384.54	357.47	321.15	298.57
25000	2254.99	1210.69	865.11	694.19	593.11	480.67	446.83	401.43	373.22
30000	2705.99	1452.82	1038.13	833.03	711.74	576.81	536.20	481.72	447.86
35000	3156.98	1694.96	1211.15	971.86	830.36	672.94	625.57	562.00	522.50
40000	3607.98	1937.10	1384.17	1110.70	948.98	769.07	714.93	642.29	597.14
45000	4058.98	2179.23	1557.19	1249.54	1067.60	865.21	804.30	722.57	671.78
46000	4149.17	2227.66	1591.80	1277.31	1091.33	884.43	822.17	738.63	686.71
47000	4239.37	2276.09	1626.40	1305.07	1115.05	903.66	840.04	754.69	701.64
48000	4329.57	2324.51	1661.00	1332.84	1138.77	922.89	857.92	770.74	716.57
49000	4419.77	2372.94	1695.61	1360.61	1162.50	942.11	875.79	786.80	731.50
50000	4509.97	2421.37	1730.21	1388.38	1186.22	961.34	893.66	802.86	746.43
51000	4600.17	2469.80	1764.82	1416.14	1209.95	980.57	911.54	818.91	761.35
52000	4690.37	2518.22	1799.42	1443.91	1233.67	999.79	929.41	834.97	776.28
53000	4780.57	2566.65	1834.02	1471.68	1257.40	1019.02	947.28	851.03	791.21
54000	4870.77	2615.08	1868.63	1499.45	1281.12	1038.25	965.15	867.08	806.14
55000	4960.97	2663.51	1903.23	1527.21	1304.85	1057.47	983.03	883.14	821.07
56000	5051.17	2711.93	1937.84	1554.98	1328.57	1076.70	1000.90	899.20	836.00
57000	5141.37	2760.36	1972.44	1582.75	1352.29	1095.93	1018.77	915.26	850.92
58000	5231.57	2808.79	2007.05	1610.52	1376.02	1115.15	1036.65	931.31	865.85
59000	5321.77	2857.21	2041.65	1638.28	1399.74	1134.38	1054.52	947.37	880.78
60000	5411.97	2905.64	2076.25	1666.05	1423.47	1153.61	1072.39	963.43	895.71
61000	5502.16	2954.07	2110.86	1693.82	1447.19	1172.83	1090.27	979.48	910.64
62000	5592.36	3002.50	2145.46	1721.59	1470.92	1192.06	1108.14	995.54	925.57
63000	5682.56	3050.92	2180.07	1749.35	1494.64	1211.29	1126.01	1011.60	940.50
64000	5772.76	3099.35	2214.67	1777.12	1518.36	1230.51	1143.89	1027.66	955.42
65000	5862.96	3147.78	2249.27	1804.89	1542.09	1249.74	1161.76	1043.71	970.35
67500	6088.46	3268.85	2335.78	1874.31	1601.40	1297.81	1206.44	1083.85	1007.67
70000	6313.96	3389.91	2422.30	1943.72	1660.71	1345.87	1251.13	1124.00	1044.99
75000	6764.96	3632.05	2595.32	2082.56	1779.33	1442.01	1340.49	1204.28	1119.64
80000	7215.95	3874.19	2768.34	2221.40	1897.95	1538.14	1429.86	1284.57	1194.28
85000	7666.95	4116.32	2941.36	2360.24	2016.58	1634.27	1519.22	1364.85	1268.92
90000	8117.95	4358.46	3114.38	2499.07	2135.20	1730.41	1608.59	1445.14	1343.56
95000	8568.94	4600.60	3287.40	2637.91	2253.82	1826.54	1697.95	1525.42	1418.20
100000	9019.94	4842.73	3460.42	2776.75	2372.44	1922.67	1787.32	1605.71	1492.85
105000	9470.94	5084.87	3633.44	2915.58	2491.06	2018.81	1876.69	1685.99	1567.49
110000	9921.93	5327.01	3806.46	3054.42	2609.69	2114.94	1966.05	1766.28	1642.13
115000	10372.93	5569.14	3979.48	3193.26	2728.31	2211.07	2055.42	1846.56	1716.77
120000	10823.93	5811.28	4152.50	3332.10	2846.93	2307.21	2144.78	1926.85	1791.41
125000	11274.92	6053.41	4325.52	3470.93	2965.55	2403.34	2234.15	2007.13	1866.06
130000	11725.92	6295.55	4498.54	3609.77	3084.17	2499.47	2323.51	2087.42	1940.70
135000	12176.92	6537.69	4671.56	3748.61	3202.79	2595.61	2412.88	2167.70	2015.34
140000	12627.91	6779.82	4844.59	3887.44	3321.42	2691.74	2502.25	2247.99	2089.98
145000	13078.91	7021.96	5017.61	4026.28	3440.04	2787.88	2591.61	2328.27	2164.63
150000	13529.91	7264.10	5190.63	4165.12	3558.66	2884.01	2680.98	2408.56	2239.27

MONTHLY PAYMENT 14⅞%
NECESSARY TO AMORTIZE A LOAN

AMOUNT	15 YEARS	18 YEARS	20 YEARS	25 YEARS	28 YEARS	29 YEARS	30 YEARS	35 YEARS	40 YEARS
$ 50	.70	.67	.66	.64	.63	.63	.63	.63	.63
100	1.40	1.34	1.31	1.28	1.26	1.26	1.26	1.25	1.25
200	2.79	2.67	2.62	2.55	2.52	2.52	2.51	2.50	2.49
300	4.18	4.00	3.93	3.82	3.78	3.78	3.77	3.74	3.73
400	5.57	5.34	5.24	5.09	5.04	5.03	5.02	4.99	4.98
500	6.96	6.67	6.54	6.36	6.30	6.29	6.28	6.24	6.22
600	8.35	8.00	7.85	7.63	7.56	7.55	7.53	7.48	7.46
700	9.74	9.33	9.16	8.90	8.82	8.80	8.79	8.73	8.71
800	11.13	10.67	10.47	10.17	10.08	10.06	10.04	9.98	9.95
900	12.52	12.00	11.77	11.45	11.34	11.32	11.30	11.22	11.19
1000	13.92	13.33	13.08	12.72	12.60	12.57	12.55	12.47	12.43
2000	27.83	26.66	26.16	25.43	25.20	25.14	25.09	24.94	24.86
3000	41.74	39.99	39.23	38.14	37.79	37.71	37.64	37.40	37.29
4000	55.65	53.31	52.31	50.85	50.39	50.28	50.18	49.87	49.72
5000	69.56	66.64	65.38	63.56	62.99	62.85	62.73	62.34	62.15
6000	83.47	79.97	78.46	76.27	75.58	75.42	75.27	74.80	74.58
7000	97.38	93.29	91.53	88.98	88.18	87.98	87.82	87.27	87.01
8000	111.29	106.62	104.61	101.70	100.78	100.55	100.36	99.74	99.44
9000	125.20	119.95	117.69	114.41	113.37	113.12	112.91	112.20	111.87
10000	139.11	133.28	130.76	127.12	125.97	125.69	125.45	124.67	124.30
15000	208.66	199.91	196.14	190.68	188.95	188.53	188.17	187.00	186.45
20000	278.21	266.55	261.52	254.23	251.94	251.38	250.90	249.33	248.59
25000	347.76	333.18	326.90	317.79	314.92	314.22	313.62	311.66	310.74
30000	417.32	399.82	392.27	381.35	377.90	377.06	376.34	374.00	372.89
35000	486.87	466.45	457.65	444.90	440.88	439.90	439.06	436.33	435.04
40000	556.42	533.09	523.03	508.46	503.87	502.75	501.79	498.66	497.18
45000	625.97	599.72	588.41	572.02	566.85	565.59	564.51	560.99	559.33
46000	639.88	613.05	601.48	584.73	579.45	578.16	577.05	573.46	571.76
47000	653.79	626.38	614.56	597.44	592.04	590.73	589.60	585.93	584.19
48000	667.70	639.70	627.64	610.15	604.64	603.30	602.14	598.39	596.62
49000	681.61	653.03	640.71	622.86	617.23	615.86	614.69	610.86	609.05
50000	695.52	666.36	653.79	635.57	629.83	628.43	627.23	623.32	621.48
51000	709.43	679.69	666.86	648.29	642.43	641.00	639.78	635.79	633.91
52000	723.34	693.01	679.94	661.00	655.02	653.57	652.32	648.26	646.34
53000	737.25	706.34	693.01	673.71	667.62	666.14	664.87	660.72	658.76
54000	751.16	719.67	706.09	686.42	680.22	678.71	677.41	673.19	671.19
55000	765.07	732.99	719.16	699.13	692.81	691.28	689.95	685.66	683.62
56000	778.98	746.32	732.24	711.84	705.41	703.84	702.50	698.12	696.05
57000	792.90	759.65	745.32	724.55	718.01	716.41	715.04	710.59	708.48
58000	806.81	772.97	758.39	737.27	730.60	728.98	727.59	723.06	720.91
59000	820.72	786.30	771.47	749.98	743.20	741.55	740.13	735.52	733.34
60000	834.63	799.63	784.54	762.69	755.80	754.12	752.68	747.99	745.77
61000	848.54	812.96	797.62	775.40	768.39	766.69	765.22	760.46	758.20
62000	862.45	826.28	810.69	788.11	780.99	779.26	777.77	772.92	770.63
63000	876.36	839.61	823.77	800.82	793.59	791.82	790.31	785.39	783.06
64000	890.27	852.94	836.85	813.53	806.18	804.39	802.86	797.85	795.49
65000	904.18	866.26	849.92	826.25	818.78	816.96	815.40	810.32	807.92
67500	938.95	899.58	882.61	858.02	850.27	848.38	846.76	841.49	838.99
70000	973.73	932.90	915.30	889.80	881.76	879.80	878.12	872.65	870.07
75000	1043.28	999.54	980.68	953.36	944.74	942.65	940.85	934.98	932.21
80000	1112.83	1066.17	1046.06	1016.92	1007.73	1005.49	1003.57	997.32	994.36
85000	1182.39	1132.81	1111.43	1080.47	1070.71	1068.33	1066.29	1059.65	1056.51
90000	1251.94	1199.44	1176.81	1144.03	1133.69	1131.18	1129.01	1121.98	1118.65
95000	1321.49	1266.08	1242.19	1207.59	1196.68	1194.02	1191.74	1184.31	1180.80
100000	1391.04	1332.71	1307.57	1271.14	1259.66	1256.86	1254.46	1246.64	1242.95
105000	1460.59	1399.35	1372.95	1334.70	1322.64	1319.70	1317.18	1308.98	1305.10
110000	1530.14	1465.98	1438.32	1398.26	1385.62	1382.55	1379.90	1371.31	1367.24
115000	1599.70	1532.62	1503.70	1461.82	1448.61	1445.39	1442.63	1433.64	1429.39
120000	1669.25	1599.25	1569.08	1525.37	1511.59	1508.23	1505.35	1495.97	1491.54
125000	1738.80	1665.89	1634.46	1588.93	1574.57	1571.08	1568.07	1558.30	1553.68
130000	1808.35	1732.52	1699.84	1652.49	1637.55	1633.92	1630.80	1620.64	1615.83
135000	1877.90	1799.16	1765.22	1716.04	1700.54	1696.76	1693.52	1682.97	1677.98
140000	1947.45	1865.79	1830.59	1779.60	1763.52	1759.60	1756.24	1745.30	1740.13
145000	2017.01	1932.43	1895.97	1843.16	1826.50	1822.45	1818.96	1807.63	1802.27
150000	2086.56	1999.07	1961.35	1906.71	1889.48	1885.29	1881.69	1869.96	1864.42

15% MONTHLY PAYMENT
NECESSARY TO AMORTIZE A LOAN

AMOUNT	1 YEAR	2 YEARS	3 YEARS	4 YEARS	5 YEARS	7 YEARS	8 YEARS	10 YEARS	12 YEARS
$ 50	4.52	2.43	1.74	1.40	1.19	.97	.90	.81	.76
100	9.03	4.85	3.47	2.79	2.38	1.93	1.80	1.62	1.51
200	18.06	9.70	6.94	5.57	4.76	3.86	3.59	3.23	3.01
300	27.08	14.55	10.40	8.35	7.14	5.79	5.39	4.85	4.51
400	36.11	19.40	13.87	11.14	9.52	7.72	7.18	6.46	6.01
500	45.13	24.25	17.34	13.92	11.90	9.65	8.98	8.07	7.51
600	54.16	29.10	20.80	16.70	14.28	11.58	10.77	9.69	9.01
700	63.19	33.95	24.27	19.49	16.66	13.51	12.57	11.30	10.51
800	72.21	38.79	27.74	22.27	19.04	15.44	14.36	12.91	12.01
900	81.24	43.64	31.20	25.05	21.42	17.37	16.16	14.53	13.51
1000	90.26	48.49	34.67	27.84	23.79	19.30	17.95	16.14	15.01
2000	180.52	96.98	69.34	55.67	47.58	38.60	35.90	32.27	30.02
3000	270.78	145.46	104.00	83.50	71.37	57.90	53.84	48.41	45.03
4000	361.04	193.95	138.67	111.33	95.16	77.19	71.79	64.54	60.04
5000	451.30	242.44	173.33	139.16	118.95	96.49	89.73	80.67	75.05
6000	541.55	290.92	208.00	166.99	142.74	115.79	107.68	96.81	90.06
7000	631.81	339.41	242.66	194.82	166.53	135.08	125.62	112.94	105.07
8000	722.07	387.90	277.33	222.65	190.32	154.38	143.57	129.07	120.08
9000	812.33	436.38	311.99	250.48	214.11	173.68	161.51	145.21	135.08
10000	902.59	484.87	346.66	278.31	237.90	192.97	179.46	161.34	150.09
15000	1353.88	727.30	519.98	417.47	356.85	289.46	269.19	242.01	225.14
20000	1805.17	969.74	693.31	556.62	475.80	385.94	358.91	322.67	300.18
25000	2256.46	1212.17	866.64	695.77	594.75	482.42	448.64	403.34	375.22
30000	2707.75	1454.60	1039.96	834.93	713.70	578.91	538.37	484.01	450.27
35000	3159.05	1697.04	1213.29	974.08	832.65	675.39	628.09	564.68	525.31
40000	3610.34	1939.47	1386.62	1113.23	951.60	771.88	717.82	645.34	600.36
45000	4061.63	2181.90	1559.94	1252.39	1070.55	868.36	807.55	726.01	675.40
46000	4151.89	2230.39	1594.61	1280.22	1094.34	887.66	825.49	742.15	690.41
47000	4242.15	2278.88	1629.28	1308.05	1118.13	906.95	843.44	758.28	705.42
48000	4332.40	2327.36	1663.94	1335.88	1141.92	926.25	861.38	774.41	720.43
49000	4422.66	2375.85	1698.61	1363.71	1165.71	945.55	879.33	790.55	735.43
50000	4512.92	2424.34	1733.27	1391.54	1189.50	964.84	897.28	806.68	750.44
51000	4603.18	2472.82	1767.94	1419.37	1213.29	984.14	915.22	822.81	765.45
52000	4693.44	2521.31	1802.60	1447.20	1237.08	1003.44	933.17	838.95	780.46
53000	4783.70	2569.80	1837.27	1475.03	1260.87	1022.73	951.11	855.08	795.47
54000	4873.95	2618.28	1871.93	1502.87	1284.66	1042.03	969.06	871.21	810.48
55000	4964.21	2666.77	1906.60	1530.70	1308.45	1061.33	987.00	887.35	825.49
56000	5054.47	2715.26	1941.26	1558.53	1332.24	1080.62	1004.95	903.48	840.50
57000	5144.73	2763.74	1975.93	1586.36	1356.03	1099.92	1022.89	919.61	855.50
58000	5234.99	2812.23	2010.59	1614.19	1379.82	1119.22	1040.84	935.75	870.51
59000	5325.25	2860.72	2045.26	1642.02	1403.61	1138.51	1058.78	951.88	885.52
60000	5415.50	2909.20	2079.92	1669.85	1427.40	1157.81	1076.73	968.01	900.53
61000	5505.76	2957.69	2114.59	1697.68	1451.19	1177.11	1094.67	984.15	915.54
62000	5596.02	3006.18	2149.26	1725.51	1474.98	1196.40	1112.62	1000.28	930.55
63000	5686.28	3054.66	2183.92	1753.34	1498.77	1215.70	1130.57	1016.42	945.56
64000	5776.54	3103.15	2218.59	1781.17	1522.56	1235.00	1148.51	1032.55	960.57
65000	5866.80	3151.64	2253.25	1809.00	1546.35	1254.29	1166.46	1048.68	975.57
67500	6092.44	3272.85	2339.91	1878.58	1605.83	1302.54	1211.32	1089.02	1013.10
70000	6318.09	3394.07	2426.58	1948.16	1665.30	1350.78	1256.18	1129.35	1050.62
75000	6769.38	3636.50	2599.90	2087.31	1784.25	1447.26	1345.91	1210.02	1125.66
80000	7220.67	3878.94	2773.23	2226.46	1903.20	1543.75	1435.64	1290.68	1200.71
85000	7671.96	4121.37	2946.56	2365.62	2022.15	1640.23	1525.36	1371.35	1275.75
90000	8123.25	4363.80	3119.88	2504.77	2141.10	1736.71	1615.09	1452.02	1350.79
95000	8574.54	4606.24	3293.21	2643.93	2260.05	1833.20	1704.82	1532.69	1425.84
100000	9025.84	4848.67	3466.54	2783.08	2379.00	1929.68	1794.55	1613.35	1500.88
105000	9477.13	5091.10	3639.86	2922.23	2497.95	2026.16	1884.27	1694.02	1575.93
110000	9928.42	5333.54	3813.19	3061.39	2616.90	2122.65	1974.00	1774.69	1650.97
115000	10379.71	5575.97	3986.52	3200.54	2735.85	2219.13	2063.73	1855.36	1726.01
120000	10831.00	5818.40	4159.84	3339.69	2854.80	2315.62	2153.45	1936.02	1801.06
125000	11282.29	6060.84	4333.17	3478.85	2973.75	2412.10	2243.18	2016.69	1876.10
130000	11733.59	6303.27	4506.50	3618.00	3092.70	2508.58	2332.91	2097.36	1951.14
135000	12184.88	6545.70	4679.82	3757.16	3211.65	2605.07	2422.63	2178.03	2026.19
140000	12636.17	6788.14	4853.15	3896.31	3330.60	2701.55	2512.36	2258.69	2101.23
145000	13087.46	7030.57	5026.48	4035.46	3449.54	2798.03	2602.09	2339.36	2176.28
150000	13538.75	7273.00	5199.80	4174.62	3568.49	2894.52	2691.82	2420.03	2251.32

132

MONTHLY PAYMENT 15%

NECESSARY TO AMORTIZE A LOAN

AMOUNT	15 YEARS	18 YEARS	20 YEARS	25 YEARS	28 YEARS	29 YEARS	30 YEARS	35 YEARS	40 YEARS
$ 50	.70	.68	.66	.65	.64	.64	.64	.63	.63
100	1.40	1.35	1.32	1.29	1.27	1.27	1.27	1.26	1.26
200	2.80	2.69	2.64	2.57	2.54	2.54	2.53	2.52	2.51
300	4.20	4.03	3.96	3.85	3.81	3.81	3.80	3.78	3.76
400	5.60	5.37	5.27	5.13	5.08	5.07	5.06	5.03	5.02
500	7.00	6.71	6.59	6.41	6.35	6.34	6.33	6.29	6.27
600	8.40	8.06	7.91	7.69	7.62	7.61	7.59	7.55	7.52
700	9.80	9.40	9.22	8.97	8.89	8.87	8.86	8.80	8.78
800	11.20	10.74	10.54	10.25	10.16	10.14	10.12	10.06	10.03
900	12.60	12.08	11.86	11.53	11.43	11.41	11.38	11.32	11.28
1000	14.00	13.42	13.17	12.81	12.70	12.67	12.65	12.57	12.54
2000	28.00	26.84	26.34	25.62	25.40	25.34	25.29	25.14	25.07
3000	41.99	40.26	39.51	38.43	38.09	38.01	37.94	37.71	37.60
4000	55.99	53.67	52.68	51.24	50.79	50.68	50.58	50.28	50.13
5000	69.98	67.09	65.84	64.05	63.48	63.34	63.23	62.85	62.67
6000	83.98	80.51	79.01	76.85	76.18	76.01	75.87	75.41	75.20
7000	97.98	93.92	92.18	89.66	88.87	88.68	88.52	87.98	87.73
8000	111.97	107.34	105.35	102.47	101.57	101.35	101.16	100.55	100.26
9000	125.97	120.76	118.52	115.28	114.26	114.02	113.80	113.12	112.80
10000	139.96	134.17	131.68	128.09	126.96	126.68	126.45	125.69	125.33
15000	209.94	201.26	197.52	192.13	190.44	190.02	189.67	188.53	187.99
20000	279.92	268.34	263.36	256.17	253.91	253.36	252.89	251.37	250.65
25000	349.90	335.43	329.20	320.21	317.39	316.70	316.12	314.21	313.31
30000	419.88	402.51	395.04	384.25	380.87	380.04	379.34	377.05	375.97
35000	489.86	469.60	460.88	448.30	444.34	443.38	442.56	439.89	438.63
40000	559.84	536.68	526.72	512.34	507.82	506.72	505.78	502.73	501.29
45000	629.82	603.77	592.56	576.38	571.30	570.06	569.00	565.57	563.96
46000	643.82	617.18	605.73	589.19	583.99	582.73	581.65	578.14	576.49
47000	657.81	630.60	618.90	602.00	596.69	595.40	594.29	590.71	589.02
48000	671.81	644.02	632.06	614.80	609.38	608.07	606.94	603.28	601.55
49000	685.80	657.43	645.23	627.61	622.08	620.74	619.58	615.84	614.08
50000	699.80	670.85	658.40	640.42	634.77	633.40	632.23	628.41	626.62
51000	713.79	684.27	671.57	653.23	647.47	646.07	644.87	640.98	639.15
52000	727.79	697.68	684.74	666.04	660.17	658.74	657.52	653.55	651.68
53000	741.79	711.10	697.90	678.85	672.86	671.41	670.16	666.12	664.21
54000	755.78	724.52	711.07	691.65	685.56	684.08	682.80	678.68	676.75
55000	769.78	737.93	724.24	704.46	698.25	696.74	695.45	691.25	689.28
56000	783.77	751.35	737.41	717.27	710.95	709.41	708.09	703.82	701.81
57000	797.77	764.77	750.58	730.08	723.64	722.08	720.74	716.39	714.34
58000	811.77	778.19	763.74	742.89	736.34	734.75	733.38	728.96	726.87
59000	825.76	791.60	776.91	755.70	749.03	747.42	746.03	741.52	739.41
60000	839.76	805.02	790.08	768.50	761.73	760.08	758.67	754.09	751.94
61000	853.75	818.44	803.25	781.31	774.42	772.75	771.32	766.66	764.47
62000	867.75	831.85	816.41	794.12	787.12	785.42	783.96	779.23	777.00
63000	881.74	845.27	829.58	806.93	799.81	798.09	796.60	791.80	789.54
64000	895.74	858.69	842.75	819.74	812.51	810.76	809.25	804.37	802.07
65000	909.74	872.10	855.92	832.54	825.21	823.42	821.89	816.93	814.60
67500	944.73	905.65	888.84	864.57	856.94	855.09	853.50	848.35	845.93
70000	979.72	939.19	921.76	896.59	888.68	886.76	885.12	879.77	877.26
75000	1049.70	1006.27	987.60	960.63	952.16	950.10	948.34	942.61	939.92
80000	1119.67	1073.36	1053.44	1024.67	1015.64	1013.44	1011.56	1005.46	1002.58
85000	1189.65	1140.44	1119.28	1088.71	1079.11	1076.78	1074.78	1068.30	1065.25
90000	1259.63	1207.53	1185.12	1152.75	1142.59	1140.12	1138.00	1131.14	1127.91
95000	1329.61	1274.61	1250.96	1216.79	1206.07	1203.46	1201.23	1193.98	1190.57
100000	1399.59	1341.70	1316.79	1280.84	1269.54	1266.80	1264.45	1256.82	1253.23
105000	1469.57	1408.78	1382.63	1344.88	1333.02	1330.14	1327.67	1319.66	1315.89
110000	1539.55	1475.86	1448.47	1408.92	1396.50	1393.48	1390.89	1382.50	1378.55
115000	1609.53	1542.95	1514.31	1472.96	1459.98	1456.82	1454.12	1445.34	1441.21
120000	1679.51	1610.03	1580.15	1537.00	1523.45	1520.16	1517.34	1508.18	1503.87
125000	1749.49	1677.12	1645.99	1601.04	1586.93	1583.50	1580.56	1571.02	1566.54
130000	1819.47	1744.20	1711.83	1665.08	1650.41	1646.84	1643.78	1633.86	1629.20
135000	1889.45	1811.29	1777.67	1729.13	1713.88	1710.18	1707.00	1696.70	1691.86
140000	1959.43	1878.37	1843.51	1793.17	1777.36	1773.52	1770.23	1759.54	1754.52
145000	2029.41	1945.46	1909.35	1857.21	1840.84	1836.86	1833.45	1822.38	1817.18
150000	2099.39	2012.54	1975.19	1921.25	1904.31	1900.20	1896.67	1885.22	1879.84

15⅛ %

MONTHLY PAYMENT
NECESSARY TO AMORTIZE A LOAN

AMOUNT	1 YEAR	2 YEARS	3 YEARS	4 YEARS	5 YEARS	7 YEARS	8 YEARS	10 YEARS	12 YEARS
$ 50	4.52	2.43	1.74	1.40	1.20	.97	.91	.82	.76
100	9.04	4.86	3.48	2.79	2.39	1.94	1.81	1.63	1.51
200	18.07	9.71	6.95	5.58	4.78	3.88	3.61	3.25	3.02
300	27.10	14.57	10.42	8.37	7.16	5.82	5.41	4.87	4.53
400	36.13	19.42	13.90	11.16	9.55	7.75	7.21	6.49	6.04
500	45.16	24.28	17.37	13.95	11.93	9.69	9.01	8.11	7.55
600	54.20	29.13	20.84	16.74	14.32	11.63	10.82	9.73	9.06
700	63.23	33.99	24.31	19.53	16.70	13.56	12.62	11.35	10.57
800	72.26	38.84	27.79	22.32	19.09	15.50	14.42	12.97	12.08
900	81.29	43.70	31.26	25.11	21.48	17.44	16.22	14.59	13.59
1000	90.32	48.55	34.73	27.90	23.86	19.37	18.02	16.22	15.09
2000	180.64	97.10	69.46	55.79	47.72	38.74	36.04	32.43	30.18
3000	270.96	145.64	104.18	83.69	71.57	58.11	54.06	48.64	45.27
4000	361.27	194.19	138.91	111.58	95.43	77.47	72.08	64.85	60.36
5000	451.59	242.74	173.64	139.48	119.28	96.84	90.09	81.06	75.45
6000	541.91	291.28	208.36	167.37	143.14	116.21	108.11	97.27	90.54
7000	632.23	339.83	243.09	195.26	166.99	135.57	126.13	113.48	105.63
8000	722.54	388.37	277.82	223.16	190.85	154.94	144.15	129.69	120.72
9000	812.86	436.92	312.54	251.05	214.71	174.31	162.17	145.90	135.81
10000	903.18	485.47	347.27	278.95	238.56	193.67	180.18	162.11	150.90
15000	1354.76	728.20	520.90	418.42	357.84	290.51	270.27	243.16	226.34
20000	1806.35	970.93	694.54	557.89	477.12	387.34	360.36	324.21	301.79
25000	2257.94	1213.66	868.17	697.36	596.39	484.18	450.45	405.26	377.24
30000	2709.52	1456.39	1041.80	836.83	715.67	581.01	540.54	486.31	452.68
35000	3161.11	1699.12	1215.44	976.30	834.95	677.85	630.63	567.36	528.13
40000	3612.70	1941.85	1389.07	1115.77	954.23	774.68	720.72	648.41	603.58
45000	4064.28	2184.58	1562.70	1255.24	1073.51	871.52	810.81	729.46	679.02
46000	4154.60	2233.12	1597.43	1283.14	1097.36	890.88	828.82	745.67	694.11
47000	4244.92	2281.67	1632.15	1311.03	1121.22	910.25	846.84	761.88	709.20
48000	4335.24	2330.22	1666.88	1338.92	1145.07	929.62	864.86	778.09	724.29
49000	4425.55	2378.76	1701.61	1366.82	1168.93	948.99	882.88	794.30	739.38
50000	4515.87	2427.31	1736.33	1394.71	1192.78	968.35	900.90	810.51	754.47
51000	4606.19	2475.85	1771.06	1422.61	1216.64	987.72	918.91	826.72	769.56
52000	4696.50	2524.40	1805.79	1450.50	1240.50	1007.09	936.93	842.93	784.65
53000	4786.82	2572.95	1840.51	1478.40	1264.35	1026.45	954.95	859.14	799.74
54000	4877.14	2621.49	1875.24	1506.29	1288.21	1045.82	972.97	875.35	814.83
55000	4967.46	2670.04	1909.97	1534.18	1312.06	1065.19	990.98	891.56	829.92
56000	5057.77	2718.58	1944.69	1562.08	1335.92	1084.55	1009.00	907.77	845.01
57000	5148.09	2767.13	1979.42	1589.97	1359.77	1103.92	1027.02	923.98	860.10
58000	5238.41	2815.68	2014.15	1617.87	1383.63	1123.29	1045.04	940.19	875.18
59000	5328.73	2864.22	2048.87	1645.76	1407.49	1142.66	1063.06	956.40	890.27
60000	5419.04	2912.77	2083.60	1673.65	1431.34	1162.02	1081.07	972.61	905.36
61000	5509.36	2961.31	2118.33	1701.55	1455.20	1181.39	1099.09	988.82	920.45
62000	5599.68	3009.86	2153.05	1729.44	1479.05	1200.76	1117.11	1005.03	935.54
63000	5690.00	3058.41	2187.78	1757.34	1502.91	1220.12	1135.13	1021.24	950.63
64000	5780.31	3106.95	2222.51	1785.23	1526.76	1239.49	1153.15	1037.45	965.72
65000	5870.63	3155.50	2257.23	1813.12	1550.62	1258.86	1171.16	1053.66	980.81
67500	6096.42	3276.86	2344.05	1882.86	1610.26	1307.27	1216.21	1094.19	1018.53
70000	6322.22	3398.23	2430.87	1952.60	1669.90	1355.69	1261.25	1134.71	1056.26
75000	6773.80	3640.96	2604.50	2092.07	1789.17	1452.53	1351.34	1215.76	1131.70
80000	7225.39	3883.69	2778.13	2231.54	1908.45	1549.36	1441.43	1296.82	1207.15
85000	7676.98	4126.42	2951.76	2371.01	2027.73	1646.20	1531.52	1377.87	1282.60
90000	8128.56	4369.15	3125.40	2510.48	2147.01	1743.03	1621.61	1458.92	1358.04
95000	8580.15	4611.88	3299.03	2649.95	2266.29	1839.87	1711.70	1539.97	1433.49
100000	9031.74	4854.61	3472.66	2789.42	2385.56	1936.70	1801.79	1621.02	1508.94
105000	9483.32	5097.34	3646.30	2928.89	2504.84	2033.54	1891.88	1702.07	1584.38
110000	9934.91	5340.07	3819.93	3068.36	2624.12	2130.37	1981.96	1783.12	1659.83
115000	10386.50	5582.80	3993.56	3207.83	2743.40	2227.20	2072.05	1864.17	1735.28
120000	10838.08	5825.53	4167.19	3347.30	2862.68	2324.04	2162.14	1945.22	1810.72
125000	11289.67	6068.26	4340.83	3486.77	2981.95	2420.87	2252.23	2026.27	1886.17
130000	11741.25	6310.99	4514.46	3626.24	3101.23	2517.71	2342.32	2107.32	1961.62
135000	12192.84	6553.72	4688.09	3765.72	3220.51	2614.54	2432.41	2188.37	2037.06
140000	12644.43	6796.45	4861.73	3905.19	3339.79	2711.38	2522.50	2269.42	2112.51
145000	13096.01	7039.18	5035.36	4044.66	3459.07	2808.21	2612.59	2350.47	2187.95
150000	13547.60	7281.91	5208.99	4184.13	3578.34	2905.05	2702.68	2431.52	2263.40

MONTHLY PAYMENT 15⅛%

NECESSARY TO AMORTIZE A LOAN

AMOUNT	15 YEARS	18 YEARS	20 YEARS	25 YEARS	28 YEARS	29 YEARS	30 YEARS	35 YEARS	40 YEARS
$ 50	.71	.68	.67	.65	.64	.64	.64	.64	.64
100	1.41	1.36	1.33	1.30	1.28	1.28	1.28	1.27	1.27
200	2.82	2.71	2.66	2.59	2.56	2.56	2.55	2.54	2.53
300	4.23	4.06	3.98	3.88	3.84	3.84	3.83	3.81	3.80
400	5.64	5.41	5.31	5.17	5.12	5.11	5.10	5.07	5.06
500	7.05	6.76	6.64	6.46	6.40	6.39	6.38	6.34	6.32
600	8.45	8.11	7.96	7.75	7.68	7.67	7.65	7.61	7.59
700	9.86	9.46	9.29	9.04	8.96	8.94	8.93	8.87	8.85
800	11.27	10.81	10.61	10.33	10.24	10.22	10.20	10.14	10.11
900	12.68	12.16	11.94	11.62	11.52	11.50	11.48	11.41	11.38
1000	14.09	13.51	13.27	12.91	12.80	12.77	12.75	12.67	12.64
2000	28.17	27.02	26.53	25.82	25.59	25.54	25.49	25.34	25.28
3000	42.25	40.53	39.79	38.72	38.39	38.31	38.24	38.01	37.91
4000	56.33	54.03	53.05	51.63	51.18	51.08	50.98	50.68	50.55
5000	70.41	67.54	66.31	64.53	63.98	63.84	63.73	63.35	63.18
6000	84.49	81.05	79.57	77.44	76.77	76.61	76.47	76.02	75.82
7000	98.58	94.55	92.83	90.34	89.57	89.38	89.22	88.69	88.45
8000	112.66	108.06	106.09	103.25	102.36	102.15	101.96	101.36	101.09
9000	126.74	121.57	119.35	116.15	115.15	114.91	114.71	114.03	113.72
10000	140.82	135.07	132.61	129.06	127.95	127.68	127.45	126.70	126.36
15000	211.23	202.61	198.91	193.59	191.92	191.52	191.17	190.05	189.53
20000	281.64	270.14	265.21	258.11	255.89	255.36	254.89	253.40	252.71
25000	352.04	337.68	331.51	322.64	319.86	319.19	318.62	316.75	315.88
30000	422.45	405.21	397.82	387.17	383.84	383.03	382.34	380.10	379.06
35000	492.86	472.75	464.12	451.69	447.81	446.87	446.06	443.45	442.23
40000	563.27	540.28	530.42	516.22	511.78	510.71	509.78	506.80	505.41
45000	633.68	607.82	596.72	580.75	575.75	574.54	573.51	570.15	568.58
46000	647.76	621.32	609.98	593.65	588.55	587.31	586.25	582.82	581.22
47000	661.84	634.83	623.24	606.56	601.34	600.08	598.99	595.49	593.86
48000	675.92	648.34	636.50	619.46	614.14	612.85	611.74	608.16	606.49
49000	690.00	661.85	649.76	632.37	626.93	625.61	624.48	620.83	619.13
50000	704.08	675.35	663.02	645.27	639.72	638.38	637.23	633.50	631.76
51000	718.17	688.86	676.28	658.18	652.52	651.15	649.97	646.17	644.40
52000	732.25	702.37	689.54	671.08	665.31	663.92	662.72	658.84	657.03
53000	746.33	715.87	702.80	683.99	678.11	676.68	675.46	671.51	669.67
54000	760.41	729.38	716.06	696.89	690.90	689.45	688.21	684.18	682.30
55000	774.49	742.89	729.32	709.80	703.70	702.22	700.95	696.85	694.94
56000	788.57	756.39	742.58	722.71	716.49	714.99	713.69	709.52	707.57
57000	802.66	769.90	755.84	735.61	729.29	727.75	726.44	722.19	720.21
58000	816.74	783.41	769.11	748.52	742.08	740.52	739.18	734.86	732.84
59000	830.82	796.91	782.37	761.42	754.87	753.29	751.93	747.53	745.48
60000	844.90	810.42	795.63	774.33	767.67	766.06	764.67	760.20	758.11
61000	858.98	823.93	808.89	787.23	780.46	778.82	777.42	772.87	770.75
62000	873.06	837.44	822.15	800.14	793.26	791.59	790.16	785.54	783.38
63000	887.14	850.94	835.41	813.04	806.05	804.36	802.91	798.21	796.02
64000	901.23	864.45	848.67	825.95	818.85	817.13	815.65	810.88	808.65
65000	915.31	877.96	861.93	838.85	831.64	829.89	828.39	823.55	821.29
67500	950.51	911.72	895.08	871.12	863.63	861.81	860.26	855.23	852.87
70000	985.72	945.49	928.23	903.38	895.61	893.73	892.12	886.90	884.46
75000	1056.12	1013.03	994.53	967.91	959.58	957.57	955.84	950.25	947.64
80000	1126.53	1080.56	1060.83	1032.43	1023.56	1021.41	1019.56	1013.60	1010.81
85000	1196.94	1148.10	1127.13	1096.96	1087.53	1085.24	1083.28	1076.95	1073.99
90000	1267.35	1215.63	1193.44	1161.49	1151.50	1149.08	1147.01	1140.30	1137.16
95000	1337.76	1283.16	1259.74	1226.01	1215.47	1212.92	1210.73	1203.65	1200.34
100000	1408.16	1350.70	1326.04	1290.54	1279.44	1276.76	1274.45	1267.00	1263.52
105000	1478.57	1418.23	1392.34	1355.07	1343.42	1340.59	1338.17	1330.35	1326.69
110000	1548.98	1485.77	1458.64	1419.60	1407.39	1404.43	1401.90	1393.70	1389.87
115000	1619.39	1553.30	1524.95	1484.12	1471.36	1468.27	1465.62	1457.05	1453.04
120000	1689.80	1620.84	1591.25	1548.65	1535.33	1532.11	1529.34	1520.40	1516.22
125000	1760.20	1688.37	1657.55	1613.18	1599.30	1595.94	1593.06	1583.75	1579.39
130000	1830.61	1755.91	1723.85	1677.70	1663.28	1659.78	1656.78	1647.10	1642.57
135000	1901.02	1823.44	1790.15	1742.23	1727.25	1723.62	1720.51	1710.45	1705.74
140000	1971.43	1890.98	1856.45	1806.76	1791.22	1787.46	1784.23	1773.80	1768.92
145000	2041.83	1958.51	1922.76	1871.28	1855.19	1851.29	1847.95	1837.15	1832.10
150000	2112.24	2026.05	1989.06	1935.81	1919.16	1915.13	1911.67	1900.50	1895.27

15¼%

MONTHLY PAYMENT
NECESSARY TO AMORTIZE A LOAN

AMOUNT	1 YEAR	2 YEARS	3 YEARS	4 YEARS	5 YEARS	7 YEARS	8 YEARS	10 YEARS	12 YEARS
$ 50	4.52	2.44	1.74	1.40	1.20	.98	.91	.82	.76
100	9.04	4.87	3.48	2.80	2.40	1.95	1.81	1.63	1.52
200	18.08	9.73	6.96	5.60	4.79	3.89	3.62	3.26	3.04
300	27.12	14.59	10.44	8.39	7.18	5.84	5.43	4.89	4.56
400	36.16	19.45	13.92	11.19	9.57	7.78	7.24	6.52	6.07
500	45.19	24.31	17.40	13.98	11.97	9.72	9.05	8.15	7.59
600	54.23	29.17	20.88	16.78	14.36	11.67	10.86	9.78	9.11
700	63.27	34.03	24.36	19.58	16.75	13.61	12.67	11.41	10.62
800	72.31	38.89	27.84	22.37	19.14	15.55	14.48	13.03	12.14
900	81.34	43.75	31.31	25.17	21.53	17.50	16.29	14.66	13.66
1000	90.38	48.61	34.79	27.96	23.93	19.44	18.10	16.29	15.18
2000	180.76	97.22	69.58	55.92	47.85	38.88	36.19	32.58	30.35
3000	271.13	145.82	104.37	83.88	71.77	58.32	54.28	48.87	45.52
4000	361.51	194.43	139.16	111.84	95.69	77.75	72.37	65.15	60.69
5000	451.89	243.03	173.94	139.79	119.61	97.19	90.46	81.44	75.86
6000	542.26	291.64	208.73	167.75	143.53	116.63	108.55	97.73	91.03
7000	632.64	340.24	243.52	195.71	167.45	136.07	126.64	114.01	106.20
8000	723.02	388.85	278.31	223.67	191.38	155.50	144.73	130.30	121.37
9000	813.39	437.45	313.10	251.62	215.30	174.94	162.82	146.59	136.54
10000	903.77	486.06	347.88	279.58	239.22	194.38	180.91	162.87	151.71
15000	1355.65	729.09	521.82	419.37	358.83	291.56	271.36	244.31	227.56
20000	1807.53	972.12	695.76	559.16	478.43	388.75	361.81	325.74	303.41
25000	2259.41	1215.14	869.70	698.95	598.04	485.94	452.26	407.18	379.26
30000	2711.29	1458.17	1043.64	838.73	717.65	583.12	542.72	488.61	455.11
35000	3163.18	1701.20	1217.58	978.52	837.25	680.31	633.17	570.05	530.96
40000	3615.06	1944.23	1391.52	1118.31	956.86	777.50	723.62	651.48	606.81
45000	4066.94	2187.25	1565.46	1258.10	1076.47	874.68	814.07	732.92	682.66
46000	4157.32	2235.86	1600.25	1286.06	1100.39	894.12	832.16	749.20	697.83
47000	4247.69	2284.46	1635.04	1314.01	1124.31	913.56	850.25	765.49	713.00
48000	4338.07	2333.07	1669.82	1341.97	1148.23	932.99	868.34	781.78	728.17
49000	4428.44	2381.68	1704.61	1369.93	1172.15	952.43	886.43	798.06	743.34
50000	4518.82	2430.28	1739.40	1397.89	1196.07	971.87	904.52	814.35	758.51
51000	4609.20	2478.89	1774.19	1425.84	1219.99	991.31	922.61	830.64	773.68
52000	4699.57	2527.49	1808.97	1453.80	1243.92	1010.74	940.70	846.93	788.85
53000	4789.95	2576.10	1843.76	1481.76	1267.84	1030.18	958.79	863.21	804.02
54000	4880.33	2624.70	1878.55	1509.72	1291.76	1049.62	976.88	879.50	819.19
55000	4970.70	2673.31	1913.34	1537.68	1315.68	1069.06	994.98	895.79	834.36
56000	5061.08	2721.91	1948.13	1565.63	1339.60	1088.49	1013.07	912.07	849.53
57000	5151.46	2770.52	1982.91	1593.59	1363.52	1107.93	1031.16	928.36	864.70
58000	5241.83	2819.12	2017.70	1621.55	1387.44	1127.37	1049.25	944.65	879.87
59000	5332.21	2867.73	2052.49	1649.51	1411.37	1146.80	1067.34	960.93	895.04
60000	5422.58	2916.34	2087.28	1677.46	1435.29	1166.24	1085.43	977.22	910.21
61000	5512.96	2964.94	2122.07	1705.42	1459.21	1185.68	1103.52	993.51	925.38
62000	5603.34	3013.55	2156.85	1733.38	1483.13	1205.12	1121.61	1009.79	940.55
63000	5693.71	3062.15	2191.64	1761.34	1507.05	1224.55	1139.70	1026.08	955.72
64000	5784.09	3110.76	2226.43	1789.29	1530.97	1243.99	1157.79	1042.37	970.89
65000	5874.47	3159.36	2261.22	1817.25	1554.89	1263.43	1175.88	1058.66	986.06
67500	6100.41	3280.88	2348.19	1887.15	1614.70	1312.02	1221.10	1099.37	1023.98
70000	6326.35	3402.39	2435.16	1957.04	1674.50	1360.61	1266.33	1140.09	1061.91
75000	6778.23	3645.42	2609.10	2096.83	1794.11	1457.80	1356.78	1221.53	1137.76
80000	7230.11	3888.45	2783.04	2236.62	1913.71	1554.99	1447.23	1302.96	1213.61
85000	7681.99	4131.47	2956.97	2376.40	2033.32	1652.17	1537.69	1384.39	1289.46
90000	8133.87	4374.50	3130.91	2516.19	2152.93	1749.36	1628.14	1465.83	1365.31
95000	8585.76	4617.53	3304.85	2655.98	2272.53	1846.55	1718.59	1547.26	1441.16
100000	9037.64	4860.56	3478.79	2795.77	2392.14	1943.73	1809.04	1628.70	1517.01
105000	9489.52	5103.58	3652.73	2935.56	2511.75	2040.92	1899.49	1710.13	1592.86
110000	9941.40	5346.61	3826.67	3075.35	2631.35	2138.11	1989.95	1791.57	1668.71
115000	10393.28	5589.64	4000.61	3215.13	2750.96	2235.29	2080.40	1873.00	1744.56
120000	10845.16	5832.67	4174.55	3354.92	2870.57	2332.48	2170.85	1954.44	1820.41
125000	11297.05	6075.69	4348.49	3494.71	2990.17	2429.67	2261.30	2035.87	1896.26
130000	11748.93	6318.72	4522.43	3634.50	3109.78	2526.85	2351.75	2117.31	1972.11
135000	12200.81	6561.75	4696.37	3774.29	3229.39	2624.04	2442.20	2198.74	2047.96
140000	12652.69	6804.78	4870.31	3914.07	3349.00	2721.22	2532.66	2280.18	2123.81
145000	13104.57	7047.80	5044.25	4053.86	3468.60	2818.41	2623.11	2361.61	2199.66
150000	13556.45	7290.83	5218.19	4193.65	3588.21	2915.60	2713.56	2443.05	2275.51

AMOUNT	15 YEARS	18 YEARS	20 YEARS	25 YEARS	28 YEARS	29 YEARS	30 YEARS	35 YEARS	40 YEARS
$ 50	.71	.68	.67	.66	.65	.65	.65	.64	.64
100	1.42	1.36	1.34	1.31	1.29	1.29	1.29	1.28	1.28
200	2.84	2.72	2.68	2.61	2.58	2.58	2.57	2.56	2.55
300	4.26	4.08	4.01	3.91	3.87	3.87	3.86	3.84	3.83
400	5.67	5.44	5.35	5.21	5.16	5.15	5.14	5.11	5.10
500	7.09	6.80	6.68	6.51	6.45	6.44	6.43	6.39	6.37
600	8.51	8.16	8.02	7.81	7.74	7.73	7.71	7.67	7.65
700	9.92	9.52	9.35	9.11	9.03	9.01	9.00	8.95	8.92
800	11.34	10.88	10.69	10.41	10.32	10.30	10.28	10.22	10.20
900	12.76	12.24	12.02	11.71	11.61	11.59	11.57	11.50	11.47
1000	14.17	13.60	13.36	13.01	12.90	12.87	12.85	12.78	12.74
2000	28.34	27.20	26.71	26.01	25.79	25.74	25.69	25.55	25.48
3000	42.51	40.80	40.06	39.01	38.69	38.61	38.54	38.32	38.22
4000	56.67	54.39	53.42	52.02	51.58	51.47	51.38	51.09	50.96
5000	70.84	67.99	66.77	65.02	64.47	64.34	64.23	63.86	63.70
6000	85.01	81.59	80.12	78.02	77.37	77.21	77.07	76.64	76.43
7000	99.18	95.19	93.48	91.02	90.26	90.08	89.92	89.41	89.17
8000	113.34	108.78	106.83	104.03	103.15	102.94	102.76	102.18	101.91
9000	127.51	122.38	120.18	117.03	116.05	115.81	115.61	114.95	114.65
10000	141.68	135.98	133.53	130.03	128.94	128.68	128.45	127.72	127.39
15000	212.52	203.96	200.30	195.04	193.41	193.01	192.67	191.58	191.08
20000	283.35	271.95	267.06	260.06	257.88	257.35	256.90	255.44	254.77
25000	354.19	339.93	333.83	325.07	322.34	321.68	321.12	319.30	318.46
30000	425.03	407.92	400.59	390.08	386.81	386.02	385.34	383.16	382.15
35000	495.87	475.91	467.36	455.10	451.28	450.36	449.57	447.02	445.84
40000	566.70	543.89	534.12	520.11	515.75	514.69	513.79	510.88	509.53
45000	637.54	611.88	600.89	585.12	580.21	579.03	578.01	574.74	573.22
46000	651.71	625.47	614.24	598.12	593.11	591.89	590.86	587.51	585.95
47000	665.88	639.07	627.60	611.13	606.00	604.76	603.70	600.28	598.69
48000	680.04	652.67	640.95	624.13	618.89	617.63	616.55	613.05	611.43
49000	694.21	666.27	654.30	637.13	631.79	630.50	629.39	625.83	624.17
50000	708.38	679.86	667.65	650.13	644.68	643.36	642.23	638.60	636.91
51000	722.55	693.46	681.01	663.14	657.57	656.23	655.08	651.37	649.64
52000	736.71	707.06	694.36	676.14	670.47	669.10	667.92	664.14	662.38
53000	750.88	720.65	707.71	689.14	683.36	681.96	680.77	676.91	675.12
54000	765.05	734.25	721.07	702.14	696.26	694.83	693.61	689.68	687.86
55000	779.22	747.85	734.42	715.15	709.15	707.70	706.46	702.46	700.60
56000	793.38	761.45	747.77	728.15	722.04	720.57	719.30	715.23	713.33
57000	807.55	775.04	761.13	741.15	734.94	733.43	732.15	728.00	726.07
58000	821.72	788.64	774.48	754.15	747.83	746.30	744.99	740.77	738.81
59000	835.89	802.24	787.83	767.16	760.72	759.17	757.84	753.54	751.55
60000	850.05	815.84	801.18	780.16	773.62	772.03	770.68	766.32	764.29
61000	864.22	829.43	814.54	793.16	786.51	784.90	783.52	779.09	777.02
62000	878.39	843.03	827.89	806.17	799.40	797.77	796.37	791.86	789.76
63000	892.56	856.63	841.24	819.17	812.30	810.64	809.21	804.63	802.50
64000	906.72	870.22	854.60	832.17	825.19	823.50	822.06	817.40	815.24
65000	920.89	883.82	867.95	845.17	838.08	836.37	834.90	830.17	827.98
67500	956.31	917.81	901.33	877.68	870.32	868.54	867.01	862.10	859.82
70000	991.73	951.81	934.71	910.19	902.55	900.71	899.13	894.03	891.67
75000	1062.57	1019.79	1001.48	975.20	967.02	965.04	963.35	957.89	955.36
80000	1133.40	1087.78	1068.24	1040.21	1031.49	1029.38	1027.57	1021.75	1019.05
85000	1204.24	1155.76	1135.01	1105.22	1095.95	1093.71	1091.79	1085.61	1082.74
90000	1275.08	1223.75	1201.77	1170.24	1160.42	1158.05	1156.02	1149.47	1146.43
95000	1345.92	1291.74	1268.54	1235.25	1224.89	1222.38	1220.24	1213.33	1210.12
100000	1416.75	1359.72	1335.30	1300.26	1289.36	1286.72	1284.46	1277.19	1273.81
105000	1487.59	1427.71	1402.07	1365.28	1353.83	1351.06	1348.69	1341.05	1337.50
110000	1558.43	1495.69	1468.83	1430.29	1418.29	1415.39	1412.91	1404.91	1401.19
115000	1629.27	1563.68	1535.60	1495.30	1482.76	1479.73	1477.13	1468.77	1464.88
120000	1700.10	1631.67	1602.36	1560.31	1547.23	1544.06	1541.36	1532.63	1528.57
125000	1770.94	1699.65	1669.13	1625.33	1611.70	1608.40	1605.58	1596.48	1592.26
130000	1841.78	1767.64	1735.89	1690.34	1676.16	1672.74	1669.80	1660.34	1655.95
135000	1912.62	1835.62	1802.66	1755.35	1740.63	1737.07	1734.02	1724.20	1719.64
140000	1983.45	1903.61	1869.42	1820.37	1805.10	1801.41	1798.25	1788.06	1783.33
145000	2054.29	1971.59	1936.19	1885.38	1869.57	1865.74	1862.47	1851.92	1847.02
150000	2125.13	2039.58	2002.95	1950.39	1934.03	1930.08	1926.69	1915.78	1910.71

15⅜% MONTHLY PAYMENT
NECESSARY TO AMORTIZE A LOAN

AMOUNT	1 YEAR	2 YEARS	3 YEARS	4 YEARS	5 YEARS	7 YEARS	8 YEARS	10 YEARS	12 YEARS
$ 50	4.53	2.44	1.75	1.41	1.20	.98	.91	.82	.77
100	9.05	4.87	3.49	2.81	2.40	1.96	1.82	1.64	1.53
200	18.09	9.74	6.97	5.61	4.80	3.91	3.64	3.28	3.06
300	27.14	14.60	10.46	8.41	7.20	5.86	5.45	4.91	4.58
400	36.18	19.47	13.94	11.21	9.60	7.81	7.27	6.55	6.11
500	45.22	24.34	17.43	14.02	12.00	9.76	9.09	8.19	7.63
600	54.27	29.20	20.91	16.82	14.40	11.71	10.90	9.82	9.16
700	63.31	34.07	24.40	19.62	16.80	13.66	12.72	11.46	10.68
800	72.35	38.94	27.88	22.42	19.19	15.61	14.54	13.10	12.21
900	81.40	43.80	31.37	25.22	21.59	17.56	16.35	14.73	13.73
1000	90.44	48.67	34.85	28.03	23.99	19.51	18.17	16.37	15.26
2000	180.88	97.34	69.70	56.05	47.98	39.02	36.33	32.73	30.51
3000	271.31	146.00	104.55	84.07	71.97	58.53	54.49	49.10	45.76
4000	361.75	194.67	139.40	112.09	95.95	78.04	72.66	65.46	61.01
5000	452.18	243.33	174.25	140.11	119.94	97.54	90.82	81.82	76.26
6000	542.62	292.00	209.10	168.13	143.93	117.05	108.98	98.19	91.51
7000	633.05	340.66	243.95	196.15	167.92	136.56	127.15	114.55	106.76
8000	723.49	389.33	278.80	224.17	191.90	156.07	145.31	130.92	122.01
9000	813.92	437.99	313.65	252.20	215.89	175.57	163.47	147.28	137.26
10000	904.36	486.66	348.50	280.22	239.88	195.08	181.64	163.64	152.51
15000	1356.54	729.98	522.74	420.32	359.81	292.62	272.45	245.46	228.77
20000	1808.71	973.31	696.99	560.43	479.75	390.16	363.27	327.28	305.02
25000	2260.89	1216.63	871.24	700.54	599.69	487.70	454.08	409.10	381.28
30000	2713.07	1459.96	1045.48	840.64	719.62	585.24	544.90	490.92	457.53
35000	3165.24	1703.28	1219.73	980.75	839.56	682.78	635.71	572.74	533.79
40000	3617.42	1946.61	1393.97	1120.85	959.49	780.31	726.53	654.56	610.04
45000	4069.60	2189.93	1568.22	1260.96	1079.43	877.85	817.34	736.38	686.30
46000	4160.03	2238.60	1603.07	1288.98	1103.42	897.36	835.51	752.74	701.55
47000	4250.47	2287.26	1637.92	1317.00	1127.40	916.87	853.67	769.11	716.80
48000	4340.90	2335.93	1672.77	1345.02	1151.39	936.38	871.83	785.47	732.05
49000	4431.34	2384.59	1707.62	1373.04	1175.38	955.88	890.00	801.84	747.30
50000	4521.77	2433.26	1742.47	1401.07	1199.37	975.39	908.16	818.20	762.55
51000	4612.21	2481.92	1777.32	1429.09	1223.35	994.90	926.32	834.56	777.80
52000	4702.64	2530.59	1812.17	1457.11	1247.34	1014.41	944.48	850.93	793.05
53000	4793.08	2579.25	1847.02	1485.13	1271.33	1033.92	962.65	867.29	808.31
54000	4883.51	2627.92	1881.86	1513.15	1295.32	1053.42	980.81	883.66	823.56
55000	4973.95	2676.58	1916.71	1541.17	1319.30	1072.93	998.97	900.02	838.81
56000	5064.39	2725.25	1951.56	1569.19	1343.29	1092.44	1017.14	916.38	854.06
57000	5154.82	2773.91	1986.41	1597.21	1367.28	1111.95	1035.30	932.75	869.31
58000	5245.26	2822.58	2021.26	1625.24	1391.26	1131.45	1053.46	949.11	884.56
59000	5335.69	2871.24	2056.11	1653.26	1415.25	1150.96	1071.63	965.48	899.81
60000	5426.13	2919.91	2090.96	1681.28	1439.24	1170.47	1089.79	981.84	915.06
61000	5516.56	2968.57	2125.81	1709.30	1463.23	1189.98	1107.95	998.20	930.31
62000	5607.00	3017.24	2160.66	1737.32	1487.21	1209.49	1126.12	1014.57	945.56
63000	5697.43	3065.90	2195.51	1765.34	1511.20	1228.99	1144.28	1030.93	960.81
64000	5787.87	3114.57	2230.36	1793.36	1535.19	1248.50	1162.44	1047.30	976.07
65000	5878.30	3163.23	2265.21	1821.38	1559.17	1268.01	1180.60	1063.66	991.32
67500	6104.39	3284.89	2352.33	1891.44	1619.14	1316.78	1226.01	1104.57	1029.44
70000	6330.48	3406.56	2439.45	1961.49	1679.11	1365.55	1271.42	1145.48	1067.57
75000	6782.66	3649.88	2613.70	2101.60	1799.05	1463.09	1362.24	1227.30	1143.83
80000	7234.83	3893.21	2787.94	2241.70	1918.98	1560.62	1453.05	1309.12	1220.08
85000	7687.01	4136.53	2962.19	2381.81	2038.92	1658.16	1543.87	1390.94	1296.34
90000	8139.19	4379.86	3136.44	2521.91	2158.86	1755.70	1634.68	1472.76	1372.59
95000	8591.36	4623.18	3310.68	2662.02	2278.79	1853.24	1725.50	1554.58	1448.84
100000	9043.54	4866.51	3484.93	2802.13	2398.73	1950.78	1816.31	1636.40	1525.10
105000	9495.72	5109.83	3659.18	2942.23	2518.66	2048.32	1907.13	1718.22	1601.35
110000	9947.89	5353.16	3833.42	3082.34	2638.60	2145.86	1997.94	1800.04	1677.61
115000	10400.07	5596.48	4007.67	3222.44	2758.54	2243.40	2088.76	1881.85	1753.86
120000	10852.25	5839.81	4181.91	3362.55	2878.47	2340.93	2179.57	1963.67	1830.12
125000	11304.42	6083.13	4356.16	3502.66	2998.41	2438.47	2270.39	2045.49	1906.37
130000	11756.60	6326.46	4530.41	3642.76	3118.34	2536.01	2361.20	2127.31	1982.63
135000	12208.78	6569.78	4704.65	3782.87	3238.28	2633.55	2452.02	2209.13	2058.88
140000	12660.96	6813.11	4878.90	3922.97	3358.22	2731.09	2542.84	2290.95	2135.14
145000	13113.13	7056.43	5053.15	4063.08	3478.15	2828.63	2633.65	2372.77	2211.39
150000	13565.31	7299.76	5227.39	4203.19	3598.09	2926.17	2724.47	2454.59	2287.65

NECESSARY TO AMORTIZE A LOAN

AMOUNT	15 YEARS	18 YEARS	20 YEARS	25 YEARS	28 YEARS	29 YEARS	30 YEARS	35 YEARS	40 YEARS
$ 50	.72	.69	.68	.66	.65	.65	.65	.65	.65
100	1.43	1.37	1.35	1.31	1.30	1.30	1.30	1.29	1.29
200	2.86	2.74	2.69	2.62	2.60	2.60	2.59	2.58	2.57
300	4.28	4.11	4.04	3.93	3.90	3.90	3.89	3.87	3.86
400	5.71	5.48	5.38	5.24	5.20	5.19	5.18	5.15	5.14
500	7.13	6.85	6.73	6.55	6.50	6.49	6.48	6.44	6.43
600	8.56	8.22	8.07	7.86	7.80	7.79	7.77	7.73	7.71
700	9.98	9.59	9.42	9.17	9.10	9.08	9.07	9.02	8.99
800	11.41	10.96	10.76	10.48	10.40	10.38	10.36	10.30	10.28
900	12.83	12.32	12.11	11.79	11.70	11.68	11.66	11.59	11.56
1000	14.26	13.69	13.45	13.10	13.00	12.97	12.95	12.88	12.85
2000	28.51	27.38	26.90	26.20	25.99	25.94	25.89	25.75	25.69
3000	42.77	41.07	40.34	39.30	38.98	38.91	38.84	38.63	38.53
4000	57.02	54.76	53.79	52.40	51.98	51.87	51.78	51.50	51.37
5000	71.27	68.44	67.23	65.50	64.97	64.84	64.73	64.37	64.21
6000	85.53	82.13	80.68	78.60	77.96	77.81	77.67	77.25	77.05
7000	99.78	95.82	94.13	91.70	90.95	90.77	90.62	90.12	89.89
8000	114.03	109.51	107.57	104.80	103.95	103.74	103.56	103.00	102.73
9000	128.29	123.19	121.02	117.90	116.94	116.71	116.51	115.87	115.57
10000	142.54	136.88	134.46	131.00	129.93	129.67	129.45	128.74	128.41
15000	213.81	205.32	201.69	196.50	194.90	194.51	194.18	193.11	192.62
20000	285.08	273.76	268.92	262.00	259.86	259.34	258.90	257.48	256.82
25000	356.35	342.19	336.15	327.50	324.82	324.18	323.63	321.85	321.03
30000	427.61	410.63	403.38	393.00	389.79	389.01	388.35	386.22	385.23
35000	498.88	479.07	470.61	458.50	454.75	453.85	453.07	450.59	449.44
40000	570.15	547.51	537.84	524.00	519.72	518.68	517.80	514.96	513.64
45000	641.42	615.95	605.07	589.50	584.68	583.52	582.52	579.33	577.85
46000	655.67	629.63	618.51	602.60	597.67	596.48	595.47	592.20	590.69
47000	669.92	643.32	631.96	615.70	610.67	609.45	608.41	605.07	603.53
48000	684.18	657.01	645.40	628.80	623.66	622.42	621.36	617.95	616.37
49000	698.43	670.70	658.85	641.90	636.65	635.38	634.30	630.82	629.21
50000	712.69	684.38	672.30	655.00	649.64	648.35	647.25	643.70	642.05
51000	726.94	698.07	685.74	668.10	662.64	661.32	660.19	656.57	654.90
52000	741.19	711.76	699.19	681.20	675.63	674.29	673.14	669.44	667.74
53000	755.45	725.45	712.63	694.30	688.62	687.25	686.08	682.32	680.58
54000	769.70	739.13	726.08	707.40	701.61	700.22	699.03	695.19	693.42
55000	783.95	752.82	739.52	720.50	714.61	713.19	711.97	708.06	706.26
56000	798.21	766.51	752.97	733.60	727.60	726.15	724.92	720.94	719.10
57000	812.46	780.20	766.42	746.70	740.59	739.12	737.86	733.81	731.94
58000	826.71	793.89	779.86	759.80	753.59	752.09	750.80	746.69	744.78
59000	840.97	807.57	793.31	772.90	766.58	765.05	763.75	759.56	757.62
60000	855.22	821.26	806.75	786.00	779.57	778.02	776.69	772.43	770.46
61000	869.47	834.95	820.20	799.10	792.56	790.99	789.64	785.31	783.31
62000	883.73	848.64	833.65	812.20	805.56	803.95	802.58	798.18	796.15
63000	897.98	862.32	847.09	825.30	818.55	816.92	815.53	811.05	808.99
64000	912.24	876.01	860.54	838.40	831.54	829.89	828.47	823.93	821.83
65000	926.49	889.70	873.98	851.50	844.54	842.86	841.42	836.80	834.67
67500	962.12	923.92	907.60	884.25	877.02	875.27	873.78	868.99	866.77
70000	997.76	958.14	941.21	917.00	909.50	907.69	906.14	901.17	898.87
75000	1069.03	1026.57	1008.44	982.50	974.46	972.52	970.87	965.54	963.08
80000	1140.29	1095.01	1075.67	1048.00	1039.43	1037.36	1035.59	1029.91	1027.28
85000	1211.56	1163.45	1142.90	1113.50	1104.39	1102.19	1100.32	1094.28	1091.49
90000	1282.83	1231.89	1210.13	1179.00	1169.35	1167.03	1165.04	1158.65	1155.69
95000	1354.10	1300.33	1277.36	1244.50	1234.32	1231.86	1229.76	1223.02	1219.90
100000	1425.37	1368.76	1344.59	1310.00	1299.28	1296.70	1294.49	1287.39	1284.10
105000	1496.63	1437.20	1411.81	1375.50	1364.25	1361.53	1359.21	1351.75	1348.31
110000	1567.90	1505.64	1479.04	1441.00	1429.21	1426.37	1423.94	1416.12	1412.51
115000	1639.17	1574.08	1546.27	1506.50	1494.17	1491.20	1488.66	1480.49	1476.72
120000	1710.44	1642.52	1613.50	1572.00	1559.14	1556.04	1553.38	1544.86	1540.92
125000	1781.71	1710.95	1680.73	1637.50	1624.10	1620.87	1618.11	1609.23	1605.13
130000	1852.97	1779.39	1747.96	1703.00	1689.07	1685.71	1682.83	1673.60	1669.33
135000	1924.24	1847.83	1815.19	1768.50	1754.03	1750.54	1747.56	1737.97	1733.54
140000	1995.51	1916.27	1882.42	1834.00	1818.99	1815.37	1812.28	1802.34	1797.74
145000	2066.78	1984.71	1949.65	1899.50	1883.96	1880.21	1877.00	1866.71	1861.95
150000	2138.05	2053.14	2016.88	1965.00	1948.92	1945.04	1941.73	1931.08	1926.15

15½% MONTHLY PAYMENT
NECESSARY TO AMORTIZE A LOAN

AMOUNT	1 YEAR	2 YEARS	3 YEARS	4 YEARS	5 YEARS	7 YEARS	8 YEARS	10 YEARS	12 YEARS
$ 50	4.53	2.44	1.75	1.41	1.21	.98	.92	.83	.77
100	9.05	4.88	3.50	2.81	2.41	1.96	1.83	1.65	1.54
200	18.10	9.75	6.99	5.62	4.82	3.92	3.65	3.29	3.07
300	27.15	14.62	10.48	8.43	7.22	5.88	5.48	4.94	4.60
400	36.20	19.49	13.97	11.24	9.63	7.84	7.30	6.58	6.14
500	45.25	24.37	17.46	14.05	12.03	9.79	9.12	8.23	7.67
600	54.30	29.24	20.95	16.86	14.44	11.75	10.95	9.87	9.20
700	63.35	34.11	24.44	19.66	16.84	13.71	12.77	11.51	10.74
800	72.40	38.98	27.93	22.47	19.25	15.67	14.59	13.16	12.27
900	81.45	43.86	31.42	25.28	21.65	17.63	16.42	14.80	13.80
1000	90.50	48.73	34.92	28.09	24.06	19.58	18.24	16.45	15.34
2000	180.99	97.45	69.83	56.17	48.11	39.16	36.48	32.89	30.67
3000	271.49	146.18	104.74	84.26	72.16	58.74	54.71	49.33	46.00
4000	361.98	194.90	139.65	112.34	96.22	78.32	72.95	65.77	61.33
5000	452.48	243.63	174.56	140.43	120.27	97.90	91.18	82.21	76.67
6000	542.97	292.35	209.47	168.51	144.32	117.48	109.42	98.65	92.00
7000	633.47	341.08	244.38	196.60	168.38	137.05	127.66	115.09	107.33
8000	723.96	389.80	279.29	224.68	192.43	156.63	145.89	131.53	122.66
9000	814.45	438.53	314.20	252.77	216.48	176.21	164.13	147.97	137.99
10000	904.95	487.25	349.11	280.85	240.54	195.79	182.36	164.42	153.33
15000	1357.42	730.87	523.67	421.28	360.80	293.69	273.54	246.62	229.99
20000	1809.89	974.50	698.22	561.70	481.07	391.57	364.72	328.83	306.65
25000	2262.37	1218.12	872.77	702.13	601.33	489.46	455.90	411.03	383.31
30000	2714.84	1461.74	1047.33	842.55	721.60	587.36	547.08	493.24	459.97
35000	3167.31	1705.36	1221.88	982.98	841.87	685.25	638.26	575.44	536.63
40000	3619.78	1948.99	1396.43	1123.40	962.13	783.14	729.44	657.65	613.29
45000	4072.25	2192.61	1570.99	1263.82	1082.40	881.03	820.62	739.85	689.95
46000	4162.75	2241.33	1605.90	1291.91	1106.45	900.61	838.86	756.29	705.28
47000	4253.24	2290.06	1640.81	1319.99	1130.50	920.19	857.09	772.73	720.61
48000	4343.74	2338.78	1675.72	1348.08	1154.56	939.77	875.33	789.18	735.94
49000	4434.23	2387.51	1710.63	1376.16	1178.61	959.34	893.57	805.62	751.28
50000	4524.73	2436.23	1745.54	1404.25	1202.66	978.92	911.80	822.06	766.61
51000	4615.22	2484.96	1780.45	1432.33	1226.72	998.50	930.04	838.50	781.94
52000	4705.71	2533.68	1815.36	1460.42	1250.77	1018.08	948.27	854.94	797.27
53000	4796.21	2582.41	1850.27	1488.50	1274.82	1037.66	966.51	871.38	812.60
54000	4886.70	2631.13	1885.18	1516.59	1298.88	1057.24	984.74	887.82	827.94
55000	4977.20	2679.85	1920.09	1544.67	1322.93	1076.81	1002.98	904.26	843.27
56000	5067.69	2728.58	1955.00	1572.76	1346.98	1096.39	1021.22	920.70	858.60
57000	5158.19	2777.30	1989.91	1600.84	1371.04	1115.97	1039.45	937.15	873.93
58000	5248.68	2826.03	2024.82	1628.93	1395.09	1135.55	1057.69	953.59	889.26
59000	5339.18	2874.75	2059.74	1657.01	1419.14	1155.13	1075.92	970.03	904.60
60000	5429.67	2923.48	2094.65	1685.10	1443.20	1174.71	1094.16	986.47	919.93
61000	5520.16	2972.20	2129.56	1713.18	1467.25	1194.28	1112.40	1002.91	935.26
62000	5610.66	3020.93	2164.47	1741.27	1491.30	1213.86	1130.63	1019.35	950.59
63000	5701.15	3069.65	2199.38	1769.35	1515.36	1233.44	1148.87	1035.79	965.92
64000	5791.65	3118.38	2234.29	1797.44	1539.41	1253.02	1167.10	1052.23	981.26
65000	5882.14	3167.10	2269.20	1825.52	1563.46	1272.60	1185.34	1068.67	996.59
67500	6108.38	3288.91	2356.48	1895.73	1623.60	1321.54	1230.93	1109.78	1034.92
70000	6334.61	3410.72	2443.75	1965.95	1683.73	1370.49	1276.52	1150.88	1073.25
75000	6787.09	3654.35	2618.31	2106.37	1803.99	1468.38	1367.70	1233.08	1149.91
80000	7239.56	3897.97	2792.86	2246.79	1924.26	1566.27	1458.88	1315.29	1226.57
85000	7692.03	4141.59	2967.41	2387.22	2044.53	1664.16	1550.06	1397.49	1303.23
90000	8144.50	4385.21	3141.97	2527.64	2164.79	1762.06	1641.24	1479.70	1379.89
95000	8596.97	4628.84	3316.52	2668.07	2285.06	1859.95	1732.42	1561.91	1456.55
100000	9049.45	4872.46	3491.07	2808.49	2405.32	1957.84	1823.60	1644.11	1533.21
105000	9501.92	5116.08	3665.63	2948.92	2525.59	2055.73	1914.78	1726.32	1609.87
110000	9954.39	5359.70	3840.18	3089.34	2645.86	2153.62	2005.96	1808.52	1686.53
115000	10406.86	5603.33	4014.73	3229.76	2766.12	2251.51	2097.14	1890.73	1763.19
120000	10859.33	5846.95	4189.29	3370.19	2886.39	2349.41	2188.32	1972.93	1839.85
125000	11311.81	6090.57	4363.84	3510.61	3006.65	2447.30	2279.50	2055.14	1916.51
130000	11764.28	6334.20	4538.39	3651.04	3126.92	2545.19	2370.67	2137.34	1993.17
135000	12216.75	6577.82	4712.95	3791.46	3247.19	2643.08	2461.85	2219.55	2069.83
140000	12669.22	6821.44	4887.50	3931.89	3367.45	2740.97	2553.03	2301.75	2146.49
145000	13121.70	7065.06	5062.05	4072.31	3487.72	2838.87	2644.21	2383.96	2223.15
150000	13574.17	7308.69	5236.61	4212.73	3607.98	2936.76	2735.39	2466.16	2299.81

140

MONTHLY PAYMENT 15½%

NECESSARY TO AMORTIZE A LOAN

AMOUNT	15 YEARS	18 YEARS	20 YEARS	25 YEARS	28 YEARS	29 YEARS	30 YEARS	35 YEARS	40 YEARS
$ 50	.72	.69	.68	.66	.66	.66	.66	.65	.65
100	1.44	1.38	1.36	1.32	1.31	1.31	1.31	1.30	1.30
200	2.87	2.76	2.71	2.64	2.62	2.62	2.61	2.60	2.59
300	4.31	4.14	4.07	3.96	3.93	3.93	3.92	3.90	3.89
400	5.74	5.52	5.42	5.28	5.24	5.23	5.22	5.20	5.18
500	7.17	6.89	6.77	6.60	6.55	6.54	6.53	6.49	6.48
600	8.61	8.27	8.13	7.92	7.86	7.85	7.83	7.79	7.77
700	10.04	9.65	9.48	9.24	9.17	9.15	9.14	9.09	9.07
800	11.48	11.03	10.84	10.56	10.48	10.46	10.44	10.39	10.36
900	12.91	12.41	12.19	11.88	11.79	11.77	11.75	11.68	11.65
1000	14.34	13.78	13.54	13.20	13.10	13.07	13.05	12.98	12.95
2000	28.68	27.56	27.08	26.40	26.19	26.14	26.10	25.96	25.89
3000	43.02	41.34	40.62	39.60	39.28	39.21	39.14	38.93	38.84
4000	57.36	55.12	54.16	52.79	52.37	52.27	52.19	51.91	51.78
5000	71.70	68.90	67.70	65.99	65.47	65.34	65.23	64.88	64.72
6000	86.04	82.67	81.24	79.19	78.56	78.41	78.28	77.86	77.67
7000	100.38	96.45	94.78	92.39	91.65	91.47	91.32	90.84	90.61
8000	114.72	110.23	108.32	105.58	104.74	104.54	104.37	103.81	103.56
9000	129.06	124.01	121.85	118.78	117.83	117.61	117.41	116.79	116.50
10000	143.40	137.79	135.39	131.98	130.93	130.67	130.46	129.76	129.44
15000	215.10	206.68	203.09	197.97	196.39	196.01	195.68	194.64	194.16
20000	286.80	275.57	270.78	263.95	261.85	261.34	260.91	259.52	258.88
25000	358.50	344.46	338.48	329.94	327.31	326.68	326.13	324.40	323.60
30000	430.20	413.35	406.17	395.93	392.77	392.01	391.36	389.28	388.32
35000	501.90	482.24	473.86	461.92	458.23	457.34	456.59	454.16	453.04
40000	573.60	551.13	541.56	527.90	523.69	522.68	521.81	519.04	517.76
45000	645.30	620.02	609.25	593.89	589.15	588.01	587.04	583.92	582.48
46000	659.64	633.80	622.79	607.09	602.24	601.08	600.08	596.89	595.43
47000	673.98	647.58	636.33	620.29	615.34	614.15	613.13	609.87	608.37
48000	688.32	661.36	649.87	633.48	628.43	627.21	626.17	622.85	621.32
49000	702.66	675.14	663.41	646.68	641.52	640.28	639.22	635.82	634.26
50000	717.00	688.91	676.95	659.88	654.61	653.35	652.26	648.80	647.20
51000	731.34	702.69	690.48	673.08	667.70	666.41	665.31	661.77	660.15
52000	745.68	716.47	704.02	686.27	680.80	679.48	678.35	674.75	673.09
53000	760.02	730.25	717.56	699.47	693.89	692.55	691.40	687.72	686.04
54000	774.36	744.03	731.10	712.67	706.98	705.61	704.44	700.70	698.98
55000	788.70	757.81	744.64	725.86	720.07	718.68	717.49	713.68	711.92
56000	803.04	771.58	758.18	739.06	733.17	731.75	730.53	726.65	724.87
57000	817.38	785.36	771.72	752.26	746.26	744.81	743.58	739.63	737.81
58000	831.72	799.14	785.26	765.46	759.35	757.88	756.62	752.60	750.76
59000	846.06	812.92	798.79	778.65	772.44	770.95	769.67	765.58	763.70
60000	860.40	826.70	812.33	791.85	785.53	784.01	782.72	778.56	776.64
61000	874.74	840.47	825.87	805.05	798.63	797.08	795.76	791.53	789.59
62000	889.08	854.25	839.41	818.25	811.72	810.15	808.81	804.51	802.53
63000	903.42	868.03	852.95	831.44	824.81	823.21	821.85	817.48	815.48
64000	917.76	881.81	866.49	844.64	837.90	836.28	834.90	830.46	828.42
65000	932.10	895.59	880.03	857.84	850.99	849.35	847.94	843.44	841.36
67500	967.95	930.03	913.87	890.83	883.73	882.01	880.55	875.87	873.72
70000	1003.80	964.48	947.72	923.83	916.46	914.68	913.17	908.31	906.08
75000	1075.50	1033.37	1015.42	989.81	981.92	980.02	978.39	973.19	970.80
80000	1147.20	1102.26	1083.11	1055.80	1047.38	1045.35	1043.62	1038.07	1035.52
85000	1218.90	1171.15	1150.80	1121.79	1112.84	1110.68	1108.84	1102.95	1100.24
90000	1290.60	1240.04	1218.50	1187.78	1178.30	1176.02	1174.07	1167.83	1164.96
95000	1362.30	1308.93	1286.19	1253.76	1243.76	1241.35	1239.30	1232.71	1229.68
100000	1434.00	1377.82	1353.89	1319.75	1309.22	1306.69	1304.52	1297.59	1294.40
105000	1505.69	1446.72	1421.58	1385.74	1374.68	1372.02	1369.75	1362.47	1359.12
110000	1577.39	1515.61	1489.27	1451.72	1440.14	1437.35	1434.97	1427.35	1423.84
115000	1649.09	1584.50	1556.97	1517.71	1505.60	1502.69	1500.20	1492.23	1488.56
120000	1720.79	1653.39	1624.66	1583.70	1571.06	1568.02	1565.43	1557.11	1553.28
125000	1792.49	1722.28	1692.36	1649.69	1636.52	1633.36	1630.65	1621.99	1618.00
130000	1864.19	1791.17	1760.05	1715.67	1701.98	1698.69	1695.88	1686.87	1682.72
135000	1935.89	1860.06	1827.74	1781.66	1767.45	1764.02	1761.10	1751.74	1747.44
140000	2007.59	1928.95	1895.44	1847.65	1832.91	1829.36	1826.33	1816.62	1812.16
145000	2079.29	1997.84	1963.13	1913.64	1898.37	1894.69	1891.55	1881.50	1876.88
150000	2150.99	2066.73	2030.83	1979.62	1963.83	1960.03	1956.78	1946.38	1941.60

141

MONTHLY PAYMENT
NECESSARY TO AMORTIZE A LOAN

AMOUNT	1 YEAR	2 YEARS	3 YEARS	4 YEARS	5 YEARS	7 YEARS	8 YEARS	10 YEARS	12 YEARS
$ 50	4.53	2.44	1.75	1.41	1.21	.99	.92	.83	.78
100	9.06	4.88	3.50	2.82	2.42	1.97	1.84	1.66	1.55
200	18.12	9.76	7.00	5.63	4.83	3.93	3.67	3.31	3.09
300	27.17	14.64	10.50	8.45	7.24	5.90	5.50	4.96	4.63
400	36.23	19.52	13.99	11.26	9.65	7.86	7.33	6.61	6.17
500	45.28	24.40	17.49	14.08	12.06	9.83	9.16	8.26	7.71
600	54.34	29.28	20.99	16.89	14.48	11.79	10.99	9.92	9.25
700	63.39	34.15	24.49	19.71	16.89	13.76	12.82	11.57	10.79
800	72.45	39.03	27.98	22.52	19.30	15.72	14.65	13.22	12.34
900	81.50	43.91	31.48	25.34	21.71	17.69	16.48	14.87	13.88
1000	90.56	48.79	34.98	28.15	24.12	19.65	18.31	16.52	15.42
2000	181.11	97.57	69.95	56.30	48.24	39.30	36.62	33.04	30.83
3000	271.67	146.36	104.92	84.45	72.36	58.95	54.93	49.56	46.24
4000	362.22	195.14	139.89	112.60	96.48	78.60	73.24	66.08	61.66
5000	452.77	243.93	174.87	140.75	120.60	98.25	91.55	82.60	77.07
6000	543.33	292.71	209.84	168.90	144.72	117.90	109.86	99.12	92.48
7000	633.88	341.49	244.81	197.05	168.84	137.55	128.17	115.63	107.90
8000	724.43	390.28	279.78	225.19	192.96	157.20	146.48	132.15	123.31
9000	814.99	439.06	314.75	253.34	217.08	176.85	164.79	148.67	138.72
10000	905.54	487.85	349.73	281.49	241.20	196.50	183.09	165.19	154.14
15000	1358.31	731.77	524.59	422.23	361.79	294.74	274.64	247.78	231.20
20000	1811.07	975.69	699.45	562.98	482.39	392.99	366.18	330.37	308.27
25000	2263.84	1219.61	874.31	703.72	602.99	491.23	457.73	412.96	385.34
30000	2716.61	1463.53	1049.17	844.46	723.58	589.48	549.27	495.56	462.40
35000	3169.38	1707.45	1224.03	985.21	844.18	687.72	640.82	578.15	539.47
40000	3622.14	1951.37	1398.89	1125.95	964.78	785.97	732.36	660.74	616.54
45000	4074.91	2195.29	1573.75	1266.69	1085.37	884.21	823.91	743.33	693.60
46000	4165.02	2244.07	1608.73	1294.84	1109.49	903.86	842.22	759.85	709.02
47000	4256.02	2292.86	1643.70	1322.99	1133.61	923.51	860.52	776.37	724.43
48000	4346.57	2341.64	1678.67	1351.14	1157.73	943.16	878.83	792.89	739.84
49000	4437.13	2390.43	1713.64	1379.29	1181.85	962.81	897.14	809.40	755.26
50000	4527.68	2439.21	1748.61	1407.43	1205.97	982.46	915.45	825.92	770.67
51000	4618.23	2488.00	1783.59	1435.58	1230.09	1002.11	933.76	842.44	786.08
52000	4708.79	2536.78	1818.56	1463.73	1254.21	1021.76	952.07	858.96	801.50
53000	4799.34	2585.56	1853.53	1491.88	1278.33	1041.41	970.38	875.48	816.91
54000	4889.89	2634.35	1888.50	1520.03	1302.44	1061.06	988.69	892.00	832.32
55000	4980.45	2683.13	1923.47	1548.18	1326.56	1080.70	1007.00	908.52	847.74
56000	5071.00	2731.92	1958.45	1576.33	1350.68	1100.35	1025.30	925.03	863.15
57000	5161.55	2780.70	1993.42	1604.47	1374.80	1120.00	1043.61	941.55	878.56
58000	5252.11	2829.48	2028.39	1632.62	1398.92	1139.65	1061.92	958.07	893.98
59000	5342.66	2878.27	2063.36	1660.77	1423.04	1159.30	1080.23	974.59	909.39
60000	5433.21	2927.05	2098.34	1688.92	1447.16	1178.95	1098.54	991.11	924.80
61000	5523.77	2975.84	2133.31	1717.07	1471.28	1198.60	1116.85	1007.63	940.22
62000	5614.32	3024.62	2168.28	1745.22	1495.40	1218.25	1135.16	1024.14	955.63
63000	5704.88	3073.40	2203.25	1773.37	1519.52	1237.90	1153.47	1040.66	971.04
64000	5795.43	3122.19	2238.22	1801.51	1543.64	1257.55	1171.78	1057.18	986.46
65000	5885.98	3170.97	2273.20	1829.66	1567.76	1277.20	1190.08	1073.70	1001.87
67500	6112.37	3292.93	2360.63	1900.03	1628.05	1326.32	1235.86	1114.99	1040.40
70000	6338.75	3414.89	2448.06	1970.41	1688.35	1375.44	1281.63	1156.29	1078.94
75000	6791.52	3658.81	2622.92	2111.15	1808.95	1473.69	1373.17	1238.88	1156.00
80000	7244.28	3902.73	2797.78	2251.89	1929.55	1571.93	1464.72	1321.47	1233.07
85000	7697.05	4146.66	2972.64	2392.64	2050.14	1670.18	1556.26	1404.07	1310.14
90000	8149.82	4390.58	3147.50	2533.38	2170.74	1768.42	1647.81	1486.66	1387.20
95000	8602.59	4634.50	3322.36	2674.12	2291.33	1866.67	1739.35	1569.25	1464.27
100000	9055.35	4878.42	3497.22	2814.86	2411.93	1964.91	1830.90	1651.84	1541.34
105000	9508.12	5122.34	3672.08	2955.61	2532.53	2063.16	1922.44	1734.43	1618.40
110000	9960.89	5366.26	3846.94	3096.35	2653.12	2161.40	2013.99	1817.03	1695.47
115000	10413.66	5610.18	4021.81	3237.09	2773.72	2259.65	2105.53	1899.62	1772.54
120000	10866.42	5854.10	4196.67	3377.84	2894.32	2357.89	2197.08	1982.21	1849.60
125000	11319.19	6098.02	4371.53	3518.58	3014.91	2456.14	2288.62	2064.80	1926.67
130000	11771.96	6341.94	4546.39	3659.32	3135.51	2554.39	2380.16	2147.39	2003.74
135000	12224.73	6585.86	4721.25	3800.06	3256.10	2652.63	2471.71	2229.98	2080.80
140000	12677.49	6829.78	4896.11	3940.81	3376.70	2750.88	2563.25	2312.58	2157.87
145000	13130.26	7073.70	5070.97	4081.55	3497.30	2849.12	2654.80	2395.17	2234.94
150000	13583.03	7317.62	5245.83	4222.29	3617.89	2947.37	2746.34	2477.76	2312.00

MONTHLY PAYMENT 15⅝%

NECESSARY TO AMORTIZE A LOAN

AMOUNT	15 YEARS	18 YEARS	20 YEARS	25 YEARS	28 YEARS	29 YEARS	30 YEARS	35 YEARS	40 YEARS
$ 50	.73	.70	.69	.67	.66	.66	.66	.66	.66
100	1.45	1.39	1.37	1.33	1.32	1.32	1.32	1.31	1.31
200	2.89	2.78	2.73	2.66	2.64	2.64	2.63	2.62	2.61
300	4.33	4.17	4.09	3.99	3.96	3.96	3.95	3.93	3.92
400	5.78	5.55	5.46	5.32	5.28	5.27	5.26	5.24	5.22
500	7.22	6.94	6.82	6.65	6.60	6.59	6.58	6.54	6.53
600	8.66	8.33	8.18	7.98	7.92	7.91	7.89	7.85	7.83
700	10.10	9.71	9.55	9.31	9.24	9.22	9.21	9.16	9.14
800	11.55	11.10	10.91	10.64	10.56	10.54	10.52	10.47	10.44
900	12.99	12.49	12.27	11.97	11.88	11.86	11.84	11.78	11.75
1000	14.43	13.87	13.64	13.30	13.20	13.17	13.15	13.08	13.05
2000	28.86	27.74	27.27	26.60	26.39	26.34	26.30	26.16	26.10
3000	43.28	41.61	40.90	39.89	39.58	39.51	39.44	39.24	39.15
4000	57.71	55.48	54.53	53.19	52.77	52.67	52.59	52.32	52.19
5000	72.14	69.35	68.16	66.48	65.96	65.84	65.73	65.39	65.24
6000	86.56	83.22	81.80	79.78	79.15	79.01	78.88	78.47	78.29
7000	100.99	97.09	95.43	93.07	92.35	92.17	92.02	91.55	91.33
8000	115.42	110.96	109.06	106.37	105.54	105.34	105.17	104.63	104.38
9000	129.84	124.83	122.69	119.66	118.73	118.51	118.32	117.71	117.43
10000	144.27	138.69	136.32	132.96	131.92	131.67	131.46	130.78	130.48
15000	216.40	208.04	204.48	199.43	197.88	197.51	197.19	196.17	195.71
20000	288.53	277.38	272.64	265.91	263.84	263.34	262.92	261.56	260.95
25000	360.66	346.73	340.80	332.38	329.80	329.18	328.65	326.95	326.18
30000	432.80	416.07	408.96	398.86	395.75	395.01	394.37	392.34	391.42
35000	504.93	485.42	477.12	465.33	461.71	460.84	460.10	457.73	456.65
40000	577.06	554.76	545.28	531.81	527.67	526.68	525.83	523.12	521.89
45000	649.19	624.11	613.44	598.28	593.63	592.51	591.56	588.51	587.12
46000	663.62	637.98	627.08	611.58	606.82	605.68	604.70	601.59	600.17
47000	678.05	651.85	640.71	624.87	620.01	618.85	617.85	614.67	613.22
48000	692.47	665.72	654.34	638.17	633.20	632.01	630.99	627.75	626.26
49000	706.90	679.59	667.97	651.47	646.40	645.18	644.14	640.82	639.31
50000	721.32	693.45	681.60	664.76	659.59	658.35	657.29	653.90	652.36
51000	735.75	707.32	695.24	678.06	672.78	671.51	670.43	666.98	665.40
52000	750.18	721.19	708.87	691.35	685.97	684.68	683.58	680.06	678.45
53000	764.60	735.06	722.50	704.65	699.16	697.85	696.72	693.14	691.50
54000	779.03	748.93	736.13	717.94	712.35	711.01	709.87	706.21	704.55
55000	793.46	762.80	749.76	731.24	725.55	724.18	723.01	719.29	717.59
56000	807.88	776.67	763.40	744.53	738.74	737.35	736.16	732.37	730.64
57000	822.31	790.54	777.03	757.83	751.93	750.51	749.31	745.45	743.69
58000	836.74	804.41	790.66	771.12	765.12	763.68	762.45	758.53	756.73
59000	851.16	818.28	804.29	784.42	778.31	776.85	775.60	771.60	769.78
60000	865.59	832.14	817.92	797.71	791.50	790.01	788.74	784.68	782.83
61000	880.02	846.01	831.56	811.01	804.70	803.18	801.89	797.76	795.88
62000	894.44	859.88	845.19	824.30	817.89	816.35	815.03	810.84	808.92
63000	908.87	873.75	858.82	837.60	831.08	829.51	828.18	823.92	821.97
64000	923.29	887.62	872.45	850.89	844.27	842.68	841.32	836.99	835.02
65000	937.72	901.49	886.08	864.19	857.46	855.85	854.47	850.07	848.06
67500	973.79	936.16	920.16	897.42	890.44	888.76	887.33	882.77	880.68
70000	1009.85	970.83	954.24	930.66	923.42	921.68	920.20	915.46	913.30
75000	1081.98	1040.18	1022.40	997.14	989.38	987.52	985.93	980.85	978.53
80000	1154.12	1109.52	1090.56	1063.61	1055.34	1053.35	1051.65	1046.24	1043.77
85000	1226.25	1178.87	1158.72	1130.09	1121.30	1119.18	1117.38	1111.63	1109.00
90000	1298.38	1248.21	1226.88	1196.56	1187.25	1185.02	1183.11	1177.02	1174.24
95000	1370.51	1317.56	1295.04	1263.04	1253.21	1250.85	1248.84	1242.41	1239.48
100000	1442.64	1386.90	1363.20	1329.52	1319.17	1316.69	1314.57	1307.80	1304.71
105000	1514.78	1456.25	1431.36	1395.99	1385.13	1382.52	1380.30	1373.19	1369.95
110000	1586.91	1525.59	1499.52	1462.47	1451.09	1448.35	1446.02	1438.58	1435.18
115000	1659.04	1594.94	1567.68	1528.94	1517.04	1514.19	1511.75	1503.97	1500.42
120000	1731.17	1664.28	1635.84	1595.42	1583.00	1580.02	1577.48	1569.36	1565.65
125000	1803.30	1733.63	1704.00	1661.89	1648.96	1645.86	1643.21	1634.75	1630.89
130000	1875.44	1802.97	1772.16	1728.37	1714.92	1711.69	1708.94	1700.14	1696.12
135000	1947.57	1872.32	1840.32	1794.84	1780.88	1777.52	1774.66	1765.53	1761.36
140000	2019.70	1941.66	1908.48	1861.32	1846.84	1843.36	1840.39	1830.92	1826.59
145000	2091.83	2011.01	1976.64	1927.80	1912.79	1909.19	1906.12	1896.31	1891.83
150000	2163.96	2080.35	2044.80	1994.27	1978.75	1975.03	1971.85	1961.70	1957.06

15¾%

MONTHLY PAYMENT
NECESSARY TO AMORTIZE A LOAN

AMOUNT	1 YEAR	2 YEARS	3 YEARS	4 YEARS	5 YEARS	7 YEARS	8 YEARS	10 YEARS	12 YEARS
$ 50	4.54	2.45	1.76	1.42	1.21	.99	.92	.83	.78
100	9.07	4.89	3.51	2.83	2.42	1.98	1.84	1.66	1.55
200	18.13	9.77	7.01	5.65	4.84	3.95	3.68	3.32	3.10
300	27.19	14.66	10.52	8.47	7.26	5.92	5.52	4.98	4.65
400	36.25	19.54	14.02	11.29	9.68	7.89	7.36	6.64	6.20
500	45.31	24.43	17.52	14.11	12.10	9.86	9.20	8.30	7.75
600	54.37	29.31	21.03	16.93	14.52	11.84	11.03	9.96	9.30
700	63.43	34.20	24.53	19.75	16.93	13.81	12.87	11.62	10.85
800	72.50	39.08	28.03	22.57	19.35	15.78	14.71	13.28	12.40
900	81.56	43.96	31.54	25.40	21.77	17.75	16.55	14.94	13.95
1000	90.62	48.85	35.04	28.22	24.19	19.72	18.39	16.60	15.50
2000	181.23	97.69	70.07	56.43	48.38	39.44	36.77	33.20	30.99
3000	271.84	146.54	105.11	84.64	72.56	59.16	55.15	49.79	46.49
4000	362.46	195.38	140.14	112.85	96.75	78.88	73.53	66.39	61.98
5000	453.07	244.22	175.17	141.07	120.93	98.60	91.92	82.98	77.48
6000	543.68	293.07	210.21	169.28	145.12	118.32	110.30	99.58	92.97
7000	634.29	341.91	245.24	197.49	169.30	138.04	128.68	116.18	108.47
8000	724.91	390.75	280.27	225.70	193.49	157.76	147.06	132.77	123.96
9000	815.52	439.60	315.31	253.92	217.67	177.48	165.44	149.37	139.46
10000	906.13	488.44	350.34	282.13	241.86	197.20	183.83	165.96	154.95
15000	1359.19	732.66	525.51	423.19	362.79	295.80	275.74	248.94	232.43
20000	1812.26	976.88	700.68	564.25	483.71	394.40	367.65	331.92	309.90
25000	2265.32	1221.10	875.85	705.32	604.64	493.00	459.56	414.90	387.37
30000	2718.38	1465.32	1051.02	846.38	725.57	591.60	551.47	497.88	464.85
35000	3171.45	1709.54	1226.19	987.44	846.49	690.20	643.38	580.86	542.32
40000	3624.51	1953.76	1401.35	1128.50	967.42	788.80	735.29	663.84	619.80
45000	4077.57	2197.97	1576.52	1269.56	1088.35	887.40	827.20	746.82	697.27
46000	4168.18	2246.82	1611.56	1297.78	1112.53	907.12	845.58	763.41	712.77
47000	4258.80	2295.66	1646.59	1325.99	1136.72	926.84	863.96	780.01	728.26
48000	4349.41	2344.50	1681.62	1354.20	1160.91	946.56	882.34	796.61	743.75
49000	4440.02	2393.35	1716.66	1382.41	1185.09	966.28	900.73	813.20	759.25
50000	4530.63	2442.19	1751.69	1410.63	1209.28	986.00	919.11	829.80	774.74
51000	4621.25	2491.04	1786.73	1438.84	1233.46	1005.72	937.49	846.39	790.24
52000	4711.86	2539.88	1821.76	1467.05	1257.65	1025.44	955.87	862.99	805.73
53000	4802.47	2588.72	1856.79	1495.26	1281.83	1045.16	974.25	879.58	821.23
54000	4893.09	2637.57	1891.83	1523.47	1306.02	1064.88	992.64	896.18	836.72
55000	4983.70	2686.41	1926.86	1551.69	1330.20	1084.60	1011.02	912.78	852.22
56000	5074.31	2735.25	1961.89	1579.90	1354.39	1104.32	1029.40	929.37	867.71
57000	5164.92	2784.10	1996.93	1608.11	1378.57	1124.04	1047.78	945.97	883.21
58000	5255.54	2832.94	2031.96	1636.32	1402.76	1143.76	1066.16	962.56	898.70
59000	5346.15	2881.79	2067.00	1664.54	1426.95	1163.48	1084.55	979.16	914.20
60000	5436.76	2930.63	2102.03	1692.75	1451.13	1183.20	1102.93	995.75	929.69
61000	5527.37	2979.47	2137.06	1720.96	1475.32	1202.92	1121.31	1012.35	945.19
62000	5617.99	3028.32	2172.10	1749.17	1499.50	1222.64	1139.69	1028.95	960.68
63000	5708.60	3077.16	2207.13	1777.39	1523.69	1242.36	1158.07	1045.54	976.18
64000	5799.21	3126.00	2242.16	1805.60	1547.87	1262.08	1176.46	1062.14	991.67
65000	5889.82	3174.85	2277.20	1833.81	1572.06	1281.80	1194.84	1078.74	1007.17
67500	6116.36	3296.96	2364.78	1904.34	1632.52	1331.10	1240.79	1120.22	1045.90
70000	6342.89	3419.07	2452.37	1974.87	1692.98	1380.40	1286.75	1161.71	1084.64
75000	6795.95	3663.29	2627.53	2115.94	1813.91	1479.00	1378.66	1244.69	1162.11
80000	7249.01	3907.50	2802.70	2257.00	1934.84	1577.60	1470.57	1327.67	1239.59
85000	7702.08	4151.72	2977.87	2398.06	2055.77	1676.20	1562.48	1410.65	1317.06
90000	8155.14	4395.94	3153.04	2539.12	2176.69	1774.80	1654.39	1493.63	1394.54
95000	8608.20	4640.16	3328.21	2680.18	2297.62	1873.40	1746.30	1576.61	1472.01
100000	9061.26	4884.38	3503.38	2821.25	2418.55	1972.00	1838.21	1659.59	1549.48
105000	9514.33	5128.60	3678.55	2962.31	2539.47	2070.60	1930.12	1742.57	1626.96
110000	9967.39	5372.82	3853.72	3103.37	2660.40	2169.20	2022.03	1825.55	1704.43
115000	10420.45	5617.04	4028.88	3244.43	2781.33	2267.80	2113.94	1908.53	1781.91
120000	10873.52	5861.25	4204.05	3385.49	2902.26	2366.40	2205.85	1991.51	1859.38
125000	11326.58	6105.47	4379.22	3526.56	3023.18	2465.00	2297.76	2074.49	1936.85
130000	11779.64	6349.69	4554.39	3667.62	3144.11	2563.60	2389.67	2157.47	2014.33
135000	12232.71	6593.91	4729.56	3808.68	3265.04	2662.20	2481.58	2240.44	2091.80
140000	12685.77	6838.13	4904.73	3949.74	3385.96	2760.80	2573.49	2323.42	2169.27
145000	13138.83	7082.35	5079.90	4090.80	3506.89	2859.40	2665.40	2406.40	2246.75
150000	13591.89	7326.57	5255.06	4231.87	3627.82	2958.00	2757.31	2489.38	2324.22

MONTHLY PAYMENT 15¾%

NECESSARY TO AMORTIZE A LOAN

AMOUNT	15 YEARS	18 YEARS	20 YEARS	25 YEARS	28 YEARS	29 YEARS	30 YEARS	35 YEARS	40 YEARS
$ 50	.73	.70	.69	.67	.67	.67	.67	.66	.66
100	1.46	1.40	1.38	1.34	1.33	1.33	1.33	1.32	1.32
200	2.91	2.80	2.75	2.68	2.66	2.66	2.65	2.64	2.64
300	4.36	4.19	4.12	4.02	3.99	3.99	3.98	3.96	3.95
400	5.81	5.59	5.50	5.36	5.32	5.31	5.30	5.28	5.27
500	7.26	6.98	6.87	6.70	6.65	6.64	6.63	6.60	6.58
600	8.71	8.38	8.24	8.04	7.98	7.97	7.95	7.91	7.90
700	10.16	9.78	9.61	9.38	9.31	9.29	9.28	9.23	9.21
800	11.62	11.17	10.99	10.72	10.64	10.62	10.60	10.55	10.53
900	13.07	12.57	12.36	12.06	11.97	11.95	11.93	11.87	11.84
1000	14.52	13.96	13.73	13.40	13.30	13.27	13.25	13.19	13.16
2000	29.03	27.92	27.46	26.79	26.59	26.54	26.50	26.37	26.31
3000	43.54	41.88	41.18	40.18	39.88	39.81	39.74	39.55	39.46
4000	58.06	55.84	54.91	53.58	53.17	53.07	52.99	52.73	52.61
5000	72.57	69.80	68.63	66.97	66.46	66.34	66.24	65.91	65.76
6000	87.08	83.76	82.36	80.36	79.75	79.61	79.48	79.09	78.91
7000	101.60	97.72	96.08	93.76	93.04	92.87	92.73	92.27	92.06
8000	116.11	111.68	109.81	107.15	106.34	106.14	105.97	105.45	105.21
9000	130.62	125.64	123.53	120.54	119.63	119.41	119.22	118.63	118.36
10000	145.14	139.60	137.26	133.93	132.92	132.67	132.47	131.81	131.51
15000	217.70	209.40	205.89	200.90	199.37	199.01	198.70	197.71	197.26
20000	290.27	279.20	274.51	267.86	265.83	265.34	264.93	263.61	263.01
25000	362.83	349.00	343.14	334.83	332.29	331.68	331.16	329.51	328.76
30000	435.40	418.80	411.77	401.79	398.74	398.01	397.39	395.41	394.51
35000	507.96	488.60	480.39	468.76	465.20	464.35	463.62	461.31	460.26
40000	580.53	558.40	549.02	535.72	531.66	530.68	529.85	527.21	526.01
45000	653.09	628.20	617.65	602.69	598.11	597.02	596.08	593.11	591.76
46000	667.61	642.16	631.37	616.08	611.40	610.28	609.33	606.29	604.91
47000	682.12	656.12	645.10	629.47	624.69	623.55	622.58	619.47	618.06
48000	696.63	670.08	658.82	642.86	637.99	636.82	635.82	632.65	631.21
49000	711.15	684.04	672.55	656.26	651.28	650.08	649.07	645.83	644.36
50000	725.66	698.00	686.27	669.65	664.57	663.35	662.31	659.01	657.51
51000	740.17	711.96	700.00	683.04	677.86	676.62	675.56	672.19	670.66
52000	754.69	725.92	713.72	696.44	691.15	689.88	688.81	685.37	683.81
53000	769.20	739.88	727.45	709.83	704.44	703.15	702.05	698.55	696.96
54000	783.71	753.84	741.17	723.22	717.73	716.42	715.30	711.73	710.11
55000	798.22	767.80	754.90	736.61	731.02	729.69	728.54	724.91	723.26
56000	812.74	781.76	768.62	750.01	744.32	742.95	741.79	738.09	736.41
57000	827.25	795.72	782.35	763.40	757.61	756.22	755.04	751.27	749.56
58000	841.76	809.68	796.07	776.79	770.90	769.49	768.28	764.45	762.71
59000	856.28	823.64	809.80	790.19	784.19	782.75	781.53	777.63	775.86
60000	870.79	837.60	823.53	803.58	797.48	796.02	794.78	790.81	789.01
61000	885.30	851.56	837.25	816.97	810.77	809.29	808.02	803.99	802.16
62000	899.82	865.52	850.98	830.36	824.06	822.55	821.27	817.17	815.31
63000	914.33	879.48	864.70	843.76	837.35	835.82	834.51	830.35	828.46
64000	928.84	893.44	878.43	857.15	850.65	849.09	847.76	843.53	841.62
65000	943.36	907.40	892.15	870.54	863.94	862.35	861.01	856.71	854.77
67500	979.64	942.30	926.47	904.03	897.17	895.52	894.12	889.66	887.64
70000	1015.92	977.20	960.78	937.51	930.39	928.69	927.24	922.61	920.52
75000	1088.49	1047.00	1029.41	1004.47	996.85	995.02	993.47	988.52	986.27
80000	1161.05	1116.80	1098.03	1071.44	1063.31	1061.36	1059.70	1054.42	1052.02
85000	1233.62	1186.60	1166.66	1138.40	1129.76	1127.69	1125.93	1120.32	1117.77
90000	1306.18	1256.40	1235.29	1205.37	1196.22	1194.03	1192.16	1186.22	1183.52
95000	1378.75	1326.20	1303.91	1272.33	1262.67	1260.36	1258.39	1252.12	1249.27
100000	1451.31	1396.00	1372.54	1339.29	1329.13	1326.70	1324.62	1318.02	1315.02
105000	1523.88	1465.80	1441.16	1406.26	1395.59	1393.03	1390.85	1383.92	1380.77
110000	1596.44	1535.60	1509.79	1473.22	1462.04	1459.37	1457.08	1449.82	1446.52
115000	1669.01	1605.40	1578.42	1540.19	1528.50	1525.70	1523.31	1515.72	1512.27
120000	1741.57	1675.20	1647.05	1607.15	1594.96	1592.04	1589.55	1581.62	1578.02
125000	1814.14	1745.00	1715.67	1674.12	1661.41	1658.37	1655.78	1647.52	1643.77
130000	1886.71	1814.80	1784.30	1741.08	1727.87	1724.70	1722.01	1713.42	1709.53
135000	1959.27	1884.60	1852.93	1808.05	1794.33	1791.04	1788.24	1779.32	1775.28
140000	2031.84	1954.40	1921.55	1875.01	1860.78	1857.37	1854.47	1845.22	1841.03
145000	2104.40	2024.20	1990.18	1941.97	1927.24	1923.71	1920.70	1911.12	1906.78
150000	2176.97	2094.00	2058.81	2008.94	1993.69	1990.04	1986.93	1977.03	1972.53

MONTHLY PAYMENT
NECESSARY TO AMORTIZE A LOAN

AMOUNT	1 YEAR	2 YEARS	3 YEARS	4 YEARS	5 YEARS	7 YEARS	8 YEARS	10 YEARS	12 YEARS
$ 50	4.54	2.45	1.76	1.42	1.22	.99	.93	.84	.78
100	9.07	4.90	3.51	2.83	2.43	1.98	1.85	1.67	1.56
200	18.14	9.79	7.02	5.66	4.86	3.96	3.70	3.34	3.12
300	27.21	14.68	10.53	8.49	7.28	5.94	5.54	5.01	4.68
400	36.27	19.57	14.04	11.32	9.71	7.92	7.39	6.67	6.24
500	45.34	24.46	17.55	14.14	12.13	9.90	9.23	8.34	7.79
600	54.41	29.35	21.06	16.97	14.56	11.88	11.08	10.01	9.35
700	63.48	34.24	24.57	19.80	16.98	13.86	12.92	11.68	10.91
800	72.54	39.13	28.08	22.63	19.41	15.84	14.77	13.34	12.47
900	81.61	44.02	31.59	25.45	21.83	17.82	16.61	15.01	14.02
1000	90.68	48.91	35.10	28.28	24.26	19.80	18.46	16.68	15.58
2000	181.35	97.81	70.20	56.56	48.51	39.59	36.92	33.35	31.16
3000	272.02	146.72	105.29	84.83	72.76	59.38	55.37	50.03	46.73
4000	362.69	195.62	140.39	113.11	97.01	79.17	73.83	66.70	62.31
5000	453.36	244.52	175.48	141.39	121.26	98.96	92.28	83.37	77.89
6000	544.04	293.43	210.58	169.66	145.52	118.75	110.74	100.05	93.46
7000	634.71	342.33	245.67	197.94	169.77	138.54	129.19	116.72	109.04
8000	725.38	391.23	280.77	226.22	194.02	158.33	147.65	133.39	124.62
9000	816.05	440.14	315.86	254.49	218.27	178.12	166.10	150.07	140.19
10000	906.72	489.04	350.96	282.77	242.52	197.91	184.56	166.74	155.77
15000	1360.08	733.56	526.44	424.15	363.78	296.87	276.84	250.11	233.65
20000	1813.44	978.07	701.91	565.53	485.04	395.82	369.11	333.47	311.53
25000	2266.80	1222.59	877.39	706.91	606.30	494.78	461.39	416.84	389.42
30000	2720.16	1467.11	1052.87	848.29	727.56	593.73	553.67	500.21	467.30
35000	3173.52	1711.62	1228.34	989.68	848.81	692.69	645.94	583.58	545.18
40000	3626.87	1956.14	1403.82	1131.06	970.07	791.64	738.22	666.94	623.06
45000	4080.23	2200.66	1579.30	1272.44	1091.33	890.60	830.50	750.31	700.94
46000	4170.90	2249.56	1614.39	1300.71	1115.58	910.39	848.95	766.99	716.52
47000	4261.58	2298.47	1649.49	1328.99	1139.83	930.18	867.41	783.66	732.10
48000	4352.25	2347.37	1684.58	1357.27	1164.09	949.97	885.86	800.33	747.67
49000	4442.92	2396.27	1719.68	1385.54	1188.34	969.76	904.32	817.01	763.25
50000	4533.59	2445.18	1754.77	1413.82	1212.59	989.55	922.77	833.68	778.83
51000	4624.26	2494.08	1789.87	1442.10	1236.84	1009.34	941.23	850.35	794.40
52000	4714.93	2542.98	1824.96	1470.37	1261.09	1029.13	959.68	867.03	809.98
53000	4805.61	2591.89	1860.06	1498.65	1285.34	1048.92	978.14	883.70	825.56
54000	4896.28	2640.79	1895.15	1526.93	1309.60	1068.72	996.59	900.37	841.13
55000	4986.95	2689.69	1930.25	1555.20	1333.85	1088.51	1015.05	917.05	856.71
56000	5077.62	2738.60	1965.34	1583.48	1358.10	1108.30	1033.50	933.72	872.29
57000	5168.29	2787.50	2000.44	1611.75	1382.35	1128.09	1051.96	950.39	887.86
58000	5258.96	2836.40	2035.54	1640.03	1406.60	1147.88	1070.42	967.07	903.44
59000	5349.64	2885.31	2070.63	1668.31	1430.85	1167.67	1088.87	983.74	919.01
60000	5440.31	2934.21	2105.73	1696.58	1455.11	1187.46	1107.33	1000.41	934.59
61000	5530.98	2983.11	2140.82	1724.86	1479.36	1207.25	1125.78	1017.09	950.17
62000	5621.65	3032.02	2175.92	1753.14	1503.61	1227.04	1144.24	1033.76	965.74
63000	5712.32	3080.92	2211.01	1781.41	1527.86	1246.83	1162.69	1050.44	981.32
64000	5802.99	3129.82	2246.11	1809.69	1552.11	1266.62	1181.15	1067.11	996.90
65000	5893.67	3178.73	2281.20	1837.96	1576.36	1286.42	1199.60	1083.78	1012.47
67500	6120.35	3300.98	2368.94	1908.66	1636.99	1335.89	1245.74	1125.47	1051.41
70000	6347.03	3423.24	2456.68	1979.35	1697.62	1385.37	1291.88	1167.15	1090.36
75000	6800.38	3667.76	2632.16	2120.73	1818.88	1484.33	1384.16	1250.52	1168.24
80000	7253.74	3912.28	2807.63	2262.11	1940.14	1583.28	1476.43	1333.88	1246.12
85000	7707.10	4156.79	2983.11	2403.49	2061.40	1682.23	1568.71	1417.25	1324.00
90000	8160.46	4401.31	3158.59	2544.87	2182.66	1781.19	1660.99	1500.62	1401.88
95000	8613.82	4645.83	3334.06	2686.25	2303.92	1880.14	1753.26	1583.99	1479.77
100000	9067.18	4890.35	3509.54	2827.64	2425.17	1979.10	1845.54	1667.35	1557.65
105000	9520.54	5134.86	3685.02	2969.02	2546.43	2078.05	1937.82	1750.72	1635.53
110000	9973.89	5379.38	3860.49	3110.40	2667.69	2177.01	2030.09	1834.09	1713.41
115000	10427.25	5623.90	4035.97	3251.78	2788.95	2275.96	2122.37	1917.46	1791.29
120000	10880.61	5868.41	4211.45	3393.16	2910.21	2374.92	2214.65	2000.82	1869.18
125000	11333.97	6112.93	4386.92	3534.54	3031.47	2473.87	2306.92	2084.19	1947.06
130000	11787.33	6357.45	4562.40	3675.92	3152.72	2572.83	2399.20	2167.56	2024.94
135000	12240.69	6601.96	4737.88	3817.31	3273.98	2671.78	2491.48	2250.93	2102.82
140000	12694.05	6846.48	4913.35	3958.69	3395.24	2770.74	2583.75	2334.29	2180.71
145000	13147.40	7091.00	5088.83	4100.07	3516.50	2869.69	2676.03	2417.66	2258.59
150000	13600.76	7335.52	5264.31	4241.45	3637.76	2968.65	2768.31	2501.03	2336.47

MONTHLY PAYMENT 15⅞%

NECESSARY TO AMORTIZE A LOAN

AMOUNT	15 YEARS	18 YEARS	20 YEARS	25 YEARS	28 YEARS	29 YEARS	30 YEARS	35 YEARS	40 YEARS
$ 50	.73	.71	.70	.68	67	67	.67	67	67
100	1.46	1.41	1.39	1.35	1.34	1.34	1.34	1.33	1.33
200	2.92	2.82	2.77	2.70	2.68	2.68	2.67	2.66	2.66
300	4.38	4.22	4.15	4.05	4.02	4.02	4.01	3.99	3.98
400	5.84	5.63	5.53	5.40	5.36	5.35	5.34	5.32	5.31
500	7.30	7.03	6.91	6.75	6.70	6.69	6.68	6.65	6.63
600	8.76	8.44	8.30	8.10	8.04	8.03	8.01	7.97	7.96
700	10.22	9.84	9.68	9.45	9.38	9.36	9.35	9.30	9.28
800	11.68	11.25	11.06	10.80	10.72	10.70	10.68	10.63	10.61
900	13.14	12.65	12.44	12.15	12.06	12.04	12.02	11.96	11.93
1000	14.60	14.06	13.82	13.50	13.40	13.37	13.35	13.29	13.26
2000	29.20	28.11	27.64	26.99	26.79	26.74	26.70	26.57	26.51
3000	43.80	42.16	41.46	40.48	40.18	40.11	40.05	39.85	39.76
4000	58.40	56.21	55.28	53.97	53.57	53.47	53.39	53.13	53.02
5000	73.00	70.26	69.10	67.46	66.96	66.84	66.74	66.42	66.27
6000	87.60	84.31	82.92	80.95	80.35	80.21	80.09	79.70	79.52
7000	102.20	98.36	96.74	94.44	93.74	93.57	93.43	92.98	92.78
8000	116.80	112.41	110.56	107.93	107.13	106.94	106.78	106.26	106.03
9000	131.40	126.47	124.37	121.42	120.52	120.31	120.13	119.55	119.28
10000	146.00	140.52	138.19	134.91	133.91	133.68	133.47	132.83	132.54
15000	219.00	210.77	207.29	202.37	200.87	200.51	200.21	199.24	198.80
20000	292.00	281.03	276.38	269.82	267.82	267.35	266.94	265.65	265.07
25000	365.00	351.28	345.48	337.28	334.78	334.18	333.68	332.06	331.34
30000	438.00	421.54	414.57	404.73	401.73	401.02	400.41	398.48	397.60
35000	511.00	491.79	483.67	472.18	468.69	467.85	467.14	464.89	463.87
40000	584.00	562.05	552.76	539.64	535.64	534.69	533.88	531.30	530.14
45000	657.00	632.31	621.85	607.09	602.60	601.53	600.61	597.71	596.40
46000	671.60	646.36	635.67	620.58	615.99	614.89	613.96	610.99	609.66
47000	686.20	660.41	649.49	634.07	629.38	628.26	627.31	624.28	622.91
48000	700.80	674.46	663.31	647.56	642.77	641.63	640.65	637.56	636.16
49000	715.40	688.51	677.13	661.06	656.16	654.99	654.00	650.84	649.42
50000	730.00	702.56	690.95	674.55	669.55	668.36	667.35	664.12	662.67
51000	744.60	716.61	704.77	688.04	682.95	681.73	680.69	677.41	675.92
52000	759.20	730.66	718.59	701.53	696.34	695.10	694.04	690.69	689.18
53000	773.80	744.71	732.40	715.02	709.73	708.46	707.39	703.97	702.43
54000	788.40	758.77	746.22	728.51	723.12	721.83	720.73	717.25	715.68
55000	803.00	772.82	760.04	742.00	736.51	735.20	734.08	730.54	728.94
56000	817.60	786.87	773.86	755.49	749.90	748.56	747.43	743.82	742.19
57000	832.20	800.92	787.68	768.98	763.29	761.93	760.77	757.10	755.44
58000	846.80	814.97	801.50	782.47	776.68	775.30	774.12	770.38	768.70
59000	861.40	829.02	815.32	795.96	790.07	788.67	787.47	783.67	781.95
60000	876.00	843.07	829.14	809.45	803.46	802.03	800.81	796.95	795.20
61000	890.60	857.12	842.96	822.95	816.86	815.40	814.16	810.23	808.46
62000	905.20	871.17	856.77	836.44	830.25	828.77	827.51	823.51	821.71
63000	919.80	885.23	870.59	849.93	843.64	842.13	840.85	836.80	834.96
64000	934.40	899.28	884.41	863.42	857.03	855.50	854.20	850.08	848.22
65000	949.00	913.33	898.23	876.91	870.42	868.87	867.55	863.36	861.47
67500	985.50	948.46	932.78	910.64	903.90	902.29	900.92	896.57	894.60
70000	1022.00	983.58	967.33	944.36	937.37	935.70	934.28	929.77	927.74
75000	1095.00	1053.84	1036.42	1011.82	1004.33	1002.54	1001.02	996.18	994.00
80000	1168.00	1124.10	1105.51	1079.27	1071.28	1069.38	1067.75	1062.60	1060.27
85000	1241.00	1194.35	1174.61	1146.73	1138.24	1136.21	1134.48	1129.01	1126.54
90000	1314.00	1264.61	1243.70	1214.18	1205.19	1203.05	1201.22	1195.42	1192.80
95000	1387.00	1334.86	1312.80	1281.63	1272.15	1269.88	1267.95	1261.83	1259.07
100000	1460.00	1405.12	1381.89	1349.09	1339.10	1336.72	1334.69	1328.24	1325.34
105000	1533.00	1475.37	1450.99	1416.54	1406.06	1403.55	1401.42	1394.66	1391.60
110000	1606.00	1545.63	1520.08	1484.00	1473.01	1470.39	1468.16	1461.07	1457.87
115000	1679.00	1615.88	1589.17	1551.45	1539.97	1537.22	1534.89	1527.48	1524.13
120000	1752.00	1686.14	1658.27	1618.90	1606.92	1604.06	1601.62	1593.89	1590.40
125000	1825.00	1756.40	1727.36	1686.36	1673.88	1670.90	1668.36	1660.30	1656.67
130000	1898.00	1826.65	1796.46	1753.81	1740.83	1737.73	1735.09	1726.71	1722.93
135000	1971.00	1896.91	1865.55	1821.27	1807.79	1804.57	1801.83	1793.13	1789.20
140000	2044.00	1967.16	1934.65	1888.72	1874.74	1871.40	1868.56	1859.54	1855.47
145000	2117.00	2037.42	2003.74	1956.17	1941.70	1938.24	1935.29	1925.95	1921.73
150000	2190.00	2107.67	2072.83	2023.63	2008.65	2005.07	2002.03	1992.36	1988.00

16% MONTHLY PAYMENT
NECESSARY TO AMORTIZE A LOAN

AMOUNT	1 YEAR	2 YEARS	3 YEARS	4 YEARS	5 YEARS	7 YEARS	8 YEARS	10 YEARS	12 YEARS
$ 50	4.54	2.45	1.76	1.42	1.22	1.00	.93	.84	.79
100	9.08	4.90	3.52	2.84	2.44	1.99	1.86	1.68	1.57
200	18.15	9.80	7.04	5.67	4.87	3.98	3.71	3.36	3.14
300	27.22	14.69	10.55	8.51	7.30	5.96	5.56	5.03	4.70
400	36.30	19.59	14.07	11.34	9.73	7.95	7.42	6.71	6.27
500	45.37	24.49	17.58	14.18	12.16	9.94	9.27	8.38	7.83
600	54.44	29.38	21.10	17.01	14.60	11.92	11.12	10.06	9.40
700	63.52	34.28	24.61	19.84	17.03	13.91	12.98	11.73	10.97
800	72.59	39.18	28.13	22.68	19.46	15.89	14.83	13.41	12.53
900	81.66	44.07	31.65	25.51	21.89	17.88	16.68	15.08	14.10
1000	90.74	48.97	35.16	28.35	24.32	19.87	18.53	16.76	15.66
2000	181.47	97.93	70.32	56.69	48.64	39.73	37.06	33.51	31.32
3000	272.20	146.89	105.48	85.03	72.96	59.59	55.59	50.26	46.98
4000	362.93	195.86	140.63	113.37	97.28	79.45	74.12	67.01	62.64
5000	453.66	244.82	175.79	141.71	121.60	99.32	92.65	83.76	78.30
6000	544.39	293.78	210.95	170.05	145.91	119.18	111.18	100.51	93.95
7000	635.12	342.75	246.10	198.39	170.23	139.04	129.71	117.26	109.61
8000	725.85	391.71	281.26	226.73	194.55	158.90	148.24	134.02	125.27
9000	816.58	440.67	316.42	255.07	218.87	178.76	166.76	150.77	140.93
10000	907.31	489.64	351.58	283.41	243.19	198.63	185.29	167.52	156.59
15000	1360.97	734.45	527.36	425.11	364.78	297.94	277.94	251.27	234.88
20000	1814.62	979.27	703.15	566.81	486.37	397.25	370.58	335.03	313.17
25000	2268.28	1224.08	878.93	708.51	607.96	496.56	463.22	418.79	391.46
30000	2721.93	1468.90	1054.72	850.21	729.55	595.87	555.87	502.54	469.75
35000	3175.59	1713.71	1230.50	991.91	851.14	695.18	648.51	586.30	548.04
40000	3629.24	1958.53	1406.29	1133.62	972.73	794.49	741.16	670.06	626.34
45000	4082.89	2203.34	1582.07	1275.32	1094.32	893.80	833.80	753.81	704.63
46000	4173.62	2252.31	1617.23	1303.66	1118.64	913.66	852.33	770.57	720.28
47000	4264.36	2301.27	1652.39	1332.00	1142.95	933.52	870.86	787.32	735.94
48000	4355.09	2350.23	1687.54	1360.34	1167.27	953.38	889.39	804.07	751.60
49000	4445.82	2399.20	1722.70	1388.68	1191.59	973.25	907.92	820.82	767.26
50000	4536.55	2448.16	1757.86	1417.02	1215.91	993.11	926.44	837.57	782.92
51000	4627.28	2497.12	1793.01	1445.36	1240.23	1012.97	944.97	854.32	798.58
52000	4718.01	2546.09	1828.17	1473.70	1264.54	1032.83	963.50	871.07	814.23
53000	4808.74	2595.05	1863.33	1502.04	1288.86	1052.69	982.03	887.82	829.89
54000	4899.47	2644.01	1898.48	1530.38	1313.18	1072.56	1000.56	904.58	845.55
55000	4990.20	2692.98	1933.64	1558.72	1337.50	1092.42	1019.09	921.33	861.21
56000	5080.93	2741.94	1968.80	1587.06	1361.82	1112.28	1037.62	938.08	876.87
57000	5171.66	2790.90	2003.96	1615.40	1386.13	1132.14	1056.15	954.83	892.53
58000	5262.39	2839.87	2039.11	1643.74	1410.45	1152.00	1074.67	971.58	908.18
59000	5353.13	2888.83	2074.27	1672.08	1434.77	1171.87	1093.20	988.33	923.84
60000	5443.86	2937.79	2109.43	1700.42	1459.09	1191.73	1111.73	1005.09	939.50
61000	5534.59	2986.75	2144.58	1728.76	1483.41	1211.59	1130.26	1021.84	955.16
62000	5625.32	3035.72	2179.74	1757.10	1507.72	1231.45	1148.79	1038.59	970.82
63000	5716.05	3084.68	2214.90	1785.44	1532.04	1251.32	1167.32	1055.34	986.47
64000	5806.78	3133.64	2250.06	1813.78	1556.36	1271.18	1185.85	1072.09	1002.13
65000	5897.51	3182.61	2285.21	1842.12	1580.68	1291.04	1204.38	1088.84	1017.79
67500	6124.34	3305.01	2373.10	1912.97	1641.47	1340.69	1250.70	1130.72	1056.94
70000	6351.17	3427.42	2461.00	1983.82	1702.27	1390.35	1297.02	1172.60	1096.08
75000	6804.82	3672.24	2636.78	2125.53	1823.86	1489.66	1389.66	1256.35	1174.37
80000	7258.47	3917.05	2812.57	2267.23	1945.45	1588.97	1482.31	1340.11	1252.67
85000	7712.13	4161.87	2988.35	2408.93	2067.04	1688.28	1574.95	1423.87	1330.96
90000	8165.78	4406.68	3164.14	2550.63	2188.63	1787.59	1667.60	1507.62	1409.25
95000	8619.44	4651.50	3339.92	2692.33	2310.22	1886.90	1760.24	1591.38	1487.54
100000	9073.09	4896.32	3515.71	2834.03	2431.81	1986.21	1852.88	1675.14	1565.83
105000	9526.75	5141.13	3691.49	2975.73	2553.40	2085.52	1945.53	1758.89	1644.12
110000	9980.40	5385.95	3867.28	3117.44	2674.99	2184.83	2038.17	1842.65	1722.41
115000	10434.05	5630.76	4043.06	3259.14	2796.58	2284.14	2130.82	1926.41	1800.70
120000	10887.71	5875.58	4218.85	3400.84	2918.17	2383.45	2223.46	2010.16	1879.00
125000	11341.36	6120.39	4394.63	3542.54	3039.76	2482.76	2316.10	2093.92	1957.29
130000	11795.02	6365.21	4570.42	3684.24	3161.35	2582.07	2408.75	2177.68	2035.58
135000	12248.67	6610.02	4746.20	3825.94	3282.94	2681.38	2501.39	2261.43	2113.87
140000	12702.33	6854.84	4921.99	3967.64	3404.53	2780.69	2594.04	2345.19	2192.16
145000	13155.98	7099.66	5097.77	4109.35	3526.12	2880.00	2686.68	2428.95	2270.45
150000	13609.63	7344.47	5273.56	4251.05	3647.71	2979.31	2779.32	2512.70	2348.74

AMOUNT	15 YEARS	18 YEARS	20 YEARS	25 YEARS	28 YEARS	29 YEARS	30 YEARS	35 YEARS	40 YEARS
$ 50	.74	.71	.70	.68	.68	.68	.68	.67	.67
100	1.47	1.42	1.40	1.36	1.35	1.35	1.35	1.34	1.34
200	2.94	2.83	2.79	2.72	2.70	2.70	2.69	2.68	2.68
300	4.41	4.25	4.18	4.08	4.05	4.05	4.04	4.02	4.01
400	5.88	5.66	5.57	5.44	5.40	5.39	5.38	5.36	5.35
500	7.35	7.08	6.96	6.80	6.75	6.74	6.73	6.70	6.68
600	8.82	8.49	8.35	8.16	8.10	8.09	8.07-	8.04	8.02
700	10.29	9.90	9.74	9.52	9.45	9.43	9.42	9.37	9.35
800	11.75	11.32	11.14	10.88	10.80	10.78	10.76	10.71	10.69
900	13.22	12.73	12.53	12.23	12.15	12.13	12.11	12.05	12.03
1000	14.69	14.15	13.92	13.59	13.50	13.47	13.45	13.39	13.36
2000	29.38	28.29	27.83	27.18	26.99	26.94	26.90	26.77	26.72
3000	44.07	42.43	41.74	40.77	40.48	40.41	40.35	40.16	40.07
4000	58.75	56.57	55.66	54.36	53.97	53.87	53.80	53.54	53.43
5000	73.44	70.72	69.57	67.95	67.46	67.34	67.24	66.93	66.79
6000	88.13	84.86	83.48	81.54	80.95	80.81	80.69	80.31	80.14
7000	102.81	99.00	97.39	95.13	94.44	94.28	94.14	93.70	93.50
8000	117.50	113.14	111.31	108.72	107.93	107.74	107.59	107.08	106.86
9000	132.19	127.29	125.22	122.30	121.42	121.21	121.03	120.47	120.21
10000	146.88	141.43	139.13	135.89	134.91	134.68	134.48	133.85	133.57
15000	220.31	212.14	208.69	203.84	202.37	202.02	201.72	200.78	200.35
20000	293.75	282.85	278.26	271.78	269.82	269.35	268.96	267.70	267.13
25000	367.18	353.57	347.82	339.73	337.28	336.69	336.19	334.62	333.92
30000	440.62	424.28	417.38	407.67	404.73	404.03	403.43	401.55	400.70
35000	514.05	494.99	486.94	475.62	472.18	471.37	470.67	468.47	467.48
40000	587.49	565.70	556.51	543.56	539.64	538.70	537.91	535.39	534.26
45000	660.92	636.42	626.07	611.50	607.09	606.04	605.15	602.32	601.05
46000	675.61	650.56	639.98	625.09	620.58	619.51	618.59	615.70	614.40
47000	690.29	664.70	653.90	638.68	634.07	632.98	632.04	629.09	627.76
48000	704.98	678.84	667.81	652.27	647.56	646.44	645.49	642.47	641.12
49000	719.67	692.99	681.72	665.86	661.06	659.91	658.94	655.86	654.47
50000	734.36	707.13	695.63	679.45	674.55	673.38	672.38	669.24	667.83
51000	749.04	721.27	709.55	693.04	688.04	686.84	685.83	682.62	681.19
52000	763.73	735.41	723.46	706.63	701.53	700.31	699.28	696.01	694.54
53000	778.42	749.56	737.37	720.22	715.02	713.78	712.73	709.39	707.90
54000	793.10	763.70	751.28	733.80	728.51	727.25	726.17	722.78	721.26
55000	807.79	777.84	765.20	747.39	742.00	740.71	739.62	736.16	734.61
56000	822.48	791.98	779.11	760.98	755.49	754.18	753.07	749.55	747.97
57000	837.16	806.13	793.02	774.57	768.98	767.65	766.52	762.93	761.32
58000	851.85	820.27	806.93	788.16	782.47	781.12	779.96	776.32	774.68
59000	866.54	834.41	820.85	801.75	795.96	794.58	793.41	789.70	788.04
60000	881.23	848.55	834.76	815.34	809.45	808.05	806.86	803.09	801.39
61000	895.91	862.70	848.67	828.93	822.95	821.52	820.31	816.47	814.75
62000	910.60	876.84	862.58	842.52	836.44	834.99	833.75	829.86	828.11
63000	925.29	890.98	876.50	856.10	849.93	848.45	847.20	843.24	841.46
64000	939.97	905.12	890.41	869.69	863.42	861.92	860.65	856.63	854.82
65000	954.66	919.27	904.32	883.28	876.91	875.39	874.10	870.01	868.18
67500	991.38	954.62	939.10	917.25	910.64	909.06	907.72	903.47	901.57
70000	1028.10	989.98	973.88	951.23	944.36	942.73	941.33	936.93	934.96
75000	1101.53	1060.69	1043.45	1019.17	1011.82	1010.06	1008.57	1003.86	1001.74
80000	1174.97	1131.40	1113.01	1087.12	1079.27	1077.40	1075.81	1070.78	1068.52
85000	1248.40	1202.12	1182.57	1155.06	1146.73	1144.74	1143.05	1137.70	1135.31
90000	1321.84	1272.83	1252.14	1223.00	1214.18	1212.08	1210.29	1204.63	1202.09
95000	1395.27	1343.54	1321.70	1290.95	1281.63	1279.41	1277.52	1271.55	1268.87
100000	1468.71	1414.25	1391.26	1358.89	1349.09	1346.75	1344.76	1338.47	1335.65
105000	1542.14	1484.96	1460.82	1426.84	1416.54	1414.09	1412.00	1405.40	1402.44
110000	1615.58	1555.68	1530.39	1494.78	1484.00	1481.42	1479.24	1472.32	1469.22
115000	1689.01	1626.39	1599.95	1562.73	1551.45	1548.76	1546.48	1539.24	1536.00
120000	1762.45	1697.10	1669.51	1630.67	1618.90	1616.10	1613.71	1606.17	1602.78
125000	1835.88	1767.81	1739.07	1698.62	1686.36	1683.44	1680.95	1673.09	1669.57
130000	1909.32	1838.53	1808.64	1766.56	1753.81	1750.77	1748.19	1740.02	1736.35
135000	1982.75	1909.24	1878.20	1834.50	1821.27	1818.11	1815.43	1806.94	1803.13
140000	2056.19	1979.95	1947.76	1902.45	1888.72	1885.45	1882.66	1873.86	1869.91
145000	2129.62	2050.66	2017.33	1970.39	1956.17	1952.78	1949.90	1940.79	1936.70
150000	2203.06	2121.38	2086.89	2038.34	2023.63	2020.12	2017.14	2007.71	2003.48

16⅛ % MONTHLY PAYMENT
NECESSARY TO AMORTIZE A LOAN

AMOUNT	1 YEAR	2 YEARS	3 YEARS	4 YEARS	5 YEARS	7 YEARS	8 YEARS	10 YEARS	12 YEARS
$ 50	4.54	2.46	1.77	1.43	1.22	1.00	.94	.85	.79
100	9.08	4.91	3.53	2.85	2.44	2.00	1.87	1.69	1.58
200	18.16	9.81	7.05	5.69	4.88	3.99	3.73	3.37	3.15
300	27.24	14.71	10.57	8.53	7.32	5.98	5.59	5.05	4.73
400	36.32	19.61	14.09	11.37	9.76	7.98	7.45	6.74	6.30
500	45.40	24.52	17.61	14.21	12.20	9.97	9.31	8.42	7.88
600	54.48	29.42	21.14	17.05	14.64	11.96	11.17	10.10	9.45
700	63.56	34.32	24.66	19.89	17.07	13.96	13.03	11.79	11.02
800	72.64	39.22	28.18	22.73	19.51	15.95	14.89	13.47	12.60
900	81.72	44.13	31.70	25.57	21.95	17.94	16.75	15.15	14.17
1000	90.80	49.03	35.22	28.41	24.39	19.94	18.61	16.83	15.75
2000	181.59	98.05	70.44	56.81	48.77	39.87	37.21	33.66	31.49
3000	272.38	147.07	105.66	85.22	73.16	59.80	55.81	50.49	47.23
4000	363.17	196.10	140.88	113.62	97.54	79.74	74.41	67.32	62.97
5000	453.96	245.12	176.10	142.03	121.93	99.67	93.02	84.15	78.71
6000	544.75	294.14	211.32	170.43	146.31	119.60	111.62	100.98	94.45
7000	635.54	343.17	246.54	198.84	170.70	139.54	130.22	117.81	110.19
8000	726.33	392.19	281.76	227.24	195.08	159.47	148.82	134.64	125.93
9000	817.12	441.21	316.97	255.64	219.47	179.40	167.43	151.47	141.67
10000	907.91	490.23	352.19	284.05	243.85	199.34	186.03	168.30	157.41
15000	1361.86	735.35	528.29	426.07	365.77	299.00	279.04	252.44	236.11
20000	1815.81	980.46	704.38	568.09	487.70	398.67	372.05	336.59	314.81
25000	2269.76	1225.58	880.47	710.11	609.62	498.34	465.06	420.74	393.51
30000	2723.71	1470.69	1056.57	852.14	731.54	598.00	558.08	504.88	472.21
35000	3177.66	1715.81	1232.66	994.16	853.46	697.67	651.09	589.03	550.91
40000	3631.61	1960.92	1408.76	1136.18	975.39	797.34	744.10	673.18	629.62
45000	4085.56	2206.03	1584.85	1278.20	1097.31	897.00	837.11	757.32	708.32
46000	4176.35	2255.06	1620.07	1306.60	1121.69	916.94	855.71	774.15	724.06
47000	4267.14	2304.08	1655.29	1335.01	1146.08	936.87	874.32	790.98	739.80
48000	4357.93	2353.10	1690.51	1363.41	1170.46	956.80	892.92	807.81	755.54
49000	4448.72	2402.13	1725.73	1391.82	1194.85	976.74	911.52	824.64	771.28
50000	4539.51	2451.15	1760.94	1420.22	1219.23	996.67	930.12	841.47	787.02
51000	4630.30	2500.17	1796.16	1448.63	1243.62	1016.60	948.73	858.30	802.76
52000	4721.09	2549.19	1831.38	1477.03	1268.00	1036.54	967.33	875.13	818.50
53000	4811.88	2598.22	1866.60	1505.44	1292.38	1056.47	985.93	891.96	834.24
54000	4902.67	2647.24	1901.82	1533.84	1316.77	1076.40	1004.53	908.79	849.98
55000	4993.46	2696.26	1937.04	1562.24	1341.15	1096.34	1023.14	925.62	865.72
56000	5084.25	2745.29	1972.26	1590.65	1365.54	1116.27	1041.74	942.45	881.46
57000	5175.04	2794.31	2007.48	1619.05	1389.92	1136.20	1060.34	959.27	897.20
58000	5265.83	2843.33	2042.69	1647.46	1414.31	1156.14	1078.94	976.10	912.94
59000	5356.62	2892.35	2077.91	1675.86	1438.69	1176.07	1097.54	992.93	928.68
60000	5447.41	2941.38	2113.13	1704.27	1463.08	1196.00	1116.15	1009.76	944.42
61000	5538.20	2990.40	2148.35	1732.67	1487.46	1215.94	1134.75	1026.59	960.16
62000	5628.99	3039.42	2183.57	1761.07	1511.85	1235.87	1153.35	1043.42	975.90
63000	5719.78	3088.45	2218.79	1789.48	1536.23	1255.80	1171.95	1060.25	991.64
64000	5810.57	3137.47	2254.01	1817.88	1560.61	1275.74	1190.56	1077.08	1007.38
65000	5901.36	3186.49	2289.23	1846.29	1585.00	1295.67	1209.16	1093.91	1023.12
67500	6128.33	3309.05	2377.27	1917.30	1645.96	1345.50	1255.66	1135.98	1062.47
70000	6355.31	3431.61	2465.32	1988.31	1706.92	1395.34	1302.17	1178.06	1101.82
75000	6809.26	3676.72	2641.41	2130.33	1828.84	1495.00	1395.18	1262.20	1180.52
80000	7263.21	3921.83	2817.51	2272.35	1950.77	1594.67	1488.19	1346.35	1259.23
85000	7717.16	4166.95	2993.60	2414.37	2072.69	1694.34	1581.21	1430.49	1337.93
90000	8171.11	4412.06	3169.69	2556.40	2194.61	1794.00	1674.22	1514.64	1416.63
95000	8625.06	4657.18	3345.79	2698.42	2316.53	1893.67	1767.23	1598.79	1495.33
100000	9079.01	4902.29	3521.88	2840.44	2438.46	1993.34	1860.24	1682.93	1574.03
105000	9532.96	5147.41	3697.98	2982.46	2560.38	2093.00	1953.25	1767.08	1652.73
110000	9986.91	5392.52	3874.07	3124.48	2682.30	2192.67	2046.27	1851.23	1731.43
115000	10440.86	5637.63	4050.16	3266.50	2804.23	2292.34	2139.28	1935.37	1810.13
120000	10894.81	5882.75	4226.26	3408.53	2926.15	2392.00	2232.29	2019.52	1888.84
125000	11348.76	6127.86	4402.35	3550.55	3048.07	2491.67	2325.30	2103.67	1967.54
130000	11802.71	6372.98	4578.45	3692.57	3169.99	2591.34	2418.31	2187.81	2046.24
135000	12256.66	6618.09	4754.54	3834.59	3291.92	2691.00	2511.32	2271.96	2124.94
140000	12710.61	6863.21	4930.63	3976.61	3413.84	2790.67	2604.34	2356.11	2203.64
145000	13164.56	7108.32	5106.73	4118.63	3535.76	2890.34	2697.35	2440.25	2282.34
150000	13618.51	7353.43	5282.82	4260.66	3657.68	2990.00	2790.36	2524.40	2361.04

150

MONTHLY PAYMENT 16⅛%

NECESSARY TO AMORTIZE A LOAN

AMOUNT	15 YEARS	18 YEARS	20 YEARS	25 YEARS	28 YEARS	29 YEARS	30 YEARS	35 YEARS	40 YEARS
$ 50	.74	.72	.71	69	68	68	68	68	68
100	1.48	1.43	1.41	1.37	1.36	1.36	1.36	1.35	1.35
200	2.96	2.85	2.81	2.74	2.72	2.72	2.71	2.70	2.70
300	4.44	4.28	4.21	4.11	4.08	4.08	4.07	4.05	4.04
400	5.91	5.70	5.61	5.48	5.44	5.43	5.42	5.40	5.39
500	7.39	7.12	7.01	6.85	6.80	6.79	6.78	6.75	6.73
600	8.87	8.55	8.41	8.22	8.16	8.15	8.13	8.10	8.08
700	10.35	9.97	9.81	9.59	9.52	9.50	9.49	9.45	9.43
800	11.82	11.39	11.21	10.95	10.88	10.86	10.84	10.79	10.77
900	13.30	12.82	12.61	12.32	12.24	12.22	12.20	12.14	12.12
1000	14.78	14.24	14.01	13.69	13.60	13.57	13.55	13.49	13.46
2000	29.55	28.47	28.02	27.38	27.19	27.14	27.10	26.98	26.92
3000	44.33	42.71	42.02	41.07	40.78	40.71	40.65	40.47	40.38
4000	59.10	56.94	56.03	54.75	54.37	54.28	54.20	53.95	53.84
5000	73.88	71.17	70.04	68.44	67.96	67.84	67.75	67.44	67.30
6000	88.65	85.41	84.04	82.13	81.55	81.41	81.30	80.93	80.76
7000	103.42	99.64	98.05	95.81	95.14	94.98	94.84	94.41	94.22
8000	118.20	113.88	112.06	109.50	108.73	108.55	108.39	107.90	107.68
9000	132.97	128.11	126.06	123.19	122.32	122.12	121.94	121.39	121.14
10000	147.75	142.34	140.07	136.88	135.91	135.68	135.49	134.88	134.60
15000	221.62	213.51	210.10	205.31	203.87	203.52	203.23	202.31	201.90
20000	295.49	284.68	280.13	273.75	271.82	271.36	270.97	269.75	269.20
25000	369.36	355.85	350.17	342.18	339.77	339.20	338.72	337.18	336.50
30000	443.23	427.02	420.20	410.62	407.73	407.04	406.46	404.62	403.80
35000	517.10	498.19	490.23	479.05	475.68	474.88	474.20	472.05	471.09
40000	590.98	569.36	560.26	547.49	543.64	542.72	541.94	539.49	538.39
45000	664.85	640.53	630.29	615.92	611.59	610.56	609.68	606.92	605.69
46000	679.62	654.77	644.30	629.61	625.18	624.13	623.23	620.41	619.15
47000	694.39	669.00	658.31	643.30	638.77	637.69	636.78	633.90	632.61
48000	709.17	683.24	672.31	656.99	652.36	651.26	650.33	647.38	646.07
49000	723.94	697.47	686.32	670.67	665.95	664.83	663.88	660.87	659.53
50000	738.72	711.70	700.33	684.36	679.54	678.40	677.43	674.36	672.99
51000	753.49	725.94	714.33	698.05	693.13	691.97	690.97	687.85	686.45
52000	768.27	740.17	728.34	711.73	706.73	705.53	704.52	701.33	699.91
53000	783.04	754.41	742.35	725.42	720.32	719.10	718.07	714.82	713.37
54000	797.81	768.64	756.35	739.11	733.91	732.67	731.62	728.31	726.83
55000	812.59	782.87	770.36	752.79	747.50	746.24	745.17	741.79	740.29
56000	827.36	797.11	784.36	766.48	761.09	759.81	758.72	755.28	753.75
57000	842.14	811.34	798.37	780.17	774.68	773.37	772.26	768.77	767.21
58000	856.91	825.58	812.38	793.86	788.27	786.94	785.81	782.25	780.67
59000	871.69	839.81	826.38	807.54	801.86	800.51	799.36	795.74	794.13
60000	886.46	854.04	840.39	821.23	815.45	814.08	812.91	809.23	807.59
61000	901.23	868.28	854.40	834.92	829.04	827.64	826.46	822.72	821.05
62000	916.01	882.51	868.40	848.60	842.63	841.21	840.01	836.20	834.51
63000	930.78	896.75	882.41	862.29	856.22	854.78	853.55	849.69	847.97
64000	945.56	910.98	896.42	875.98	869.81	868.35	867.10	863.18	861.43
65000	960.33	925.21	910.42	889.67	883.41	881.92	880.65	876.66	874.89
67500	997.27	960.80	945.44	923.88	917.38	915.84	914.52	910.38	908.54
70000	1034.20	996.38	980.45	958.10	951.36	949.76	948.39	944.10	942.18
75000	1108.07	1067.55	1050.49	1026.54	1019.31	1017.59	1016.14	1011.54	1009.48
80000	1181.95	1138.72	1120.52	1094.97	1087.27	1085.43	1083.88	1078.97	1076.78
85000	1255.82	1209.89	1190.55	1163.41	1155.22	1153.27	1151.62	1146.41	1144.08
90000	1329.69	1281.06	1260.58	1231.84	1223.17	1221.11	1219.36	1213.84	1211.38
95000	1403.56	1352.23	1330.62	1300.28	1291.13	1288.95	1287.10	1281.28	1278.68
100000	1477.43	1423.40	1400.65	1368.71	1359.08	1356.79	1354.85	1348.71	1345.98
105000	1551.30	1494.57	1470.68	1437.15	1427.04	1424.63	1422.59	1416.15	1413.27
110000	1625.17	1565.74	1540.71	1505.58	1494.99	1492.47	1490.33	1483.58	1480.57
115000	1699.04	1636.91	1610.74	1574.02	1562.94	1560.31	1558.07	1551.02	1547.87
120000	1772.92	1708.08	1680.78	1642.46	1630.90	1628.15	1625.81	1618.45	1615.17
125000	1846.79	1779.25	1750.81	1710.89	1698.85	1695.99	1693.56	1685.89	1682.47
130000	1920.66	1850.42	1820.84	1779.33	1766.81	1763.83	1761.30	1753.32	1749.77
135000	1994.53	1921.59	1890.87	1847.76	1834.76	1831.67	1829.04	1820.76	1817.07
140000	2068.40	1992.76	1960.90	1916.20	1902.71	1899.51	1896.78	1888.19	1884.36
145000	2142.27	2063.93	2030.94	1984.63	1970.67	1967.35	1964.52	1955.63	1951.66
150000	2216.14	2135.10	2100.97	2053.07	2038.62	2035.18	2032.27	2023.07	2018.96

MONTHLY PAYMENT
NECESSARY TO AMORTIZE A LOAN

AMOUNT	1 YEAR	2 YEARS	3 YEARS	4 YEARS	5 YEARS	7 YEARS	8 YEARS	10 YEARS	12 YEARS
$ 50	4.55	2.46	1.77	1.43	1.23	1.01	.94	.85	.80
100	9.09	4.91	3.53	2.85	2.45	2.01	1.87	1.70	1.59
200	18.17	9.82	7.06	5.70	4.90	4.01	3.74	3.39	3.17
300	27.26	14.73	10.59	8.55	7.34	6.01	5.61	5.08	4.75
400	36.34	19.64	14.12	11.39	9.79	8.01	7.48	6.77	6.33
500	45.43	24.55	17.65	14.24	12.23	10.01	9.34	8.46	7.92
600	54.51	29.45	21.17	17.09	14.68	12.01	11.21	10.15	9.50
700	63.60	34.36	24.70	19.93	17.12	14.01	13.08	11.84	11.08
800	72.68	39.27	28.23	22.78	19.57	16.01	14.95	13.53	12.66
900	81.77	44.18	31.76	25.63	22.01	18.01	16.81	15.22	14.25
1000	90.85	49.09	35.29	28.47	24.46	20.01	18.68	16.91	15.83
2000	181.70	98.17	70.57	56.94	48.91	40.01	37.36	33.82	31.65
3000	272.55	147.25	105.85	85.41	73.36	60.02	56.03	50.73	47.47
4000	363.40	196.34	141.13	113.88	97.81	80.02	74.71	67.63	63.29
5000	454.25	245.42	176.41	142.35	122.26	100.03	93.39	84.54	79.12
6000	545.10	294.50	211.69	170.82	146.71	120.03	112.06	101.45	94.94
7000	635.95	343.58	246.97	199.28	171.16	140.04	130.74	118.36	110.76
8000	726.80	392.67	282.25	227.75	195.61	160.04	149.41	135.26	126.58
9000	817.65	441.75	317.53	256.22	220.06	180.05	168.09	152.17	142.41
10000	908.50	490.83	352.81	284.69	244.52	200.05	186.77	169.08	158.23
15000	1362.74	736.24	529.21	427.03	366.77	300.08	280.15	253.62	237.34
20000	1816.99	981.66	705.62	569.37	489.03	400.10	373.53	338.15	316.45
25000	2271.24	1227.07	882.02	711.72	611.28	500.12	466.91	422.69	395.57
30000	2725.48	1472.48	1058.42	854.06	733.54	600.15	560.29	507.23	474.68
35000	3179.73	1717.90	1234.83	996.40	855.79	700.17	653.67	591.77	553.79
40000	3633.97	1963.31	1411.23	1138.74	978.05	800.19	747.05	676.30	632.90
45000	4088.22	2208.72	1587.63	1281.09	1100.30	900.22	840.43	760.84	712.01
46000	4179.07	2257.81	1622.91	1309.56	1124.76	920.22	859.11	777.75	727.84
47000	4269.92	2306.89	1658.19	1338.02	1149.21	940.23	877.78	794.65	743.66
48000	4360.77	2355.97	1693.47	1366.49	1173.66	960.23	896.46	811.56	759.48
49000	4451.62	2405.05	1728.75	1394.96	1198.11	980.24	915.13	828.47	775.30
50000	4542.47	2454.14	1764.03	1423.43	1222.56	1000.24	933.81	845.38	791.13
51000	4633.31	2503.22	1799.31	1451.90	1247.01	1020.25	952.49	862.28	806.95
52000	4724.16	2552.30	1834.60	1480.37	1271.46	1040.25	971.16	879.19	822.77
53000	4815.01	2601.39	1869.88	1508.83	1295.91	1060.25	989.84	896.10	838.59
54000	4905.86	2650.47	1905.16	1537.30	1320.36	1080.26	1008.51	913.01	854.42
55000	4996.71	2699.55	1940.44	1565.77	1344.81	1100.26	1027.19	929.91	870.24
56000	5087.56	2748.63	1975.72	1594.24	1369.27	1120.27	1045.87	946.82	886.06
57000	5178.41	2797.72	2011.00	1622.71	1393.72	1140.27	1064.54	963.73	901.88
58000	5269.26	2846.80	2046.28	1651.18	1418.17	1160.28	1083.22	980.64	917.71
59000	5360.11	2895.88	2081.56	1679.65	1442.62	1180.28	1101.89	997.54	933.53
60000	5450.96	2944.96	2116.84	1708.11	1467.07	1200.29	1120.57	1014.45	949.35
61000	5541.81	2994.05	2152.12	1736.58	1491.52	1220.29	1139.25	1031.36	965.17
62000	5632.66	3043.13	2187.40	1765.05	1515.97	1240.30	1157.92	1048.27	981.00
63000	5723.50	3092.21	2222.68	1793.52	1540.42	1260.30	1176.60	1065.17	996.82
64000	5814.35	3141.29	2257.96	1821.99	1564.87	1280.31	1195.27	1082.08	1012.64
65000	5905.20	3190.38	2293.24	1850.46	1589.33	1300.31	1213.95	1098.99	1028.46
67500	6132.33	3313.08	2381.44	1921.63	1650.45	1350.32	1260.64	1141.26	1068.02
70000	6359.45	3435.79	2469.65	1992.80	1711.58	1400.33	1307.33	1183.53	1107.58
75000	6813.70	3681.20	2646.05	2135.14	1833.84	1500.36	1400.71	1268.06	1186.69
80000	7267.94	3926.62	2822.45	2277.48	1956.09	1600.38	1494.09	1352.60	1265.80
85000	7722.19	4172.03	2998.85	2419.83	2078.35	1700.41	1587.47	1437.14	1344.91
90000	8176.43	4417.44	3175.26	2562.17	2200.60	1800.43	1680.85	1521.67	1424.02
95000	8630.68	4662.86	3351.66	2704.51	2322.86	1900.45	1774.23	1606.21	1503.14
100000	9084.93	4908.27	3528.06	2846.85	2445.11	2000.48	1867.61	1690.75	1582.25
105000	9539.17	5153.68	3704.47	2939.20	2567.37	2100.50	1960.99	1775.29	1661.36
110000	9993.42	5399.10	3880.87	3131.54	2689.62	2200.52	2054.37	1859.82	1740.47
115000	10447.66	5644.51	4057.27	3273.88	2811.88	2300.55	2147.76	1944.36	1819.59
120000	10901.91	5889.92	4233.67	3416.22	2934.14	2400.57	2241.14	2028.90	1898.70
125000	11356.16	6135.34	4410.08	3558.57	3056.39	2500.59	2334.52	2113.44	1977.81
130000	11810.40	6380.75	4586.48	3700.91	3178.65	2600.62	2427.90	2197.97	2056.92
135000	12264.65	6626.16	4762.88	3843.25	3300.90	2700.64	2521.28	2282.51	2136.03
140000	12718.89	6871.58	4939.29	3985.59	3423.16	2800.66	2614.66	2367.05	2215.15
145000	13173.14	7116.99	5115.69	4127.93	3545.41	2900.69	2708.04	2451.58	2294.26
150000	13627.39	7362.40	5292.09	4270.28	3667.67	3000.71	2801.42	2536.12	2373.37

MONTHLY PAYMENT 16¼%

NECESSARY TO AMORTIZE A LOAN

AMOUNT	15 YEARS	18 YEARS	20 YEARS	25 YEARS	28 YEARS	29 YEARS	30 YEARS	35 YEARS	40 YEARS
$ 50	.75	.72	.71	69	69	69	69	68	68
100	1.49	1.44	1.42	1.38	1.37	1.37	1.37	1.36	1.36
200	2.98	2.87	2.83	2.76	2.74	2.74	2.73	2.72	2.72
300	4.46	4.30	4.24	4.14	4.11	4.11	4.10	4.08	4.07
400	5.95	5.74	5.65	5.52	5.48	5.47	5.46	5.44	5.43
500	7.44	7.17	7.06	6.90	6.85	6.84	6.83	6.80	6.79
600	8.92	8.60	8.47	8.28	8.22	8.21	8.19	8.16	8.14
700	10.41	10.03	9.88	9.65	9.59	9.57	9.56	9.52	9.50
800	11.89	11.47	11.29	11.03	10.96	10.94	10.92	10.88	10.86
900	13.38	12.90	12.70	12.41	12.33	12.31	12.29	12.24	12.21
1000	14.87	14.33	14.11	13.79	13.70	13.67	13.65	13.59	13.57
2000	29.73	28.66	28.21	27.58	27.39	27.34	27.30	27.18	27.13
3000	44.59	42.98	42.31	41.36	41.08	41.01	40.95	40.77	40.69
4000	59.45	57.31	56.41	55.15	54.77	54.68	54.60	54.36	54.26
5000	74.31	71.63	70.51	68.93	68.46	68.35	68.25	67.95	67.82
6000	89.18	85.96	84.61	82.72	82.15	82.02	81.90	81.54	81.38
7000	104.04	100.28	98.71	96.50	95.84	95.68	95.55	95.13	94.95
8000	118.90	114.61	112.81	110.29	109.53	109.35	109.20	108.72	108.51
9000	133.76	128.94	126.91	124.07	123.22	123.02	122.85	122.31	122.07
10000	148.62	143.26	141.01	137.86	136.91	136.69	136.50	135.90	135.63
15000	222.93	214.89	211.51	206.79	205.37	205.03	204.75	203.85	203.45
20000	297.24	286.52	282.01	275.71	273.82	273.37	272.99	271.79	271.26
25000	371.55	358.15	352.52	344.64	342.28	341.71	341.24	339.74	339.08
30000	445.86	429.78	423.02	413.57	410.73	410.06	409.49	407.69	406.89
35000	520.16	501.40	493.52	482.49	479.18	478.40	477.73	475.64	474.71
40000	594.47	573.03	564.02	551.42	547.64	546.74	545.98	543.58	542.52
45000	668.78	644.66	634.53	620.35	616.09	615.08	614.23	611.53	610.34
46000	683.64	658.99	648.63	634.13	629.78	628.75	627.87	625.12	623.90
47000	698.50	673.31	662.73	647.92	643.47	642.42	641.52	638.71	637.46
48000	713.37	687.64	676.83	661.70	657.16	656.09	655.17	652.30	651.03
49000	728.23	701.96	690.93	675.49	670.86	669.76	668.82	665.89	664.59
50000	743.09	716.29	705.03	689.28	684.55	683.42	682.47	679.48	678.15
51000	757.95	730.62	719.13	703.06	698.24	697.09	696.12	693.07	691.72
52000	772.81	744.94	733.23	716.85	711.93	710.76	709.77	706.66	705.28
53000	787.67	759.27	747.33	730.63	725.62	724.43	723.42	720.25	718.84
54000	802.54	773.59	761.43	744.42	739.31	738.10	737.07	733.84	732.41
55000	817.40	787.92	775.53	758.20	753.00	751.77	750.72	747.43	745.97
56000	832.26	802.24	789.63	771.99	766.69	765.43	764.37	761.02	759.53
57000	847.12	816.57	803.73	785.77	780.38	779.10	778.02	774.61	773.09
58000	861.98	830.89	817.83	799.56	794.07	792.77	791.67	788.20	786.66
59000	876.84	845.22	831.93	813.34	807.76	806.44	805.32	801.79	800.22
60000	891.71	859.55	846.03	827.13	821.45	820.11	818.97	815.37	813.78
61000	906.57	873.87	860.13	840.92	835.15	833.78	832.62	828.96	827.35
62000	921.43	888.20	874.23	854.70	848.84	847.44	846.26	842.55	840.91
63000	936.29	902.52	888.33	868.49	862.53	861.11	859.91	856.14	854.47
64000	951.15	916.85	902.43	882.27	876.22	874.78	873.56	869.73	868.03
65000	966.01	931.17	916.53	896.06	889.91	888.45	887.21	883.32	881.60
67500	1003.17	966.99	951.79	930.52	924.14	922.62	921.34	917.30	915.51
70000	1040.32	1002.80	987.04	964.98	958.36	956.79	955.46	951.27	949.41
75000	1114.63	1074.43	1057.54	1033.91	1026.82	1025.13	1023.71	1019.22	1017.23
80000	1188.94	1146.06	1128.04	1102.84	1095.27	1093.48	1091.95	1087.16	1085.04
85000	1263.25	1217.69	1198.54	1171.77	1163.73	1161.82	1160.20	1155.11	1152.86
90000	1337.56	1289.32	1269.05	1240.69	1232.18	1230.16	1228.45	1223.06	1220.67
95000	1411.86	1360.95	1339.55	1309.62	1300.63	1298.50	1296.69	1291.01	1288.49
100000	1486.17	1432.57	1410.05	1378.55	1369.09	1366.84	1364.94	1358.95	1356.30
105000	1560.48	1504.20	1480.55	1447.47	1437.54	1435.19	1433.19	1426.90	1424.12
110000	1634.79	1575.83	1551.06	1516.40	1506.00	1503.53	1501.43	1494.85	1491.93
115000	1709.10	1647.46	1621.56	1585.33	1574.45	1571.87	1569.68	1562.80	1559.75
120000	1783.41	1719.09	1692.06	1654.25	1642.90	1640.21	1637.93	1630.74	1627.56
125000	1857.72	1790.72	1762.56	1723.18	1711.36	1708.55	1706.17	1698.69	1695.38
130000	1932.02	1862.34	1833.06	1792.11	1779.81	1776.89	1774.42	1766.64	1763.19
135000	2006.33	1933.97	1903.57	1861.04	1848.27	1845.24	1842.67	1834.59	1831.01
140000	2080.64	2005.60	1974.07	1929.96	1916.72	1913.58	1910.91	1902.53	1898.82
145000	2154.95	2077.23	2044.57	1998.89	1985.17	1981.92	1979.16	1970.48	1966.64
150000	2229.26	2148.86	2115.07	2067.82	2053.63	2050.26	2047.41	2038.43	2034.45

153

16⅜% MONTHLY PAYMENT
NECESSARY TO AMORTIZE A LOAN

AMOUNT	1 YEAR	2 YEARS	3 YEARS	4 YEARS	5 YEARS	7 YEARS	8 YEARS	10 YEARS	12 YEARS
$ 50	4.55	2.46	1.77	1.43	1.23	1.01	.94	.85	.80
100	9.10	4.92	3.54	2.86	2.46	2.01	1.88	1.70	1.60
200	18.19	9.83	7.07	5.71	4.91	4.02	3.75	3.40	3.19
300	27.28	14.75	10.61	8.56	7.36	6.03	5.63	5.10	4.78
400	36.37	19.66	14.14	11.42	9.81	8.04	7.50	6.80	6.37
500	45.46	24.58	17.68	14.27	12.26	10.04	9.38	8.50	7.96
600	54.55	29.49	21.21	17.12	14.72	12.05	11.25	10.20	9.55
700	63.64	34.40	24.74	19.98	17.17	14.06	13.13	11.90	11.14
800	72.73	39.32	28.28	22.83	19.62	16.07	15.00	13.59	12.73
900	81.82	44.23	31.81	25.68	22.07	18.07	16.88	15.29	14.32
1000	90.91	49.15	35.35	28.54	24.52	20.08	18.75	16.99	15.91
2000	181.82	98.29	70.69	57.07	49.04	40.16	37.50	33.98	31.81
3000	272.73	147.43	106.03	85.60	73.56	60.23	56.25	50.96	47.72
4000	363.64	196.57	141.37	114.14	98.08	80.31	75.00	67.95	63.62
5000	454.55	245.72	176.72	142.67	122.59	100.39	93.75	84.93	79.53
6000	545.46	294.86	212.06	171.20	147.11	120.46	112.50	101.92	95.43
7000	636.36	344.00	247.40	199.73	171.63	140.54	131.25	118.91	111.34
8000	727.27	393.14	282.74	228.27	196.15	160.61	150.00	135.89	127.24
9000	818.18	442.29	318.09	256.80	220.66	180.69	168.75	152.88	143.15
10000	909.09	491.43	353.43	285.33	245.18	200.77	187.50	169.86	159.05
15000	1363.63	737.14	530.14	428.00	367.77	301.15	281.25	254.79	238.58
20000	1818.17	982.85	706.85	570.66	490.36	401.53	375.00	339.72	318.10
25000	2272.72	1228.57	883.57	713.32	612.95	501.91	468.75	424.65	397.62
30000	2727.26	1474.28	1060.28	855.99	735.54	602.29	562.50	509.58	477.15
35000	3181.80	1719.99	1236.99	998.65	858.13	702.67	656.25	594.51	556.67
40000	3636.34	1965.70	1413.70	1141.31	980.72	803.05	750.00	679.44	636.20
45000	4090.88	2211.42	1590.42	1283.98	1103.30	903.44	843.75	764.36	715.72
46000	4181.79	2260.56	1625.76	1312.51	1127.82	923.51	862.50	781.35	731.63
47000	4272.70	2309.70	1661.10	1341.04	1152.34	943.59	881.25	798.34	747.53
48000	4363.61	2358.84	1696.44	1369.57	1176.86	963.66	900.00	815.32	763.44
49000	4454.52	2407.99	1731.79	1398.11	1201.38	983.74	918.75	832.31	779.34
50000	4545.43	2457.13	1767.13	1426.64	1225.89	1003.82	937.50	849.29	795.24
51000	4636.33	2506.27	1802.47	1455.17	1250.41	1023.89	956.25	866.28	811.15
52000	4727.24	2555.41	1837.81	1483.71	1274.93	1043.97	975.00	883.26	827.05
53000	4818.15	2604.56	1873.15	1512.24	1299.45	1064.05	993.75	900.25	842.96
54000	4909.06	2653.70	1908.50	1540.77	1323.96	1084.12	1012.50	917.24	858.86
55000	4999.97	2702.84	1943.84	1569.30	1348.48	1104.20	1031.25	934.22	874.77
56000	5090.88	2751.98	1979.18	1597.84	1373.00	1124.27	1050.00	951.21	890.67
57000	5181.78	2801.13	2014.52	1626.37	1397.52	1144.35	1068.75	968.19	906.58
58000	5272.69	2850.27	2049.87	1654.90	1422.03	1164.43	1087.50	985.18	922.48
59000	5363.60	2899.41	2085.21	1683.43	1446.55	1184.50	1106.25	1002.16	938.39
60000	5454.51	2948.55	2120.55	1711.97	1471.07	1204.58	1125.00	1019.15	954.29
61000	5545.42	2997.70	2155.89	1740.50	1495.59	1224.66	1143.75	1036.14	970.20
62000	5636.33	3046.84	2191.24	1769.03	1520.11	1244.73	1162.50	1053.12	986.10
63000	5727.23	3095.98	2226.58	1797.57	1544.62	1264.81	1181.25	1070.11	1002.01
64000	5818.14	3145.12	2261.92	1826.10	1569.14	1284.88	1200.00	1087.09	1017.91
65000	5909.05	3194.27	2297.26	1854.63	1593.66	1304.96	1218.75	1104.08	1033.82
67500	6136.32	3317.12	2385.62	1925.96	1654.95	1355.15	1265.63	1146.54	1073.58
70000	6363.59	3439.98	2473.98	1997.29	1716.25	1405.34	1312.50	1189.01	1113.34
75000	6818.14	3685.69	2650.69	2139.96	1838.84	1505.72	1406.25	1273.94	1192.86
80000	7272.68	3931.40	2827.40	2282.62	1961.43	1606.10	1500.00	1358.87	1272.39
85000	7727.22	4177.12	3004.11	2425.28	2084.01	1706.49	1593.75	1443.79	1351.91
90000	8181.76	4422.83	3180.83	2567.95	2206.60	1806.87	1687.50	1528.72	1431.44
95000	8636.30	4668.54	3357.54	2710.61	2329.19	1907.25	1781.25	1613.65	1510.96
100000	9090.85	4914.25	3534.25	2853.28	2451.78	2007.63	1875.00	1698.58	1590.48
105000	9545.39	5159.97	3710.96	2995.94	2574.37	2108.01	1968.75	1783.51	1670.01
110000	9999.93	5405.68	3887.67	3138.60	2696.96	2208.39	2062.50	1868.44	1749.53
115000	10454.47	5651.39	4064.39	3281.27	2819.55	2308.77	2156.25	1953.37	1829.06
120000	10909.01	5897.10	4241.10	3423.93	2942.14	2409.15	2250.00	2038.30	1908.58
125000	11363.56	6142.81	4417.81	3566.59	3064.72	2509.53	2343.75	2123.22	1988.10
130000	11818.10	6388.53	4594.52	3709.26	3187.31	2609.92	2437.50	2208.15	2067.63
135000	12272.64	6634.24	4771.24	3851.92	3309.90	2710.30	2531.25	2293.08	2147.15
140000	12727.18	6879.95	4947.95	3994.58	3432.49	2810.68	2625.00	2378.01	2226.68
145000	13181.72	7125.66	5124.66	4137.25	3555.08	2911.06	2718.75	2462.94	2306.20
150000	13636.27	7371.38	5301.37	4279.91	3677.67	3011.44	2812.50	2547.87	2385.72

154

MONTHLY PAYMENT 16⅜%
NECESSARY TO AMORTIZE A LOAN

AMOUNT	15 YEARS	18 YEARS	20 YEARS	25 YEARS	28 YEARS	29 YEARS	30 YEARS	35 YEARS	40 YEARS
$ 50	.75	.73	.71	.70	.69	.69	.69	.69	.69
100	1.50	1.45	1.42	1.39	1.38	1.38	1.38	1.37	1.37
200	2.99	2.89	2.84	2.78	2.76	2.76	2.76	2.74	2.74
300	4.49	4.33	4.26	4.17	4.14	4.14	4.13	4.11	4.10
400	5.98	5.77	5.68	5.56	5.52	5.51	5.51	5.48	5.47
500	7.48	7.21	7.10	6.95	6.90	6.89	6.88	6.85	6.84
600	8.97	8.66	8.52	8.34	8.28	8.27	8.26	8.22	8.20
700	10.47	10.10	9.94	9.72	9.66	9.64	9.63	9.59	9.57
800	11.96	11.54	11.36	11.11	11.04	11.02	11.01	10.96	10.94
900	13.46	12.98	12.78	12.50	12.42	12.40	12.38	12.33	12.30
1000	14.95	14.42	14.20	13.89	13.80	13.77	13.76	13.70	13.67
2000	29.90	28.84	28.39	27.77	27.59	27.54	27.51	27.39	27.34
3000	44.85	43.26	42.59	41.66	41.38	41.31	41.26	41.08	41.00
4000	59.80	57.68	56.78	55.54	55.17	55.08	55.01	54.77	54.67
5000	74.75	72.09	70.98	69.42	68.96	68.85	68.76	68.46	68.34
6000	89.70	86.51	85.17	83.31	82.75	82.62	82.51	82.16	82.00
7000	104.65	100.93	99.37	97.19	96.54	96.39	96.26	95.85	95.67
8000	119.60	115.35	113.56	111.08	110.33	110.16	110.01	109.54	109.34
9000	134.55	129.76	127.76	124.96	124.12	123.93	123.76	123.23	123.00
10000	149.50	144.18	141.95	138.84	137.91	137.69	137.51	136.92	136.67
15000	224.24	216.27	212.92	208.26	206.87	206.54	206.26	205.38	205.00
20000	298.99	288.36	283.90	277.68	275.82	275.38	275.01	273.84	273.33
25000	373.74	360.44	354.87	347.10	344.78	344.23	343.76	342.30	341.66
30000	448.48	432.53	425.84	416.52	413.73	413.07	412.52	410.76	409.99
35000	523.23	504.62	496.82	485.94	482.69	481.92	481.27	479.22	478.32
40000	597.98	576.71	567.79	555.36	551.64	550.76	550.02	547.68	546.66
45000	672.72	648.80	638.76	624.78	620.60	619.61	618.77	616.14	614.99
46000	687.67	663.21	652.96	638.66	634.39	633.38	632.52	629.84	628.65
47000	702.62	677.63	667.15	652.55	648.18	647.15	646.27	643.53	642.32
48000	717.57	692.05	681.35	666.43	661.97	660.92	660.02	657.22	655.99
49000	732.52	706.47	695.54	680.31	675.76	674.69	673.77	670.91	669.65
50000	747.47	720.88	709.74	694.20	689.55	688.45	687.52	684.60	683.32
51000	762.42	735.30	723.93	708.08	703.35	702.22	701.27	698.30	696.98
52000	777.37	749.72	738.13	721.97	717.14	715.99	715.02	711.99	710.65
53000	792.32	764.14	752.32	735.85	730.93	729.76	728.77	725.68	724.32
54000	807.27	778.55	766.52	749.73	744.72	743.53	742.52	739.37	737.98
55000	822.22	792.97	780.71	763.62	758.51	757.30	756.28	753.06	751.65
56000	837.17	807.39	794.91	777.50	772.30	771.07	770.03	766.76	765.32
57000	852.11	821.81	809.10	791.39	786.09	784.84	783.78	780.45	778.98
58000	867.06	836.22	823.29	805.27	799.88	798.61	797.53	794.14	792.65
59000	882.01	850.64	837.49	819.15	813.67	812.38	811.28	807.83	806.31
60000	896.96	865.06	851.68	833.04	827.46	826.14	825.03	821.52	819.98
61000	911.91	879.48	865.88	846.92	841.26	839.91	838.78	835.22	833.65
62000	926.86	893.89	880.07	860.80	855.05	853.68	852.53	848.91	847.31
63000	941.81	908.31	894.27	874.69	868.84	867.45	866.28	862.60	860.98
64000	956.76	922.73	908.46	888.57	882.63	881.22	880.03	876.29	874.65
65000	971.71	937.15	922.66	902.46	896.42	894.99	893.78	889.98	888.31
67500	1009.08	973.19	958.14	937.17	930.90	929.41	928.15	924.21	922.48
70000	1046.46	1009.23	993.63	971.88	965.37	963.83	962.53	958.44	956.64
75000	1121.20	1081.32	1064.60	1041.30	1034.33	1032.68	1031.28	1026.90	1024.97
80000	1195.95	1153.41	1135.58	1110.71	1103.28	1101.52	1100.03	1095.36	1093.31
85000	1270.69	1225.50	1206.55	1180.13	1172.24	1170.37	1168.79	1163.82	1161.64
90000	1345.44	1297.59	1277.52	1249.55	1241.19	1239.21	1237.54	1232.28	1229.97
95000	1420.19	1369.67	1348.50	1318.97	1310.15	1308.06	1306.29	1300.74	1298.30
100000	1494.93	1441.76	1419.47	1388.39	1379.10	1376.90	1375.04	1369.20	1366.63
105000	1569.68	1513.85	1490.44	1457.81	1448.06	1445.75	1443.79	1437.66	1434.96
110000	1644.43	1585.94	1561.42	1527.23	1517.01	1514.59	1512.55	1506.12	1503.29
115000	1719.17	1658.02	1632.39	1596.65	1585.97	1583.44	1581.30	1574.58	1571.63
120000	1793.92	1730.11	1703.36	1666.07	1654.92	1652.28	1650.05	1643.04	1639.96
125000	1868.67	1802.20	1774.34	1735.49	1723.88	1721.13	1718.80	1711.50	1708.29
130000	1943.41	1874.29	1845.31	1804.91	1792.83	1789.97	1787.55	1779.96	1776.62
135000	2018.16	1946.38	1916.28	1874.33	1861.79	1858.82	1856.30	1848.42	1844.95
140000	2092.91	2018.46	1987.26	1943.75	1930.74	1927.66	1925.06	1916.88	1913.28
145000	2167.65	2090.55	2058.23	2013.17	1999.70	1996.51	1993.81	1985.34	1981.61
150000	2242.40	2162.64	2129.20	2082.59	2068.65	2065.35	2062.56	2053.80	2049.94

16½% MONTHLY PAYMENT
NECESSARY TO AMORTIZE A LOAN

AMOUNT	1 YEAR	2 YEARS	3 YEARS	4 YEARS	5 YEARS	7 YEARS	8 YEARS	10 YEARS	12 YEARS
$ 50	4.55	2.47	1.78	1.43	1.23	1.01	.95	.86	.80
100	9.10	4.93	3.55	2.86	2.46	2.02	1.89	1.71	1.60
200	18.20	9.85	7.09	5.72	4.92	4.03	3.77	3.42	3.20
300	27.30	14.77	10.63	8.58	7.38	6.05	5.65	5.12	4.80
400	36.39	19.69	14.17	11.44	9.84	8.06	7.53	6.83	6.40
500	45.49	24.61	17.71	14.30	12.30	10.08	9.42	8.54	8.00
600	54.59	29.53	21.25	17.16	14.76	12.09	11.30	10.24	9.60
700	63.68	34.45	24.79	20.02	17.21	14.11	13.18	11.95	11.20
800	72.78	39.37	28.33	22.88	19.67	16.12	15.06	13.66	12.79
900	81.88	44.29	31.87	25.74	22.13	18.14	16.95	15.36	14.39
1000	90.97	49.21	35.41	28.60	24.59	20.15	18.83	17.07	15.99
2000	181.94	98.41	70.81	57.20	49.17	40.30	37.65	34.13	31.98
3000	272.91	147.61	106.22	85.80	73.76	60.45	56.48	51.20	47.97
4000	363.88	196.81	141.62	114.39	98.34	80.60	75.30	68.26	63.95
5000	454.84	246.02	177.03	142.99	122.93	100.74	94.12	85.33	79.94
6000	545.81	295.22	212.43	171.59	147.51	120.89	112.95	102.39	95.93
7000	636.78	344.42	247.84	200.18	172.10	141.04	131.77	119.45	111.92
8000	727.75	393.62	283.24	228.78	196.68	161.19	150.60	136.52	127.90
9000	818.71	442.83	318.64	257.38	221.27	181.34	169.42	153.58	143.89
10000	909.68	492.03	354.05	285.98	245.85	201.48	188.24	170.65	159.88
15000	1364.52	738.04	531.07	428.96	368.77	302.22	282.36	255.97	239.82
20000	1819.36	984.05	708.09	571.95	491.70	402.96	376.48	341.29	319.75
25000	2274.20	1230.06	885.11	714.93	614.62	503.70	470.60	426.61	399.69
30000	2729.03	1476.08	1062.14	857.92	737.54	604.44	564.72	511.93	479.63
35000	3183.87	1722.09	1239.16	1000.90	860.47	705.18	658.84	597.25	559.56
40000	3638.71	1968.10	1416.18	1143.89	983.39	805.92	752.96	682.57	639.50
45000	4093.55	2214.11	1593.20	1286.87	1106.31	906.66	847.08	767.90	719.44
46000	4184.52	2263.31	1628.61	1315.47	1130.89	926.81	865.91	784.96	735.42
47000	4275.48	2312.52	1664.01	1344.06	1155.48	946.96	884.73	802.02	751.41
48000	4366.45	2361.72	1699.42	1372.66	1180.06	967.10	903.56	819.09	767.40
49000	4457.42	2410.92	1734.82	1401.26	1204.65	987.25	922.38	836.15	783.38
50000	4548.39	2460.12	1770.22	1429.86	1229.23	1007.40	941.20	853.22	799.37
51000	4639.35	2509.32	1805.63	1458.45	1253.82	1027.55	960.03	870.28	815.36
52000	4730.32	2558.53	1841.03	1487.05	1278.40	1047.70	978.85	887.34	831.35
53000	4821.29	2607.73	1876.44	1515.65	1302.98	1067.84	997.68	904.41	847.33
54000	4912.26	2656.93	1911.84	1544.24	1327.57	1087.99	1016.50	921.47	863.32
55000	5003.23	2706.14	1947.25	1572.84	1352.15	1108.14	1035.32	938.54	879.31
56000	5094.19	2755.34	1982.65	1601.44	1376.74	1128.29	1054.15	955.60	895.30
57000	5185.16	2804.54	2018.05	1630.03	1401.32	1148.43	1072.97	972.67	911.28
58000	5276.13	2853.74	2053.46	1658.63	1425.91	1168.58	1091.80	989.73	927.27
59000	5367.10	2902.94	2088.86	1687.23	1450.49	1188.73	1110.62	1006.79	943.26
60000	5458.06	2952.15	2124.27	1715.83	1475.08	1208.88	1129.44	1023.86	959.25
61000	5549.03	3001.35	2159.67	1744.42	1499.66	1229.03	1148.27	1040.92	975.23
62000	5640.00	3050.55	2195.08	1773.02	1524.25	1249.17	1167.09	1057.99	991.22
63000	5730.97	3099.75	2230.48	1801.62	1548.83	1269.32	1185.92	1075.05	1007.21
64000	5821.93	3148.96	2265.89	1830.21	1573.41	1289.47	1204.74	1092.12	1023.19
65000	5912.90	3198.16	2301.29	1858.81	1598.00	1309.62	1223.56	1109.18	1039.18
67500	6140.32	3321.16	2389.80	1930.30	1659.46	1359.99	1270.62	1151.84	1079.15
70000	6367.74	3444.17	2478.31	2001.80	1720.92	1410.36	1317.68	1194.50	1119.12
75000	6822.58	3690.18	2655.33	2144.78	1843.84	1511.10	1411.80	1279.82	1199.06
80000	7277.42	3936.19	2832.36	2287.77	1966.77	1611.84	1505.92	1365.14	1278.99
85000	7732.25	4182.20	3009.38	2430.75	2089.69	1712.58	1600.04	1450.46	1358.93
90000	8187.09	4428.22	3186.40	2573.74	2212.61	1813.32	1694.16	1535.79	1438.87
95000	8641.93	4674.23	3363.42	2716.72	2335.53	1914.05	1788.28	1621.11	1518.80
100000	9096.77	4920.24	3540.44	2859.71	2458.46	2014.79	1882.40	1706.43	1598.74
105000	9551.61	5166.25	3717.47	3002.69	2581.38	2115.53	1976.52	1791.75	1678.68
110000	10006.45	5412.26	3894.49	3145.68	2704.30	2216.27	2070.64	1877.07	1758.61
115000	10461.28	5658.28	4071.51	3288.66	2827.22	2317.01	2164.76	1962.39	1838.55
120000	10916.12	5904.29	4248.53	3431.65	2950.15	2417.75	2258.88	2047.71	1918.49
125000	11370.96	6150.30	4425.55	3574.63	3073.07	2518.49	2353.00	2133.03	1998.42
130000	11825.80	6396.31	4602.57	3717.62	3195.99	2619.23	2447.12	2218.35	2078.36
135000	12280.64	6642.32	4779.60	3860.60	3318.92	2719.97	2541.24	2303.68	2158.30
140000	12735.47	6888.33	4956.62	4003.59	3441.84	2820.71	2635.36	2389.00	2238.23
145000	13190.31	7134.35	5133.64	4146.57	3564.76	2921.45	2729.48	2474.32	2318.17
150000	13645.15	7380.36	5310.66	4289.56	3687.68	3022.19	2823.60	2559.64	2398.11

156

MONTHLY PAYMENT 16½%

NECESSARY TO AMORTIZE A LOAN

AMOUNT	15 YEARS	18 YEARS	20 YEARS	25 YEARS	28 YEARS	29 YEARS	30 YEARS	35 YEARS	40 YEARS
$ 50	.76	.73	.72	.70	.70	.70	.70	.69	.69
100	1.51	1.46	1.43	1.40	1.40	1.39	1.39	1.38	1.38
200	3.01	2.91	2.86	2.80	2.78	2.78	2.78	2.76	2.76
300	4.52	4.36	4.29	4.20	4.17	4.17	4.16	4.14	4.14
400	6.02	5.81	5.72	5.60	5.56	5.55	5.55	5.52	5.51
500	7.52	7.26	7.15	7.00	6.95	6.94	6.93	6.90	6.89
600	9.03	8.71	8.58	8.39	8.34	8.33	8.32	8.28	8.27
700	10.53	10.16	10.01	9.79	9.73	9.71	9.70	9.66	9.64
800	12.03	11.61	11.44	11.19	11.12	11.10	11.09	11.04	11.02
900	13.54	13.06	12.87	12.59	12.51	12.49	12.47	12.42	12.40
1000	15.04	14.51	14.29	13.99	13.90	13.87	13.86	13.80	13.77
2000	30.08	29.02	28.58	27.97	27.79	27.74	27.71	27.59	27.54
3000	45.12	43.53	42.87	41.95	41.68	41.61	41.56	41.39	41.31
4000	60.15	58.04	57.16	55.93	55.57	55.48	55.41	55.18	55.08
5000	75.19	72.55	71.45	69.92	69.46	69.35	69.26	68.98	68.85
6000	90.23	87.06	85.74	83.90	83.35	83.22	83.11	82.77	82.62
7000	105.26	101.57	100.03	97.88	97.24	97.09	96.97	96.57	96.39
8000	120.30	116.08	114.32	111.86	111.13	110.96	110.82	110.36	110.16
9000	135.34	130.59	128.61	125.85	125.03	124.83	124.67	124.16	123.93
10000	150.38	145.10	142.90	139.83	138.92	138.70	138.52	137.95	137.70
15000	225.56	217.65	214.34	209.74	208.37	208.05	207.78	206.92	206.55
20000	300.75	290.20	285.79	279.65	277.83	277.40	277.03	275.90	275.40
25000	375.93	362.75	357.23	349.57	347.29	346.75	346.29	344.87	344.24
30000	451.12	435.29	428.68	419.48	416.74	416.10	415.55	413.84	413.09
35000	526.30	507.84	500.12	489.39	486.20	485.44	484.81	482.81	481.94
40000	601.49	580.39	571.57	559.30	555.65	554.79	554.06	551.79	550.79
45000	676.67	652.94	643.01	629.22	625.11	624.14	623.32	620.76	619.64
46000	691.71	667.45	657.30	643.20	639.00	638.01	637.17	634.55	633.41
47000	706.75	681.96	671.59	657.18	652.89	651.88	651.02	648.35	647.18
48000	721.79	696.47	685.88	671.16	666.78	665.75	664.88	662.14	660.95
49000	736.82	710.98	700.17	685.14	680.68	679.62	678.73	675.94	674.72
50000	751.86	725.49	714.46	699.13	694.57	693.49	692.58	689.73	688.48
51000	766.90	739.99	728.74	713.11	708.46	707.36	706.43	703.53	702.25
52000	781.93	754.50	743.03	727.09	722.35	721.23	720.28	717.32	716.02
53000	796.97	769.01	757.32	741.07	736.24	735.10	734.13	731.12	729.79
54000	812.01	783.52	771.61	755.06	750.13	748.97	747.98	744.91	743.56
55000	827.04	798.03	785.90	769.04	764.02	762.84	761.84	758.70	757.33
56000	842.08	812.54	800.19	783.02	777.91	776.71	775.69	772.50	771.10
57000	857.12	827.05	814.48	797.00	791.81	790.58	789.54	786.29	784.87
58000	872.16	841.56	828.77	810.99	805.70	804.45	803.39	800.09	798.64
59000	887.19	856.07	843.06	824.97	819.59	818.32	817.24	813.88	812.41
60000	902.23	870.58	857.35	838.95	833.48	832.19	831.09	827.68	826.18
61000	917.27	885.09	871.63	852.93	847.37	846.06	844.95	841.47	839.95
62000	932.30	899.60	885.92	866.92	861.26	859.93	858.80	855.27	853.72
63000	947.34	914.11	900.21	880.90	875.15	873.80	872.65	869.06	867.49
64000	962.38	928.62	914.50	894.88	889.04	887.67	886.50	882.86	881.26
65000	977.42	943.13	928.79	908.86	902.94	901.54	900.35	896.65	895.03
67500	1015.01	979.40	964.51	943.82	937.66	936.21	934.98	931.14	929.45
70000	1052.60	1015.68	1000.24	978.78	972.39	970.88	969.61	965.62	963.88
75000	1127.79	1088.23	1071.68	1048.69	1041.85	1040.23	1038.87	1034.60	1032.72
80000	1202.97	1160.77	1143.13	1118.60	1111.30	1109.58	1108.12	1103.57	1101.57
85000	1278.16	1233.32	1214.57	1188.51	1180.76	1178.93	1177.38	1172.54	1170.42
90000	1353.34	1305.87	1286.02	1258.43	1250.22	1248.28	1246.64	1241.51	1239.27
95000	1428.53	1378.42	1357.46	1328.34	1319.67	1317.63	1315.90	1310.49	1308.12
100000	1503.71	1450.97	1428.91	1398.25	1389.13	1386.98	1385.15	1379.46	1376.96
105000	1578.90	1523.51	1500.35	1468.16	1458.59	1456.33	1454.41	1448.43	1445.81
110000	1654.08	1596.06	1571.80	1538.07	1528.04	1525.67	1523.67	1517.40	1514.66
115000	1729.27	1668.61	1643.24	1607.99	1597.50	1595.02	1592.93	1586.38	1583.51
120000	1804.46	1741.16	1714.69	1677.90	1666.95	1664.37	1662.18	1655.35	1652.36
125000	1879.64	1813.71	1786.13	1747.81	1736.41	1733.72	1731.44	1724.32	1721.20
130000	1954.83	1886.25	1857.58	1817.72	1805.87	1803.07	1800.70	1793.30	1790.05
135000	2030.01	1958.80	1929.02	1887.64	1875.32	1872.42	1869.95	1862.27	1858.90
140000	2105.20	2031.35	2000.47	1957.55	1944.78	1941.76	1939.21	1931.24	1927.75
145000	2180.38	2103.90	2071.91	2027.46	2014.24	2011.11	2008.47	2000.21	1996.60
150000	2255.57	2176.45	2143.36	2097.37	2083.69	2080.46	2077.73	2069.19	2065.44

16⅝% MONTHLY PAYMENT
NECESSARY TO AMORTIZE A LOAN

AMOUNT	1 YEAR	2 YEARS	3 YEARS	4 YEARS	5 YEARS	7 YEARS	8 YEARS	10 YEARS	12 YEARS
$ 50	4.56	2.47	1.78	1.44	1.24	1.02	.95	.86	.81
100	9.11	4.93	3.55	2.87	2.47	2.03	1.89	1.72	1.61
200	18.21	9.86	7.10	5.74	4.94	4.05	3.78	3.43	3.22
300	27.31	14.78	10.64	8.60	7.40	6.07	5.67	5.15	4.83
400	36.42	19.71	14.19	11.47	9.87	8.09	7.56	6.86	6.43
500	45.52	24.64	17.74	14.34	12.33	10.11	9.45	8.58	8.04
600	54.62	29.56	21.28	17.20	14.80	12.14	11.34	10.29	9.65
700	63.72	34.49	24.83	20.07	17.26	14.16	13.23	12.01	11.25
800	72.83	39.41	28.38	22.93	19.73	16.18	15.12	13.72	12.86
900	81.93	44.34	31.92	25.80	22.19	18.20	17.01	15.43	14.47
1000	91.03	49.27	35.47	28.67	24.66	20.22	18.90	17.15	16.08
2000	182.06	98.53	70.94	57.33	49.31	40.44	37.80	34.29	32.15
3000	273.09	147.79	106.40	85.99	73.96	60.66	56.70	51.43	48.22
4000	364.11	197.05	141.87	114.65	98.61	80.88	75.60	68.58	64.29
5000	455.14	246.32	177.34	143.31	123.26	101.10	94.50	85.72	80.36
6000	546.17	295.58	212.80	171.97	147.91	121.32	113.39	102.86	96.43
7000	637.19	344.84	248.27	200.63	172.56	141.54	132.29	120.01	112.50
8000	728.22	394.10	283.74	229.30	197.22	161.76	151.19	137.15	128.57
9000	819.25	443.37	319.20	257.96	221.87	181.98	170.09	154.29	144.64
10000	910.27	492.63	354.67	286.62	246.52	202.20	188.99	171.43	160.71
15000	1365.41	738.94	532.00	429.93	369.78	303.30	283.48	257.15	241.06
20000	1820.54	985.25	709.33	573.23	493.03	404.40	377.97	342.86	321.41
25000	2275.68	1231.56	886.66	716.54	616.29	505.50	472.46	428.58	401.76
30000	2730.81	1477.87	1064.00	859.85	739.55	606.60	566.95	514.29	482.11
35000	3185.95	1724.18	1241.33	1003.15	862.80	707.69	661.44	600.01	562.46
40000	3641.08	1970.50	1418.66	1146.46	986.06	808.79	755.93	685.72	642.81
45000	4096.21	2216.81	1595.99	1289.77	1109.32	909.89	850.42	771.43	723.16
46000	4187.24	2266.07	1631.46	1318.43	1133.97	930.11	869.32	788.58	739.23
47000	4278.27	2315.33	1666.92	1347.09	1158.62	950.33	888.22	805.72	755.30
48000	4369.30	2364.59	1702.39	1375.75	1183.27	970.55	907.12	822.86	771.37
49000	4460.32	2413.86	1737.86	1404.41	1207.92	990.77	926.01	840.01	787.44
50000	4551.35	2463.12	1773.32	1433.07	1232.57	1010.99	944.91	857.15	803.51
51000	4642.38	2512.38	1808.79	1461.74	1257.23	1031.21	963.81	874.29	819.58
52000	4733.40	2561.64	1844.26	1490.40	1281.88	1051.43	982.71	891.43	835.65
53000	4824.43	2610.91	1879.72	1519.06	1306.53	1071.65	1001.61	908.58	851.72
54000	4915.46	2660.17	1915.19	1547.72	1331.18	1091.87	1020.50	925.72	867.79
55000	5006.48	2709.43	1950.66	1576.38	1355.83	1112.09	1039.40	942.86	883.86
56000	5097.51	2758.69	1986.12	1605.04	1380.48	1132.31	1058.30	960.01	899.93
57000	5188.54	2807.95	2021.59	1633.70	1405.13	1152.53	1077.20	977.15	916.00
58000	5279.56	2857.22	2057.05	1662.37	1429.79	1172.75	1096.10	994.29	932.07
59000	5370.59	2906.48	2092.52	1691.03	1454.44	1192.97	1114.99	1011.43	948.14
60000	5461.62	2955.74	2127.99	1719.69	1479.09	1213.19	1133.89	1028.58	964.21
61000	5552.64	3005.00	2163.45	1748.35	1503.74	1233.41	1152.79	1045.72	980.28
62000	5643.67	3054.27	2198.92	1777.01	1528.39	1253.62	1171.69	1062.86	996.35
63000	5734.70	3103.53	2234.39	1805.67	1553.04	1273.84	1190.59	1080.01	1012.42
64000	5825.73	3152.79	2269.85	1834.33	1577.69	1294.06	1209.49	1097.15	1028.49
65000	5916.75	3202.05	2305.32	1863.00	1602.35	1314.28	1228.38	1114.29	1044.56
67500	6144.32	3325.21	2393.99	1934.65	1663.97	1364.83	1275.63	1157.15	1084.73
70000	6371.89	3448.36	2482.65	2006.30	1725.60	1415.38	1322.87	1200.01	1124.91
75000	6827.02	3694.67	2659.98	2149.61	1848.86	1516.48	1417.36	1285.72	1205.26
80000	7282.16	3940.99	2837.32	2292.92	1972.12	1617.58	1511.86	1371.43	1285.61
85000	7737.29	4187.30	3014.65	2436.22	2095.37	1718.68	1606.35	1457.15	1365.96
90000	8192.42	4433.61	3191.98	2579.53	2218.63	1819.78	1700.84	1542.86	1446.31
95000	8647.56	4679.92	3369.31	2722.84	2341.89	1920.87	1795.33	1628.58	1526.66
100000	9102.69	4926.23	3546.64	2866.14	2465.14	2021.97	1889.82	1714.29	1607.01
105000	9557.83	5172.54	3723.97	3009.45	2588.40	2123.07	1984.31	1800.01	1687.36
110000	10012.96	5418.85	3901.31	3152.76	2711.66	2224.17	2078.80	1885.72	1767.71
115000	10468.10	5665.17	4078.64	3296.07	2834.91	2325.27	2173.29	1971.44	1848.06
120000	10923.23	5911.48	4255.97	3439.37	2958.17	2426.37	2267.78	2057.15	1928.41
125000	11378.37	6157.79	4433.30	3582.68	3081.43	2527.46	2362.27	2142.86	2008.76
130000	11833.50	6404.10	4610.63	3725.99	3204.69	2628.56	2456.76	2228.58	2089.11
135000	12288.63	6650.41	4787.97	3869.29	3327.94	2729.66	2551.25	2314.29	2169.46
140000	12743.77	6896.72	4965.30	4012.60	3451.20	2830.76	2645.74	2400.01	2249.81
145000	13198.90	7143.03	5142.63	4155.91	3574.46	2931.86	2740.23	2485.72	2330.16
150000	13654.04	7389.34	5319.96	4299.21	3697.71	3032.96	2834.72	2571.44	2410.51

MONTHLY PAYMENT 16⅝%

NECESSARY TO AMORTIZE A LOAN

AMOUNT	15 YEARS	18 YEARS	20 YEARS	25 YEARS	28 YEARS	29 YEARS	30 YEARS	35 YEARS	40 YEARS
50	.76	.74	.72	.71	.70	.70	.70	.70	.70
100	1.52	1.47	1.44	1.41	1.40	1.40	1.40	1.39	1.39
200	3.03	2.93	2.88	2.82	2.80	2.80	2.80	2.78	2.78
300	4.54	4.39	4.32	4.23	4.20	4.20	4.19	4.17	4.17
400	6.06	5.85	5.76	5.64	5.60	5.59	5.59	5.56	5.55
500	7.57	7.31	7.20	7.05	7.00	6.99	6.98	6.95	6.94
600	9.08	8.77	8.64	8.45	8.40	8.39	8.38	8.34	8.33
700	10.59	10.23	10.07	9.86	9.80	9.78	9.77	9.73	9.72
800	12.11	11.69	11.51	11.27	11.20	11.18	11.17	11.12	11.10
900	13.62	13.15	12.95	12.68	12.60	12.58	12.56	12.51	12.49
1000	15.13	14.61	14.39	14.09	14.00	13.98	13.96	13.90	13.88
2000	30.26	29.21	28.77	28.17	27.99	27.95	27.91	27.80	27.75
3000	45.38	43.81	43.16	42.25	41.98	41.92	41.86	41.70	41.62
4000	60.51	58.41	57.54	56.33	55.97	55.89	55.82	55.59	55.50
5000	75.63	73.01	71.92	70.41	69.96	69.86	69.77	69.49	69.37
6000	90.76	87.62	86.31	84.49	83.95	83.83	83.72	83.39	83.24
7000	105.88	102.22	100.69	98.57	97.95	97.80	97.67	97.28	97.12
8000	121.01	116.82	115.07	112.65	111.94	111.77	111.63	111.18	110.99
9000	136.13	131.42	129.46	126.74	125.93	125.74	125.58	125.08	124.86
10000	151.26	146.02	143.84	140.82	139.92	139.71	139.53	138.98	138.73
15000	226.88	219.03	215.76	211.22	209.88	209.56	209.30	208.46	208.10
20000	302.51	292.04	287.68	281.63	279.84	279.42	279.06	277.95	277.46
25000	378.13	365.05	359.59	352.03	349.80	349.27	348.82	347.43	346.83
30000	453.76	438.06	431.51	422.44	419.75	419.12	418.59	416.92	416.19
35000	529.38	511.07	503.43	492.85	489.71	488.97	488.35	486.40	485.56
40000	605.01	584.08	575.35	563.25	559.67	558.83	558.11	555.89	554.92
45000	680.63	657.09	647.26	633.66	629.63	628.68	627.88	625.38	624.29
46000	695.76	671.69	661.65	647.74	643.62	642.65	641.83	639.27	638.16
47000	710.88	686.29	676.03	661.82	657.61	656.62	655.78	653.17	652.03
48000	726.01	700.89	690.41	675.90	671.60	670.59	669.73	667.07	665.91
49000	741.13	715.49	704.80	689.98	685.59	684.56	683.69	680.96	679.78
50000	756.26	730.10	719.18	704.06	699.59	698.53	697.64	694.86	693.65
51000	771.38	744.70	733.56	718.14	713.58	712.50	711.59	708.76	707.53
52000	786.51	759.30	747.95	732.22	727.57	726.47	725.54	722.66	721.40
53000	801.63	773.90	762.33	746.31	741.56	740.44	739.50	736.55	735.27
54000	816.76	788.50	776.72	760.39	755.55	754.41	753.45	750.45	749.14
55000	831.88	803.11	791.10	774.47	769.54	768.38	767.40	764.35	763.02
56000	847.01	817.71	805.48	788.55	783.53	782.35	781.35	778.24	776.89
57000	862.13	832.31	819.87	802.63	797.53	796.32	795.31	792.14	790.76
58000	877.26	846.91	834.25	816.71	811.52	810.29	809.26	806.04	804.64
59000	892.38	861.51	848.63	830.79	825.51	824.27	823.21	819.94	818.51
60000	907.51	876.11	863.02	844.87	839.50	838.24	837.17	833.83	832.38
61000	922.63	890.72	877.40	858.96	853.49	852.21	851.12	847.73	846.26
62000	937.76	905.32	891.78	873.04	867.48	866.18	865.07	861.63	860.13
63000	952.88	919.92	906.17	887.12	881.48	880.15	879.02	875.52	874.00
64000	968.01	934.52	920.55	901.20	895.47	894.12	892.98	889.42	887.87
65000	983.13	949.12	934.93	915.28	909.46	908.09	906.93	903.32	901.75
67500	1020.95	985.63	970.89	950.48	944.44	943.01	941.81	938.06	936.43
70000	1058.76	1022.13	1006.85	985.69	979.42	977.94	976.69	972.80	971.11
75000	1134.38	1095.14	1078.77	1056.09	1049.38	1047.79	1046.46	1042.29	1040.48
80000	1210.01	1168.15	1150.69	1126.50	1119.33	1117.65	1116.22	1111.78	1109.84
85000	1285.64	1241.16	1222.60	1196.90	1189.29	1187.50	1185.98	1181.26	1179.21
90000	1361.26	1314.17	1294.52	1267.31	1259.25	1257.35	1255.75	1250.75	1248.57
95000	1436.89	1387.18	1366.44	1337.71	1329.21	1327.20	1325.51	1320.23	1317.94
100000	1512.51	1460.19	1438.36	1408.12	1399.17	1397.06	1395.27	1389.72	1387.30
105000	1588.14	1533.20	1510.27	1478.53	1469.12	1466.91	1465.04	1459.20	1456.67
110000	1663.76	1606.21	1582.19	1548.93	1539.08	1536.76	1534.80	1528.69	1526.03
115000	1739.39	1679.21	1654.11	1619.34	1609.04	1606.61	1604.56	1598.18	1595.40
120000	1815.01	1752.22	1726.03	1689.74	1679.00	1676.47	1674.33	1667.66	1664.76
125000	1890.64	1825.23	1797.95	1760.15	1748.96	1746.32	1744.09	1737.15	1734.12
130000	1966.26	1898.24	1869.86	1830.55	1818.91	1816.17	1813.85	1806.63	1803.49
135000	2041.89	1971.25	1941.78	1900.96	1888.87	1886.02	1883.62	1876.12	1872.85
140000	2117.51	2044.26	2013.70	1971.37	1958.83	1955.88	1953.38	1945.60	1942.22
145000	2193.14	2117.27	2085.62	2041.77	2028.79	2025.73	2023.14	2015.09	2011.58
150000	2268.76	2190.28	2157.53	2112.18	2098.75	2095.58	2092.91	2084.58	2080.95

159

16¾%   MONTHLY PAYMENT
NECESSARY TO AMORTIZE A LOAN

AMOUNT	1 YEAR	2 YEARS	3 YEARS	4 YEARS	5 YEARS	7 YEARS	8 YEARS	10 YEARS	12 YEARS
$ 50	4.56	2.47	1.78	1.44	1.24	1.02	95	.87	.81
100	9.11	4.94	3.56	2.88	2.48	2.03	1.90	1.73	1.62
200	18.22	9.87	7.11	5.75	4.95	4.06	3.80	3.45	3.24
300	27.33	14.80	10.66	8.62	7.42	6.09	5.70	5.17	4.85
400	36.44	19.73	14.22	11.50	9.89	8.12	7.59	6.89	6.47
500	45.55	24.67	17.77	14.37	12.36	10.15	9.49	8.62	8.08
600	54.66	29.60	21.32	17.24	14.84	12.18	11.39	10.34	9.70
700	63.77	34.53	24.87	20.11	17.31	14.21	13.29	12.06	11.31
800	72.87	39.46	28.43	22.99	19.78	16.24	15.18	13.78	12.93
900	81.98	44.40	31.98	25.86	22.25	18.27	17.08	15.50	14.54
1000	91.09	49.33	35.53	28.73	24.72	20.30	18.98	17.23	16.16
2000	182.18	98.65	71.06	57.46	49.44	40.59	37.95	34.45	32.31
3000	273.26	147.97	106.59	86.18	74.16	60.88	56.92	51.67	48.46
4000	364.35	197.29	142.12	114.91	98.88	81.17	75.89	68.89	64.62
5000	455.44	246.62	177.65	143.63	123.60	101.46	94.87	86.11	80.77
6000	546.52	295.94	213.18	172.36	148.32	121.75	113.84	103.34	96.92
7000	637.61	345.26	248.70	201.09	173.03	142.05	132.81	120.56	113.08
8000	728.69	394.58	284.23	229.81	197.75	162.34	151.78	137.78	129.23
9000	819.78	443.91	319.76	258.54	222.47	182.63	170.76	155.00	145.38
10000	910.87	493.23	355.29	287.26	247.19	202.92	189.73	172.22	161.53
15000	1366.30	739.84	532.93	430.89	370.78	304.38	284.59	258.33	242.30
20000	1821.73	986.45	710.57	574.52	494.37	405.84	379.45	344.44	323.06
25000	2277.16	1233.06	888.22	718.15	617.96	507.29	474.32	430.55	403.83
30000	2732.59	1479.67	1065.86	861.78	741.56	608.75	569.18	516.66	484.59
35000	3188.02	1726.28	1243.50	1005.41	865.15	710.21	664.04	602.76	565.36
40000	3643.45	1972.89	1421.14	1149.04	988.74	811.67	758.90	688.87	646.12
45000	4098.88	2219.51	1598.78	1292.67	1112.33	913.13	853.76	774.98	726.89
46000	4189.97	2268.83	1634.31	1321.39	1137.05	933.42	872.74	792.20	743.04
47000	4281.05	2318.15	1669.84	1350.12	1161.77	953.71	891.71	809.42	759.19
48000	4372.14	2367.47	1705.37	1378.85	1186.49	974.00	910.68	826.65	775.35
49000	4463.23	2416.79	1740.90	1407.57	1211.20	994.29	929.65	843.87	791.50
50000	4554.31	2466.12	1776.43	1436.30	1235.92	1014.58	948.63	861.09	807.65
51000	4645.40	2515.44	1811.95	1465.02	1260.64	1034.88	967.60	878.31	823.80
52000	4736.48	2564.76	1847.48	1493.75	1285.36	1055.17	986.57	895.53	839.96
53000	4827.57	2614.08	1883.01	1522.48	1310.08	1075.46	1005.54	912.75	856.11
54000	4918.66	2663.41	1918.54	1551.20	1334.80	1095.75	1024.52	929.98	872.26
55000	5009.74	2712.73	1954.07	1579.93	1359.51	1116.04	1043.49	947.20	888.42
56000	5100.83	2762.05	1989.60	1608.65	1384.23	1136.33	1062.46	964.42	904.57
57000	5191.92	2811.37	2025.13	1637.38	1408.95	1156.63	1081.43	981.64	920.72
58000	5283.00	2860.69	2060.65	1666.11	1433.67	1176.92	1100.41	998.86	936.88
59000	5374.09	2910.02	2096.18	1694.83	1458.39	1197.21	1119.38	1016.08	953.03
60000	5465.17	2959.34	2131.71	1723.56	1483.11	1217.50	1138.35	1033.31	969.18
61000	5556.26	3008.66	2167.24	1752.28	1507.82	1237.79	1157.32	1050.53	985.33
62000	5647.35	3057.98	2202.77	1781.01	1532.54	1258.08	1176.30	1067.75	1001.49
63000	5738.43	3107.31	2238.30	1809.73	1557.26	1278.37	1195.27	1084.97	1017.64
64000	5829.52	3156.63	2273.82	1838.46	1581.98	1298.67	1214.24	1102.19	1033.79
65000	5920.60	3205.95	2309.35	1867.19	1606.70	1318.96	1233.21	1119.41	1049.95
67500	6148.32	3329.26	2398.17	1939.00	1668.49	1369.69	1280.64	1162.47	1090.33
70000	6376.04	3452.56	2487.00	2010.82	1730.29	1420.42	1328.07	1205.52	1130.71
75000	6831.47	3699.17	2664.64	2154.44	1853.88	1521.87	1422.94	1291.63	1211.48
80000	7286.90	3945.78	2842.28	2298.07	1977.47	1623.33	1517.80	1377.74	1292.24
85000	7742.33	4192.39	3019.92	2441.70	2101.06	1724.79	1612.66	1463.85	1373.00
90000	8197.76	4439.01	3197.56	2585.33	2224.66	1826.25	1707.52	1549.96	1453.77
95000	8653.19	4685.62	3375.21	2728.96	2348.25	1927.71	1802.39	1636.06	1534.53
100000	9108.62	4932.23	3552.85	2872.59	2471.84	2029.16	1897.25	1722.17	1615.30
105000	9564.05	5178.84	3730.49	3016.22	2595.43	2130.62	1992.11	1808.28	1696.06
110000	10019.48	5425.45	3908.13	3159.85	2719.02	2232.08	2086.97	1894.39	1776.83
115000	10474.91	5672.06	4085.77	3303.48	2842.62	2333.54	2181.83	1980.50	1857.59
120000	10930.34	5918.67	4263.42	3447.11	2966.21	2435.00	2276.70	2066.61	1938.36
125000	11385.77	6165.28	4441.06	3590.74	3089.80	2536.45	2371.56	2152.71	2019.12
130000	11841.20	6411.89	4618.70	3734.37	3213.39	2637.91	2466.42	2238.82	2099.89
135000	12296.64	6658.51	4796.34	3878.00	3336.98	2739.37	2561.28	2324.93	2180.65
140000	12752.07	6905.12	4973.99	4021.63	3460.57	2840.83	2656.14	2411.04	2261.42
145000	13207.50	7151.73	5151.63	4165.26	3584.17	2942.29	2751.01	2497.15	2342.18
150000	13662.93	7398.34	5329.27	4308.88	3707.76	3043.74	2845.87	2583.26	2422.95

MONTHLY PAYMENT 16¾%
NECESSARY TO AMORTIZE A LOAN

AMOUNT	15 YEARS	18 YEARS	20 YEARS	25 YEARS	28 YEARS	29 YEARS	30 YEARS	35 YEARS	40 YEARS
$ 50	.77	.74	.73	.71	.71	.71	.71	.70	.70
100	1.53	1.47	1.45	1.42	1.41	1.41	1.41	1.40	1.40
200	3.05	2.94	2.90	2.84	2.82	2.82	2.82	2.80	2.80
300	4.57	4.41	4.35	4.26	4.23	4.23	4.22	4.20	4.20
400	6.09	5.88	5.80	5.68	5.64	5.64	5.63	5.60	5.60
500	7.61	7.35	7.24	7.09	7.05	7.04	7.03	7.00	6.99
600	9.13	8.82	8.69	8.51	8.46	8.45	8.44	8.40	8.39
700	10.65	10.29	10.14	9.93	9.87	9.85	9.84	9.80	9.79
800	12.18	11.76	11.59	11.35	11.28	11.26	11.25	11.20	11.19
900	13.70	13.23	13.04	12.77	12.69	12.67	12.65	12.60	12.58
1000	15.22	14.70	14.48	14.18	14.10	14.08	14.06	14.00	13.98
2000	30.43	29.39	28.96	28.36	28.19	28.15	28.11	28.00	27.96
3000	45.64	44.09	43.44	42.54	42.28	42.22	42.17	42.00	41.93
4000	60.86	58.78	57.92	56.72	56.37	56.29	56.22	56.00	55.91
5000	76.07	73.48	72.40	70.90	70.47	70.36	70.27	70.00	69.89
6000	91.28	88.17	86.87	85.08	84.56	84.43	84.33	84.00	83.86
7000	106.50	102.86	101.35	99.26	98.65	98.50	98.38	98.00	97.84
8000	121.71	117.56	115.83	113.44	112.74	112.58	112.44	112.00	111.82
9000	136.92	132.25	130.31	127.62	126.83	126.65	126.49	126.00	125.79
10000	152.14	146.95	144.79	141.80	140.93	140.72	140.54	140.00	139.77
15000	228.20	220.42	217.18	212.70	211.39	211.08	210.81	210.00	209.65
20000	304.27	293.89	289.57	283.60	281.85	281.43	281.08	280.00	279.53
25000	380.34	367.36	361.96	354.50	352.31	351.79	351.35	350.00	349.41
30000	456.40	440.83	434.35	425.40	422.77	422.15	421.62	420.00	419.30
35000	532.47	514.30	506.74	496.30	493.23	492.50	491.89	490.00	489.18
40000	608.53	587.77	579.13	567.20	563.69	562.86	562.16	560.00	559.06
45000	684.60	661.24	651.52	638.10	634.15	633.22	632.43	630.00	628.94
46000	699.81	675.94	666.00	652.28	648.24	647.29	646.49	644.00	642.92
47000	715.03	690.63	680.48	666.46	662.33	661.36	660.54	658.00	656.89
48000	730.24	705.33	694.96	680.64	676.42	675.43	674.59	672.00	670.87
49000	745.45	720.02	709.44	694.82	690.52	689.50	688.65	686.00	684.85
50000	760.67	734.72	723.91	709.00	704.61	703.58	702.70	699.99	698.82
51000	775.88	749.41	738.39	723.18	718.70	717.65	716.76	713.99	712.80
52000	791.09	764.10	752.87	737.36	732.79	731.72	730.81	727.99	726.78
53000	806.31	778.80	767.35	751.54	746.88	745.79	744.86	741.99	740.75
54000	821.52	793.49	781.83	765.72	760.98	759.86	758.92	755.99	754.73
55000	836.73	808.19	796.31	779.90	775.07	773.93	772.97	769.99	768.70
56000	851.94	822.88	810.78	794.08	789.16	788.00	787.03	783.99	782.68
57000	867.16	837.57	825.26	808.26	803.25	802.07	801.08	797.99	796.66
58000	882.37	852.27	839.74	822.44	817.34	816.15	815.13	811.99	810.63
59000	897.58	866.96	854.22	836.62	831.44	830.22	829.19	825.99	824.61
60000	912.80	881.66	868.70	850.80	845.53	844.29	843.24	839.99	838.59
61000	928.01	896.35	883.17	864.98	859.62	858.36	857.30	853.99	852.56
62000	943.22	911.05	897.65	879.16	873.71	872.43	871.35	867.99	866.54
63000	958.44	925.74	912.13	893.34	887.80	886.50	885.40	881.99	880.52
64000	973.65	940.43	926.61	907.52	901.90	900.57	899.46	895.99	894.49
65000	988.86	955.13	941.09	921.70	915.99	914.65	913.51	909.99	908.47
67500	1026.90	991.86	977.28	957.15	951.22	949.82	948.65	944.99	943.41
70000	1064.93	1028.60	1013.48	992.60	986.45	985.00	983.78	979.99	978.35
75000	1141.00	1102.07	1085.87	1063.50	1056.91	1055.36	1054.05	1049.99	1048.23
80000	1217.06	1175.54	1158.26	1134.40	1127.37	1125.72	1124.32	1119.99	1118.11
85000	1293.13	1249.01	1230.65	1205.30	1197.83	1196.07	1194.59	1189.99	1187.99
90000	1369.19	1322.48	1303.04	1276.20	1268.29	1266.43	1264.86	1259.99	1257.88
95000	1445.26	1395.95	1375.43	1347.10	1338.75	1336.79	1335.13	1329.99	1327.76
100000	1521.33	1469.43	1447.82	1418.00	1409.21	1407.15	1405.40	1399.98	1397.64
105000	1597.39	1542.90	1520.22	1488.90	1479.67	1477.50	1475.67	1469.98	1467.52
110000	1673.46	1616.37	1592.61	1559.80	1550.13	1547.86	1545.94	1539.98	1537.40
115000	1749.52	1689.84	1665.00	1630.70	1620.59	1618.22	1616.21	1609.98	1607.29
120000	1825.59	1763.31	1737.39	1701.60	1691.05	1688.57	1686.48	1679.98	1677.17
125000	1901.66	1836.78	1809.78	1772.50	1761.51	1758.93	1756.75	1749.98	1747.05
130000	1977.72	1910.25	1882.17	1843.40	1831.97	1829.29	1827.02	1819.98	1816.93
135000	2053.79	1983.72	1954.56	1914.30	1902.43	1899.64	1897.29	1889.98	1886.81
140000	2129.85	2057.19	2026.95	1985.20	1972.89	1970.00	1967.56	1959.98	1956.69
145000	2205.92	2130.66	2099.34	2056.10	2043.35	2040.36	2037.83	2029.98	2026.58
150000	2281.99	2204.14	2171.73	2127.00	2113.81	2110.72	2108.10	2099.97	2096.46

16⅞% MONTHLY PAYMENT
NECESSARY TO AMORTIZE A LOAN

AMOUNT	1 YEAR	2 YEARS	3 YEARS	4 YEARS	5 YEARS	7 YEARS	8 YEARS	10 YEARS	12 YEARS
$ 50	4.56	2.47	1.78	1.44	1.24	1.02	.96	.87	.82
100	9.12	4.94	3.56	2.88	2.48	2.04	1.91	1.74	1.63
200	18.23	9.88	7.12	5.76	4.96	4.08	3.81	3.47	3.25
300	27.35	14.82	10.68	8.64	7.44	6.11	5.72	5.20	4.88
400	36.46	19.76	14.24	11.52	9.92	8.15	7.62	6.93	6.50
500	45.58	24.70	17.80	14.40	12.40	10.19	9.53	8.66	8.12
600	54.69	29.63	21.36	17.28	14.88	12.22	11.43	10.39	9.75
700	63.81	34.57	24.92	20.16	17.35	14.26	13.34	12.12	11.37
800	72.92	39.51	28.48	23.04	19.83	16.30	15.24	13.85	12.99
900	82.04	44.45	32.04	25.92	22.31	18.33	17.15	15.58	14.62
1000	91.15	49.39	35.60	28.80	24.79	20.37	19.05	17.31	16.24
2000	182.30	98.77	71.19	57.59	49.58	40.73	38.10	34.61	32.48
3000	273.44	148.15	106.78	86.38	74.36	61.10	57.15	51.91	48.71
4000	364.59	197.53	142.37	115.17	99.15	81.46	76.19	69.21	64.95
5000	455.73	246.92	177.96	143.96	123.93	101.82	95.24	86.51	81.18
6000	546.88	296.30	213.55	172.75	148.72	122.19	114.29	103.81	97.42
7000	638.02	345.68	249.14	201.54	173.50	142.55	133.33	121.11	113.66
8000	729.17	395.06	284.73	230.33	198.29	162.91	152.38	138.41	129.89
9000	820.31	444.45	320.32	259.12	223.07	183.28	171.43	155.71	146.13
10000	911.46	493.83	355.91	287.91	247.86	203.64	190.47	173.01	162.36
15000	1367.19	740.74	533.86	431.86	371.79	305.46	285.71	259.51	243.54
20000	1822.91	987.65	711.82	575.81	495.71	407.28	380.94	346.02	324.72
25000	2278.64	1234.56	889.77	719.77	619.64	509.10	476.18	432.52	405.90
30000	2734.37	1481.47	1067.72	863.72	743.57	610.91	571.41	519.02	487.08
35000	3190.10	1728.38	1245.67	1007.67	867.49	712.73	666.65	605.53	568.26
40000	3645.82	1975.29	1423.63	1151.62	991.42	814.55	761.88	692.03	649.44
45000	4101.55	2222.21	1601.58	1295.57	1115.35	916.37	857.11	778.53	730.62
46000	4192.70	2271.59	1637.17	1324.36	1140.13	936.73	876.16	795.83	746.86
47000	4283.84	2320.97	1672.76	1353.15	1164.92	957.10	895.21	813.13	763.10
48000	4374.99	2370.35	1708.35	1381.94	1189.70	977.46	914.25	830.44	779.33
49000	4466.13	2419.73	1743.94	1410.74	1214.49	997.82	933.30	847.74	795.57
50000	4557.28	2469.12	1779.53	1439.53	1239.28	1018.19	952.35	865.04	811.80
51000	4648.42	2518.50	1815.12	1468.32	1264.06	1038.55	971.40	882.34	828.04
52000	4739.57	2567.88	1850.71	1497.11	1288.85	1058.91	990.44	899.64	844.28
53000	4830.71	2617.26	1886.30	1525.90	1313.63	1079.28	1009.49	916.94	860.51
54000	4921.84	2666.65	1921.89	1554.69	1338.42	1099.64	1028.54	934.24	876.75
55000	5013.00	2716.03	1957.49	1583.48	1363.20	1120.00	1047.58	951.54	892.98
56000	5104.15	2765.41	1993.08	1612.27	1387.99	1140.37	1066.63	968.84	909.22
57000	5195.30	2814.79	2028.67	1641.06	1412.77	1160.73	1085.68	986.14	925.46
58000	5286.44	2864.17	2064.26	1669.85	1437.56	1181.10	1104.72	1003.44	941.69
59000	5377.59	2913.56	2099.85	1698.64	1462.34	1201.46	1123.77	1020.74	957.93
60000	5468.73	2962.94	2135.44	1727.43	1487.13	1221.82	1142.82	1038.04	974.16
61000	5559.88	3012.32	2171.03	1756.22	1511.92	1242.19	1161.86	1055.34	990.40
62000	5651.02	3061.70	2206.62	1785.01	1536.70	1262.55	1180.91	1072.64	1006.64
63000	5742.17	3111.09	2242.21	1813.80	1561.49	1282.91	1199.96	1089.95	1022.87
64000	5833.31	3160.47	2277.80	1842.59	1586.27	1303.28	1219.00	1107.25	1039.11
65000	5924.46	3209.85	2313.39	1871.38	1611.06	1323.64	1238.05	1124.55	1055.34
67500	6152.32	3333.31	2402.37	1943.36	1673.02	1374.55	1285.67	1167.80	1095.93
70000	6380.19	3456.76	2491.34	2015.33	1734.98	1425.46	1333.29	1211.05	1136.52
75000	6835.91	3703.67	2669.30	2159.29	1858.91	1527.28	1428.52	1297.55	1217.70
80000	7291.64	3950.58	2847.25	2303.24	1982.84	1629.10	1523.75	1384.06	1298.88
85000	7747.37	4197.49	3025.20	2447.19	2106.77	1730.91	1618.99	1470.56	1380.06
90000	8203.09	4444.41	3203.15	2591.14	2230.69	1832.73	1714.22	1557.06	1461.24
95000	8658.82	4691.32	3381.11	2735.09	2354.62	1934.55	1809.46	1643.57	1542.42
100000	9114.55	4938.23	3559.06	2879.05	2478.55	2036.37	1904.69	1730.07	1623.60
105000	9570.28	5185.14	3737.01	3023.00	2602.47	2138.19	1999.93	1816.57	1704.78
110000	10026.01	5432.05	3914.96	3166.95	2726.40	2240.00	2095.16	1903.08	1785.96
115000	10481.73	5678.96	4092.92	3310.90	2850.33	2341.82	2190.39	1989.58	1867.14
120000	10937.46	5925.87	4270.87	3454.85	2974.25	2443.64	2285.63	2076.08	1948.32
125000	11393.19	6172.78	4448.82	3598.81	3098.18	2545.46	2380.86	2162.58	2029.50
130000	11848.91	6419.69	4626.78	3742.76	3222.11	2647.28	2476.10	2249.09	2110.68
135000	12304.64	6666.61	4804.73	3886.71	3346.04	2749.10	2571.33	2335.59	2191.86
140000	12760.37	6913.52	4982.68	4030.66	3469.96	2850.91	2666.57	2422.09	2273.04
145000	13216.09	7160.43	5160.63	4174.61	3593.89	2952.73	2761.80	2508.60	2354.22
150000	13671.82	7407.34	5338.59	4318.57	3717.82	3054.55	2857.04	2595.10	2435.40

MONTHLY PAYMENT 16⅞%

NECESSARY TO AMORTIZE A LOAN

AMOUNT	15 YEARS	18 YEARS	20 YEARS	25 YEARS	28 YEARS	29 YEARS	30 YEARS	35 YEARS	40 YEARS
$ 50	.77	.74	.73	.72	.71	.71	.71	.71	.71
100	1.54	1.48	1.46	1.43	1.42	1.42	1.42	1.42	1.41
200	3.07	2.96	2.92	2.86	2.84	2.84	2.84	2.83	2.82
300	4.60	4.44	4.38	4.29	4.26	4.26	4.25	4.24	4.23
400	6.13	5.92	5.83	5.72	5.68	5.67	5.67	5.65	5.64
500	7.66	7.40	7.29	7.14	7.10	7.09	7.08	7.06	7.04
600	9.19	8.88	8.75	8.57	8.52	8.51	8.50	8.47	8.45
700	10.72	10.36	10.21	10.00	9.94	9.93	9.91	9.88	9.86
800	12.25	11.83	11.66	11.43	11.36	11.34	11.33	11.29	11.27
900	13.78	13.31	13.12	12.86	12.78	12.76	12.74	12.70	12.68
1000	15.31	14.79	14.58	14.28	14.20	14.18	14.16	14.11	14.08
2000	30.61	29.58	29.15	28.56	28.39	28.35	28.32	28.21	28.16
3000	45.91	44.37	43.72	42.84	42.58	42.52	42.47	42.31	42.24
4000	61.21	59.15	58.30	57.12	56.78	56.69	56.63	56.42	56.32
5000	76.51	73.94	72.87	71.40	70.97	70.87	70.78	70.52	70.40
6000	91.81	88.73	87.44	85.68	85.16	85.04	84.94	84.62	84.48
7000	107.12	103.51	102.02	99.96	99.35	99.21	99.09	98.72	98.56
8000	122.42	118.30	116.59	114.24	113.55	113.38	113.25	112.83	112.64
9000	137.72	133.09	131.16	128.52	127.74	127.56	127.40	126.93	126.72
10000	153.02	147.87	145.74	142.79	141.93	141.73	141.56	141.03	140.80
15000	229.53	221.81	218.60	214.19	212.89	212.59	212.33	211.54	211.20
20000	306.04	295.74	291.47	285.58	283.86	283.45	283.11	282.06	281.60
25000	382.54	369.67	364.33	356.98	354.82	354.31	353.89	352.57	352.00
30000	459.05	443.61	437.20	428.37	425.78	425.18	424.66	423.08	422.40
35000	535.56	517.54	510.06	499.77	496.75	496.04	495.44	493.59	492.80
40000	612.07	591.48	582.93	571.16	567.71	566.90	566.22	564.11	563.20
45000	688.57	665.41	655.79	642.56	638.67	637.76	636.99	634.62	633.60
46000	703.88	680.20	670.36	656.83	652.87	651.93	651.15	648.72	647.67
47000	719.18	694.98	684.94	671.11	667.06	666.11	665.30	662.82	661.75
48000	734.48	709.77	699.51	685.39	681.25	680.28	679.46	676.93	675.83
49000	749.78	724.56	714.08	699.67	695.44	694.45	693.62	691.03	689.91
50000	765.08	739.34	728.66	713.95	709.64	708.62	707.77	705.13	703.99
51000	780.38	754.13	743.23	728.23	723.83	722.80	721.93	719.23	718.07
52000	795.69	768.92	757.80	742.51	738.02	736.97	736.08	733.34	732.15
53000	810.99	783.70	772.38	756.79	752.21	751.14	750.24	747.44	746.23
54000	826.29	798.49	786.95	771.07	766.41	765.31	764.39	761.54	760.31
55000	841.59	813.28	801.52	785.35	780.60	779.49	778.55	775.64	774.39
56000	856.89	828.06	816.09	799.62	794.79	793.66	792.70	789.75	788.47
57000	872.19	842.85	830.67	813.90	808.98	807.83	806.86	803.85	802.55
58000	887.49	857.64	845.24	828.18	823.18	822.00	821.01	817.95	816.63
59000	902.80	872.42	859.81	842.46	837.37	836.18	835.17	832.05	830.71
60000	918.10	887.21	874.39	856.74	851.56	850.35	849.32	846.16	844.79
61000	933.40	902.00	888.96	871.02	865.75	864.52	863.48	860.26	858.87
62000	948.70	916.78	903.53	885.30	879.95	878.69	877.63	874.36	872.95
63000	964.00	931.57	918.11	899.58	894.14	892.86	891.79	888.46	887.03
64000	979.30	946.36	932.68	913.86	908.33	907.04	905.95	902.57	901.11
65000	994.61	961.14	947.25	928.13	922.52	921.21	920.10	916.67	915.19
67500	1032.86	998.11	983.68	963.83	958.01	956.64	955.49	951.92	950.39
70000	1071.11	1035.08	1020.12	999.53	993.49	992.07	990.88	987.18	985.59
75000	1147.62	1109.01	1092.98	1070.92	1064.45	1062.93	1061.65	1057.69	1055.99
80000	1224.13	1182.95	1165.85	1142.32	1135.41	1133.80	1132.43	1128.21	1126.39
85000	1300.64	1256.88	1238.71	1213.71	1206.38	1204.66	1203.21	1198.72	1196.79
90000	1377.14	1330.81	1311.58	1285.11	1277.34	1275.52	1273.98	1269.23	1267.19
95000	1453.65	1404.75	1384.44	1356.50	1348.30	1346.38	1344.76	1339.74	1337.58
100000	1530.16	1478.68	1457.31	1427.90	1419.27	1417.24	1415.54	1410.26	1407.98
105000	1606.67	1552.61	1530.17	1499.29	1490.23	1488.10	1486.31	1480.77	1478.38
110000	1683.17	1626.55	1603.04	1570.69	1561.19	1558.97	1557.09	1551.28	1548.78
115000	1759.68	1700.48	1675.90	1642.08	1632.16	1629.83	1627.87	1621.79	1619.18
120000	1836.19	1774.42	1748.77	1713.47	1703.12	1700.69	1698.64	1692.31	1689.58
125000	1912.70	1848.35	1821.63	1784.87	1774.08	1771.55	1769.42	1762.82	1759.98
130000	1989.21	1922.28	1894.50	1856.26	1845.04	1842.41	1840.20	1833.33	1830.38
135000	2065.71	1996.22	1967.36	1927.66	1916.01	1913.28	1910.97	1903.84	1900.78
140000	2142.22	2070.15	2040.23	1999.05	1986.97	1984.14	1981.75	1974.36	1971.17
145000	2218.73	2144.08	2113.09	2070.45	2057.93	2055.00	2052.53	2044.87	2041.57
150000	2295.24	2218.02	2185.96	2141.84	2128.90	2125.86	2123.30	2115.38	2111.97

17% MONTHLY PAYMENT
NECESSARY TO AMORTIZE A LOAN

AMOUNT	1 YEAR	2 YEARS	3 YEARS	4 YEARS	5 YEARS	7 YEARS	8 YEARS	10 YEARS	12 YEARS
$ 50	4.57	2.48	1.79	1.45	1.25	1.03	.96	.87	.82
100	9.13	4.95	3.57	2.89	2.49	2.05	1.92	1.74	1.64
200	18.25	9.89	7.14	5.78	4.98	4.09	3.83	3.48	3.27
300	27.37	14.84	10.70	8.66	7.46	6.14	5.74	5.22	4.90
400	36.49	19.78	14.27	11.55	9.95	8.18	7.65	6.96	6.53
500	45.61	24.73	17.83	14.43	12.43	10.22	9.57	8.69	8.16
600	54.73	29.67	21.40	17.32	14.92	12.27	11.48	10.43	9.80
700	63.85	34.61	24.96	20.20	17.40	14.31	13.39	12.17	11.43
800	72.97	39.56	28.53	23.09	19.89	16.35	15.30	13.91	13.06
900	82.09	44.50	32.09	25.97	22.37	18.40	17.21	15.65	14.69
1000	91.21	49.45	35.66	28.86	24.86	20.44	19.13	17.38	16.32
2000	182.41	98.89	71.31	57.72	49.71	40.88	38.25	34.76	32.64
3000	273.62	148.33	106.96	86.57	74.56	61.31	57.37	52.14	48.96
4000	364.82	197.77	142.62	115.43	99.42	81.75	76.49	69.52	65.28
5000	456.03	247.22	178.27	144.28	124.27	102.18	95.61	86.90	81.60
6000	547.23	296.66	213.92	173.14	149.12	122.62	114.73	104.28	97.92
7000	638.44	346.10	249.57	201.99	173.97	143.06	133.86	121.66	114.24
8000	729.64	395.54	285.23	230.85	198.83	163.49	152.98	139.04	130.56
9000	820.85	444.99	320.88	259.70	223.68	183.93	172.10	156.42	146.88
10000	912.05	494.43	356.53	288.56	248.53	204.36	191.22	173.80	163.20
15000	1368.08	741.64	534.80	432.83	372.79	306.54	286.83	260.70	244.79
20000	1824.10	988.85	713.06	577.11	497.06	408.72	382.43	347.60	326.39
25000	2280.12	1236.06	891.32	721.38	621.32	510.90	478.04	434.50	407.99
30000	2736.15	1483.27	1069.59	865.66	745.58	613.08	573.65	521.40	489.58
35000	3192.17	1730.48	1247.85	1009.93	869.85	715.26	669.26	608.30	571.18
40000	3648.20	1977.70	1426.11	1154.21	994.11	817.44	764.86	695.20	652.77
45000	4104.22	2224.91	1604.38	1298.48	1118.37	919.62	860.47	782.09	734.37
46000	4195.42	2274.35	1640.03	1327.34	1143.22	940.05	879.59	799.47	750.69
47000	4286.63	2323.79	1675.68	1356.19	1168.08	960.49	898.71	816.85	767.01
48000	4377.83	2373.23	1711.34	1385.05	1192.93	980.92	917.83	834.23	783.33
49000	4469.04	2422.68	1746.99	1413.90	1217.78	1001.36	936.96	851.61	799.65
50000	4560.24	2472.12	1782.64	1442.76	1242.63	1021.80	956.08	868.99	815.97
51000	4651.45	2521.56	1818.29	1471.61	1267.49	1042.23	975.20	886.37	832.29
52000	4742.65	2571.00	1853.95	1500.47	1292.34	1062.67	994.32	903.75	848.60
53000	4833.86	2620.44	1889.60	1529.32	1317.19	1083.10	1013.44	921.13	864.92
54000	4925.06	2669.89	1925.25	1558.18	1342.04	1103.54	1032.56	938.51	881.24
55000	5016.27	2719.33	1960.91	1587.03	1366.90	1123.97	1051.68	955.89	897.56
56000	5107.47	2768.77	1996.56	1615.89	1391.75	1144.41	1070.81	973.27	913.88
57000	5198.68	2818.21	2032.21	1644.74	1416.60	1164.85	1089.93	990.65	930.20
58000	5289.88	2867.66	2067.86	1673.60	1441.45	1185.28	1109.05	1008.03	946.52
59000	5381.09	2917.10	2103.52	1702.45	1466.31	1205.72	1128.17	1025.41	962.84
60000	5472.29	2966.54	2139.17	1731.31	1491.16	1226.15	1147.29	1042.79	979.16
61000	5563.49	3015.98	2174.82	1760.16	1516.01	1246.59	1166.41	1060.17	995.48
62000	5654.70	3065.43	2210.47	1789.02	1540.86	1267.02	1185.54	1077.55	1011.80
63000	5745.90	3114.87	2246.13	1817.87	1565.72	1287.46	1204.66	1094.93	1028.12
64000	5837.11	3164.31	2281.78	1846.73	1590.57	1307.90	1223.78	1112.31	1044.44
65000	5928.31	3213.75	2317.43	1875.58	1615.42	1328.33	1242.90	1129.69	1060.75
67500	6156.33	3337.36	2406.56	1947.72	1677.55	1379.42	1290.70	1173.14	1101.55
70000	6384.34	3460.96	2495.70	2019.86	1739.69	1430.51	1338.51	1216.59	1142.35
75000	6840.36	3708.17	2673.96	2164.13	1863.95	1532.69	1434.11	1303.49	1223.95
80000	7296.39	3955.39	2852.22	2308.41	1988.21	1634.87	1529.72	1390.39	1305.54
85000	7752.41	4202.60	3030.49	2452.68	2112.47	1737.05	1625.33	1477.29	1387.14
90000	8208.43	4449.81	3208.75	2596.96	2236.74	1839.23	1720.94	1564.18	1468.74
95000	8664.46	4697.02	3387.01	2741.23	2361.00	1941.41	1816.54	1651.08	1550.33
100000	9120.48	4944.23	3565.28	2885.51	2485.26	2043.59	1912.15	1737.98	1631.93
105000	9576.50	5191.44	3743.54	3029.78	2609.53	2145.76	2007.76	1824.88	1713.52
110000	10032.53	5438.65	3921.81	3174.06	2733.79	2247.94	2103.36	1911.78	1795.12
115000	10488.55	5685.87	4100.07	3318.33	2858.05	2350.12	2198.97	1998.68	1876.72
120000	10944.58	5933.08	4278.33	3462.61	2982.31	2452.30	2294.58	2085.58	1958.31
125000	11400.60	6180.29	4456.60	3606.89	3106.58	2554.48	2390.19	2172.48	2039.91
130000	11856.62	6427.50	4634.86	3751.16	3230.84	2656.66	2485.79	2259.37	2121.50
135000	12312.65	6674.71	4813.12	3895.44	3355.10	2758.84	2581.40	2346.27	2203.10
140000	12768.67	6921.92	4991.39	4039.71	3479.37	2861.02	2677.01	2433.17	2284.70
145000	13224.69	7169.13	5169.65	4183.99	3603.63	2963.20	2772.62	2520.07	2366.29
150000	13680.72	7416.34	5347.91	4328.26	3727.89	3065.38	2868.22	2606.97	2447.89

MONTHLY PAYMENT

17%

NECESSARY TO AMORTIZE A LOAN

AMOUNT	15 YEARS	18 YEARS	20 YEARS	25 YEARS	28 YEARS	29 YEARS	30 YEARS	35 YEARS	40 YEARS
$ 50	.77	.75	.74	.72	.72	.72	.72	.72	.71
100	1.54	1.49	1.47	1.44	1.43	1.43	1.43	1.43	1.42
200	3.08	2.98	2.94	2.88	2.86	2.86	2.86	2.85	2.84
300	4.62	4.47	4.41	4.32	4.29	4.29	4.28	4.27	4.26
400	6.16	5.96	5.87	5.76	5.72	5.71	5.71	5.69	5.68
500	7.70	7.44	7.34	7.19	7.15	7.14	7.13	7.11	7.10
600	9.24	8.93	8.81	8.63	8.58	8.57	8.56	8.53	8.51
700	10.78	10.42	10.27	10.07	10.01	10.00	9.98	9.95	9.93
800	12.32	11.91	11.74	11.51	11.44	11.42	11.41	11.37	11.35
900	13.86	13.40	13.21	12.95	12.87	12.85	12.84	12.79	12.77
1000	15.40	14.88	14.67	14.38	14.30	14.28	14.26	14.21	14.19
2000	30.79	29.76	29.34	28.76	28.59	28.55	28.52	28.42	28.37
3000	46.18	44.64	44.01	43.14	42.88	42.83	42.78	42.62	42.55
4000	61.57	59.52	58.68	57.52	57.18	57.10	57.03	56.83	56.74
5000	76.96	74.40	73.35	71.89	71.47	71.37	71.29	71.03	70.92
6000	92.35	89.28	88.01	86.27	85.76	85.65	85.55	85.24	85.10
7000	107.74	104.16	102.68	100.65	100.06	99.92	99.80	99.44	99.29
8000	123.13	119.04	117.35	115.03	114.35	114.19	114.06	113.65	113.47
9000	138.52	133.92	132.02	129.41	128.64	128.47	128.32	127.85	127.65
10000	153.91	148.80	146.69	143.78	142.94	142.74	142.57	142.06	141.84
15000	230.86	223.20	220.03	215.67	214.40	214.11	213.86	213.08	212.75
20000	307.81	297.59	293.37	287.56	285.87	285.47	285.14	284.11	283.67
25000	384.76	371.99	366.71	359.45	357.34	356.84	356.42	355.14	354.59
30000	461.71	446.39	440.05	431.34	428.80	428.21	427.71	426.16	425.50
35000	538.66	520.79	513.39	503.23	500.27	499.58	498.99	497.19	496.42
40000	615.61	595.18	586.73	575.12	571.74	570.94	570.28	568.22	567.33
45000	692.56	669.58	660.07	647.01	643.20	642.31	641.56	639.24	638.25
46000	707.95	684.46	674.73	661.39	657.49	656.58	655.82	653.45	652.43
47000	723.34	699.34	689.40	675.77	671.79	670.86	670.07	667.65	666.62
48000	738.73	714.22	704.07	690.15	686.08	685.13	684.33	681.86	680.80
49000	754.12	729.10	718.74	704.53	700.37	699.40	698.59	696.06	694.98
50000	769.51	743.98	733.41	718.90	714.67	713.68	712.84	710.27	709.17
51000	784.90	758.86	748.07	733.28	728.96	727.95	727.10	724.47	723.35
52000	800.29	773.74	762.74	747.66	743.25	742.22	741.36	738.68	737.53
53000	815.68	788.62	777.41	762.04	757.55	756.50	755.61	752.88	751.72
54000	831.07	803.50	792.08	776.42	771.84	770.77	769.87	767.09	765.90
55000	846.46	818.38	806.75	790.79	786.13	785.04	784.13	781.29	780.08
56000	861.85	833.26	821.41	805.17	800.43	799.32	798.38	795.50	794.27
57000	877.24	848.13	836.08	819.55	814.72	813.59	812.64	809.70	808.45
58000	892.63	863.01	850.75	833.93	829.01	827.86	826.90	823.91	822.63
59000	908.02	877.89	865.42	848.30	843.31	842.14	841.15	838.12	836.82
60000	923.41	892.77	880.09	862.68	857.60	856.41	855.41	852.32	851.00
61000	938.80	907.65	894.75	877.06	871.89	870.69	869.67	866.53	865.18
62000	954.19	922.53	909.42	891.44	886.19	884.96	883.92	880.73	879.37
63000	969.58	937.41	924.09	905.82	900.48	899.23	898.18	894.94	893.55
64000	984.97	952.29	938.76	920.19	914.77	913.51	912.44	909.14	907.73
65000	1000.36	967.17	953.43	934.57	929.07	927.78	926.69	923.35	921.92
67500	1038.83	1004.37	990.10	970.52	964.80	963.46	962.34	958.86	957.37
70000	1077.31	1041.57	1026.77	1006.46	1000.53	999.15	997.98	994.37	992.83
75000	1154.26	1115.97	1100.11	1078.35	1072.00	1070.51	1069.26	1065.40	1063.75
80000	1231.21	1190.36	1173.45	1150.24	1143.47	1141.88	1140.55	1136.43	1134.66
85000	1308.16	1264.76	1246.79	1222.13	1214.93	1213.25	1211.83	1207.45	1205.58
90000	1385.11	1339.16	1320.13	1294.02	1286.40	1284.62	1283.11	1278.48	1276.50
95000	1462.06	1413.55	1393.47	1365.91	1357.86	1355.98	1354.40	1349.50	1347.41
100000	1539.01	1487.95	1466.81	1437.80	1429.33	1427.35	1425.68	1420.53	1418.33
105000	1615.96	1562.35	1540.15	1509.69	1500.80	1498.72	1496.96	1491.56	1489.24
110000	1692.91	1636.75	1613.49	1581.58	1572.26	1570.08	1568.25	1562.58	1560.16
115000	1769.86	1711.14	1686.83	1653.47	1643.73	1641.45	1639.53	1633.61	1631.08
120000	1846.81	1785.54	1760.17	1725.36	1715.20	1712.82	1710.82	1704.64	1701.99
125000	1923.76	1859.94	1833.51	1797.25	1786.66	1784.19	1782.10	1775.66	1772.91
130000	2000.71	1934.34	1906.85	1869.14	1858.13	1855.55	1853.38	1846.69	1843.83
135000	2077.66	2008.73	1980.19	1941.03	1929.59	1926.92	1924.67	1917.72	1914.74
140000	2154.61	2083.13	2053.53	2012.92	2001.06	1998.29	1995.95	1988.74	1985.66
145000	2231.56	2157.53	2126.87	2084.81	2072.53	2069.65	2067.23	2059.77	2056.57
150000	2308.51	2231.93	2200.21	2156.70	2143.99	2141.02	2138.52	2130.79	2127.49

17⅛% MONTHLY PAYMENT
NECESSARY TO AMORTIZE A LOAN

AMOUNT	1 YEAR	2 YEARS	3 YEARS	4 YEARS	5 YEARS	7 YEARS	8 YEARS	10 YEARS	12 YEARS
$ 50	4.57	2.48	1.79	1.45	1.25	1.03	.96	.88	.83
100	9.13	4.96	3.58	2.90	2.50	2.06	1.92	1.75	1.65
200	18.26	9.91	7.15	5.79	4.99	4.11	3.84	3.50	3.29
300	27.38	14.86	10.72	8.68	7.48	6.16	5.76	5.24	4.93
400	36.51	19.81	14.29	11.57	9.97	8.21	7.68	6.99	6.57
500	45.64	24.76	17.86	14.46	12.46	10.26	9.60	8.73	8.21
600	54.76	29.71	21.43	17.36	14.96	12.31	11.52	10.48	9.85
700	63.89	34.66	25.01	20.25	17.45	14.36	13.44	12.23	11.49
800	73.02	39.61	28.58	23.14	19.94	16.41	15.36	13.97	13.13
900	82.14	44.56	32.15	26.03	22.43	18.46	17.28	15.72	14.77
1000	91.27	49.51	35.72	28.92	24.92	20.51	19.20	17.46	16.41
2000	182.53	99.01	71.43	57.84	49.84	41.02	38.40	34.92	32.81
3000	273.80	148.51	107.15	86.76	74.76	61.53	57.59	52.38	49.21
4000	365.06	198.01	142.86	115.68	99.68	82.04	76.79	69.84	65.62
5000	456.33	247.52	178.58	144.60	124.60	102.55	95.99	87.30	82.02
6000	547.59	297.02	214.29	173.52	149.52	123.05	115.18	104.76	98.42
7000	638.85	346.52	250.01	202.44	174.44	143.56	134.38	122.22	114.82
8000	730.12	396.02	285.72	231.36	199.36	164.07	153.57	139.68	131.23
9000	821.38	445.53	321.44	260.28	224.28	184.58	172.77	157.14	147.63
10000	912.65	495.03	357.15	289.20	249.20	205.09	191.97	174.60	164.03
15000	1368.97	742.54	535.73	433.80	373.80	307.63	287.95	261.89	246.04
20000	1825.29	990.05	714.30	578.40	498.40	410.17	383.93	349.19	328.06
25000	2281.61	1237.56	892.88	723.00	623.00	512.71	479.91	436.48	410.07
30000	2737.93	1485.08	1071.45	867.60	747.60	615.25	575.89	523.78	492.08
35000	3194.25	1732.59	1250.03	1012.20	872.20	717.79	671.87	611.07	574.10
40000	3650.57	1980.10	1428.60	1156.80	996.80	820.33	767.85	698.37	656.11
45000	4106.89	2227.61	1607.18	1301.39	1121.40	922.87	863.83	785.66	738.12
46000	4198.15	2277.11	1642.89	1330.31	1146.32	943.38	883.03	803.12	754.53
47000	4289.42	2326.62	1678.61	1359.23	1171.24	963.89	902.23	820.58	770.93
48000	4380.68	2376.12	1714.32	1388.15	1196.16	984.39	921.42	838.04	787.33
49000	4471.95	2425.62	1750.04	1417.07	1221.08	1004.90	940.62	855.50	803.73
50000	4563.21	2475.12	1785.75	1445.99	1246.00	1025.41	959.81	872.96	820.14
51000	4654.47	2524.62	1821.47	1474.91	1270.92	1045.92	979.01	890.42	836.54
52000	4745.74	2574.13	1857.18	1503.83	1295.84	1066.43	998.21	907.88	852.94
53000	4837.00	2623.63	1892.90	1532.75	1320.76	1086.93	1017.40	925.33	869.34
54000	4928.27	2673.13	1928.61	1561.67	1345.68	1107.44	1036.60	942.79	885.75
55000	5019.53	2722.63	1964.33	1590.59	1370.60	1127.95	1055.79	960.25	902.15
56000	5110.79	2772.14	2000.04	1619.51	1395.52	1148.46	1074.99	977.71	918.55
57000	5202.06	2821.64	2035.76	1648.43	1420.44	1168.97	1094.19	995.17	934.96
58000	5293.32	2871.14	2071.47	1677.35	1445.36	1189.48	1113.38	1012.63	951.36
59000	5384.59	2920.64	2107.19	1706.27	1470.28	1209.98	1132.58	1030.09	967.76
60000	5475.85	2970.15	2142.90	1735.19	1495.20	1230.49	1151.78	1047.55	984.16
61000	5567.11	3019.65	2178.62	1764.11	1520.12	1251.00	1170.97	1065.01	1000.57
62000	5658.38	3069.15	2214.33	1793.03	1545.03	1271.51	1190.17	1082.47	1016.97
63000	5749.64	3118.65	2250.05	1821.95	1569.95	1292.02	1209.36	1099.93	1033.37
64000	5840.91	3168.16	2285.76	1850.87	1594.87	1312.52	1228.56	1117.38	1049.77
65000	5932.17	3217.66	2321.48	1879.79	1619.79	1333.03	1247.76	1134.84	1066.18
67500	6160.33	3341.41	2410.77	1952.09	1682.09	1384.30	1295.75	1178.49	1107.18
70000	6388.49	3465.17	2500.05	2024.39	1744.39	1435.57	1343.74	1222.14	1148.19
75000	6844.81	3712.68	2678.63	2168.99	1868.99	1538.11	1439.72	1309.43	1230.20
80000	7301.13	3960.19	2857.20	2313.59	1993.59	1640.65	1535.70	1396.73	1312.22
85000	7757.45	4207.70	3035.78	2458.18	2118.19	1743.19	1631.68	1484.02	1394.23
90000	8213.77	4455.22	3214.35	2602.78	2242.79	1845.73	1727.66	1571.32	1476.24
95000	8670.09	4702.73	3392.93	2747.38	2367.39	1948.28	1823.64	1658.62	1558.26
100000	9126.41	4950.24	3571.50	2891.98	2491.99	2050.82	1919.62	1745.91	1640.27
105000	9582.73	5197.75	3750.08	3036.58	2616.59	2153.36	2015.60	1833.21	1722.28
110000	10039.05	5445.26	3928.65	3181.18	2741.19	2255.90	2111.58	1920.50	1804.29
115000	10495.37	5692.77	4107.23	3325.78	2865.79	2358.44	2207.57	2007.80	1886.31
120000	10951.70	5940.29	4285.80	3470.38	2990.39	2460.98	2303.55	2095.09	1968.32
125000	11408.02	6187.80	4464.38	3614.97	3114.98	2563.52	2399.53	2182.39	2050.33
130000	11864.34	6435.31	4642.95	3759.57	3239.58	2666.06	2495.51	2269.68	2132.35
135000	12320.66	6682.82	4821.53	3904.17	3364.18	2768.60	2591.49	2356.98	2214.36
140000	12776.98	6930.33	5000.10	4048.77	3488.78	2871.14	2687.47	2444.27	2296.37
145000	13233.30	7177.85	5178.68	4193.37	3613.38	2973.68	2783.45	2531.57	2378.39
150000	13689.62	7425.36	5357.25	4337.97	3737.98	3076.22	2879.43	2618.86	2460.40

MONTHLY PAYMENT 17⅛%

NECESSARY TO AMORTIZE A LOAN

AMOUNT	15 YEARS	18 YEARS	20 YEARS	25 YEARS	28 YEARS	29 YEARS	30 YEARS	35 YEARS	40 YEARS
$ 50	.78	.75	.74	.73	.72	.72	.72	.72	.72
100	1.55	1.50	1.48	1.45	1.44	1.44	1.44	1.44	1.43
200	3.10	3.00	2.96	2.90	2.88	2.88	2.88	2.87	2.86
300	4.65	4.50	4.43	4.35	4.32	4.32	4.31	4.30	4.29
400	6.20	5.99	5.91	5.80	5.76	5.75	5.75	5.73	5.72
500	7.74	7.49	7.39	7.24	7.20	7.19	7.18	7.16	7.15
600	9.29	8.99	8.86	8.69	8.64	8.63	8.62	8.59	8.58
700	10.84	10.49	10.34	10.14	10.08	10.07	10.06	10.02	10.01
800	12.39	11.98	11.82	11.59	11.52	11.50	11.49	11.45	11.43
900	13.94	13.48	13.29	13.03	12.96	12.94	12.93	12.88	12.86
1000	15.48	14.98	14.77	14.48	14.40	14.38	14.36	14.31	14.29
2000	30.96	29.95	29.53	28.96	28.79	28.75	28.72	28.62	28.58
3000	46.44	44.92	44.29	43.44	43.19	43.13	43.08	42.93	42.87
4000	61.92	59.89	59.06	57.91	57.58	57.50	57.44	57.24	57.15
5000	77.40	74.87	73.82	72.39	71.97	71.88	71.80	71.55	71.44
6000	92.88	89.84	88.58	86.87	86.37	86.25	86.15	85.85	85.73
7000	108.36	104.81	103.35	101.34	100.76	100.63	100.51	100.16	100.01
8000	123.83	119.78	118.11	115.82	115.16	115.00	114.87	114.47	114.30
9000	139.31	134.76	132.87	130.30	129.55	129.38	129.23	128.78	128.59
10000	154.79	149.73	147.64	144.78	143.94	143.75	143.59	143.09	142.87
15000	232.19	224.59	221.45	217.16	215.91	215.62	215.38	214.63	214.31
20000	309.58	299.45	295.27	289.55	287.88	287.50	287.17	286.17	285.74
25000	386.97	374.31	369.08	361.93	359.85	359.37	358.96	357.71	357.17
30000	464.37	449.18	442.90	434.32	431.82	431.24	430.75	429.25	428.61
35000	541.76	524.04	516.71	506.70	503.79	503.12	502.54	500.79	500.04
40000	619.15	598.90	590.53	579.09	575.76	574.99	574.34	572.33	571.47
45000	696.55	673.76	664.35	651.48	647.73	646.86	646.13	643.87	642.91
46000	712.03	688.73	679.11	665.95	662.13	661.24	660.49	658.18	657.19
47000	727.50	703.71	693.87	680.43	676.52	675.61	674.84	672.48	671.48
48000	742.98	718.68	708.64	694.91	690.92	689.99	689.20	686.79	685.77
49000	758.46	733.65	723.40	709.38	705.31	704.36	703.56	701.10	700.05
50000	773.94	748.62	738.16	723.86	719.70	718.73	717.92	715.41	714.34
51000	789.42	763.59	752.93	738.34	734.10	733.11	732.28	729.72	728.63
52000	804.90	778.57	767.69	752.82	748.49	747.48	746.63	744.02	742.91
53000	820.38	793.54	782.45	767.29	762.89	761.86	760.99	758.33	757.20
54000	835.86	808.51	797.21	781.77	777.28	776.23	775.35	772.64	771.49
55000	851.33	823.48	811.98	796.25	791.67	790.61	789.71	786.95	785.77
56000	866.81	838.46	826.74	810.72	806.07	804.98	804.07	801.26	800.06
57000	882.29	853.43	841.50	825.20	820.46	819.36	818.43	815.56	814.35
58000	897.77	868.40	856.27	839.68	834.86	833.73	832.78	829.87	828.63
59000	913.25	883.37	871.03	854.16	849.25	848.11	847.14	844.18	842.92
60000	928.73	898.35	885.79	868.63	863.64	862.48	861.50	858.49	857.21
61000	944.21	913.32	900.56	883.11	878.04	876.86	875.86	872.80	871.49
62000	959.69	928.29	915.32	897.59	892.43	891.23	890.22	887.11	885.78
63000	975.16	943.26	930.08	912.06	906.83	905.60	904.58	901.41	900.07
64000	990.64	958.24	944.85	926.54	921.22	919.98	918.93	915.72	914.36
65000	1006.12	973.21	959.61	941.02	935.61	934.35	933.29	930.03	928.64
67500	1044.82	1010.64	996.52	977.21	971.60	970.29	969.19	965.80	964.36
70000	1083.52	1048.07	1033.42	1013.40	1007.58	1006.23	1005.08	1001.57	1000.08
75000	1160.91	1122.93	1107.24	1085.79	1079.55	1078.10	1076.88	1073.11	1071.51
80000	1238.30	1197.79	1181.06	1158.18	1151.52	1149.97	1148.67	1144.65	1142.94
85000	1315.70	1272.65	1254.87	1230.56	1223.49	1221.85	1220.46	1216.19	1214.38
90000	1393.09	1347.52	1328.69	1302.95	1295.46	1293.72	1292.25	1287.73	1285.81
95000	1470.48	1422.38	1402.50	1375.33	1367.43	1365.59	1364.04	1359.27	1357.24
100000	1547.88	1497.24	1476.32	1447.72	1439.40	1437.46	1435.83	1430.81	1428.68
105000	1625.27	1572.10	1550.13	1520.10	1511.37	1509.34	1507.62	1502.35	1500.11
110000	1702.66	1646.96	1623.95	1592.49	1583.34	1581.21	1579.41	1573.89	1571.54
115000	1780.06	1721.83	1697.77	1664.88	1655.31	1653.08	1651.21	1645.43	1642.98
120000	1857.45	1796.69	1771.58	1737.26	1727.28	1724.96	1723.00	1716.97	1714.41
125000	1934.85	1871.55	1845.40	1809.65	1799.25	1796.83	1794.79	1788.51	1785.85
130000	2012.24	1946.41	1919.21	1882.03	1871.22	1868.70	1866.58	1860.05	1857.28
135000	2089.63	2021.27	1993.03	1954.42	1943.19	1940.57	1938.37	1931.59	1928.71
140000	2167.03	2096.13	2066.84	2026.80	2015.16	2012.45	2010.16	2003.13	2000.15
145000	2244.42	2171.00	2140.66	2099.19	2087.13	2084.32	2081.95	2074.67	2071.58
150000	2321.81	2245.86	2214.48	2171.58	2159.10	2156.19	2153.75	2146.21	2143.01

17¼%

MONTHLY PAYMENT
NECESSARY TO AMORTIZE A LOAN

AMOUNT	1 YEAR	2 YEARS	3 YEARS	4 YEARS	5 YEARS	7 YEARS	8 YEARS	10 YEARS	12 YEARS
$ 50	4.57	2.48	1.79	1.45	1.25	1.03	.97	.88	.83
100	9.14	4.96	3.58	2.90	2.50	2.06	1.93	1.76	1.65
200	18.27	9.92	7.16	5.80	5.00	4.12	3.86	3.51	3.30
300	27.40	14.87	10.74	8.70	7.50	6.18	5.79	5.27	4.95
400	36.53	19.83	14.32	11.60	10.00	8.24	7.71	7.02	6.60
500	45.67	24.79	17.89	14.50	12.50	10.30	9.64	8.77	8.25
600	54.80	29.74	21.47	17.40	15.00	12.35	11.57	10.53	9.90
700	63.93	34.70	25.05	20.29	17.50	14.41	13.49	12.28	11.55
800	73.06	39.65	28.63	23.19	19.99	16.47	15.42	14.04	13.19
900	82.20	44.61	32.20	26.09	22.49	18.53	17.35	15.79	14.84
1000	91.33	49.57	35.78	28.99	24.99	20.59	19.28	17.54	16.49
2000	182.65	99.13	71.56	57.97	49.98	41.17	38.55	35.08	32.98
3000	273.98	148.69	107.34	86.96	74.97	61.75	57.82	52.62	49.46
4000	365.30	198.25	143.11	115.94	99.95	82.33	77.09	70.16	65.95
5000	456.62	247.82	178.89	144.93	124.94	102.91	96.36	87.70	82.44
6000	547.95	297.38	214.67	173.91	149.93	123.49	115.63	105.24	98.92
7000	639.27	346.94	250.45	202.90	174.92	144.07	134.90	122.77	115.41
8000	730.59	396.50	286.22	231.88	199.90	164.65	154.17	140.31	131.89
9000	821.92	446.07	322.00	260.87	224.89	185.23	173.44	157.85	148.38
10000	913.24	495.63	357.78	289.85	249.88	205.81	192.72	175.39	164.87
15000	1369.86	743.44	536.66	434.77	374.81	308.71	289.07	263.08	247.30
20000	1826.47	991.25	715.55	579.70	499.75	411.62	385.43	350.78	329.73
25000	2283.09	1239.07	894.44	724.62	624.68	514.52	481.78	438.47	412.16
30000	2739.71	1486.88	1073.32	869.54	749.62	617.42	578.14	526.16	494.59
35000	3196.33	1734.69	1252.21	1014.46	874.56	720.32	674.49	613.85	577.02
40000	3652.94	1982.50	1431.10	1159.39	999.49	823.23	770.85	701.55	659.45
45000	4109.56	2230.32	1609.98	1304.31	1124.43	926.13	867.20	789.24	741.88
46000	4200.88	2279.88	1645.76	1333.29	1149.42	946.71	886.47	806.78	758.37
47000	4292.21	2329.44	1681.54	1362.28	1174.40	967.29	905.74	824.31	774.86
48000	4383.53	2379.00	1717.31	1391.26	1199.39	987.87	925.02	841.85	791.34
49000	4474.85	2428.57	1753.09	1420.25	1224.38	1008.45	944.29	859.39	807.83
50000	4566.18	2478.13	1788.87	1449.23	1249.36	1029.03	963.56	876.93	824.32
51000	4657.50	2527.69	1824.65	1478.22	1274.35	1049.61	982.83	894.47	840.80
52000	4748.82	2577.25	1860.42	1507.20	1299.34	1070.19	1002.10	912.01	857.29
53000	4840.15	2626.82	1896.20	1536.19	1324.33	1090.77	1021.37	929.55	873.77
54000	4931.47	2676.38	1931.98	1565.17	1349.31	1111.35	1040.64	947.08	890.26
55000	5022.79	2725.94	1967.75	1594.16	1374.30	1131.93	1059.91	964.62	906.75
56000	5114.12	2775.50	2003.53	1623.14	1399.29	1152.52	1079.18	982.16	923.23
57000	5205.44	2825.07	2039.31	1652.12	1424.28	1173.10	1098.45	999.70	939.72
58000	5296.76	2874.63	2075.09	1681.11	1449.26	1193.68	1117.73	1017.24	956.21
59000	5388.09	2924.19	2110.86	1710.09	1474.25	1214.26	1137.00	1034.78	972.69
60000	5479.41	2973.75	2146.64	1739.08	1499.24	1234.84	1156.27	1052.32	989.18
61000	5570.73	3023.32	2182.42	1768.06	1524.22	1255.42	1175.54	1069.85	1005.66
62000	5662.06	3072.88	2218.20	1797.05	1549.21	1276.00	1194.81	1087.39	1022.15
63000	5753.38	3122.44	2253.97	1826.03	1574.20	1296.58	1214.08	1104.93	1038.64
64000	5844.70	3172.00	2289.75	1855.02	1599.19	1317.16	1233.35	1122.47	1055.12
65000	5936.03	3221.57	2325.53	1884.00	1624.17	1337.74	1252.62	1140.01	1071.61
67500	6164.34	3345.47	2414.97	1956.46	1686.64	1389.19	1300.80	1183.85	1112.82
70000	6392.65	3469.38	2504.41	2028.92	1749.11	1440.64	1348.98	1227.70	1154.04
75000	6849.26	3717.19	2683.30	2173.85	1874.04	1543.55	1445.33	1315.39	1236.47
80000	7305.88	3965.00	2862.19	2318.77	1998.98	1646.45	1541.69	1403.09	1318.90
85000	7762.50	4212.82	3041.07	2463.69	2123.92	1749.35	1638.04	1490.78	1401.33
90000	8219.11	4460.63	3219.96	2608.61	2248.85	1852.25	1734.40	1578.47	1483.76
95000	8675.73	4708.44	3398.85	2753.54	2373.79	1955.16	1830.75	1666.16	1566.19
100000	9132.35	4956.25	3577.73	2898.46	2498.72	2058.06	1927.11	1753.86	1648.63
105000	9588.97	5204.06	3756.62	3043.38	2623.66	2160.96	2023.47	1841.55	1731.06
110000	10045.58	5451.88	3935.50	3188.31	2748.60	2263.86	2119.82	1929.24	1813.49
115000	10502.20	5699.69	4114.39	3333.23	2873.53	2366.77	2216.18	2016.93	1895.92
120000	10958.82	5947.50	4293.28	3478.15	2998.47	2469.67	2312.53	2104.63	1978.35
125000	11415.43	6195.31	4472.16	3623.07	3123.40	2572.57	2408.89	2192.32	2060.78
130000	11872.05	6443.13	4651.05	3768.00	3248.34	2675.48	2505.24	2280.01	2143.21
135000	12328.67	6690.94	4829.94	3912.92	3373.28	2778.38	2601.60	2367.70	2225.64
140000	12785.29	6938.75	5008.82	4057.84	3498.21	2881.28	2697.95	2455.40	2308.07
145000	13241.90	7186.56	5187.71	4202.76	3623.15	2984.18	2794.31	2543.09	2390.51
150000	13698.52	7434.38	5366.60	4347.69	3748.08	3087.09	2890.66	2630.78	2472.94

NECESSARY TO AMORTIZE A LOAN

AMOUNT	15 YEARS	18 YEARS	20 YEARS	25 YEARS	28 YEARS	29 YEARS	30 YEARS	35 YEARS	40 YEARS
$ 50	.78	.76	.75	.73	.73	.73	.73	.73	.72
100	1.56	1.51	1.49	1.46	1.45	1.45	1.45	1.45	1.44
200	3.12	3.02	2.98	2.92	2.90	2.90	2.90	2.89	2.88
300	4.68	4.52	4.46	4.38	4.35	4.35	4.34	4.33	4.32
400	6.23	6.03	5.95	5.84	5.80	5.80	5.79	5.77	5.76
500	7.79	7.54	7.43	7.29	7.25	7.24	7.23	7.21	7.20
600	9.35	9.04	8.92	8.75	8.70	8.69	8.68	8.65	8.64
700	10.90	10.55	10.41	10.21	10.15	10.14	10.13	10.09	10.08
800	12.46	12.06	11.89	11.67	11.60	11.59	11.57	11.53	11.52
900	14.02	13.56	13.38	13.12	13.05	13.03	13.02	12.97	12.96
1000	15.57	15.07	14.86	14.58	14.50	14.48	14.46	14.42	14.40
2000	31.14	30.14	29.72	29.16	28.99	28.96	28.92	28.83	28.79
3000	46.71	45.20	44.58	43.73	43.49	43.43	43.38	43.24	43.18
4000	62.28	60.27	59.44	58.31	57.98	57.91	57.84	57.65	57.57
5000	77.84	75.33	74.30	72.89	72.48	72.38	72.30	72.06	71.96
6000	93.41	90.40	89.16	87.46	86.97	86.86	86.76	86.47	86.35
7000	108.98	105.46	104.01	102.04	101.47	101.34	101.22	100.88	100.74
8000	124.55	120.53	118.87	116.62	115.96	115.81	115.68	115.29	115.13
9000	140.11	135.59	133.73	131.19	130.46	130.29	130.14	129.70	129.52
10000	155.68	150.66	148.59	145.77	144.95	144.76	144.60	144.11	143.91
15000	233.52	225.99	222.88	218.65	217.43	217.14	216.90	216.17	215.86
20000	311.36	301.31	297.17	291.53	289.90	289.52	289.20	288.22	287.81
25000	389.19	376.64	371.47	364.42	362.38	361.90	361.50	360.28	359.76
30000	467.03	451.97	445.76	437.30	434.85	434.28	433.80	432.33	431.71
35000	544.87	527.29	520.05	510.18	507.32	506.66	506.10	504.39	503.66
40000	622.71	602.62	594.34	583.06	579.80	579.04	578.40	576.44	575.61
45000	700.55	677.95	668.63	655.94	652.27	651.42	650.70	648.50	647.57
46000	716.11	693.01	683.49	670.52	666.77	665.89	665.16	662.91	661.96
47000	731.68	708.08	698.35	685.10	681.26	680.37	679.62	677.32	676.35
48000	747.25	723.14	713.21	699.67	695.76	694.84	694.08	691.73	690.74
49000	762.82	738.21	728.07	714.25	710.25	709.32	708.54	706.14	705.13
50000	778.38	753.27	742.93	728.83	724.75	723.80	723.00	720.55	719.52
51000	793.95	768.34	757.78	743.40	739.24	738.27	737.46	734.96	733.91
52000	809.52	783.41	772.64	757.98	753.74	752.75	751.92	749.37	748.30
53000	825.09	798.47	787.50	772.55	768.23	767.22	766.38	763.78	762.69
54000	840.65	813.54	802.36	787.13	782.72	781.70	780.84	778.19	777.08
55000	856.22	828.60	817.22	801.71	797.22	796.18	795.30	792.61	791.47
56000	871.79	843.67	832.08	816.28	811.71	810.65	809.76	807.02	805.86
57000	887.36	858.73	846.93	830.86	826.21	825.13	824.22	821.43	820.25
58000	902.92	873.80	861.79	845.44	840.70	839.60	838.68	835.84	834.64
59000	918.49	888.86	876.65	860.01	855.20	854.08	853.14	850.25	849.03
60000	934.06	903.93	891.51	874.59	869.69	868.55	867.60	864.66	863.42
61000	949.63	918.99	906.37	889.17	884.19	883.03	882.06	879.07	877.81
62000	965.19	934.06	921.23	903.74	898.68	897.51	896.52	893.48	892.20
63000	980.76	949.12	936.09	918.32	913.18	911.98	910.98	907.89	906.59
64000	996.33	964.19	950.94	932.90	927.67	926.46	925.44	922.30	920.98
65000	1011.90	979.26	965.80	947.47	942.17	940.93	939.90	936.71	935.37
67500	1050.82	1016.92	1002.95	983.91	978.40	977.12	976.05	972.74	971.35
70000	1089.73	1054.58	1040.09	1020.35	1014.64	1013.31	1012.20	1008.77	1007.32
75000	1167.57	1129.91	1114.39	1093.24	1087.12	1085.69	1084.49	1080.82	1079.27
80000	1245.41	1205.24	1188.68	1166.12	1159.59	1158.07	1156.79	1152.88	1151.22
85000	1323.25	1280.56	1262.97	1239.00	1232.06	1230.45	1229.09	1224.93	1223.17
90000	1401.09	1355.89	1337.26	1311.88	1304.54	1302.83	1301.39	1296.99	1295.13
95000	1478.92	1431.22	1411.55	1384.76	1377.01	1375.21	1373.69	1369.04	1367.08
100000	1556.76	1506.54	1485.85	1457.65	1449.49	1447.59	1445.99	1441.10	1439.03
105000	1634.60	1581.87	1560.14	1530.53	1521.96	1519.97	1518.29	1513.15	1510.98
110000	1712.44	1657.20	1634.43	1603.41	1594.43	1592.35	1590.59	1585.21	1582.93
115000	1790.28	1732.53	1708.72	1676.29	1666.91	1664.72	1662.89	1657.26	1654.88
120000	1868.11	1807.85	1783.02	1749.17	1739.38	1737.10	1735.19	1729.32	1726.83
125000	1945.95	1883.18	1857.31	1822.06	1811.86	1809.48	1807.49	1801.37	1798.78
130000	2023.79	1958.51	1931.60	1894.94	1884.33	1881.86	1879.79	1873.42	1870.74
135000	2101.63	2033.83	2005.89	1967.82	1956.80	1954.24	1952.09	1945.48	1942.69
140000	2179.46	2109.16	2080.18	2040.70	2029.28	2026.62	2024.39	2017.53	2014.64
145000	2257.30	2184.49	2154.48	2113.59	2101.75	2099.00	2096.68	2089.59	2086.59
150000	2335.14	2259.81	2228.77	2186.47	2174.23	2171.38	2168.98	2161.64	2158.54

17⅜% MONTHLY PAYMENT
NECESSARY TO AMORTIZE A LOAN

AMOUNT	1 YEAR	2 YEARS	3 YEARS	4 YEARS	5 YEARS	7 YEARS	8 YEARS	10 YEARS	12 YEARS
$ 50	4.57	2.49	1.80	1.46	1.26	1.04	.97	.89	.83
100	9.14	4.97	3.59	2.91	2.51	2.07	1.94	1.77	1.66
200	18.28	9.93	7.17	5.81	5.02	4.14	3.87	3.53	3.32
300	27.42	14.89	10.76	8.72	7.52	6.20	5.81	5.29	4.98
400	36.56	19.85	14.34	11.62	10.03	8.27	7.74	7.05	6.63
500	45.70	24.82	17.92	14.53	12.53	10.33	9.68	8.81	8.29
600	54.83	29.78	21.51	17.43	15.04	12.40	11.61	10.58	9.95
700	63.97	34.74	25.09	20.34	17.54	14.46	13.55	12.34	11.60
800	73.11	39.70	28.68	23.24	20.05	16.53	15.48	14.10	13.26
900	82.25	44.67	32.26	26.15	22.55	18.59	17.42	15.86	14.92
1000	91.39	49.63	35.84	29.05	25.06	20.66	19.35	17.62	16.57
2000	182.77	99.25	71.68	58.10	50.11	41.31	38.70	35.24	33.14
3000	274.15	148.87	107.52	87.15	75.17	61.96	58.04	52.86	49.71
4000	365.54	198.50	143.36	116.20	100.22	82.62	77.39	70.48	66.28
5000	456.92	248.12	179.20	145.25	125.28	103.27	96.74	88.10	82.85
6000	548.30	297.74	215.04	174.30	150.33	123.92	116.08	105.71	99.42
7000	639.68	347.36	250.88	203.35	175.39	144.58	135.43	123.33	115.99
8000	731.07	396.99	286.72	232.40	200.44	165.23	154.77	140.95	132.56
9000	822.45	446.61	322.56	261.45	225.50	185.88	174.12	158.57	149.13
10000	913.83	496.23	358.40	290.50	250.55	206.54	193.47	176.19	165.70
15000	1370.75	744.34	537.60	435.75	375.82	309.80	290.20	264.28	248.55
20000	1827.66	992.46	716.80	580.99	501.10	413.07	386.93	352.37	331.40
25000	2284.58	1240.57	896.00	726.24	626.37	516.33	483.66	440.46	414.25
30000	2741.49	1488.68	1075.19	871.49	751.64	619.60	580.39	528.55	497.10
35000	3198.40	1736.80	1254.39	1016.73	876.92	722.86	677.12	616.64	579.95
40000	3655.32	1984.91	1433.59	1161.98	1002.19	826.13	773.85	704.73	662.80
45000	4112.23	2233.02	1612.79	1307.23	1127.46	929.39	870.58	792.82	745.65
46000	4203.61	2282.65	1648.63	1336.28	1152.52	950.05	889.92	810.44	762.22
47000	4295.00	2332.27	1684.47	1365.33	1177.57	970.70	909.27	828.06	778.79
48000	4386.38	2381.89	1720.31	1394.38	1202.63	991.35	928.62	845.67	795.36
49000	4477.76	2431.51	1756.15	1423.43	1227.68	1012.01	947.96	863.29	811.93
50000	4569.15	2481.14	1791.99	1452.48	1252.74	1032.66	967.31	880.91	828.50
51000	4660.53	2530.76	1827.83	1481.53	1277.79	1053.31	986.65	898.53	845.07
52000	4751.91	2580.38	1863.67	1510.57	1302.85	1073.97	1006.00	916.15	861.64
53000	4843.29	2630.00	1899.51	1539.62	1327.90	1094.62	1025.35	933.76	878.21
54000	4934.68	2679.63	1935.35	1568.67	1352.96	1115.27	1044.69	951.38	894.78
55000	5026.06	2729.25	1971.19	1597.72	1378.01	1135.93	1064.04	969.00	911.35
56000	5117.44	2778.87	2007.02	1626.77	1403.07	1156.58	1083.38	986.62	927.92
57000	5208.83	2828.50	2042.86	1655.82	1428.12	1177.23	1102.73	1004.24	944.49
58000	5300.21	2878.12	2078.70	1684.87	1453.18	1197.88	1122.08	1021.86	961.06
59000	5391.59	2927.74	2114.54	1713.92	1478.23	1218.54	1141.42	1039.47	977.63
60000	5482.97	2977.36	2150.38	1742.97	1503.28	1239.19	1160.77	1057.09	994.20
61000	5574.36	3026.99	2186.22	1772.02	1528.34	1259.84	1180.11	1074.71	1010.77
62000	5665.74	3076.61	2222.06	1801.07	1553.39	1280.50	1199.46	1092.33	1027.34
63000	5757.12	3126.23	2257.90	1830.12	1578.45	1301.15	1218.81	1109.95	1043.91
64000	5848.50	3175.85	2293.74	1859.17	1603.50	1321.80	1238.15	1127.56	1060.48
65000	5939.89	3225.48	2329.58	1888.22	1628.56	1342.46	1257.50	1145.18	1077.05
67500	6168.34	3349.53	2419.18	1960.84	1691.19	1394.09	1305.86	1189.23	1118.48
70000	6396.80	3473.59	2508.78	2033.46	1753.83	1445.72	1354.23	1233.27	1159.90
75000	6853.72	3721.70	2687.98	2178.71	1879.10	1548.99	1450.96	1321.36	1242.75
80000	7310.63	3969.82	2867.18	2323.96	2004.38	1652.25	1547.69	1409.45	1325.60
85000	7767.54	4217.93	3046.37	2469.21	2129.65	1755.52	1644.42	1497.54	1408.45
90000	8224.46	4466.04	3225.57	2614.45	2254.92	1858.78	1741.15	1585.63	1491.30
95000	8681.37	4714.16	3404.77	2759.70	2380.20	1962.05	1837.88	1673.73	1574.15
100000	9138.29	4962.27	3583.97	2904.95	2505.47	2065.32	1934.61	1761.82	1657.00
105000	9595.20	5210.38	3763.17	3050.19	2630.74	2168.58	2031.34	1849.91	1739.85
110000	10052.11	5458.50	3942.37	3195.44	2756.02	2271.85	2128.07	1938.00	1822.70
115000	10509.03	5706.61	4121.56	3340.69	2881.29	2375.11	2224.80	2026.09	1905.55
120000	10965.94	5954.72	4300.76	3485.94	3006.56	2478.38	2321.53	2114.18	1988.40
125000	11422.86	6202.83	4479.96	3631.18	3131.84	2581.64	2418.26	2202.27	2071.25
130000	11879.77	6450.95	4659.16	3776.43	3257.11	2684.91	2514.99	2290.36	2154.10
135000	12336.68	6699.06	4838.36	3921.68	3382.38	2788.17	2611.72	2378.45	2236.95
140000	12793.60	6947.17	5017.55	4066.92	3507.66	2891.44	2708.45	2466.54	2319.80
145000	13250.51	7195.29	5196.75	4212.17	3632.93	2994.70	2805.18	2554.63	2402.65
150000	13707.43	7443.40	5375.95	4357.42	3758.20	3097.97	2901.91	2642.72	2485.50

170

AMOUNT	15 YEARS	18 YEARS	20 YEARS	25 YEARS	28 YEARS	29 YEARS	30 YEARS	35 YEARS	40 YEARS
$ 50	.79	.76	.75	.74	.73	.73	.73	.73	.73
100	1.57	1.52	1.50	1.47	1.46	1.46	1.46	1.46	1.45
200	3.14	3.04	3.00	2.94	2.92	2.92	2.92	2.91	2.90
300	4.70	4.55	4.49	4.41	4.38	4.38	4.37	4.36	4.35
400	6.27	6.07	5.99	5.88	5.84	5.84	5.83	5.81	5.80
500	7.83	7.58	7.48	7.34	7.30	7.29	7.29	7.26	7.25
600	9.40	9.10	8.98	8.81	8.76	8.75	8.74	8.71	8.70
700	10.96	10.62	10.47	10.28	10.22	10.21	10.20	10.16	10.15
800	12.53	12.13	11.97	11.75	11.68	11.67	11.65	11.62	11.60
900	14.10	13.65	13.46	13.21	13.14	13.12	13.11	13.07	13.05
1000	15.66	15.16	14.96	14.68	14.60	14.58	14.57	14.52	14.50
2000	31.32	30.32	29.91	29.36	29.20	29.16	29.13	29.03	28.99
3000	46.97	45.48	44.87	44.03	43.79	43.74	43.69	43.55	43.49
4000	62.63	60.64	59.82	58.71	58.39	58.31	58.25	58.06	57.98
5000	78.29	75.80	74.77	73.38	72.98	72.89	72.81	72.57	72.47
6000	93.94	90.96	89.73	88.06	87.58	87.47	87.37	87.09	86.97
7000	109.60	106.12	104.68	102.74	102.18	102.04	101.94	101.60	101.46
8000	125.26	121.27	119.64	117.41	116.77	116.62	116.50	116.12	115.96
9000	140.91	136.43	134.59	132.09	131.37	131.20	131.06	130.63	130.45
10000	156.57	151.59	149.54	146.76	145.96	145.78	145.62	145.14	144.94
15000	234.85	227.38	224.31	220.14	218.94	218.66	218.43	217.71	217.41
20000	313.14	303.18	299.08	293.52	291.92	291.55	291.24	290.28	289.88
25000	391.42	378.97	373.85	366.90	364.90	364.43	364.04	362.85	362.35
30000	469.70	454.76	448.62	440.28	437.88	437.32	436.85	435.42	434.82
35000	547.99	530.56	523.39	513.66	510.86	510.20	509.66	507.99	507.29
40000	626.27	606.35	598.16	587.04	583.83	583.09	582.47	580.56	579.76
45000	704.55	682.14	672.93	660.42	656.81	655.98	655.27	653.13	652.22
46000	720.21	697.30	687.88	675.09	671.41	670.55	669.83	667.64	666.72
47000	735.86	712.46	702.84	689.77	686.00	685.13	684.40	682.15	681.21
48000	751.52	727.62	717.79	704.44	700.60	699.71	698.96	696.67	695.71
49000	767.18	742.78	732.74	719.12	715.20	714.28	713.52	711.18	710.20
50000	782.83	757.93	747.70	733.80	729.79	728.86	728.08	725.70	724.69
51000	798.49	773.09	762.65	748.47	744.39	743.44	742.64	740.21	739.19
52000	814.15	788.25	777.61	763.15	758.98	758.02	757.20	754.72	753.68
53000	829.80	803.41	792.56	777.82	773.58	772.59	771.77	769.24	768.17
54000	845.46	818.57	807.51	792.50	788.17	787.17	786.33	783.75	782.67
55000	861.12	833.73	822.47	807.17	802.77	801.75	800.89	798.26	797.16
56000	876.77	848.89	837.42	821.85	817.37	816.32	815.45	812.78	811.66
57000	892.43	864.04	852.37	836.53	831.96	830.90	830.01	827.29	826.15
58000	908.09	879.20	867.33	851.20	846.56	845.48	844.57	841.81	840.64
59000	923.74	894.36	882.28	865.88	861.15	860.06	859.13	856.32	855.14
60000	939.40	909.52	897.24	880.55	875.75	874.63	873.70	870.83	869.63
61000	955.06	924.68	912.19	895.23	890.34	889.21	888.26	885.35	884.13
62000	970.71	939.84	927.14	909.90	904.94	903.79	902.82	899.86	898.62
63000	986.37	955.00	942.10	924.58	919.54	918.36	917.38	914.38	913.11
64000	1002.03	970.15	957.05	939.26	934.13	932.94	931.94	928.89	927.61
65000	1017.68	985.31	972.01	953.93	948.73	947.52	946.50	943.40	942.10
67500	1056.82	1023.21	1009.39	990.62	985.22	983.96	982.91	979.69	978.33
70000	1095.97	1061.11	1046.77	1027.31	1021.71	1020.40	1019.31	1015.97	1014.57
75000	1174.25	1136.90	1121.54	1100.69	1094.68	1093.29	1092.12	1088.54	1087.04
80000	1252.53	1212.69	1196.31	1174.07	1167.66	1166.18	1164.93	1161.11	1159.51
85000	1330.82	1288.49	1271.08	1247.45	1240.64	1239.06	1237.73	1233.68	1231.98
90000	1409.10	1364.28	1345.85	1320.83	1313.62	1311.95	1310.54	1306.25	1304.44
95000	1487.38	1440.07	1420.62	1394.21	1386.60	1384.83	1383.35	1378.82	1376.91
100000	1565.66	1515.86	1495.39	1467.59	1459.58	1457.72	1456.16	1451.39	1449.38
105000	1643.95	1591.66	1570.16	1540.96	1532.56	1530.60	1528.96	1523.96	1521.85
110000	1722.23	1667.45	1644.93	1614.34	1605.53	1603.49	1601.77	1596.52	1594.32
115000	1800.51	1743.24	1719.70	1687.72	1678.51	1676.37	1674.58	1669.09	1666.79
120000	1878.80	1819.04	1794.47	1761.10	1751.49	1749.26	1747.39	1741.66	1739.26
125000	1957.08	1894.83	1869.24	1834.48	1824.47	1822.15	1820.19	1814.23	1811.73
130000	2035.36	1970.62	1944.01	1907.86	1897.45	1895.03	1893.00	1886.80	1884.20
135000	2113.64	2046.42	2018.77	1981.24	1970.43	1967.92	1965.81	1959.37	1956.66
140000	2191.93	2122.21	2093.54	2054.62	2043.41	2040.80	2038.62	2031.94	2029.13
145000	2270.21	2198.00	2168.31	2128.00	2116.38	2113.69	2111.43	2104.51	2101.60
150000	2348.49	2273.79	2243.08	2201.38	2189.36	2186.57	2184.23	2177.08	2174.07

17½% MONTHLY PAYMENT
NECESSARY TO AMORTIZE A LOAN

AMOUNT	1 YEAR	2 YEARS	3 YEARS	4 YEARS	5 YEARS	7 YEARS	8 YEARS	10 YEARS	12 YEARS
$ 50	4.58	2.49	1.80	1.46	1.26	1.04	.98	.89	.84
100	9.15	4.97	3.60	2.92	2.52	2.08	1.95	1.77	1.67
200	18.29	9.94	7.19	5.83	5.03	4.15	3.89	3.54	3.34
300	27.44	14.91	10.78	8.74	7.54	6.22	5.83	5.31	5.00
400	36.58	19.88	14.37	11.65	10.05	8.30	7.77	7.08	6.67
500	45.73	24.85	17.96	14.56	12.57	10.37	9.72	8.85	8.33
600	54.87	29.81	21.55	17.47	15.08	12.44	11.66	10.62	10.00
700	64.01	34.78	25.14	20.39	17.59	14.51	13.60	12.39	11.66
800	73.16	39.75	28.73	23.30	20.10	16.59	15.54	14.16	13.33
900	82.30	44.72	32.32	26.21	22.61	18.66	17.48	15.93	14.99
1000	91.45	49.69	35.91	29.12	25.13	20.73	19.43	17.70	16.66
2000	182.89	99.37	71.81	58.23	50.25	41.46	38.85	35.40	33.31
3000	274.33	149.05	107.71	87.35	75.37	62.18	58.27	53.10	49.97
4000	365.77	198.74	143.61	116.46	100.49	82.91	77.69	70.80	66.62
5000	457.22	248.42	179.52	145.58	125.62	103.63	97.11	88.49	83.27
6000	548.66	298.10	215.42	174.69	150.74	124.36	116.53	106.19	99.93
7000	640.10	347.78	251.32	203.81	175.86	145.09	135.95	123.89	116.58
8000	731.54	397.47	287.22	232.92	200.98	165.81	155.37	141.59	133.24
9000	822.98	447.15	323.12	262.03	226.10	186.54	174.80	159.29	149.89
10000	914.43	496.83	359.03	291.15	251.23	207.26	194.22	176.98	166.54
15000	1371.64	745.25	538.54	436.72	376.84	310.89	291.32	265.47	249.81
20000	1828.85	993.66	718.05	582.29	502.45	414.52	388.43	353.96	333.08
25000	2286.06	1242.08	897.56	727.86	628.06	518.15	485.54	442.45	416.35
30000	2743.27	1490.49	1077.07	873.44	753.67	621.78	582.64	530.94	499.62
35000	3200.48	1738.90	1256.58	1019.01	879.28	725.41	679.75	619.43	582.89
40000	3657.69	1987.32	1436.09	1164.58	1004.89	829.04	776.85	707.92	666.16
45000	4114.90	2235.73	1615.60	1310.15	1130.50	932.67	873.96	796.41	749.43
46000	4206.35	2285.42	1651.50	1339.27	1155.63	953.39	893.38	814.11	766.08
47000	4297.79	2335.10	1687.40	1368.38	1180.75	974.12	912.80	831.81	782.74
48000	4389.23	2384.78	1723.30	1397.49	1205.87	994.84	932.22	849.50	799.39
49000	4480.67	2434.46	1759.21	1426.61	1230.99	1015.57	951.64	867.20	816.04
50000	4572.12	2484.15	1795.11	1455.72	1256.12	1036.29	971.07	884.90	832.70
51000	4663.56	2533.83	1831.01	1484.84	1281.24	1057.02	990.49	902.60	849.35
52000	4755.00	2583.51	1866.91	1513.95	1306.36	1077.75	1009.91	920.29	866.01
53000	4846.44	2633.20	1902.81	1543.07	1331.48	1098.47	1029.33	937.99	882.66
54000	4937.88	2682.88	1938.72	1572.18	1356.60	1119.20	1048.75	955.69	899.31
55000	5029.33	2732.56	1974.62	1601.30	1381.73	1139.92	1068.17	973.39	915.97
56000	5120.77	2782.24	2010.52	1630.41	1406.85	1160.65	1087.59	991.09	932.62
57000	5212.21	2831.93	2046.42	1659.52	1431.97	1181.38	1107.01	1008.78	949.28
58000	5303.65	2881.61	2082.32	1688.64	1457.09	1202.10	1126.44	1026.48	965.93
59000	5395.10	2931.29	2118.23	1717.75	1482.22	1222.83	1145.86	1044.18	982.58
60000	5486.54	2980.98	2154.13	1746.87	1507.34	1243.55	1165.28	1061.88	999.24
61000	5577.98	3030.66	2190.03	1775.98	1532.46	1264.28	1184.70	1079.58	1015.89
62000	5669.42	3080.34	2225.93	1805.10	1557.58	1285.00	1204.12	1097.27	1032.54
63000	5760.86	3130.02	2261.84	1834.21	1582.70	1305.73	1223.54	1114.97	1049.20
64000	5852.31	3179.71	2297.74	1863.32	1607.83	1326.46	1242.96	1132.67	1065.85
65000	5943.75	3229.39	2333.64	1892.44	1632.95	1347.18	1262.38	1150.37	1082.51
67500	6172.35	3353.60	2423.39	1965.23	1695.75	1399.00	1310.94	1194.61	1124.14
70000	6400.96	3477.80	2513.15	2038.01	1758.56	1450.81	1359.49	1238.86	1165.78
75000	6858.17	3726.22	2692.66	2183.58	1884.17	1554.44	1456.60	1327.35	1249.05
80000	7315.38	3974.63	2872.17	2329.15	2009.78	1658.07	1553.70	1415.84	1332.31
85000	7772.59	4223.05	3051.68	2474.73	2135.39	1761.70	1650.81	1504.32	1415.58
90000	8229.80	4471.46	3231.19	2620.30	2261.00	1865.33	1747.91	1592.81	1498.85
95000	8687.01	4719.88	3410.70	2765.87	2386.62	1968.96	1845.02	1681.30	1582.12
100000	9144.23	4968.29	3590.21	2911.44	2512.23	2072.58	1942.13	1769.79	1665.39
105000	9601.44	5216.70	3769.72	3057.01	2637.84	2176.21	2039.23	1858.28	1748.66
110000	10058.65	5465.12	3949.23	3202.59	2763.45	2279.84	2136.34	1946.77	1831.93
115000	10515.86	5713.53	4128.74	3348.16	2889.06	2383.47	2233.44	2035.26	1915.20
120000	10973.07	5961.95	4308.25	3493.73	3014.67	2487.10	2330.55	2123.75	1998.47
125000	11430.28	6210.36	4487.76	3639.30	3140.28	2590.73	2427.66	2212.24	2081.74
130000	11887.49	6458.78	4667.27	3784.87	3265.89	2694.36	2524.76	2300.73	2165.01
135000	12344.70	6707.19	4846.78	3930.45	3391.50	2797.99	2621.87	2389.22	2248.28
140000	12801.91	6955.60	5026.29	4076.02	3517.11	2901.62	2718.97	2477.71	2331.55
145000	13259.12	7204.02	5205.80	4221.59	3642.73	3005.25	2816.08	2566.20	2414.82
150000	13716.34	7452.43	5385.31	4367.16	3768.34	3108.87	2913.19	2654.69	2498.09

MONTHLY PAYMENT 17½%

NECESSARY TO AMORTIZE A LOAN

AMOUNT	15 YEARS	18 YEARS	20 YEARS	25 YEARS	28 YEARS	29 YEARS	30 YEARS	35 YEARS	40 YEARS
$ 50	.79	.77	.76	.74	.74	.74	.74	.74	.73
100	1.58	1.53	1.51	1.48	1.47	1.47	1.47	1.47	1.46
200	3.15	3.06	3.01	2.96	2.94	2.94	2.94	2.93	2.92
300	4.73	4.58	4.52	4.44	4.41	4.41	4.40	4.39	4.38
400	6.30	6.11	6.02	5.92	5.88	5.88	5.87	5.85	5.84
500	7.88	7.63	7.53	7.39	7.35	7.34	7.34	7.31	7.30
600	9.45	9.16	9.03	8.87	8.82	8.81	8.80	8.78	8.76
700	11.03	10.68	10.54	10.35	10.29	10.28	10.27	10.24	10.22
800	12.60	12.21	12.04	11.83	11.76	11.75	11.74	11.70	11.68
900	14.18	13.73	13.55	13.30	13.23	13.22	13.20	13.16	13.14
1000	15.75	15.26	15.05	14.78	14.70	14.68	14.67	14.62	14.60
2000	31.50	30.51	30.10	29.56	29.40	29.36	29.33	29.24	29.20
3000	47.24	45.76	45.15	44.33	44.10	44.04	43.99	43.86	43.80
4000	62.99	61.01	60.20	59.11	58.79	58.72	58.66	58.47	58.39
5000	78.73	76.26	75.25	73.88	73.49	73.40	73.32	73.09	72.99
6000	94.48	91.52	90.30	88.66	88.19	88.08	87.98	87.71	87.59
7000	110.23	106.77	105.35	103.43	102.88	102.75	102.65	102.32	102.19
8000	125.97	122.02	120.40	118.21	117.58	117.43	117.31	116.94	116.78
9000	141.72	137.27	135.45	132.98	132.28	132.11	131.97	131.56	131.38
10000	157.46	152.52	150.50	147.76	146.97	146.79	146.64	146.17	145.98
15000	236.19	228.78	225.75	221.63	220.46	220.18	219.95	219.26	218.97
20000	314.92	305.04	300.99	295.51	293.94	293.58	293.27	292.34	291.95
25000	393.65	381.30	376.24	369.39	367.42	366.97	366.59	365.42	364.94
30000	472.38	457.56	451.49	443.26	440.91	440.36	439.90	438.51	437.93
35000	551.11	533.82	526.73	517.14	514.39	513.75	513.22	511.59	510.91
40000	629.84	610.08	601.98	591.02	587.87	587.15	586.54	584.68	583.90
45000	708.57	686.34	677.23	664.89	661.36	660.54	659.85	657.76	656.89
46000	724.31	701.59	692.28	679.67	676.05	675.22	674.51	672.38	671.48
47000	740.06	716.85	707.33	694.44	690.75	689.90	689.18	686.99	686.08
48000	755.80	732.10	722.38	709.22	705.45	704.57	703.84	701.61	700.68
49000	771.55	747.35	737.43	723.99	720.14	719.25	718.50	716.23	715.27
50000	787.29	762.60	752.48	738.77	734.84	733.93	733.17	730.84	729.87
51000	803.04	777.85	767.53	753.55	749.54	748.61	747.83	745.46	744.47
52000	818.79	793.11	782.57	768.32	764.23	763.29	762.49	760.08	759.07
53000	834.53	808.36	797.62	783.10	778.93	777.97	777.16	774.69	773.66
54000	850.28	823.61	812.67	797.87	793.63	792.64	791.82	789.31	788.26
55000	866.02	838.86	827.72	812.65	808.32	807.32	806.48	803.93	802.86
56000	881.77	854.11	842.77	827.42	823.02	822.00	821.15	818.54	817.46
57000	897.51	869.37	857.82	842.20	837.72	836.68	835.81	833.16	832.05
58000	913.26	884.62	872.87	856.97	852.41	851.36	850.47	847.78	846.65
59000	929.01	899.87	887.92	871.75	867.11	866.04	865.14	862.39	861.25
60000	944.75	915.12	902.97	886.52	881.81	880.72	879.80	877.01	875.85
61000	960.50	930.37	918.02	901.30	896.50	895.39	894.46	891.63	890.44
62000	976.24	945.63	933.07	916.07	911.20	910.07	909.13	906.24	905.04
63000	991.99	960.88	948.12	930.85	925.90	924.75	923.79	920.86	919.64
64000	1007.74	976.13	963.17	945.62	940.59	939.43	938.45	935.48	934.23
65000	1023.48	991.38	978.22	960.40	955.29	954.11	953.12	950.09	948.83
67500	1062.85	1029.51	1015.84	997.34	992.03	990.80	989.77	986.64	985.33
70000	1102.21	1067.64	1053.46	1034.28	1028.78	1027.50	1026.43	1023.18	1021.82
75000	1180.94	1143.90	1128.71	1108.15	1102.26	1100.89	1099.75	1096.26	1094.81
80000	1259.67	1220.16	1203.96	1182.03	1175.74	1174.29	1173.07	1169.35	1167.79
85000	1338.40	1296.42	1279.21	1255.91	1249.23	1247.68	1246.38	1242.43	1240.78
90000	1417.13	1372.68	1354.45	1329.78	1322.71	1321.07	1319.70	1315.51	1313.77
95000	1495.85	1448.94	1429.70	1403.66	1396.19	1394.46	1393.01	1388.60	1386.75
100000	1574.58	1525.20	1504.95	1477.53	1469.68	1467.86	1466.33	1461.68	1459.74
105000	1653.31	1601.46	1580.19	1551.41	1543.16	1541.25	1539.65	1534.76	1532.73
110000	1732.04	1677.72	1655.44	1625.29	1616.64	1614.64	1612.96	1607.85	1605.71
115000	1810.77	1753.98	1730.69	1699.16	1690.13	1688.03	1686.28	1680.93	1678.70
120000	1889.50	1830.24	1805.94	1773.04	1763.61	1761.43	1759.60	1754.02	1751.69
125000	1968.23	1906.50	1881.18	1846.92	1837.09	1834.82	1832.91	1827.10	1824.67
130000	2046.96	1982.76	1956.43	1920.79	1910.58	1908.21	1906.23	1900.18	1897.66
135000	2125.69	2059.02	2031.68	1994.67	1984.06	1981.60	1979.54	1973.27	1970.65
140000	2204.41	2135.28	2106.92	2068.55	2057.55	2055.00	2052.86	2046.35	2043.63
145000	2283.14	2211.54	2182.17	2142.42	2131.03	2128.39	2126.18	2119.43	2116.62
150000	2361.87	2287.80	2257.42	2216.30	2204.51	2201.78	2199.49	2192.52	2189.61

17⅝% MONTHLY PAYMENT
NECESSARY TO AMORTIZE A LOAN

AMOUNT	1 YEAR	2 YEARS	3 YEARS	4 YEARS	5 YEARS	7 YEARS	8 YEARS	10 YEARS	12 YEARS
$ 50	4.58	2.49	1.80	1.46	1.26	1.04	.98	89	.84
100	9.16	4.98	3.60	2.92	2.52	2.08	1.95	1.78	1.68
200	18.31	9.95	7.20	5.84	5.04	4.16	3.90	3.56	3.35
300	27.46	14.93	10.79	8.76	7.56	6.24	5.85	5.34	5.03
400	36.61	19.90	14.39	11.68	10.08	8.32	7.80	7.12	6.70
500	45.76	24.88	17.99	14.59	12.60	10.40	9.75	8.89	8.37
600	54.91	29.85	21.58	17.51	15.12	12.48	11.70	10.67	10.05
700	64.06	34.83	25.18	20.43	17.64	14.56	13.65	12.45	11.72
800	73.21	39.80	28.78	23.35	20.16	16.64	15.60	14.23	13.40
900	82.36	44.77	32.37	26.27	22.68	18.72	17.55	16.01	15.07
1000	91.51	49.75	35.97	29.18	25.19	20.80	19.50	17.78	16.74
2000	183.01	99.49	71.93	58.36	50.38	41.60	39.00	35.56	33.48
3000	274.51	149.23	107.90	87.54	75.57	62.40	58.49	53.34	50.22
4000	366.01	198.98	143.86	116.72	100.76	83.20	77.99	71.12	66.96
5000	457.51	248.72	179.83	145.90	125.95	104.00	97.49	88.89	83.69
6000	549.01	298.46	215.79	175.08	151.14	124.80	116.98	106.67	100.43
7000	640.52	348.21	251.76	204.26	176.33	145.60	136.48	124.45	117.17
8000	732.02	397.95	287.72	233.44	201.52	166.39	155.98	142.23	133.91
9000	823.52	447.69	323.69	262.62	226.71	187.19	175.47	160.01	150.65
10000	915.02	497.44	359.65	291.80	251.90	207.99	194.97	177.78	167.38
15000	1372.53	746.15	539.47	437.70	377.85	311.98	292.45	266.67	251.07
20000	1830.04	994.87	719.30	583.59	503.80	415.98	389.94	355.56	334.76
25000	2287.55	1243.58	899.12	729.49	629.75	519.97	487.42	444.45	418.45
30000	2745.05	1492.30	1078.94	875.39	755.70	623.96	584.90	533.34	502.14
35000	3202.56	1741.01	1258.76	1021.28	881.65	727.96	682.38	622.23	585.83
40000	3660.07	1989.73	1438.59	1167.18	1007.60	831.95	779.87	711.12	669.52
45000	4117.58	2238.44	1618.41	1313.08	1133.55	935.94	877.35	800.01	753.21
46000	4209.08	2288.19	1654.37	1342.26	1158.74	956.74	896.84	817.78	769.95
47000	4300.58	2337.93	1690.34	1371.44	1183.93	977.54	916.34	835.56	786.69
48000	4392.08	2387.67	1726.30	1400.62	1209.12	998.33	935.84	853.34	803.43
49000	4483.58	2437.42	1762.27	1429.80	1234.31	1019.14	955.33	871.12	820.16
50000	4575.09	2487.16	1798.23	1458.98	1259.50	1039.94	974.83	888.90	836.90
51000	4666.59	2536.90	1834.20	1488.15	1284.69	1060.73	994.33	906.67	853.64
52000	4758.09	2586.65	1870.16	1517.33	1309.88	1081.53	1013.82	924.45	870.38
53000	4849.59	2636.39	1906.13	1546.51	1335.07	1102.33	1033.32	942.23	887.12
54000	4941.09	2686.13	1942.09	1575.69	1360.26	1123.13	1052.82	960.01	903.85
55000	5032.59	2735.88	1978.06	1604.87	1385.45	1143.93	1072.31	977.78	920.59
56000	5124.10	2785.62	2014.02	1634.05	1410.64	1164.73	1091.81	995.56	937.33
57000	5215.60	2835.36	2049.98	1663.23	1435.83	1185.53	1111.31	1013.34	954.07
58000	5307.10	2885.10	2085.95	1692.41	1461.02	1206.32	1130.80	1031.12	970.81
59000	5398.60	2934.85	2121.91	1721.59	1486.21	1227.12	1150.30	1048.90	987.54
60000	5490.10	2984.59	2157.88	1750.77	1511.40	1247.92	1169.80	1066.67	1004.28
61000	5581.60	3034.33	2193.84	1779.95	1536.59	1268.72	1189.29	1084.45	1021.02
62000	5673.11	3084.08	2229.81	1809.13	1561.78	1289.52	1208.79	1102.23	1037.76
63000	5764.61	3133.82	2265.77	1838.31	1586.97	1310.32	1228.28	1120.01	1054.50
64000	5856.11	3183.56	2301.74	1867.49	1612.16	1331.12	1247.78	1137.78	1071.23
65000	5947.61	3233.31	2337.70	1896.67	1637.35	1351.91	1267.28	1155.56	1087.97
67500	6176.36	3357.66	2427.61	1969.62	1700.32	1403.91	1316.02	1200.01	1129.82
70000	6405.12	3482.02	2517.52	2042.56	1763.30	1455.91	1364.76	1244.45	1171.66
75000	6862.63	3730.74	2697.35	2188.46	1889.25	1559.90	1462.24	1333.34	1255.35
80000	7320.13	3979.45	2877.17	2334.36	2015.19	1663.89	1559.73	1422.23	1339.04
85000	7777.64	4228.17	3056.99	2480.25	2141.14	1767.89	1657.21	1511.12	1422.73
90000	8235.15	4476.88	3236.81	2626.15	2267.09	1871.88	1754.69	1600.01	1506.42
95000	8692.66	4725.60	3416.64	2772.05	2393.04	1975.87	1852.17	1688.90	1590.11
100000	9150.17	4974.31	3596.46	2917.95	2518.99	2079.87	1949.66	1777.79	1673.80
105000	9607.68	5223.03	3776.28	3063.84	2644.94	2183.86	2047.14	1866.67	1757.49
110000	10065.18	5471.75	3956.11	3209.74	2770.89	2287.85	2144.62	1955.56	1841.18
115000	10522.69	5720.46	4135.93	3355.64	2896.84	2391.85	2242.10	2044.45	1924.87
120000	10980.20	5969.18	4315.75	3501.53	3022.79	2495.84	2339.59	2133.34	2008.56
125000	11437.71	6217.89	4495.57	3647.43	3148.74	2599.83	2437.07	2222.23	2092.25
130000	11895.22	6466.61	4675.40	3793.33	3274.69	2703.82	2534.55	2311.12	2175.94
135000	12352.72	6715.32	4855.22	3939.23	3400.64	2807.82	2632.03	2400.01	2259.63
140000	12810.23	6964.04	5035.04	4085.12	3526.59	2911.81	2729.52	2488.90	2343.32
145000	13267.74	7212.75	5214.87	4231.02	3652.54	3015.80	2827.00	2577.79	2427.01
150000	13725.25	7461.47	5394.69	4376.92	3778.49	3119.80	2924.48	2666.68	2510.70

174

MONTHLY PAYMENT 17⅝%
NECESSARY TO AMORTIZE A LOAN

AMOUNT	15 YEARS	18 YEARS	20 YEARS	25 YEARS	28 YEARS	29 YEARS	30 YEARS	35 YEARS	40 YEARS
$ 50	.80	.77	.76	.75	.74	.74	.74	.74	.74
100	1.59	1.54	1.52	1.49	1.48	1.48	1.48	1.48	1.48
200	3.17	3.07	3.03	2.98	2.96	2.96	2.96	2.95	2.95
300	4.76	4.61	4.55	4.47	4.44	4.44	4.43	4.42	4.42
400	6.34	6.14	6.06	5.95	5.92	5.92	5.91	5.89	5.89
500	7.92	7.68	7.58	7.44	7.40	7.39	7.39	7.36	7.36
600	9.51	9.21	9.09	8.93	8.88	8.87	8.86	8.84	8.83
700	11.09	10.75	10.61	10.42	10.36	10.35	10.34	10.31	10.30
800	12.67	12.28	12.12	11.90	11.84	11.83	11.82	11.78	11.77
900	14.26	13.82	13.64	13.39	13.32	13.31	13.29	13.25	13.24
1000	15.84	15.35	15.15	14.88	14.80	14.78	14.77	14.72	14.71
2000	31.68	30.70	30.30	29.75	29.60	29.56	29.54	29.44	29.41
3000	47.51	46.04	45.44	44.63	44.40	44.34	44.30	44.16	44.11
4000	63.35	61.39	60.59	59.50	59.20	59.12	59.07	58.88	58.81
5000	79.18	76.73	75.73	74.38	73.99	73.90	73.83	73.60	73.51
6000	95.02	92.08	90.88	89.25	88.79	88.68	88.60	88.32	88.21
7000	110.85	107.42	106.02	104.13	103.59	103.46	103.36	103.04	102.91
8000	126.69	122.77	121.17	119.00	118.39	118.24	118.13	117.76	117.61
9000	142.52	138.11	136.31	133.88	133.19	133.02	132.89	132.48	132.31
10000	158.36	153.46	151.46	148.75	147.98	147.80	147.66	147.20	147.01
15000	237.53	230.19	227.18	223.13	221.97	221.70	221.48	220.80	220.52
20000	316.71	306.91	302.91	297.50	295.96	295.60	295.31	294.40	294.02
25000	395.88	383.64	378.63	371.88	369.95	369.50	369.13	368.00	367.53
30000	475.06	460.37	454.36	446.25	443.94	443.40	442.96	441.60	441.03
35000	554.23	537.10	530.08	520.63	517.93	517.30	516.78	515.20	514.54
40000	633.41	613.82	605.81	595.00	591.92	591.20	590.61	588.79	588.04
45000	712.59	690.55	681.54	669.38	665.91	665.10	664.43	662.39	661.55
46000	728.42	705.90	696.68	684.25	680.70	679.88	679.20	677.11	676.25
47000	744.26	721.24	711.83	699.13	695.50	694.66	693.96	691.83	690.95
48000	760.09	736.59	726.97	714.00	710.30	709.44	708.73	706.55	705.65
49000	775.93	751.93	742.12	728.87	725.10	724.22	723.49	721.27	720.35
50000	791.76	767.28	757.26	743.75	739.89	739.00	738.26	735.99	735.05
51000	807.60	782.62	772.41	758.62	754.69	753.78	753.02	750.71	749.75
52000	823.43	797.97	787.55	773.50	769.49	768.56	767.79	765.43	764.45
53000	839.27	813.31	802.70	788.37	784.29	783.34	782.55	780.15	779.15
54000	855.10	828.66	817.84	803.25	799.09	798.12	797.32	794.87	793.85
55000	870.94	844.01	832.99	818.12	813.88	812.90	812.08	809.59	808.56
56000	886.77	859.35	848.13	833.00	828.68	827.68	826.85	824.31	823.26
57000	902.61	874.70	863.28	847.87	843.48	842.46	841.61	839.03	837.96
58000	918.44	890.04	878.42	862.75	858.28	857.24	856.38	853.75	852.66
59000	934.28	905.39	893.57	877.62	873.07	872.02	871.14	868.47	867.36
60000	950.11	920.73	908.71	892.50	887.87	886.80	885.91	883.19	882.06
61000	965.95	936.08	923.86	907.37	902.67	901.58	900.67	897.91	896.76
62000	981.78	951.42	939.00	922.25	917.47	916.36	915.44	912.63	911.46
63000	997.62	966.77	954.15	937.12	932.27	931.14	930.20	927.35	926.16
64000	1013.45	982.11	969.29	952.00	947.06	945.92	944.97	942.07	940.86
65000	1029.29	997.46	984.44	966.87	961.86	960.70	959.73	956.79	955.56
67500	1068.88	1035.82	1022.30	1004.06	998.86	997.65	996.65	993.59	992.32
70000	1108.46	1074.19	1060.16	1041.25	1035.85	1034.60	1033.56	1030.39	1029.07
75000	1187.64	1150.91	1135.89	1115.62	1109.84	1108.50	1107.38	1103.99	1102.57
80000	1266.82	1227.64	1211.62	1190.00	1183.83	1182.40	1181.21	1177.58	1176.08
85000	1345.99	1304.37	1287.34	1264.37	1257.82	1256.30	1255.03	1251.18	1249.58
90000	1425.17	1381.10	1363.07	1338.75	1331.81	1330.20	1328.86	1324.78	1323.09
95000	1504.34	1457.82	1438.79	1413.12	1405.80	1404.10	1402.69	1398.38	1396.59
100000	1583.52	1534.55	1514.52	1487.49	1479.78	1478.00	1476.51	1471.98	1470.10
105000	1662.69	1611.28	1590.24	1561.87	1553.77	1551.90	1550.34	1545.58	1543.60
110000	1741.87	1688.01	1665.97	1636.24	1627.76	1625.80	1624.16	1619.18	1617.11
115000	1821.05	1764.73	1741.70	1710.62	1701.75	1699.70	1697.99	1692.77	1690.61
120000	1900.22	1841.46	1817.42	1784.99	1775.74	1773.60	1771.81	1766.37	1764.12
125000	1979.40	1918.19	1893.15	1859.37	1849.73	1847.50	1845.64	1839.97	1837.62
130000	2058.57	1994.92	1968.87	1933.74	1923.72	1921.40	1919.46	1913.57	1911.12
135000	2137.75	2071.64	2044.60	2008.12	1997.71	1995.30	1993.29	1987.17	1984.63
140000	2216.92	2148.37	2120.32	2082.49	2071.70	2069.20	2067.11	2060.77	2058.13
145000	2296.10	2225.10	2196.05	2156.86	2145.68	2143.10	2140.94	2134.37	2131.64
150000	2375.28	2301.82	2271.78	2231.24	2219.67	2217.00	2214.76	2207.97	2205.14

175

17¾%　　MONTHLY PAYMENT
NECESSARY TO AMORTIZE A LOAN

AMOUNT	1 YEAR	2 YEARS	3 YEARS	4 YEARS	5 YEARS	7 YEARS	8 YEARS	10 YEARS	12 YEARS
$ 50	4.58	2.50	1.81	1.47	1.27	1.05	.98	.90	.85
100	9.16	4.99	3.61	2.93	2.53	2.09	1.96	1.79	1.69
200	18.32	9.97	7.21	5.85	5.06	4.18	3.92	3.58	3.37
300	27.47	14.95	10.81	8.78	7.58	6.27	5.88	5.36	5.05
400	36.63	19.93	14.42	11.70	10.11	8.35	7.83	7.15	6.73
500	45.79	24.91	18.02	14.63	12.63	10.44	9.79	8.93	8.42
600	54.94	29.89	21.62	17.55	15.16	12.53	11.75	10.72	10.10
700	64.10	34.87	25.22	20.48	17.69	14.62	13.71	12.51	11.78
800	73.25	39.85	28.83	23.40	20.21	16.70	15.66	14.29	13.46
900	82.41	44.83	32.43	26.33	22.74	18.79	17.62	16.08	15.14
1000	91.57	49.81	36.03	29.25	25.26	20.88	19.58	17.86	16.83
2000	183.13	99.61	72.06	58.49	50.52	41.75	39.15	35.72	33.65
3000	274.69	149.42	108.09	87.74	75.78	62.62	58.72	53.58	50.47
4000	366.25	199.22	144.11	116.98	101.04	83.49	78.29	71.44	67.29
5000	457.81	249.02	180.14	146.23	126.29	104.36	97.86	89.29	84.12
6000	549.37	298.83	216.17	175.47	151.55	125.23	117.44	107.15	100.94
7000	640.93	348.63	252.19	204.72	176.81	146.11	137.01	125.01	117.76
8000	732.49	398.43	288.22	233.96	202.07	166.98	156.58	142.87	134.58
9000	824.05	448.24	324.25	263.21	227.32	187.85	176.15	160.73	151.40
10000	915.62	498.04	360.28	292.45	252.58	208.72	195.72	178.58	168.23
15000	1373.42	747.06	540.41	438.67	378.87	313.08	293.58	267.87	252.34
20000	1831.23	996.07	720.55	584.90	505.16	417.44	391.44	357.16	336.45
25000	2289.03	1245.09	900.68	731.12	631.45	521.79	489.30	446.45	420.56
30000	2746.84	1494.11	1080.82	877.34	757.73	626.15	587.16	535.74	504.67
35000	3204.64	1743.12	1260.95	1023.56	884.02	730.51	685.02	625.03	588.78
40000	3662.45	1992.14	1441.09	1169.79	1010.31	834.87	782.88	714.32	672.89
45000	4120.25	2241.16	1621.22	1316.01	1136.60	939.23	880.74	803.61	757.00
46000	4211.81	2290.96	1657.25	1345.25	1161.86	960.10	900.31	821.47	773.83
47000	4303.37	2340.76	1693.28	1374.50	1187.11	980.97	919.89	839.33	790.65
48000	4394.94	2390.57	1729.31	1403.74	1212.37	1001.84	939.46	857.18	807.47
49000	4486.50	2440.37	1765.33	1432.99	1237.63	1022.71	959.03	875.04	824.29
50000	4578.06	2490.37	1801.36	1462.23	1262.89	1043.58	978.60	892.90	841.12
51000	4669.62	2539.98	1837.39	1491.48	1288.14	1064.45	998.17	910.76	857.94
52000	4761.18	2589.78	1873.41	1520.72	1313.40	1085.33	1017.75	928.61	874.76
53000	4852.74	2639.58	1909.44	1549.96	1338.66	1106.20	1037.32	946.47	891.58
54000	4944.30	2689.39	1945.47	1579.21	1363.92	1127.07	1056.89	964.33	908.40
55000	5035.86	2739.19	1981.50	1608.45	1389.17	1147.94	1076.46	982.19	925.23
56000	5127.42	2788.99	2017.52	1637.70	1414.43	1168.81	1096.03	1000.05	942.05
57000	5218.99	2838.80	2053.55	1666.94	1439.69	1189.68	1115.61	1017.90	958.87
58000	5310.55	2888.60	2089.58	1696.19	1464.95	1210.56	1135.18	1035.76	975.69
59000	5402.11	2938.41	2125.60	1725.43	1490.20	1231.43	1154.75	1053.62	992.51
60000	5493.67	2988.21	2161.63	1754.68	1515.46	1252.30	1174.32	1071.48	1009.34
61000	5585.23	3038.01	2197.66	1783.92	1540.72	1273.17	1193.89	1089.34	1026.16
62000	5676.79	3087.82	2233.69	1813.17	1565.98	1294.04	1213.46	1107.19	1042.98
63000	5768.35	3137.62	2269.71	1842.41	1591.24	1314.91	1233.04	1125.05	1059.80
64000	5859.91	3187.42	2305.74	1871.65	1616.49	1335.78	1252.61	1142.91	1076.63
65000	5951.47	3237.23	2341.77	1900.90	1641.75	1356.66	1272.18	1160.77	1093.45
67500	6180.38	3361.73	2431.83	1974.01	1704.89	1408.84	1321.11	1205.41	1135.50
70000	6409.28	3486.24	2521.90	2047.12	1768.04	1461.01	1370.04	1250.06	1177.56
75000	6867.08	3735.26	2702.04	2193.34	1894.33	1565.37	1467.90	1339.35	1261.67
80000	7324.89	3984.28	2882.17	2339.57	2020.61	1669.73	1565.76	1428.64	1345.78
85000	7782.69	4233.29	3062.31	2485.79	2146.90	1774.09	1663.62	1517.93	1429.89
90000	8240.50	4482.31	3242.44	2632.01	2273.19	1878.45	1761.48	1607.21	1514.00
95000	8698.31	4731.33	3422.58	2778.23	2399.48	1982.80	1859.34	1696.50	1598.11
100000	9156.11	4980.34	3602.72	2924.46	2525.77	2087.16	1957.20	1785.79	1682.23
105000	9613.92	5229.36	3782.85	3070.68	2652.06	2191.52	2055.06	1875.08	1766.34
110000	10071.72	5478.38	3962.99	3216.90	2778.34	2295.88	2152.92	1964.37	1850.45
115000	10529.53	5727.39	4143.12	3363.13	2904.63	2400.23	2250.78	2053.66	1934.56
120000	10987.33	5976.41	4323.26	3509.35	3030.92	2504.59	2348.64	2142.95	2018.67
125000	11445.14	6225.43	4503.39	3655.57	3157.21	2608.95	2446.50	2232.24	2102.78
130000	11902.94	6474.45	4683.53	3801.79	3283.50	2713.31	2544.36	2321.53	2186.89
135000	12360.75	6723.46	4863.66	3948.02	3409.78	2817.67	2642.22	2410.82	2271.00
140000	12818.55	6972.48	5043.80	4094.24	3536.07	2922.02	2740.08	2500.11	2355.11
145000	13276.36	7221.50	5223.94	4240.46	3662.36	3026.38	2837.94	2589.40	2439.22
150000	13734.16	7470.51	5404.07	4386.68	3788.65	3130.74	2935.79	2678.69	2523.34

176

MONTHLY PAYMENT   17¾%
NECESSARY TO AMORTIZE A LOAN

AMOUNT	15 YEARS	18 YEARS	20 YEARS	25 YEARS	28 YEARS	29 YEARS	30 YEARS	35 YEARS	40 YEARS
$ 50	.80	.78	.77	.75	.75	.75	.75	.75	.75
100	1.60	1.55	1.53	1.50	1.49	1.49	1.49	1.49	1.49
200	3.19	3.09	3.05	3.00	2.98	2.98	2.98	2.97	2.97
300	4.78	4.64	4.58	4.50	4.47	4.47	4.47	4.45	4.45
400	6.37	6.18	6.10	5.99	5.96	5.96	5.95	5.93	5.93
500	7.97	7.72	7.63	7.49	7.45	7.45	7.44	7.42	7.41
600	9.56	9.27	9.15	8.99	8.94	8.93	8.93	8.90	8.89
700	11.15	10.81	10.67	10.49	10.43	10.42	10.41	10.38	10.37
800	12.74	12.36	12.20	11.98	11.92	11.91	11.90	11.86	11.85
900	14.34	13.90	13.72	13.48	13.41	13.40	13.39	13.35	13.33
1000	15.93	15.44	15.25	14.98	14.90	14.89	14.87	14.83	14.81
2000	31.85	30.88	30.49	29.95	29.80	29.77	29.74	29.65	29.61
3000	47.78	46.32	45.73	44.93	44.70	44.65	44.61	44.47	44.42
4000	63.70	61.76	60.97	59.90	59.60	59.53	59.47	59.30	59.22
5000	79.63	77.20	76.21	74.88	74.50	74.41	74.34	74.12	74.03
6000	95.55	92.64	91.45	89.85	89.40	89.29	89.21	88.94	88.83
7000	111.48	108.08	106.69	104.83	104.30	104.18	104.07	103.76	103.64
8000	127.40	123.52	121.93	119.80	119.20	119.06	118.94	118.59	118.44
9000	143.33	138.96	137.17	134.78	134.10	133.94	133.81	133.41	133.25
10000	159.25	154.40	152.41	149.75	148.99	148.82	148.67	148.23	148.05
15000	238.87	231.59	228.62	224.62	223.49	223.23	223.01	222.35	222.07
20000	318.50	308.79	304.82	299.50	297.98	297.64	297.34	296.46	296.10
25000	398.12	385.98	381.03	374.37	372.48	372.04	371.68	370.57	370.12
30000	477.74	463.18	457.23	449.24	446.97	446.45	446.01	444.69	444.14
35000	557.37	540.37	533.44	524.12	521.47	520.86	520.35	518.80	518.16
40000	636.99	617.57	609.64	598.99	595.96	595.27	594.68	592.92	592.19
45000	716.61	694.77	685.85	673.86	670.46	669.67	669.02	667.03	666.21
46000	732.54	710.20	701.09	688.84	685.36	684.55	683.88	681.85	681.01
47000	748.46	725.64	716.33	703.81	700.26	699.44	698.75	696.67	695.82
48000	764.39	741.08	731.57	718.79	715.15	714.32	713.62	711.50	710.62
49000	780.31	756.52	746.81	733.76	730.05	729.20	728.48	726.32	725.43
50000	796.24	771.96	762.05	748.73	744.95	744.08	743.35	741.14	740.23
51000	812.16	787.40	777.30	763.71	759.85	758.96	758.22	755.97	755.04
52000	828.09	802.84	792.54	778.68	774.75	773.84	773.08	770.79	769.84
53000	844.01	818.28	807.78	793.66	789.65	788.73	787.95	785.61	784.65
54000	859.94	833.72	823.02	808.63	804.55	803.61	802.82	800.43	799.45
55000	875.86	849.16	838.26	823.61	819.45	818.49	817.69	815.26	814.25
56000	891.79	864.60	853.50	838.58	834.35	833.37	832.55	830.08	829.06
57000	907.71	880.04	868.74	853.56	849.24	848.25	847.42	844.90	843.86
58000	923.64	895.47	883.98	868.53	864.14	863.13	862.29	859.72	858.67
59000	939.56	910.91	899.22	883.51	879.04	878.01	877.15	874.55	873.47
60000	955.48	926.35	914.46	898.48	893.94	892.90	892.02	889.37	888.28
61000	971.41	941.79	929.71	913.46	908.84	907.78	906.89	904.19	903.08
62000	987.33	957.23	944.95	928.43	923.74	922.66	921.75	919.02	917.89
63000	1003.26	972.67	960.19	943.40	938.64	937.54	936.62	933.84	932.69
64000	1019.18	988.11	975.43	958.38	953.54	952.42	951.49	948.66	947.50
65000	1035.11	1003.55	990.67	973.35	968.44	967.30	966.35	963.48	962.30
67500	1074.92	1042.15	1028.77	1010.79	1005.68	1004.51	1003.52	1000.54	999.31
70000	1114.73	1080.74	1066.87	1048.23	1042.93	1041.71	1040.69	1037.60	1036.32
75000	1194.35	1157.94	1143.08	1123.10	1117.43	1116.12	1115.02	1111.71	1110.35
80000	1273.98	1235.14	1219.28	1197.97	1191.92	1190.53	1189.36	1185.83	1184.37
85000	1353.60	1312.33	1295.49	1272.85	1266.42	1264.93	1263.69	1259.94	1258.39
90000	1433.22	1389.53	1371.69	1347.72	1340.91	1339.34	1338.03	1334.05	1332.41
95000	1512.85	1466.72	1447.90	1422.59	1415.40	1413.75	1412.36	1408.17	1406.44
100000	1592.47	1543.92	1524.10	1497.46	1489.90	1488.16	1486.70	1482.28	1480.46
105000	1672.09	1621.11	1600.31	1572.34	1564.39	1562.56	1561.03	1556.39	1554.48
110000	1751.72	1698.31	1676.51	1647.21	1638.89	1636.97	1635.37	1630.51	1628.50
115000	1831.34	1775.50	1752.72	1722.08	1713.38	1711.38	1709.70	1704.62	1702.53
120000	1910.96	1852.70	1828.92	1796.96	1787.88	1785.79	1784.04	1778.74	1776.55
125000	1990.59	1929.90	1905.13	1871.83	1862.37	1860.19	1858.37	1852.85	1850.57
130000	2070.21	2007.09	1981.33	1946.70	1936.87	1934.60	1932.70	1926.96	1924.59
135000	2149.83	2084.29	2057.54	2021.58	2011.36	2009.01	2007.04	2001.08	1998.62
140000	2229.46	2161.48	2133.74	2096.45	2085.86	2083.42	2081.37	2075.19	2072.64
145000	2309.08	2238.68	2209.95	2171.32	2160.35	2157.82	2155.71	2149.30	2146.66
150000	2388.70	2315.87	2286.15	2246.19	2234.85	2232.23	2230.04	2223.42	2220.69

MONTHLY PAYMENT
NECESSARY TO AMORTIZE A LOAN

AMOUNT	1 YEAR	2 YEARS	3 YEARS	4 YEARS	5 YEARS	7 YEARS	8 YEARS	10 YEARS	12 YEARS
$ 50	4.59	2.50	1.81	1.47	1.27	1.05	.99	.90	.85
100	9.17	4.99	3.61	2.94	2.54	2.10	1.97	1.80	1.70
200	18.33	9.98	7.22	5.87	5.07	4.19	3.93	3.59	3.39
300	27.49	14.96	10.83	8.80	7.60	6.29	5.90	5.39	5.08
400	36.65	19.95	14.44	11.73	10.14	8.38	7.86	7.18	6.77
500	45.82	24.94	18.05	14.66	12.67	10.48	9.83	8.97	8.46
600	54.98	29.92	21.66	17.59	15.20	12.57	11.79	10.77	10.15
700	64.14	34.91	25.27	20.52	17.73	14.67	13.76	12.56	11.84
800	73.30	39.90	28.88	23.45	20.27	16.76	15.72	14.36	13.53
900	82.46	44.88	32.49	26.38	22.80	18.86	17.69	16.15	15.22
1000	91.63	49.87	36.09	29.31	25.33	20.95	19.65	17.94	16.91
2000	183.25	99.73	72.18	58.62	50.66	41.89	39.30	35.88	33.82
3000	274.87	149.60	108.27	87.93	75.98	62.84	58.95	53.82	50.72
4000	366.49	199.46	144.36	117.24	101.31	83.78	78.60	71.76	67.63
5000	458.11	249.32	180.45	146.55	126.63	104.73	98.24	89.70	84.54
6000	549.73	299.19	216.54	175.86	151.96	125.67	117.89	107.63	101.44
7000	641.35	349.05	252.63	205.17	177.28	146.62	137.54	125.57	118.35
8000	732.97	398.91	288.72	234.48	202.61	167.56	157.19	143.51	135.26
9000	824.59	448.78	324.81	263.79	227.93	188.51	176.83	161.45	152.16
10000	916.21	498.64	360.90	293.10	253.26	209.45	196.48	179.39	169.07
15000	1374.31	747.96	541.35	439.65	379.89	314.17	294.72	269.08	253.60
20000	1832.42	997.28	721.80	586.20	506.51	418.90	392.96	358.77	338.14
25000	2290.52	1246.60	902.25	732.75	633.14	523.62	491.19	448.46	422.67
30000	2748.62	1495.92	1082.70	879.30	759.77	628.34	589.43	538.15	507.20
35000	3206.72	1745.24	1263.15	1025.85	886.40	733.07	687.67	627.84	591.74
40000	3664.83	1994.55	1443.59	1172.39	1013.02	837.79	785.91	717.53	676.27
45000	4122.93	2243.87	1624.04	1318.94	1139.65	942.51	884.14	807.22	760.80
46000	4214.55	2293.74	1660.13	1348.25	1164.98	963.46	903.79	825.16	777.71
47000	4306.17	2343.60	1696.22	1377.56	1190.30	984.40	923.44	843.10	794.62
48000	4397.79	2393.46	1732.31	1406.87	1215.63	1005.35	943.09	861.03	811.52
49000	4489.41	2443.33	1768.40	1436.18	1240.95	1026.29	962.73	878.97	828.43
50000	4581.03	2493.19	1804.49	1465.49	1266.28	1047.24	982.38	896.91	845.34
51000	4672.65	2543.06	1840.58	1494.80	1291.60	1068.18	1002.03	914.85	862.24
52000	4764.27	2592.92	1876.67	1524.11	1316.93	1089.13	1021.68	932.79	879.15
53000	4855.89	2642.78	1912.76	1553.42	1342.26	1110.07	1041.32	950.73	896.06
54000	4947.51	2692.65	1948.85	1582.73	1367.58	1131.02	1060.97	968.66	912.96
55000	5039.13	2742.51	1984.94	1612.04	1392.91	1151.96	1080.62	986.60	929.87
56000	5130.75	2792.37	2021.03	1641.35	1418.23	1172.90	1100.27	1004.54	946.78
57000	5222.37	2842.24	2057.12	1670.66	1443.56	1193.85	1119.91	1022.48	963.68
58000	5313.99	2892.10	2093.21	1699.97	1468.88	1214.79	1139.56	1040.42	980.59
59000	5405.62	2941.96	2129.30	1729.28	1494.21	1235.74	1159.21	1058.35	997.50
60000	5497.24	2991.83	2165.39	1758.59	1519.53	1256.68	1178.86	1076.29	1014.40
61000	5588.86	3041.69	2201.48	1787.90	1544.86	1277.63	1198.50	1094.23	1031.31
62000	5680.48	3091.56	2237.57	1817.21	1570.18	1298.57	1218.15	1112.17	1048.22
63000	5772.10	3141.42	2273.66	1846.52	1595.51	1319.52	1237.80	1130.11	1065.12
64000	5863.72	3191.28	2309.75	1875.83	1620.84	1340.46	1257.45	1148.04	1082.03
65000	5955.34	3241.15	2345.84	1905.14	1646.16	1361.41	1277.09	1165.98	1098.94
67500	6184.39	3365.81	2436.06	1978.41	1709.47	1413.77	1326.21	1210.83	1141.20
70000	6413.44	3490.47	2526.29	2051.69	1772.79	1466.13	1375.33	1255.67	1183.47
75000	6871.54	3739.78	2706.73	2198.23	1899.42	1570.85	1473.57	1345.36	1268.00
80000	7329.65	3989.10	2887.18	2344.78	2026.04	1675.58	1571.81	1435.05	1352.53
85000	7787.75	4238.42	3067.63	2491.33	2152.67	1780.30	1670.04	1524.75	1437.07
90000	8245.85	4487.74	3248.08	2637.88	2279.30	1885.02	1768.28	1614.44	1521.60
95000	8703.95	4737.06	3428.53	2784.43	2405.93	1989.75	1866.52	1704.13	1606.13
100000	9162.06	4986.38	3608.98	2930.98	2532.55	2094.47	1964.76	1793.82	1690.67
105000	9620.16	5235.70	3789.43	3077.53	2659.18	2199.19	2062.99	1883.51	1775.20
110000	10078.26	5485.01	3969.87	3224.07	2785.81	2303.91	2161.23	1973.20	1859.73
115000	10536.36	5734.33	4150.32	3370.62	2912.43	2408.64	2259.47	2062.89	1944.27
120000	10994.47	5983.65	4330.77	3517.17	3039.06	2513.36	2357.71	2152.58	2028.80
125000	11452.57	6232.97	4511.22	3663.72	3165.69	2618.08	2455.94	2242.27	2113.33
130000	11910.67	6482.29	4691.67	3810.27	3292.32	2722.81	2554.18	2331.96	2197.87
135000	12368.77	6731.61	4872.12	3956.82	3418.94	2827.53	2652.42	2421.65	2282.40
140000	12826.88	6980.93	5052.57	4103.37	3545.57	2932.25	2750.66	2511.34	2366.93
145000	13284.98	7230.25	5233.01	4249.91	3672.20	3036.98	2848.89	2601.03	2451.46
150000	13743.08	7479.56	5413.46	4396.46	3798.83	3141.70	2947.13	2690.72	2536.00

MONTHLY PAYMENT 17⅞%

NECESSARY TO AMORTIZE A LOAN

AMOUNT	15 YEARS	18 YEARS	20 YEARS	25 YEARS	28 YEARS	29 YEARS	30 YEARS	35 YEARS	40 YEARS
$ 50	.81	.78	.77	.76	.76	.75	.75	.75	.75
100	1.61	1.56	1.54	1.51	1.51	1.50	1.50	1.50	1.50
200	3.21	3.11	3.07	3.02	3.01	3.00	3.00	2.99	2.99
300	4.81	4.66	4.61	4.53	4.51	4.50	4.50	4.48	4.48
400	6.41	6.22	6.14	6.03	6.01	6.00	5.99	5.98	5.97
500	8.01	7.77	7.67	7.54	7.51	7.50	7.49	7.47	7.46
600	9.61	9.32	9.21	9.05	9.01	8.99	8.99	8.96	8.95
700	11.22	10.88	10.74	10.56	10.51	10.49	10.48	10.45	10.44
800	12.82	12.43	12.27	12.06	12.01	11.99	11.98	11.95	11.93
900	14.42	13.98	13.81	13.57	13.51	13.49	13.48	13.44	13.42
1000	16.02	15.54	15.34	15.08	15.01	14.99	14.97	14.93	14.91
2000	32.03	31.07	30.68	30.15	30.01	29.97	29.94	29.86	29.82
3000	48.05	46.60	46.02	45.23	45.01	44.95	44.91	44.78	44.73
4000	64.06	62.14	61.35	60.30	60.01	59.94	59.88	59.71	59.64
5000	80.08	77.67	76.69	75.38	75.01	74.92	74.85	74.63	74.55
6000	96.09	93.20	92.03	90.45	90.01	89.90	89.82	89.56	89.45
7000	112.11	108.74	107.36	105.53	105.01	104.89	104.79	104.49	104.36
8000	128.12	124.27	122.70	120.60	120.01	119.87	119.76	119.41	119.27
9000	144.13	139.80	138.04	135.67	135.01	134.85	134.72	134.34	134.18
10000	160.15	155.33	153.37	150.75	150.01	149.84	149.69	149.26	149.09
15000	240.22	233.00	230.06	226.12	225.01	224.75	224.54	223.89	223.63
20000	320.29	310.66	306.74	301.49	300.01	299.67	299.38	298.52	298.17
25000	400.36	388.33	383.43	376.86	375.01	374.58	374.23	373.15	372.71
30000	480.44	465.99	460.11	452.24	450.01	449.50	449.07	447.78	447.25
35000	560.51	543.66	536.80	527.61	525.01	524.41	523.91	522.41	521.79
40000	640.58	621.32	613.48	602.98	600.01	599.33	598.76	597.04	596.33
45000	720.65	698.99	690.17	678.35	675.01	674.25	673.60	671.67	670.87
46000	736.67	714.52	705.51	693.43	690.01	689.23	688.57	686.59	685.78
47000	752.68	730.05	720.84	708.50	705.01	704.21	703.54	701.52	700.69
48000	768.69	745.59	736.18	723.58	720.01	719.19	718.51	716.44	715.60
49000	784.71	761.12	751.52	738.65	735.01	734.18	733.48	731.37	730.51
50000	800.72	776.65	766.85	753.72	750.01	749.16	748.45	746.30	745.41
51000	816.74	792.19	782.19	768.80	765.01	764.14	763.42	761.22	760.32
52000	832.75	807.72	797.53	783.87	780.01	779.13	778.39	776.15	775.23
53000	848.77	823.25	812.87	798.95	795.01	794.11	793.35	791.07	790.14
54000	864.78	838.78	828.20	814.02	810.01	809.09	808.32	806.00	805.05
55000	880.79	854.32	843.54	829.10	825.01	824.08	823.29	820.93	819.95
56000	896.81	869.85	858.88	844.17	840.02	839.06	838.26	835.85	834.86
57000	912.82	885.38	874.21	859.25	855.02	854.04	853.23	850.78	849.77
58000	928.84	900.92	889.55	874.32	870.02	869.03	868.20	865.70	864.68
59000	944.85	916.45	904.89	889.39	885.02	884.01	883.17	880.63	879.59
60000	960.87	931.98	920.22	904.47	900.02	898.99	898.14	895.55	894.50
61000	976.88	947.51	935.56	919.54	915.02	913.98	913.11	910.48	909.40
62000	992.90	963.05	950.90	934.62	930.02	928.96	928.07	925.41	924.31
63000	1008.91	978.58	966.24	949.69	945.02	943.94	943.04	940.33	939.22
64000	1024.92	994.11	981.57	964.77	960.02	958.92	958.01	955.26	954.13
65000	1040.94	1009.65	996.91	979.84	975.02	973.91	972.98	970.18	969.04
67500	1080.97	1048.48	1035.25	1017.53	1012.52	1011.37	1010.40	1007.50	1006.31
70000	1121.01	1087.31	1073.59	1055.21	1050.02	1048.82	1047.82	1044.81	1043.58
75000	1201.08	1164.98	1150.28	1130.58	1125.02	1123.74	1122.67	1119.44	1118.12
80000	1281.15	1242.64	1226.96	1205.96	1200.00	1198.65	1197.51	1194.07	1192.66
85000	1361.23	1320.31	1303.65	1281.33	1275.02	1273.57	1272.36	1268.70	1267.20
90000	1441.30	1397.97	1380.33	1356.70	1350.02	1348.49	1347.20	1343.33	1341.74
95000	1521.37	1475.63	1457.02	1432.07	1425.02	1423.40	1422.05	1417.96	1416.28
100000	1601.44	1553.30	1533.70	1507.44	1500.02	1498.32	1496.89	1492.59	1490.82
105000	1681.51	1630.96	1610.39	1582.82	1575.02	1573.23	1571.73	1567.22	1565.36
110000	1761.58	1708.63	1687.07	1658.19	1650.02	1648.15	1646.58	1641.85	1639.90
115000	1841.66	1786.29	1763.76	1733.56	1725.03	1723.06	1721.42	1716.47	1714.44
120000	1921.73	1863.96	1840.44	1808.93	1800.03	1797.98	1796.27	1791.10	1788.99
125000	2001.80	1941.62	1917.13	1884.30	1875.03	1872.89	1871.11	1865.73	1863.53
130000	2081.87	2019.29	1993.81	1959.68	1950.03	1947.81	1945.96	1940.36	1938.07
135000	2161.94	2096.95	2070.50	2035.05	2025.03	2022.73	2020.80	2014.99	2012.61
140000	2242.01	2174.62	2147.18	2110.42	2100.03	2097.64	2095.64	2089.62	2087.15
145000	2322.09	2252.28	2223.87	2185.79	2175.03	2172.56	2170.49	2164.25	2161.69
150000	2402.16	2329.95	2300.55	2261.16	2250.03	2247.47	2245.33	2238.88	2236.23

18% MONTHLY PAYMENT
NECESSARY TO AMORTIZE A LOAN

AMOUNT	1 YEAR	2 YEARS	3 YEARS	4 YEARS	5 YEARS	7 YEARS	8 YEARS	10 YEARS	12 YEARS
$ 50	4.59	2.50	1.81	1.47	1.27	1.06	.99	.91	.85
100	9.17	5.00	3.62	2.94	2.54	2.11	1.98	1.81	1.70
200	18.34	9.99	7.24	5.88	5.08	4.21	3.95	3.61	3.40
300	27.51	14.98	10.85	8.82	7.62	6.31	5.92	5.41	5.10
400	36.68	19.97	14.47	11.75	10.16	8.41	7.89	7.21	6.80
500	45.84	24.97	18.08	14.69	12.70	10.51	9.87	9.01	8.50
600	55.01	29.96	21.70	17.63	15.24	12.62	11.84	10.82	10.20
700	64.18	34.95	25.31	20.57	17.78	14.72	13.81	12.62	11.90
800	73.35	39.94	28.93	23.50	20.32	16.82	15.78	14.42	13.60
900	82.52	44.94	32.54	26.44	22.86	18.92	17.76	16.22	15.30
1000	91.68	49.93	36.16	29.38	25.40	21.02	19.73	18.02	17.00
2000	183.36	99.85	72.31	58.75	50.79	42.04	39.45	36.04	33.99
3000	275.04	149.78	108.46	88.13	76.19	63.06	59.17	54.06	50.98
4000	366.72	199.70	144.61	117.50	101.58	84.08	78.90	72.08	67.97
5000	458.40	249.63	180.77	146.88	126.97	105.09	98.62	90.10	84.96
6000	550.08	299.55	216.92	176.25	152.37	126.11	118.34	108.12	101.95
7000	641.76	349.47	253.07	205.63	177.76	147.13	138.07	126.13	118.94
8000	733.44	399.40	289.22	235.00	203.15	168.15	157.79	144.15	135.93
9000	825.12	449.32	325.38	264.38	228.55	189.17	177.51	162.17	152.93
10000	916.80	499.25	361.53	293.75	253.94	210.18	197.24	180.19	169.92
15000	1375.20	748.87	542.29	440.63	380.91	315.27	295.85	270.28	254.87
20000	1833.60	998.49	723.05	587.50	507.87	420.36	394.47	360.38	339.83
25000	2292.00	1248.11	903.81	734.38	634.84	525.45	493.09	450.47	424.78
30000	2750.40	1497.73	1084.58	881.25	761.81	630.54	591.70	540.56	509.74
35000	3208.80	1747.35	1265.34	1028.13	888.77	735.63	690.32	630.65	594.70
40000	3667.20	1996.97	1446.10	1175.00	1015.74	840.72	788.93	720.75	679.65
45000	4125.60	2246.59	1626.86	1321.88	1142.71	945.81	887.55	810.84	764.61
46000	4217.28	2296.51	1663.02	1351.25	1168.10	966.83	907.27	828.86	781.60
47000	4308.96	2346.44	1699.17	1380.63	1193.50	987.84	927.00	846.88	798.59
48000	4400.64	2396.36	1735.32	1410.00	1218.89	1008.86	946.72	864.89	815.58
49000	4492.32	2446.29	1771.47	1439.38	1244.28	1029.88	966.44	882.91	832.57
50000	4584.00	2496.21	1807.62	1468.75	1269.68	1050.90	986.17	900.93	849.56
51000	4675.68	2546.13	1843.78	1498.13	1295.07	1071.91	1005.89	918.95	866.56
52000	4767.36	2596.06	1879.93	1527.50	1320.46	1092.93	1025.61	936.97	883.55
53000	4859.04	2645.98	1916.08	1556.88	1345.86	1113.95	1045.34	954.99	900.54
54000	4950.72	2695.91	1952.23	1586.25	1371.25	1134.97	1065.06	973.01	917.53
55000	5042.40	2745.83	1988.39	1615.63	1396.64	1155.99	1084.78	991.02	934.52
56000	5134.08	2795.75	2024.54	1645.00	1422.04	1177.00	1104.50	1009.04	951.51
57000	5225.76	2845.68	2060.69	1674.38	1447.43	1198.02	1124.23	1027.06	968.50
58000	5317.44	2895.60	2096.84	1703.75	1472.82	1219.04	1143.95	1045.08	985.49
59000	5409.12	2945.53	2133.00	1733.13	1498.22	1240.06	1163.67	1063.10	1002.49
60000	5500.80	2995.45	2169.15	1762.50	1523.61	1261.08	1183.40	1081.12	1019.48
61000	5592.48	3045.38	2205.30	1791.88	1549.00	1282.09	1203.12	1099.13	1036.47
62000	5684.16	3095.30	2241.45	1821.25	1574.40	1303.11	1222.84	1117.15	1053.46
63000	5775.84	3145.22	2277.61	1850.63	1599.79	1324.13	1242.57	1135.17	1070.45
64000	5867.52	3195.15	2313.76	1880.00	1625.18	1345.15	1262.29	1153.19	1087.44
65000	5959.20	3245.07	2349.91	1909.38	1650.58	1366.16	1282.01	1171.21	1104.43
67500	6188.40	3369.88	2440.29	1982.82	1714.06	1418.71	1331.32	1216.26	1146.91
70000	6417.60	3494.69	2530.67	2056.25	1777.54	1471.25	1380.63	1261.30	1189.39
75000	6876.00	3744.31	2711.43	2203.13	1904.51	1576.34	1479.25	1351.39	1274.34
80000	7334.40	3993.93	2892.20	2350.00	2031.48	1681.43	1577.86	1441.49	1359.30
85000	7792.80	4243.55	3072.96	2496.88	2158.45	1786.52	1676.48	1531.58	1444.26
90000	8251.20	4493.17	3253.72	2643.75	2285.41	1891.61	1775.09	1621.67	1529.21
95000	8709.60	4742.79	3434.48	2790.63	2412.38	1996.70	1873.71	1711.76	1614.17
100000	9168.00	4992.42	3615.24	2937.50	2539.35	2101.79	1972.33	1801.86	1699.12
105000	9626.40	5242.04	3796.01	3084.38	2666.31	2206.88	2070.94	1891.95	1784.08
110000	10084.80	5491.66	3976.77	3231.25	2793.28	2311.97	2169.56	1982.04	1869.04
115000	10543.20	5741.28	4157.53	3378.13	2920.25	2417.06	2268.17	2072.13	1953.99
120000	11001.60	5990.90	4338.29	3525.00	3047.22	2522.15	2366.79	2162.23	2038.95
125000	11460.00	6240.52	4519.05	3671.88	3174.18	2627.23	2465.41	2252.32	2123.90
130000	11918.40	6490.14	4699.82	3818.75	3301.15	2732.32	2564.02	2342.41	2208.86
135000	12376.80	6739.76	4880.58	3965.63	3428.12	2837.41	2662.64	2432.51	2293.82
140000	12835.20	6989.38	5061.34	4112.50	3555.08	2942.50	2761.25	2522.60	2378.77
145000	13293.60	7239.00	5242.10	4259.38	3682.05	3047.59	2859.87	2612.69	2463.73
150000	13752.00	7488.62	5422.86	4406.25	3809.02	3152.68	2958.49	2702.78	2548.68

MONTHLY PAYMENT 18%

NECESSARY TO AMORTIZE A LOAN

AMOUNT	15 YEARS	18 YEARS	20 YEARS	25 YEARS	28 YEARS	29 YEARS	30 YEARS	35 YEARS	40 YEARS
$ 50	.81	.79	.78	.76	.76	.76	.76	.76	.76
100	1.62	1.57	1.55	1.52	1.52	1.51	1.51	1.51	1.51
200	3.23	3.13	3.09	3.04	3.03	3.02	3.02	3.01	3.01
300	4.84	4.69	4.63	4.56	4.54	4.53	4.53	4.51	4.51
400	6.45	6.26	6.18	6.07	6.05	6.04	6.03	6.02	6.01
500	8.06	7.82	7.72	7.59	7.56	7.55	7.54	7.52	7.51
600	9.67	9.38	9.26	9.11	9.07	9.06	9.05	9.02	9.01
700	11.28	10.94	10.81	10.63	10.58	10.56	10.55	10.53	10.51
800	12.89	12.51	12.35	12.14	12.09	12.07	12.06	12.03	12.01
900	14.50	14.07	13.89	13.66	13.60	13.58	13.57	13.53	13.52
1000	16.11	15.63	15.44	15.18	15.11	15.09	15.08	15.03	15.02
2000	32.21	31.26	30.87	30.35	30.21	30.17	30.15	30.06	30.03
3000	48.32	46.89	46.30	45.53	45.31	45.26	45.22	45.09	45.04
4000	64.42	62.51	61.74	60.70	60.41	60.34	60.29	60.12	60.05
5000	80.53	78.14	77.17	75.88	75.51	75.43	75.36	75.15	75.06
6000	96.63	93.77	92.60	91.05	90.61	90.51	90.43	90.18	90.08
7000	112.73	109.39	108.04	106.23	105.72	105.60	105.50	105.21	105.09
8000	128.84	125.02	123.47	121.40	120.82	120.68	120.57	120.24	120.10
9000	144.94	140.65	138.90	136.57	135.92	135.77	135.64	135.27	135.11
10000	161.05	156.27	154.34	151.75	151.02	150.85	150.71	150.29	150.12
15000	241.57	234.41	231.50	227.62	226.53	226.28	226.07	225.44	225.18
20000	322.09	312.54	308.67	303.49	302.03	301.70	301.42	300.58	300.24
25000	402.61	390.68	385.83	379.36	377.54	377.12	376.78	375.73	375.30
30000	483.13	468.81	463.00	455.23	453.05	452.55	452.13	450.87	450.36
35000	563.65	546.95	540.16	531.11	528.56	527.97	527.48	526.02	525.42
40000	644.17	625.08	617.33	606.98	604.06	603.40	602.84	601.16	600.48
45000	724.69	703.22	694.50	682.85	679.57	678.82	678.19	676.31	675.54
46000	740.80	718.84	709.93	698.02	694.67	693.91	693.26	691.34	690.55
47000	756.90	734.47	725.36	713.20	709.78	708.99	708.34	706.36	705.56
48000	773.01	750.10	740.79	728.37	724.88	724.08	723.41	721.39	720.57
49000	789.11	765.72	756.23	743.55	739.98	739.16	738.48	736.42	735.58
50000	805.22	781.35	771.66	758.72	755.08	754.24	753.55	751.45	750.60
51000	821.32	796.98	787.09	773.89	770.18	769.33	768.62	766.48	765.61
52000	837.42	812.60	802.53	789.07	785.28	784.41	783.69	781.51	780.62
53000	853.53	828.23	817.96	804.24	800.38	799.50	798.76	796.54	795.63
54000	869.63	843.86	833.39	819.42	815.49	814.58	813.83	811.57	810.64
55000	885.74	859.49	848.83	834.59	830.59	829.67	828.90	826.60	825.66
56000	901.84	875.11	864.26	849.77	845.69	844.75	843.97	841.62	840.67
57000	917.94	890.74	879.69	864.94	860.79	859.84	859.04	856.65	855.68
58000	934.05	906.37	895.13	880.11	875.89	874.92	874.11	871.68	870.69
59000	950.15	921.99	910.56	895.29	890.99	890.01	889.19	886.71	885.70
60000	966.26	937.62	925.99	910.46	906.09	905.09	904.26	901.74	900.71
61000	982.36	953.25	941.43	925.64	921.20	920.18	919.33	916.77	915.73
62000	998.47	968.87	956.86	940.81	936.30	935.26	934.40	931.80	930.74
63000	1014.57	984.50	972.29	955.99	951.40	950.35	949.47	946.83	945.75
64000	1030.67	1000.13	987.72	971.16	966.50	965.43	964.54	961.86	960.76
65000	1046.78	1015.75	1003.16	986.33	981.60	980.52	979.61	976.88	975.77
67500	1087.04	1054.82	1041.74	1024.27	1019.36	1018.23	1017.29	1014.46	1013.30
70000	1127.30	1093.89	1080.32	1062.21	1057.11	1055.94	1054.96	1052.03	1050.83
75000	1207.82	1172.02	1157.49	1138.08	1132.62	1131.36	1130.32	1127.17	1125.89
80000	1288.34	1250.16	1234.65	1213.95	1208.12	1206.79	1205.67	1202.32	1200.95
85000	1368.86	1328.29	1311.82	1289.82	1283.63	1282.21	1281.03	1277.46	1276.01
90000	1449.38	1406.43	1388.99	1365.69	1359.14	1357.64	1356.38	1352.61	1351.07
95000	1529.90	1484.56	1466.15	1441.56	1434.65	1433.06	1431.74	1427.75	1426.13
100000	1610.43	1562.70	1543.32	1517.43	1510.15	1508.48	1507.09	1502.90	1501.19
105000	1690.95	1640.83	1620.48	1593.31	1585.66	1583.91	1582.44	1578.04	1576.25
110000	1771.47	1718.97	1697.65	1669.18	1661.17	1659.33	1657.80	1653.19	1651.31
115000	1851.99	1797.10	1774.81	1745.05	1736.68	1734.76	1733.15	1728.33	1726.36
120000	1932.51	1875.23	1851.98	1820.92	1812.18	1810.18	1808.51	1803.48	1801.42
125000	2013.03	1953.37	1929.14	1896.79	1887.69	1885.60	1883.86	1878.62	1876.48
130000	2093.55	2031.50	2006.31	1972.66	1963.20	1961.03	1959.22	1953.76	1951.54
135000	2174.07	2109.64	2083.48	2048.54	2038.71	2036.45	2034.57	2028.91	2026.60
140000	2254.59	2187.77	2160.64	2124.41	2114.21	2111.88	2109.92	2104.05	2101.66
145000	2335.12	2265.91	2237.81	2200.28	2189.72	2187.30	2185.28	2179.20	2176.72
150000	2415.64	2344.04	2314.97	2276.15	2265.23	2262.72	2260.63	2254.34	2251.78

POINTS DISCOUNT
TABLES

POINTS DISCOUNT TABLE

SHOWS APR FOR DISCLOSURE WHEN POINTS ARE CHARGED

INTEREST RATE	POINTS	TERMS								
		5 YEARS	7 YEARS	10 YEARS	15 YEARS	20 YEARS	25 YEARS	30 YEARS	35 YEARS	40 YEARS
7%	1	7.42	7.31	7.23	7.16	7.13	7.11	7.10	7.09	7.09
	1½	7.64	7.47	7.34	7.24	7.20	7.17	7.15	7.14	7.13
	2	7.85	7.63	7.46	7.33	7.26	7.23	7.20	7.19	7.17
	2½	8.07	7.79	7.57	7.41	7.33	7.28	7.25	7.23	7.22
	3	8.29	7.95	7.69	7.49	7.40	7.34	7.30	7.28	7.26
	4	8.73	8.27	7.93	7.66	7.53	7.46	7.41	7.38	7.35
	5	9.17	8.60	8.17	7.83	7.67	7.58	7.52	7.48	7.45
	6	9.63	8.93	8.41	8.01	7.81	7.70	7.62	7.58	7.54
	7	10.09	9.27	8.66	8.19	7.96	7.82	7.74	7.68	7.64
	8	10.56	9.62	8.91	8.37	8.10	7.95	7.85	7.78	7.73
7⅛%	1	7.55	7.44	7.35	7.29	7.26	7.24	7.23	7.22	7.21
	1½	7.76	7.59	7.47	7.37	7.32	7.29	7.28	7.26	7.26
	2	7.98	7.75	7.58	7.45	7.39	7.35	7.33	7.31	7.30
	2½	8.19	7.91	7.70	7.54	7.46	7.41	7.38	7.36	7.35
	3	8.41	8.07	7.82	7.62	7.52	7.47	7.43	7.41	7.39
	4	8.85	8.40	8.06	7.79	7.66	7.59	7.54	7.51	7.48
	5	9.30	8.73	8.30	7.96	7.80	7.71	7.65	7.60	7.58
	6	9.76	9.06	8.54	8.14	7.94	7.83	7.75	7.71	7.67
	7	10.22	9.40	8.79	8.32	8.09	7.95	7.87	7.81	7.77
	8	10.69	9.75	9.04	8.50	8.23	8.08	7.98	7.91	7.87
7¼%	1	7.67	7.56	7.48	7.41	7.38	7.36	7.35	7.34	7.34
	1½	7.89	7.72	7.59	7.50	7.45	7.42	7.40	7.39	7.38
	2	8.10	7.88	7.71	7.58	7.51	7.48	7.45	7.44	7.43
	2½	8.32	8.04	7.83	7.66	7.58	7.54	7.51	7.49	7.47
	3	8.54	8.20	7.94	7.75	7.65	7.59	7.56	7.54	7.52
	4	8.98	8.53	8.18	7.92	7.79	7.71	7.67	7.63	7.61
	5	9.43	8.86	8.42	8.09	7.93	7.83	7.77	7.73	7.71
	6	9.89	9.19	8.67	8.27	8.07	7.96	7.88	7.84	7.80
	7	10.35	9.53	8.92	8.45	8.21	8.08	8.00	7.94	7.90
	8	10.82	9.88	9.17	8.63	8.36	8.21	8.11	8.05	8.00
7⅜%	1	7.80	7.69	7.60	7.54	7.51	7.49	7.48	7.47	7.46
	1½	8.01	7.85	7.72	7.62	7.57	7.55	7.53	7.52	7.51
	2	8.23	8.00	7.84	7.70	7.64	7.60	7.58	7.57	7.55
	2½	8.45	8.16	7.95	7.79	7.71	7.66	7.63	7.61	7.60
	3	8.67	8.33	8.07	7.87	7.78	7.72	7.69	7.66	7.65
	4	9.11	8.65	8.31	8.05	7.92	7.84	7.79	7.76	7.74
	5	9.56	8.98	8.55	8.22	8.06	7.96	7.90	7.86	7.84
	6	10.01	9.32	8.80	8.40	8.20	8.09	8.01	7.97	7.93
	7	10.48	9.66	9.05	8.58	8.34	8.21	8.13	8.07	8.03
	8	10.95	10.01	9.30	8.76	8.49	8.34	8.24	8.18	8.13
7½%	1	7.92	7.81	7.73	7.66	7.63	7.61	7.60	7.60	7.59
	1½	8.14	7.97	7.84	7.75	7.70	7.67	7.66	7.64	7.64
	2	8.36	8.13	7.96	7.83	7.77	7.73	7.71	7.69	7.68
	2½	8.57	8.29	8.08	7.92	7.84	7.79	7.76	7.74	7.73
	3	8.79	8.45	8.20	8.00	7.90	7.85	7.81	7.79	7.77
	4	9.24	8.78	8.44	8.17	8.04	7.97	7.92	7.89	7.87
	5	9.69	9.11	8.68	8.35	8.19	8.09	8.03	7.99	7.97
	6	10.14	9.45	8.93	8.52	8.33	8.22	8.14	8.10	8.06
	7	10.61	9.79	9.18	8.70	8.47	8.34	8.26	8.20	8.16
	8	11.08	10.14	9.43	8.89	8.62	8.47	8.37	8.31	8.27
7⅝%	1	8.05	7.94	7.85	7.79	7.76	7.74	7.73	7.72	7.72
	1½	8.27	8.10	7.97	7.87	7.83	7.80	7.78	7.77	7.76
	2	8.48	8.26	8.09	7.96	7.89	7.86	7.83	7.82	7.81
	2½	8.70	8.42	8.21	8.04	7.96	7.92	7.89	7.87	7.85
	3	8.92	8.58	8.32	8.13	8.03	7.98	7.94	7.92	7.90
	4	9.36	8.91	8.56	8.30	8.17	8.10	8.05	8.02	8.00
	5	9.81	9.24	8.81	8.48	8.31	8.22	8.16	8.12	8.09
	6	10.27	9.58	9.05	8.65	8.46	8.35	8.27	8.23	8.19
	7	10.73	9.92	9.31	8.83	8.60	8.47	8.39	8.33	8.30
	8	11.21	10.27	9.56	9.02	8.75	8.60	8.51	8.44	8.40

POINTS DISCOUNT TABLE

SHOWS APR FOR DISCLOSURE WHEN POINTS ARE CHARGED

INTEREST RATE	POINTS	TERMS 5 YEARS	7 YEARS	10 YEARS	15 YEARS	20 YEARS	25 YEARS	30 YEARS	35 YEARS	40 YEARS
7¾%	1	8.18	8.06	7.98	7.92	7.88	7.87	7.85	7.85	7.84
	1½	8.39	8.22	8.10	8.00	7.95	7.92	7.91	7.90	7.89
	2	8.61	8.38	8.21	8.08	8.02	7.98	7.96	7.95	7.93
	2½	8.83	8.54	8.33	8.17	8.09	8.04	8.01	8.00	7.98
	3	9.05	8.71	8.45	8.25	8.16	8.10	8.07	8.05	8.03
	4	9.49	9.03	8.69	8.43	8.30	8.23	8.18	8.15	8.13
	5	9.94	9.37	8.94	8.60	8.44	8.35	8.29	8.25	8.22
	6	10.40	9.70	9.18	8.78	8.59	8.47	8.40	8.36	8.32
	7	10.86	10.05	9.44	8.96	8.73	8.60	8.52	8.46	8.43
	8	11.33	10.40	9.69	9.15	8.88	8.73	8.64	8.57	8.53
7⅞%	1	8.30	8.19	8.11	8.04	8.01	7.99	7.98	7.97	7.97
	1½	8.52	8.35	8.22	8.13	8.08	8.05	8.03	8.02	8.01
	2	8.73	8.51	8.34	8.21	8.15	8.11	8.09	8.07	8.06
	2½	8.95	8.67	8.46	8.30	8.22	8.17	8.14	8.12	8.11
	3	9.17	8.83	8.58	8.38	8.29	8.23	8.20	8.17	8.16
	4	9.62	9.16	8.82	8.56	8.43	8.35	8.31	8.28	8.26
	5	10.07	9.49	9.06	8.73	8.57	8.48	8.42	8.38	8.35
	6	10.53	9.83	9.31	8.91	8.72	8.60	8.53	8.49	8.46
	7	10.99	10.18	9.56	9.09	8.86	8.73	8.65	8.60	8.56
	8	11.46	10.53	9.82	9.28	9.02	8.86	8.77	8.71	8.66
8%	1	8.43	8.32	8.23	8.17	8.14	8.12	8.11	8.10	8.09
	1½	8.64	8.47	8.35	8.25	8.20	8.18	8.16	8.15	8.14
	2	8.86	8.63	8.47	8.34	8.27	8.24	8.21	8.20	8.19
	2½	9.08	8.80	8.58	8.42	8.34	8.30	8.27	8.25	8.24
	3	9.30	8.96	8.70	8.51	8.41	8.36	8.32	8.30	8.29
	4	9.74	9.29	8.95	8.68	8.55	8.48	8.44	8.40	8.38
	5	10.20	9.62	9.19	8.86	8.70	8.61	8.55	8.51	8.48
	6	10.65	9.96	9.44	9.04	8.85	8.73	8.66	8.62	8.59
	7	11.12	10.31	9.69	9.22	8.99	8.86	8.78	8.73	8.69
	8	11.59	10.65	9.95	9.41	9.15	9.00	8.90	8.84	8.80
8⅛%	1	8.55	8.44	8.36	8.29	8.26	8.24	8.23	8.22	8.22
	1½	8.77	8.60	8.47	8.38	8.33	8.30	8.29	8.27	8.27
	2	8.99	8.76	8.59	8.46	8.40	8.36	8.34	8.33	8.32
	2½	9.20	8.92	8.71	8.55	8.47	8.42	8.40	8.38	8.36
	3	9.43	9.09	8.83	8.63	8.54	8.49	8.45	8.43	8.41
	4	9.87	9.42	9.07	8.81	8.68	8.61	8.56	8.53	8.51
	5	10.32	9.75	9.32	8.99	8.83	8.74	8.68	8.64	8.61
	6	10.78	10.09	9.57	9.17	8.98	8.86	8.79	8.75	8.72
	7	11.25	10.43	9.82	9.35	9.13	8.99	8.91	8.86	8.82
	8	11.72	10.78	10.08	9.54	9.28	9.13	9.03	8.97	8.93
8¼%	1	8.68	8.57	8.48	8.42	8.39	8.37	8.36	8.35	8.35
	1½	8.89	8.73	8.60	8.50	8.46	8.43	8.41	8.40	8.39
	2	9.11	8.89	8.72	8.59	8.53	8.49	8.47	8.45	8.44
	2½	9.33	9.05	8.84	8.67	8.60	8.55	8.52	8.50	8.49
	3	9.55	9.21	8.96	8.76	8.67	8.61	8.58	8.56	8.54
	4	10.00	9.54	9.20	8.94	8.81	8.74	8.69	8.66	8.64
	5	10.45	9.88	9.45	9.12	8.96	8.86	8.81	8.77	8.74
	6	10.91	10.22	9.70	9.30	9.10	8.99	8.92	8.88	8.85
	7	11.38	10.56	9.95	9.48	9.26	9.13	9.04	8.99	8.95
	8	11.85	10.91	10.21	9.67	9.41	9.26	9.17	9.10	9.06
8⅜%	1	8.80	8.69	8.61	8.54	8.51	8.49	8.48	8.48	8.47
	1½	9.02	8.85	8.73	8.63	8.58	8.56	8.54	8.53	8.52
	2	9.24	9.01	8.84	8.71	8.65	8.62	8.59	8.58	8.57
	2½	9.46	9.18	8.96	8.80	8.72	8.68	8.65	8.63	8.62
	3	9.68	9.34	9.08	8.89	8.79	8.74	8.71	8.68	8.67
	4	10.13	9.67	9.33	9.07	8.94	8.87	8.82	8.79	8.77
	5	10.58	10.01	9.58	9.24	9.08	8.99	8.94	8.90	8.87
	6	11.04	10.35	9.83	9.43	9.23	9.12	9.06	9.01	8.98
	7	11.51	10.69	10.08	9.61	9.39	9.26	9.18	9.12	9.09
	8	11.98	11.04	10.34	9.80	9.54	9.39	9.30	9.24	9.20

POINTS DISCOUNT TABLE

SHOWS APR FOR DISCLOSURE WHEN POINTS ARE CHARGED

INTEREST RATE	POINTS	TERMS								
		5 YEARS	7 YEARS	10 YEARS	15 YEARS	20 YEARS	25 YEARS	30 YEARS	35 YEARS	40 YEARS
8½%	1	8.93	8.82	8.73	8.67	8.64	8.62	8.61	8.60	8.60
	1½	9.15	8.98	8.85	8.75	8.71	8.68	8.66	8.65	8.65
	2	9.36	9.14	8.97	8.84	8.78	8.74	8.72	8.71	8.70
	2½	9.58	9.30	9.09	8.93	8.85	8.80	8.78	8.76	8.75
	3	9.80	9.47	9.21	9.02	8.92	8.87	8.83	8.81	8.80
	4	10.25	9.80	9.46	9.19	9.07	8.99	8.95	8.92	8.90
	5	10.71	10.13	9.70	9.37	9.21	9.12	9.07	9.03	9.00
	6	11.17	10.47	9.95	9.56	9.36	9.25	9.19	9.14	9.11
	7	11.64	10.82	10.21	9.74	9.52	9.39	9.31	9.25	9.22
	8	12.11	11.17	10.47	9.93	9.67	9.52	9.43	9.37	9.33
8⅝%	1	9.05	8.94	8.86	8.79	8.76	8.75	8.74	8.73	8.72
	1½	9.27	9.10	8.98	8.88	8.83	8.81	8.79	8.78	8.77
	2	9.49	9.27	9.10	8.97	8.90	8.87	8.85	8.83	8.82
	2½	9.71	9.43	9.22	9.05	8.98	8.93	8.90	8.89	8.87
	3	9.93	9.59	9.34	9.14	9.05	8.99	8.96	8.94	8.92
	4	10.38	9.92	9.58	9.32	9.19	9.12	9.08	9.05	9.03
	5	10.83	10.26	9.83	9.50	9.34	9.25	9.20	9.16	9.13
	6	11.30	10.60	10.08	9.68	9.49	9.38	9.32	9.27	9.24
	7	11.76	10.95	10.34	9.87	9.65	9.52	9.44	9.39	9.35
	8	12.24	11.30	10.60	10.06	9.80	9.65	9.56	9.50	9.46
8¾%	1	9.18	9.07	8.98	8.92	8.89	8.87	8.86	8.85	8.85
	1½	9.40	9.23	9.10	9.01	8.96	8.93	8.92	8.91	8.90
	2	9.62	9.39	9.22	9.09	9.03	9.00	8.97	8.96	8.95
	2½	9.84	9.55	9.34	9.18	9.10	9.06	9.03	9.01	9.00
	3	10.06	9.72	9.46	9.27	9.18	9.12	9.09	9.07	9.05
	4	10.51	10.05	9.71	9.45	9.32	9.25	9.21	9.18	9.16
	5	10.96	10.39	9.96	9.63	9.47	9.38	9.32	9.29	9.26
	6	11.42	10.73	10.21	9.81	9.62	9.51	9.45	9.40	9.37
	7	11.89	11.08	10.47	10.00	9.78	9.65	9.57	9.52	9.48
	8	12.37	11.43	10.73	10.19	9.93	9.79	9.69	9.64	9.60
8⅞%	1	9.31	9.19	9.11	9.05	9.02	9.00	8.99	8.98	8.98
	1½	9.52	9.35	9.23	9.13	9.09	9.06	9.04	9.03	9.03
	2	9.74	9.52	9.35	9.22	9.16	9.12	9.10	9.09	9.08
	2½	9.96	9.68	9.47	9.31	9.23	9.19	9.16	9.14	9.13
	3	10.18	9.85	9.59	9.40	9.30	9.25	9.22	9.20	9.18
	4	10.63	10.18	9.84	9.58	9.45	9.38	9.33	9.31	9.29
	5	11.09	10.52	10.09	9.76	9.60	9.51	9.45	9.42	9.39
	6	11.55	10.86	10.34	9.94	9.75	9.64	9.58	9.53	9.50
	7	12.02	11.21	10.60	10.13	9.91	9.78	9.70	9.65	9.62
	8	12.50	11.56	10.86	10.32	10.06	9.92	9.83	9.77	9.73
9%	1	9.43	9.32	9.24	9.17	9.14	9.12	9.11	9.11	9.10
	1½	9.65	9.48	9.35	9.26	9.21	9.19	9.17	9.16	9.15
	2	9.87	9.64	9.48	9.35	9.28	9.25	9.23	9.21	9.20
	2½	10.09	9.81	9.60	9.43	9.36	9.31	9.29	9.27	9.26
	3	10.31	9.97	9.72	9.52	9.43	9.38	9.34	9.32	9.31
	4	10.76	10.31	9.96	9.70	9.58	9.51	9.46	9.43	9.42
	5	11.22	10.64	10.21	9.89	9.73	9.64	9.58	9.55	9.52
	6	11.68	10.99	10.47	10.07	9.88	9.77	9.71	9.66	9.64
	7	12.15	11.34	10.73	10.26	10.04	9.91	9.83	9.78	9.75
	8	12.63	11.69	10.99	10.45	10.19	10.05	9.96	9.90	9.86
9⅛%	1	9.56	9.44	9.36	9.30	9.27	9.25	9.24	9.23	9.23
	1½	9.77	9.61	9.48	9.38	9.34	9.31	9.30	9.29	9.28
	2	9.99	9.77	9.60	9.47	9.41	9.38	9.35	9.34	9.33
	2½	10.21	9.93	9.72	9.56	9.48	9.44	9.41	9.40	9.38
	3	10.44	10.10	9.84	9.65	9.56	9.50	9.47	9.45	9.44
	4	10.89	10.43	10.09	9.83	9.71	9.63	9.59	9.56	9.54
	5	11.34	10.77	10.34	10.01	9.86	9.77	9.71	9.68	9.65
	6	11.81	11.12	10.60	10.20	10.01	9.90	9.84	9.79	9.77
	7	12.28	11.47	10.86	10.39	10.17	10.04	9.96	9.91	9.88
	8	12.76	11.82	11.12	10.58	10.33	10.18	10.09	10.03	10.00

POINTS DISCOUNT TABLE

SHOWS APR FOR DISCLOSURE WHEN POINTS ARE CHARGED

INTEREST RATE	POINTS	TERMS								
		5 YEARS	7 YEARS	10 YEARS	15 YEARS	20 YEARS	25 YEARS	30 YEARS	35 YEARS	40 YEARS
9¼%	1	9.68	9.57	9.49	9.42	9.39	9.38	9.36	9.36	9.35
	1½	9.90	9.73	9.61	9.51	9.46	9.44	9.42	9.41	9.41
	2	10.12	9.90	9.73	9.60	9.54	9.50	9.48	9.47	9.46
	2½	10.34	10.06	9.85	9.69	9.61	9.57	9.54	9.52	9.51
	3	10.56	10.23	9.97	9.78	9.68	9.63	9.60	9.58	9.56
	4	11.01	10.56	10.22	9.96	9.83	9.76	9.72	9.69	9.67
	5	11.47	10.90	10.47	10.14	9.99	9.90	9.84	9.81	9.78
	6	11.94	11.24	10.73	10.33	10.14	10.03	9.97	9.93	9.90
	7	12.41	11.59	10.99	10.52	10.30	10.17	10.09	10.05	10.01
	8	12.89	11.95	11.25	10.71	10.46	10.31	10.22	10.17	10.13
9⅜%	1	9.81	9.70	9.61	9.55	9.52	9.50	9.49	9.48	9.48
	1½	10.03	9.86	9.73	9.64	9.59	9.56	9.55	9.54	9.53
	2	10.25	10.02	9.85	9.73	9.66	9.63	9.61	9.59	9.59
	2½	10.47	10.19	9.98	9.81	9.74	9.69	9.67	9.65	9.64
	3	10.69	10.35	10.10	9.90	9.81	9.76	9.73	9.71	9.69
	4	11.14	10.69	10.35	10.09	9.96	9.89	9.85	9.82	9.80
	5	11.60	11.03	10.60	10.27	10.11	10.03	9.97	9.94	9.91
	6	12.07	11.37	10.85	10.46	10.27	10.16	10.10	10.06	10.03
	7	12.54	11.72	11.12	10.65	10.43	10.30	10.23	10.18	10.15
	8	13.02	12.08	11.38	10.84	10.59	10.44	10.36	10.30	10.26
9½%	1	9.93	9.82	9.74	9.67	9.64	9.63	9.62	9.61	9.61
	1½	10.15	9.98	9.86	9.76	9.72	9.69	9.68	9.66	9.66
	2	10.37	10.15	9.98	9.85	9.79	9.76	9.73	9.72	9.71
	2½	10.59	10.31	10.10	9.94	9.86	9.82	9.79	9.78	9.77
	3	10.82	10.48	10.22	10.03	9.94	9.89	9.85	9.83	9.82
	4	11.27	10.81	10.47	10.21	10.09	10.02	9.98	9.95	9.93
	5	11.73	11.16	10.73	10.40	10.24	10.16	10.10	10.07	10.05
	6	12.19	11.50	10.98	10.59	10.40	10.29	10.23	10.19	10.16
	7	12.67	11.85	11.24	10.78	10.56	10.43	10.36	10.31	10.28
	8	13.15	12.21	11.51	10.97	10.72	10.58	10.49	10.43	10.40
9⅝%	1	10.06	9.95	9.86	9.80	9.77	9.75	9.74	9.74	9.73
	1½	10.28	10.11	9.98	9.89	9.84	9.82	9.80	9.79	9.78
	2	10.50	10.27	10.11	9.98	9.92	9.88	9.86	9.85	9.84
	2½	10.72	10.44	10.23	10.07	9.99	9.95	9.92	9.90	9.89
	3	10.94	10.61	10.35	10.16	10.07	10.01	9.98	9.96	9.95
	4	11.40	10.94	10.60	10.34	10.22	10.15	10.11	10.08	10.06
	5	11.86	11.28	10.85	10.53	10.37	10.28	10.23	10.20	10.18
	6	12.32	11.63	11.11	10.72	10.53	10.42	10.36	10.32	10.29
	7	12.80	11.98	11.37	10.91	10.69	10.56	10.49	10.44	10.41
	8	13.28	12.34	11.64	11.11	10.85	10.71	10.62	10.57	10.53
9¾%	1	10.18	10.07	9.99	9.93	9.90	9.88	9.87	9.86	9.86
	1½	10.40	10.24	10.11	10.01	9.97	9.94	9.93	9.92	9.91
	2	10.62	10.40	10.23	10.10	10.04	10.01	9.99	9.97	9.97
	2½	10.85	10.57	10.35	10.19	10.12	10.07	10.05	10.03	10.02
	3	11.07	10.73	10.48	10.29	10.19	10.14	10.11	10.09	10.08
	4	11.52	11.07	10.73	10.47	10.35	10.28	10.23	10.21	10.19
	5	11.98	11.41	10.98	10.66	10.50	10.41	10.36	10.33	10.31
	6	12.45	11.76	11.24	10.85	10.66	10.55	10.49	10.45	10.42
	7	12.92	12.11	11.50	11.04	10.82	10.70	10.62	10.57	10.54
	8	13.41	12.47	11.77	11.24	10.98	10.84	10.76	10.70	10.67
9⅞%	1	10.31	10.20	10.11	10.05	10.02	10.00	9.99	9.99	9.98
	1½	10.53	10.36	10.24	10.14	10.10	10.07	10.05	10.04	10.04
	2	10.75	10.53	10.36	10.23	10.17	10.14	10.11	10.10	10.09
	2½	10.97	10.69	10.48	10.32	10.24	10.20	10.18	10.16	10.15
	3	11.20	10.86	10.61	10.41	10.32	10.27	10.24	10.22	10.21
	4	11.65	11.20	10.86	10.60	10.47	10.40	10.36	10.34	10.32
	5	12.11	11.54	11.11	10.78	10.63	10.54	10.49	10.46	10.44
	6	12.58	11.89	11.37	10.98	10.79	10.68	10.62	10.58	10.55
	7	13.05	12.24	11.63	11.17	10.95	10.83	10.75	10.71	10.68
	8	13.53	12.60	11.90	11.37	11.11	10.97	10.89	10.83	10.80

POINTS DISCOUNT TABLE

SHOWS APR FOR DISCLOSURE WHEN POINTS ARE CHARGED

INTEREST RATE	POINTS	TERMS								
		5 YEARS	7 YEARS	10 YEARS	15 YEARS	20 YEARS	25 YEARS	30 YEARS	35 YEARS	40 YEARS
10%	1	10.43	10.32	10.24	10.18	10.15	10.13	10.12	10.11	10.11
	1½	10.65	10.49	10.36	10.27	10.22	10.20	10.18	10.17	10.16
	2	10.88	10.65	10.48	10.36	10.30	10.26	10.24	10.23	10.22
	2½	11.10	10.82	10.61	10.45	10.37	10.33	10.30	10.29	10.28
	3	11.32	10.99	10.73	10.54	10.45	10.40	10.37	10.35	10.33
	4	11.78	11.32	10.98	10.72	10.60	10.53	10.49	10.47	10.45
	5	12.24	11.67	11.24	10.91	10.76	10.67	10.62	10.59	10.57
	6	12.71	12.02	11.50	11.10	10.92	10.81	10.75	10.71	10.69
	7	13.18	12.37	11.76	11.30	11.08	10.96	10.88	10.84	10.81
	8	13.66	12.73	12.03	11.50	11.25	11.11	11.02	10.97	10.93
10⅛%	1	10.56	10.45	10.37	10.30	10.27	10.26	10.25	10.24	10.24
	1½	10.78	10.61	10.49	10.39	10.35	10.32	10.31	10.30	10.29
	2	11.00	10.78	10.61	10.48	10.42	10.39	10.37	10.36	10.35
	2½	11.23	10.94	10.73	10.57	10.50	10.46	10.43	10.41	10.40
	3	11.45	11.11	10.86	10.67	10.57	10.52	10.49	10.47	10.46
	4	11.90	11.45	11.11	10.85	10.73	10.66	10.62	10.59	10.58
	5	12.37	11.79	11.37	11.04	10.89	10.80	10.75	10.72	10.70
	6	12.84	12.14	11.63	11.23	11.05	10.94	10.88	10.84	10.82
	7	13.31	12.50	11.89	11.43	11.21	11.09	11.02	10.97	10.94
	8	13.79	12.86	12.16	11.63	11.38	11.24	11.15	11.10	11.07
10¼%	1	10.69	10.57	10.49	10.43	10.40	10.38	10.37	10.37	10.36
	1½	10.91	10.74	10.61	10.52	10.47	10.45	10.43	10.42	10.42
	2	11.13	10.90	10.74	10.61	10.55	10.52	10.50	10.48	10.47
	2½	11.35	11.07	10.86	10.70	10.63	10.58	10.56	10.54	10.53
	3	11.58	11.24	10.99	10.79	10.70	10.65	10.62	10.60	10.59
	4	12.03	11.58	11.24	10.98	10.86	10.79	10.75	10.72	10.71
	5	12.49	11.92	11.50	11.17	11.02	10.93	10.88	10.85	10.83
	6	12.96	12.27	11.76	11.36	11.18	11.07	11.01	10.97	10.95
	7	13.44	12.63	12.02	11.56	11.34	11.22	11.15	11.10	11.07
	8	13.92	12.99	12.29	11.76	11.51	11.37	11.29	11.23	11.20
10⅜%	1	10.81	10.70	10.62	10.55	10.52	10.51	10.50	10.49	10.49
	1½	11.03	10.86	10.74	10.64	10.60	10.57	10.56	10.55	10.54
	2	11.25	11.03	10.86	10.74	10.68	10.64	10.62	10.61	10.60
	2½	11.48	11.20	10.99	10.83	10.75	10.71	10.69	10.67	10.66
	3	11.70	11.37	11.11	10.92	10.83	10.78	10.75	10.73	10.72
	4	12.16	11.71	11.37	11.11	10.99	10.92	10.88	10.85	10.84
	5	12.62	12.05	11.62	11.30	11.15	11.06	11.01	10.98	10.96
	6	13.09	12.40	11.88	11.49	11.31	11.20	11.14	11.11	11.08
	7	13.57	12.76	12.15	11.69	11.47	11.35	11.28	11.24	11.21
	8	14.05	13.12	12.42	11.89	11.64	11.50	11.42	11.37	11.34
10½%	1	10.94	10.83	10.74	10.68	10.65	10.63	10.62	10.62	10.61
	1½	11.16	10.99	10.87	10.77	10.73	10.70	10.69	10.68	10.67
	2	11.38	11.16	10.99	10.86	10.80	10.77	10.75	10.74	10.73
	2½	11.60	11.32	11.11	10.95	10.88	10.84	10.81	10.80	10.79
	3	11.83	11.49	11.24	11.05	10.96	10.91	10.88	10.86	10.85
	4	12.29	11.83	11.49	11.24	11.11	11.05	11.01	10.98	10.97
	5	12.75	12.18	11.75	11.43	11.27	11.19	11.14	11.11	11.09
	6	13.22	12.53	12.01	11.62	11.44	11.34	11.27	11.24	11.21
	7	13.70	12.89	12.28	11.82	11.60	11.48	11.41	11.37	11.34
	8	14.18	13.25	12.55	12.02	11.77	11.63	11.55	11.50	11.47
10⅝%	1	11.06	10.95	10.87	10.81	10.78	10.76	10.75	10.74	10.74
	1½	11.28	11.12	10.99	10.90	10.85	10.83	10.81	10.80	10.80
	2	11.51	11.28	11.12	10.99	10.93	10.90	10.88	10.86	10.86
	2½	11.73	11.45	11.24	11.08	11.01	10.96	10.94	10.92	10.91
	3	11.96	11.62	11.37	11.17	11.08	11.03	11.00	10.99	10.97
	4	12.41	11.96	11.62	11.36	11.24	11.18	11.14	11.11	11.10
	5	12.88	12.31	11.88	11.56	11.40	11.32	11.27	11.24	11.22
	6	13.35	12.66	12.14	11.75	11.57	11.47	11.41	11.37	11.34
	7	13.83	13.01	12.41	11.95	11.73	11.61	11.54	11.50	11.47
	8	14.31	13.38	12.68	12.15	11.90	11.77	11.69	11.64	11.60

POINTS DISCOUNT TABLE

SHOWS APR FOR DISCLOSURE WHEN POINTS ARE CHARGED

INTEREST RATE	POINTS	5 YEARS	7 YEARS	10 YEARS	15 YEARS	20 YEARS	25 YEARS	30 YEARS	35 YEARS	40 YEARS
10¾%	1	11.19	11.08	10.99	10.93	10.90	10.89	10.88	10.87	10.87
	1½	11.41	11.24	11.12	11.02	10.98	10.95	10.94	10.93	10.92
	2	11.63	11.41	11.24	11.11	11.06	11.02	11.00	10.99	10.98
	2½	11.86	11.58	11.37	11.21	11.13	11.09	11.07	11.05	11.04
	3	12.08	11.75	11.49	11.30	11.21	11.16	11.13	11.11	11.10
	4	12.54	12.09	11.75	11.49	11.37	11.30	11.26	11.24	11.22
	5	13.01	12.43	12.01	11.68	11.53	11.45	11.40	11.37	11.35
	6	13.48	12.79	12.27	11.88	11.70	11.60	11.54	11.50	11.48
	7	13.96	13.14	12.54	12.08	11.86	11.75	11.68	11.63	11.61
	8	14.44	13.51	12.81	12.28	12.03	11.90	11.82	11.77	11.74
10⅞%	1	11.31	11.20	11.12	11.06	11.03	11.01	11.00	11.00	10.99
	1½	11.54	11.37	11.24	11.15	11.10	11.08	11.07	11.06	11.05
	2	11.76	11.53	11.37	11.24	11.18	11.15	11.13	11.12	11.11
	2½	11.98	11.70	11.49	11.33	11.26	11.22	11.19	11.18	11.17
	3	12.21	11.87	11.62	11.43	11.34	11.29	11.26	11.24	11.23
	4	12.67	12.21	11.88	11.62	11.50	11.43	11.39	11.37	11.35
	5	13.13	12.56	12.14	11.81	11.66	11.58	11.53	11.50	11.48
	6	13.61	12.91	12.40	12.01	11.83	11.73	11.67	11.63	11.61
	7	14.08	13.27	12.67	12.21	12.00	11.88	11.81	11.77	11.74
	8	14.57	13.64	12.94	12.41	12.17	12.03	11.95	11.90	11.87
11%	1	11.44	11.33	11.25	11.18	11.15	11.14	11.13	11.12	11.12
	1½	11.66	11.49	11.37	11.27	11.23	11.21	11.19	11.18	11.18
	2	11.88	11.66	11.49	11.37	11.31	11.28	11.26	11.24	11.24
	2½	12.11	11.83	11.62	11.46	11.39	11.35	11.32	11.31	11.30
	3	12.34	12.00	11.75	11.56	11.47	11.42	11.39	11.37	11.36
	4	12.80	12.34	12.00	11.75	11.63	11.56	11.52	11.50	11.48
	5	13.26	12.69	12.26	11.94	11.79	11.71	11.66	11.63	11.61
	6	13.73	13.04	12.53	12.14	11.96	11.86	11.80	11.76	11.74
	7	14.21	13.40	12.80	12.34	12.13	12.01	11.94	11.90	11.87
	8	14.70	13.77	13.07	12.54	12.30	12.16	12.08	12.04	12.01
11⅛%	1	11.56	11.45	11.37	11.31	11.28	11.26	11.25	11.25	11.24
	1½	11.79	11.62	11.50	11.40	11.36	11.33	11.32	11.31	11.30
	2	12.01	11.79	11.62	11.49	11.43	11.40	11.38	11.37	11.36
	2½	12.24	11.96	11.75	11.59	11.51	11.47	11.45	11.43	11.43
	3	12.46	12.13	11.87	11.68	11.59	11.54	11.52	11.50	11.49
	4	12.92	12.47	12.13	11.88	11.76	11.69	11.65	11.63	11.61
	5	13.39	12.82	12.39	12.07	11.92	11.84	11.79	11.76	11.74
	6	13.86	13.17	12.66	12.27	12.09	11.99	11.93	11.89	11.87
	7	14.34	13.53	12.93	12.47	12.26	12.14	12.07	12.03	12.00
	8	14.83	13.90	13.20	12.68	12.43	12.30	12.22	12.17	12.14
11¼%	1	11.69	11.58	11.50	11.43	11.40	11.39	11.38	11.37	11.37
	1½	11.91	11.75	11.62	11.53	11.48	11.46	11.44	11.44	11.43
	2	12.14	11.91	11.75	11.62	11.56	11.53	11.51	11.50	11.49
	2½	12.36	12.08	11.87	11.71	11.64	11.60	11.58	11.56	11.55
	3	12.59	12.25	12.00	11.81	11.72	11.67	11.64	11.63	11.62
	4	13.05	12.60	12.26	12.00	11.88	11.82	11.78	11.76	11.74
	5	13.52	12.95	12.52	12.20	12.05	11.97	11.92	11.89	11.87
	6	13.99	13.30	12.79	12.40	12.22	12.12	12.06	12.03	12.00
	7	14.47	13.66	13.06	12.60	12.39	12.27	12.20	12.16	12.14
	8	14.96	14.03	13.33	12.81	12.56	12.43	12.35	12.30	12.28
11⅜%	1	11.82	11.70	11.62	11.56	11.53	11.51	11.50	11.50	11.50
	1½	12.04	11.87	11.75	11.65	11.61	11.58	11.57	11.56	11.56
	2	12.26	12.04	11.87	11.75	11.69	11.66	11.64	11.63	11.62
	2½	12.49	12.21	12.00	11.84	11.77	11.73	11.70	11.69	11.68
	3	12.72	12.38	12.13	11.94	11.85	11.80	11.77	11.75	11.74
	4	13.18	12.72	12.39	12.13	12.01	11.95	11.91	11.89	11.87
	5	13.64	13.07	12.65	12.33	12.18	12.10	12.05	12.02	12.00
	6	14.12	13.43	12.92	12.53	12.35	12.25	12.19	12.16	12.14
	7	14.60	13.79	13.19	12.73	12.52	12.40	12.34	12.30	12.27
	8	15.09	14.16	13.46	12.94	12.69	12.56	12.48	12.44	12.41

POINTS DISCOUNT TABLE

SHOWS APR FOR DISCLOSURE WHEN POINTS ARE CHARGED

INTEREST RATE	POINTS	TERMS								
		5 YEARS	7 YEARS	10 YEARS	15 YEARS	20 YEARS	25 YEARS	30 YEARS	35 YEARS	40 YEARS
11½%	1	11.94	11.83	11.75	11.69	11.66	11.64	11.63	11.63	11.62
	1½	12.16	12.00	11.87	11.78	11.74	11.71	11.70	11.69	11.68
	2	12.39	12.17	12.00	11.87	11.81	11.78	11.76	11.75	11.75
	2½	12.62	12.33	12.13	11.97	11.89	11.86	11.83	11.82	11.81
	3	12.84	12.51	12.25	12.06	11.98	11.93	11.90	11.88	11.87
	4	13.30	12.85	12.51	12.26	12.14	12.08	12.04	12.02	12.00
	5	13.77	13.20	12.78	12.46	12.31	12.23	12.18	12.15	12.13
	6	14.25	13.56	13.04	12.66	12.48	12.38	12.32	12.29	12.27
	7	14.73	13.92	13.32	12.86	12.65	12.54	12.47	12.43	12.40
	8	15.22	14.29	13.59	13.07	12.83	12.69	12.62	12.57	12.54
11⅝%	1	12.07	11.96	11.87	11.81	11.78	11.77	11.76	11.75	11.75
	1½	12.29	12.12	12.00	11.90	11.86	11.84	11.82	11.82	11.81
	2	12.51	12.29	12.13	12.00	11.94	11.91	11.89	11.88	11.87
	2½	12.74	12.46	12.25	12.10	12.02	11.98	11.96	11.95	11.94
	3	12.97	12.63	12.38	12.19	12.10	12.06	12.03	12.01	12.00
	4	13.43	12.98	12.64	12.39	12.27	12.20	12.17	12.14	12.13
	5	13.90	13.33	12.90	12.58	12.44	12.36	12.31	12.28	12.26
	6	14.38	13.69	13.17	12.79	12.61	12.51	12.45	12.42	12.40
	7	14.86	14.05	13.45	12.99	12.78	12.67	12.60	12.56	12.54
	8	15.35	14.42	13.72	13.20	12.96	12.83	12.75	12.71	12.68
11¾%	1	12.19	12.08	12.00	11.94	11.91	11.89	11.88	11.88	11.87
	1½	12.42	12.25	12.12	12.03	11.99	11.96	11.95	11.94	11.94
	2	12.64	12.42	12.25	12.13	12.07	12.04	12.02	12.01	12.00
	2½	12.87	12.59	12.38	12.22	12.15	12.11	12.09	12.07	12.06
	3	13.10	12.76	12.51	12.32	12.23	12.18	12.16	12.14	12.13
	4	13.56	13.11	12.77	12.51	12.40	12.33	12.30	12.27	12.26
	5	14.03	13.46	13.03	12.71	12.57	12.49	12.44	12.41	12.39
	6	14.50	13.81	13.30	12.92	12.74	12.64	12.58	12.55	12.53
	7	14.99	14.18	13.57	13.12	12.91	12.80	12.73	12.69	12.67
	8	15.48	14.55	13.85	13.33	13.09	12.96	12.88	12.84	12.81
11⅞%	1	12.32	12.21	12.12	12.06	12.03	12.02	12.01	12.00	12.00
	1½	12.54	12.37	12.25	12.16	12.11	12.09	12.08	12.07	12.06
	2	12.77	12.54	12.38	12.25	12.19	12.16	12.15	12.13	12.13
	2½	12.99	12.71	12.51	12.35	12.28	12.24	12.21	12.20	12.19
	3	13.22	12.89	12.63	12.45	12.36	12.31	12.28	12.27	12.26
	4	13.69	13.23	12.90	12.64	12.52	12.46	12.43	12.40	12.39
	5	14.16	13.59	13.16	12.84	12.69	12.62	12.57	12.54	12.53
	6	14.63	13.94	13.43	13.05	12.87	12.77	12.72	12.68	12.66
	7	15.12	14.31	13.70	13.25	13.04	12.93	12.87	12.83	12.80
	8	15.61	14.68	13.98	13.46	13.22	13.09	13.02	12.97	12.95
12%	1	12.44	12.33	12.25	12.19	12.16	12.14	12.13	12.13	12.13
	1½	12.67	12.50	12.38	12.28	12.24	12.22	12.20	12.20	12.19
	2	12.89	12.67	12.50	12.38	12.32	12.29	12.27	12.26	12.25
	2½	13.12	12.84	12.63	12.48	12.40	12.36	12.34	12.33	12.32
	3	13.35	13.01	12.76	12.57	12.49	12.44	12.41	12.40	12.39
	4	13.81	13.36	13.02	12.77	12.65	12.59	12.55	12.53	12.52
	5	14.28	13.71	13.29	12.97	12.82	12.74	12.70	12.67	12.66
	6	14.76	14.07	13.56	13.17	13.00	12.90	12.85	12.81	12.80
	7	15.25	14.44	13.83	13.38	13.17	13.06	13.00	12.96	12.94
	8	15.74	14.81	14.11	13.59	13.35	13.22	13.15	13.11	13.08
12⅛%	1	12.57	12.46	12.38	12.31	12.29	12.27	12.26	12.26	12.25
	1½	12.79	12.63	12.50	12.41	12.37	12.34	12.33	12.32	12.32
	2	13.02	12.80	12.63	12.51	12.45	12.42	12.40	12.39	12.38
	2½	13.25	12.97	12.76	12.60	12.53	12.49	12.47	12.46	12.45
	3	13.48	13.14	12.89	12.70	12.61	12.57	12.54	12.52	12.51
	4	13.94	13.49	13.15	12.90	12.78	12.72	12.68	12.66	12.65
	5	14.41	13.84	13.42	13.10	12.95	12.87	12.83	12.80	12.79
	6	14.89	14.20	13.69	13.30	13.13	13.03	12.98	12.95	12.93
	7	15.37	14.56	13.96	13.51	13.30	13.19	13.13	13.09	13.07
	8	15.87	14.94	14.24	13.72	13.49	13.36	13.29	13.24	13.22

POINTS DISCOUNT TABLE

SHOWS APR FOR DISCLOSURE WHEN POINTS ARE CHARGED

INTEREST RATE	POINTS	TERMS								
		5 YEARS	7 YEARS	10 YEARS	15 YEARS	20 YEARS	25 YEARS	30 YEARS	35 YEARS	40 YEARS
12¼%	1	12.69	12.58	12.50	12.44	12.41	12.40	12.39	12.38	12.38
	1½	12.92	12.75	12.63	12.54	12.49	12.47	12.46	12.45	12.44
	2	13.15	12.92	12.76	12.63	12.57	12.54	12.53	12.52	12.51
	2½	13.37	13.09	12.89	12.73	12.66	12.62	12.60	12.58	12.58
	3	13.60	13.27	13.02	12.83	12.74	12.69	12.67	12.65	12.64
	4	14.07	13.61	13.28	13.03	12.91	12.85	12.81	12.79	12.78
	5	14.54	13.97	13.55	13.23	13.08	13.00	12.96	12.93	12.92
	6	15.02	14.33	13.82	13.43	13.26	13.16	13.11	13.08	13.06
	7	15.50	14.69	14.09	13.64	13.44	13.33	13.26	13.23	13.20
	8	16.00	15.07	14.37	13.86	13.62	13.49	13.42	13.38	13.35
12⅜%	1	12.82	12.71	12.63	12.57	12.54	12.52	12.51	12.51	12.50
	1½	13.04	12.88	12.75	12.66	12.62	12.60	12.58	12.57	12.57
	2	13.27	13.05	12.88	12.76	12.70	12.67	12.65	12.64	12.64
	2½	13.50	13.22	13.01	12.86	12.78	12.75	12.72	12.71	12.70
	3	13.73	13.39	13.14	12.95	12.87	12.82	12.80	12.78	12.77
	4	14.19	13.74	13.41	13.15	13.04	12.98	12.94	12.92	12.91
	5	14.67	14.10	13.67	13.36	13.21	13.13	13.09	13.06	13.05
	6	15.15	14.46	13.95	13.56	13.39	13.29	13.24	13.21	13.19
	7	15.63	14.82	14.22	13.77	13.57	13.46	13.40	13.36	13.34
	8	16.13	15.20	14.50	13.99	13.75	13.62	13.55	13.51	13.49
12½%	1	12.95	12.83	12.75	12.69	12.66	12.65	12.64	12.63	12.63
	1½	13.17	13.00	12.88	12.79	12.74	12.72	12.71	12.70	12.70
	2	13.40	13.17	13.01	12.88	12.83	12.80	12.78	12.77	12.76
	2½	13.63	13.35	13.14	12.98	12.91	12.87	12.85	12.84	12.83
	3	13.86	13.52	13.27	13.08	13.00	12.95	12.92	12.91	12.90
	4	14.32	13.87	13.53	13.28	13.17	13.11	13.07	13.05	13.04
	5	14.79	14.22	13.80	13.49	13.34	13.26	13.22	13.19	13.18
	6	15.27	14.59	14.08	13.69	13.52	13.42	13.37	13.34	13.32
	7	15.76	14.95	14.35	13.90	13.70	13.59	13.53	13.49	13.47
	8	16.26	15.33	14.63	14.12	13.88	13.76	13.69	13.64	13.62
12⅝%	1	13.07	12.96	12.88	12.82	12.79	12.77	12.76	12.76	12.76
	1½	13.30	13.13	13.01	12.91	12.87	12.85	12.84	12.83	12.82
	2	13.52	13.30	13.14	13.01	12.95	12.92	12.91	12.90	12.89
	2½	13.75	13.47	13.27	13.11	13.04	13.00	12.98	12.97	12.96
	3	13.98	13.65	13.40	13.21	13.12	13.08	13.05	13.04	13.03
	4	14.45	14.00	13.66	13.41	13.30	13.23	13.20	13.18	13.17
	5	14.92	14.35	13.93	13.61	13.47	13.39	13.35	13.33	13.31
	6	15.40	14.71	14.20	13.82	13.65	13.56	13.50	13.47	13.46
	7	15.89	15.08	14.48	14.03	13.83	13.72	13.66	13.62	13.60
	8	16.39	15.46	14.77	14.25	14.01	13.89	13.82	13.78	13.76
12¾%	1	13.20	13.09	13.00	12.94	12.91	12.90	12.89	12.89	12.88
	1½	13.42	13.26	13.13	13.04	13.00	12.97	12.96	12.95	12.95
	2	13.65	13.43	13.26	13.14	13.08	13.05	13.03	13.02	13.02
	2½	13.88	13.60	13.39	13.24	13.17	13.13	13.11	13.09	13.09
	3	14.11	13.77	13.52	13.34	13.25	13.21	13.18	13.17	13.16
	4	14.58	14.12	13.79	13.54	13.42	13.36	13.33	13.31	13.30
	5	15.05	14.48	14.06	13.74	13.60	13.52	13.48	13.46	13.44
	6	15.53	14.84	14.33	13.95	13.78	13.69	13.64	13.61	13.59
	7	16.02	15.21	14.61	14.16	13.96	13.85	13.79	13.76	13.74
	8	16.52	15.59	14.90	14.38	14.15	14.02	13.95	13.91	13.89
12⅞%	1	13.32	13.21	13.13	13.07	13.04	13.03	13.02	13.01	13.01
	1½	13.55	13.38	13.26	13.17	13.12	13.10	13.09	13.08	13.08
	2	13.78	13.55	13.39	13.26	13.21	13.18	13.16	13.15	13.15
	2½	14.01	13.73	13.52	13.36	13.29	13.26	13.23	13.22	13.22
	3	14.24	13.90	13.65	13.46	13.38	13.33	13.31	13.29	13.29
	4	14.70	14.25	13.92	13.67	13.55	13.49	13.46	13.44	13.43
	5	15.18	14.61	14.19	13.87	13.73	13.65	13.61	13.59	13.57
	6	15.66	14.97	14.46	14.08	13.91	13.82	13.77	13.74	13.72
	7	16.15	15.34	14.74	14.30	14.09	13.99	13.93	13.89	13.87
	8	16.65	15.72	15.03	14.51	14.28	14.16	14.09	14.05	14.03

POINTS DISCOUNT TABLE

SHOWS APR FOR DISCLOSURE WHEN POINTS ARE CHARGED

INTEREST RATE	POINTS	TERMS								
		5 YEARS	7 YEARS	10 YEARS	15 YEARS	20 YEARS	25 YEARS	30 YEARS	35 YEARS	40 YEARS
13%	1	13.45	13.34	13.26	13.19	13.17	13.15	13.14	13.14	13.14
	1½	13.67	13.51	13.38	13.29	13.25	13.23	13.22	13.21	13.20
	2	13.90	13.68	13.51	13.39	13.33	13.30	13.29	13.28	13.27
	2½	14.13	13.85	13.65	13.49	13.42	13.38	13.36	13.35	13.34
	3	14.36	14.03	13.78	13.59	13.51	13.46	13.44	13.42	13.41
	4	14.83	14.38	14.04	13.79	13.68	13.62	13.59	13.57	13.56
	5	15.31	14.74	14.32	14.00	13.86	13.78	13.74	13.72	13.70
	6	15.79	15.10	14.59	14.21	14.04	13.95	13.90	13.87	13.85
	7	16.28	15.47	14.87	14.43	14.22	14.12	14.06	14.02	14.00
	8	16.77	15.84	15.16	14.64	14.41	14.29	14.22	14.18	14.16
13⅛%	1	13.57	13.46	13.38	13.32	13.29	13.28	13.27	13.26	13.26
	1½	13.80	13.63	13.51	13.42	13.38	13.35	13.34	13.33	13.33
	2	14.03	13.81	13.64	13.52	13.46	13.43	13.42	13.41	13.40
	2½	14.26	13.98	13.77	13.62	13.55	13.51	13.49	13.48	13.47
	3	14.49	14.15	13.90	13.72	13.63	13.59	13.56	13.55	13.54
	4	14.96	14.51	14.17	13.92	13.81	13.75	13.72	13.70	13.69
	5	15.43	14.86	14.44	14.13	13.99	13.91	13.87	13.85	13.83
	6	15.92	15.23	14.72	14.34	14.17	14.08	14.03	14.00	13.98
	7	16.41	15.60	15.00	14.56	14.35	14.25	14.19	14.16	14.14
	8	16.90	15.97	15.29	14.78	14.54	14.42	14.35	14.32	14.29
13¼%	1	13.70	13.59	13.51	13.45	13.42	13.40	13.39	13.39	13.39
	1½	13.93	13.76	13.64	13.54	13.50	13.48	13.47	13.46	13.46
	2	14.15	13.93	13.77	13.64	13.59	13.56	13.54	13.53	13.53
	2½	14.38	14.11	13.90	13.74	13.67	13.64	13.62	13.61	13.60
	3	14.62	14.28	14.03	13.85	13.76	13.72	13.69	13.68	13.67
	4	15.09	14.63	14.30	14.05	13.94	13.88	13.85	13.83	13.82
	5	15.56	14.99	14.57	14.26	14.12	14.04	14.00	13.98	13.97
	6	16.04	15.36	14.85	14.47	14.30	14.21	14.16	14.13	14.12
	7	16.54	15.73	15.13	14.69	14.48	14.38	14.32	14.29	14.27
	8	17.03	16.11	15.42	14.91	14.68	14.56	14.49	14.45	14.43
13⅜%	1	13.82	13.71	13.63	13.57	13.54	13.53	13.52	13.52	13.51
	1½	14.05	13.89	13.76	13.67	13.63	13.61	13.59	13.59	13.58
	2	14.28	14.06	13.89	13.77	13.71	13.69	13.67	13.66	13.66
	2½	14.51	14.23	14.02	13.87	13.80	13.76	13.74	13.73	13.73
	3	14.74	14.41	14.16	13.97	13.89	13.85	13.82	13.81	13.80
	4	15.21	14.76	14.43	14.18	14.07	14.01	13.98	13.96	13.95
	5	15.69	15.12	14.70	14.39	14.25	14.17	14.13	14.11	14.10
	6	16.17	15.49	14.98	14.60	14.43	14.34	14.29	14.26	14.25
	7	16.66	15.86	15.26	14.82	14.62	14.51	14.46	14.42	14.41
	8	17.16	16.24	15.55	15.04	14.81	14.69	14.62	14.59	14.56
13½%	1	13.95	13.84	13.76	13.70	13.67	13.65	13.65	13.64	13.64
	1½	14.18	14.01	13.89	13.80	13.75	13.73	13.72	13.71	13.71
	2	14.41	14.18	14.02	13.90	13.84	13.81	13.80	13.79	13.78
	2½	14.64	14.36	14.15	14.00	13.93	13.89	13.87	13.86	13.85
	3	14.87	14.53	14.28	14.10	14.02	13.97	13.95	13.94	13.93
	4	15.34	14.89	14.55	14.31	14.19	14.14	14.10	14.09	14.08
	5	15.82	15.25	14.83	14.52	14.38	14.30	14.26	14.24	14.23
	6	16.30	15.62	15.11	14.73	14.56	14.47	14.42	14.40	14.38
	7	16.79	15.99	15.39	14.95	14.75	14.65	14.59	14.56	14.54
	8	17.29	16.37	15.68	15.17	14.94	14.82	14.76	14.72	14.70
13⅝%	1	14.08	13.96	13.88	13.82	13.80	13.78	13.77	13.77	13.77
	1½	14.30	14.14	14.01	13.92	13.88	13.86	13.85	13.84	13.84
	2	14.53	14.31	14.15	14.02	13.97	13.94	13.92	13.91	13.91
	2½	14.76	14.48	14.28	14.12	14.06	14.02	14.00	13.99	13.98
	3	15.00	14.66	14.41	14.23	14.14	14.10	14.08	14.06	14.06
	4	15.47	15.02	14.68	14.43	14.32	14.27	14.23	14.22	14.21
	5	15.94	15.38	14.96	14.65	14.51	14.43	14.39	14.37	14.36
	6	16.43	15.74	15.24	14.86	14.69	14.60	14.56	14.53	14.51
	7	16.92	16.12	15.52	15.08	14.88	14.78	14.72	14.69	14.67
	8	17.42	16.50	15.81	15.30	15.07	14.95	14.89	14.85	14.83

POINTS DISCOUNT TABLE

SHOWS APR FOR DISCLOSURE WHEN POINTS ARE CHARGED

INTEREST RATE	POINTS	TERMS								
		5 YEARS	7 YEARS	10 YEARS	15 YEARS	20 YEARS	25 YEARS	30 YEARS	35 YEARS	40 YEARS
13¾%	1	14.20	14.09	14.01	13.95	13.92	13.91	13.90	13.89	13.89
	1½	14.43	14.26	14.14	14.05	14.01	13.99	13.97	13.97	13.96
	2	14.66	14.44	14.27	14.15	14.09	14.07	14.05	14.04	14.04
	2½	14.89	14.61	14.40	14.25	14.18	14.15	14.13	14.12	14.11
	3	15.12	14.79	14.54	14.35	14.27	14.23	14.21	14.19	14.18
	4	15.59	15.14	14.81	14.56	14.45	14.39	14.36	14.35	14.34
	5	16.07	15.51	15.09	14.77	14.63	14.56	14.52	14.50	14.49
	6	16.56	15.87	15.37	14.99	14.82	14.73	14.69	14.66	14.65
	7	17.05	16.25	15.65	15.21	15.01	14.91	14.85	14.82	14.81
	8	17.55	16.63	15.94	15.43	15.21	15.09	15.02	14.99	14.97
13⅞%	1	14.33	14.22	14.13	14.07	14.05	14.03	14.03	14.02	14.02
	1½	14.55	14.39	14.27	14.17	14.13	14.11	14.10	14.09	14.09
	2	14.78	14.56	14.40	14.28	14.22	14.19	14.18	14.17	14.16
	2½	15.02	14.74	14.53	14.38	14.31	14.27	14.26	14.24	14.24
	3	15.25	14.91	14.67	14.48	14.40	14.36	14.33	14.32	14.31
	4	15.72	15.27	14.94	14.69	14.58	14.52	14.49	14.47	14.47
	5	16.20	15.63	15.21	14.90	14.76	14.69	14.65	14.63	14.62
	6	16.69	16.00	15.49	15.12	14.95	14.87	14.82	14.79	14.78
	7	17.18	16.38	15.78	15.34	15.14	15.04	14.99	14.96	14.94
	8	17.68	16.76	16.07	15.56	15.34	15.22	15.16	15.12	15.10
14%	1	14.45	14.34	14.26	14.20	14.17	14.16	14.15	14.15	14.14
	1½	14.68	14.51	14.39	14.30	14.26	14.24	14.23	14.22	14.22
	2	14.91	14.69	14.52	14.40	14.35	14.32	14.30	14.30	14.29
	2½	15.14	14.86	14.66	14.51	14.44	14.40	14.38	14.37	14.37
	3	15.38	15.04	14.79	14.61	14.53	14.48	14.46	14.45	14.44
	4	15.85	15.40	15.07	14.82	14.71	14.65	14.62	14.60	14.60
	5	16.33	15.76	15.34	15.03	14.89	14.82	14.78	14.76	14.75
	6	16.82	16.13	15.62	15.25	15.08	15.00	14.95	14.93	14.91
	7	17.31	16.50	15.91	15.47	15.27	15.17	15.12	15.09	15.07
	8	17.81	16.89	16.20	15.70	15.47	15.36	15.29	15.26	15.24
14⅛%	1	14.58	14.47	14.39	14.33	14.30	14.28	14.28	14.27	14.27
	1½	14.81	14.64	14.52	14.43	14.39	14.37	14.35	14.35	14.34
	2	15.04	14.81	14.65	14.53	14.48	14.45	14.43	14.42	14.42
	2½	15.27	14.99	14.78	14.63	14.56	14.53	14.51	14.50	14.49
	3	15.50	15.17	14.92	14.74	14.65	14.61	14.59	14.58	14.57
	4	15.98	15.53	15.19	14.95	14.84	14.78	14.75	14.73	14.72
	5	16.46	15.89	15.47	15.16	15.02	14.95	14.92	14.89	14.88
	6	16.94	16.26	15.75	15.38	15.21	15.13	15.08	15.06	15.04
	7	17.44	16.63	16.04	15.60	15.41	15.31	15.25	15.22	15.21
	8	17.94	17.02	16.33	15.83	15.60	15.49	15.43	15.39	15.38
14¼%	1	14.70	14.59	14.51	14.45	14.42	14.41	14.40	14.40	14.40
	1½	14.93	14.77	14.64	14.55	14.51	14.49	14.48	14.47	14.47
	2	15.16	14.94	14.78	14.66	14.60	14.57	14.56	14.55	14.55
	2½	15.40	15.12	14.91	14.76	14.69	14.66	14.64	14.63	14.62
	3	15.63	15.29	15.05	14.86	14.78	14.74	14.72	14.71	14.70
	4	16.10	15.65	15.32	15.08	14.97	14.91	14.88	14.86	14.85
	5	16.58	16.02	15.60	15.29	15.15	15.08	15.05	15.02	15.01
	6	17.07	16.39	15.88	15.51	15.34	15.26	15.21	15.19	15.18
	7	17.57	16.76	16.17	15.73	15.54	15.44	15.39	15.36	15.34
	8	18.07	17.15	16.46	15.96	15.74	15.62	15.56	15.53	15.51
14⅜%	1	14.83	14.72	14.64	14.58	14.55	14.54	14.53	14.53	14.52
	1½	15.06	14.89	14.77	14.68	14.64	14.62	14.61	14.60	14.60
	2	15.29	15.07	14.90	14.78	14.73	14.70	14.69	14.68	14.67
	2½	15.52	15.24	15.04	14.89	14.82	14.78	14.77	14.76	14.75
	3	15.76	15.42	15.17	14.99	14.91	14.87	14.85	14.83	14.83
	4	16.23	15.78	15.45	15.20	15.09	15.04	15.01	14.99	14.98
	5	16.71	16.15	15.73	15.42	15.28	15.21	15.18	15.16	15.14
	6	17.20	16.52	16.01	15.64	15.47	15.39	15.35	15.32	15.31
	7	17.70	16.89	16.30	15.86	15.67	15.57	15.52	15.49	15.47
	8	18.20	17.28	16.59	16.09	15.87	15.76	15.70	15.66	15.65

POINTS DISCOUNT TABLE

SHOWS APR FOR DISCLOSURE WHEN POINTS ARE CHARGED

INTEREST RATE	POINTS	TERMS								
		5 YEARS	7 YEARS	10 YEARS	15 YEARS	20 YEARS	25 YEARS	30 YEARS	35 YEARS	40 YEARS
14½%	1	14.95	14.84	14.76	14.70	14.68	14.66	14.66	14.65	14.65
	1½	15.18	15.02	14.90	14.81	14.77	14.75	14.73	14.73	14.72
	2	15.42	15.19	15.03	14.91	14.86	14.83	14.81	14.81	14.80
	2½	15.65	15.37	15.16	15.01	14.95	14.91	14.89	14.88	14.88
	3	15.88	15.55	15.30	15.12	15.04	15.00	14.97	14.96	14.96
	4	16.36	15.91	15.58	15.33	15.22	15.17	15.14	15.12	15.11
	5	16.84	16.27	15.86	15.55	15.41	15.34	15.31	15.29	15.28
	6	17.33	16.65	16.14	15.77	15.60	15.52	15.48	15.45	15.44
	7	17.83	17.02	16.43	15.99	15.80	15.70	15.65	15.62	15.61
	8	18.33	17.41	16.72	16.22	16.00	15.89	15.83	15.80	15.78
14⅝%	1	15.08	14.97	14.89	14.83	14.80	14.79	14.78	14.78	14.78
	1½	15.31	15.14	15.02	14.93	14.89	14.87	14.86	14.85	14.85
	2	15.54	15.32	15.16	15.04	14.98	14.96	14.94	14.93	14.93
	2½	15.77	15.50	15.29	15.14	15.07	15.04	15.02	15.01	15.01
	3	16.01	15.67	15.43	15.25	15.17	15.12	15.10	15.09	15.08
	4	16.49	16.04	15.70	15.46	15.35	15.30	15.27	15.25	15.24
	5	16.97	16.40	15.98	15.68	15.54	15.47	15.44	15.42	15.41
	6	17.46	16.77	16.27	15.90	15.74	15.65	15.61	15.59	15.57
	7	17.96	17.15	16.56	16.12	15.93	15.84	15.78	15.76	15.74
	8	18.46	17.54	16.85	16.35	16.13	16.02	15.96	15.93	15.92
14¾%	1	15.21	15.10	15.01	14.95	14.93	14.91	14.91	14.90	14.90
	1½	15.44	15.27	15.15	15.06	15.02	15.00	14.99	14.98	14.98
	2	15.67	15.45	15.28	15.16	15.11	15.08	15.07	15.06	15.06
	2½	15.90	15.62	15.42	15.27	15.20	15.17	15.15	15.14	15.13
	3	16.14	15.80	15.55	15.37	15.29	15.25	15.23	15.22	15.21
	4	16.61	16.16	15.83	15.59	15.48	15.43	15.40	15.38	15.37
	5	17.10	16.53	16.11	15.81	15.67	15.60	15.57	15.55	15.54
	6	17.59	16.90	16.40	16.03	15.87	15.78	15.74	15.72	15.71
	7	18.08	17.28	16.69	16.26	16.06	15.97	15.92	15.89	15.88
	8	18.59	17.67	16.99	16.49	16.27	16.16	16.10	16.07	16.05
14⅞%	1	15.33	15.22	15.14	15.08	15.05	15.04	15.03	15.03	15.03
	1½	15.56	15.40	15.27	15.18	15.14	15.12	15.11	15.11	15.11
	2	15.79	15.57	15.41	15.29	15.24	15.21	15.20	15.19	15.18
	2½	16.03	15.75	15.54	15.39	15.33	15.29	15.28	15.27	15.26
	3	16.26	15.93	15.68	15.50	15.42	15.38	15.36	15.35	15.34
	4	16.74	16.29	15.96	15.72	15.61	15.56	15.53	15.51	15.50
	5	17.22	16.66	16.24	15.94	15.80	15.73	15.70	15.68	15.67
	6	17.72	17.03	16.53	16.16	16.00	15.92	15.87	15.85	15.84
	7	18.21	17.41	16.82	16.39	16.20	16.10	16.05	16.02	16.01
	8	18.72	17.80	17.12	16.62	16.40	16.29	16.23	16.20	16.19
15%	1	15.46	15.35	15.27	15.21	15.18	15.17	15.16	15.16	15.15
	1½	15.69	15.52	15.40	15.31	15.27	15.25	15.24	15.23	15.23
	2	15.92	15.70	15.54	15.42	15.36	15.34	15.32	15.31	15.31
	2½	16.15	15.88	15.67	15.52	15.46	15.42	15.40	15.40	15.39
	3	16.39	16.06	15.81	15.63	15.55	15.51	15.49	15.48	15.47
	4	16.87	16.42	16.09	15.84	15.74	15.68	15.66	15.64	15.63
	5	17.35	16.79	16.37	16.07	15.93	15.86	15.83	15.81	15.80
	6	17.84	17.16	16.66	16.29	16.13	16.05	16.00	15.98	15.97
	7	18.34	17.54	16.95	16.52	16.33	16.23	16.18	16.16	16.14
	8	18.85	17.93	17.25	16.75	16.53	16.42	16.37	16.34	16.32
15⅛%	1	15.58	15.47	15.39	15.33	15.31	15.29	15.29	15.28	15.28
	1½	15.81	15.65	15.53	15.44	15.40	15.38	15.37	15.36	15.36
	2	16.05	15.82	15.66	15.54	15.49	15.46	15.45	15.44	15.44
	2½	16.28	16.00	15.80	15.65	15.58	15.55	15.53	15.52	15.52
	3	16.52	16.18	15.94	15.76	15.68	15.64	15.62	15.61	15.60
	4	16.99	16.55	16.22	15.97	15.87	15.81	15.79	15.77	15.76
	5	17.48	16.91	16.50	16.19	16.06	15.99	15.96	15.94	15.93
	6	17.97	17.29	16.79	16.42	16.26	16.18	16.14	16.11	16.10
	7	18.47	17.67	17.08	16.65	16.46	16.37	16.32	16.29	16.28
	8	18.98	18.06	17.38	16.88	16.66	16.56	16.50	16.47	16.46

POINTS DISCOUNT TABLE

SHOWS APR FOR DISCLOSURE WHEN POINTS ARE CHARGED

INTEREST RATE	POINTS	TERMS								
		5 YEARS	7 YEARS	10 YEARS	15 YEARS	20 YEARS	25 YEARS	30 YEARS	35 YEARS	40 YEARS
15¼%	1	15.71	15.60	15.52	15.46	15.43	15.42	15.41	15.41	15.41
	1½	15.94	15.77	15.65	15.56	15.52	15.50	15.49	15.49	15.49
	2	16.17	15.95	15.79	15.67	15.62	15.59	15.58	15.57	15.57
	2½	16.41	16.13	15.92	15.78	15.71	15.68	15.66	15.65	15.65
	3	16.64	16.31	16.06	15.88	15.80	15.77	15.74	15.73	15.73
	4	17.12	16.67	16.34	16.10	16.00	15.94	15.92	15.90	15.89
	5	17.61	17.04	16.63	16.32	16.19	16.12	16.09	16.07	16.06
	6	18.10	17.42	16.92	16.55	16.39	16.31	16.27	16.25	16.24
	7	18.60	17.80	17.21	16.78	16.59	16.50	16.45	16.43	16.41
	8	19.11	18.19	17.51	17.01	16.80	16.69	16.64	16.61	16.59
15⅜%	1	15.83	15.72	15.64	15.58	15.56	15.54	15.54	15.53	15.53
	1½	16.06	15.90	15.78	15.69	15.65	15.63	15.62	15.62	15.61
	2	16.30	16.08	15.91	15.80	15.74	15.72	15.70	15.70	15.69
	2½	16.53	16.26	16.05	15.90	15.84	15.80	15.79	15.78	15.77
	3	16.77	16.44	16.19	16.01	15.93	15.89	15.87	15.86	15.86
	4	17.25	16.80	16.47	16.23	16.12	16.07	16.05	16.03	16.02
	5	17.74	17.17	16.76	16.45	16.32	16.26	16.22	16.20	16.19
	6	18.23	17.55	17.05	16.68	16.52	16.44	16.40	16.38	16.37
	7	18.73	17.93	17.34	16.91	16.72	16.63	16.58	16.56	16.55
	8	19.24	18.32	17.64	17.15	16.93	16.82	16.77	16.74	16.73
15½%	1	15.96	15.85	15.77	15.71	15.68	15.67	15.66	15.66	15.66
	1½	16.19	16.03	15.90	15.82	15.78	15.76	15.75	15.74	15.74
	2	16.42	16.20	16.04	15.92	15.87	15.84	15.83	15.82	15.82
	2½	16.66	16.38	16.18	16.03	15.96	15.93	15.92	15.91	15.90
	3	16.90	16.56	16.32	16.14	16.06	16.02	16.00	15.99	15.99
	4	17.38	16.93	16.60	16.36	16.25	16.20	16.17	16.16	16.15
	5	17.86	17.30	16.88	16.58	16.45	16.39	16.35	16.33	16.33
	6	18.36	17.68	17.17	16.81	16.65	16.57	16.53	16.51	16.50
	7	18.86	18.06	17.47	17.04	16.86	16.76	16.72	16.69	16.68
	8	19.37	18.45	17.77	17.28	17.06	16.96	16.90	16.88	16.86
15⅝%	1	16.08	15.97	15.89	15.83	15.81	15.80	15.79	15.79	15.78
	1½	16.32	16.15	16.03	15.94	15.90	15.88	15.87	15.87	15.87
	2	16.55	16.33	16.17	16.05	16.00	15.97	15.96	15.95	15.95
	2½	16.79	16.51	16.31	16.16	16.09	16.06	16.04	16.03	16.03
	3	17.02	16.69	16.44	16.27	16.19	16.15	16.13	16.12	16.11
	4	17.50	17.06	16.73	16.49	16.38	16.33	16.30	16.29	16.28
	5	17.99	17.43	17.01	16.71	16.58	16.52	16.48	16.47	16.46
	6	18.49	17.80	17.30	16.94	16.78	16.70	16.66	16.64	16.63
	7	18.99	18.19	17.60	17.17	16.99	16.90	16.85	16.83	16.81
	8	19.50	18.58	17.90	17.41	17.20	17.09	17.04	17.01	17.00
15¾%	1	16.21	16.10	16.02	15.96	15.94	15.92	15.92	15.91	15.91
	1½	16.44	16.28	16.16	16.07	16.03	16.01	16.00	16.00	15.99
	2	16.68	16.46	16.29	16.18	16.12	16.10	16.09	16.08	16.08
	2½	16.91	16.64	16.43	16.28	16.22	16.19	16.17	16.16	16.16
	3	17.15	16.82	16.57	16.39	16.32	16.28	16.26	16.25	16.24
	4	17.63	17.18	16.85	16.61	16.51	16.46	16.43	16.42	16.41
	5	18.12	17.56	17.14	16.84	16.71	16.65	16.61	16.60	16.59
	6	18.62	17.93	17.43	17.07	16.91	16.84	16.80	16.78	16.77
	7	19.12	18.32	17.73	17.30	17.12	17.03	16.98	16.96	16.95
	8	19.63	18.71	18.03	17.54	17.33	17.23	17.17	17.15	17.13
15⅞%	1	16.34	16.23	16.15	16.09	16.06	16.05	16.04	16.04	16.04
	1½	16.57	16.40	16.28	16.19	16.16	16.14	16.13	16.12	16.12
	2	16.80	16.58	16.42	16.30	16.25	16.23	16.21	16.21	16.20
	2½	17.04	16.76	16.56	16.41	16.35	16.32	16.30	16.29	16.29
	3	17.28	16.94	16.70	16.52	16.44	16.41	16.39	16.38	16.37
	4	17.76	17.31	16.98	16.74	16.64	16.59	16.56	16.55	16.54
	5	18.25	17.68	17.27	16.97	16.84	16.78	16.74	16.73	16.72
	6	18.74	18.06	17.56	17.20	17.04	16.97	16.93	16.91	16.90
	7	19.25	18.45	17.86	17.43	17.25	17.16	17.12	17.09	17.08
	8	19.76	18.84	18.16	17.67	17.46	17.36	17.31	17.28	17.27

POINTS DISCOUNT TABLE

SHOWS APR FOR DISCLOSURE WHEN POINTS ARE CHARGED

INTEREST RATE	POINTS	TERMS								
		5 YEARS	7 YEARS	10 YEARS	15 YEARS	20 YEARS	25 YEARS	30 YEARS	35 YEARS	40 YEARS
16%	1	16.46	16.35	16.27	16.21	16.19	16.17	16.17	16.17	16.16
	1½	16.69	16.53	16.41	16.32	16.28	16.25	16.25	16.25	16.25
	2	16.93	16.71	16.55	16.43	16.38	16.35	16.34	16.33	16.33
	2½	17.17	16.89	16.69	16.54	16.47	16.44	16.43	16.42	16.41
	3	17.40	17.07	16.83	16.65	16.57	16.53	16.51	16.51	16.50
	4	17.89	17.44	17.11	16.87	16.77	16.72	16.69	16.68	16.67
	5	18.38	17.81	17.40	17.10	16.97	16.91	16.88	16.86	16.85
	6	18.87	18.19	17.69	17.33	17.17	17.10	17.06	17.04	17.03
	7	19.38	18.58	17.99	17.57	17.38	17.29	17.25	17.23	17.22
	8	19.89	18.97	18.29	17.81	17.60	17.49	17.44	17.42	17.40
16⅛%	1	16.59	16.48	16.40	16.34	16.31	16.30	16.29	16.29	16.29
	1½	16.82	16.65	16.53	16.45	16.41	16.39	16.38	16.38	16.37
	2	17.06	16.83	16.67	16.56	16.50	16.48	16.47	16.46	16.46
	2½	17.29	17.01	16.81	16.66	16.60	16.57	16.55	16.55	16.54
	3	17.53	17.20	16.95	16.78	16.70	16.66	16.64	16.63	16.63
	4	18.01	17.57	17.24	17.00	16.90	16.85	16.82	16.81	16.80
	5	18.50	17.94	17.53	17.23	17.10	17.04	17.01	16.99	16.98
	6	19.00	18.32	17.82	17.46	17.31	17.23	17.19	17.17	17.16
	7	19.51	18.71	18.12	17.70	17.51	17.43	17.38	17.36	17.35
	8	20.02	19.10	18.42	17.94	17.73	17.63	17.58	17.55	17.54
16¼%	1	16.71	16.60	16.52	16.46	16.44	16.43	16.42	16.42	16.42
	1½	16.95	16.78	16.66	16.57	16.53	16.52	16.51	16.50	16.50
	2	17.18	16.96	16.80	16.68	16.63	16.61	16.59	16.59	16.58
	2½	17.42	17.14	16.94	16.79	16.73	16.70	16.68	16.67	16.67
	3	17.66	17.32	17.08	16.90	16.83	16.79	16.77	16.76	16.76
	4	18.14	17.69	17.37	17.13	17.03	16.98	16.95	16.94	16.93
	5	18.63	18.07	17.66	17.36	17.23	17.17	17.14	17.12	17.11
	6	19.13	18.45	17.95	17.59	17.44	17.36	17.32	17.31	17.30
	7	19.64	18.84	18.25	17.83	17.65	17.56	17.52	17.49	17.48
	8	20.15	19.23	18.56	18.07	17.86	17.76	17.71	17.69	17.67
16⅜%	1	16.84	16.73	16.65	16.59	16.56	16.55	16.55	16.54	16.54
	1½	17.07	16.91	16.79	16.70	16.66	16.64	16.63	16.63	16.63
	2	17.31	17.09	16.93	16.81	16.76	16.73	16.72	16.72	16.71
	2½	17.54	17.27	17.07	16.92	16.86	16.83	16.81	16.80	16.80
	3	17.78	17.45	17.21	17.03	16.95	16.92	16.90	16.89	16.89
	4	18.27	17.82	17.49	17.26	17.16	17.11	17.08	17.07	17.06
	5	18.76	18.20	17.78	17.49	17.36	17.30	17.27	17.25	17.24
	6	19.26	18.58	18.08	17.72	17.57	17.49	17.46	17.44	17.43
	7	19.77	18.97	18.38	17.96	17.78	17.69	17.65	17.63	17.62
	8	20.28	19.36	18.69	18.20	17.99	17.90	17.85	17.82	17.81
16½%	1	16.96	16.85	16.77	16.72	16.69	16.68	16.67	16.67	16.67
	1½	17.20	17.03	16.91	16.82	16.79	16.77	16.76	16.76	16.75
	2	17.43	17.21	17.05	16.93	16.89	16.86	16.85	16.84	16.84
	2½	17.67	17.39	17.19	17.05	16.98	16.95	16.94	16.93	16.93
	3	17.91	17.58	17.33	17.16	17.08	17.05	17.03	17.02	17.01
	4	18.40	17.95	17.62	17.38	17.28	17.24	17.21	17.20	17.19
	5	18.89	18.32	17.91	17.62	17.49	17.43	17.40	17.38	17.38
	6	19.39	18.71	18.21	17.85	17.70	17.63	17.59	17.57	17.56
	7	19.89	19.09	18.51	18.09	17.91	17.83	17.78	17.76	17.75
	8	20.41	19.49	18.82	18.33	18.13	18.03	17.98	17.96	17.95
16⅝%	1	17.09	16.98	16.90	16.84	16.82	16.80	16.80	16.80	16.79
	1½	17.32	17.16	17.04	16.95	16.91	16.90	16.89	16.88	16.88
	2	17.56	17.34	17.18	17.06	17.01	16.99	16.98	16.97	16.97
	2½	17.80	17.52	17.32	17.17	17.11	17.08	17.07	17.06	17.05
	3	18.04	17.70	17.46	17.29	17.21	17.17	17.16	17.15	17.14
	4	18.52	18.08	17.75	17.51	17.41	17.37	17.34	17.33	17.32
	5	19.02	18.45	18.04	17.75	17.62	17.56	17.53	17.51	17.51
	6	19.52	18.84	18.34	17.98	17.83	17.76	17.72	17.70	17.69
	7	20.02	19.22	18.64	18.22	18.04	17.96	17.92	17.90	17.89
	8	20.54	19.62	18.95	18.47	18.26	18.16	18.12	18.09	18.08

POINTS DISCOUNT TABLE

SHOWS APR FOR DISCLOSURE WHEN POINTS ARE CHARGED

INTEREST RATE	POINTS	TERMS								
		5 YEARS	7 YEARS	10 YEARS	15 YEARS	20 YEARS	25 YEARS	30 YEARS	35 YEARS	40 YEARS
16¾%	1	17.21	17.11	17.03	16.97	16.94	16.93	16.93	16.92	16.92
	1½	17.45	17.28	17.16	17.08	17.04	17.02	17.01	17.01	17.01
	2	17.69	17.47	17.30	17.19	17.14	17.12	17.10	17.10	17.09
	2½	17.92	17.65	17.45	17.30	17.24	17.21	17.19	17.19	17.18
	3	18.16	17.83	17.59	17.41	17.34	17.30	17.29	17.28	17.27
	4	18.65	18.20	17.88	17.64	17.54	17.49	17.47	17.46	17.45
	5	19.14	18.58	18.17	17.87	17.75	17.69	17.66	17.65	17.64
	6	19.64	18.96	18.47	18.11	17.96	17.89	17.85	17.84	17.83
	7	20.15	19.35	18.77	18.35	18.18	18.09	18.05	18.03	18.02
	8	20.67	19.75	19.08	18.60	18.39	18.30	18.25	18.23	18.22
16⅞%	1	17.34	17.23	17.15	17.09	17.07	17.06	17.05	17.05	17.05
	1½	17.58	17.41	17.29	17.20	17.17	17.15	17.14	17.14	17.13
	2	17.81	17.59	17.43	17.31	17.27	17.24	17.23	17.22	17.22
	2½	18.05	17.77	17.57	17.43	17.37	17.34	17.32	17.31	17.31
	3	18.29	17.96	17.72	17.54	17.47	17.43	17.41	17.41	17.40
	4	18.78	18.33	18.00	17.77	17.67	17.62	17.60	17.59	17.58
	5	19.27	18.71	18.30	18.00	17.88	17.82	17.79	17.78	17.77
	6	19.77	19.09	18.60	18.24	18.09	18.02	17.99	17.97	17.96
	7	20.28	19.48	18.90	18.48	18.31	18.22	18.18	18.16	18.15
	8	20.80	19.88	19.21	18.73	18.53	18.43	18.39	18.36	18.35
17%	1	17.47	17.36	17.28	17.22	17.19	17.18	17.18	17.17	17.17
	1½	17.70	17.54	17.42	17.33	17.29	17.28	17.27	17.26	17.26
	2	17.94	17.72	17.56	17.44	17.39	17.37	17.36	17.35	17.35
	2½	18.18	17.90	17.70	17.55	17.49	17.46	17.45	17.44	17.44
	3	18.42	18.09	17.84	17.67	17.59	17.56	17.54	17.53	17.53
	4	18.90	18.46	18.13	17.90	17.80	17.75	17.73	17.72	17.71
	5	19.40	18.84	18.43	18.13	18.01	17.95	17.92	17.91	17.90
	6	19.90	19.22	18.73	18.37	18.22	18.15	18.12	18.10	18.09
	7	20.41	19.61	19.03	18.61	18.44	18.36	18.32	18.30	18.29
	8	20.93	20.01	19.34	18.86	18.66	18.57	18.52	18.50	18.49
17⅛%	1	17.59	17.48	17.40	17.34	17.32	17.31	17.30	17.30	17.30
	1½	17.83	17.66	17.54	17.46	17.42	17.40	17.39	17.39	17.39
	2	18.06	17.84	17.68	17.57	17.52	17.50	17.49	17.48	17.48
	2½	18.30	18.03	17.83	17.68	17.62	17.59	17.58	17.57	17.57
	3	18.54	18.21	17.97	17.80	17.72	17.69	17.67	17.66	17.66
	4	19.03	18.59	18.26	18.03	17.93	17.88	17.86	17.85	17.84
	5	19.53	18.97	18.56	18.26	18.14	18.08	18.05	18.04	18.03
	6	20.03	19.35	18.86	18.50	18.35	18.28	18.25	18.23	18.23
	7	20.54	19.74	19.16	18.75	18.57	18.49	18.45	18.43	18.42
	8	21.06	20.14	19.47	18.99	18.79	18.70	18.66	18.63	18.62
17¼%	1	17.72	17.61	17.53	17.47	17.45	17.44	17.43	17.43	17.43
	1½	17.95	17.79	17.67	17.58	17.55	17.53	17.52	17.52	17.51
	2	18.19	17.97	17.81	17.70	17.65	17.62	17.61	17.61	17.60
	2½	18.43	18.15	17.95	17.81	17.75	17.72	17.71	17.70	17.70
	3	18.67	18.34	18.10	17.92	17.85	17.82	17.80	17.79	17.79
	4	19.16	18.71	18.39	18.16	18.06	18.01	17.99	17.98	17.97
	5	19.66	19.09	18.68	18.39	18.27	18.21	18.18	18.17	18.16
	6	20.16	19.48	18.99	18.63	18.48	18.42	18.38	18.37	18.36
	7	20.67	19.87	19.29	18.88	18.70	18.62	18.58	18.57	18.56
	8	21.19	20.27	19.60	19.13	18.93	18.83	18.79	18.77	18.76
17⅜%	1	17.84	17.73	17.65	17.60	17.57	17.56	17.56	17.55	17.55
	1½	18.08	17.91	17.79	17.71	17.67	17.66	17.65	17.64	17.64
	2	18.32	18.10	17.94	17.82	17.77	17.75	17.74	17.73	17.73
	2½	18.56	18.28	18.08	17.94	17.88	17.85	17.83	17.83	17.82
	3	18.80	18.47	18.22	18.05	17.98	17.94	17.93	17.92	17.92
	4	19.29	18.84	18.52	18.28	18.19	18.14	18.12	18.11	18.10
	5	19.78	19.22	18.81	18.52	18.40	18.34	18.31	18.30	18.30
	6	20.29	19.61	19.12	18.76	18.62	18.55	18.51	18.50	18.49
	7	20.80	20.00	19.42	19.01	18.84	18.76	18.72	18.70	18.69
	8	21.32	20.40	19.73	19.26	19.06	18.97	18.93	18.90	18.89

POINTS DISCOUNT TABLE

SHOWS APR FOR DISCLOSURE WHEN POINTS ARE CHARGED

INTEREST RATE	POINTS	TERMS								
		5 YEARS	7 YEARS	10 YEARS	15 YEARS	20 YEARS	25 YEARS	30 YEARS	35 YEARS	40 YEARS
17½%	1	17.97	17.86	17.78	17.72	17.70	17.69	17.68	17.68	17.68
	1½	18.20	18.04	17.92	17.83	17.80	17.78	17.77	17.77	17.77
	2	18.44	18.22	18.06	17.95	17.90	17.88	17.87	17.86	17.86
	2½	18.68	18.41	18.21	18.06	18.00	17.97	17.96	17.95	17.95
	3	18.92	18.59	18.35	18.18	18.11	18.07	18.06	18.05	18.04
	4	19.41	18.97	18.64	18.41	18.32	18.27	18.25	18.24	18.23
	5	19.91	19.35	18.94	18.65	18.53	18.47	18.45	18.43	18.43
	6	20.42	19.74	19.24	18.89	18.75	18.68	18.65	18.63	18.62
	7	20.93	20.13	19.55	19.14	18.97	18.89	18.85	18.83	18.82
	8	21.45	20.53	19.87	19.39	19.19	19.10	19.06	19.04	19.03
17⅝%	1	18.09	17.98	17.90	17.85	17.82	17.81	17.81	17.81	17.80
	1½	18.33	18.17	18.05	17.96	17.93	17.91	17.90	17.90	17.90
	2	18.57	18.35	18.19	18.08	18.03	18.01	17.99	17.99	17.99
	2½	18.81	18.53	18.33	18.19	18.13	18.10	18.09	18.08	18.08
	3	19.05	18.72	18.48	18.31	18.23	18.20	18.18	18.18	18.17
	4	19.54	19.10	18.77	18.54	18.44	18.40	18.38	18.37	18.36
	5	20.04	19.48	19.07	18.78	18.66	18.60	18.58	18.56	18.56
	6	20.54	19.87	19.37	19.02	18.88	18.81	18.78	18.76	18.76
	7	21.06	20.26	19.68	19.27	19.10	19.02	18.98	18.97	18.96
	8	21.58	20.66	20.00	19.52	19.33	19.24	19.20	19.18	19.17
17¾%	1	18.22	18.11	18.03	17.97	17.95	17.94	17.93	17.93	17.93
	1½	18.46	18.29	18.17	18.09	18.05	18.04	18.03	18.02	18.02
	2	18.70	18.48	18.32	18.20	18.15	18.13	18.12	18.12	18.11
	2½	18.94	18.66	18.46	18.32	18.26	18.23	18.22	18.21	18.21
	3	19.18	18.85	18.61	18.43	18.36	18.33	18.31	18.31	18.30
	4	19.67	19.22	18.90	18.67	18.57	18.53	18.51	18.50	18.49
	5	20.17	19.61	19.20	18.91	18.79	18.73	18.71	18.70	18.69
	6	20.67	20.00	19.50	19.15	19.01	18.94	18.91	18.90	18.89
	7	21.19	20.39	19.81	19.40	19.23	19.16	19.12	19.10	19.09
	8	21.71	20.79	20.13	19.66	19.46	19.37	19.33	19.31	19.30
17⅞%	1	18.34	18.24	18.16	18.10	18.08	18.07	18.06	18.06	18.06
	1½	18.58	18.42	18.30	18.21	18.18	18.16	18.15	18.15	18.15
	2	18.82	18.60	18.44	18.33	18.28	18.26	18.25	18.24	18.24
	2½	19.06	18.79	18.59	18.44	18.39	18.36	18.34	18.34	18.34
	3	19.31	18.97	18.73	18.56	18.49	18.46	18.44	18.43	18.43
	4	19.80	19.35	19.03	18.80	18.70	18.66	18.64	18.63	18.62
	5	20.30	19.74	19.33	19.04	18.92	18.86	18.84	18.83	18.82
	6	20.80	20.13	19.63	19.28	19.14	19.07	19.04	19.03	19.02
	7	21.32	20.52	19.94	19.53	19.37	19.29	19.25	19.23	19.23
	8	21.84	20.92	20.26	19.79	19.59	19.51	19.47	19.45	19.44
18%	1	18.47	18.36	18.28	18.23	18.20	18.19	18.19	18.18	18.18
	1½	18.71	18.54	18.42	18.34	18.30	18.29	18.28	18.28	18.28
	2	18.95	18.73	18.57	18.46	18.41	18.39	18.38	18.37	18.37
	2½	19.19	18.91	18.71	18.57	18.51	18.49	18.47	18.47	18.46
	3	19.43	19.10	18.86	18.69	18.62	18.59	18.57	18.56	18.56
	4	19.92	19.48	19.16	18.93	18.83	18.79	18.77	18.76	18.75
	5	20.42	19.86	19.46	19.17	19.05	19.00	18.97	18.96	18.95
	6	20.93	20.25	19.76	19.41	19.27	19.21	19.18	19.16	19.15
	7	21.45	20.65	20.07	19.67	19.50	19.42	19.39	19.37	19.36
	8	21.97	21.05	20.39	19.92	19.73	19.64	19.60	19.58	19.57

LOAN PROGRESS
CHARTS

LOAN PROGRESS CHART

Showing the dollar balance remaining on a $1,000 loan

INTEREST RATE	ORIG TERM	ELAPSED TERM IN YEARS									
		3	4	5	8	10	12	15	18	20	25
7%	10	769	681	586	259						
	15	874	826	774	596	454	291				
	20	923	894	863	754	668	569	392	173		
	25	951	932	912	842	786	723	609	468	357	
	30	967	955	941	895	858	816	740	647	573	336
7⅛%	10	770	682	588	260						
	15	875	827	776	598	456	293				
	20	924	895	864	756	670	572	394	175		
	25	952	933	913	844	789	726	612	472	360	
	30	968	956	943	897	861	819	744	651	577	339
7¼%	10	772	684	589	262						
	15	876	829	778	600	458	295				
	20	925	897	866	759	673	574	397	176		
	25	952	934	915	846	792	729	616	475	363	
	30	969	957	944	899	863	822	747	655	581	342
7⅜%	10	773	685	591	263						
	15	877	830	779	602	460	296				
	20	926	898	867	761	676	577	399	178		
	25	953	935	916	848	795	732	619	478	366	
	30	969	958	945	901	866	825	751	659	585	346
7½%	10	774	687	592	264						
	15	878	832	781	604	463	298				
	20	927	899	869	763	679	580	402	179		
	25	954	936	917	851	797	735	623	482	369	
	30	970	959	946	903	868	827	754	663	589	349
7⅝%	10	775	688	594	265						
	15	880	833	783	607	465	300				
	20	928	901	871	766	681	583	405	180		
	25	955	938	919	853	800	738	626	485	372	
	30	971	960	947	905	870	830	758	666	593	352
7¾%	10	776	689	595	266						
	15	881	834	784	609	467	301				
	20	929	902	872	768	684	586	407	182		
	25	956	939	920	855	802	741	629	489	375	
	30	971	960	948	907	873	833	761	670	597	355
7⅞%	10	777	691	597	267						
	15	882	836	786	611	469	303				
	20	930	903	874	770	687	589	410	183		
	25	957	940	921	857	805	744	633	492	378	
	30	972	961	950	908	875	836	764	674	601	359
8%	10	778	692	598	268						
	15	883	837	788	613	471	305				
	20	931	904	875	773	689	592	413	185		
	25	957	941	923	859	808	747	636	495	381	
	30	973	962	951	910	877	839	768	678	605	362
8⅛%	10	780	693	600	269						
	15	884	839	789	615	473	307				
	20	932	906	877	775	692	595	415	186		
	25	958	942	924	861	810	750	639	499	384	
	30	973	963	952	912	879	841	771	682	609	365
8¼%	10	781	695	601	271						
	15	885	840	791	617	476	308				
	20	933	907	878	777	695	597	418	188		
	25	959	943	925	863	813	753	643	502	387	
	30	974	964	953	914	882	844	774	685	613	368

LOAN PROGRESS CHART

Showing the dollar balance remaining on a $1,000 loan

INTEREST RATE	ORIG TERM	ELAPSED TERM IN YEARS									
		3	4	5	8	10	12	15	18	20	25
8⅜%	10	782	696	603	272						
	15	886	841	793	620	478	310				
	20	934	908	880	780	697	600	420	189		
	25	960	934	927	865	815	756	646	505	390	
	30	975	965	954	915	884	847	778	689	616	372
8½%	10	783	697	604	273						
	15	887	843	794	622	480	312				
	20	935	909	881	782	700	603	423	191		
	25	960	945	928	867	818	759	649	508	392	
	30	975	966	955	917	886	849	781	693	620	375
8⅝%	10	784	699	606	274						
	15	888	844	796	624	482	314				
	20	936	910	883	784	703	606	426	192		
	25	961	946	929	869	820	762	653	512	395	
	30	976	966	956	919	888	852	784	696	624	378
8¾%	10	785	700	607	275						
	15	889	845	797	626	484	315				
	20	937	912	884	786	705	609	428	194		
	25	962	947	930	871	823	765	656	515	398	
	30	976	967	957	920	890	854	787	700	628	381
8⅞%	10	786	701	609	276						
	15	890	847	799	628	486	317				
	20	938	913	886	788	707	611	431	195		
	25	963	948	932	873	825	767	659	518	401	
	30	977	968	958	922	892	857	790	703	631	384
9%	10	787	703	610	277						
	15	891	848	801	630	489	319				
	20	938	914	887	791	710	614	433	197		
	25	963	949	933	875	827	770	662	522	404	
	30	978	969	959	924	894	859	793	707	635	388
9⅛%	10	788	704	612	278						
	15	892	849	802	633	491	321				
	20	939	915	888	793	713	617	436	198		
	25	964	950	934	877	830	773	666	525	407	
	30	978	969	960	925	896	862	796	711	639	391
9¼%	10	790	705	613	280						
	15	893	851	804	635	493	322				
	20	940	916	890	795	715	620	439	200		
	25	965	951	935	879	832	776	669	528	410	
	30	979	970	961	927	898	864	799	714	643	394
9⅜%	10	791	707	615	281						
	15	894	852	805	637	495	324				
	20	941	917	891	797	718	622	441	201		
	25	965	951	936	881	834	778	672	531	413	
	30	979	971	962	928	900	866	802	717	646	397
9½%	10	792	708	616	282						
	15	895	853	807	639	497	326				
	20	942	918	893	799	720	625	444	203		
	25	966	952	937	883	837	781	675	535	416	
	30	980	971	962	930	902	869	805	721	650	400
9⅝%	10	793	709	618	283						
	15	896	855	809	641	499	328				
	20	943	919	894	801	723	628	446	205		
	25	967	953	938	885	839	784	678	538	419	
	30	980	972	963	931	904	871	808	724	653	404

LOAN PROGRESS CHART

Showing the dollar balance remaining on a $1,000 loan

INTEREST RATE	ORIG TERM	ELAPSED TERM IN YEARS									
		3	4	5	8	10	12	15	18	20	25
9¾%	10	794	711	619	284						
	15	897	856	810	643	501	330				
	20	943	921	895	803	725	631	449	206		
	25	967	954	940	886	841	786	681	541	422	
	30	981	973	964	933	906	873	811	728	657	407
9⅞%	10	795	712	621	285						
	15	898	857	812	645	504	331				
	20	944	922	897	805	728	633	452	208		
	25	968	955	941	888	843	789	685	544	425	
	30	981	973	965	934	908	876	814	731	661	410
10%	10	796	713	622	286						
	15	899	858	813	647	506	333				
	20	945	923	898	807	730	636	454	209		
	25	969	956	942	890	846	792	688	547	428	
	30	982	974	966	935	909	878	817	734	664	413
10⅛%	10	797	715	623	288						
	15	900	860	815	649	508	335				
	20	946	924	899	810	733	639	457	211		
	25	969	957	943	892	848	794	691	551	431	
	30	982	975	967	937	911	880	819	738	668	416
10¼%	10	798	716	625	289						
	15	901	861	816	651	510	337				
	20	947	925	901	812	735	641	459	212		
	25	970	957	944	893	850	797	694	554	433	
	30	982	975	967	938	913	882	822	741	671	419
10⅜%	10	799	717	626	290						
	15	902	862	818	654	512	338				
	20	947	926	902	814	738	644	462	214		
	25	970	958	945	895	852	799	697	557	436	
	30	983	976	968	939	915	884	825	744	674	422
10½%	10	800	719	628	291						
	15	903	863	819	656	514	340				
	20	948	927	903	816	740	647	464	215		
	25	971	959	946	897	854	802	700	560	439	
	30	983	976	969	941	916	886	828	747	678	426
10⅝%	10	801	720	629	292						
	15	904	865	821	658	516	342				
	20	949	928	904	818	742	649	467	217		
	25	971	960	947	898	856	804	703	563	442	
	30	984	977	970	942	918	888	830	750	681	429
10¾%	10	802	721	631	293						
	15	905	866	822	660	519	344				
	20	950	929	906	820	745	652	470	218		
	25	972	960	948	900	858	807	706	566	445	
	30	984	978	970	943	919	890	833	754	685	432
10⅞%	10	803	722	632	294						
	15	906	867	824	662	521	345				
	20	950	930	907	821	747	654	472	220		
	25	973	961	949	901	860	809	709	569	448	
	30	984	978	971	944	921	892	835	757	688	435
11%	10	805	724	634	296						
	15	907	868	825	664	523	347				
	20	951	931	908	823	749	657	475	221		
	25	973	962	950	903	862	812	712	572	451	
	30	985	979	972	945	923	894	838	760	691	438

LOAN PROGRESS CHART

Showing the dollar balance remaining on a $1,000 loan

INTEREST RATE	ORIG TERM	ELAPSED TERM IN YEARS									
		3	4	5	8	10	12	15	18	20	25
11⅛%	10	806	725	635	297						
	15	908	869	827	666	525	349				
	20	952	932	909	825	752	660	477	223		
	25	974	963	950	905	864	814	714	575	454	
	30	985	979	972	947	924	896	840	763	695	441
11¼%	10	807	726	636	298						
	15	909	871	828	668	527	351				
	20	952	933	911	827	754	662	480	225		
	25	974	963	951	906	866	816	717	579	456	
	30	986	980	973	948	926	898	843	766	698	444
11⅜%	10	808	728	638	299						
	15	909	872	829	670	529	352				
	20	953	934	912	829	756	665	482	226		
	25	975	964	952	908	868	819	720	582	459	
	30	986	980	974	949	927	900	845	769	701	447
11½%	10	809	729	639	300						
	15	910	873	831	672	531	354				
	20	954	935	913	831	759	667	485	228		
	25	975	965	953	909	870	821	723	585	462	
	30	986	981	974	950	929	902	848	772	704	450
11⅝%	10	810	730	641	301						
	15	911	874	832	674	533	356				
	20	954	935	914	833	761	670	487	229		
	25	976	965	954	911	872	823	726	588	465	
	30	987	981	975	951	930	903	850	775	708	453
11¾%	10	811	731	642	302						
	15	912	875	834	676	535	358				
	20	955	936	915	835	763	672	490	231		
	25	976	966	955	912	874	826	729	591	468	
	30	987	982	975	952	931	905	852	777	711	456
11⅞%	10	812	733	644	304						
	15	913	876	835	678	537	360				
	20	956	937	916	837	765	675	492	232		
	25	977	967	956	913	876	828	731	594	471	
	30	987	982	976	953	933	907	855	780	714	459
12%	10	813	734	645	305						
	15	914	877	837	680	540	361				
	20	956	938	917	838	767	677	495	234		
	25	977	967	957	915	878	830	734	597	473	
	30	988	982	977	954	934	909	857	783	717	462
12⅛%	10	814	735	646	306						
	15	915	879	838	682	542	363				
	20	957	939	919	840	770	680	498	235		
	25	978	968	957	916	879	832	737	600	476	
	30	988	983	977	955	936	910	859	786	720	465
12¼%	10	815	736	648	307						
	15	915	880	839	684	544	365				
	20	958	940	920	842	772	682	500	237		
	25	978	969	958	918	881	835	740	603	479	
	30	988	983	978	956	937	912	862	789	723	468
12⅜%	10	816	738	649	308						
	15	916	881	841	686	546	367				
	20	958	941	921	844	774	685	503	239		
	25	978	969	959	919	883	837	742	605	482	
	30	989	984	978	957	938	914	864	791	726	471

LOAN PROGRESS CHART

Showing the dollar balance remaining on a $1,000 loan

INTEREST RATE	ORIG TERM	ELAPSED TERM IN YEARS									
		3	4	5	8	10	12	15	18	20	25
12½%	10	817	739	651	309						
	15	917	882	842	688	548	368				
	20	959	942	922	845	776	687	505	240		
	25	979	970	960	920	885	839	745	608	485	
	30	989	984	979	958	939	915	866	794	729	474
12⅝%	10	818	740	652	311						
	15	918	883	843	690	550	370				
	20	960	942	923	847	778	690	507	242		
	25	979	970	960	922	886	841	748	611	487	
	30	989	985	980	959	941	917	868	797	732	477
12¾%	10	819	741	653	312						
	15	919	884	845	692	552	372				
	20	960	943	924	849	780	692	510	243		
	25	980	971	961	923	888	843	750	614	490	
	30	989	985	980	960	942	918	870	800	735	480
12⅞%	10	820	743	655	313						
	15	920	885	846	694	554	374				
	20	961	944	925	851	783	695	512	245		
	25	980	972	962	924	890	845	753	617	493	
	30	990	985	980	961	943	920	872	802	738	483
13%	10	821	744	656	314						
	15	920	886	847	695	556	376				
	20	961	945	926	852	785	697	515	246		
	25	981	972	963	926	891	847	755	620	496	
	30	990	986	981	962	944	922	874	805	741	486
13⅛%	10	822	745	658	315						
	15	921	887	849	697	558	377				
	20	962	946	927	854	787	699	517	248		
	25	981	973	963	927	893	849	758	623	498	
	30	990	986	981	963	945	923	876	807	744	489
13¼%	10	823	746	659	316						
	15	922	888	850	699	560	379				
	20	963	946	928	856	789	702	520	250		
	25	981	973	964	928	895	851	760	626	501	
	30	991	986	982	963	946	924	878	810	747	492
13⅜%	10	824	747	660	318						
	15	923	889	851	701	562	381				
	20	963	947	929	857	791	704	522	251		
	25	982	974	965	929	896	853	763	628	504	
	30	991	987	982	964	948	926	880	812	749	495
13½%	10	825	749	662	319						
	15	924	890	853	703	564	383				
	20	964	948	930	859	793	707	525	253		
	25	982	974	965	930	898	855	765	631	507	
	30	991	987	983	965	949	927	882	815	752	498
13⅝%	10	826	750	663	320						
	15	924	892	854	705	566	384				
	20	964	949	931	861	795	709	527	254		
	25	982	975	966	932	899	857	768	634	509	
	30	991	987	983	966	950	929	884	817	755	501
13¾%	10	827	751	665	321						
	15	925	893	855	707	568	386				
	20	965	949	931	862	797	711	530	256		
	25	983	975	967	933	901	859	770	637	512	
	30	991	988	983	967	951	930	886	820	758	504

LOAN PROGRESS CHART

Showing the dollar balance remaining on a $1,000 loan

INTEREST RATE	ORIG TERM	ELAPSED TERM IN YEARS									
		3	4	5	8	10	12	15	18	20	25
13⅞%	10	828	752	666	322						
	15	926	894	856	709	570	388				
	20	965	950	933	864	799	714	532	257		
	25	983	976	967	934	902	861	773	640	515	
	30	992	988	984	967	952	931	888	822	760	506
14%	10	829	754	667	323						
	15	927	895	858	711	572	390				
	20	966	951	934	865	801	716	534	259		
	25	984	976	968	935	904	863	775	642	517	
	30	992	988	984	968	953	933	890	824	763	509
14⅛%	10	829	755	669	325						
	15	927	896	859	712	574	391				
	20	966	952	935	867	803	718	537	261		
	25	984	977	969	936	905	865	778	645	520	
	30	992	989	985	969	954	934	892	827	766	512
14¼%	10	830	756	670	326						
	15	928	897	860	714	576	393				
	20	967	952	936	868	805	720	539	262		
	25	984	977	969	937	907	867	780	648	523	
	30	992	989	985	970	955	935	893	829	768	515
14⅜%	10	831	757	671	327						
	15	929	898	861	716	578	395				
	20	967	953	936	870	807	723	542	264		
	25	985	978	970	938	908	868	782	650	525	
	30	993	989	985	970	956	937	895	831	771	518
14½%	10	832	758	673	328						
	15	930	899	863	718	580	397				
	20	968	954	937	871	809	725	544	265		
	25	985	978	970	939	910	870	785	653	528	
	30	993	990	986	971	957	938	897	834	774	520
14⅝%	10	833	759	674	329						
	15	930	900	864	720	582	398				
	20	968	954	938	873	811	727	546	267		
	25	985	979	971	940	911	872	787	656	531	
	30	993	990	986	972	958	939	898	836	776	523
14¾%	10	834	761	675	330						
	15	931	901	865	722	584	400				
	20	969	955	939	874	812	729	549	268		
	25	985	979	972	941	912	874	789	658	533	
	30	993	990	987	972	959	940	900	838	779	526
14⅞%	10	835	762	677	332						
	15	932	901	866	723	586	402				
	20	969	956	940	876	814	732	551	270		
	25	986	979	972	942	914	875	792	661	536	
	30	993	990	987	973	959	941	902	840	781	529
15%	10	836	763	678	333						
	15	933	902	868	725	588	404				
	20	970	956	941	877	816	734	554	272		
	25	986	980	973	943	915	877	794	664	538	
	30	993	991	987	973	960	942	903	842	784	532
15⅛%	10	837	764	680	334						
	15	933	903	869	727	590	405				
	20	970	957	942	879	818	736	556	273		
	25	986	980	973	944	916	879	796	666	541	
	30	994	991	988	974	961	944	905	845	786	534

LOAN PROGRESS CHART

Showing the dollar balance remaining on a $1,000 loan

INTEREST RATE	ORIG TERM	ELAPSED TERM IN YEARS									
		3	4	5	8	10	12	15	18	20	25
15¼%	10	838	765	681	335						
	15	934	904	870	729	592	407				
	20	971	958	943	880	820	738	558	275		
	25	987	981	974	945	918	880	798	669	544	
	30	994	991	988	975	962	945	907	847	789	537
15⅜%	10	839	766	682	336						
	15	935	905	871	731	594	409				
	20	971	958	943	882	822	740	561	276		
	25	987	981	974	946	919	882	801	672	546	
	30	994	991	988	975	963	946	908	849	791	540
15½%	10	840	768	684	337						
	15	935	906	872	732	596	411				
	20	972	959	944	883	823	742	563	278		
	25	987	981	975	947	920	884	803	674	549	
	30	994	992	988	976	964	947	910	851	793	542
15⅝%	10	841	769	685	339						
	15	936	907	873	734	598	413				
	20	972	960	945	884	825	745	565	279		
	25	988	982	975	948	922	885	805	677	551	
	30	994	992	989	976	964	948	911	853	796	545
15¾%	10	842	770	686	340						
	15	937	908	875	736	600	414				
	20	973	960	946	886	827	747	568	281		
	25	988	982	976	949	923	887	807	679	554	
	30	994	992	989	977	965	949	913	855	798	548
15⅞%	10	842	771	688	341						
	15	937	909	876	738	602	416				
	20	973	961	947	887	829	749	570	283		
	25	988	983	976	950	924	889	809	682	556	
	30	995	992	989	977	966	950	914	857	800	550
16%	10	843	772	689	342						
	15	938	910	877	739	604	418				
	20	973	961	947	889	831	751	572	284		
	25	988	983	977	951	925	890	811	684	559	
	30	995	992	990	978	967	951	916	859	803	553
16⅛%	10	844	773	690	343						
	15	939	911	878	741	606	419				
	20	974	962	948	890	832	753	574	286		
	25	989	983	977	952	926	892	813	687	561	
	30	995	993	990	979	967	952	917	861	805	556
16¼%	10	845	775	691	344						
	15	939	912	879	743	608	421				
	20	974	963	949	891	834	755	577	287		
	25	989	984	978	953	928	893	815	689	564	
	30	995	993	990	979	968	953	918	863	807	558
16⅜%	10	846	776	693	346						
	15	940	912	880	745	610	423				
	20	975	963	950	892	836	757	579	289		
	25	989	984	978	953	929	895	817	692	566	
	30	995	993	990	980	969	954	920	865	810	561
16½%	10	847	777	694	347						
	15	941	913	881	746	612	425				
	20	975	964	950	894	837	759	581	290		
	25	989	984	979	954	930	896	819	694	569	
	30	995	993	991	980	969	955	921	866	812	563

LOAN PROGRESS CHART

Showing the dollar balance remaining on a $1,000 loan

INTEREST RATE	ORIG TERM	ELAPSED TERM IN YEARS									
		3	4	5	8	10	12	15	18	20	25
16⅝%	10	848	778	695	348						
	15	941	914	882	748	614	426				
	20	976	964	951	895	839	761	583	292		
	25	989	985	979	955	931	898	821	696	571	
	30	995	993	991	980	970	956	922	868	814	566
16¾%	10	849	779	697	349						
	15	942	915	883	750	615	428				
	20	976	965	952	896	841	763	586	294		
	25	990	985	979	956	932	899	823	699	574	
	30	996	994	991	981	971	956	924	870	816	569
16⅞%	10	850	780	698	350						
	15	942	916	884	751	617	430				
	20	976	965	952	898	842	765	588	295		
	25	990	985	980	957	933	900	825	701	576	
	30	996	994	991	981	971	957	925	872	818	571
17%	10	850	781	699	352						
	15	943	917	886	753	619	432				
	20	977	966	953	899	844	767	590	297		
	25	990	986	980	957	934	902	827	704	579	
	30	996	994	992	982	972	958	926	874	820	574
17⅛%	10	851	782	701	353						
	15	944	918	887	755	621	433				
	20	977	966	954	900	846	769	592	298		
	25	990	986	981	958	935	903	829	706	581	
	30	996	994	992	982	973	959	928	875	822	576
17¼%	10	852	783	702	354						
	15	944	918	888	756	623	435				
	20	977	967	954	901	847	771	595	300		
	25	991	986	981	959	936	905	831	708	583	
	30	996	994	992	983	973	960	929	877	824	579
17⅜%	10	853	785	703	355						
	15	945	919	889	758	625	437				
	20	978	967	955	902	849	773	597	301		
	25	991	987	981	960	937	906	833	711	586	
	30	996	994	992	983	974	961	930	879	827	581
17½%	10	854	786	704	356						
	15	945	920	890	760	627	439				
	20	978	968	956	904	850	775	599	303		
	25	991	987	982	960	938	907	835	713	588	
	30	996	995	992	983	974	961	931	880	829	584
17⅝%	10	855	787	706	357						
	15	946	921	891	761	629	440				
	20	978	968	956	905	852	777	601	304		
	25	991	987	982	961	939	909	837	715	591	
	30	996	995	993	984	975	962	932	882	831	586
17¾%	10	856	788	707	359						
	15	947	922	892	763	630	442				
	20	979	969	957	906	853	779	603	306		
	25	991	987	983	962	940	910	839	717	593	
	30	996	995	993	984	975	963	934	884	833	589
18%	10	857	790	710	361						
	15	948	923	894	766	634	445				
	20	980	970	958	908	857	782	608	309		
	25	992	988	983	963	942	912	842	722	598	
	30	997	995	993	985	977	964	936	887	836	593

207

BASIC PAYMENT TABLES
CONSTANT PERCENT TABLES
DOWN PAYMENT TABLES

BASIC QUARTERLY PAYMENTS
FOR A $1000 LOAN

TERM YRS	MOS	PERS	7%	7⅛%	7¼%	7⅜%	7½%	7⅝%	7¾%	7⅞%
1	0	4	261.04	261.24	261.43	261.63	261.83	262.03	262.23	262.43
1	6	6	177.03	177.22	177.40	177.59	177.78	177.97	178.15	178.34
2	0	8	135.05	135.23	135.41	135.60	135.78	135.96	136.15	136.33
2	6	10	109.88	110.06	110.24	110.42	110.60	110.79	110.97	111.15
3	0	12	93.12	93.30	93.48	93.66	93.84	94.02	94.20	94.38
3	6	14	81.16	81.34	81.52	81.70	81.88	82.06	82.24	82.43
4	0	16	72.20	72.39	72.57	72.75	72.93	73.11	73.29	73.47
4	6	18	65.25	65.43	65.61	65.79	65.98	66.16	66.34	66.52
5	0	20	59.70	59.88	60.06	60.24	60.43	60.61	60.79	60.98
5	6	22	55.16	55.34	55.53	55.71	55.90	56.08	56.27	56.45
6	0	24	51.39	51.58	51.76	51.94	52.13	52.32	52.50	52.69
6	6	26	48.21	48.39	48.58	48.77	48.95	49.14	49.33	49.52
7	0	28	45.49	45.67	45.86	46.05	46.24	46.43	46.62	46.80
7	6	30	43.13	43.32	43.51	43.70	43.89	44.08	44.27	44.46
8	0	32	41.08	41.27	41.46	41.65	41.85	42.04	42.23	42.42
8	6	34	39.28	39.47	39.66	39.85	40.05	40.24	40.43	40.63
9	0	36	37.68	37.87	38.07	38.26	38.45	38.65	38.85	39.04
9	6	38	36.25	36.45	36.64	36.84	37.04	37.23	37.43	37.63
10	0	40	34.98	35.17	35.37	35.57	35.76	35.96	36.16	36.36
10	6	42	33.83	34.02	34.22	34.42	34.62	34.82	35.02	35.22
11	0	44	32.78	32.98	33.18	33.38	33.58	33.78	33.99	34.19
11	6	46	31.84	32.04	32.24	32.44	32.64	32.84	33.05	33.25
12	0	48	30.97	31.17	31.38	31.58	31.78	31.99	32.19	32.40
12	6	50	30.18	30.38	30.59	30.79	31.00	31.20	31.41	31.62
13	0	52	29.45	29.66	29.86	30.07	30.28	30.49	30.69	30.90
13	6	54	28.78	28.99	29.20	29.40	29.61	29.82	30.03	30.25
14	0	56	28.16	28.37	28.58	28.79	29.00	29.21	29.42	29.64
14	6	58	27.59	27.80	28.01	28.22	28.43	28.65	28.86	29.08
15	0	60	27.06	27.27	27.48	27.70	27.91	28.12	28.34	28.56
15	6	62	26.56	26.78	26.99	27.21	27.42	27.64	27.85	28.07
16	0	64	26.10	26.32	26.53	26.75	26.97	27.18	27.40	27.62
16	6	66	25.67	25.89	26.11	26.32	26.54	26.76	26.98	27.20
17	0	68	25.27	25.49	25.71	25.93	26.15	26.37	26.59	26.81
17	6	70	24.89	25.11	25.33	25.55	25.78	26.00	26.22	26.45
18	0	72	24.54	24.76	24.98	25.21	25.43	25.65	25.88	26.10
18	6	74	24.21	24.43	24.65	24.88	25.10	25.33	25.56	25.78
19	0	76	23.90	24.12	24.34	24.57	24.80	25.02	25.25	25.48
19	6	78	23.60	23.83	24.05	24.28	24.51	24.74	24.97	25.20
20	0	80	23.33	23.55	23.78	24.01	24.24	24.47	24.70	24.93
20	6	82	23.06	23.29	23.52	23.75	23.98	24.21	24.45	24.68
21	0	84	22.82	23.05	23.28	23.51	23.74	23.97	24.21	24.44
21	6	86	22.58	22.81	23.05	23.28	23.51	23.75	23.98	24.22
22	0	88	22.36	22.59	22.83	23.06	23.30	23.53	23.77	24.01
22	6	90	22.15	22.39	22.62	22.86	23.09	23.33	23.57	23.81
23	0	92	21.95	22.19	22.42	22.66	22.90	23.14	23.38	23.62
23	6	94	21.77	22.00	22.24	22.48	22.72	22.96	23.20	23.44
24	0	96	21.59	21.82	22.06	22.30	22.54	22.79	23.03	23.27
24	6	98	21.42	21.65	21.89	22.14	22.38	22.62	22.87	23.11
25	0	100	21.25	21.49	21.74	21.98	22.22	22.47	22.71	22.96
25	6	102	21.10	21.34	21.58	21.83	22.07	22.32	22.57	22.81
26	0	104	20.95	21.20	21.44	21.69	21.93	22.18	22.43	22.68
26	6	106	20.81	21.06	21.30	21.55	21.80	22.05	22.30	22.55
27	0	108	20.68	20.93	21.17	21.42	21.67	21.92	22.17	22.42
27	6	110	20.55	20.80	21.05	21.30	21.55	21.80	22.05	22.30
28	0	112	20.43	20.68	20.93	21.18	21.43	21.68	21.94	22.19
28	6	114	20.32	20.56	20.82	21.07	21.32	21.57	21.83	22.08
29	0	116	20.20	20.46	20.71	20.96	21.21	21.47	21.72	21.98
29	6	118	20.10	20.35	20.60	20.86	21.11	21.37	21.63	21.88
30	0	120	20.00	20.25	20.50	20.76	21.02	21.27	21.53	21.79

BASIC QUARTERLY PAYMENTS
FOR A $1000 LOAN

TERM YRS	MOS	PERS	8%	8⅛%	8¼%	8⅜%	8½%	8⅝%	8¾%	8⅞%
1	0	4	262.63	262.83	263.03	263.23	263.43	263.63	263.82	264.02
1	6	6	178.53	178.72	178.91	179.10	179.28	179.47	179.66	179.85
2	0	8	136.51	136.70	136.88	137.07	137.25	137.44	137.62	137.80
2	6	10	111.33	111.51	111.70	111.88	112.06	112.24	112.43	112.61
3	0	12	94.56	94.75	94.93	95.11	95.29	95.47	95.66	95.84
3	6	14	82.61	82.79	82.97	83.15	83.34	83.52	83.70	83.88
4	0	16	73.66	73.84	74.02	74.20	74.39	74.57	74.75	74.94
4	6	18	66.71	66.89	67.07	67.26	67.44	67.63	67.81	68.00
5	0	20	61.16	61.35	61.53	61.72	61.90	62.09	62.27	62.46
5	6	22	56.64	56.82	57.01	57.20	57.38	57.57	57.76	57.94
6	0	24	52.88	53.06	53.25	53.44	53.63	53.82	54.01	54.20
6	6	26	49.70	49.89	50.08	50.27	50.46	50.65	50.84	51.03
7	0	28	46.99	47.19	47.38	47.57	47.76	47.95	48.14	48.34
7	6	30	44.65	44.85	45.04	45.23	45.43	45.62	45.81	46.01
8	0	32	42.62	42.81	43.00	43.20	43.39	43.59	43.79	43.98
8	6	34	40.82	41.02	41.22	41.41	41.61	41.81	42.00	42.20
9	0	36	39.24	39.44	39.63	39.83	40.03	40.23	40.43	40.63
9	6	38	37.83	38.02	38.22	38.42	38.62	38.83	39.03	39.23
10	0	40	36.56	36.76	36.96	37.16	37.37	37.57	37.77	37.98
10	6	42	35.42	35.62	35.83	36.03	36.24	36.44	36.65	36.85
11	0	44	34.39	34.60	34.80	35.01	35.21	35.42	35.63	35.84
11	6	46	33.46	33.66	33.87	34.08	34.29	34.49	34.70	34.91
12	0	48	32.61	32.81	33.02	33.23	33.44	33.65	33.86	34.07
12	6	50	31.83	32.04	32.25	32.46	32.67	32.88	33.10	33.31
13	0	52	31.11	31.33	31.54	31.75	31.96	32.18	32.39	32.61
13	6	54	30.46	30.67	30.88	31.10	31.31	31.53	31.75	31.96
14	0	56	29.85	30.07	30.28	30.50	30.71	30.93	31.15	31.37
14	6	58	29.29	29.51	29.73	29.94	30.16	30.38	30.60	30.82
15	0	60	28.77	28.99	29.21	29.43	29.65	29.87	30.09	30.32
15	6	62	28.29	28.51	28.73	28.95	29.18	29.40	29.62	29.85
16	0	64	27.84	28.07	28.29	28.51	28.73	28.96	29.19	29.41
16	6	66	27.43	27.65	27.87	28.10	28.32	28.55	28.78	29.01
17	0	68	27.04	27.26	27.49	27.71	27.94	28.17	28.40	28.63
17	6	70	26.67	26.90	27.13	27.35	27.58	27.81	28.05	28.28
18	0	72	26.33	26.56	26.79	27.02	27.25	27.48	27.71	27.95
18	6	74	26.01	26.24	26.47	26.70	26.94	27.17	27.40	27.64
19	0	76	25.71	25.94	26.18	26.41	26.64	26.88	27.11	27.35
19	6	78	25.43	25.66	25.90	26.13	26.37	26.61	26.84	27.08
20	0	80	25.17	25.40	25.64	25.87	26.11	26.35	26.59	26.83
20	6	82	24.92	25.15	25.39	25.63	25.87	26.11	26.35	26.59
21	0	84	24.68	24.92	25.16	25.40	25.64	25.88	26.12	26.36
21	6	86	24.46	24.70	24.94	25.18	25.42	25.66	25.91	26.15
22	0	88	24.25	24.49	24.73	24.97	25.22	25.46	25.71	25.95
22	6	90	24.05	24.29	24.54	24.78	25.03	25.27	25.52	25.77
23	0	92	23.86	24.11	24.35	24.60	24.84	25.09	25.34	25.59
23	6	94	23.69	23.93	24.18	24.42	24.67	24.92	25.17	25.42
24	0	96	23.52	23.76	24.01	24.26	24.51	24.76	25.01	25.27
24	6	98	23.36	23.61	23.86	24.11	24.36	24.61	24.86	25.12
25	0	100	23.21	23.46	23.71	23.96	24.21	24.46	24.72	24.97
25	6	102	23.06	23.31	23.57	23.82	24.07	24.33	24.58	24.84
26	0	104	22.93	23.18	23.43	23.69	23.94	24.20	24.46	24.71
26	6	106	22.80	23.05	23.31	23.56	23.82	24.08	24.33	24.59
27	0	108	22.68	22.93	23.19	23.44	23.70	23.96	24.22	24.48
27	6	110	22.56	22.81	23.07	23.33	23.59	23.85	24.11	24.37
28	0	112	22.45	22.70	22.96	23.22	23.48	23.74	24.01	24.27
28	6	114	22.34	22.60	22.86	23.12	23.38	23.64	23.91	24.17
29	0	116	22.24	22.50	22.76	23.02	23.29	23.55	23.81	24.08
29	6	118	22.14	22.41	22.67	22.93	23.19	23.46	23.73	23.99
30	0	120	22.05	22.32	22.58	22.84	23.11	23.37	23.64	23.91

BASIC QUARTERLY PAYMENTS
FOR A $1000 LOAN

YRS	MOS	PERS	9%	9⅛%	9¼%	9⅜%	9½%	9⅝%	9¾%	9⅞%
1	0	4	264.22	264.42	264.62	264.82	265.02	265.22	265.42	265.62
1	6	6	180.04	180.23	180.42	180.61	180.80	180.99	181.18	181.37
2	0	8	137.99	138.17	138.36	138.54	138.73	138.92	139.10	139.29
2	6	10	112.79	112.98	113.16	113.34	113.53	113.71	113.90	114.08
3	0	12	96.02	96.21	96.39	96.57	96.76	96.94	97.12	97.31
3	6	14	84.07	84.25	84.43	84.62	84.80	84.99	85.17	85.36
4	0	16	75.12	75.31	75.49	75.68	75.86	76.05	76.23	76.42
4	6	18	68.18	68.37	68.55	68.74	68.93	69.11	69.30	69.49
5	0	20	62.65	62.83	63.02	63.21	63.40	63.59	63.77	63.96
5	6	22	58.13	58.32	58.51	58.70	58.89	59.08	59.27	59.46
6	0	24	54.39	54.58	54.77	54.96	55.15	55.34	55.53	55.72
6	6	26	51.23	51.42	51.61	51.80	52.00	52.19	52.38	52.58
7	0	28	48.53	48.72	48.92	49.11	49.31	49.50	49.70	49.90
7	6	30	46.20	46.40	46.60	46.79	46.99	47.19	47.39	47.58
8	0	32	44.18	44.38	44.57	44.77	44.97	45.17	45.37	45.57
8	6	34	42.40	42.60	42.80	43.00	43.20	43.40	43.61	43.81
9	0	36	40.83	41.03	41.23	41.44	41.64	41.84	42.05	42.25
9	6	38	39.43	39.64	39.84	40.04	40.25	40.46	40.66	40.87
10	0	40	38.18	38.39	38.59	38.80	39.01	39.21	39.42	39.63
10	6	42	37.06	37.27	37.47	37.68	37.89	38.10	38.31	38.52
11	0	44	36.04	36.25	36.46	36.67	36.88	37.10	37.31	37.52
11	6	46	35.12	35.34	35.55	35.76	35.97	36.19	36.40	36.62
12	0	48	34.29	34.50	34.71	34.93	35.14	35.36	35.58	35.79
12	6	50	33.52	33.74	33.95	34.17	34.39	34.61	34.82	35.04
13	0	52	32.82	33.04	33.26	33.48	33.70	33.92	34.14	34.36
13	6	54	32.18	32.40	32.62	32.84	33.06	33.28	33.51	33.73
14	0	56	31.59	31.81	32.03	32.25	32.48	32.70	32.93	33.15
14	6	58	31.04	31.27	31.49	31.72	31.94	32.17	32.39	32.62
15	0	60	30.54	30.76	30.99	31.22	31.44	31.67	31.90	32.13
15	6	62	30.07	30.30	30.53	30.75	30.98	31.21	31.44	31.67
16	0	64	29.64	29.87	30.10	30.33	30.56	30.79	31.02	31.25
16	6	66	29.24	29.47	29.70	29.93	30.16	30.39	30.63	30.86
17	0	68	28.86	29.09	29.32	29.56	29.79	30.03	30.26	30.50
17	6	70	28.51	28.74	28.98	29.21	29.45	29.69	29.92	30.16
18	0	72	28.18	28.42	28.65	28.89	29.13	29.37	29.61	29.85
18	6	74	27.88	28.11	28.35	28.59	28.83	29.07	29.31	29.55
19	0	76	27.59	27.83	28.07	28.31	28.55	28.79	29.04	29.28
19	6	78	27.32	27.56	27.80	28.05	28.29	28.53	28.78	29.02
20	0	80	27.07	27.31	27.55	27.80	28.04	28.29	28.54	28.78
20	6	82	26.83	27.08	27.32	27.57	27.81	28.06	28.31	28.56
21	0	84	26.61	26.85	27.10	27.35	27.60	27.85	28.10	28.35
21	6	86	26.40	26.65	26.89	27.14	27.39	27.64	27.90	28.15
22	0	88	26.20	26.45	26.70	26.95	27.20	27.45	27.71	27.96
22	6	90	26.02	26.27	26.52	26.77	27.02	27.28	27.53	27.79
23	0	92	25.84	26.09	26.34	26.60	26.85	27.11	27.36	27.62
23	6	94	25.68	25.93	26.18	26.44	26.69	26.95	27.21	27.47
24	0	96	25.52	25.77	26.03	26.29	26.54	26.80	27.06	27.32
24	6	98	25.37	25.63	25.88	26.14	26.40	26.66	26.92	27.18
25	0	100	25.23	25.49	25.75	26.01	26.27	26.53	26.79	27.05
25	6	102	25.10	25.36	25.62	25.88	26.14	26.40	26.67	26.93
26	0	104	24.97	25.23	25.49	25.76	26.02	26.28	26.55	26.81
26	6	106	24.85	25.12	25.38	25.64	25.91	26.17	26.44	26.71
27	0	108	24.74	25.01	25.27	25.53	25.80	26.07	26.33	26.60
27	6	110	24.64	24.90	25.16	25.43	25.70	25.97	26.23	26.50
28	0	112	24.53	24.80	25.07	25.33	25.60	25.87	26.14	26.41
28	6	114	24.44	24.71	24.97	25.24	25.51	25.78	26.05	26.33
29	0	116	24.35	24.62	24.88	25.15	25.42	25.70	25.97	26.24
29	6	118	24.26	24.53	24.80	25.07	25.34	25.62	25.89	26.16
30	0	120	24.18	24.45	24.72	24.99	25.27	25.54	25.81	26.09

BASIC QUARTERLY PAYMENTS
FOR A $1000 LOAN

TERM YRS	MOS	PERS	10%	10⅛%	10¼%	10⅜%	10½%	10⅝%	10¾%	10⅞%
1	0	4	265.82	266.02	266.22	266.42	266.62	266.82	267.02	267.23
1	6	6	181.55	181.74	181.93	182.12	182.31	182.50	182.70	182.89
2	0	8	139.47	139.66	139.84	140.03	140.22	140.40	140.59	140.78
2	6	10	114.26	114.45	114.63	114.82	115.00	115.19	115.37	115.56
3	0	12	97.49	97.68	97.86	98.05	98.23	98.42	98.60	98.79
3	6	14	85.54	85.73	85.91	86.10	86.28	86.47	86.66	86.84
4	0	16	76.60	76.79	76.98	77.16	77.35	77.54	77.73	77.91
4	6	18	69.68	69.86	70.05	70.24	70.43	70.62	70.81	71.00
5	0	20	64.15	64.34	64.53	64.72	64.91	65.10	65.29	65.49
5	6	22	59.65	59.84	60.03	60.23	60.42	60.61	60.80	61.00
6	0	24	55.92	56.11	56.30	56.50	56.69	56.89	57.08	57.28
6	6	26	52.77	52.97	53.16	53.36	53.56	53.75	53.95	54.15
7	0	28	50.09	50.29	50.49	50.69	50.88	51.08	51.28	51.48
7	6	30	47.78	47.98	48.18	48.38	48.58	48.78	48.99	49.19
8	0	32	45.77	45.97	46.18	46.38	46.58	46.79	46.99	47.19
8	6	34	44.01	44.22	44.42	44.62	44.83	45.03	45.24	45.45
9	0	36	42.46	42.66	42.87	43.08	43.28	43.49	43.70	43.91
9	6	38	41.08	41.28	41.49	41.70	41.91	42.12	42.33	42.54
10	0	40	39.84	40.05	40.26	40.47	40.68	40.90	41.11	41.32
10	6	42	38.73	38.95	39.16	39.37	39.59	39.80	40.02	40.23
11	0	44	37.74	37.95	38.16	38.38	38.60	38.81	39.03	39.25
11	6	46	36.83	37.05	37.27	37.48	37.70	37.92	38.14	38.36
12	0	48	36.01	36.23	36.45	36.67	36.89	37.11	37.33	37.55
12	6	50	35.26	35.48	35.70	35.93	36.15	36.37	36.60	36.82
13	0	52	34.58	34.80	35.03	35.25	35.47	35.70	35.93	36.15
13	6	54	33.95	34.18	34.40	34.63	34.86	35.08	35.31	35.54
14	0	56	33.38	33.60	33.83	34.06	34.29	34.52	34.75	34.98
14	6	58	32.85	33.08	33.31	33.54	33.77	34.00	34.23	34.46
15	0	60	32.36	32.59	32.82	33.05	33.29	33.52	33.75	33.99
15	6	62	31.91	32.14	32.37	32.61	32.84	33.08	33.31	33.55
16	0	64	31.49	31.72	31.96	32.19	32.43	32.67	32.91	33.15
16	6	66	31.10	31.34	31.57	31.81	32.05	32.29	32.53	32.77
17	0	68	30.74	30.98	31.22	31.46	31.70	31.94	32.18	32.42
17	6	70	30.40	30.64	30.88	31.13	31.37	31.61	31.86	32.10
18	0	72	30.09	30.33	30.57	30.82	31.06	31.31	31.55	31.80
18	6	74	29.80	30.04	30.29	30.53	30.78	31.03	31.27	31.52
19	0	76	29.52	29.77	30.02	30.26	30.51	30.76	31.01	31.26
19	6	78	29.27	29.52	29.77	30.01	30.26	30.52	30.77	31.02
20	0	80	29.03	29.28	29.53	29.78	30.03	30.29	30.54	30.79
20	6	82	28.81	29.06	29.31	29.56	29.82	30.07	30.33	30.58
21	0	84	28.60	28.85	29.10	29.36	29.61	29.87	30.13	30.38
21	6	86	28.40	28.66	28.91	29.17	29.42	29.68	29.94	30.20
22	0	88	28.22	28.47	28.73	28.99	29.25	29.50	29.76	30.03
22	6	90	28.04	28.30	28.56	28.82	29.08	29.34	29.60	29.86
23	0	92	27.88	28.14	28.40	28.66	28.92	29.18	29.45	29.71
23	6	94	27.73	27.99	28.25	28.51	28.77	29.04	29.30	29.57
24	0	96	27.58	27.84	28.11	28.37	28.63	28.90	29.17	29.43
24	6	98	27.45	27.71	27.97	28.24	28.50	28.77	29.04	29.31
25	0	100	27.32	27.58	27.85	28.11	28.38	28.65	28.92	29.19
25	0	102	27.20	27.46	27.73	28.00	28.27	28.54	28.81	29.08
26	0	104	27.08	27.35	27.62	27.89	28.16	28.43	28.70	28.97
26	6	106	26.97	27.24	27.51	27.78	28.05	28.33	28.60	28.87
27	0	108	26.87	27.14	27.41	27.68	27.96	28.23	28.51	28.78
27	6	110	26.78	27.05	27.32	27.59	27.87	28.14	28.42	28.69
28	0	112	26.68	26.96	27.23	27.50	27.78	28.06	28.33	28.61
28	6	114	26.60	26.87	27.15	27.42	27.70	27.98	28.25	28.53
29	0	116	26.52	26.79	27.07	27.34	27.62	27.90	28.18	28.46
29	6	118	26.44	26.72	26.99	27.27	27.55	27.83	28.11	28.39
30	0	120	26.37	26.64	26.92	27.20	27.48	27.76	28.04	28.33

BASIC QUARTERLY PAYMENTS
FOR A $1000 LOAN

YRS	TERM MOS	PERS	11%	11⅛%	11¼%	11⅜%	11½%	11⅝%	11¾%	11⅞%
1	0	4	267.43	267.63	267.83	268.03	268.23	268.43	268.63	268.83
1	6	6	183.08	183.27	183.46	183.65	183.84	184.03	184.22	184.41
2	0	8	140.96	141.15	141.34	141.52	141.71	141.90	142.09	142.27
2	6	10	115.74	115.93	116.12	116.30	116.49	116.68	116.86	117.05
3	0	12	98.97	99.16	99.35	99.53	99.72	99.91	100.09	100.28
3	6	14	87.03	87.22	87.40	87.59	87.78	87.97	88.15	88.34
4	0	16	78.10	78.29	78.48	78.67	78.86	79.05	79.24	79.43
4	6	18	71.19	71.38	71.57	71.76	71.95	72.14	72.33	72.52
5	0	20	65.68	65.87	66.06	66.25	66.45	66.64	66.83	67.03
5	6	22	61.19	61.39	61.58	61.77	61.97	62.16	62.36	62.56
6	0	24	57.47	57.67	57.87	58.06	58.26	58.46	58.66	58.85
6	6	26	54.35	54.54	54.74	54.94	55.14	55.34	55.54	55.74
7	0	28	51.68	51.88	52.08	52.29	52.49	52.69	52.89	53.09
7	6	30	49.39	49.59	49.80	50.00	50.20	50.41	50.61	50.82
8	0	32	47.40	47.60	47.81	48.01	48.22	48.43	48.64	48.84
8	6	34	45.65	45.86	46.07	46.28	46.49	46.70	46.91	47.12
9	0	36	44.12	44.33	44.54	44.75	44.96	45.17	45.38	45.60
9	6	38	42.75	42.96	43.18	43.39	43.60	43.82	44.03	44.25
10	0	40	41.54	41.75	41.97	42.18	42.40	42.61	42.83	43.05
10	6	42	40.45	40.66	40.88	41.10	41.32	41.54	41.76	41.98
11	0	44	39.47	39.69	39.90	40.12	40.35	40.57	40.79	41.01
11	6	46	38.58	38.80	39.02	39.25	39.47	39.69	39.92	40.14
12	0	48	37.78	38.00	38.22	38.45	38.67	38.90	39.13	39.35
12	6	50	37.05	37.27	37.50	37.73	37.95	38.18	38.41	38.64
13	0	52	36.38	36.61	36.84	37.07	37.30	37.53	37.76	37.99
13	6	54	35.77	36.00	36.23	36.46	36.69	36.93	37.16	37.40
14	0	56	35.21	35.44	35.68	35.91	36.14	36.38	36.62	36.85
14	6	58	34.70	34.93	35.17	35.40	35.64	35.88	36.12	36.35
15	0	60	34.23	34.46	34.70	34.94	35.18	35.42	35.66	35.90
15	6	62	33.79	34.03	34.27	34.51	34.75	34.99	35.23	35.48
16	0	64	33.39	33.63	33.87	34.11	34.35	34.60	34.84	35.09
16	6	66	33.01	33.26	33.50	33.74	33.99	34.23	34.48	34.73
17	0	68	32.67	32.91	33.16	33.40	33.65	33.90	34.15	34.40
17	6	70	32.35	32.59	32.84	33.09	33.34	33.59	33.84	34.09
18	0	72	32.05	32.30	32.55	32.80	33.05	33.30	33.55	33.81
18	6	74	31.77	32.02	32.27	32.53	32.78	33.03	33.29	33.54
19	0	76	31.51	31.77	32.02	32.27	32.53	32.78	33.04	33.30
19	6	78	31.27	31.53	31.78	32.04	32.29	32.55	32.81	33.07
20	0	80	31.05	31.30	31.56	31.82	32.08	32.34	32.60	32.86
20	6	82	30.84	31.10	31.35	31.61	31.87	32.13	32.40	32.66
21	0	84	30.64	30.90	31.16	31.42	31.68	31.95	32.21	32.47
21	6	86	30.46	30.72	30.98	31.24	31.51	31.77	32.04	32.30
22	0	88	30.29	30.55	30.81	31.08	31.34	31.61	31.87	32.14
22	6	90	30.13	30.39	30.66	30.92	31.19	31.45	31.72	31.99
23	0	92	29.98	30.24	30.51	30.77	31.04	31.31	31.58	31.85
23	6	94	29.83	30.10	30.37	30.64	30.91	31.18	31.45	31.72
24	0	96	29.70	29.97	30.24	30.51	30.78	31.05	31.32	31.60
24	6	98	29.58	29.85	30.12	30.39	30.66	30.93	31.21	31.48
25	0	100	29.46	29.73	30.00	30.28	30.55	30.82	31.10	31.38
25	6	102	29.35	29.62	29.90	30.17	30.44	30.72	31.00	31.27
26	0	104	29.25	29.52	29.79	30.07	30.35	30.62	30.90	31.18
26	6	106	29.15	29.42	29.70	29.98	30.25	30.53	30.81	31.09
27	0	108	29.06	29.33	29.61	29.89	30.17	30.45	30.73	31.01
27	6	110	28.97	29.25	29.53	29.81	30.09	30.37	30.65	30.93
28	0	112	28.89	29.17	29.45	29.73	30.01	30.29	30.57	30.86
28	6	114	28.81	29.09	29.37	29.66	29.94	30.22	30.50	30.79
29	0	116	28.74	29.02	29.30	29.59	29.87	30.15	30.44	30.72
29	6	118	28.67	28.95	29.24	29.52	29.81	30.09	30.38	30.66
30	0	120	28.61	28.89	29.18	29.46	29.75	30.03	30.32	30.61

BASIC QUARTERLY PAYMENTS
FOR A $1000 LOAN

TERM YRS	MOS	PERS	12%	12⅛%	12¼%	12⅜%	12½%	12⅝%	12¾%	12⅞%
1	0	4	269.03	269.23	269.43	269.64	269.84	270.04	270.24	270.44
1	6	6	184.60	184.79	184.99	185.18	185.37	185.56	185.75	185.94
2	0	8	142.46	142.65	142.84	143.03	143.21	143.40	143.59	143.78
2	6	10	117.24	117.42	117.61	117.80	117.98	118.17	118.36	118.55
3	0	12	100.47	100.65	100.84	101.03	101.22	101.41	101.59	101.78
3	6	14	88.53	88.72	88.91	89.10	89.29	89.48	89.67	89.86
4	0	16	79.62	79.81	80.00	80.19	80.38	80.57	80.76	80.95
4	6	18	72.71	72.91	73.10	73.29	73.48	73.68	73.87	74.07
5	0	20	67.22	67.42	67.61	67.80	68.00	68.20	68.39	68.59
5	6	22	62.75	62.95	63.15	63.34	63.54	63.74	63.94	64.14
6	0	24	59.05	59.25	59.45	59.65	59.85	60.05	60.25	60.45
6	6	26	55.94	56.14	56.35	56.55	56.75	56.95	57.16	57.36
7	0	28	53.30	53.50	53.71	53.91	54.12	54.32	54.53	54.73
7	6	30	51.02	51.23	51.44	51.64	51.85	52.06	52.27	52.48
8	0	32	49.05	49.26	49.47	49.68	49.89	50.10	50.31	50.52
8	6	34	47.33	47.54	47.75	47.96	48.18	48.39	48.60	48.82
9	0	36	45.81	46.02	46.24	46.45	46.67	46.88	47.10	47.32
9	6	38	44.46	44.68	44.90	45.11	45.33	45.55	45.77	45.99
10	0	40	43.27	43.49	43.71	43.93	44.15	44.37	44.59	44.81
10	6	42	42.20	42.42	42.64	42.86	43.09	43.31	43.53	43.76
11	0	44	41.23	41.46	41.68	41.91	42.13	42.36	42.59	42.81
11	6	46	40.37	40.59	40.82	41.05	41.28	41.50	41.73	41.96
12	0	48	39.58	39.81	40.04	40.27	40.50	40.73	40.96	41.20
12	6	50	38.87	39.10	39.33	39.57	39.80	40.03	40.27	40.50
13	0	52	38.22	38.46	38.69	38.92	39.16	39.39	39.63	39.87
13	6	54	37.63	37.87	38.10	38.34	38.58	38.81	39.05	39.29
14	0	56	37.09	37.33	37.57	37.80	38.04	38.29	38.53	38.77
14	6	58	36.59	36.83	37.07	37.32	37.56	37.80	38.04	38.29
15	0	60	36.14	36.38	36.62	36.87	37.11	37.36	37.60	37.85
15	6	62	35.72	35.96	36.21	36.45	36.70	36.95	37.20	37.44
16	0	64	35.33	35.58	35.83	36.07	36.32	36.57	36.82	37.07
16	6	66	34.98	35.22	35.47	35.72	35.97	36.23	36.48	36.73
17	0	68	34.65	34.90	35.15	35.40	35.65	35.91	36.16	36.42
17	6	70	34.34	34.59	34.85	35.10	35.36	35.61	35.87	36.12
18	0	72	34.06	34.31	34.57	34.82	35.08	35.34	35.60	35.86
18	6	74	33.80	34.05	34.31	34.57	34.83	35.09	35.35	35.61
19	0	76	33.55	33.81	34.07	34.33	34.59	34.85	35.11	35.38
19	6	78	33.33	33.59	33.85	34.11	34.37	34.64	34.90	35.16
20	0	80	33.12	33.38	33.64	33.90	34.17	34.43	34.70	34.97
20	6	82	32.92	33.18	33.45	33.71	33.98	34.25	34.51	34.78
21	0	84	32.74	33.00	33.27	33.54	33.80	34.07	34.34	34.61
21	6	86	32.57	32.83	33.10	33.37	33.64	33.91	34.18	34.45
22	0	88	32.41	32.68	32.95	33.22	33.49	33.76	34.03	34.30
22	6	90	32.26	32.53	32.80	33.07	33.35	33.62	33.89	34.17
23	0	92	32.12	32.39	32.67	32.94	33.21	33.49	33.76	34.04
23	6	94	31.99	32.27	32.54	32.81	33.09	33.36	33.64	33.92
24	0	96	31.87	32.15	32.42	32.70	32.97	33.25	33.53	33.81
24	6	98	31.76	32.03	32.31	32.59	32.87	33.14	33.42	33.70
25	0	100	31.65	31.93	32.21	32.49	32.76	33.04	33.33	33.61
25	6	102	31.55	31.83	32.11	32.39	32.67	32.95	33.23	33.52
26	0	104	31.46	31.74	32.02	32.30	32.58	32.87	33.15	33.43
26	6	106	31.37	31.65	31.93	32.22	32.50	32.78	33.07	33.35
27	0	108	31.29	31.57	31.86	32.14	32.42	32.71	32.99	33.28
27	6	110	31.21	31.50	31.78	32.07	32.35	32.64	32.92	33.21
28	0	112	31.14	31.43	31.71	32.00	32.28	32.57	32.86	33.15
28	6	114	31.07	31.36	31.65	31.93	32.22	32.51	32.80	33.09
29	0	116	31.01	31.30	31.58	31.87	32.16	32.45	32.74	33.03
29	6	118	30.95	31.24	31.53	31.82	32.11	32.40	32.69	32.98
30	0	120	30.89	31.18	31.47	31.76	32.05	32.34	32.64	32.93

BASIC QUARTERLY PAYMENTS
FOR A $1000 LOAN

TERM YRS	MOS	PERS	13%	13⅛%	13¼%	13⅜%	13½%	13⅝%	13¾%	13⅞%
1	0	4	270.64	270.84	271.05	271.25	271.45	271.65	271.85	272.05
1	6	6	186.13	186.33	186.52	186.71	186.90	187.10	187.29	187.48
2	0	8	143.97	144.16	144.35	144.53	144.72	144.91	145.10	145.29
2	6	10	118.74	118.92	119.11	119.30	119.49	119.68	119.87	120.06
3	0	12	101.97	102.16	102.35	102.54	102.73	102.92	103.11	103.30
3	6	14	90.05	90.24	90.43	90.62	90.81	91.00	91.19	91.38
4	0	16	81.15	81.34	81.53	81.72	81.92	82.11	82.30	82.50
4	6	18	74.26	74.45	74.65	74.84	75.04	75.23	75.43	75.63
5	0	20	68.78	68.98	69.18	69.37	69.57	69.77	69.97	70.17
5	6	22	64.33	64.53	64.73	64.93	65.13	65.33	65.53	65.74
6	0	24	60.65	60.86	61.06	61.26	61.46	61.67	61.87	62.07
6	6	26	57.56	57.77	57.97	58.18	58.38	58.59	58.80	59.00
7	0	28	54.94	55.15	55.35	55.56	55.77	55.98	56.19	56.40
7	6	30	52.69	52.90	53.11	53.32	53.53	53.74	53.95	54.16
8	0	32	50.73	50.95	51.16	51.37	51.59	51.80	52.02	52.23
8	6	34	49.03	49.25	49.46	49.68	49.89	50.11	50.33	50.55
9	0	36	47.53	47.75	47.97	48.19	48.41	48.63	48.85	49.07
9	6	38	46.21	46.43	46.65	46.87	47.09	47.32	47.54	47.76
10	0	40	45.03	45.26	45.48	45.70	45.93	46.15	46.38	46.61
10	6	42	43.98	44.21	44.43	44.66	44.89	45.12	45.34	45.57
11	0	44	43.04	43.27	43.50	43.73	43.96	44.19	44.42	44.65
11	6	46	42.19	42.42	42.66	42.89	43.12	43.35	43.59	43.82
12	0	48	41.43	41.66	41.90	42.13	42.37	42.60	42.84	43.07
12	6	50	40.74	40.97	41.21	41.44	41.68	41.92	42.16	42.40
13	0	52	40.11	40.34	40.58	40.82	41.06	41.30	41.54	41.79
13	6	54	39.53	39.77	40.02	40.26	40.50	40.74	40.99	41.23
14	0	56	39.01	39.25	39.50	39.74	39.99	40.23	40.48	40.72
14	6	58	38.53	38.78	39.02	39.27	39.52	39.77	40.01	40.26
15	0	60	38.09	38.34	38.59	38.84	39.09	39.34	39.59	39.84
15	6	62	37.69	37.94	38.19	38.44	38.70	38.95	39.20	39.46
16	0	64	37.32	37.58	37.83	38.08	38.34	38.59	38.85	39.10
16	6	66	36.98	37.24	37.49	37.75	38.00	38.26	38.52	38.78
17	0	68	36.67	36.93	37.18	37.44	37.70	37.96	38.22	38.48
17	6	70	36.38	36.64	36.90	37.16	37.42	37.68	37.94	38.20
18	0	72	36.12	36.38	36.64	36.90	37.16	37.42	37.69	37.95
18	6	74	35.87	36.13	36.39	36.66	36.92	37.19	37.45	37.72
19	0	76	35.64	35.90	36.17	36.43	36.70	36.97	37.23	37.50
19	6	78	35.43	35.69	35.96	36.23	36.50	36.76	37.03	37.30
20	0	80	35.23	35.50	35.77	36.04	36.31	36.58	36.85	37.12
20	6	82	35.05	35.32	35.59	35.86	36.13	36.40	36.67	36.95
21	0	84	34.88	35.15	35.42	35.70	35.97	36.24	36.52	36.79
21	6	86	34.72	35.00	35.27	35.54	35.82	36.09	36.37	36.64
22	0	88	34.58	34.85	35.13	35.40	35.68	35.95	36.23	36.51
22	6	90	34.44	34.72	34.99	35.27	35.55	35.83	36.10	36.38
23	0	92	34.31	34.59	34.87	35.15	35.43	35.71	35.99	36.27
23	6	94	34.20	34.47	34.75	35.03	35.31	35.59	35.88	36.16
24	0	96	34.09	34.37	34.65	34.93	35.21	35.49	35.77	36.06
24	6	98	33.98	34.27	34.55	34.83	35.11	35.40	35.68	35.96
25	0	100	33.89	34.17	34.45	34.74	35.02	35.31	35.59	35.88
25	6	102	33.80	34.08	34.37	34.65	34.94	35.22	35.51	35.80
26	0	104	33.72	34.00	34.29	34.57	34.86	35.15	35.43	35.72
26	6	106	33.64	33.92	34.21	34.50	34.79	35.07	35.36	35.65
27	0	108	33.57	33.85	34.14	34.43	34.72	35.01	35.30	35.59
27	6	110	33.50	33.79	34.08	34.36	34.65	34.94	35.24	35.53
28	0	112	33.43	33.72	34.01	34.30	34.60	34.89	35.18	35.47
28	6	114	33.38	33.67	33.96	34.25	34.54	34.83	35.13	35.42
29	0	116	33.32	33.61	33.90	34.20	34.49	34.78	35.08	35.37
29	6	118	33.27	33.56	33.85	34.15	34.44	34.73	35.03	35.32
30	0	120	33.22	33.51	33.81	34.10	34.40	34.69	34.99	35.28

BASIC QUARTERLY PAYMENTS
FOR A $1000 LOAN

TERM YRS MOS PERS			14%	14⅛%	14¼%	14⅜%	14½%	14⅝%	14¾%	14⅞%
1	0	4	272.26	272.46	272.66	272.86	273.06	273.27	273.47	273.67
1	6	6	187.67	187.87	188.06	188.25	188.44	188.64	188.83	189.02
2	0	8	145.48	145.67	145.86	146.05	146.24	146.43	146.62	146.81
2	6	10	120.25	120.44	120.63	120.82	121.01	121.20	121.39	121.58
3	0	12	103.49	103.68	103.87	104.06	104.25	104.44	104.63	104.83
3	6	14	91.58	91.77	91.96	92.15	92.35	92.54	92.73	92.92
4	0	16	82.69	82.88	83.08	83.27	83.47	83.66	83.86	84.05
4	6	18	75.82	76.02	76.22	76.41	76.61	76.81	77.01	77.20
5	0	20	70.37	70.57	70.76	70.96	71.16	71.36	71.57	71.77
5	6	22	65.94	66.14	66.34	66.54	66.75	66.95	67.15	67.36
6	0	24	62.28	62.48	62.69	62.89	63.10	63.30	63.51	63.72
6	6	26	59.21	59.42	59.63	59.83	60.04	60.25	60.46	60.67
7	0	28	56.61	56.82	57.03	57.24	57.45	57.66	57.87	58.09
7	6	30	54.38	54.59	54.80	55.02	55.23	55.45	55.66	55.88
8	0	32	52.45	52.66	52.88	53.10	53.31	53.53	53.75	53.97
8	6	34	50.76	50.98	51.20	51.42	51.64	51.86	52.08	52.31
9	0	36	49.29	49.51	49.73	49.96	50.18	50.40	50.63	50.85
9	6	38	47.99	48.21	48.44	48.66	48.89	49.11	49.34	49.57
10	0	40	46.83	47.06	47.29	47.52	47.74	47.97	48.20	48.43
10	6	42	45.80	46.03	46.26	46.49	46.73	46.96	47.19	47.42
11	0	44	44.88	45.12	45.35	45.58	45.82	46.05	46.29	46.52
11	6	46	44.06	44.29	44.53	44.76	45.00	45.24	45.48	45.72
12	0	48	43.31	43.55	43.79	44.03	44.27	44.51	44.75	44.99
12	6	50	42.64	42.88	43.12	43.36	43.60	43.85	44.09	44.33
13	0	52	42.03	42.27	42.52	42.76	43.01	43.25	43.50	43.74
13	6	54	41.48	41.72	41.97	42.21	42.46	42.71	42.96	43.21
14	0	56	40.97	41.22	41.47	41.72	41.97	42.22	42.47	42.72
14	6	58	40.51	40.76	41.01	41.27	41.52	41.77	42.02	42.28
15	0	60	40.09	40.35	40.60	40.85	41.11	41.36	41.62	41.87
15	6	62	39.71	39.96	40.22	40.48	40.73	40.99	41.25	41.51
16	0	64	39.36	39.62	39.87	40.13	40.39	40.65	40.91	41.17
16	6	66	39.04	39.29	39.55	39.81	40.08	40.34	40.60	40.86
17	0	68	38.74	39.00	39.26	39.52	39.79	40.05	40.32	40.58
17	6	70	38.47	38.73	38.99	39.26	39.52	39.79	40.06	40.32
18	0	72	38.21	38.48	38.75	39.01	39.28	39.55	39.82	40.08
18	6	74	37.98	38.25	38.52	38.79	39.06	39.33	39.60	39.87
19	0	76	37.77	38.04	38.31	38.58	38.85	39.12	39.39	39.67
19	6	78	37.57	37.84	38.11	38.39	38.66	38.93	39.21	39.48
20	0	80	37.39	37.66	37.94	38.21	38.48	38.76	39.03	39.31
20	6	82	37.22	37.50	37.77	38.05	38.32	38.60	38.88	39.15
21	0	84	37.07	37.34	37.62	37.89	38.17	38.45	38.73	39.01
21	6	86	36.92	37.20	37.48	37.75	38.03	38.31	38.59	38.87
22	0	88	36.79	37.07	37.35	37.63	37.91	38.19	38.47	38.75
22	6	90	36.66	36.94	37.22	37.51	37.79	38.07	38.35	38.64
23	0	92	36.55	36.83	37.11	37.39	37.68	37.96	38.25	38.53
23	6	94	36.44	36.72	37.01	37.29	37.58	37.86	38.15	38.43
24	0	96	36.34	36.63	36.91	37.20	37.48	37.77	38.06	38.34
24	6	98	36.25	36.54	36.82	37.11	37.40	37.68	37.97	38.26
25	0	100	36.16	36.45	36.74	37.03	37.32	37.60	37.89	38.18
25	6	102	36.08	36.37	36.66	36.95	37.24	37.53	37.82	38.11
26	0	104	36.01	36.30	36.59	36.88	37.17	37.46	37.75	38.05
26	6	106	35.94	36.23	36.52	36.81	37.11	37.40	37.69	37.98
27	0	108	35.88	36.17	36.46	36.75	37.05	37.34	37.63	37.93
27	6	110	35.82	36.11	36.40	36.70	36.99	37.29	37.58	37.87
28	0	112	35.76	36.06	36.35	36.64	36.94	37.23	37.53	37.83
28	6	114	35.71	36.01	36.30	36.60	36.89	37.19	37.48	37.78
29	0	116	35.66	35.96	36.25	36.55	36.85	37.14	37.44	37.74
29	6	118	35.62	35.92	36.21	36.51	36.81	37.10	37.40	37.70
30	0	120	35.58	35.87	36.17	36.47	36.77	37.07	37.36	37.66

BASIC QUARTERLY PAYMENTS
FOR A $1000 LOAN

YRS	MOS	PERS	15%	15⅛%	15¼%	15⅜%	15½%	15⅝%	15¾%	15⅞%
1	0	4	273.87	274.08	274.28	274.48	274.68	274.89	275.09	275.29
1	6	6	189.22	189.41	189.60	189.80	189.99	190.19	190.38	190.57
2	0	8	147.00	147.19	147.39	147.58	147.77	147.96	148.15	148.34
2	6	10	121.77	121.96	122.15	122.34	122.53	122.72	122.91	123.10
3	0	12	105.02	105.21	105.40	105.59	105.79	105.98	106.17	106.36
3	6	14	93.12	93.31	93.51	93.70	93.89	94.09	94.28	94.48
4	0	16	84.25	84.45	84.64	84.84	85.04	85.23	85.43	85.63
4	6	18	77.40	77.60	77.80	78.00	78.20	78.40	78.60	78.80
5	0	20	71.97	72.17	72.37	72.57	72.77	72.98	73.18	73.38
5	6	22	67.56	67.76	67.97	68.17	68.38	68.59	68.79	69.00
6	0	24	63.92	64.13	64.34	64.55	64.76	64.96	65.17	65.38
6	6	26	60.88	61.09	61.30	61.51	61.72	61.93	62.15	62.36
7	0	28	58.30	58.51	58.73	58.94	59.15	59.37	59.59	59.80
7	6	30	56.09	56.31	56.53	56.74	56.96	57.18	57.40	57.62
8	0	32	54.19	54.41	54.63	54.85	55.07	55.29	55.51	55.73
8	6	34	52.53	52.75	52.97	53.20	53.42	53.64	53.87	54.09
9	0	36	51.08	51.30	51.53	51.75	51.98	52.21	52.44	52.66
9	6	38	49.80	50.02	50.25	50.48	50.71	50.94	51.17	51.41
10	0	40	48.66	48.90	49.13	49.36	49.59	49.83	50.06	50.29
10	6	42	47.66	47.89	48.13	48.36	48.60	48.83	49.07	49.31
11	0	44	46.76	47.00	47.23	47.47	47.71	47.95	48.19	48.43
11	6	46	45.95	46.19	46.43	46.68	46.92	47.16	47.40	47.64
12	0	48	45.23	45.47	45.72	45.96	46.20	46.45	46.69	46.94
12	6	50	44.58	44.82	45.07	45.32	45.56	45.81	46.06	46.31
13	0	52	43.99	44.24	44.49	44.73	44.98	45.23	45.48	45.74
13	6	54	43.46	43.71	43.96	44.21	44.46	44.71	44.97	45.22
14	0	56	42.97	43.23	43.48	43.73	43.99	44.24	44.50	44.75
14	6	58	42.53	42.79	43.04	43.30	43.56	43.81	44.07	44.33
15	0	60	42.13	42.39	42.65	42.91	43.16	43.42	43.68	43.95
15	6	62	41.77	42.03	42.29	42.55	42.81	43.07	43.33	43.60
16	0	64	41.43	41.69	41.96	42.22	42.48	42.75	43.01	43.28
16	6	66	41.13	41.39	41.65	41.92	42.19	42.45	42.72	42.99
17	0	68	40.85	41.11	41.38	41.65	41.91	42.18	42.45	42.72
17	6	70	40.59	40.86	41.13	41.40	41.67	41.94	42.21	42.48
18	0	72	40.35	40.62	40.89	41.17	41.44	41.71	41.98	42.26
18	6	74	40.14	40.41	40.68	40.96	41.23	41.50	41.78	42.05
19	0	76	39.94	40.21	40.49	40.76	41.04	41.31	41.59	41.87
19	6	78	39.76	40.03	40.31	40.58	40.86	41.14	41.42	41.70
20	0	80	39.59	39.86	40.14	40.42	40.70	40.98	41.26	41.54
20	6	82	39.43	39.71	39.99	40.27	40.55	40.83	41.11	41.39
21	0	84	39.29	39.57	39.85	40.13	40.41	40.70	40.98	41.26
21	6	86	39.16	39.44	39.72	40.00	40.29	40.57	40.85	41.14
22	0	88	39.03	39.32	39.60	39.89	40.17	40.46	40.74	41.03
22	6	90	38.92	39.21	39.49	39.78	40.06	40.35	40.64	40.92
23	0	92	38.82	39.10	39.39	39.68	39.96	40.25	40.54	40.83
23	6	94	38.72	39.01	39.30	39.58	39.87	40.16	40.45	40.74
24	0	96	38.63	38.92	39.21	39.50	39.79	40.08	40.37	40.66
24	6	98	38.55	38.84	39.13	39.42	39.71	40.00	40.30	40.59
25	0	100	38.47	38.76	39.06	39.35	39.64	39.93	40.23	40.52
25	6	102	38.40	38.70	38.99	39.28	39.58	39.87	40.16	40.46
26	0	104	38.34	38.63	38.92	39.22	39.51	39.81	40.10	40.40
26	6	106	38.28	38.57	38.87	39.16	39.46	39.75	40.05	40.34
27	0	108	38.22	38.52	38.81	39.11	39.40	39.70	40.00	40.29
27	6	110	38.17	38.47	38.76	39.06	39.36	39.65	39.95	40.25
28	0	112	38.12	38.42	38.72	39.01	39.31	39.61	39.91	40.21
28	6	114	38.08	38.38	38.67	38.97	39.27	39.57	39.87	40.17
29	0	116	38.04	38.33	38.63	38.93	39.23	39.53	39.83	40.13
29	6	118	38.00	38.30	38.60	38.90	39.20	39.50	39.80	40.10
30	0	120	37.96	38.26	38.56	38.86	39.16	39.46	39.77	40.07

BASIC QUARTERLY PAYMENTS
FOR A $1000 LOAN

YRS	MOS	PERS	16%	16⅛%	16¼%	16⅜%	16½%	16⅝%	16¾%	16⅞%
1	0	4	275.50	275.70	275.90	276.10	276.31	276.51	276.71	276.92
1	6	6	190.77	190.96	191.16	191.35	191.54	191.74	191.93	192.13
2	0	8	148.53	148.72	148.92	149.11	149.30	149.49	149.68	149.88
2	6	10	123.30	123.49	123.68	123.87	124.06	124.26	124.45	124.64
3	0	12	106.56	106.75	106.94	107.14	107.33	107.53	107.72	107.91
3	6	14	94.67	94.87	95.07	95.26	95.46	95.65	95.85	96.05
4	0	16	85.82	86.02	86.22	86.42	86.62	86.82	87.02	87.22
4	6	18	79.00	79.20	79.40	79.60	79.80	80.00	80.21	80.41
5	0	20	73.59	73.79	73.99	74.20	74.40	74.61	74.81	75.02
5	6	22	69.20	69.41	69.62	69.83	70.03	70.24	70.45	70.66
6	0	24	65.59	65.80	66.01	66.22	66.43	66.65	66.86	67.07
6	6	26	62.57	62.79	63.00	63.21	63.43	63.64	63.86	64.07
7	0	28	60.02	60.23	60.45	60.67	60.89	61.10	61.32	61.54
7	6	30	57.84	58.05	58.27	58.50	58.72	58.94	59.16	59.38
8	0	32	55.95	56.18	56.40	56.62	56.85	57.07	57.30	57.52
8	6	34	54.32	54.55	54.77	55.00	55.23	55.45	55.68	55.91
9	0	36	52.89	53.12	53.35	53.58	53.81	54.04	54.27	54.50
9	6	38	51.64	51.87	52.10	52.33	52.57	52.80	53.04	53.27
10	0	40	50.53	50.76	51.00	51.24	51.47	51.71	51.95	52.18
10	6	42	49.55	49.78	50.02	50.26	50.50	50.74	50.98	51.22
11	0	44	48.67	48.91	49.15	49.39	49.64	49.88	50.12	50.37
11	6	46	47.89	48.13	48.38	48.62	48.87	49.11	49.36	49.61
12	0	48	47.19	47.43	47.68	47.93	48.18	48.42	48.67	48.92
12	6	50	46.56	46.80	47.05	47.31	47.56	47.81	48.06	48.31
13	0	52	45.99	46.24	46.49	46.74	47.00	47.25	47.51	47.76
13	6	54	45.47	45.73	45.98	46.24	46.50	46.75	47.01	47.27
14	0	56	45.01	45.27	45.52	45.78	46.04	46.30	46.56	46.82
14	6	58	44.59	44.85	45.11	45.37	45.63	45.89	46.15	46.42
15	0	60	44.21	44.47	44.73	44.99	45.26	45.52	45.79	46.05
15	6	62	43.86	44.12	44.39	44.65	44.92	45.19	45.45	45.72
16	0	64	43.54	43.81	44.08	44.34	44.61	44.88	45.15	45.42
16	6	66	43.25	43.52	43.79	44.06	44.33	44.60	44.87	45.14
17	0	68	42.99	43.26	43.53	43.80	44.08	44.35	44.62	44.90
17	6	70	42.75	43.02	43.30	43.57	43.84	44.12	44.39	44.67
18	0	72	42.53	42.80	43.08	43.35	43.63	43.91	44.18	44.46
18	6	74	42.33	42.60	42.88	43.16	43.44	43.71	43.99	44.27
19	0	76	42.14	42.42	42.70	42.98	43.26	43.54	43.82	44.10
19	6	78	41.97	42.25	42.53	42.82	43.10	43.38	43.66	43.94
20	0	80	41.82	42.10	42.38	42.66	42.95	43.23	43.51	43.80
20	6	82	41.68	41.96	42.24	42.53	42.81	43.10	43.38	43.67
21	0	84	41.55	41.83	42.11	42.40	42.69	42.97	43.26	43.55
21	6	86	41.43	41.71	42.00	42.28	42.57	42.86	43.15	43.44
22	0	88	41.31	41.60	41.89	42.18	42.47	42.75	43.04	43.33
22	6	90	41.21	41.50	41.79	42.08	42.37	42.66	42.95	43.24
23	0	92	41.12	41.41	41.70	41.99	42.28	42.57	42.86	43.16
23	6	94	41.03	41.32	41.62	41.91	42.20	42.49	42.78	43.08
24	0	96	40.95	41.25	41.54	41.83	42.12	42.42	42.71	43.01
24	6	98	40.88	41.17	41.47	41.76	42.06	42.35	42.65	42.94
25	0	100	40.81	41.11	41.40	41.70	41.99	42.29	42.58	42.88
25	6	102	40.75	41.05	41.34	41.64	41.93	42.23	42.53	42.83
26	0	104	40.69	40.99	41.29	41.58	41.88	42.18	42.48	42.77
26	6	106	40.64	40.94	41.24	41.53	41.83	42.13	42.43	42.73
27	0	108	40.59	40.89	41.19	41.49	41.79	42.09	42.38	42.68
27	6	110	40.55	40.85	41.15	41.44	41.74	42.04	42.34	42.65
28	0	112	40.51	40.81	41.11	41.41	41.71	42.01	42.31	42.61
28	6	114	40.47	40.77	41.07	41.37	41.67	41.97	42.27	42.58
29	0	116	40.43	40.73	41.03	41.34	41.64	41.94	42.24	42.54
29	6	118	40.40	40.70	41.00	41.31	41.61	41.91	42.21	42.52
30	0	120	40.37	40.67	40.97	41.28	41.58	41.88	42.19	42.49

BASIC QUARTERLY PAYMENTS
FOR A $1000 LOAN

YRS	MOS	PERS	17%	17⅛%	17¼%	17⅜%	17½%	17⅝%	17¾%	18%
1	0	4	277.12	277.32	277.53	277.73	277.93	278.14	278.34	278.75
1	6	6	192.32	192.52	192.71	192.91	193.10	193.30	193.49	193.88
2	0	8	150.07	150.26	150.46	150.65	150.84	151.03	151.23	151.61
2	6	10	124.84	125.03	125.22	125.41	125.61	125.80	126.00	126.38
3	0	12	108.11	108.30	108.50	108.69	108.89	109.08	109.28	109.67
3	6	14	96.24	96.44	96.64	96.83	97.03	97.23	97.43	97.83
4	0	16	87.42	87.62	87.82	88.02	88.22	88.42	88.62	89.02
4	6	18	80.61	80.81	81.02	81.22	81.42	81.63	81.83	82.24
5	0	20	75.22	75.43	75.64	75.84	76.05	76.26	76.47	76.88
5	6	22	70.87	71.08	71.29	71.50	71.71	71.92	72.13	72.55
6	0	24	67.28	67.49	67.71	67.92	68.13	68.35	68.56	68.99
6	6	26	64.29	64.50	64.72	64.94	65.15	65.37	65.59	66.03
7	0	28	61.76	61.98	62.20	62.42	62.64	62.86	63.08	63.53
7	6	30	59.60	59.83	60.05	60.27	60.50	60.72	60.95	61.40
8	0	32	57.75	57.97	58.20	58.43	58.65	58.88	59.11	59.57
8	6	34	56.14	56.37	56.60	56.83	57.06	57.29	57.52	57.99
9	0	36	54.74	54.97	55.20	55.44	55.67	55.90	56.14	56.61
9	6	38	53.51	53.74	53.98	54.22	54.45	54.69	54.93	55.41
10	0	40	52.42	52.66	52.90	53.14	53.38	53.62	53.86	54.35
10	6	42	51.46	51.71	51.95	52.19	52.44	52.68	52.92	53.41
11	0	44	50.61	50.86	51.10	51.35	51.60	51.84	52.09	52.59
11	6	46	49.85	50.10	50.35	50.60	50.85	51.10	51.35	51.85
12	0	48	49.17	49.42	49.68	49.93	50.18	50.43	50.69	51.19
12	6	50	48.57	48.82	49.07	49.33	49.58	49.84	50.09	50.61
13	0	52	48.02	48.27	48.53	48.79	49.05	49.30	49.56	50.08
13	6	54	47.53	47.78	48.04	48.30	48.56	48.82	49.09	49.61
14	0	56	47.08	47.34	47.60	47.87	48.13	48.39	48.66	49.19
14	6	58	46.68	46.94	47.21	47.47	47.74	48.00	48.27	48.80
15	0	60	46.32	46.58	46.85	47.12	47.38	47.65	47.92	48.46
15	6	62	45.99	46.26	46.52	46.79	47.06	47.33	47.60	48.15
16	0	64	45.69	45.96	46.23	46.50	46.77	47.05	47.32	47.87
16	6	66	45.42	45.69	45.96	46.24	46.51	46.78	47.06	47.61
17	0	68	45.17	45.44	45.72	45.99	46.27	46.55	46.82	47.38
17	6	70	44.94	45.22	45.50	45.78	46.05	46.33	46.61	47.17
18	0	72	44.74	45.02	45.30	45.58	45.86	46.14	46.42	46.98
18	6	74	44.55	44.83	45.11	45.39	45.68	45.96	46.24	46.81
19	0	76	44.38	44.66	44.95	45.23	45.51	45.80	46.08	46.65
19	6	78	44.23	44.51	44.79	45.08	45.36	45.65	45.93	46.51
20	0	80	44.08	44.37	44.65	44.94	45.23	45.51	45.80	46.38
20	6	82	43.95	44.24	44.53	44.81	45.10	45.39	45.68	46.26
21	0	84	43.83	44.12	44.41	44.70	44.99	45.28	45.57	46.15
21	6	86	43.72	44.01	44.30	44.59	44.88	45.18	45.47	46.05
22	0	88	43.62	43.92	44.21	44.50	44.79	45.08	45.37	45.96
22	6	90	43.53	43.82	44.12	44.41	44.70	45.00	45.29	45.88
23	0	92	43.45	43.74	44.04	44.33	44.62	44.92	45.21	45.80
23	6	94	43.37	43.67	43.96	44.26	44.55	44.85	45.14	45.73
24	0	96	43.30	43.60	43.89	44.19	44.48	44.78	45.08	45.67
24	6	98	43.24	43.53	43.83	44.13	44.42	44.72	45.02	45.62
25	0	100	43.18	43.47	43.77	44.07	44.37	44.67	44.97	45.56
25	6	102	43.12	43.42	43.72	44.02	44.32	44.62	44.92	45.52
26	0	104	43.07	43.37	43.67	43.97	44.27	44.57	44.87	45.47
26	6	106	43.03	43.33	43.63	43.93	44.23	44.53	44.83	45.43
27	0	108	42.98	43.29	43.59	43.89	44.19	44.49	44.79	45.40
27	6	110	42.95	43.25	43.55	43.85	44.15	44.45	44.76	45.36
28	0	112	42.91	43.21	43.51	43.82	44.12	44.42	44.73	45.33
28	6	114	42.88	43.18	43.48	43.79	44.09	44.39	44.70	45.30
29	0	116	42.85	43.15	43.45	43.76	44.06	44.37	44.67	45.28
29	6	118	42.82	43.12	43.43	43.73	44.04	44.34	44.65	45.26
30	0	120	42.79	43.10	43.40	43.71	44.01	44.32	44.62	45.23

BASIC SEMIANNUAL PAYMENTS
FOR A $1000 LOAN

TERM YRS	MOS	PERS	7%	7⅛%	7¼%	7⅜%	7½%	7⅝%	7¾%	7⅞%
1	0	2	526.41	526.88	527.35	527.83	528.30	528.78	529.25	529.73
1	6	3	356.94	357.37	357.79	358.22	358.65	359.07	359.50	359.93
2	0	4	272.26	272.66	273.06	273.47	273.87	274.28	274.68	275.09
2	6	5	221.49	221.88	222.27	222.66	223.06	223.45	223.84	224.24
3	0	6	187.67	188.06	188.44	188.83	189.22	189.60	189.99	190.38
3	6	7	163.55	163.93	164.31	164.70	165.08	165.46	165.85	166.23
4	0	8	145.48	145.86	146.24	146.62	147.00	147.39	147.77	148.15
4	6	9	131.45	131.83	132.21	132.59	132.97	133.35	133.73	134.12
5	0	10	120.25	120.63	121.01	121.39	121.77	122.15	122.53	122.91
5	6	11	111.10	111.48	111.86	112.24	112.62	113.00	113.39	113.77
6	0	12	103.49	103.87	104.25	104.63	105.02	105.40	105.79	106.17
6	6	13	97.07	97.45	97.83	98.22	98.60	98.99	99.37	99.76
7	0	14	91.58	91.96	92.35	92.73	93.12	93.51	93.89	94.28
7	6	15	86.83	87.22	87.60	87.99	88.38	88.77	89.16	89.55
8	0	16	82.69	83.08	83.47	83.86	84.25	84.64	85.04	85.43
8	6	17	79.05	79.44	79.83	80.22	80.62	81.01	81.41	81.81
9	0	18	75.82	76.22	76.61	77.01	77.40	77.80	78.20	78.60
9	6	19	72.95	73.34	73.74	74.14	74.54	74.94	75.34	75.74
10	0	20	70.37	70.76	71.16	71.57	71.97	72.37	72.77	73.18
10	6	21	68.04	68.44	68.85	69.25	69.65	70.06	70.47	70.88
11	0	22	65.94	66.34	66.75	67.15	67.56	67.97	68.38	68.79
11	6	23	64.02	64.43	64.84	65.25	65.66	66.07	66.48	66.90
12	0	24	62.28	62.69	63.10	63.51	63.92	64.34	64.76	65.17
12	6	25	60.68	61.09	61.51	61.92	62.34	62.75	63.17	63.59
13	0	26	59.21	59.63	60.04	60.46	60.88	61.30	61.72	62.15
13	6	27	57.86	58.28	58.69	59.12	59.54	59.96	60.39	60.82
14	0	28	56.61	57.03	57.45	57.87	58.30	58.73	59.16	59.59
14	6	29	55.45	55.87	56.30	56.73	57.15	57.59	58.02	58.45
15	0	30	54.38	54.80	55.23	55.66	56.09	56.53	56.96	57.40
15	6	31	53.38	53.81	54.24	54.67	55.11	55.54	55.98	56.42
16	0	32	52.45	52.88	53.31	53.75	54.19	54.63	55.07	55.51
16	6	33	51.58	52.01	52.45	52.89	53.33	53.77	54.22	54.66
17	0	34	50.76	51.20	51.64	52.08	52.53	52.97	53.42	53.87
17	6	35	50.00	50.44	50.89	51.33	51.78	52.23	52.68	53.13
18	0	36	49.29	49.73	50.18	50.63	51.08	51.53	51.98	52.44
18	6	37	48.62	49.06	49.51	49.96	50.42	50.87	51.33	51.78
19	0	38	47.99	48.44	48.89	49.34	49.80	50.25	50.71	51.17
19	6	39	47.39	47.84	48.30	48.76	49.21	49.67	50.14	50.60
20	0	40	46.83	47.29	47.74	48.20	48.66	49.13	49.59	50.06
20	6	41	46.30	46.76	47.22	47.68	48.15	48.61	49.08	49.55
21	0	42	45.80	46.26	46.73	47.19	47.66	48.13	48.60	49.07
21	6	43	45.33	45.79	46.26	46.73	47.20	47.67	48.14	48.62
22	0	44	44.88	45.35	45.82	46.29	46.76	47.23	47.71	48.19
22	6	45	44.46	44.93	45.40	45.87	46.35	46.82	47.30	47.78
23	0	46	44.06	44.53	45.00	45.48	45.95	46.43	46.92	47.40
23	6	47	43.67	44.15	44.62	45.10	45.58	46.07	46.55	47.04
24	0	48	43.31	43.79	44.27	44.75	45.23	45.72	46.20	46.69
24	6	49	42.97	43.45	43.93	44.41	44.90	45.38	45.88	46.37
25	0	50	42.64	43.12	43.60	44.09	44.58	45.07	45.56	46.06
25	6	51	42.33	42.81	43.30	43.79	44.28	44.77	45.27	45.76
26	0	52	42.03	42.52	43.01	43.50	43.99	44.49	44.98	45.48
26	6	53	41.75	42.24	42.73	43.22	43.72	44.22	44.72	45.22
27	0	54	41.48	41.97	42.46	42.96	43.46	43.96	44.46	44.97
27	6	55	41.22	41.71	42.21	42.71	43.21	43.71	44.22	44.73
28	0	56	40.97	41.47	41.97	42.47	42.97	43.48	43.99	44.50
28	6	57	40.74	41.24	41.74	42.24	42.75	43.26	43.77	44.28
29	0	58	40.51	41.01	41.52	42.02	42.53	43.04	43.56	44.07
29	6	59	40.30	40.80	41.31	41.82	42.33	42.84	43.36	43.87
30	0	60	40.09	40.60	41.11	41.62	42.13	42.65	43.16	43.68

BASIC SEMIANNUAL PAYMENTS
FOR A $1000 LOAN

TERM YRS	MOS	PERS	8%	8⅛%	8¼%	8⅜%	8½%	8⅝%	8¾%	8⅞%
1	0	2	530.20	530.68	531.15	531.63	532.10	532.58	533.05	533.53
1	6	3	360.35	360.78	361.21	361.64	362.06	362.49	362.92	363.35
2	0	4	275.50	275.90	276.31	276.71	277.12	277.53	277.93	278.34
2	6	5	224.63	225.03	225.42	225.82	226.21	226.61	227.00	227.40
3	0	6	190.77	191.16	191.54	191.93	192.32	192.71	193.10	193.49
3	6	7	166.61	167.00	167.39	167.77	168.16	168.54	168.93	169.32
4	0	8	148.53	148.92	149.30	149.68	150.07	150.46	150.84	151.23
4	6	9	134.50	134.88	135.27	135.65	136.03	136.42	136.81	137.19
5	0	10	123.30	123.68	124.06	124.45	124.84	125.22	125.61	126.00
5	6	11	114.15	114.54	114.92	115.31	115.70	116.09	116.47	116.86
6	0	12	106.56	106.94	107.33	107.72	108.11	108.50	108.89	109.28
6	6	13	100.15	100.54	100.93	101.32	101.71	102.10	102.49	102.89
7	0	14	94.67	95.07	95.46	95.85	96.24	96.64	97.03	97.43
7	6	15	89.95	90.34	90.73	91.13	91.53	91.92	92.32	92.72
8	0	16	85.82	86.22	86.62	87.02	87.42	87.82	88.22	88.62
8	6	17	82.20	82.60	83.00	83.40	83.81	84.21	84.61	85.02
9	0	18	79.00	79.40	79.80	80.21	80.61	81.02	81.42	81.83
9	6	19	76.14	76.55	76.95	77.36	77.77	78.18	78.59	79.00
10	0	20	73.59	73.99	74.40	74.81	75.22	75.64	76.05	76.47
10	6	21	71.29	71.70	72.11	72.52	72.94	73.35	73.77	74.19
11	0	22	69.20	69.62	70.03	70 45	70.87	71.29	71.71	72.13
11	6	23	67.31	67.73	68.15	68 57	68.99	69.41	69.84	70.26
12	0	24	65.59	66.01	66.43	66.86	67.28	67.71	68.13	68.56
12	6	25	64.02	64.44	64.87	65.29	65.72	66.15	66.58	67.01
13	0	26	62.57	63.00	63.43	63.86	64.29	64.72	65.15	65.59
13	6	27	61.24	61.67	62.11	62.54	62.97	63.41	63.85	64.28
14	0	28	60.02	60.45	60.89	61.32	61.76	62.20	62.64	63.08
14	6	29	58.88	59.32	59.76	60.20	60.64	61.08	61.53	61.97
15	0	30	57.84	58.27	58.72	59.16	59.60	60.05	60.50	60.95
15	6	31	56.86	57.30	57.75	58.19	58.64	59.09	59.54	59.99
16	0	32	55.95	56.40	56.85	57.30	57.75	58.20	58.65	59.11
16	6	33	55.11	55.56	56.01	56.46	56.92	57.37	57.83	58.29
17	0	34	54.32	54.77	55.23	55.68	56.14	56.60	57.06	57.52
17	6	35	53.58	54.04	54.50	54.95	55.41	55.88	56.34	56.81
18	0	36	52.89	53.35	53.81	54.27	54.74	55.20	55.67	56.14
18	6	37	52.24	52.71	53.17	53.64	54.10	54.57	55.04	55.51
19	0	38	51.64	52.10	52.57	53.04	53.51	53.98	54.45	54.93
19	6	39	51.07	51.53	52.00	52.48	52.95	53.42	53.90	54.38
20	0	40	50.53	51.00	51.47	51.95	52.42	52.90	53.38	53.86
20	6	41	50.02	50.50	50.97	51.45	51.93	52.41	52.89	53.38
21	0	42	49.55	50.02	50.50	50.98	51.46	51.95	52.44	52.92
21	6	43	49.09	49.57	50.06	50.54	51.03	51.51	52.00	52.49
22	0	44	48.67	49.15	49.64	50.12	50.61	51.10	51.60	52.09
22	6	45	48.27	48.75	49.24	49.73	50.22	50.72	51.21	51.71
23	0	46	47.89	48.38	48.87	49.36	49.85	50.35	50.85	51.35
23	6	47	47.53	48.02	48.51	49.01	49.50	50.00	50.50	51.01
24	0	48	47.19	47.68	48.18	48.67	49.17	49.68	50.18	50.69
24	6	49	46.86	47.36	47.86	48.36	48.86	49.37	49.87	50.38
25	0	50	46.56	47.05	47.56	48.06	48.57	49.07	49.58	50.09
25	6	51	46.26	46.77	47.27	47.78	48.28	48.79	49.31	49.82
26	0	52	45.99	46.49	47.00	47.51	48.02	48.53	49.05	49.56
26	6	53	45.72	46.23	46.74	47.25	47.77	48.28	48.80	49.32
27	0	54	45.47	45.98	46.50	47.01	47.53	48.04	48.56	49.09
27	6	55	45.24	45.75	46.26	46.78	47.30	47.82	48.34	48.87
28	0	56	45.01	45.52	46.04	46.56	47.08	47.60	48.13	48.66
28	6	57	44.79	45.31	45.83	46.35	46.88	47.40	47.93	48.46
29	0	58	44.59	45.11	45.63	46.15	46.68	47.21	47.74	48.27
29	6	59	44.39	44.92	45.44	45.97	46.49	47.02	47.56	48.09
30	0	60	44.21	44.73	45.26	45.79	46.32	46.85	47.38	47.92

BASIC SEMIANNUAL PAYMENTS
FOR A $1000 LOAN

YRS	MOS	PERS	9%	9⅛%	9¼%	9⅜%	9½%	9⅝%	9¾%	9⅞%
1	0	2	534.00	534.48	534.95	535.43	535.91	536.38	536.86	537.33
1	6	3	363.78	364.21	364.64	365.07	365.49	365.92	366.35	366.78
2	0	4	278.75	279.16	279.56	279.97	280.38	280.79	281.20	281.61
2	6	5	227.80	228.19	228.59	228.99	229.39	229.78	230.18	230.58
3	0	6	193.88	194.27	194.67	195.06	195.45	195.84	196.24	196.63
3	6	7	169.71	170.09	170.48	170.87	171.26	171.65	172.04	172.43
4	0	8	151.61	152.00	152.39	152.78	153.17	153.56	153.95	154.34
4	6	9	137.58	137.97	138.36	138.74	139.13	139.52	139.91	140.30
5	0	10	126.38	126.77	127.16	127.55	127.94	128.33	128.72	129.12
5	6	11	117.25	117.64	118.03	118.43	118.82	119.21	119.60	120.00
6	0	12	109.67	110.06	110.46	110.85	111.25	111.64	112.04	112.43
6	6	13	103.28	103.68	104.07	104.47	104.86	105.26	105.66	106.06
7	0	14	97.83	98.22	98.62	99.02	99.42	99.82	100.22	100.63
7	6	15	93.12	93.52	93.92	94.32	94.73	95.13	95.53	95.94
8	0	16	89.02	89.42	89.83	90.23	90.64	91.05	91.46	91.86
8	6	17	85.42	85.83	86.24	86.65	87.06	87.47	87.88	88.29
9	0	18	82.24	82.65	83.06	83.48	83.89	84.30	84.72	85.13
9	6	19	79.41	79.83	80.24	80.66	81.07	81.49	81.91	82.33
10	0	20	76.88	77.30	77.72	78.14	78.56	78.98	79.40	79.82
10	6	21	74.61	75.03	75.45	75.87	76.29	76.72	77.15	77.57
11	0	22	72.55	72.97	73.40	73.83	74.25	74.68	75.11	75.54
11	6	23	70.69	71.11	71.54	71.97	72.40	72.84	73.27	73.71
12	0	24	68.99	69.42	69.86	70.29	70.72	71.16	71.60	72.04
12	6	25	67.44	67.88	68.31	68.75	69.19	69.63	70.07	70.51
13	0	26	66.03	66.46	66.90	67.34	67.79	68.23	68.68	69.12
13	6	27	64.72	65.17	65.61	66.05	66.50	66.95	67.40	67.85
14	0	28	63.53	63.97	64.42	64.87	65.32	65.77	66.22	66.67
14	6	29	62.42	62.87	63.32	63.77	64.22	64.68	65.13	65.59
15	0	30	61.40	61.85	62.30	62.76	63.21	63.67	64.13	64.59
15	6	31	60.45	60.90	61.36	61.82	62.28	62.74	63.21	63.67
16	0	32	59.57	60.03	60.49	60.95	61.41	61.88	62.35	62.82
16	6	33	58.75	59.21	59.68	60.14	60.61	61.08	61.55	62.02
17	0	34	57.99	58.45	58.92	59.39	59.86	60.33	60.81	61.28
17	6	35	57.28	57.74	58.22	58.69	59.16	59.64	60.12	60.60
18	0	36	56.61	57.08	57.56	58.03	58.51	58.99	59.47	59.96
18	6	37	55.99	56.47	56.94	57.42	57.90	58.39	58.87	59.36
19	0	38	55.41	55.89	56.37	56.85	57.33	57.82	58.31	58.80
19	6	39	54.86	55.34	55.83	56.31	56.80	57.29	57.78	58.28
20	0	40	54.35	54.83	55.32	55.81	56.30	56.79	57.29	57.79
20	6	41	53.87	54.36	54.85	55.34	55.83	56.33	56.83	57.33
21	0	42	53.41	53.91	54.40	54.90	55.39	55.89	56.39	56.90
21	6	43	52.99	53.48	53.98	54.48	54.98	55.48	55.98	56.49
22	0	44	52.59	53.08	53.58	54.09	54.59	55.09	55.60	56.11
22	6	45	52.21	52.71	53.21	53.72	54.22	54.73	55.24	55.75
23	0	46	51.85	52.35	52.86	53.37	53.88	54.39	54.90	55.42
23	6	47	51.51	52.02	52.53	53.04	53.55	54.07	54.58	55.10
24	0	48	51.19	51.70	52.22	52.73	53.24	53.76	54.28	54.80
24	6	49	50.89	51.40	51.92	52.44	52.95	53.47	54.00	54.52
25	0	50	50.61	51.12	51.64	52.16	52.68	53.20	53.73	54.25
25	6	51	50.34	50.86	51.38	51.90	52.42	52.95	53.47	54.00
26	0	52	50.08	50.60	51.13	51.65	52.18	52.70	53.23	53.77
26	6	53	49.84	50.36	50.89	51.42	51.94	52.48	53.01	53.54
27	0	54	49.61	50.14	50.66	51.19	51.73	52.26	52.79	53.33
27	6	55	49.39	49.92	50.45	50.98	51.52	52.05	52.59	53.13
28	0	56	49.19	49.72	50.25	50.78	51.32	51.86	52.40	52.94
28	6	57	48.99	49.52	50.06	50.60	51.13	51.68	52.22	52.76
29	0	58	48.80	49.34	49.88	50.42	50.96	51.50	52.05	52.59
29	6	59	48.63	49.17	49.71	50.25	50.79	51.34	51.88	52.43
30	0	60	48.46	49.00	49.54	50.09	50.63	51.18	51.73	52.28

BASIC SEMIANNUAL PAYMENTS
FOR A $1000 LOAN

TERM YRS	MOS	PERS	10%	10⅛%	10¼%	10⅜%	10½%	10⅝%	10¾%	10⅞%
1	0	2	537.81	538.29	538.76	539.24	539.72	540.19	540.67	541.15
1	6	3	367.21	367.64	368.07	368.50	368.94	369.37	369.80	370.23
2	0	4	282.02	282.43	282.84	283.25	283.66	284.07	284.48	284.89
2	6	5	230.98	231.38	231.78	232.18	232.58	232.98	233.38	233.78
3	0	6	197.02	197.42	197.81	198.21	198.60	199.00	199.39	199.79
3	6	7	172.82	173.22	173.61	174.00	174.39	174.79	175.18	175.57
4	0	8	154.73	155.12	155.51	155.90	156.29	156.69	157.08	157.47
4	6	9	140.70	141.09	141.48	141.87	142.27	142.66	143.05	143.45
5	0	10	129.51	129.90	130.30	130.69	131.09	131.48	131.88	132.28
5	6	11	120.39	120.79	121.19	121.58	121.98	122.38	122.78	123.18
6	0	12	112.83	113.23	113.63	114.03	114.43	114.83	115.23	115.63
6	6	13	106.46	106.86	107.26	107.67	108.07	108.47	108.88	109.28
7	0	14	101.03	101.43	101.84	102.24	102.65	103.06	103.47	103.87
7	6	15	96.35	96.75	97.16	97.57	97.98	98.39	98.80	99.22
8	0	16	92.27	92.69	93.10	93.51	93.92	94.34	94.75	95.17
8	6	17	88.70	89.12	89.53	89.95	90.37	90.79	91.21	91.63
9	0	18	85.55	85.97	86.39	86.81	87.23	87.65	88.08	88.50
9	6	19	82.75	83.17	83.60	84.02	84.44	84.87	85.30	85.73
10	0	20	80.25	80.67	81.10	81.53	81.96	82.39	82.82	83.25
10	6	21	78.00	78.43	78.86	79.29	79.73	80.16	80.60	81.03
11	0	22	75.98	76.41	76.84	77.28	77.72	78.15	78.59	79.03
11	6	23	74.14	74.58	75.02	75.46	75.90	76.34	76.78	77.23
12	0	24	72.48	72.92	73.36	73.80	74.25	74.69	75.14	75.59
12	6	25	70.96	71.40	71.85	72.30	72.75	73.20	73.65	74.10
13	0	26	69.57	70.02	70.47	70.92	71.37	71.83	72.28	72.74
13	6	27	68.30	68.75	69.20	69.66	70.12	70.57	71.03	71.50
14	0	28	67.13	67.58	68.04	68.50	68.96	69.42	69.89	70.35
14	6	29	66.05	66.51	66.97	67.44	67.90	68.37	68.83	69.30
15	0	30	65.06	65.52	65.99	66.45	66.92	67.39	67.86	68.34
15	6	31	64.14	64.61	65.07	65.55	66.02	66.49	66.97	67.44
16	0	32	63.29	63.76	64.23	64.70	65.18	65.66	66.14	66.62
16	6	33	62.50	62.97	63.45	63.93	64.41	64.89	65.37	65.85
17	0	34	61.76	62.24	62.72	63.20	63.69	64.17	64.66	65.15
17	6	35	61.08	61.56	62.04	62.53	63.02	63.50	63.99	64.49
18	0	36	60.44	60.93	61.41	61.90	62.39	62.89	63.38	63.87
18	6	37	59.84	60.33	60.83	61.32	61.81	62.31	62.81	63.30
19	0	38	59.29	59.78	60.28	60.77	61.27	61.77	62.27	62.77
19	6	39	58.77	59.27	59.76	60.26	60.76	61.27	61.77	62.28
20	0	40	58.28	58.78	59.28	59.79	60.29	60.80	61.31	61.81
20	6	41	57.83	58.33	58.83	59.34	59.85	60.36	60.87	61.38
21	0	42	57.40	57.91	58.41	58.92	59.43	59.95	60.46	60.98
21	6	43	57.00	57.51	58.02	58.53	59.05	59.56	60.08	60.60
22	0	44	56.62	57.13	57.65	58.16	58.68	59.20	59.72	60.24
22	6	45	56.27	56.78	57.30	57.82	58.34	58.86	59.38	59.91
23	0	46	55.93	56.45	56.97	57.49	58.02	58.54	59.07	59.60
23	6	47	55.62	56.14	56.66	57.19	57.71	58.24	58.77	59.30
24	0	48	55.32	55.85	56.37	56.90	57.43	57.96	58.49	59.03
24	6	49	55.04	55.57	56.10	56.63	57.16	57.70	58.23	58.77
25	0	50	54.78	55.31	55.84	56.38	56.91	57.45	57.99	58.53
25	6	51	54.53	55.07	55.60	56.14	56.67	57.21	57.75	58.30
26	0	52	54.30	54.83	55.37	55.91	56.45	56.99	57.54	58.08
26	6	53	54.08	54.62	55.16	55.70	56.24	56.78	57.33	57.88
27	0	54	53.87	54.41	54.95	55.50	56.04	56.59	57.14	57.69
27	6	55	53.67	54.21	54.76	55.31	55.85	56.40	56.95	57.51
28	0	56	53.49	54.03	54.58	55.13	55.68	56.23	56.78	57.34
28	6	57	53.31	53.86	54.41	54.96	55.51	56.06	56.62	57.18
29	0	58	53.14	53.69	54.24	54.80	55.35	55.91	56.46	57.02
29	6	59	52.98	53.54	54.09	54.64	55.20	55.76	56.32	56.88
30	0	60	52.83	53.39	53.94	54.50	55.06	55.62	56.18	56.75

BASIC SEMIANNUAL PAYMENTS
FOR A $1000 LOAN

TERM YRS	MOS	PERS	11%	11⅛%	11¼%	11⅜%	11½%	11⅝%	11¾%	11⅞%
1	0	2	541.62	542.10	542.58	543.05	543.53	544.01	544.49	544.96
1	6	3	370.66	371.09	371.52	371.95	372.39	372.82	373.25	373.68
2	0	4	285.30	285.71	286.12	286.53	286.95	287.36	287.77	288.18
2	6	5	234.18	234.58	234.98	235.39	235.79	236.19	236.59	237.00
3	0	6	200.18	200.58	200.98	201.38	201.77	202.17	202.57	202.97
3	6	7	175.97	176.36	176.76	177.16	177.55	177.95	178.34	178.74
4	0	8	157.87	158.26	158.66	159.06	159.45	159.85	160.25	160.64
4	6	9	143.84	144.24	144.64	145.03	145.43	145.83	146.23	146.63
5	0	10	132.67	133.07	133.47	133.87	134.27	134.67	135.07	135.47
5	6	11	123.58	123.98	124.38	124.78	125.18	125.58	125.99	126.39
6	0	12	116.03	116.44	116.84	117.25	117.65	118.06	118.47	118.87
6	6	13	109.69	110.10	110.50	110.91	111.32	111.73	112.14	112.55
7	0	14	104.28	104.69	105.11	105.52	105.93	106.34	106.76	107.17
7	6	15	99.63	100.04	100.46	100.88	101.29	101.71	102.13	102.55
8	0	16	95.59	96.01	96.42	96.84	97.27	97.69	98.11	98.53
8	6	17	92.05	92.47	92.89	93.32	93.74	94.17	94.59	95.02
9	0	18	88.92	89.35	89.78	90.21	90.64	91.07	91.50	91.93
9	6	19	86.16	86.59	87.02	87.45	87.88	88.32	88.75	89.19
10	0	20	83.68	84.12	84.55	84.99	85.43	85.87	86.31	86.75
10	6	21	81.47	81.91	82.35	82.79	83.23	83.67	84.12	84.56
11	0	22	79.48	79.92	80.36	80.81	81.25	81.70	82.15	82.60
11	6	23	77.67	78.12	78.57	79.02	79.47	79.92	80.37	80.83
12	0	24	76.04	76.49	76.94	77.40	77.85	78.31	78.77	79.22
12	6	25	74.55	75.01	75.47	75.92	76.38	76.84	77.30	77.77
13	0	26	73.20	73.66	74.12	74.58	75.04	75.51	75.97	76.44
13	6	27	71.96	72.42	72.89	73.35	73.82	74.29	74.76	75.23
14	0	28	70.82	71.29	71.76	72.23	72.70	73.17	73.65	74.12
14	6	29	69.77	70.25	70.72	71.19	71.67	72.15	72.62	73.10
15	0	30	68.81	69.29	69.76	70.24	70.72	71.20	71.68	72.17
15	6	31	67.92	68.40	68.88	69.36	69.85	70.33	70.82	71.31
16	0	32	67.10	67.58	68.07	68.55	69.04	69.53	70.02	70.51
16	6	33	66.34	66.83	67.32	67.81	68.30	68.79	69.28	69.78
17	0	34	65.63	66.13	66.62	67.11	67.61	68.10	68.60	69.10
17	6	35	64.98	65.47	65.97	66.47	66.97	67.47	67.97	68.47
18	0	36	64.37	64.87	65.37	65.87	66.37	66.88	67.38	67.89
18	6	37	63.80	64.31	64.81	65.32	65.82	66.33	66.84	67.35
19	0	38	63.28	63.78	64.29	64.80	65.31	65.82	66.33	66.85
19	6	39	62.78	63.29	63.80	64.32	64.83	65.35	65.86	66.38
20	0	40	62.33	62.84	63.35	63.87	64.38	64.90	65.42	65.94
20	6	41	61.90	62.41	62.93	63.45	63.97	64.49	65.01	65.54
21	0	42	61.49	62.01	62.53	63.06	63.58	64.10	64.63	65.16
21	6	43	61.12	61.64	62.16	62.69	63.22	63.74	64.27	64.81
22	0	44	60.77	61.29	61.82	62.35	62.88	63.41	63.94	64.48
22	6	45	60.44	60.96	61.49	62.03	62.56	63.09	63.63	64.17
23	0	46	60.13	60.66	61.19	61.73	62.26	62.80	63.34	63.88
23	6	47	59.84	60.37	60.91	61.44	61.98	62.52	63.06	63.61
24	0	48	59.56	60.10	60.64	61.18	61.72	62.26	62.81	63.36
24	6	49	59.31	59.85	60.39	60.93	61.48	62.02	62.57	63.12
25	0	50	59.07	59.61	60.15	60.70	61.25	61.79	62.35	62.90
25	6	51	58.84	59.39	59.93	60.48	61.03	61.58	62.13	62.69
26	0	52	58.63	59.17	59.72	60.28	60.83	61.38	61.94	62.49
26	6	53	58.43	58.98	59.53	60.08	60.64	61.19	61.75	62.31
27	0	54	58.24	58.79	59.34	59.90	60.46	61.02	61.58	62.14
27	6	55	58.06	58.61	59.17	59.73	60.29	60.85	61.41	61.98
28	0	56	57.89	58.45	59.01	59.57	60.13	60.69	61.26	61.83
28	6	57	57.73	58.29	58.86	59.42	59.98	60.55	61.11	61.68
29	0	58	57.59	58.15	58.71	59.28	59.84	60.41	60.98	61.55
29	6	59	57.44	58.01	58.57	59.14	59.71	60.28	60.85	61.42
30	0	60	57.31	57.88	58.45	59.02	59.59	60.16	60.73	61.31

BASIC SEMIANNUAL PAYMENTS

FOR A $1000 LOAN

TERM YRS MOS PERS	12%	12⅛%	12¼%	12⅜%	12½%	12⅝%	12¾%	12⅞%
1 0 2	545.44	545.92	546.40	546.88	547.35	547.83	548.31	548.79
1 6 3	374.11	374.55	374.98	375.41	375.85	376.28	376.71	377.15
2 0 4	288.60	289.01	289.42	289.84	290.25	290.66	291.08	291.49
2 6 5	237.40	237.81	238.21	238.61	239.02	239.42	239.83	240.23
3 0 6	203.37	203.77	204.17	204.57	204.97	205.37	205.77	206.17
3 6 7	179.14	179.54	179.94	180.34	180.73	181.13	181.53	181.94
4 0 8	161.04	161.44	161.84	162.24	162.64	163.04	163.44	163.84
4 6 9	147.03	147.43	147.83	148.23	148.63	149.03	149.44	149.84
5 0 10	135.87	136.28	136.68	137.08	137.49	137.89	138.30	138.70
5 6 11	126.80	127.20	127.61	128.02	128.42	128.83	129.24	129.65
6 0 12	119.28	119.69	120.10	120.51	120.92	121.33	121.75	122.16
6 6 13	112.97	113.38	113.79	114.21	114.62	115.04	115.45	115.87
7 0 14	107.59	108.01	108.42	108.84	109.26	109.68	110.10	110.52
7 6 15	102.97	103.39	103.81	104.23	104.66	105.08	105.51	105.93
8 0 16	98.96	99.38	99.81	100.24	100.66	101.09	101.52	101.95
8 6 17	95.45	95.88	96.31	96.74	97.17	97.61	98.04	98.48
9 0 18	92.36	92.80	93.23	93.67	94.10	94.54	94.98	95.42
9 6 19	89.63	90.06	90.50	90.94	91.39	91.83	92.27	92.72
10 0 20	87.19	87.63	88.08	88.52	88.97	89.41	89.86	90.31
10 6 21	85.01	85.46	85.91	86.35	86.81	87.26	87.71	88.16
11 0 22	83.05	83.50	83.96	84.41	84.86	85.32	85.78	86.24
11 6 23	81.28	81.74	82.20	82.66	83.12	83.58	84.04	84.50
12 0 24	79.68	80.14	80.61	81.07	81.53	82.00	82.47	82.93
12 6 25	78.23	78.70	79.16	79.63	80.10	80.57	81.04	81.51
13 0 26	76.91	77.38	77.85	78.32	78.79	79.27	79.74	80.22
13 6 27	75.70	76.18	76.65	77.13	77.61	78.08	78.56	79.05
14 0 28	74.60	75.08	75.56	76.04	76.52	77.00	77.49	77.97
14 6 29	73.58	74.07	74.55	75.04	75.52	76.01	76.50	76.99
15 0 30	72.65	73.14	73.63	74.12	74.61	75.10	75.59	76.09
15 6 31	71.80	72.29	72.78	73.27	73.77	74.26	74.76	75.26
16 0 32	71.01	71.50	72.00	72.50	72.99	73.49	74.00	74.50
16 6 33	70.28	70.78	71.28	71.78	72.28	72.78	73.29	73.80
17 0 34	69.60	70.11	70.61	71.11	71.62	72.13	72.64	73.15
17 6 35	68.98	69.49	69.99	70.50	71.01	71.52	72.04	72.55
18 0 36	68.40	68.91	69.42	69.93	70.45	70.96	71.48	72.00
18 6 37	67.86	68.38	68.89	69.41	69.93	70.44	70.97	71.49
19 0 38	67.36	67.88	68.40	68.92	69.44	69.96	70.49	71.01
19 6 39	66.90	67.42	67.94	68.47	68.99	69.52	70.04	70.57
20 0 40	66.47	66.99	67.52	68.04	68.57	69.10	69.63	70.16
20 6 41	66.06	66.59	67.12	67.65	68.18	68.72	69.25	69.79
21 0 42	65.69	66.22	66.75	67.29	67.82	68.36	68.89	69.43
21 6 43	65.34	65.87	66.41	66.94	67.48	68.02	68.56	69.11
22 0 44	65.01	65.55	66.09	66.63	67.17	67.71	68.25	68.80
22 6 45	64.71	65.25	65.79	66.33	66.87	67.42	67.97	68.52
23 0 46	64.42	64.96	65.51	66.05	66.60	67.15	67.70	68.25
23 6 47	64.15	64.70	65.25	65.79	66.34	66.90	67.45	68.00
24 0 48	63.90	64.45	65.00	65.55	66.11	66.66	67.22	67.77
24 6 49	63.67	64.22	64.77	65.33	65.88	66.44	67.00	67.56
25 0 50	63.45	64.00	64.56	65.12	65.67	66.23	66.79	67.36
25 6 51	63.24	63.80	64.36	64.92	65.48	66.04	66.60	67.17
26 0 52	63.05	63.61	64.17	64.73	65.30	65.86	66.43	66.99
26 6 53	62.87	63.43	64.00	64.56	65.12	65.69	66.26	66.83
27 0 54	62.70	63.27	63.83	64.40	64.96	65.53	66.10	66.68
27 6 55	62.54	63.11	63.68	64.24	64.81	65.39	65.96	66.53
28 0 56	62.39	62.96	63.53	64.10	64.67	65.25	65.82	66.40
28 6 57	62.25	62.82	63.39	63.97	64.54	65.12	65.69	66.27
29 0 58	62.12	62.69	63.27	63.84	64.42	65.00	65.57	66.15
29 6 59	62.00	62.57	63.15	63.72	64.30	64.88	65.46	66.04
30 0 60	61.88	62.46	63.04	63.61	64.19	64.78	65.36	65.94

BASIC SEMIANNUAL PAYMENTS
FOR A $1000 LOAN

TERM YRS	MOS	PERS	13%	13⅛%	13¼%	13⅜%	13½%	13⅝%	13¾%	13⅞%
1	0	2	549.27	549.74	550.22	550.70	551.18	551.66	552.14	552.62
1	6	3	377.58	378.01	378.45	378.88	379.32	379.75	380.19	380.62
2	0	4	291.91	292.32	292.74	293.15	293.57	293.98	294.40	294.82
2	6	5	240.64	241.05	241.45	241.86	242.27	242.67	243.08	243.49
3	0	6	206.57	206.98	207.38	207.78	208.18	208.59	208.99	209.40
3	6	7	182.34	182.74	183.14	183.54	183.94	184.35	184.75	185.15
4	0	8	164.24	164.64	165.05	165.45	165.85	166.26	166.66	167.07
4	6	9	150.24	150.65	151.05	151.46	151.86	152.27	152.68	153.08
5	0	10	139.11	139.52	139.92	140.33	140.74	141.15	141.56	141.97
5	6	11	130.06	130.47	130.88	131.29	131.71	132.12	132.53	132.95
6	0	12	122.57	122.99	123.40	123.82	124.23	124.65	125.07	125.49
6	6	13	116.29	116.71	117.13	117.55	117.97	118.39	118.81	119.23
7	0	14	110.95	111.37	111.79	112.22	112.64	113.07	113.49	113.92
7	6	15	106.36	106.79	107.21	107.64	108.07	108.50	108.93	109.37
8	0	16	102.38	102.81	103.25	103.68	104.12	104.55	104.99	105.42
8	6	17	98.91	99.35	99.79	100.22	100.66	101.10	101.55	101.99
9	0	18	95.86	96.30	96.74	97.19	97.63	98.08	98.52	98.97
9	6	19	93.16	93.61	94.05	94.50	94.95	95.40	95.85	96.31
10	0	20	90.76	91.21	91.66	92.12	92.57	93.03	93.48	93.94
10	6	21	88.62	89.07	89.53	89.99	90.45	90.91	91.37	91.83
11	0	22	86.70	87.16	87.62	88.08	88.55	89.01	89.48	89.94
11	6	23	84.97	85.43	85.90	86.37	86.83	87.30	87.77	88.25
12	0	24	83.40	83.87	84.34	84.82	85.29	85.76	86.24	86.72
12	6	25	81.99	82.46	82.94	83.41	83.89	84.37	84.85	85.33
13	0	26	80.70	81.18	81.66	82.14	82.62	83.11	83.59	84.08
13	6	27	79.53	80.01	80.50	80.98	81.47	81.96	82.45	82.94
14	0	28	78.46	78.95	79.44	79.93	80.42	80.91	81.41	81.90
14	6	29	77.48	77.97	78.47	78.96	79.46	79.95	80.45	80.95
15	0	30	76.58	77.08	77.58	78.08	78.58	79.08	79.58	80.09
15	6	31	75.76	76.26	76.76	77.27	77.77	78.28	78.78	79.29
16	0	32	75.00	75.51	76.01	76.52	77.03	77.54	78.05	78.56
16	6	33	74.30	74.81	75.32	75.84	76.35	76.86	77.38	77.90
17	0	34	73.66	74.17	74.69	75.20	75.72	76.24	76.76	77.28
17	6	35	73.07	73.58	74.10	74.62	75.14	75.67	76.19	76.71
18	0	36	72.52	73.04	73.56	74.08	74.61	75.14	75.66	76.19
18	6	37	72.01	72.53	73.06	73.59	74.12	74.65	75.18	75.71
19	0	38	71.54	72.07	72.60	73.13	73.66	74.19	74.73	75.26
19	6	39	71.10	71.64	72.17	72.70	73.24	73.77	74.31	74.85
20	0	40	70.70	71.23	71.77	72.31	72.85	73.39	73.93	74.47
20	6	41	70.32	70.86	71.40	71.94	72.48	73.03	73.57	74.12
21	0	42	69.97	70.52	71.06	71.60	72.15	72.69	73.24	73.79
21	6	43	69.65	70.19	70.74	71.29	71.83	72.38	72.94	73.49
22	0	44	69.35	69.89	70.44	70.99	71.54	72.10	72.65	73.21
22	6	45	69.06	69.62	70.17	70.72	71.28	71.83	72.39	72.95
23	0	46	68.80	69.36	69.91	70.47	71.02	71.58	72.14	72.70
23	6	47	68.56	69.11	69.67	70.23	70.79	71.35	71.91	72.48
24	0	48	68.33	68.89	69.45	70.01	70.57	71.14	71.70	72.27
24	6	49	68.12	68.68	69.24	69.81	70.37	70.94	71.51	72.07
25	0	50	67.92	68.48	69.05	69.62	70.18	70.75	71.32	71.89
25	6	51	67.73	68.30	68.87	69.44	70.01	70.58	71.15	71.72
26	0	52	67.56	68.13	68.70	69.27	69.84	70.42	70.99	71.57
26	6	53	67.40	67.97	68.54	69.12	69.69	70.27	70.84	71.42
27	0	54	67.25	67.82	68.40	68.97	69.55	70.13	70.71	71.29
27	6	55	67.11	67.68	68.26	68.84	69.42	70.00	70.58	71.16
28	0	56	66.97	67.55	68.13	68.71	69.29	69.87	70.46	71.04
28	6	57	66.85	67.43	68.01	68.59	69.18	69.76	70.34	70.93
29	0	58	66.73	67.32	67.90	68.48	69.07	69.65	70.24	70.83
29	6	59	66.63	67.21	67.79	68.38	68.97	69.55	70.14	70.73
30	0	60	66.53	67.11	67.70	68.28	68.87	69.46	70.05	70.64

BASIC SEMIANNUAL PAYMENTS
FOR A $1000 LOAN

YRS	MOS	PERS	14%	14⅛%	14¼%	14⅜%	14½%	14⅝%	14¾%	14⅞%
1	0	2	553.10	553.58	554.06	554.53	555.01	555.49	555.97	556.45
1	6	3	381.06	381.49	381.93	382.36	382.80	383.23	383.67	384.11
2	0	4	295.23	295.65	296.07	296.48	296.90	297.32	297.74	298.15
2	6	5	243.90	244.30	244.71	245.12	245.53	245.94	246.35	246.76
3	0	6	209.80	210.21	210.61	211.02	211.42	211.83	212.24	212.64
3	6	7	185.56	185.96	186.37	186.77	187.18	187.58	187.99	188.40
4	0	8	167.47	167.88	168.28	168.69	169.10	169.51	169.91	170.32
4	6	9	153.49	153.90	154.31	154.72	155.13	155.54	155.95	156.36
5	0	10	142.38	142.79	143.21	143.62	144.03	144.45	144.86	145.28
5	6	11	133.36	133.78	134.19	134.61	135.03	135.45	135.86	136.28
6	0	12	125.91	126.33	126.75	127.17	127.59	128.01	128.43	128.86
6	6	13	119.66	120.08	120.50	120.93	121.36	121.78	122.21	122.64
7	0	14	114.35	114.78	115.21	115.64	116.07	116.50	116.93	117.37
7	6	15	109.80	110.23	110.67	111.10	111.54	111.98	112.41	112.85
8	0	16	105.86	106.30	106.74	107.18	107.62	108.06	108.51	108.95
8	6	17	102.43	102.87	103.32	103.76	104.21	104.66	105.11	105.56
9	0	18	99.42	99.87	100.32	100.77	101.22	101.67	102.12	102.58
9	6	19	96.76	97.21	97.67	98.12	98.58	99.04	99.50	99.96
10	0	20	94.40	94.86	95.32	95.78	96.24	96.70	97.17	97.63
10	6	21	92.29	92.76	93.22	93.69	94.16	94.62	95.09	95.56
11	0	22	90.41	90.88	91.35	91.82	92.29	92.77	93.24	93.72
11	6	23	88.72	89.19	89.67	90.14	90.62	91.10	91.58	92.06
12	0	24	87.19	87.67	88.15	88.63	89.12	89.60	90.08	90.57
12	6	25	85.82	86.30	86.78	87.27	87.76	88.24	88.73	89.22
13	0	26	84.57	85.05	85.54	86.03	86.53	87.02	87.51	88.01
13	6	27	83.43	83.92	84.42	84.91	85.41	85.91	86.41	86.91
14	0	28	82.40	82.89	83.39	83.89	84.39	84.90	85.40	85.90
14	6	29	81.45	81.96	82.46	82.96	83.47	83.98	84.48	84.99
15	0	30	80.59	81.10	81.61	82.11	82.62	83.14	83.65	84.16
15	6	31	79.80	80.31	80.82	81.34	81.85	82.37	82.88	83.40
16	0	32	79.08	79.59	80.11	80.63	81.15	81.66	82.19	82.71
16	6	33	78.41	78.93	79.45	79.97	80.50	81.02	81.55	82.07
17	0	34	77.80	78.32	78.85	79.37	79.90	80.43	80.96	81.49
17	6	35	77.24	77.77	78.29	78.82	79.35	79.89	80.42	80.95
18	0	36	76.72	77.25	77.78	78.32	78.85	79.39	79.92	80.46
18	6	37	76.24	76.78	77.31	77.85	78.39	78.93	79.47	80.01
19	0	38	75.80	76.34	76.88	77.42	77.96	78.50	79.05	79.59
19	6	39	75.39	75.93	76.48	77.02	77.56	78.11	78.66	79.21
20	0	40	75.01	75.56	76.11	76.65	77.20	77.75	78.30	78.85
20	6	41	74.66	75.21	75.76	76.31	76.86	77.42	77.97	78.53
21	0	42	74.34	74.89	75.44	76.00	76.55	77.11	77.67	78.22
21	6	43	74.04	74.60	75.15	75.71	76.27	76.82	77.38	77.94
22	0	44	73.76	74.32	74.88	75.44	76.00	76.56	77.12	77.69
22	6	45	73.50	74.06	74.63	75.19	75.75	76.32	76.88	77.45
23	0	46	73.26	73.83	74.39	74.96	75.52	76.09	76.66	77.23
23	6	47	73.04	73.61	74.17	74.74	75.31	75.88	76.45	77.02
24	0	48	72.84	73.40	73.97	74.54	75.11	75.69	76.26	76.83
24	6	49	72.64	73.21	73.79	74.36	74.93	75.51	76.08	76.66
25	0	50	72.46	73.04	73.61	74.19	74.76	75.34	75.92	76.50
25	6	51	72.30	72.87	73.45	74.03	74.61	75.19	75.77	76.35
26	0	52	72.14	72.72	73.30	73.88	74.46	75.04	75.62	76.21
26	6	53	72.00	72.58	73.16	73.74	74.32	74.91	75.49	76.08
27	0	54	71.87	72.45	73.03	73.61	74.20	74.78	75.37	75.96
27	6	55	71.74	72.33	72.91	73.50	74.08	74.67	75.26	75.85
28	0	56	71.63	72.21	72.80	73.38	73.97	74.56	75.15	75.74
28	6	57	71.52	72.10	72.69	73.28	73.87	74.46	75.05	75.65
29	0	58	71.42	72.01	72.60	73.19	73.78	74.37	74.96	75.56
29	6	59	71.32	71.91	72.50	73.10	73.69	74.28	74.88	75.48
30	0	60	71.23	71.83	72.42	73.01	73.61	74.20	74.80	75.40

BASIC SEMIANNUAL PAYMENTS
FOR A $1000 LOAN

TERM YRS	MOS	PERS	15%	15⅛%	15¼%	15⅜%	15½%	15⅝%	15¾%	15⅞%
1	0	2	556.93	557.41	557.89	558.37	558.85	559.33	559.81	560.29
1	6	3	384.54	384.98	385.42	385.85	386.29	386.73	387.16	387.60
2	0	4	298.57	298.99	299.41	299.83	300.25	300.67	301.09	301.51
2	6	5	247.17	247.58	247.99	248.40	248.81	249.22	249.64	250.05
3	0	6	213.05	213.46	213.87	214.27	214.68	215.09	215.50	215.91
3	6	7	188.81	189.21	189.62	190.03	190.44	190.85	191.26	191.67
4	0	8	170.73	171.14	171.55	171.96	172.37	172.78	173.20	173.61
4	6	9	156.71	157.18	157.60	158.01	158.42	158.84	159.25	159.67
5	0	10	145.69	146.11	146.52	146.94	147.36	147.78	148.20	148.61
5	6	11	136.70	137.12	137.54	137.97	138.39	138.81	139.23	139.66
6	0	12	129.28	129.71	130.13	130.56	130.99	131.41	131.84	132.27
6	6	13	123.07	123.50	123.93	124.36	124.79	125.23	125.66	126.09
7	0	14	117.80	118.24	118.67	119.11	119.55	119.98	120.42	120.86
7	6	15	113.29	113.73	114.17	114.61	115.06	115.50	115.94	116.39
8	0	16	109.40	109.84	110.29	110.73	111.18	111.63	112.08	112.53
8	6	17	106.01	106.46	106.91	107.36	107.81	108.27	108.72	109.18
9	0	18	103.03	103.49	103.95	104.40	104.86	105.32	105.78	106.24
9	6	19	100.42	100.88	101.34	101.80	102.27	102.73	103.20	103.66
10	0	20	98.10	98.56	99.03	99.50	99.97	100.44	100.91	101.38
10	6	21	96.03	96.51	96.98	97.45	97.93	98.40	98.88	99.36
11	0	22	94.19	94.67	95.15	95.63	96.11	96.59	97.07	97.55
11	6	23	92.54	93.02	93.51	93.99	94.48	94.96	95.45	95.94
12	0	24	91.06	91.54	92.03	92.52	93.01	93.50	93.99	94.49
12	6	25	89.72	90.21	90.70	91.20	91.69	92.19	92.69	93.18
13	0	26	88.50	89.00	89.50	90.00	90.50	91.00	91.50	92.01
13	6	27	87.41	87.91	88.41	88.92	89.42	89.93	90.44	90.94
14	0	28	86.41	86.92	87.42	87.93	88.44	88.95	89.47	89.98
14	6	29	85.50	86.01	86.53	87.04	87.55	88.07	88.59	89.10
15	0	30	84.68	85.19	85.71	86.23	86.75	87.27	87.79	88.31
15	6	31	83.92	84.44	84.96	85.48	86.01	86.53	87.06	87.58
16	0	32	83.23	83.76	84.28	84.81	85.33	85.86	86.39	86.92
16	6	33	82.60	83.13	83.66	84.19	84.72	85.25	85.79	86.32
17	0	34	82.02	82.55	83.09	83.62	84.16	84.69	85.23	85.77
17	6	35	81.49	82.02	82.56	83.10	83.64	84.18	84.72	85.26
18	0	36	81.00	81.54	82.08	82.62	83.17	83.71	84.26	84.80
18	6	37	80.55	81.09	81.64	82.18	82.73	83.28	83.83	84.38
19	0	38	80.14	80.68	81.23	81.78	82.33	82.88	83.44	83.99
19	6	39	79.76	80.31	80.86	81.41	81.96	82.52	83.08	83.63
20	0	40	79.41	79.96	80.51	81.07	81.63	82.19	82.74	83.30
20	6	41	79.08	79.64	80.20	80.76	81.32	81.88	82.44	83.00
21	0	42	78.78	79.34	79.90	80.47	81.03	81.59	82.16	82.72
21	6	43	78.51	79.07	79.63	80.20	80.77	81.33	81.90	82.47
22	0	44	78.25	78.82	79.38	79.95	80.52	81.09	81.66	82.23
22	6	45	78.02	78.59	79.15	79.73	80.30	80.87	81.44	82.02
23	0	46	77.80	78.37	78.94	79.52	80.09	80.66	81.24	81.82
23	6	47	77.60	78.17	78.75	79.32	79.90	80.48	81.05	81.63
24	0	48	77.41	77.99	78.56	79.14	79.72	80.30	80.88	81.46
24	6	49	77.24	77.82	78.40	78.98	79.56	80.14	80.72	81.31
25	0	50	77.08	77.66	78.24	78.82	79.41	79.99	80.58	81.16
25	6	51	76.93	77.51	78.10	78.68	79.27	79.85	80.44	81.03
26	0	52	76.79	77.38	77.96	78.55	79.14	79.73	80.31	80.90
26	6	53	76.66	77.25	77.84	78.43	79.02	79.61	80.20	80.79
27	0	54	76.55	77.13	77.72	78.32	78.91	79.50	80.09	80.68
27	6	55	76.44	77.03	77.62	78.21	78.80	79.40	79.99	80.59
28	0	56	76.33	76.93	77.52	78.11	78.71	79.30	79.90	80.50
28	6	57	76.24	76.83	77.43	78.02	78.62	79.22	79.82	80.41
29	0	58	76.15	76.75	77.35	77.94	78.54	79.14	79.74	80.34
29	6	59	76.07	76.67	77.27	77.87	78.46	79.06	79.66	80.27
30	0	60	76.00	76.59	77.19	77.79	78.39	79.00	79.60	80.20

BASIC SEMIANNUAL PAYMENTS
FOR A $1000 LOAN

TERM YRS	MOS	PERS	16%	16⅛%	16¼%	16⅜%	16½%	16⅝%	16¾%	16⅞%
1	0	2	560.77	561.25	561.74	562.22	562.70	563.18	563.66	564.14
1	6	3	388.04	388.48	388.91	389.35	389.79	390.23	390.67	391.11
2	0	4	301.93	302.35	302.77	303.19	303.61	304.03	304.45	304.87
2	6	5	250.46	250.87	251.29	251.70	252.11	252.53	252.94	253.36
3	0	6	216.32	216.73	217.14	217.55	217.96	218.38	218.79	219.20
3	6	7	192.08	192.49	192.90	193.31	193.72	194.14	194.55	194.96
4	0	8	174.02	174.43	174.85	175.26	175.67	176.09	176.50	176.92
4	6	9	160.08	160.50	160.92	161.34	161.75	162.17	162.59	163.01
5	0	10	149.03	149.45	149.88	150.30	150.72	151.14	151.56	151.99
5	6	11	140.08	140.51	140.93	141.36	141.78	142.21	142.64	143.07
6	0	12	132.70	133.13	133.56	133.99	134.42	134.86	135.29	135.72
6	6	13	126.53	126.96	127.40	127.83	128.27	128.71	129.15	129.59
7	0	14	121.30	121.74	122.18	122.63	123.07	123.51	123.96	124.40
7	6	15	116.83	117.28	117.73	118.18	118.62	119.07	119.52	119.97
8	0	16	112.98	113.43	113.89	114.34	114.79	115.25	115.70	116.16
8	6	17	109.63	110.09	110.55	111.01	111.47	111.93	112.39	112.85
9	0	18	106.71	107.17	107.63	108.10	108.56	109.03	109.50	109.97
9	6	19	104.13	104.60	105.07	105.54	106.01	106.48	106.96	107.43
10	0	20	101.86	102.33	102.81	103.28	103.76	104.24	104.72	105.20
10	6	21	99.84	100.32	100.80	101.28	101.76	102.24	102.73	103.21
11	0	22	98.04	98.52	99.01	99.50	99.98	100.47	100.96	101.45
11	6	23	96.43	96.92	97.41	97.90	98.39	98.89	99.38	99.88
12	0	24	94.98	95.48	95.98	96.47	96.97	97.47	97.97	98.47
12	6	25	93.68	94.18	94.69	95.19	95.69	96.20	96.70	97.21
13	0	26	92.51	93.02	93.52	94.03	94.54	95.05	95.56	96.07
13	6	27	91.45	91.96	92.48	92.99	93.50	94.02	94.53	95.05
14	0	28	90.49	91.01	91.53	92.04	92.56	93.08	93.60	94.12
14	6	29	89.62	90.14	90.66	91.19	91.71	92.23	92.76	93.28
15	0	30	88.83	89.36	89.88	90.41	90.94	91.46	91.99	92.52
15	6	31	88.11	88.64	89.17	89.70	90.23	90.77	91.30	91.83
16	0	32	87.46	87.99	88.52	89.06	89.59	90.13	90.67	91.21
16	6	33	86.86	87.39	87.93	88.47	89.01	89.55	90.09	90.64
17	0	34	86.31	86.85	87.39	87.94	88.48	89.02	89.57	90.12
17	6	35	85.81	86.35	86.90	87.45	87.99	88.54	89.09	89.64
18	0	36	85.35	85.90	86.45	87.00	87.55	88.10	88.66	89.21
18	6	37	84.93	85.48	86.03	86.59	87.14	87.70	88.26	88.81
19	0	38	84.54	85.10	85.66	86.21	86.77	87.33	87.89	88.45
19	6	39	84.19	84.75	85.31	85.87	86.43	86.99	87.56	88.12
20	0	40	83.87	84.43	84.99	85.55	86.12	86.68	87.25	87.82
20	6	41	83.57	84.13	84.70	85.26	85.83	86.40	86.97	87.54
21	0	42	83.29	83.86	84.43	85.00	85.57	86.14	86.71	87.29
21	6	43	83.04	83.61	84.18	84.75	85.33	85.90	86.48	87.05
22	0	44	82.81	83.38	83.95	84.53	85.11	85.68	86.26	86.84
22	6	45	82.59	83.17	83.75	84.32	84.90	85.48	86.06	86.64
23	0	46	82.39	82.97	83.55	84.13	84.71	85.30	85.88	86.46
23	6	47	82.21	82.79	83.38	83.96	84.54	85.13	85.71	86.30
24	0	48	82.05	82.63	83.21	83.80	84.38	84.97	85.56	86.14
24	6	49	81.89	82.48	83.06	83.65	84.24	84.83	85.41	86.00
25	0	50	81.75	82.34	82.92	83.51	84.10	84.69	85.28	85.88
25	6	51	81.62	82.21	82.80	83.39	83.98	84.57	85.16	85.76
26	0	52	81.49	82.09	82.68	83.27	83.86	84.46	85.05	85.65
26	6	53	81.38	81.98	82.57	83.16	83.76	84.35	84.95	85.55
27	0	54	81.28	81.87	82.47	83.07	83.66	84.26	84.86	85.46
27	6	55	81.18	81.78	82.38	82.97	83.57	84.17	84.77	85.37
28	0	56	81.09	81.69	82.29	82.89	83.49	84.09	84.69	85.29
28	6	57	81.01	81.61	82.21	82.81	83.41	84.02	84.62	85.22
29	0	58	80.94	81.54	82.14	82.74	83.34	83.95	84.55	85.16
29	6	59	80.87	81.47	82.07	82.68	83.28	83.88	84.49	85.09
30	0	60	80.80	81.41	82.01	82.62	83.22	83.83	84.43	85.04

BASIC SEMIANNUAL PAYMENTS
FOR A $1000 LOAN

TERM YRS	MOS	PERS	17%	17⅛%	17¼%	17⅜%	17½%	17⅝%	17¾%	18%
1	0	2	564.62	565.10	565.58	566.07	566.55	567.03	567.51	568.47
1	6	3	391.54	391.98	392.42	392.86	393.30	393.74	394.18	395.06
2	0	4	305.29	305.71	306.14	306.56	306.98	307.40	307.83	308.67
2	6	5	253.77	254.19	254.60	255.02	255.43	255.85	256.26	257.10
3	0	6	219.61	220.03	220.44	220.85	221.27	221.68	222.09	222.92
3	6	7	195.37	195.79	196.20	196.62	197.03	197.45	197.86	198.70
4	0	8	177.34	177.75	178.17	178.59	179.00	179.42	179.84	180.68
4	6	9	163.43	163.85	164.27	164.69	165.11	165.53	165.96	166.80
5	0	10	152.41	152.84	153.26	153.69	154.11	154.54	154.97	155.83
5	6	11	143.50	143.93	144.36	144.79	145.22	145.65	146.08	146.95
6	0	12	136.16	136.59	137.03	137.46	137.90	138.34	138.78	139.66
6	6	13	130.03	130.47	130.91	131.35	131.79	132.24	132.68	133.57
7	0	14	124.85	125.29	125.74	126.19	126.64	127.09	127.54	128.44
7	6	15	120.43	120.88	121.33	121.78	122.24	122.69	123.15	124.06
8	0	16	116.62	117.08	117.54	118.00	118.46	118.92	119.38	120.30
8	6	17	113.32	113.78	114.25	114.71	115.18	115.64	116.11	117.05
9	0	18	110.44	110.91	111.38	111.85	112.32	112.79	113.27	114.22
9	6	19	107.91	108.38	108.86	109.34	109.81	110.29	110.77	111.74
10	0	20	105.68	106.16	106.64	107.12	107.61	108.09	108.58	109.55
10	6	21	103.70	104.19	104.68	105.16	105.65	106.14	106.64	107.62
11	0	22	101.94	102.44	102.93	103.42	103.92	104.42	104.91	105.91
11	6	23	100.38	100.87	101.37	101.87	102.37	102.88	103.38	104.39
12	0	24	98.97	99.48	99.98	100.49	100.99	101.50	102.01	103.03
12	6	25	97.72	98.23	98.73	99.25	99.76	100.27	100.78	101.81
13	0	26	96.59	97.10	97.61	98.13	98.65	99.16	99.68	100.72
13	6	27	95.57	96.08	96.60	97.12	97.64	98.17	98.69	99.74
14	0	28	94.64	95.17	95.69	96.22	96.74	97.27	97.80	98.86
14	6	29	93.81	94.34	94.87	95.40	95.93	96.46	96.99	98.06
15	0	30	93.06	93.59	94.12	94.66	95.19	95.73	96.26	97.34
15	6	31	92.37	92.91	93.44	93.98	94.52	95.06	95.60	96.69
16	0	32	91.75	92.29	92.83	93.37	93.92	94.46	95.01	96.10
16	6	33	91.18	91.73	92.27	92.82	93.37	93.92	94.46	95.57
17	0	34	90.66	91.21	91.76	92.31	92.87	93.42	93.97	95.08
17	6	35	90.19	90.75	91.30	91.86	92.41	92.97	93.52	94.64
18	0	36	89.77	90.32	90.88	91.44	92.00	92.56	93.12	94.24
18	6	37	89.37	89.93	90.49	91.05	91.62	92.18	92.74	93.88
19	0	38	89.01	89.58	90.14	90.71	91.27	91.84	92.41	93.54
19	6	39	88.69	89.25	89.82	90.39	90.96	91.53	92.10	93.24
20	0	40	88.39	88.96	89.53	90.10	90.67	91.24	91.82	92.96
20	6	41	88.11	88.68	89.26	89.83	90.41	90.98	91.56	92.71
21	0	42	87.86	88.44	89.01	89.59	90.17	90.74	91.32	92.48
21	6	43	87.63	88.21	88.79	89.37	89.95	90.53	91.11	92.27
22	0	44	87.42	88.00	88.58	89.16	89.74	90.33	90.91	92.08
22	6	45	87.22	87.81	88.39	88.97	89.56	90.15	90.73	91.91
23	0	46	87.05	87.63	88.22	88.80	89.39	89.98	90.57	91.75
23	6	47	86.88	87.47	88.06	88.65	89.24	89.83	90.42	91.60
24	0	48	86.73	87.32	87.91	88.50	89.09	89.69	90.28	91.47
24	6	49	86.60	87.19	87.78	88.37	88.96	89.56	90.15	91.34
25	0	50	86.47	87.06	87.66	88.25	88.85	89.44	90.04	91.23
25	6	51	86.35	86.95	87.54	88.14	88.74	89.33	89.93	91.13
26	0	52	86.24	86.84	87.44	88.04	88.64	89.23	89.83	91.04
26	6	53	86.15	86.74	87.34	87.94	88.54	89.14	89.75	90.95
27	0	54	86.06	86.66	87.26	87.86	88.46	89.06	89.66	90.87
27	6	55	85.97	86.57	87.18	87.78	88.38	88.98	89.59	90.80
28	0	56	85.90	86.50	87.10	87.71	88.31	88.92	89.52	90.73
28	6	57	85.83	86.43	87.03	87.64	88.24	88.85	89.46	90.67
29	0	58	85.76	86.37	86.97	87.58	88.18	88.79	89.40	90.62
29	6	59	85.70	86.31	86.91	87.52	88.13	88.74	89.35	90.57
30	0	60	85.65	86.25	86.86	87.47	88.08	88.69	89.30	90.52

BASIC ANNUAL PAYMENTS
FOR A $1000 LOAN

TERM YRS	MOS	PERS	7%	7⅛%	7¼%	7⅜%	7½%	7⅝%	7¾%	7⅞%
2	0	2	553.10	554.06	555.01	555.97	556.93	557.89	558.85	559.81
3	0	3	381.06	381.93	382.80	383.67	384.54	385.42	386.29	387.16
4	0	4	295.23	296.07	296.90	297.74	298.57	299.41	300.25	301.09
5	0	5	243.90	244.71	245.53	246.35	247.17	247.99	248.81	249.64
6	0	6	209.80	210.61	211.42	212.24	213.05	213.87	214.68	215.50
7	0	7	185.56	186.37	187.18	187.99	188.81	189.62	190.44	191.26
8	0	8	167.47	168.28	169.10	169.91	170.73	171.55	172.37	173.20
9	0	9	153.49	154.31	155.13	155.95	156.77	157.60	158.42	159.25
10	0	10	142.38	143.21	144.03	144.86	145.69	146.52	147.36	148.20
11	0	11	133.36	134.19	135.03	135.86	136.70	137.54	138.39	139.23
12	0	12	125.91	126.75	127.59	128.43	129.28	130.13	130.99	131.84
13	0	13	119.66	120.50	121.36	122.21	123.07	123.93	124.79	125.66
14	0	14	114.35	115.21	116.07	116.93	117.80	118.67	119.55	120.42
15	0	15	109.80	110.67	111.54	112.41	113.29	114.17	115.06	115.94
16	0	16	105.86	106.74	107.62	108.51	109.40	110.29	111.18	112.08
17	0	17	102.43	103.32	104.21	105.11	106.01	106.91	107.81	108.72
18	0	18	99.42	100.32	101.22	102.12	103.03	103.95	104.86	105.78
19	0	19	96.76	97.67	98.58	99.50	100.42	101.34	102.27	103.20
20	0	20	94.40	95.32	96.24	97.17	98.10	99.03	99.97	100.91
21	0	21	92.29	93.22	94.16	95.09	96.03	96.98	97.93	98.88
22	0	22	90.41	91.35	92.29	93.24	94.19	95.15	96.11	97.07
23	0	23	88.72	89.67	90.62	91.58	92.54	93.51	94.48	95.45
24	0	24	87.19	88.15	89.12	90.08	91.06	92.03	93.01	93.99
25	0	25	85.82	86.78	87.76	88.73	89.72	90.70	91.69	92.69
26	0	26	84.57	85.54	86.53	87.51	88.50	89.50	90.50	91.50
27	0	27	83.43	84.42	85.41	86.41	87.41	88.41	89.42	90.44
28	0	28	82.40	83.39	84.39	85.40	86.41	87.42	88.44	89.47
29	0	29	81.45	82.46	83.47	84.48	85.50	86.53	87.55	88.59
30	0	30	80.59	81.61	82.62	83.65	84.68	85.71	86.75	87.79
31	0	31	79.80	80.82	81.85	82.88	83.92	84.96	86.01	87.06
32	0	32	79.08	80.11	81.15	82.19	83.23	84.28	85.33	86.39
33	0	33	78.41	79.45	80.50	81.55	82.60	83.66	84.72	85.79
34	0	34	77.80	78.85	79.90	80.96	82.02	83.09	84.16	85.23
35	0	35	77.24	78.29	79.35	80.42	81.49	82.56	83.64	84.72
36	0	36	76.72	77.78	78.85	79.92	81.00	82.08	83.17	84.26
37	0	37	76.24	77.31	78.39	79.47	80.55	81.64	82.73	83.83
38	0	38	75.80	76.88	77.96	79.05	80.14	81.23	82.33	83.44
39	0	39	75.39	76.48	77.56	78.66	79.76	80.86	81.96	83.08
40	0	40	75.01	76.11	77.20	78.30	79.41	80.51	81.63	82.74
41	0	41	74.66	75.76	76.86	77.97	79.08	80.20	81.32	82.44
42	0	42	74.34	75.44	76.55	77.67	78.78	79.90	81.03	82.16
43	0	43	74.04	75.15	76.27	77.38	78.51	79.63	80.77	81.90
44	0	44	73.76	74.88	76.00	77.12	78.25	79.38	80.52	81.66
45	0	45	73.50	74.63	75.75	76.88	78.02	79.15	80.30	81.44
46	0	46	73.26	74.39	75.52	76.66	77.80	78.94	80.09	81.24
47	0	47	73.04	74.17	75.31	76.45	77.60	78.75	79.90	81.05
48	0	48	72.84	73.97	75.11	76.26	77.41	78.56	79.72	80.88
49	0	49	72.64	73.79	74.93	76.08	77.24	78.40	79.56	80.72
50	0	50	72.46	73.61	74.76	75.92	77.08	78.24	79.41	80.58
51	0	51	72.30	73.45	74.61	75.77	76.93	78.10	79.27	80.44
52	0	52	72.14	73.30	74.46	75.62	76.79	77.96	79.14	80.31
53	0	53	72.00	73.16	74.32	75.49	76.66	77.84	79.02	80.20
54	0	54	71.87	73.03	74.20	75.37	76.55	77.72	78.91	80.09
55	0	55	71.74	72.91	74.08	75.26	76.44	77.62	78.80	79.99
56	0	56	71.63	72.80	73.97	75.15	76.33	77.52	78.71	79.90
57	0	57	71.52	72.69	73.87	75.05	76.24	77.43	78.62	79.82
58	0	58	71.42	72.60	73.78	74.96	76.15	77.35	78.54	79.74
59	0	59	71.32	72.50	73.69	74.88	76.07	77.27	78.46	79.66
60	0	60	71.23	72.42	73.61	74.80	76.00	77.19	78.39	79.60

BASIC ANNUAL PAYMENTS
FOR A $1000 LOAN

TERM YRS	MOS	PERS	8%	8⅛%	8¼%	8⅜%	8½%	8⅝%	8¾%	8⅞%
2	0	2	560.77	561.74	562.70	563.66	564.62	565.58	566.55	567.51
3	0	3	388.04	388.91	389.79	390.67	391.54	392.42	393.30	394.18
4	0	4	301.93	302.77	303.61	304.45	305.29	306.14	306.98	307.83
5	0	5	250.46	251.29	252.11	252.94	253.77	254.60	255.43	256.26
6	0	6	216.32	217.14	217.96	218.79	219.61	220.44	221.27	222.09
7	0	7	192.08	192.90	193.72	194.55	195.37	196.20	197.03	197.86
8	0	8	174.02	174.85	175.67	176.50	177.34	178.17	179.00	179.84
9	0	9	160.08	160.92	161.75	162.59	163.43	164.27	165.11	165.96
10	0	10	149.03	149.88	150.72	151.56	152.41	153.26	154.11	154.97
11	0	11	140.08	140.93	141.78	142.64	143.50	144.36	145.22	146.08
12	0	12	132.70	133.56	134.42	135.29	136.16	137.03	137.90	138.78
13	0	13	126.53	127.40	128.27	129.15	130.03	130.91	131.79	132.68
14	0	14	121.30	122.18	123.07	123.96	124.85	125.74	126.64	127.54
15	0	15	116.83	117.73	118.62	119.52	120.43	121.33	122.24	123.15
16	0	16	112.98	113.89	114.79	115.70	116.62	117.54	118.46	119.38
17	0	17	109.63	110.55	111.47	112.39	113.32	114.25	115.18	116.11
18	0	18	106.71	107.63	108.56	109.50	110.44	111.38	112.32	113.27
19	0	19	104.13	105.07	106.01	106.96	107.91	108.86	109.81	110.77
20	0	20	101.86	102.81	103.76	104.72	105.68	106.64	107.61	108.58
21	0	21	99.84	100.80	101.76	102.73	103.70	104.68	105.65	106.64
22	0	22	98.04	99.01	99.98	100.96	101.94	102.93	103.92	104.91
23	0	23	96.43	97.41	98.39	99.38	100.38	101.37	102.37	103.38
24	0	24	94.98	95.98	96.97	97.97	98.97	99.98	100.99	102.01
25	0	25	93.68	94.69	95.69	96.70	97.72	98.73	99.76	100.78
26	0	26	92.51	93.52	94.54	95.56	96.59	97.61	98.65	99.68
27	0	27	91.45	92.48	93.50	94.53	95.57	96.60	97.64	98.69
28	0	28	90.49	91.53	92.56	93.60	94.64	95.69	96.74	97.80
29	0	29	89.62	90.66	91.71	92.76	93.81	94.87	95.93	96.99
30	0	30	88.83	89.88	90.94	91.99	93.06	94.12	95.19	96.26
31	0	31	88.11	89.17	90.23	91.30	92.37	93.44	94.52	95.60
32	0	32	87.46	88.52	89.59	90.67	91.75	92.83	93.92	95.01
33	0	33	86.86	87.93	89.01	90.09	91.18	92.27	93.37	94.46
34	0	34	86.31	87.39	88.48	89.57	90.66	91.76	92.87	93.97
35	0	35	85.81	86.90	87.99	89.09	90.19	91.30	92.41	93.52
36	0	36	85.35	86.45	87.55	88.66	89.77	90.88	92.00	93.12
37	0	37	84.93	86.03	87.14	88.26	89.37	90.49	91.62	92.74
38	0	38	84.54	85.66	86.77	87.89	89.01	90.14	91.27	92.41
39	0	39	84.19	85.31	86.43	87.56	88.69	89.82	90.96	92.10
40	0	40	83.87	84.99	86.12	87.25	88.39	89.53	90.67	91.82
41	0	41	83.57	84.70	85.83	86.97	88.11	89.26	90.41	91.56
42	0	42	83.29	84.43	85.57	86.71	87.86	89.01	90.17	91.32
43	0	43	83.04	84.18	85.33	86.48	87.63	88.79	89.95	91.11
44	0	44	82.81	83.95	85.11	86.26	87.42	88.58	89.74	90.91
45	0	45	82.59	83.75	84.90	86.06	87.22	88.39	89.56	90.73
46	0	46	82.39	83.55	84.71	85.88	87.05	88.22	89.39	90.57
47	0	47	82.21	83.38	84.54	85.71	86.88	88.06	89.24	90.42
48	0	48	82.05	83.21	84.38	85.56	86.73	87.91	89.09	90.28
49	0	49	81.89	83.06	84.24	85.41	86.60	87.78	88.96	90.15
50	0	50	81.75	82.92	84.10	85.28	86.47	87.66	88.85	90.04
51	0	51	81.62	82.80	83.98	85.16	86.35	87.54	88.74	89.93
52	0	52	81.49	82.68	83.86	85.05	86.24	87.44	88.64	89.83
53	0	53	81.38	82.57	83.76	84.95	86.15	87.34	88.54	89.75
54	0	54	81.28	82.47	83.66	84.86	86.06	87.26	88.46	89.66
55	0	55	81.18	82.38	83.57	84.77	85.97	87.18	88.38	89.59
56	0	56	81.09	82.29	83.49	84.69	85.90	87.10	88.31	89.52
57	0	57	81.01	82.21	83.41	84.62	85.83	87.03	88.24	89.46
58	0	58	80.94	82.14	83.34	84.55	85.76	86.97	88.18	89.40
59	0	59	80.87	82.07	83.28	84.49	85.70	86.91	88.13	89.35
60	0	60	80.80	82.01	83.22	84.43	85.65	86.86	88.08	89.30

BASIC ANNUAL PAYMENTS
FOR A $1000 LOAN

TERM YRS	MOS	PERS	9%	9⅛%	9¼%	9⅜%	9½%	9⅝%	9¾%	9⅞%
2	0	2	568.47	569.44	570.40	571.37	572.33	573.30	574.26	575.23
3	0	3	395.06	395.94	396.82	397.70	398.58	399.47	400.35	401.24
4	0	4	308.67	309.52	310.37	311.22	312.07	312.92	313.77	314.62
5	0	5	257.10	257.93	258.77	259.60	260.44	261.28	262.12	262.96
6	0	6	222.92	223.76	224.59	225.42	226.26	227.09	227.93	228.77
7	0	7	198.70	199.53	200.37	201.20	202.04	202.88	203.72	204.57
8	0	8	180.68	181.52	182.36	183.21	184.05	184.90	185.75	186.60
9	0	9	166.80	167.65	168.50	169.36	170.21	171.07	171.92	172.78
10	0	10	155.83	156.68	157.54	158.41	159.27	160.14	161.01	161.88
11	0	11	146.95	147.82	148.69	149.57	150.44	151.32	152.20	153.08
12	0	12	139.66	140.54	141.42	142.30	143.19	144.08	144.98	145.87
13	0	13	133.57	134.46	135.36	136.26	137.16	138.06	138.97	139.87
14	0	14	128.44	129.34	130.25	131.16	132.07	132.99	133.91	134.83
15	0	15	124.06	124.98	125.90	126.82	127.75	128.68	129.61	130.54
16	0	16	120.30	121.23	122.17	123.10	124.04	124.98	125.92	126.87
17	0	17	117.05	117.99	118.94	119.89	120.84	121.79	122.75	123.71
18	0	18	114.22	115.17	116.13	117.09	118.05	119.02	119.99	120.96
19	0	19	111.74	112.70	113.67	114.64	115.62	116.60	117.58	118.56
20	0	20	109.55	110.53	111.51	112.49	113.48	114.47	115.47	116.46
21	0	21	107.62	108.61	109.60	110.60	111.60	112.60	113.61	114.62
22	0	22	105.91	106.91	107.91	108.92	109.93	110.95	111.96	112.99
23	0	23	104.39	105.40	106.41	107.43	108.45	109.48	110.51	111.54
24	0	24	103.03	104.05	105.08	106.11	107.14	108.18	109.21	110.26
25	0	25	101.81	102.84	103.88	104.92	105.96	107.01	108.06	109.12
26	0	26	100.72	101.76	102.81	103.86	104.91	105.97	107.03	108.10
27	0	27	99.74	100.79	101.85	102.91	103.97	105.04	106.11	107.19
28	0	28	98.86	99.92	100.99	102.06	103.13	104.21	105.29	106.37
29	0	29	98.06	99.13	100.21	101.29	102.37	103.46	104.54	105.64
30	0	30	97.34	98.42	99.51	100.59	101.69	102.78	103.88	104.98
31	0	31	96.69	97.78	98.87	99.97	101.07	102.17	103.28	104.39
32	0	32	96.10	97.20	98.30	99.40	100.51	101.62	102.74	103.86
33	0	33	95.57	96.67	97.78	98.89	100.01	101.13	102.25	103.38
34	0	34	95.08	96.19	97.31	98.43	99.55	100.68	101.81	102.94
35	0	35	94.64	95.76	96.89	98.01	99.14	100.28	101.41	102.55
36	0	36	94.24	95.37	96.50	97.63	98.77	99.91	101.05	102.20
37	0	37	93.88	95.01	96.15	97.29	98.43	99.58	100.73	101.88
38	0	38	93.54	94.68	95.83	96.97	98.12	99.28	100.43	101.59
39	0	39	93.24	94.39	95.54	96.69	97.85	99.00	100.17	101.33
40	0	40	92.96	94.12	95.27	96.43	97.59	98.76	99.92	101.09
41	0	41	92.71	93.87	95.03	96.20	97.36	98.53	99.70	100.88
42	0	42	92.48	93.65	94.81	95.98	97.15	98.33	99.50	100.68
43	0	43	92.27	93.44	94.61	95.79	96.96	98.14	99.32	100.51
44	0	44	92.08	93.25	94.43	95.61	96.79	97.97	99.16	100.35
45	0	45	91.91	93.08	94.26	95.45	96.63	97.82	99.01	100.20
46	0	46	91.75	92.93	94.11	95.30	96.49	97.68	98.87	100.07
47	0	47	91.60	92.79	93.97	95.17	96.36	97.55	98.75	99.95
48	0	48	91.47	92.66	93.85	95.04	96.24	97.44	98.64	99.84
49	0	49	91.34	92.54	93.73	94.93	96.13	97.33	98.54	99.74
50	0	50	91.23	92.43	93.63	94.83	96.03	97.24	98.44	99.65
51	0	51	91.13	92.33	93.53	94.74	95.94	97.15	98.36	99.57
52	0	52	91.04	92.24	93.44	94.65	95.86	97.07	98.28	99.50
53	0	53	90.95	92.16	93.36	94.57	95.79	97.00	98.21	99.43
54	0	54	90.87	92.08	93.29	94.50	95.72	96.93	98.15	99.37
55	0	55	90.80	92.01	93.22	94.44	95.65	96.87	98.09	99.31
56	0	56	90.73	91.95	93.16	94.38	95.60	96.82	98.04	99.26
57	0	57	90.67	91.89	93.11	94.33	95.55	96.77	97.99	99.22
58	0	58	90.62	91.83	93.05	94.28	95.50	96.72	97.95	99.18
59	0	59	90.57	91.79	93.01	94.23	95.46	96.68	97.91	99.14
60	0	60	90.52	91.74	92.97	94.19	95.42	96.64	97.87	99.10

BASIC ANNUAL PAYMENTS
FOR A $1000 LOAN

YRS	MOS	PERS	10%	10⅛%	10¼%	10⅜%	10½%	10⅝%	10¾%	10⅞%
2	0	2	576.20	577.16	578.13	579.10	580.06	581.03	582.00	582.97
3	0	3	402.12	403.01	403.89	404.78	405.66	406.55	407.44	408.33
4	0	4	315.48	316.33	317.18	318.04	318.90	319.75	320.61	321.47
5	0	5	263.80	264.65	265.49	266.33	267.18	268.03	268.88	269.73
6	0	6	229.61	230.45	231.30	232.14	232.99	233.83	234.68	235.53
7	0	7	205.41	206.26	207.10	207.95	208.80	209.66	210.51	211.36
8	0	8	187.45	188.30	189.16	190.02	190.87	191.73	192.60	193.46
9	0	9	173.65	174.51	175.37	176.24	177.11	177.98	178.86	179.73
10	0	10	162.75	163.63	164.50	165.38	166.26	167.15	168.03	168.92
11	0	11	153.97	154.86	155.74	156.64	157.53	158.43	159.32	160.22
12	0	12	146.77	147.67	148.57	149.47	150.38	151.29	152.20	153.12
13	0	13	140.78	141.70	142.61	143.53	144.45	145.37	146.30	147.23
14	0	14	135.75	136.68	137.61	138.54	139.47	140.41	141.35	142.29
15	0	15	131.48	132.42	133.36	134.31	135.25	136.20	137.16	138.11
16	0	16	127.82	128.77	129.73	130.69	131.65	132.61	133.58	134.55
17	0	17	124.67	125.63	126.60	127.58	128.55	129.53	130.51	131.49
18	0	18	121.94	122.91	123.90	124.88	125.87	126.86	127.85	128.85
19	0	19	119.55	120.54	121.54	122.54	123.54	124.54	125.55	126.56
20	0	20	117.46	118.47	119.48	120.49	121.50	122.51	123.53	124.56
21	0	21	115.63	116.65	117.66	118.69	119.71	120.74	121.77	122.81
22	0	22	114.01	115.04	116.07	117.10	118.14	119.18	120.22	121.27
23	0	23	112.58	113.62	114.66	115.70	116.75	117.80	118.86	119.92
24	0	24	111.30	112.35	113.41	114.46	115.52	116.59	117.65	118.72
25	0	25	110.17	111.23	112.30	113.36	114.43	115.51	116.58	117.66
26	0	26	109.16	110.23	111.31	112.39	113.47	114.55	115.64	116.73
27	0	27	108.26	109.34	110.43	111.51	112.60	113.70	114.79	115.89
28	0	28	107.46	108.55	109.64	110.74	111.83	112.94	114.04	115.15
29	0	29	106.73	107.83	108.93	110.04	111.15	112.26	113.37	114.49
30	0	30	106.08	107.19	108.30	109.42	110.53	111.65	112.78	113.90
31	0	31	105.50	106.62	107.74	108.86	109.98	111.11	112.24	113.38
32	0	32	104.98	106.10	107.23	108.36	109.49	110.63	111.76	112.90
33	0	33	104.50	105.64	106.77	107.91	109.05	110.19	111.34	112.48
34	0	34	104.08	105.22	106.36	107.50	108.65	109.80	110.95	112.11
35	0	35	103.69	104.84	105.99	107.14	108.29	109.45	110.61	111.77
36	0	36	103.35	104.50	105.65	106.81	107.97	109.13	110.30	111.47
37	0	37	103.03	104.19	105.35	106.52	107.68	108.85	110.02	111.19
38	0	38	102.75	103.92	105.08	106.25	107.42	108.60	109.77	110.95
39	0	39	102.50	103.67	104.84	106.01	107.19	108.37	109.55	110.73
40	0	40	102.26	103.44	104.62	105.79	106.98	108.16	109.35	110.53
41	0	41	102.05	103.23	104.42	105.60	106.79	107.97	109.16	110.36
42	0	42	101.86	103.05	104.24	105.42	106.61	107.81	109.00	110.20
43	0	43	101.69	102.88	104.07	105.26	106.46	107.66	108.85	110.05
44	0	44	101.54	102.73	103.92	105.12	106.32	107.52	108.72	109.93
45	0	45	101.40	102.59	103.79	104.99	106.19	107.40	108.60	109.81
46	0	46	101.27	102.47	103.67	104.87	106.08	107.29	108.49	109.71
47	0	47	101.15	102.36	103.56	104.77	105.98	107.19	108.40	109.61
48	0	48	101.05	102.25	103.46	104.67	105.88	107.10	108.31	109.53
49	0	49	100.95	102.16	103.37	104.58	105.80	107.01	108.23	109.45
50	0	50	100.86	102.08	103.29	104.51	105.72	106.94	108.16	109.38
51	0	51	100.79	102.00	103.22	104.43	105.65	106.87	108.10	109.32
52	0	52	100.71	101.93	103.15	104.37	105.59	106.82	108.04	109.26
53	0	53	100.65	101.87	103.09	104.31	105.54	106.76	107.99	109.21
54	0	54	100.59	101.81	103.04	104.26	105.49	106.71	107.94	109.17
55	0	55	100.54	101.76	102.99	104.21	105.44	106.67	107.90	109.13
56	0	56	100.49	101.71	102.94	104.17	105.40	106.63	107.86	109.09
57	0	57	100.44	101.67	102.90	104.13	105.36	106.59	107.82	109.06
58	0	58	100.40	101.63	102.86	104.09	105.33	106.56	107.79	109.03
59	0	59	100.37	101.60	102.83	104.06	105.30	106.53	107.77	109.00
60	0	60	100.33	101.57	102.80	104.03	105.27	106.50	107.74	108.98

BASIC ANNUAL PAYMENTS

FOR A $1000 LOAN

YRS	MOS	PERS	11%	11⅛%	11¼%	11⅜%	11½%	11⅝%	11¾%	11⅞%
2	0	2	583.94	584.91	585.88	586.85	587.82	588.79	589.76	590.73
3	0	3	409.22	410.11	411.00	411.89	412.78	413.67	414.57	415.46
4	0	4	322.33	323.19	324.05	324.92	325.78	326.64	327.51	328.37
5	0	5	270.58	271.43	272.28	273.13	273.99	274.84	275.70	276.56
6	0	6	236.38	237.23	238.09	238.94	239.80	240.65	241.51	242.37
7	0	7	212.22	213.08	213.94	214.80	215.66	216.52	217.39	218.25
8	0	8	194.33	195.19	196.06	196.93	197.80	198.68	199.55	200.43
9	0	9	180.61	181.49	182.37	183.25	184.13	185.02	185.90	186.79
10	0	10	169.81	170.70	171.59	172.49	173.38	174.28	175.18	176.08
11	0	11	161.13	162.03	162.94	163.85	164.76	165.67	166.58	167.50
12	0	12	154.03	154.95	155.87	156.79	157.72	158.65	159.58	160.51
13	0	13	148.16	149.09	150.02	150.96	151.90	152.84	153.79	154.73
14	0	14	143.23	144.18	145.13	146.08	147.04	147.99	148.95	149.91
15	0	15	139.07	140.03	140.99	141.96	142.93	143.90	144.87	145.85
16	0	16	135.52	136.50	137.47	138.45	139.44	140.42	141.41	142.40
17	0	17	132.48	133.47	134.46	135.45	136.45	137.45	138.45	139.45
18	0	18	129.85	130.85	131.85	132.86	133.87	134.89	135.90	136.92
19	0	19	127.57	128.58	129.60	130.62	131.65	132.67	133.70	134.73
20	0	20	125.58	126.61	127.64	128.67	129.71	130.75	131.79	132.84
21	0	21	123.84	124.88	125.93	126.97	128.02	129.07	130.13	131.19
22	0	22	122.32	123.37	124.43	125.48	126.54	127.61	128.67	129.74
23	0	23	120.98	122.04	123.11	124.18	125.25	126.32	127.40	128.48
24	0	24	119.79	120.87	121.94	123.02	124.11	125.19	126.28	127.37
25	0	25	118.75	119.83	120.92	122.01	123.10	124.20	125.30	126.40
26	0	26	117.82	118.91	120.01	121.11	122.22	123.32	124.43	125.54
27	0	27	116.99	118.10	119.21	120.32	121.43	122.55	123.66	124.79
28	0	28	116.26	117.38	118.49	119.61	120.73	121.86	122.99	124.12
29	0	29	115.61	116.73	117.86	118.99	120.12	121.25	122.39	123.52
30	0	30	115.03	116.16	117.29	118.43	119.57	120.71	121.85	123.00
31	0	31	114.51	115.65	116.79	117.94	119.08	120.23	121.38	122.54
32	0	32	114.05	115.19	116.34	117.49	118.65	119.80	120.96	122.12
33	0	33	113.63	114.79	115.94	117.10	118.26	119.42	120.59	121.76
34	0	34	113.26	114.42	115.59	116.75	117.92	119.09	120.26	121.43
35	0	35	112.93	114.10	115.27	116.44	117.61	118.78	119.96	121.14
36	0	36	112.64	113.81	114.98	116.16	117.34	118.52	119.70	120.88
37	0	37	112.37	113.55	114.73	115.91	117.09	118.28	119.46	120.65
38	0	38	112.13	113.31	114.50	115.68	116.87	118.06	119.26	120.45
39	0	39	111.92	113.10	114.29	115.48	116.68	117.87	119.07	120.27
40	0	40	111.72	112.92	114.11	115.30	116.50	117.70	118.90	120.10
41	0	41	111.55	112.75	113.95	115.14	116.35	117.55	118.75	119.96
42	0	42	111.40	112.60	113.80	115.00	116.21	117.41	118.62	119.83
43	0	43	111.26	112.46	113.67	114.87	116.08	117.29	118.50	119.72
44	0	44	111.13	112.34	113.55	114.76	115.97	117.18	118.40	119.61
45	0	45	111.02	112.23	113.44	114.65	115.87	117.09	118.30	119.52
46	0	46	110.92	112.13	113.35	114.56	115.78	117.00	118.22	119.44
47	0	47	110.83	112.04	113.26	114.48	115.70	116.92	118.14	119.37
48	0	48	110.74	111.96	113.18	114.40	115.63	116.85	118.08	119.30
49	0	49	110.67	111.89	113.11	114.34	115.56	116.79	118.02	119.24
50	0	50	110.60	111.83	113.05	114.28	115.50	116.73	117.96	119.19
51	0	51	110.54	111.77	113.00	114.22	115.45	116.68	117.91	119.14
52	0	52	110.49	111.72	112.95	114.18	115.41	116.64	117.87	119.10
53	0	53	110.44	111.67	112.90	114.13	115.37	116.60	117.83	119.07
54	0	54	110.40	111.63	112.86	114.09	115.33	116.56	117.80	119.03
55	0	55	110.36	111.59	112.83	114.06	115.29	116.53	117.77	119.00
56	0	56	110.32	111.56	112.79	114.03	115.26	116.50	117.74	118.98
57	0	57	110.29	111.53	112.76	114.00	115.24	116.48	117.71	118.95
58	0	58	110.26	111.50	112.74	113.98	115.21	116.45	117.69	118.93
59	0	59	110.24	111.48	112.71	113.95	115.19	116.43	117.67	118.91
60	0	60	110.22	111.45	112.69	113.93	115.17	116.41	117.65	118.90

BASIC ANNUAL PAYMENTS
FOR A $1000 LOAN

TERM YRS	MOS	PERS	12%	12⅛%	12¼%	12⅜%	12½%	12⅝%	12¾%	12⅞%
2	0	2	591.70	592.68	593.65	594.62	595.59	596.57	597.54	598.51
3	0	3	416.35	417.25	418.14	419.04	419.94	420.83	421.73	422.63
4	0	4	329.24	330.11	330.97	331.84	332.71	333.58	334.45	335.33
5	0	5	277.41	278.27	279.13	280.00	280.86	281.72	282.59	283.45
6	0	6	243.23	244.09	244.96	245.82	246.68	247.55	248.42	249.29
7	0	7	219.12	219.99	220.86	221.73	222.61	223.48	224.36	225.24
8	0	8	201.31	202.19	203.07	203.95	204.84	205.72	206.61	207.50
9	0	9	187.68	188.58	189.47	190.37	191.27	192.16	193.07	193.97
10	0	10	176.99	177.90	178.80	179.71	180.63	181.54	182.46	183.37
11	0	11	168.42	169.34	170.26	171.19	172.12	173.05	173.98	174.91
12	0	12	161.44	162.38	163.32	164.26	165.20	166.14	167.09	168.04
13	0	13	155.68	156.63	157.59	158.54	159.50	160.46	161.42	162.39
14	0	14	150.88	151.84	152.81	153.78	154.76	155.73	156.71	157.69
15	0	15	146.83	147.81	148.79	149.78	150.77	151.76	152.75	153.75
16	0	16	143.40	144.39	145.39	146.39	147.39	148.40	149.41	150.42
17	0	17	140.46	141.47	142.48	143.50	144.52	145.54	146.56	147.59
18	0	18	137.94	138.97	139.99	141.02	142.05	143.09	144.12	145.16
19	0	19	135.77	136.81	137.85	138.89	139.93	140.98	142.03	143.08
20	0	20	133.88	134.93	135.99	137.04	138.10	139.16	140.22	141.29
21	0	21	132.25	133.31	134.37	135.44	136.51	137.58	138.66	139.74
22	0	22	130.82	131.89	132.97	134.05	135.13	136.21	137.30	138.39
23	0	23	129.56	130.65	131.74	132.83	133.92	135.02	136.12	137.22
24	0	24	128.47	129.57	130.66	131.77	132.87	133.98	135.09	136.20
25	0	25	127.50	128.61	129.72	130.83	131.95	133.07	134.18	135.31
26	0	26	126.66	127.77	128.89	130.01	131.14	132.27	133.39	134.53
27	0	27	125.91	127.04	128.16	129.29	130.43	131.56	132.70	133.84
28	0	28	125.25	126.38	127.52	128.66	129.80	130.95	132.09	133.24
29	0	29	124.67	125.81	126.95	128.10	129.25	130.40	131.56	132.71
30	0	30	124.15	125.30	126.45	127.61	128.77	129.92	131.09	132.25
31	0	31	123.69	124.85	126.01	127.17	128.34	129.50	130.67	131.84
32	0	32	123.29	124.45	125.62	126.79	127.96	129.13	130.31	131.48
33	0	33	122.93	124.10	125.27	126.45	127.62	128.80	129.98	131.17
34	0	34	122.61	123.78	124.96	126.14	127.33	128.51	129.70	130.89
35	0	35	122.32	123.50	124.69	125.88	127.06	128.25	129.45	130.64
36	0	36	122.07	123.26	124.45	125.64	126.83	128.03	129.22	130.42
37	0	37	121.84	123.04	124.23	125.43	126.63	127.83	129.03	130.23
38	0	38	121.64	122.84	124.04	125.24	126.44	127.65	128.85	130.06
39	0	39	121.47	122.67	123.87	125.08	126.28	127.49	128.70	129.91
40	0	40	121.31	122.51	123.72	124.93	126.14	127.35	128.56	129.78
41	0	41	121.17	122.38	123.59	124.80	126.01	127.23	128.44	129.66
42	0	42	121.04	122.25	123.47	124.68	125.90	127.12	128.34	129.56
43	0	43	120.93	122.15	123.36	124.58	125.80	127.02	128.24	129.46
44	0	44	120.83	122.05	123.27	124.49	125.71	126.93	128.16	129.38
45	0	45	120.74	121.96	123.18	124.41	125.63	126.86	128.08	129.31
46	0	46	120.66	121.89	123.11	124.34	125.56	126.79	128.02	129.25
47	0	47	120.59	121.82	123.04	124.27	125.50	126.73	127.96	129.19
48	0	48	120.53	121.76	122.98	124.21	125.44	126.68	127.91	129.14
49	0	49	120.47	121.70	122.93	124.16	125.40	126.63	127.86	129.10
50	0	50	120.42	121.65	122.89	124.12	125.35	126.59	127.82	129.06
51	0	51	120.38	121.61	122.84	124.08	125.31	126.55	127.79	129.02
52	0	52	120.34	121.57	122.81	124.04	125.28	126.52	127.75	128.99
53	0	53	120.30	121.54	122.77	124.01	125.25	126.49	127.73	128.97
54	0	54	120.27	121.51	122.74	123.98	125.22	126.46	127.70	128.94
55	0	55	120.24	121.48	122.72	123.96	125.20	126.44	127.68	128.92
56	0	56	120.22	121.46	122.69	123.94	125.18	126.42	127.66	128.90
57	0	57	120.19	121.43	122.67	123.92	125.16	126.40	127.64	128.88
58	0	58	120.17	121.41	122.66	123.90	125.14	126.38	127.63	128.87
59	0	59	120.15	121.40	122.64	123.88	125.13	126.37	127.61	128.86
60	0	60	120.14	121.38	122.62	123.87	125.11	126.36	127.60	128.84

BASIC ANNUAL PAYMENTS

FOR A $1000 LOAN

TERM YRS	MOS	PERS	13%	13⅛%	13¼%	13⅜%	13½%	13⅝%	13¾%	13⅞%
2	0	2	599.49	600.46	601.44	602.41	603.39	604.37	605.34	606.32
3	0	3	423.53	424.43	425.33	426.23	427.13	428.03	428.93	429.83
4	0	4	336.20	337.07	337.95	338.82	339.70	340.57	341.45	342.33
5	0	5	284.32	285.19	286.06	286.93	287.80	288.67	289.54	290.41
6	0	6	250.16	251.03	251.90	252.78	253.65	254.53	255.40	256.28
7	0	7	226.12	227.00	227.88	228.76	229.65	230.53	231.42	232.31
8	0	8	208.39	209.28	210.18	211.07	211.97	212.87	213.77	214.67
9	0	9	194.87	195.78	196.69	197.60	198.51	199.42	200.34	201.26
10	0	10	184.29	185.22	186.14	187.06	187.99	188.92	189.85	190.78
11	0	11	175.85	176.78	177.72	178.66	179.61	180.55	181.50	182.45
12	0	12	168.99	169.94	170.90	171.86	172.82	173.78	174.74	175.71
13	0	13	163.36	164.32	165.30	166.27	167.24	168.22	169.20	170.18
14	0	14	158.67	159.66	160.64	161.63	162.63	163.62	164.62	165.61
15	0	15	154.75	155.75	156.75	157.75	158.76	159.77	160.78	161.80
16	0	16	151.43	152.45	153.46	154.48	155.51	156.53	157.56	158.59
17	0	17	148.61	149.64	150.68	151.71	152.75	153.79	154.83	155.87
18	0	18	146.21	147.25	148.30	149.35	150.40	151.45	152.51	153.57
19	0	19	144.14	145.20	146.26	147.32	148.38	149.45	150.52	151.59
20	0	20	142.36	143.43	144.50	145.58	146.66	147.74	148.82	149.90
21	0	21	140.82	141.90	142.99	144.08	145.17	146.26	147.35	148.45
22	0	22	139.48	140.58	141.68	142.78	143.88	144.98	146.09	147.20
23	0	23	138.32	139.43	140.54	141.65	142.76	143.88	144.99	146.11
24	0	24	137.31	138.43	139.55	140.67	141.79	142.92	144.05	145.18
25	0	25	136.43	137.56	138.69	139.82	140.95	142.09	143.22	144.36
26	0	26	135.66	136.80	137.93	139.07	140.22	141.36	142.51	143.65
27	0	27	134.98	136.13	137.28	138.42	139.57	140.73	141.88	143.04
28	0	28	134.39	135.54	136.70	137.86	139.02	140.18	141.34	142.50
29	0	29	133.87	135.03	136.20	137.36	138.53	139.69	140.86	142.04
30	0	30	133.42	134.58	135.75	136.92	138.10	139.27	140.45	141.63
31	0	31	133.01	134.19	135.36	136.54	137.72	138.90	140.09	141.27
32	0	32	132.66	133.84	135.02	136.21	137.39	138.58	139.77	140.96
33	0	33	132.35	133.54	134.72	135.91	137.10	138.30	139.49	140.69
34	0	34	132.08	133.27	134.46	135.66	136.85	138.05	139.25	140.45
35	0	35	131.83	133.03	134.23	135.43	136.63	137.83	139.04	140.24
36	0	36	131.62	132.82	134.02	135.23	136.43	137.64	138.85	140.06
37	0	37	131.43	132.64	133.85	135.05	136.26	137.47	138.68	139.90
38	0	38	131.27	132.48	133.69	134.90	136.11	137.33	138.54	139.76
39	0	39	131.12	132.33	133.55	134.76	135.98	137.20	138.42	139.63
40	0	40	130.99	132.21	133.42	134.64	135.86	137.08	138.30	139.53
41	0	41	130.88	132.10	133.32	134.54	135.76	136.98	138.21	139.43
42	0	42	130.78	132.00	133.22	134.44	135.67	136.90	138.12	139.35
43	0	43	130.69	131.91	133.14	134.36	135.59	136.82	138.05	139.28
44	0	44	130.61	131.84	133.06	134.29	135.52	136.75	137.98	139.21
45	0	45	130.54	131.77	133.00	134.23	135.46	136.69	137.92	139.16
46	0	46	130.48	131.71	132.94	134.17	135.40	136.64	137.87	139.11
47	0	47	130.42	131.66	132.89	134.12	135.36	136.59	137.83	139.06
48	0	48	130.37	131.61	132.84	134.08	135.32	136.55	137.79	139.03
49	0	49	130.33	131.57	132.80	134.04	135.28	136.52	137.75	138.99
50	0	50	130.29	131.53	132.77	134.01	135.25	136.48	137.72	138.96
51	0	51	130.26	131.50	132.74	133.98	135.22	136.46	137.70	138.94
52	0	52	130.23	131.47	132.71	133.95	135.19	136.43	137.67	138.92
53	0	53	130.21	131.45	132.69	133.93	135.17	136.41	137.65	138.90
54	0	54	130.18	131.42	132.67	133.91	135.15	136.39	137.64	138.88
55	0	55	130.16	131.40	132.65	133.89	135.13	136.38	137.62	138.86
56	0	56	130.14	131.39	132.63	133.87	135.12	136.36	137.61	138.85
57	0	57	130.13	131.37	132.62	133.86	135.10	136.35	137.59	138.84
58	0	58	130.11	131.36	132.60	133.85	135.09	136.34	137.58	138.83
59	0	59	130.10	131.35	132.59	133.84	135.08	136.33	137.57	138.82
60	0	60	130.09	131.34	132.58	133.83	135.07	136.32	137.57	138.81

BASIC ANNUAL PAYMENTS
FOR A $1000 LOAN

YRS	MOS	PERS	14%	14⅛%	14¼%	14⅜%	14½%	14⅝%	14¾%	14⅞%
2	0	2	607.29	608.27	609.25	610.23	611.21	612.18	613.16	614.14
3	0	3	430.74	431.64	432.54	433.45	434.35	435.26	436.17	437.07
4	0	4	343.21	344.09	344.97	345.85	346.73	347.62	348.50	349.39
5	0	5	291.29	292.16	293.04	293.92	294.80	295.68	296.56	297.44
6	0	6	257.16	258.04	258.93	259.81	260.69	261.58	262.47	263.35
7	0	7	233.20	234.09	234.98	235.88	236.77	237.67	238.57	239.46
8	0	8	215.58	216.48	217.39	218.29	219.20	220.11	221.03	221.94
9	0	9	202.17	203.09	204.01	204.94	205.86	206.79	207.72	208.65
10	0	10	191.72	192.65	193.59	194.53	195.47	196.42	197.36	198.31
11	0	11	183.40	184.35	185.31	186.26	187.22	188.18	189.14	190.11
12	0	12	176.67	177.64	178.62	179.59	180.56	181.54	182.52	183.50
13	0	13	171.17	172.15	173.14	174.13	175.13	176.12	177.12	178.12
14	0	14	166.61	167.62	168.62	169.63	170.64	171.65	172.66	173.68
15	0	15	162.81	163.83	164.85	165.88	166.90	167.93	168.96	169.99
16	0	16	159.62	160.65	161.69	162.73	163.77	164.81	165.86	166.90
17	0	17	156.92	157.97	159.02	160.07	161.13	162.19	163.25	164.31
18	0	18	154.63	155.69	156.75	157.82	158.89	159.96	161.04	162.11
19	0	19	152.67	153.74	154.82	155.90	156.99	158.07	159.16	160.25
20	0	20	150.99	152.08	153.17	154.27	155.36	156.46	157.56	158.66
21	0	21	149.55	150.65	151.76	152.86	153.97	155.08	156.19	157.31
22	0	22	148.31	149.42	150.54	151.65	152.77	153.89	155.02	156.14
23	0	23	147.24	148.36	149.49	150.61	151.74	152.88	154.01	155.15
24	0	24	146.31	147.44	148.58	149.72	150.86	152.00	153.14	154.29
25	0	25	145.50	146.65	147.79	148.94	150.09	151.24	152.39	153.55
26	0	26	144.81	145.96	147.11	148.27	149.43	150.59	151.75	152.91
27	0	27	144.20	145.36	146.52	147.68	148.85	150.02	151.19	152.36
28	0	28	143.67	144.84	146.01	147.18	148.35	149.53	150.70	151.88
29	0	29	143.21	144.38	145.56	146.74	147.92	149.10	150.29	151.47
30	0	30	142.81	143.99	145.17	146.36	147.54	148.73	149.92	151.11
31	0	31	142.46	143.65	144.83	146.03	147.22	148.41	149.61	150.80
32	0	32	142.15	143.35	144.54	145.74	146.93	148.13	149.33	150.53
33	0	33	141.88	143.08	144.28	145.48	146.69	147.89	149.10	150.30
34	0	34	141.65	142.85	144.06	145.26	146.47	147.68	148.89	150.10
35	0	35	141.45	142.65	143.86	145.07	146.28	147.50	148.71	149.92
36	0	36	141.27	142.48	143.69	144.91	146.12	147.34	148.55	149.77
37	0	37	141.11	142.33	143.54	144.76	145.98	147.20	148.42	149.64
38	0	38	140.97	142.19	143.41	144.63	145.85	147.08	148.30	149.52
39	0	39	140.86	142.08	143.30	144.52	145.75	146.97	148.20	149.42
40	0	40	140.75	141.97	143.20	144.43	145.65	146.88	148.11	149.34
41	0	41	140.66	141.88	143.11	144.34	145.57	146.80	148.03	149.26
42	0	42	140.58	141.81	143.04	144.27	145.50	146.73	147.96	149.20
43	0	43	140.51	141.74	142.97	144.20	145.44	146.67	147.90	149.14
44	0	44	140.45	141.68	142.91	144.15	145.38	146.62	147.85	149.09
45	0	45	140.39	141.63	142.86	144.10	145.33	146.57	147.81	149.05
46	0	46	140.34	141.58	142.82	144.05	145.29	146.53	147.77	149.01
47	0	47	140.30	141.54	142.78	144.02	145.26	146.49	147.73	148.98
48	0	48	140.27	141.50	142.74	143.98	145.22	146.46	147.71	148.95
49	0	49	140.23	141.47	142.71	143.95	145.20	146.44	147.68	148.92
50	0	50	140.21	141.45	142.69	143.93	145.17	146.41	147.66	148.90
51	0	51	140.18	141.42	142.66	143.91	145.15	146.39	147.64	148.88
52	0	52	140.16	141.40	142.64	143.89	145.13	146.38	147.62	148.86
53	0	53	140.14	141.38	142.63	143.87	145.12	146.36	147.61	148.85
54	0	54	140.12	141.37	142.61	143.86	145.10	146.35	147.59	148.84
55	0	55	140.11	141.35	142.60	143.84	145.09	146.34	147.58	148.83
56	0	56	140.10	141.34	142.59	143.83	145.08	146.33	147.57	148.82
57	0	57	140.08	141.33	142.58	143.82	145.07	146.32	147.56	148.81
58	0	58	140.08	141.32	142.57	143.81	145.06	146.31	147.56	148.80
59	0	59	140.07	141.31	142.56	143.81	145.05	146.30	147.55	148.80
60	0	60	140.06	141.31	142.55	143.80	145.05	146.30	147.54	148.79

BASIC ANNUAL PAYMENTS

FOR A $1000 LOAN

YRS	TERM MOS	PERS	15%	15⅛%	15¼%	15⅜%	15½%	15⅝%	15¾%	15⅞%
2	0	2	615.12	616.10	617.08	618.06	619.04	620.02	621.00	621.99
3	0	3	437.98	438.89	439.80	440.71	441.62	442.53	443.44	444.35
4	0	4	350.27	351.16	352.04	352.93	353.82	354.71	355.60	356.49
5	0	5	298.32	299.20	300.09	300.97	301.86	302.75	303.64	304.52
6	0	6	264.24	265.13	266.02	266.92	267.81	268.70	269.60	270.50
7	0	7	240.37	241.27	242.17	243.08	243.98	244.89	245.80	246.71
8	0	8	222.86	223.77	224.69	225.61	226.53	227.45	228.38	229.30
9	0	9	209.58	210.51	211.45	212.38	213.32	214.26	215.20	216.14
10	0	10	199.26	200.21	201.16	202.11	203.07	204.03	204.98	205.94
11	0	11	191.07	192.04	193.01	193.98	194.96	195.93	196.91	197.89
12	0	12	184.49	185.47	186.46	187.45	188.44	189.43	190.43	191.42
13	0	13	179.12	180.12	181.12	182.13	183.14	184.15	185.16	186.17
14	0	14	174.69	175.71	176.73	177.76	178.78	179.81	180.84	181.87
15	0	15	171.02	172.06	173.10	174.13	175.18	176.22	177.27	178.31
16	0	16	167.95	169.00	170.06	171.11	172.17	173.23	174.29	175.35
17	0	17	165.37	166.44	167.51	168.58	169.65	170.72	171.80	172.88
18	0	18	163.19	164.27	165.35	166.44	167.52	168.61	169.70	170.80
19	0	19	161.34	162.44	163.53	164.63	165.73	166.83	167.93	169.04
20	0	20	159.77	160.87	161.98	163.09	164.20	165.32	166.43	167.55
21	0	21	158.42	159.54	160.66	161.78	162.91	164.03	165.16	166.29
22	0	22	157.27	158.40	159.53	160.66	161.80	162.94	164.08	165.22
23	0	23	156.28	157.42	158.56	159.71	160.85	162.00	163.15	164.30
24	0	24	155.43	156.58	157.74	158.89	160.04	161.20	162.36	163.52
25	0	25	154.70	155.86	157.02	158.18	159.35	160.51	161.68	162.85
26	0	26	154.07	155.24	156.41	157.58	158.75	159.92	161.10	162.27
27	0	27	153.53	154.71	155.88	157.06	158.24	159.42	160.60	161.78
28	0	28	153.06	154.24	155.43	156.61	157.80	158.98	160.17	161.36
29	0	29	152.66	153.84	155.03	156.22	157.42	158.61	159.80	161.00
30	0	30	152.31	153.50	154.69	155.89	157.09	158.29	159.49	160.69
31	0	31	152.00	153.20	154.40	155.60	156.81	158.01	159.21	160.42
32	0	32	151.74	152.94	154.15	155.35	156.56	157.77	158.98	160.19
33	0	33	151.51	152.72	153.93	155.14	156.35	157.56	158.78	159.99
34	0	34	151.31	152.52	153.74	154.95	156.17	157.39	158.60	159.82
35	0	35	151.14	152.36	153.57	154.79	156.01	157.23	158.45	159.67
36	0	36	150.99	152.21	153.43	154.65	155.88	157.10	158.32	159.55
37	0	37	150.86	152.08	153.31	154.53	155.76	156.98	158.21	159.44
38	0	38	150.75	151.97	153.20	154.43	155.66	156.89	158.11	159.34
39	0	39	150.65	151.88	153.11	154.34	155.57	156.80	158.03	159.26
40	0	40	150.57	151.80	153.03	154.26	155.49	156.73	157.96	159.19
41	0	41	150.49	151.73	152.96	154.19	155.43	156.66	157.90	159.13
42	0	42	150.43	151.66	152.90	154.13	155.37	156.61	157.84	159.08
43	0	43	150.37	151.61	152.85	154.08	155.32	156.56	157.80	159.04
44	0	44	150.33	151.56	152.80	154.04	155.28	156.52	157.76	159.00
45	0	45	150.28	151.52	152.76	154.00	155.24	156.48	157.72	158.96
46	0	46	150.25	151.49	152.73	153.97	155.21	156.45	157.69	158.94
47	0	47	150.22	151.46	152.70	153.94	155.18	156.43	157.67	158.91
48	0	48	150.19	151.43	152.67	153.92	155.16	156.40	157.65	158.89
49	0	49	150.16	151.41	152.65	153.89	155.14	156.38	157.63	158.87
50	0	50	150.14	151.39	152.63	153.88	155.12	156.37	157.61	158.86
51	0	51	150.13	151.37	152.61	153.86	155.10	156.35	157.60	158.84
52	0	52	150.11	151.35	152.60	153.85	155.09	156.34	157.58	158.83
53	0	53	150.10	151.34	152.59	153.83	155.08	156.33	157.57	158.82
54	0	54	150.08	151.33	152.58	153.82	155.07	156.32	157.56	158.81
55	0	55	150.07	151.32	152.57	153.81	155.06	156.31	157.56	158.80
56	0	56	150.06	151.31	152.56	153.81	155.05	156.30	157.55	158.80
57	0	57	150.06	151.30	152.55	153.80	155.05	156.29	157.54	158.79
58	0	58	150.05	151.30	152.55	153.79	155.04	156.29	157.54	158.79
59	0	59	150.04	151.29	152.54	153.79	155.04	156.28	157.53	158.78
60	0	60	150.04	151.29	152.54	153.78	155.03	156.28	157.53	158.78

BASIC ANNUAL PAYMENTS
FOR A $1000 LOAN

YRS	TERM MOS	PERS	16%	16⅛%	16¼%	16⅜%	16½%	16⅝%	16¾%	16⅞%
2	0	2	622.97	623.95	624.93	625.92	626.90	627.88	628.87	629.85
3	0	3	445.26	446.18	447.09	448.00	448.92	449.83	450.75	451.66
4	0	4	357.38	358.27	359.17	360.06	360.95	361.85	362.74	363.64
5	0	5	305.41	306.31	307.20	308.09	308.98	309.88	310.77	311.67
6	0	6	271.39	272.29	273.19	274.10	275.00	275.90	276.81	277.71
7	0	7	247.62	248.53	249.44	250.36	251.27	252.19	253.11	254.03
8	0	8	230.23	231.16	232.09	233.02	233.95	234.88	235.82	236.76
9	0	9	217.09	218.03	218.98	219.93	220.88	221.83	222.78	223.74
10	0	10	206.91	207.87	208.84	209.80	210.77	211.74	212.71	213.69
11	0	11	198.87	199.85	200.83	201.82	202.80	203.79	204.78	205.78
12	0	12	192.42	193.42	194.42	195.43	196.43	197.44	198.45	199.46
13	0	13	187.19	188.21	189.23	190.25	191.27	192.30	193.32	194.35
14	0	14	182.90	183.94	184.97	186.01	187.05	188.10	189.14	190.19
15	0	15	179.36	180.41	181.47	182.52	183.58	184.64	185.70	186.76
16	0	16	176.42	177.49	178.55	179.63	180.70	181.77	182.85	183.93
17	0	17	173.96	175.04	176.12	177.21	178.30	179.39	180.48	181.57
18	0	18	171.89	172.99	174.08	175.18	176.29	177.39	178.49	179.60
19	0	19	170.15	171.26	172.37	173.48	174.60	175.71	176.83	177.95
20	0	20	168.67	169.79	170.92	172.04	173.17	174.30	175.43	176.56
21	0	21	167.42	168.55	169.69	170.83	171.96	173.10	174.25	175.39
22	0	22	166.36	167.50	168.65	169.79	170.94	172.09	173.25	174.40
23	0	23	165.45	166.61	167.76	168.92	170.08	171.24	172.40	173.56
24	0	24	164.68	165.84	167.01	168.17	169.34	170.51	171.68	172.85
25	0	25	164.02	165.19	166.36	167.54	168.71	169.89	171.07	172.25
26	0	26	163.45	164.63	165.81	166.99	168.18	169.36	170.55	171.73
27	0	27	162.97	164.15	165.34	166.53	167.72	168.91	170.10	171.30
28	0	28	162.55	163.75	164.94	166.13	167.33	168.53	169.73	170.93
29	0	29	162.20	163.39	164.59	165.79	167.00	168.20	169.40	170.61
30	0	30	161.89	163.09	164.30	165.50	166.71	167.92	169.13	170.34
31	0	31	161.63	162.84	164.05	165.26	166.47	167.68	168.89	170.11
32	0	32	161.40	162.61	163.83	165.04	166.26	167.48	168.69	169.91
33	0	33	161.21	162.42	163.64	164.86	166.08	167.30	168.52	169.74
34	0	34	161.04	162.26	163.48	164.70	165.93	167.15	168.38	169.60
35	0	35	160.90	162.12	163.35	164.57	165.80	167.02	168.25	169.48
36	0	36	160.77	162.00	163.23	164.45	165.68	166.91	168.14	169.37
37	0	37	160.67	161.90	163.13	164.36	165.59	166.82	168.05	169.28
38	0	38	160.58	161.81	163.04	164.27	165.50	166.74	167.97	169.21
39	0	39	160.50	161.73	162.96	164.20	165.43	166.67	167.90	169.14
40	0	40	160.43	161.66	162.90	164.14	165.37	166.61	167.85	169.09
41	0	41	160.37	161.61	162.84	164.08	165.32	166.56	167.80	169.04
42	0	42	160.32	161.56	162.80	164.04	165.28	166.52	167.76	169.00
43	0	43	160.28	161.52	162.76	164.00	165.24	166.48	167.72	168.96
44	0	44	160.24	161.48	162.72	163.96	165.20	166.45	167.69	168.93
45	0	45	160.21	161.45	162.69	163.93	165.18	166.42	167.66	168.91
46	0	46	160.18	161.42	162.66	163.91	165.15	166.40	167.64	168.88
47	0	47	160.15	161.40	162.64	163.89	165.13	166.38	167.62	168.87
48	0	48	160.13	161.38	162.62	163.87	165.11	166.36	167.60	168.85
49	0	49	160.12	161.36	162.61	163.85	165.10	166.34	167.59	168.84
50	0	50	160.10	161.35	162.59	163.84	165.08	166.33	167.58	168.82
51	0	51	160.09	161.33	162.58	163.83	165.07	166.32	167.57	168.81
52	0	52	160.08	161.32	162.57	163.82	165.06	166.31	167.56	168.81
53	0	53	160.07	161.31	162.56	163.81	165.06	166.30	167.55	168.80
54	0	54	160.06	161.31	162.55	163.80	165.05	166.30	167.54	168.79
55	0	55	160.05	161.30	162.55	163.79	165.04	166.29	167.54	168.79
56	0	56	160.04	161.29	162.54	163.79	165.04	166.29	167.53	168.78
57	0	57	160.04	161.29	162.54	163.78	165.03	166.28	167.53	168.78
58	0	58	160.03	161.28	162.53	163.78	165.03	166.28	167.53	168.77
59	0	59	160.03	161.28	162.53	163.78	165.03	166.27	167.52	168.77
60	0	60	160.03	161.28	162.52	163.77	165.02	166.27	167.52	168.77

BASIC ANNUAL PAYMENTS
FOR A $1000 LOAN

YRS	TERM MOS	PERS	17%	17⅛%	17¼%	17⅜%	17½%	17⅝%	17¾%	18%
2	0	2	630.83	631.82	632.80	633.79	634.78	635.76	636.75	638.72
3	0	3	452.58	453.50	454.41	455.33	456.25	457.17	458.09	459.93
4	0	4	364.54	365.44	366.34	367.23	368.14	369.04	369.94	371.74
5	0	5	312.57	313.47	314.37	315.27	316.17	317.07	317.97	319.78
6	0	6	278.62	279.53	280.44	281.35	282.26	283.17	284.08	285.92
7	0	7	254.95	255.87	256.80	257.72	258.65	259.58	260.51	262.37
8	0	8	237.69	238.63	239.58	240.52	241.46	242.41	243.35	245.25
9	0	9	224.70	225.65	226.61	227.57	228.54	229.50	230.46	232.40
10	0	10	214.66	215.64	216.62	217.60	218.58	219.56	220.55	222.52
11	0	11	206.77	207.77	208.76	209.76	210.76	211.76	212.77	214.78
12	0	12	200.47	201.48	202.50	203.52	204.54	205.56	206.58	208.63
13	0	13	195.38	196.42	197.45	198.49	199.52	200.56	201.60	203.69
14	0	14	191.24	192.29	193.34	194.39	195.45	196.50	197.56	199.68
15	0	15	187.83	188.89	189.96	191.03	192.10	193.18	194.25	196.41
16	0	16	185.01	186.09	187.18	188.26	189.35	190.44	191.53	193.72
17	0	17	182.67	183.76	184.86	185.96	187.06	188.17	189.27	191.49
18	0	18	180.71	181.82	182.93	184.05	185.16	186.28	187.40	189.64
19	0	19	179.07	180.20	181.32	182.45	183.58	184.71	185.84	188.11
20	0	20	177.70	178.83	179.97	181.11	182.25	183.39	184.53	186.82
21	0	21	176.54	177.68	178.83	179.98	181.13	182.28	183.44	185.75
22	0	22	175.56	176.71	177.87	179.03	180.19	181.35	182.52	184.85
23	0	23	174.73	175.89	177.06	178.23	179.40	180.57	181.74	184.10
24	0	24	174.02	175.20	176.38	177.55	178.73	179.91	181.09	183.46
25	0	25	173.43	174.61	175.79	176.98	178.17	179.35	180.54	182.92
26	0	26	172.92	174.11	175.30	176.50	177.69	178.88	180.08	182.47
27	0	27	172.49	173.69	174.89	176.08	177.28	178.48	179.69	182.09
28	0	28	172.13	173.33	174.53	175.74	176.94	178.15	179.35	181.77
29	0	29	171.81	173.02	174.23	175.44	176.65	177.86	179.07	181.50
30	0	30	171.55	172.76	173.97	175.19	176.40	177.62	178.83	181.27
31	0	31	171.32	172.54	173.76	174.97	176.19	177.41	178.63	181.08
32	0	32	171.13	172.35	173.57	174.79	176.02	177.24	178.46	180.91
33	0	33	170.97	172.19	173.41	174.64	175.86	177.09	178.32	180.77
34	0	34	170.83	172.05	173.28	174.51	175.74	176.96	178.19	180.65
35	0	35	170.71	171.94	173.16	174.40	175.63	176.86	178.09	180.56
36	0	36	170.60	171.84	173.07	174.30	175.53	176.77	178.00	180.47
37	0	37	170.52	171.75	172.98	174.22	175.45	176.69	177.93	180.40
38	0	38	170.44	171.68	172.91	174.15	175.39	176.62	177.86	180.34
39	0	39	170.38	171.62	172.85	174.09	175.33	176.57	177.81	180.29
40	0	40	170.32	171.56	172.80	174.04	175.28	176.52	177.76	180.25
41	0	41	170.28	171.52	172.76	174.00	175.24	176.48	177.72	180.21
42	0	42	170.24	171.48	172.72	173.96	175.21	176.45	177.69	180.18
43	0	43	170.20	171.45	172.69	173.93	175.18	176.42	177.66	180.15
44	0	44	170.18	171.42	172.66	173.91	175.15	176.39	177.64	180.13
45	0	45	170.15	171.39	172.64	173.88	175.13	176.37	177.62	180.11
46	0	46	170.13	171.37	172.62	173.86	175.11	176.36	177.60	180.09
47	0	47	170.11	171.36	172.60	173.85	175.09	176.34	177.59	180.08
48	0	48	170.10	171.34	172.59	173.83	175.08	176.33	177.57	180.07
49	0	49	170.08	171.33	172.58	173.82	175.07	176.32	177.56	180.06
50	0	50	170.07	171.32	172.57	173.81	175.06	176.31	177.56	180.05
51	0	51	170.06	171.31	172.56	173.80	175.05	176.30	177.55	180.04
52	0	52	170.05	171.30	172.55	173.80	175.04	176.29	177.54	180.04
53	0	53	170.05	171.29	172.54	173.79	175.04	176.29	177.54	180.03
54	0	54	170.04	171.29	172.54	173.79	175.03	176.28	177.53	180.03
55	0	55	170.04	171.28	172.53	173.78	175.03	176.28	177.53	180.03
56	0	56	170.03	171.28	172.53	173.78	175.03	176.27	177.52	180.02
57	0	57	170.03	171.28	172.52	173.77	175.02	176.27	177.52	180.02
58	0	58	170.02	171.27	172.52	173.77	175.02	176.27	177.52	180.02
59	0	59	170.02	171.27	172.52	173.77	175.02	176.27	177.52	180.02
60	0	60	170.02	171.27	172.52	173.77	175.02	176.27	177.51	180.01

1/10% MONTHLY PAYMENTS
FOR A $1000 LOAN

TERM YRS	MOS	PERS	8%	8.1%	8.2%	8.3%	8.4%	8.5%	8.6%	8.7%
1	0	12	86.99	87.04	87.09	87.13	87.18	87.22	87.27	87.32
1	6	18	59.15	59.19	59.24	59.28	59.33	59.37	59.42	59.47
2	0	24	45.23	45.28	45.32	45.37	45.41	45.46	45.51	45.55
2	6	30	36.89	36.94	36.99	37.03	37.08	37.12	37.17	37.21
3	0	36	31.34	31.39	31.43	31.48	31.53	31.57	31.62	31.67
3	6	42	27.38	27.43	27.48	27.52	27.57	27.62	27.66	27.71
4	0	48	24.42	24.46	24.51	24.56	24.61	24.65	24.70	24.75
4	6	54	22.12	22.16	22.21	22.26	22.31	22.36	22.40	22.45
5	0	60	20.28	20.33	20.38	20.43	20.47	20.52	20.57	20.62
5	6	66	18.78	18.83	18.88	18.93	18.98	19.03	19.07	19.12
6	0	72	17.54	17.59	17.64	17.69	17.73	17.78	17.83	17.88
6	6	78	16.49	16.54	16.59	16.64	16.69	16.74	16.79	16.84
7	0	84	15.59	15.64	15.69	15.74	15.79	15.84	15.89	15.94
7	6	90	14.82	14.87	14.92	14.97	15.02	15.07	15.12	15.17
8	0	96	14.14	14.19	14.24	14.29	14.35	14.40	14.45	14.50
8	6	102	13.55	13.60	13.65	13.70	13.75	13.81	13.86	13.91
9	0	108	13.02	13.08	13.13	13.18	13.23	13.28	13.34	13.39
9	6	114	12.56	12.61	12.66	12.71	12.77	12.82	12.87	12.93
10	0	120	12.14	12.19	12.24	12.30	12.35	12.40	12.46	12.51
10	6	126	11.76	11.81	11.87	11.92	11.98	12.03	12.08	12.14
11	0	132	11.42	11.47	11.53	11.58	11.64	11.69	11.75	11.80
11	6	138	11.11	11.17	11.22	11.27	11.33	11.38	11.44	11.50
12	0	144	10.83	10.88	10.94	10.99	11.05	11.11	11.16	11.22
12	6	150	10.57	10.63	10.68	10.74	10.79	10.85	10.91	10.96
13	0	156	10.34	10.39	10.45	10.50	10.56	10.62	10.67	10.73
13	6	162	10.12	10.17	10.23	10.29	10.34	10.40	10.46	10.52
14	0	168	9.92	9.98	10.03	10.09	10.15	10.20	10.26	10.32
14	6	174	9.73	9.79	9.85	9.91	9.96	10.02	10.08	10.14
15	0	180	9.56	9.62	9.68	9.74	9.79	9.85	9.91	9.97
15	6	186	9.40	9.46	9.52	9.58	9.64	9.70	9.75	9.81
16	0	192	9.25	9.31	9.37	9.43	9.49	9.55	9.61	9.67
16	6	198	9.12	9.18	9.23	9.29	9.35	9.41	9.47	9.53
17	0	204	8.99	9.05	9.11	9.17	9.23	9.29	9.35	9.41
17	6	210	8.87	8.93	8.99	9.05	9.11	9.17	9.23	9.29
18	0	216	8.75	8.82	8.88	8.94	9.00	9.06	9.12	9.18
18	6	222	8.65	8.71	8.77	8.83	8.89	8.96	9.02	9.08
19	0	228	8.55	8.61	8.67	8.74	8.80	8.86	8.92	8.98
19	6	234	8.46	8.52	8.58	8.64	8.71	8.77	8.83	8.89
20	0	240	8.37	8.43	8.49	8.56	8.62	8.68	8.75	8.81
20	6	246	8.29	8.35	8.41	8.48	8.54	8.60	8.67	8.73
21	0	252	8.21	8.27	8.34	8.40	8.46	8.53	8.59	8.66
21	6	258	8.14	8.20	8.26	8.33	8.39	8.46	8.52	8.59
22	0	264	8.07	8.13	8.20	8.26	8.32	8.39	8.45	8.52
22	6	270	8.00	8.07	8.13	8.20	8.26	8.33	8.39	8.46
23	0	276	7.94	8.00	8.07	8.13	8.20	8.27	8.33	8.40
23	6	282	7.88	7.95	8.01	8.08	8.14	8.21	8.28	8.34
24	0	288	7.83	7.89	7.96	8.02	8.09	8.16	8.22	8.29
24	6	294	7.77	7.84	7.91	7.97	8.04	8.11	8.17	8.24
25	0	300	7.72	7.79	7.86	7.92	7.99	8.06	8.12	8.19
25	6	306	7.68	7.74	7.81	7.88	7.94	8.01	8.08	8.15
26	0	312	7.63	7.70	7.77	7.83	7.90	7.97	8.04	8.11
26	6	318	7.59	7.66	7.72	7.79	7.86	7.93	8.00	8.07
27	0	324	7.55	7.62	7.68	7.75	7.82	7.89	7.96	8.03
27	6	330	7.51	7.58	7.65	7.71	7.78	7.85	7.92	7.99
28	0	336	7.47	7.54	7.61	7.68	7.75	7.82	7.89	7.96
28	6	342	7.44	7.51	7.58	7.64	7.71	7.78	7.85	7.92
29	0	348	7.40	7.47	7.54	7.61	7.68	7.75	7.82	7.89
29	6	354	7.37	7.44	7.51	7.58	7.65	7.72	7.79	7.86
30	0	360	7.34	7.41	7.48	7.55	7.62	7.69	7.77	7.84

1/10% MONTHLY PAYMENTS
FOR A $1000 LOAN

TERM YRS MOS PERS			8.8%	8.9%	9%	9.1%	9.2%	9.3%	9.4%	9.5%
1	0	12	87.36	87.41	87.46	87.50	87.55	87.60	87.64	87.69
1	6	18	59.51	59.56	59.60	59.65	59.69	59.74	59.79	59.83
2	0	24	45.60	45.64	45.69	45.74	45.78	45.83	45.87	45.92
2	6	30	37.26	37.31	37.35	37.40	37.45	37.49	37.54	37.58
3	0	36	31.71	31.76	31.80	31.85	31.90	31.94	31.99	32.04
3	6	42	27.76	27.80	27.85	27.90	27.94	27.99	28.04	28.09
4	0	48	24.80	24.84	24.89	24.94	24.99	25.03	25.08	25.13
4	6	54	22.50	22.55	22.59	22.64	22.69	22.74	22.79	22.84
5	0	60	20.67	20.71	20.76	20.81	20.86	20.91	20.96	21.01
5	6	66	19.17	19.22	19.27	19.32	19.37	19.42	19.47	19.52
6	0	72	17.93	17.98	18.03	18.08	18.13	18.18	18.23	18.28
6	6	78	16.89	16.94	16.99	17.04	17.09	17.14	17.19	17.24
7	0	84	15.99	16.04	16.09	16.14	16.20	16.25	16.30	16.35
7	6	90	15.22	15.27	15.32	15.38	15.43	15.48	15.53	15.58
8	0	96	14.55	14.60	14.65	14.71	14.76	14.81	14.86	14.92
8	6	102	13.96	14.02	14.07	14.12	14.17	14.23	14.28	14.33
9	0	108	13.44	13.49	13.55	13.60	13.65	13.71	13.76	13.81
9	6	114	12.98	13.03	13.09	13.14	13.19	13.25	13.30	13.36
10	0	120	12.56	12.62	12.67	12.73	12.78	12.84	12.89	12.94
10	6	126	12.19	12.25	12.30	12.36	12.41	12.47	12.52	12.58
11	0	132	11.86	11.91	11.97	12.02	12.08	12.13	12.19	12.24
11	6	138	11.55	11.61	11.66	11.72	11.77	11.83	11.89	11.94
12	0	144	11.27	11.33	11.39	11.44	11.50	11.55	11.61	11.67
12	6	150	11.02	11.08	11.13	11.19	11.25	11.30	11.36	11.42
13	0	156	10.79	10.84	10.90	10.96	11.02	11.07	11.13	11.19
13	6	162	10.57	10.63	10.69	10.75	10.81	10.86	10.92	10.98
14	0	168	10.38	10.44	10.49	10.55	10.61	10.67	10.73	10.79
14	6	174	10.20	10.26	10.31	10.37	10.43	10.49	10.55	10.61
15	0	180	10.03	10.09	10.15	10.21	10.27	10.33	10.39	10.45
15	6	186	9.87	9.93	9.99	10.05	10.11	10.17	10.23	10.30
16	0	192	9.73	9.79	9.85	9.91	9.97	10.03	10.09	10.15
16	6	198	9.60	9.66	9.72	9.78	9.84	9.90	9.96	10.02
17	0	204	9.47	9.53	9.59	9.65	9.72	9.78	9.84	9.90
17	6	210	9.35	9.42	9.48	9.54	9.60	9.66	9.73	9.79
18	0	216	9.24	9.31	9.37	9.43	9.49	9.56	9.62	9.68
18	6	222	9.14	9.21	9.27	9.33	9.39	9.46	9.52	9.59
19	0	228	9.05	9.11	9.17	9.24	9.30	9.37	9.43	9.49
19	6	234	8.96	9.02	9.09	9.15	9.21	9.28	9.34	9.41
20	0	240	8.87	8.94	9.00	9.07	9.13	9.20	9.26	9.33
20	6	246	8.80	8.86	8.92	8.99	9.05	9.12	9.18	9.25
21	0	252	8.72	8.79	8.85	8.92	8.98	9.05	9.11	9.18
21	6	258	8.65	8.72	8.78	8.85	8.91	8.98	9.05	9.11
22	0	264	8.59	8.65	8.72	8.78	8.85	8.92	8.98	9.05
22	6	270	8.52	8.59	8.66	8.72	8.79	8.86	8.92	8.99
23	0	276	8.46	8.53	8.60	8.66	8.73	8.80	8.87	8.93
23	6	282	8.41	8.48	8.54	8.61	8.68	8.75	8.81	8.88
24	0	288	8.36	8.42	8.49	8.56	8.63	8.70	8.76	8.83
24	6	294	8.31	8.37	8.44	8.51	8.58	8.65	8.72	8.79
25	0	300	8.26	8.33	8.40	8.47	8.53	8.60	8.67	8.74
25	6	306	8.22	8.28	8.35	8.42	8.49	8.56	8.63	8.70
26	0	312	8.17	8.24	8.31	8.38	8.45	8.52	8.59	8.66
26	6	318	8.13	8.20	8.27	8.34	8.41	8.48	8.55	8.62
27	0	324	8.10	8.17	8.24	8.31	8.38	8.45	8.52	8.59
27	6	330	8.06	8.13	8.20	8.27	8.34	8.41	8.48	8.56
28	0	336	8.03	8.10	8.17	8.24	8.31	8.38	8.45	8.52
28	6	342	7.99	8.07	8.14	8.21	8.28	8.35	8.42	8.49
29	0	348	7.96	8.04	8.11	8.18	8.25	8.32	8.39	8.47
29	6	354	7.94	8.01	8.08	8.15	8.22	8.29	8.37	8.44
30	0	360	7.91	7.98	8.05	8.12	8.20	8.27	8.34	8.41

1/10% MONTHLY PAYMENTS
FOR A $1000 LOAN

TERM YRS	MOS	PERS	9.6%	9.7%	9.8%	9.9%	10%	10.1%	10.2%	10.3%
1	0	12	87.73	87.78	87.83	87.87	87.92	87.97	88.01	88.06
1	6	18	59.88	59.92	59.97	60.02	60.06	60.11	60.15	60.20
2	0	24	45.97	46.01	46.06	46.10	46.15	46.20	46.24	46.29
2	6	30	37.63	37.68	37.72	37.77	37.82	37.86	37.91	37.96
3	0	36	32.08	32.13	32.18	32.23	32.27	32.32	32.37	32.41
3	6	42	28.13	28.18	28.23	28.27	28.32	28.37	28.42	28.46
4	0	48	25.18	25.22	25.27	25.32	25.37	25.42	25.46	25.51
4	6	54	22.88	22.93	22.98	23.03	23.08	23.13	23.17	23.22
5	0	60	21.06	21.10	21.15	21.20	21.25	21.30	21.35	21.40
5	6	66	19.57	19.62	19.67	19.71	19.76	19.81	19.86	19.91
6	0	72	18.33	18.38	18.43	18.48	18.53	18.58	18.63	18.68
6	6	78	17.29	17.34	17.39	17.44	17.49	17.54	17.59	17.65
7	0	84	16.40	16.45	16.50	16.55	16.61	16.66	16.71	16.76
7	6	90	15.63	15.69	15.74	15.79	15.84	15.90	15.95	16.00
8	0	96	14.97	15.02	15.07	15.13	15.18	15.23	15.29	15.34
8	6	102	14.38	14.44	14.49	14.54	14.60	14.65	14.70	14.76
9	0	108	13.87	13.92	13.98	14.03	14.08	14.14	14.19	14.25
9	6	114	13.41	13.46	13.52	13.57	13.63	13.68	13.74	13.79
10	0	120	13.00	13.05	13.11	13.16	13.22	13.28	13.33	13.39
10	6	126	12.63	12.69	12.74	12.80	12.85	12.91	12.97	13.02
11	0	132	12.30	12.36	12.41	12.47	12.52	12.58	12.64	12.70
11	6	138	12.00	12.06	12.11	12.17	12.23	12.28	12.34	12.40
12	0	144	11.73	11.78	11.84	11.90	11.96	12.01	12.07	12.13
12	6	150	11.48	11.53	11.59	11.65	11.71	11.77	11.83	11.88
13	0	156	11.25	11.31	11.37	11.42	11.48	11.54	11.60	11.66
13	6	162	11.04	11.10	11.16	11.22	11.28	11.34	11.40	11.46
14	0	168	10.85	10.91	10.97	11.03	11.09	11.15	11.21	11.27
14	6	174	10.67	10.73	10.79	10.85	10.91	10.97	11.03	11.09
15	0	180	10.51	10.57	10.63	10.69	10.75	10.81	10.87	10.94
15	6	186	10.36	10.42	10.48	10.54	10.60	10.66	10.73	10.79
16	0	192	10.22	10.28	10.34	10.40	10.46	10.53	10.59	10.65
16	6	198	10.09	10.15	10.21	10.27	10.34	10.40	10.46	10.53
17	0	204	9.97	10.03	10.09	10.15	10.22	10.28	10.34	10.41
17	6	210	9.85	9.92	9.98	10.04	10.11	10.17	10.23	10.30
18	0	216	9.75	9.81	9.88	9.94	10.00	10.07	10.13	10.20
18	6	222	9.65	9.71	9.78	9.84	9.91	9.97	10.04	10.10
19	0	228	9.56	9.62	9.69	9.75	9.82	9.88	9.95	10.01
19	6	234	9.47	9.54	9.60	9.67	9.73	9.80	9.87	9.93
20	0	240	9.39	9.46	9.52	9.59	9.66	9.72	9.79	9.85
20	6	246	9.32	9.38	9.45	9.52	9.58	9.65	9.72	9.78
21	0	252	9.25	9.31	9.38	9.45	9.51	9.58	9.65	9.72
21	6	258	9.18	9.25	9.31	9.38	9.45	9.52	9.58	9.65
22	0	264	9.12	9.18	9.25	9.32	9.39	9.46	9.52	9.59
22	6	270	9.06	9.13	9.19	9.26	9.33	9.40	9.47	9.54
23	0	276	9.00	9.07	9.14	9.21	9.28	9.35	9.41	9.48
23	6	282	8.95	9.02	9.09	9.16	9.23	9.30	9.37	9.44
24	0	288	8.90	8.97	9.04	9.11	9.18	9.25	9.32	9.39
24	6	294	8.86	8.92	8.99	9.06	9.13	9.20	9.27	9.35
25	0	300	8.81	8.88	8.95	9.02	9.09	9.16	9.23	9.30
25	6	306	8.77	8.84	8.91	8.98	9.05	9.12	9.19	9.27
26	0	312	8.73	8.80	8.87	8.94	9.01	9.09	9.16	9.23
26	6	318	8.69	8.77	8.84	8.91	8.98	9.05	9.12	9.20
27	0	324	8.66	8.73	8.80	8.87	8.95	9.02	9.09	9.16
27	6	330	8.63	8.70	8.77	8.84	8.91	8.99	9.06	9.13
28	0	336	8.60	8.67	8.74	8.81	8.88	8.96	9.03	9.10
28	6	342	8.57	8.64	8.71	8.78	8.86	8.93	9.00	9.08
29	0	348	8.54	8.61	8.68	8.76	8.83	8.90	8.98	9.05
29	6	354	8.51	8.58	8.66	8.73	8.80	8.88	8.95	9.03
30	0	360	8.49	8.56	8.63	8.71	8.78	8.85	8.93	9.00

1/10% MONTHLY PAYMENTS
FOR A $1000 LOAN

TERM YRS	MOS	PERS	10.4%	10.5%	10.6%	10.7%	10.8%	10.9%	11%	11.1%
1	0	12	88.11	88.15	88.20	88.25	88.29	88.34	88.39	88.43
1	6	18	60.25	60.29	60.34	60.38	60.43	60.48	60.52	60.57
2	0	24	46.33	46.38	46.43	46.47	46.52	46.57	46.61	46.66
2	6	30	38.00	38.05	38.10	38.14	38.19	38.24	38.28	38.33
3	0	36	32.46	32.51	32.55	32.60	32.65	32.70	32.74	32.79
3	6	42	28.51	28.56	28.61	28.66	28.70	28.75	28.80	28.85
4	0	48	25.56	25.61	25.66	25.71	25.75	25.80	25.85	25.90
4	6	54	23.27	23.32	23.37	23.42	23.47	23.52	23.57	23.62
5	0	60	21.45	21.50	21.55	21.60	21.65	21.70	21.75	21.80
5	6	66	19.96	20.01	20.06	20.12	20.17	20.22	20.27	20.32
6	0	72	18.73	18.78	18.83	18.89	18.94	18.99	19.04	19.09
6	6	78	17.70	17.75	17.80	17.85	17.90	17.95	18.01	18.06
7	0	84	16.81	16.87	16.92	16.97	17.02	17.07	17.13	17.18
7	6	90	16.05	16.11	16.16	16.21	16.26	16.32	16.37	16.42
8	0	96	15.39	15.45	15.50	15.55	15.61	15.66	15.71	15.77
8	6	102	14.81	14.87	14.92	14.97	15.03	15.08	15.14	15.19
9	0	108	14.30	14.36	14.41	14.47	14.52	14.58	14.63	14.69
9	6	114	13.85	13.90	13.96	14.01	14.07	14.13	14.18	14.24
10	0	120	13.44	13.50	13.55	13.61	13.67	13.72	13.78	13.84
10	6	126	13.08	13.14	13.19	13.25	13.31	13.36	13.42	13.48
11	0	132	12.75	12.81	12.87	12.92	12.98	13.04	13.10	13.16
11	6	138	12.46	12.51	12.57	12.63	12.69	12.75	12.81	12.86
12	0	144	12.19	12.25	12.30	12.36	12.42	12.48	12.54	12.60
12	6	150	11.94	12.00	12.06	12.12	12.18	12.24	12.30	12.36
13	0	156	11.72	11.78	11.84	11.90	11.96	12.02	12.08	12.14
13	6	162	11.52	11.58	11.64	11.70	11.76	11.82	11.88	11.94
14	0	168	11.33	11.39	11.45	11.51	11.57	11.63	11.70	11.76
14	6	174	11.16	11.22	11.28	11.34	11.40	11.46	11.53	11.59
15	0	180	11.00	11.06	11.12	11.18	11.25	11.31	11.37	11.43
15	6	186	10.85	10.91	10.98	11.04	11.10	11.16	11.23	11.29
16	0	192	10.71	10.78	10.84	10.90	10.97	11.03	11.10	11.16
16	6	198	10.59	10.65	10.72	10.78	10.84	10.91	10.97	11.04
17	0	204	10.47	10.54	10.60	10.66	10.73	10.79	10.86	10.92
17	6	210	10.36	10.43	10.49	10.56	10.62	10.69	10.75	10.82
18	0	216	10.26	10.33	10.39	10.46	10.52	10.59	10.66	10.72
18	6	222	10.17	10.23	10.30	10.37	10.43	10.50	10.56	10.63
19	0	228	10.08	10.15	10.21	10.28	10.35	10.41	10.48	10.55
19	6	234	10.00	10.06	10.13	10.20	10.27	10.33	10.40	10.47
20	0	240	9.92	9.99	10.06	10.12	10.19	10.26	10.33	10.40
20	6	246	9.85	9.92	9.99	10.05	10.12	10.19	10.26	10.33
21	0	252	9.78	9.85	9.92	9.99	10.06	10.12	10.19	10.26
21	6	258	9.72	9.79	9.86	9.93	10.00	10.06	10.13	10.20
22	0	264	9.66	9.73	9.80	9.87	9.94	10.01	10.08	10.15
22	6	270	9.61	9.68	9.74	9.81	9.88	9.95	10.02	10.09
23	0	276	9.55	9.62	9.69	9.76	9.83	9.90	9.98	10.05
23	6	282	9.51	9.58	9.65	9.72	9.79	9.86	9.93	10.00
24	0	288	9.46	9.53	9.60	9.67	9.74	9.81	9.89	9.96
24	6	294	9.42	9.49	9.56	9.63	9.70	9.77	9.84	9.92
25	0	300	9.38	9.45	9.52	9.59	9.66	9.73	9.81	9.88
25	6	306	9.34	9.41	9.48	9.55	9.63	9.70	9.77	9.84
26	0	312	9.30	9.37	9.45	9.52	9.59	9.66	9.74	9.81
26	6	318	9.27	9.34	9.41	9.49	9.56	9.63	9.70	9.78
27	0	324	9.24	9.31	9.38	9.45	9.53	9.60	9.67	9.75
27	6	330	9.21	9.28	9.35	9.42	9.50	9.57	9.65	9.72
28	0	336	9.18	9.25	9.32	9.40	9.47	9.55	9.62	9.69
28	6	342	9.15	9.22	9.30	9.37	9.45	9.52	9.59	9.67
29	0	348	9.12	9.20	9.27	9.35	9.42	9.50	9.57	9.65
29	6	354	9.10	9.17	9.25	9.32	9.40	9.47	9.55	9.62
30	0	360	9.08	9.15	9.23	9.30	9.38	9.45	9.53	9.60

1/10% MONTHLY PAYMENTS
FOR A $1000 LOAN

YRS	MOS	PERS	11.2%	11.3%	11.4%	11.5%	11.6%	11.7%	11.8%	11.9%
1	0	12	88.48	88.53	88.57	88.62	88.67	88.71	88.76	88.81
1	6	18	60.62	60.66	60.71	60.76	60.80	60.85	60.89	60.94
2	0	24	46.71	46.75	46.80	46.85	46.89	46.94	46.99	47.03
2	6	30	38.38	38.42	38.47	38.52	38.56	38.61	38.66	38.71
3	0	36	32.84	32.89	32.93	32.98	33.03	33.08	33.12	33.17
3	6	42	28.89	28.94	28.99	29.04	29.09	29.14	29.18	29.23
4	0	48	25.95	26.00	26.05	26.09	26.14	26.19	26.24	26.29
4	6	54	23.67	23.71	23.76	23.81	23.86	23.91	23.96	24.01
5	0	60	21.85	21.90	21.95	22.00	22.05	22.10	22.15	22.20
5	6	66	20.37	20.42	20.47	20.52	20.57	20.62	20.67	20.72
6	0	72	19.14	19.19	19.24	19.30	19.35	19.40	19.45	19.50
6	6	78	18.11	18.16	18.21	18.27	18.32	18.37	18.42	18.48
7	0	84	17.23	17.29	17.34	17.39	17.44	17.50	17.55	17.60
7	6	90	16.48	16.53	16.58	16.64	16.69	16.75	16.80	16.85
8	0	96	15.82	15.88	15.93	15.98	16.04	16.09	16.15	16.20
8	6	102	15.25	15.30	15.36	15.41	15.47	15.52	15.58	15.63
9	0	108	14.74	14.80	14.85	14.91	14.96	15.02	15.08	15.13
9	6	114	14.29	14.35	14.41	14.46	14.52	14.58	14.63	14.69
10	0	120	13.89	13.95	14.01	14.06	14.12	14.18	14.24	14.29
10	6	126	13.54	13.59	13.65	13.71	13.77	13.82	13.88	13.94
11	0	132	13.21	13.27	13.33	13.39	13.45	13.51	13.56	13.62
11	6	138	12.92	12.98	13.04	13.10	13.16	13.22	13.28	13.34
12	0	144	12.66	12.72	12.78	12.84	12.90	12.96	13.02	13.08
12	6	150	12.42	12.48	12.54	12.60	12.66	12.72	12.78	12.84
13	0	156	12.20	12.26	12.32	12.38	12.45	12.51	12.57	12.63
13	6	162	12.00	12.06	12.12	12.19	12.25	12.31	12.37	12.43
14	0	168	11.82	11.88	11.94	12.01	12.07	12.13	12.19	12.26
14	6	174	11.65	11.71	11.78	11.84	11.90	11.97	12.03	12.09
15	0	180	11.50	11.56	11.62	11.69	11.75	11.81	11.88	11.94
15	6	186	11.35	11.42	11.48	11.55	11.61	11.67	11.74	11.80
16	0	192	11.22	11.29	11.35	11.42	11.48	11.55	11.61	11.68
16	6	198	11.10	11.17	11.23	11.30	11.36	11.43	11.49	11.56
17	0	204	10.99	11.05	11.12	11.19	11.25	11.32	11.38	11.45
17	6	210	10.88	10.95	11.02	11.08	11.15	11.22	11.28	11.35
18	0	216	10.79	10.85	10.92	10.99	11.05	11.12	11.19	11.26
18	6	222	10.70	10.76	10.83	10.90	10.97	11.03	11.10	11.17
19	0	228	10.61	10.68	10.75	10.82	10.89	10.95	11.02	11.09
19	6	234	10.54	10.60	10.67	10.74	10.81	10.88	10.95	11.02
20	0	240	10.46	10.53	10.60	10.67	10.74	10.81	10.88	10.95
20	6	246	10.40	10.46	10.53	10.60	10.67	10.74	10.81	10.88
21	0	252	10.33	10.40	10.47	10.54	10.61	10.68	10.75	10.82
21	6	258	10.27	10.34	10.41	10.48	10.55	10.62	10.69	10.77
22	0	264	10.22	10.29	10.36	10.43	10.50	10.57	10.64	10.71
22	6	270	10.17	10.24	10.31	10.38	10.45	10.52	10.59	10.66
23	0	276	10.12	10.19	10.26	10.33	10.40	10.47	10.55	10.62
23	6	282	10.07	10.14	10.21	10.29	10.36	10.43	10.50	10.58
24	0	288	10.03	10.10	10.17	10.25	10.32	10.39	10.46	10.54
24	6	294	9.99	10.06	10.13	10.21	10.28	10.35	10.43	10.50
25	0	300	9.95	10.02	10.10	10.17	10.24	10.32	10.39	10.46
25	6	306	9.92	9.99	10.06	10.14	10.21	10.28	10.36	10.43
26	0	312	9.88	9.96	10.03	10.10	10.18	10.25	10.33	10.40
26	6	318	9.85	9.93	10.00	10.07	10.15	10.22	10.30	10.37
27	0	324	9.82	9.90	9.97	10.05	10.12	10.19	10.27	10.34
27	6	330	9.79	9.87	9.94	10.02	10.09	10.17	10.24	10.32
28	0	336	9.77	9.84	9.92	9.99	10.07	10.14	10.22	10.30
28	6	342	9.74	9.82	9.89	9.97	10.05	10.12	10.20	10.27
29	0	348	9.72	9.80	9.87	9.95	10.02	10.10	10.18	10.25
29	6	354	9.70	9.78	9.85	9.93	10.00	10.08	10.16	10.23
30	0	360	9.68	9.76	9.83	9.91	9.98	10.06	10.14	10.21

TERM YRS MOS PERS			12%	12.1%	12.2%	12.3%	12.4%	12.5%	12.6%	12.7%
1	0	12	88.85	88.90	88.95	88.99	89.04	89.09	89.13	89.18
1	6	18	60.99	61.03	61.08	61.13	61.17	61.22	61.27	61.31
2	0	24	47.08	47.13	47.17	47.22	47.27	47.31	47.36	47.41
2	6	30	38.75	38.80	38.85	38.89	38.94	38.99	39.04	39.08
3	0	36	33.22	33.27	33.31	33.36	33.41	33.46	33.51	33.55
3	6	42	29.28	29.33	29.38	29.43	29.47	29.52	29.57	29.62
4	0	48	26.34	26.39	26.44	26.49	26.54	26.58	26.63	26.68
4	6	54	24.06	24.11	24.16	24.21	24.26	24.31	24.36	24.41
5	0	60	22.25	22.30	22.35	22.40	22.45	22.50	22.55	22.60
5	6	66	20.78	20.83	20.88	20.93	20.98	21.03	21.08	21.14
6	C	72	19.56	19.61	19.66	19.71	19.76	19.82	19.87	19.92
6	6	78	18.53	18.58	18.64	18.69	18.74	18.79	18.85	18.90
7	0	84	17.66	17.71	17.76	17.82	17.87	17.93	17.98	18.03
7	6	90	16.91	16.96	17.02	17.07	17.13	17.18	17.24	17.29
8	0	96	16.26	16.31	16.37	16.42	16.48	16.53	16.59	16.64
8	6	102	15.69	15.75	15.80	15.86	15.91	15.97	16.03	16.08
9	0	108	15.19	15.25	15.30	15.36	15.42	15.47	15.53	15.59
9	6	114	14.75	14.80	14.86	14.92	14.98	15.03	15.09	15.15
10	0	120	14.35	14.41	14.47	14.53	14.58	14.64	14.70	14.76
10	6	126	14.00	14.06	14.12	14.18	14.23	14.29	14.35	14.41
11	0	132	13.68	13.74	13.80	13.86	13.92	13.98	14.04	14.10
11	6	138	13.40	13.46	13.52	13.58	13.64	13.70	13.76	13.82
12	0	144	13.14	13.20	13.26	13.32	13.38	13.44	13.50	13.57
12	6	150	12.90	12.97	13.03	13.09	13.15	13.21	13.27	13.34
13	0	156	12.69	12.75	12.82	12.88	12.94	13.00	13.07	13.13
13	6	162	12.50	12.56	12.62	12.69	12.75	12.81	12.87	12.94
14	0	168	12.32	12.38	12.45	12.51	12.57	12.64	12.70	12.76
14	6	174	12.16	12.22	12.28	12.35	12.41	12.48	12.54	12.61
15	0	180	12.01	12.07	12.14	12.20	12.27	12.33	12.40	12.46
15	6	186	11.87	11.93	12.00	12.06	12.13	12.20	12.26	12.33
16	0	192	11.74	11.81	11.87	11.94	12.01	12.07	12.14	12.20
16	6	198	11.63	11.69	11.76	11.82	11.89	11.96	12.02	12.09
17	0	204	11.52	11.58	11.65	11.72	11.78	11.85	11.92	11.99
17	6	210	11.42	11.48	11.55	11.62	11.69	11.75	11.82	11.89
18	0	216	11.32	11.39	11.46	11.53	11.60	11.67	11.73	11.80
18	6	222	11.24	11.31	11.38	11.44	11.51	11.58	11.65	11.72
19	0	228	11.16	11.23	11.30	11.37	11.44	11.50	11.57	11.64
19	6	234	11.08	11.15	11.22	11.29	11.36	11.43	11.50	11.57
20	0	240	11.02	11.09	11.16	11.23	11.30	11.37	11.44	11.51
20	6	246	10.95	11.02	11.09	11.16	11.23	11.30	11.38	11.45
21	0	252	10.89	10.96	11.03	11.10	11.18	11.25	11.32	11.39
21	6	258	10.84	10.91	10.98	11.05	11.12	11.19	11.27	11.34
22	0	264	10.78	10.86	10.93	11.00	11.07	11.14	11.22	11.29
22	6	270	10.74	10.81	10.88	10.95	11.02	11.10	11.17	11.24
23	0	276	10.69	10.76	10.84	10.91	10.98	11.05	11.13	11.20
23	6	282	10.65	10.72	10.79	10.87	10.94	11.01	11.09	11.16
24	0	288	10.61	10.68	10.76	10.83	10.90	10.98	11.05	11.12
24	6	294	10.57	10.65	10.72	10.79	10.87	10.94	11.02	11.09
25	0	300	10.54	10.61	10.69	10.76	10.83	10.91	10.98	11.06
25	6	306	10.50	10.58	10.65	10.73	10.80	10.88	10.95	11.03
26	0	312	10.47	10.55	10.62	10.70	10.77	10.85	10.92	11.00
26	6	318	10.45	10.52	10.60	10.67	10.75	10.82	10.90	10.97
27	0	324	10.42	10.49	10.57	10.65	10.72	10.80	10.87	10.95
27	6	330	10.39	10.47	10.55	10.62	10.70	10.77	10.85	10.93
28	0	336	10.37	10.45	10.52	10.60	10.68	10.75	10.83	10.91
28	6	342	10.35	10.43	10.50	10.58	10.65	10.73	10.81	10.89
29	0	348	10.33	10.41	10.48	10.56	10.64	10.71	10.79	10.87
29	6	354	10.31	10.39	10.46	10.54	10.62	10.69	10.77	10.85
30	0	360	10.29	10.37	10.45	10.52	10.60	10.68	10.76	10.83

1/10% MONTHLY PAYMENTS
FOR A $1000 LOAN

TERM YRS MOS PERS	12.8%	12.9%	13%	13.1%	13.2%	13.3%	13.4%	13.5%
1 0 12	89.23	89.28	89.32	89.37	89.42	89.46	89.51	89.56
1 6 18	61.36	61.41	61.45	61.50	61.55	61.59	61.64	61.69
2 0 24	47.45	47.50	47.55	47.59	47.64	47.69	47.73	47.78
2 6 30	39.13	39.18	39.23	39.27	39.32	39.37	39.42	39.46
3 0 36	33.60	33.65	33.70	33.75	33.80	33.84	33.89	33.94
3 6 42	29.67	29.72	29.77	29.82	29.86	29.91	29.96	30.01
4 0 48	26.73	26.78	26.83	26.88	26.93	26.98	27.03	27.08
4 6 54	24.46	24.51	24.56	24.61	24.66	24.71	24.76	24.82
5 0 60	22.66	22.71	22.76	22.81	22.86	22.91	22.96	23.01
5 6 66	21.19	21.24	21.29	21.34	21.40	21.45	21.50	21.55
6 0 72	19.97	20.03	20.08	20.13	20.18	20.24	20.29	20.34
6 6 78	18.95	19.01	19.06	19.12	19.17	19.22	19.28	19.33
7 0 84	18.09	18.14	18.20	18.25	18.31	18.36	18.42	18.47
7 6 90	17.34	17.40	17.45	17.51	17.57	17.62	17.68	17.73
8 0 96	16.70	16.76	16.81	16.87	16.92	16.98	17.04	17.09
8 6 102	16.14	16.19	16.25	16.31	16.37	16.42	16.48	16.54
9 0 108	15.64	15.70	15.76	15.82	15.87	15.93	15.99	16.05
9 6 114	15.21	15.26	15.32	15.38	15.44	15.50	15.56	15.62
10 0 120	14.82	14.88	14.94	15.00	15.05	15.11	15.17	15.23
10 6 126	14.47	14.53	14.59	14.65	14.71	14.77	14.83	14.89
11 0 132	14.16	14.22	14.28	14.34	14.40	14.46	14.52	14.58
11 6 138	13.88	13.94	14.00	14.06	14.13	14.19	14.25	14.31
12 0 144	13.63	13.69	13.75	13.81	13.88	13.94	14.00	14.06
12 6 150	13.40	13.46	13.52	13.59	13.65	13.71	13.77	13.84
13 0 156	13.19	13.25	13.32	13.38	13.44	13.51	13.57	13.63
13 6 162	13.00	13.07	13.13	13.19	13.26	13.32	13.39	13.45
14 0 168	12.83	12.89	12.96	13.02	13.09	13.15	13.22	13.28
14 6 174	12.67	12.74	12.80	12.87	12.93	13.00	13.06	13.13
15 0 180	12.53	12.59	12.66	12.72	12.79	12.86	12.92	12.99
15 6 186	12.39	12.46	12.53	12.59	12.66	12.73	12.79	12.86
16 0 192	12.27	12.34	12.40	12.47	12.54	12.61	12.67	12.74
16 6 198	12.16	12.23	12.29	12.36	12.43	12.50	12.57	12.63
17 0 204	12.06	12.12	12.19	12.26	12.33	12.40	12.46	12.53
17 6 210	11.96	12.03	12.10	12.17	12.23	12.30	12.37	12.44
18 0 216	11.87	11.94	12.01	12.08	12.15	12.22	12.29	12.36
18 6 222	11.79	11.86	11.93	12.00	12.07	12.14	12.21	12.28
19 0 228	11.71	11.78	11.85	11.92	11.99	12.07	12.14	12.21
19 6 234	11.64	11.71	11.78	11.86	11.93	12.00	12.07	12.14
20 0 240	11.58	11.65	11.72	11.79	11.86	11.94	12.01	12.08
20 6 246	11.52	11.59	11.66	11.73	11.81	11.88	11.95	12.02
21 0 252	11.46	11.53	11.61	11.68	11.75	11.82	11.90	11.97
21 6 258	11.41	11.48	11.55	11.63	11.70	11.77	11.85	11.92
22 0 264	11.36	11.43	11.51	11.58	11.65	11.73	11.80	11.87
22 6 270	11.32	11.39	11.46	11.54	11.61	11.68	11.76	11.83
23 0 276	11.27	11.35	11.42	11.50	11.57	11.64	11.72	11.79
23 6 282	11.24	11.31	11.38	11.46	11.53	11.61	11.68	11.76
24 0 288	11.20	11.27	11.35	11.42	11.50	11.57	11.65	11.72
24 6 294	11.16	11.24	11.31	11.39	11.46	11.54	11.62	11.69
25 0 300	11.13	11.21	11.28	11.36	11.43	11.51	11.59	11.66
25 6 306	11.10	11.18	11.25	11.33	11.41	11.48	11.56	11.63
26 0 312	11.08	11.15	11.23	11.30	11.38	11.46	11.53	11.61
26 6 318	11.05	11.13	11.20	11.28	11.36	11.43	11.51	11.59
27 0 324	11.03	11.10	11.18	11.26	11.33	11.41	11.49	11.56
27 6 330	11.00	11.08	11.16	11.23	11.31	11.39	11.47	11.54
28 0 336	10.98	11.06	11.14	11.21	11.29	11.37	11.45	11.52
28 6 342	10.96	11.04	11.12	11.19	11.27	11.35	11.43	11.51
29 0 348	10.94	11.02	11.10	11.18	11.25	11.33	11.41	11.49
29 6 354	10.93	11.00	11.08	11.16	11.24	11.32	11.40	11.47
30 0 360	10.91	10.99	11.07	11.15	11.22	11.30	11.38	11.46

1/10% MONTHLY PAYMENTS
FOR A $1000 LOAN

TERM YRS	MOS	PERS	13.6%	13.7%	13.8%	13.9%	14%	14.1%	14.2%	14.3%
1	0	12	89.60	89.65	89.70	89.75	89.79	89.84	89.89	89.93
1	6	18	61.73	61.78	61.83	61.87	61.92	61.97	62.01	62.06
2	0	24	47.83	47.88	47.92	47.97	48.02	48.07	48.11	48.16
2	6	30	39.51	39.56	39.61	39.66	39.70	39.75	39.80	39.85
3	0	36	33.99	34.04	34.09	34.13	34.18	34.23	34.28	34.33
3	6	42	30.06	30.11	30.16	30.21	30.26	30.31	30.36	30.41
4	0	48	27.13	27.18	27.23	27.28	27.33	27.38	27.43	27.48
4	6	54	24.87	24.92	24.97	25.02	25.07	25.12	25.17	25.22
5	0	60	23.07	23.12	23.17	23.22	23.27	23.33	23.38	23.43
5	6	66	21.60	21.66	21.71	21.76	21.82	21.87	21.92	21.97
6	0	72	20.40	20.45	20.50	20.56	20.61	20.66	20.72	20.77
6	6	78	19.38	19.44	19.49	19.55	19.60	19.66	19.71	19.76
7	0	84	18.52	18.58	18.63	18.69	18.75	18.80	18.86	18.91
7	6	90	17.79	17.84	17.90	17.96	18.01	18.07	18.12	18.18
8	0	96	17.15	17.21	17.26	17.32	17.38	17.43	17.49	17.55
8	6	102	16.59	16.65	16.71	16.77	16.82	16.88	16.94	17.00
9	0	108	16.11	16.16	16.22	16.28	16.34	16.40	16.46	16.51
9	6	114	15.67	15.73	15.79	15.85	15.91	15.97	16.03	16.09
10	0	120	15.29	15.35	15.41	15.47	15.53	15.59	15.65	15.71
10	6	126	14.95	15.01	15.07	15.13	15.19	15.25	15.32	15.38
11	0	132	14.65	14.71	14.77	14.83	14.89	14.95	15.02	15.08
11	6	138	14.37	14.43	14.50	14.56	14.62	14.68	14.75	14.81
12	0	144	14.12	14.19	14.25	14.31	14.38	14.44	14.50	14.57
12	6	150	13.90	13.96	14.03	14.09	14.16	14.22	14.28	14.35
13	0	156	13.70	13.76	13.83	13.89	13.96	14.02	14.09	14.15
13	6	162	13.51	13.58	13.64	13.71	13.77	13.84	13.91	13.97
14	0	168	13.35	13.41	13.48	13.54	13.61	13.68	13.74	13.81
14	6	174	13.19	13.26	13.33	13.39	13.46	13.53	13.59	13.66
15	0	180	13.05	13.12	13.19	13.26	13.32	13.39	13.46	13.52
15	6	186	12.93	12.99	13.06	13.13	13.20	13.26	13.33	13.40
16	0	192	12.81	12.88	12.95	13.01	13.08	13.15	13.22	13.29
16	6	198	12.70	12.77	12.84	12.91	12.98	13.05	13.11	13.18
17	0	204	12.60	12.67	12.74	12.81	12.88	12.95	13.02	13.09
17	6	210	12.51	12.58	12.65	12.72	12.79	12.86	12.93	13.00
18	0	216	12.43	12.50	12.57	12.64	12.71	12.78	12.85	12.92
18	6	222	12.35	12.42	12.49	12.56	12.63	12.70	12.78	12.85
19	0	228	12.28	12.35	12.42	12.49	12.56	12.64	12.71	12.78
19	6	234	12.21	12.28	12.36	12.43	12.50	12.57	12.64	12.72
20	0	240	12.15	12.22	12.30	12.37	12.44	12.51	12.59	12.66
20	6	246	12.09	12.17	12.24	12.31	12.39	12.46	12.53	12.61
21	0	252	12.04	12.11	12.19	12.26	12.33	12.41	12.48	12.56
21	6	258	11.99	12.07	12.14	12.21	12.29	12.36	12.44	12.51
22	0	264	11.95	12.02	12.10	12.17	12.24	12.32	12.39	12.47
22	6	270	11.91	11.98	12.05	12.13	12.20	12.28	12.35	12.43
23	0	276	11.87	11.94	12.02	12.09	12.17	12.24	12.32	12.39
23	6	282	11.83	11.91	11.98	12.06	12.13	12.21	12.28	12.36
24	0	288	11.80	11.87	11.95	12.02	12.10	12.18	12.25	12.33
24	6	294	11.77	11.84	11.92	11.99	12.07	12.15	12.22	12.30
25	0	300	11.74	11.81	11.89	11.97	12.04	12.12	12.20	12.27
25	6	306	11.71	11.79	11.86	11.94	12.02	12.09	12.17	12.25
26	0	312	11.69	11.76	11.84	11.92	11.99	12.07	12.15	12.22
26	6	318	11.66	11.74	11.82	11.89	11.97	12.05	12.13	12.20
27	0	324	11.64	11.72	11.80	11.87	11.95	12.03	12.11	12.18
27	6	330	11.62	11.70	11.78	11.85	11.93	12.01	12.09	12.17
28	0	336	11.60	11.68	11.76	11.84	11.91	11.99	12.07	12.15
28	6	342	11.58	11.66	11.74	11.82	11.90	11.98	12.05	12.13
29	0	348	11.57	11.65	11.72	11.80	11.88	11.96	12.04	12.12
29	6	354	11.55	11.63	11.71	11.79	11.87	11.95	12.03	12.10
30	0	360	11.54	11.62	11.70	11.77	11.85	11.93	12.01	12.09

1/10% MONTHLY PAYMENTS

FOR A $1000 LOAN

TERM YRS	MOS	PERS	14.4%	14.5%	14.6%	14.7%	14.8%	14.9%	15%	15.1%
1	0	12	89.98	90.03	90.07	90.12	90.17	90.22	90.26	90.31
1	6	18	62.11	62.15	62.20	62.25	62.30	62.34	62.39	62.44
2	0	24	48.21	48.25	48.30	48.35	48.40	48.44	48.49	48.54
2	6	30	39.90	39.94	39.99	40.04	40.09	40.14	40.18	40.23
3	0	36	34.38	34.43	34.47	34.52	34.57	34.62	34.67	34.72
3	6	42	30.46	30.51	30.56	30.60	30.65	30.70	30.75	30.80
4	0	48	27.53	27.58	27.63	27.68	27.73	27.79	27.84	27.89
4	6	54	25.27	25.33	25.38	25.43	25.48	25.53	25.58	25.63
5	0	60	23.48	23.53	23.59	23.64	23.69	23.74	23.79	23.85
5	6	66	22.03	22.08	22.13	22.19	22.24	22.29	22.35	22.40
6	0	72	20.83	20.88	20.93	20.99	21.04	21.10	21.15	21.20
6	6	78	19.82	19.87	19.93	19.98	20.04	20.09	20.15	20.20
7	0	84	18.97	19.02	19.08	19.13	19.19	19.25	19.30	19.36
7	6	90	18.24	18.29	18.35	18.41	18.46	18.52	18.58	18.63
8	0	96	17.60	17.66	17.72	17.78	17.83	17.89	17.95	18.01
8	6	102	17.06	17.11	17.17	17.23	17.29	17.35	17.41	17.46
9	0	108	16.57	16.63	16.69	16.75	16.81	16.87	16.93	16.99
9	6	114	16.15	16.21	16.27	16.33	16.39	16.45	16.51	16.57
10	0	120	15.77	15.83	15.89	15.96	16.02	16.08	16.14	16.20
10	6	126	15.44	15.50	15.56	15.62	15.68	15.75	15.81	15.87
11	0	132	15.14	15.20	15.26	15.33	15.39	15.45	15.51	15.58
11	6	138	14.87	14.93	15.00	15.06	15.12	15.19	15.25	15.31
12	0	144	14.63	14.69	14.76	14.82	14.89	14.95	15.01	15.08
12	6	150	14.41	14.48	14.54	14.61	14.67	14.74	14.80	14.87
13	0	156	14.22	14.28	14.35	14.41	14.48	14.54	14.61	14.67
13	6	162	14.04	14.10	14.17	14.23	14.30	14.37	14.43	14.50
14	0	168	13.87	13.94	14.01	14.07	14.14	14.21	14.28	14.34
14	6	174	13.73	13.79	13.86	13.93	14.00	14.06	14.13	14.20
15	0	180	13.59	13.66	13.73	13.80	13.86	13.93	14.00	14.07
15	6	186	13.47	13.54	13.61	13.67	13.74	13.81	13.88	13.95
16	0	192	13.36	13.43	13.49	13.56	13.63	13.70	13.77	13.84
16	6	198	13.25	13.32	13.39	13.46	13.53	13.60	13.67	13.74
17	0	204	13.16	13.23	13.30	13.37	13.44	13.51	13.58	13.65
17	6	210	13.07	13.14	13.21	13.28	13.36	13.43	13.50	13.57
18	0	216	12.99	13.06	13.14	13.21	13.28	13.35	13.42	13.49
18	6	222	12.92	12.99	13.06	13.13	13.21	13.28	13.35	13.42
19	0	228	12.85	12.92	13.00	13.07	13.14	13.21	13.29	13.36
19	6	234	12.79	12.86	12.93	13.01	13.08	13.15	13.23	13.30
20	0	240	12.73	12.80	12.88	12.95	13.03	13.10	13.17	13.25
20	6	246	12.68	12.75	12.83	12.90	12.97	13.05	13.12	13.20
21	0	252	12.63	12.70	12.78	12.85	12.93	13.00	13.08	13.15
21	6	258	12.58	12.66	12.73	12.81	12.88	12.96	13.03	13.11
22	0	264	12.54	12.62	12.69	12.77	12.84	12.92	12.99	13.07
22	6	270	12.50	12.58	12.65	12.73	12.81	12.88	12.96	13.03
23	0	276	12.47	12.54	12.62	12.70	12.77	12.85	12.92	13.00
23	6	282	12.44	12.51	12.59	12.66	12.74	12.82	12.89	12.97
24	0	288	12.40	12.48	12.56	12.63	12.71	12.79	12.86	12.94
24	6	294	12.38	12.45	12.53	12.61	12.68	12.76	12.84	12.92
25	0	300	12.35	12.43	12.50	12.58	12.66	12.74	12.81	12.89
25	6	306	12.33	12.40	12.48	12.56	12.64	12.71	12.79	12.87
26	0	312	12.30	12.38	12.46	12.54	12.61	12.69	12.77	12.85
26	6	318	12.28	12.36	12.44	12.52	12.59	12.67	12.75	12.83
27	0	324	12.26	12.34	12.42	12.50	12.58	12.65	12.73	12.81
27	6	330	12.24	12.32	12.40	12.48	12.56	12.64	12.72	12.79
28	0	336	12.23	12.31	12.38	12.46	12.54	12.62	12.70	12.78
28	6	342	12.21	12.29	12.37	12.45	12.53	12.61	12.69	12.77
29	0	348	12.20	12.28	12.36	12.43	12.51	12.59	12.67	12.75
29	6	354	12.18	12.26	12.34	12.42	12.50	12.58	12.66	12.74
30	0	360	12.17	12.25	12.33	12.41	12.49	12.57	12.65	12.73

1/10% MONTHLY PAYMENTS
FOR A $1000 LOAN

TERM YRS MOS PERS			15.2%	15.3%	15.4%	15.5%	15.6%	15.7%	15.8%	15.9%
1	0	12	90.36	90.40	90.45	90.50	90.55	90.59	90.64	90.69
1	6	18	62.48	62.53	62.58	62.63	62.67	62.72	62.77	62.81
2	0	24	48.59	48.63	48.68	48.73	48.78	48.82	48.87	48.92
2	6	30	40.28	40.33	40.38	40.42	40.47	40.52	40.57	40.62
3	0	36	34.77	34.82	34.87	34.92	34.96	35.01	35.06	35.11
3	6	42	30.85	30.90	30.95	31.00	31.05	31.10	31.15	31.20
4	0	48	27.94	27.99	28.04	28.09	28.14	28.19	28.24	28.29
4	6	54	25.69	25.74	25.79	25.84	25.89	25.95	26.00	26.05
5	0	60	23.90	23.95	24.01	24.06	24.11	24.16	24.22	24.27
5	6	66	22.45	22.51	22.56	22.61	22.67	22.72	22.78	22.83
6	0	72	21.26	21.31	21.37	21.42	21.48	21.53	21.59	21.64
6	6	78	20.26	20.32	20.37	20.43	20.48	20.54	20.59	20.65
7	0	84	19.41	19.47	19.53	19.58	19.64	19.70	19.75	19.81
7	6	90	18.69	18.75	18.81	18.86	18.92	18.98	19.04	19.09
8	0	96	18.07	18.12	18.18	18.24	18.30	18.36	18.42	18.48
8	6	102	17.52	17.58	17.64	17.70	17.76	17.82	17.88	17.94
9	0	108	17.05	17.11	17.17	17.23	17.29	17.35	17.41	17.47
9	6	114	16.63	16.69	16.75	16.81	16.87	16.94	17.00	17.06
10	0	120	16.26	16.32	16.38	16.45	16.51	16.57	16.63	16.69
10	6	126	15.93	16.00	16.06	16.12	16.18	16.25	16.31	16.37
11	0	132	15.64	15.70	15.77	15.83	15.89	15.96	16.02	16.08
11	6	138	15.38	15.44	15.51	15.57	15.63	15.70	15.76	15.83
12	0	144	15.14	15.21	15.27	15.34	15.40	15.47	15.53	15.60
12	6	150	14.93	15.00	15.06	15.13	15.19	15.26	15.33	15.39
13	0	156	14.74	14.81	14.87	14.94	15.00	15.07	15.14	15.21
13	6	162	14.57	14.63	14.70	14.77	14.83	14.90	14.97	15.04
14	0	168	14.41	14.48	14.55	14.61	14.68	14.75	14.82	14.89
14	6	174	14.27	14.34	14.40	14.47	14.54	14.61	14.68	14.75
15	0	180	14.14	14.21	14.28	14.34	14.41	14.48	14.55	14.62
15	6	186	14.02	14.09	14.16	14.23	14.30	14.37	14.44	14.51
16	0	192	13.91	13.98	14.05	14.12	14.19	14.26	14.33	14.41
16	6	198	13.81	13.88	13.96	14.03	14.10	14.17	14.24	14.31
17	0	204	13.72	13.80	13.87	13.94	14.01	14.08	14.15	14.22
17	6	210	13.64	13.71	13.79	13.86	13.93	14.00	14.07	14.15
18	0	216	13.57	13.64	13.71	13.78	13.86	13.93	14.00	14.07
18	6	222	13.50	13.57	13.64	13.72	13.79	13.86	13.94	14.01
19	0	228	13.43	13.51	13.58	13.65	13.73	13.80	13.87	13.95
19	6	234	13.37	13.45	13.52	13.60	13.67	13.74	13.82	13.89
20	0	240	13.32	13.40	13.47	13.54	13.62	13.69	13.77	13.84
20	6	246	13.27	13.35	13.42	13.50	13.57	13.65	13.72	13.80
21	0	252	13.23	13.30	13.38	13.45	13.53	13.60	13.68	13.75
21	6	258	13.18	13.26	13.33	13.41	13.49	13.56	13.64	13.71
22	0	264	13.15	13.22	13.30	13.37	13.45	13.53	13.60	13.68
22	6	270	13.11	13.19	13.26	13.34	13.42	13.49	13.57	13.65
23	0	276	13.08	13.15	13.23	13.31	13.38	13.46	13.54	13.61
23	6	282	13.05	13.12	13.20	13.28	13.35	13.43	13.51	13.59
24	0	288	13.02	13.10	13.17	13.25	13.33	13.41	13.48	13.56
24	6	294	12.99	13.07	13.15	13.23	13.30	13.38	13.46	13.54
25	0	300	12.97	13.05	13.12	13.20	13.28	13.36	13.44	13.52
25	6	306	12.95	13.02	13.10	13.18	13.26	13.34	13.42	13.50
26	0	312	12.93	13.00	13.08	13.16	13.24	13.32	13.40	13.48
26	6	318	12.91	12.99	13.06	13.14	13.22	13.30	13.38	13.46
27	0	324	12.89	12.97	13.05	13.13	13.21	13.29	13.36	13.44
27	6	330	12.87	12.95	13.03	13.11	13.19	13.27	13.35	13.43
28	0	336	12.86	12.94	13.02	13.10	13.18	13.26	13.34	13.42
28	6	342	12.85	12.92	13.00	13.08	13.16	13.24	13.32	13.40
29	0	348	12.83	12.91	12.99	13.07	13.15	13.23	13.31	13.39
29	6	354	12.82	12.90	12.98	13.06	13.14	13.22	13.30	13.38
30	0	360	12.81	12.89	12.97	13.05	13.13	13.21	13.29	13.37

CONSTANT ANNUAL PERCENT - MONTHLY

DIVIDE BY 12 TO DETERMINE MONTHLY PAYMENT

INTEREST RATE	5 YEARS	10 YEARS	15 YEARS	20 YEARS	25 YEARS	30 YEARS	35 YEARS	40 YEARS
13	27.31	17.92	15.19	14.06	13.54	13.28	13.15	13.08
1/8	27.39	18.01	15.29	14.17	13.65	13.40	13.27	13.20
1/4	27.46	18.10	15.39	14.28	13.77	13.51	13.39	13.32
3/8	27.54	18.19	15.49	14.39	13.88	13.63	13.51	13.45
1/2	27.62	18.28	15.58	14.49	13.99	13.75	13.63	13.57
5/8	27.69	18.37	15.68	14.60	14.11	13.87	13.75	13.69
3/4	27.77	18.46	15.78	14.71	14.22	13.99	13.87	13.81
7/8	27.85	18.55	15.89	14.82	14.34	14.10	13.99	13.94
14	27.93	18.64	15.99	14.93	14.45	14.22	14.11	14.06
1/8	28.00	18.73	16.09	15.04	14.57	14.34	14.23	14.18
1/4	28.08	18.82	16.19	15.15	14.68	14.46	14.36	14.30
3/8	28.16	18.91	16.29	15.26	14.80	14.58	14.48	14.43
1/2	28.24	19.00	16.39	15.36	14.91	14.70	14.60	14.55
5/8	28.32	19.09	16.49	15.48	15.03	14.82	14.72	14.67
3/4	28.40	19.18	16.60	15.59	15.14	14.94	14.84	14.80
7/8	28.47	19.27	16.70	15.70	15.26	15.06	14.96	14.92
15	28.55	19.37	16.80	15.81	15.37	15.18	15.09	15.04
1/8	28.63	19.46	16.90	15.92	15.49	15.30	15.21	15.17
1/4	28.71	19.55	17.01	16.03	15.61	15.42	15.33	15.29
3/8	28.79	19.64	17.11	16.14	15.72	15.54	15.45	15.41
1/2	28.87	19.73	17.21	16.25	15.84	15.66	15.58	15.54
5/8	28.95	19.83	17.32	16.36	15.96	15.78	15.70	15.66
3/4	29.03	19.92	17.42	16.48	16.08	15.90	15.82	15.79
7/8	29.11	20.01	17.52	16.59	16.19	16.02	15.94	15.91
16	29.19	20.11	17.63	16.70	16.31	16.14	16.07	16.03
1/4	29.35	20.29	17.84	16.93	16.55	16.38	16.31	16.28
1/2	29.51	20.48	18.05	17.15	16.78	16.63	16.56	16.53
3/4	29.67	20.67	18.26	17.38	17.02	16.87	16.80	16.78
17	29.83	20.86	18.47	17.61	17.26	17.11	17.05	17.02
1/4	29.99	21.05	18.69	17.84	17.50	17.36	17.30	17.27
1/2	30.15	21.24	18.90	18.06	17.74	17.60	17.55	17.52
3/4	30.31	21.43	19.11	18.29	17.97	17.85	17.79	17.77
18	30.48	21.63	19.33	18.52	18.21	18.09	18.04	18.02
1/4	30.64	21.82	19.55	18.76	18.45	18.34	18.29	18.27
1/2	30.80	22.01	19.76	18.99	18.69	18.58	18.54	18.52
3/4	30.97	22.21	19.98	19.22	18.94	18.83	18.78	18.77
19	31.13	22.41	20.20	19.45	19.18	19.07	19.03	19.02
1/4	31.30	22.60	20.42	19.69	19.42	19.32	19.28	19.26
1/2	31.46	22.80	20.64	19.92	19.66	19.56	19.53	19.51
3/4	31.63	23.00	20.86	20.16	19.90	19.81	19.78	19.76
20	31.80	23.20	21.08	20.39	20.15	20.06	20.02	20.01
1/4	31.96	23.39	21.30	20.63	20.39	20.30	20.27	20.26
1/2	32.13	23.59	21.53	20.86	20.63	20.55	20.52	20.51
3/4	32.30	23.80	21.75	21.10	20.88	20.80	20.77	20.76
21	32.47	24.00	21.97	21.34	21.12	21.05	21.02	21.01
1/4	32.64	24.20	22.20	21.57	21.37	21.29	21.27	21.26
1/2	32.81	24.40	22.42	21.81	21.61	21.54	21.52	21.51
3/4	32.98	24.60	22.65	22.05	21.85	21.79	21.77	21.76
22	33.15	24.81	22.87	22.29	22.10	22.04	22.02	22.01
1/4	33.32	25.01	23.10	22.53	22.35	22.28	22.26	22.26
1/2	33.49	25.22	23.33	22.77	22.59	22.53	22.51	22.51
3/4	33.66	25.42	23.56	23.01	22.84	22.78	22.76	22.76
23	33.83	25.63	23.78	23.25	23.08	23.03	23.01	23.01
1/2	34.18	26.05	24.24	23.73	23.58	23.53	23.51	23.51
24	34.53	26.46	24.70	24.21	24.07	24.02	24.01	24.01
1/2	34.88	26.88	25.17	24.70	24.56	24.52	24.51	24.51
25	35.23	27.30	25.63	25.18	25.06	25.02	25.01	25.01

PERCENT DOWN PAYMENT

Appraised Value	15%	20%	25%	30%	33⅓%	35%	40%
15000	2.250	3.000	3.750	4.500	5.000	5.250	6.000
15500	2.325	3.100	3.875	4.650	5.167	5.425	6.200
16000	2.400	3.200	4.000	4.800	5.333	5.600	6.400
16500	2.475	3.300	4.125	4.950	5.500	5.775	6.600
17000	2.550	3.400	4.250	5.100	5.667	5.950	6.800
17500	2.625	3.500	4.375	5.250	5.833	6.125	7.000
18000	2.700	3.600	4.500	5.400	6.000	6.300	7.200
18500	2.775	3.700	4.625	5.550	6.167	6.475	7.400
19000	2.850	3.800	4.750	5.700	6.333	6.650	7.600
19500	2.925	3.900	4.875	5.850	6.500	6.825	7.800
20000	3.000	4.000	5.000	6.000	6.667	7.000	8.000
20500	3.075	4.100	5.125	6.150	6.833	7.175	8.200
21000	3.150	4.200	5.250	6.300	7.000	7.350	8.400
21500	3.225	4.300	5.375	6.450	7.167	7.525	8.600
22000	3.300	4.400	5.500	6.600	7.333	7.700	8.800
22500	3.375	4.500	5.625	6.750	7.500	7.875	9.000
23000	3.450	4.600	5.750	6.900	7.667	8.050	9.200
23500	3.525	4.700	5.875	7.050	7.833	8.225	9.400
24000	3.600	4.800	6.000	7.200	8.000	8.400	9.600
24500	3.675	4.900	6.125	7.350	8.167	8.575	9.800
25000	3.750	5.000	6.250	7.500	8.333	8.750	10.000
25500	3.825	5.100	6.375	7.650	8.500	8.925	10.200
26000	3.900	5.200	6.500	7.800	8.667	9.100	10.400
26500	3.975	5.300	6.625	7.950	8.833	9.275	10.600
27000	4.050	5.400	6.750	8.100	9.000	9.450	10.800
27500	4.125	5.500	6.875	8.250	9.167	9.625	11.000
28000	4.200	5.600	7.000	8.400	9.333	9.800	11.200
28500	4.275	5.700	7.125	8.550	9.500	9.975	11.400
29000	4.350	5.800	7.250	8.700	9.667	10.150	11.600
29500	4.425	5.900	7.375	8.850	9.833	10.325	11.800
30000	4.500	6.000	7.500	9.000	10.000	10.500	12.000
30500	4.575	6.100	7.625	9.150	10.167	10.675	12.200
31000	4.650	6.200	7.750	9.300	10.333	10.850	12.400
31500	4.725	6.300	7.875	9.450	10.500	11.025	12.600
32000	4.800	6.400	8.000	9.600	10.667	11.200	12.800
32500	4.875	6.500	8.125	9.750	10.833	11.375	13.000
33000	4.950	6.600	8.250	9.900	11.000	11.550	13.200
33500	5.025	6.700	8.375	10.050	11.167	11.725	13.400
34000	5.100	6.800	8.500	10.200	11.333	11.900	13.600
34500	5.175	6.900	8.625	10.350	11.500	12.075	13.800
35000	5.250	7.000	8.750	10.500	11.667	12.250	14.000
35500	5.325	7.100	8.875	10.650	11.833	12.425	14.200
36000	5.400	7.200	9.000	10.800	12.000	12.600	14.400
36500	5.475	7.300	9.125	10.950	12.167	12.775	14.600
37000	5.550	7.400	9.250	11.100	12.333	12.950	14.800
37500	5.625	7.500	9.375	11.250	12.500	13.125	15.000
38000	5.700	7.600	9.500	11.400	12.667	13.300	15.200
38500	5.775	7.700	9.625	11.550	12.833	13.475	15.400
39000	5.850	7.800	9.750	11.700	13.000	13.650	15.600
40000	6.000	8.000	10.000	12.000	13.333	14.000	16.000
41000	6.150	8.200	10.250	12.300	13.667	14.350	16.400
42000	6.300	8.400	10.500	12.600	14.000	14.700	16.800
43000	6.450	8.600	10.750	12.900	14.333	15.050	17.200
44000	6.600	8.800	11.000	13.200	14.667	15.400	17.600
45000	6.750	9.000	11.250	13.500	15.000	15.750	18.000
50000	7.500	10.000	12.500	15.000	16.667	17.500	20.000
55000	8.250	11.000	13.750	16.500	18.333	19.250	22.000
60000	9.000	12.000	15.000	18.000	20.000	21.000	24.000
65000	9.750	13.000	16.250	19.500	21.667	22.750	26.000
70000	10.500	14.000	17.500	21.000	23.333	24.500	28.000
75000	11.250	15.000	18.750	22.500	25.000	26.250	30.000
100000	15.000	20.000	25.000	30.000	33.333	35.000	40.000